The English Legal System in Action

THE
ENGLISH LEGAL SYSTEM
IN ACTION

THE ADMINISTRATION OF JUSTICE

THIRD EDITION

Robin C. A. White

OXFORD
UNIVERSITY PRESS

Oxford University Press, Great Clarendon Street, Oxford OX2 6DP

Oxford New York

Athens Auckland Bangkok Bogotá Buenos Aires Calcutta
Cape Town Chennai Dar es Salaam Delhi Florence Hong Kong Istanbul
Karachi Kuala Lumpur Madrid Melbourne Mexico City Mumbai
Nairobi Paris São Paulo Singapore Taipei Tokyo Toronto Warsaw
and associated companies in Berlin Ibadan

Oxford is a registered trade mark of Oxford University Press

Published in the United States
by Oxford University Press Inc., New York

British Library Cataloguing in Publication Data
Data available

Library of Congress Cataloging in Publication Data
White, Robin C. A.
The administration of justice / Robin C. A. White. — 3rd ed.
p.   cm.
Includes index.
1. Law—Great Britain.   2. Justice, Administration of—Great
Britain.   I. Title.
KD660.W45   1998
347.41—dc21   98–37658
ISBN 0–19–876494–4
ISBN 0–19–876493–6 (pbk.)

1 3 5 7 9 10 8 6 4 2

Typeset in Minion
by Graphicraft Limited, Hong Kong
Printed in Great Britain
on acid-free paper by
Bookcraft Ltd., Midsomer Norton, Somerset

Contents

Preface

This is the third edition of this book, which was previously published by Black-wells. It is now published under a new title (in order to make it clearer to browsers what the book is about) and with a new publisher. The opportunity has been taken to move from the Harvard system of referencing to the more traditional foot-noting system. Such is the pace of change that virtually all chapters have been substantially rewritten.

In preparing the new edition, I have tried to keep faith with the objectives stated in the Preface to the first edition. Firstly, I have tried to deliver to those with no prior detailed knowledge of the legal system a readable and lively account of those parts of the system with which the ordinary citizen is most likely to come into con-tact. Secondly, I have adopted a consumer-oriented perspective on the legal system in order to illustrate the difficulties users of the legal system might experience. Thirdly, I have sought to offer some critique of the system where the result of my first two endeavours has been the frequent conclusion that there is a gap between the law in the books and the law in action.

The book recognises how deeply European law now shapes and influences our legal system. The penetration of European Union law into the national legal order is by now well known and acknowledged, and is to be joined by the newly in-corporated European Convention on Human Rights. I have accordingly included a new chapter providing an overview of European Union law and the law of the European Convention on Human Rights. In particular, the rights in the European Convention will be used within the national legal order to benchmark the work of both civil courts and tribunals, and the criminal courts, as well as other institu-tions such as the police and Government agencies. The chapters on understanding the criminal justice system and the new chapter on understanding the civil justice system appear at the start of their respective sections as a means of providing an agenda for consideration as readers absorb the detailed workings of the two sys-tems which are described in the ensuing chapters.

It is trite to say that our legal system develops at a rapid pace, but the changes, both implemented since the last edition in 1991 and planned for the coming years, are as remarkable as anything which has gone before. There has been a Royal Commission on Criminal Justice to see how the criminal justice system can avoid the string of miscarriages of justice which were such an embarrassment to most of the institutions which make up the criminal justice system. The Woolf reforms look likely to reshape the operation of the civil justice system. The notion of propor-tional procedures also appears to be influencing changes planned for the two sets of tribunals considered in this book. The Lord Chancellor's 'modernisation' of the legal aid system suggests that funding legal services will change dramatically with consequences for the organisation of the legal profession. In turn, the legal profession is wrestling with issues of organisation and regulation as the homogeneity of earlier years is replaced by the heterogeneity of modern legal practice.

The manuscript for this edition was delivered to the publishers in late June 1998. The delay in the finalisation of the Human Rights Act 1998 has been a little problematic. However, by the time proofs were returned, the Bill was looking in something like its final state, and the risk has been taken that the numbers of the clauses in the July 1998 version of the Bill will reflect section numbers in the Act. Readers should, however, cross-check the references to section numbers in the Human Rights Act 1998 appearing in this book against a Queen's Printer's copy of the statute after Royal Assent.

Over the years many colleagues have responded to queries and ideas which can be found in this book, and thanks are due to them all. Particular mention should be made of my colleagues, Tony Bradney and Fiona Cownie, who have shared the teaching of legal system with me at Leicester University for a number of years, and whose work on their own legal system book has challenged my own thinking about the subject. Thanks also go to the generations of students who have used earlier editions of this book and told me what they think of them.

Terrific support and encouragement has been provided by Michaela Coulthard and Myf Milton at Oxford University Press. Elizabeth Davison did a wonderful job of copy-editing the text, and Robert Spicer has produced the index. Many thanks to all of them.

I have tried to state the law as at 1 July 1998, though the opportunity has been taken to include reference to changes known to be taking effect at a later date. These relate primarily to the incorporation of the European Convention on Human Rights by the Human Rights Act 1998, but also include developments to be found in provisions of the Crime and Disorder Act 1998, the Employment Rights (Dispute Resolution) Act 1998, the Magistrates' Courts (Procedure) Act 1998 and the Social Security Act 1998.

Robin C. A. White
Leicester University
October 1998

Table of Cases

United Kingdom courts

United States

Court of Human Rights

Court of Justice of the European Communities

Table of Statutes

Table of Statutory Instruments

Table of Other Documents

Secondary legislation of the European Communities

Treaties

Abbreviations

AC	Appeal Cases
ADR	alternative dispute resolution
All ER	All England Law Reports
Archbold 1998	*Archbold, Criminal Pleading, Evidence and Practice 1998* (London: Sweet & Maxwell, 1998)
Brit. J of Crim.	*British Journal of Criminology*
Cd.	Command Papers (1900–1918)
Ch.	Chancery Division
CLJ	*Cambridge Law Journal*
CLP	*Current Legal Problems*
Cm.	Command Papers (1987 onwards)
Cmd.	Command Papers (1919–1956)
Cmnd.	Command Papers (1956–1986)
Cox CC	Cox's Criminal Cases
CPS	Crown Prosecution Service
Cr. App. R	Criminal Appeal Reports
Crim. LR	*Criminal Law Review*
DAT	Disability Appeal Tribunal
EAT	Employment Appeal Tribunal
EC	European Communities
EC Treaty	Treaty establishing the European Community
ECHR	European Convention on Human Rights
ECR	European Court Reports
ECSC Treaty	Treaty establishing the European Coal and Steel Community
EEC	European Economic Community
EHRLR	*European Human Rights Law Review*
EHRR	European Human Rights Reports
ELRev	*European Law Review*
Euratom Treaty	Treaty establishing the European Atomic Energy Community
HCP	House of Commons Sessional Papers
HL	House of Lords
HLR	Housing Law Reports
HMSO	Her Majesty's Stationery Office
J of Crim. Law and Criminology	*Journal of Criminal Law and Criminology*
J of Law and Soc.	*Journal of Law and Society*
KB	King's Bench
LAG Bulletin	*Legal Action Group Bulletin*
Law and Soc. Rev.	*Law and Society Review*

MAT	Medical Appeal Tribunal
MLR	*Modern Law Review*
NCCL	National Council for Civil Liberties
OFT	Office of Fair Trading
OJ	Official Journal of European Communities
PACE	Police and Criminal Evidence Act 1984, as amended
PL	*Public Law*
PNLR	Professional Negligence Law Reports
QB	Queen's Bench Division
SPTL	Society of Public Teachers of Law
SSAT	Social Security Appeal Tribunal
WLR	Weekly Law Reports

List of Figures

PART 1

INSTITUTIONS AND PROCESSES

1

INSTITUTIONS AND PROCESSES

Introduction

It is a truism to say that we live in an ordered society and that social interaction requires a degree of predictability. Law and the legal process contribute to the stable functioning of society by providing a framework of rules governing a multitude of activities. The reach of the law into everyday lives continues to increase, so that there are today few activities wholly unregulated by the law. This does not necessarily mean that there has been an increasing flood of legal disputes. Dispute resolution is just one of the functions of legal processes. It would certainly be a mistake to assume that it was always the intervention of lawyers or adjudication by courts or tribunals which resolved peoples' problems—and it is primarily about the legal problems of individuals rather than business enterprises that this book is concerned. Very frequently disputes are resolved outside the courtroom by the operation of self-help, legal advice and sometimes even by default. The bulk of lawyers' work is not concerned with court work, but with advice to clients to enable disputes to be settled amicably without litigation, and with the implementation of clients' wishes concerning their property. Examples are the buying and selling of property (conveyancing) and the drafting of wills and the administration of the estates of people who have died (probate).

Disputes arise where parties involved in some interaction disagree as to some fact or point of law involved in the interaction. Such disputes are likely to be resolved in one of the following ways:

- abandonment or concession;
- enquiry;
- negotiation;
- conciliation or mediation;
- arbitration;
- adjudication.

All these options may be followed as self-help processes where no legal advice is sought from persons with specialised knowledge, or on advice from an adviser with specialised knowledge. The adviser may or may not be a professionally qualified lawyer, such as a solicitor. Where arbitration or adjudication is involved, the parties are often represented by lawyers.

Let us attempt a working definition of each of the above methods of settlement.

Abandonment or concession occurs where one or other party regards the matter as insignificant and chooses not to pursue it. Alternatively, one or other party may feel powerless to act or act in ignorance in not pursuing the matter.

Enquiry is used to resolve some uncertainty about the facts or the relevant law. Once the uncertainty is resolved the matter may move to one of the other methods of settlement, including the abandoning of the claim by one party. The person conducting the enquiry is usually chosen by agreement between the parties.

Negotiation is a process of bargaining on the basis of asserted positions which are not subjected to independent adjudication. Negotiation usually involves compromise; each side makes concessions to the other in order to resolve the dispute by agreement. Such settlements are often made without any admission of liability. Negotiation enables the parties to keep the outcome of the dispute private.

Conciliation or mediation is rather like negotiation but a third party is brought in to help the parties come to an agreed settlement. The process is seen as important where a continuing relationship exists between the parties, as in family or employment disputes. It is invariably a private process.

Arbitration involves each side putting its case to an independent third party chosen by agreement of the parties to the dispute, who then makes a decision between them. It is of particular importance in commercial matters where complex technical and financial detail is involved. Arbitration is usually the result of agreement made in advance of the dispute arising. For example, a commercial contract may provide that any disputes that arise under the contract which cannot be resolved by agreement between the parties shall be referred to arbitration. Such clauses are binding. Arbitration normally takes place in private. Small claims in the county court are often said to be settled by arbitration, but the process is more in the nature of a special form of adjudication.[1]

Adjudication involves each side putting its case to a court or tribunal, which makes a decision between the parties. The placing of the matter in the hands of the court or tribunal can usually be achieved by unilateral act of one of the parties. The type of business with which particular courts and tribunals can deal is limited by their jurisdiction, which is usually determined by reference to geographical limitations, or the monetary value or seriousness of the dispute, or the nature of the dispute. Adjudication normally takes place in public and a decision is given in open court.

Lawyers have an important role to play in all forms of dispute settlement, and indeed perhaps have an even more important role as preventers of disputes, provided, of course, that advice is sought at a sufficiently early stage. Though the above processes seem more naturally to apply to disputes between individuals or business entities, they can have an application in criminal proceedings.[2]

[1] See Ch. 13.   [2] See Part 2.

This range of approaches to dispute resolution shows that adjudication is just one of many options. It is also the most formal remedy, where concession and compromise have little role to play. But it is important to realise that the various means of dispute resolution do not exist in isolation. Negotiation between parties who have embarked on the process of adjudication often continues right up to the door of the courtroom. Some procedures of adjudication have conciliation or mediation built into them in the hope of avoiding the confrontation inherent in adjudication. It is probably true to say that adjudication has a greater importance than other forms of dispute resolution because the outcome of adjudication is normally public and the reasons for a judge's or tribunal's decisions, when treated cumulatively, have an influence on the way in which similar disputes are resolved, whatever the means of resolution. For this reason lawyers tend to have a court-centred view of the legal system.

The court-centred view of the legal system is, however, being challenged by the official encouragement of dispute resolution other than through adjudication in the courts. The term 'alternative dispute resolution' or 'ADR' is now widely used to to refer, somewhat loosely, to such arrangements.[3]

Distinguishing between Civil and Criminal Proceedings

Understanding the distinction between civil and criminal proceedings is fundamental to an understanding of the English legal system. Different courts and procedures are used for civil and criminal proceedings, though some judges sit in both civil and criminal courts. The distinction between civil and criminal proceedings resides, somewhat unhelpfully, in the legal consequences that follow a particular act. Appreciation of the nature of the distinction and of the terminology associated with it will avoid some serious confusions about the role of various courts in the system.

Civil law and civil proceedings

Civil law and civil proceedings aim to determine the rights and obligations of individuals as between each other. Examples are the determination of rights arising under a contract, of obligations to pay damages for torts, such as negligence, nuisance or defamation, of rights in property and of succession, and of questions of status, such as divorce, adoption and the custody of children. Most of these rights are of a private nature, and are said to belong to the area of private law. There is also a body of civil law of a public nature, such as questions of taxation or questions

---

[3] This theme is taken up in Ch. 10.

concerning planning or compulsory purchase; these are said to belong to the area of public law.[4]

In most civil proceedings the person beginning the proceedings is the plaintiff who sues or brings an action against a defendant. The plaintiff will be seeking a remedy, usually in the form of damages (money compensation), but possibly also in the form of an injunction (an order prohibiting the defendant from committing or continuing to commit some wrongful act). There are other remedies that may be appropriate in particular cases, such as a declaration of parties' legal rights and responsibilities. Most civil proceedings are heard by a judge sitting alone; only very rarely (usually in defamation cases) will there be a jury in civil proceedings. The judge hears the action and delivers a judgment.

In some proceedings the terminology is different but it is not appropriate to list all the variations here. For example, in divorce proceedings the party asking for the marriage to be dissolved is the petitioner, who petitions for a decree against the respondent.

In civil proceedings, the plaintiff usually has the burden of proof; this means that the plaintiff must prove the facts on which the claim is based. The burden of proof in civil cases is said to be on the balance of probabilities: in other words the plaintiff must adduce admissible evidence to satisfy the judge that it is more probable than not that what the plaintiff alleges is true.

Criminal law and criminal proceedings

Criminal law and criminal proceedings are concerned with wrongs regarded as committed by the individual against society for which guilty individuals must be punished. In some circumstances even companies can commit criminal offences.[5] Whereas the objective of civil proceedings is to provide a remedy for the person wronged, usually in the form of damages, the objective of criminal proceedings is to determine the guilt or innocence of the accused person and, if that person is found to be guilty, to punish the wrongdoer and to protect society. Part of the purpose of the penalty is also seen as seeking to rehabilitate the wrongdoer. Debates about the purposes of sentencing form a distinct basis of study known generally as penology, which is itself often associated with criminology.[6]

In criminal proceedings a prosecutor, initially the police but subsequently the Crown Prosecutor, institutes a prosecution against a defendant or accused person (sometimes referred to simply as the accused). The outcome is a determination of guilt or innocence (by verdict if the trial is by jury). A finding that the accused person is not guilty is termed an acquittal. If the offence is proved, the court imposes

---

[4] For an example of a case where the distinction was important, see *Roy* v. *Kensington and Chelsea and Westminster Family Practitioners Committee* [1992] 1 AC 624; [1992] 1 All ER 705, especially the opinion of Lord Lowry.

[5] For an exploration of the issues, see C. Clarkson, 'Kicking Corporate Bodies and Damning their Souls' (1996) 59 MLR 557.

[6] Broadly defined as the scientific study of crime, it can perhaps more easily be thought of as the study of the anthropology, economics, politics, psychology, sociology and theory of criminal justice.

a sentence (usually either a fine or a term of imprisonment) or makes some other order (such as a probation order or community service order).

The prosecutor almost invariably has the burden of proof, which is said to be beyond all reasonable doubt. The prosecutor must adduce admissible evidence to prove that there is no doubt that the defendant committed the offence charged and this involves satisfying the magistrates or jury (known as the tribunal of fact) that every essential element of the offence is proved and that the acts of the defendant[7] were done with the requisite intent.[8] When certain defences are raised, such as insanity, the defendant has the burden of proof on the balance of probabilities. In other words, if insanity is raised as a defence, the prosecutor does not have to prove beyond all reasonable doubt that the defendant was sane, but rather the defendant must prove that on the balance of probabilities he or she is insane within the legal definition of that term.

The same set of facts may give rise to both civil and criminal proceedings. The most common example is the motor accident where someone is injured because of a driver's bad driving. A civil action by the injured person often follows as well as a prosecution for a driving offence. Another example of overlap might occur in the case of persons who sell dishonestly goods which are in their possession for repair. Such action amounts to (a) breach of contract (a civil wrong), (b) the tort of conversion (a civil wrong), and (c) theft (a crime).

Appeals

When both civil and criminal cases go on appeal, the terminology again changes. The party appealing is called the appellant and the other party who responds to the appeal is called the respondent. Appeals to the House of Lords are by petition and the Law Lords give opinions rather than deliver judgments. In all courts there are fairly strict time limits for entering appeals.

Sometimes appeals are available as of right. This means that an unsuccessful litigant does not need any permission to raise the matter before an appeal court. In other cases, a court's permission, known as leave to appeal is needed. Leave is often required where it is felt that there must be present some wider general interest than the dissatisfaction of one of the parties before the matter should be brought before an appellate court, or where a filter is needed to decide which appeals are meritorious.

Appeals serve a variety of purposes. In broad general terms, appeals can be divided into those concerned with the merits of the decision under appeal and those concerned with the legality of the process by which that decision was reached. A litigant is entitled not only to a fair and proper decision on the merits, but also to a decision arrived at by due process of law.

---

[7] Usually referred to by the Latin tag, *actus reus*, translating as 'the guilty act'.
[8] Usually referred to by the Latin tag, *mens rea*, translating as 'the guilty mind'.

Institutions

Some classifications of courts

A clear pecking order of courts exists which is of great importance in studying the doctrine of precedent, since decisions of courts higher in the hierarchy are generally binding on those lower in the hierarchy. Lower courts must follow the decisions of higher courts in similar cases unless there is some ground for distinguishing the earlier case. In the tribunal system the doctrine of precedent is not as fully developed but decisions of courts exercising appellate or supervisory jurisdiction[9] are binding on tribunals. Where there is a tribunal which itself hears appeals from tribunals lower in the hierarchy, decisions of the appellate tribunal normally bind the lower tribunal.

Courts are sometimes classified as superior or inferior courts, though this classification is not one which has a clearly defined basis. The distinction can have practical importance in defining a court's powers in the face of an act considered to be contempt of court, and in determining whether the High Court (a superior court) can exercise its supervisory jurisdiction in relation to the inferior court.[10] The nature of superior courts is that their jurisdiction is limited neither geographically nor in money terms, whereas it is a characteristic of inferior courts that their jurisdiction is both local and limited. The proceedings of inferior courts are not recorded verbatim but those of superior courts usually are. Inferior courts are also subject to what is known as the supervisory jurisdiction of the High Court. Magistrates courts and county courts are inferior courts, while other courts are superior courts. The Crown Court is a hybrid, because when it is hearing appeals from magistrates' courts it is deemed to be an inferior court, though for all other purposes it is a superior court. The Supreme Court of Judicature is the collective title given to the Court of Appeal, the High Court and the Crown Court.

Types of jurisdiction

Reference has been made above to appellate and supervisory jurisdiction. Jurisdiction can be divided into three types as follows:

Original jurisdiction indicates that the court or tribunal has jurisdiction to try a case; this is sometimes described as the court or tribunal of first instance.

Appellate jurisdiction indicates the court with jurisdiction to review either the decision of the court of first instance or the decision of an appellate court lower in the hierarchy. An example of the latter is the House of Lords reviewing a decision of the Court of Appeal. The exercise of appellate jurisdiction is concerned with the merits of the decision, though appeal to the House of Lords will only be allowed

---

[9] See below.
[10] See *Attorney-General* v. *BBC* [1981] AC 303; [1980] 3 WLR 109, HL, which concerned a local valuation court, and *R* v. *Cripps, ex parte Muldoon* [1984] QB 68; [1984] 3 WLR 53, which concerned an election court.

if the case raises a point of law of general public importance beyond the dispute between the litigants in the case.

Supervisory jurisdiction refers to the exercise of the jurisdiction of the High Court to ensure that inferior courts and tribunals do not act wrongly in law, in excess of their jurisdiction or otherwise unfairly. Supervisory jurisdiction is exercised either on application for judicial review or by way of case stated. The exercise of supervisory jurisdiction is primarily concerned with the legality of the process by which the decision was reached.

Some important institutions

A thumbnail sketch of the courts having jurisdiction in the main areas of civil and criminal law covered in this book will give a slightly more detailed picture of the legal system.

The main courts having jurisdiction in civil cases in contract and tort are the county courts and the Queen's Bench Division of the High Court, with appeal lying to the Court of Appeal, Civil Division, and then to the House of Lords. This is represented in diagrammatic form in Figure 1.1. The Final Report of the Civil Justice Review[11] abandoned a suggestion that the county courts and the High Court should become a unified court; now all but the most important and complex cases in contract and tort are heard by county courts.

In criminal cases, there are two entirely separate forms of trial: summary trial before magistrates and trial on indictment in the Crown Court. Trial on indictment in the Crown Court is reserved for the more serious criminal offences, though, where a defendant retains the right to refuse trial in the magistrates' court, minor

Figure 1.1. **Courts having jurisdiction in contract and tort**

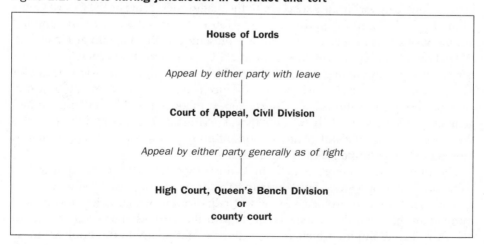

House of Lords

Appeal by either party with leave

Court of Appeal, Civil Division

Appeal by either party generally as of right

High Court, Queen's Bench Division
or
county court

---

[11] *Civil Justice Review: Report of the Review Body on Civil Justice* (London: HMSO, 1988, Cm. 394).

Figure 1.2. **Summary trial**

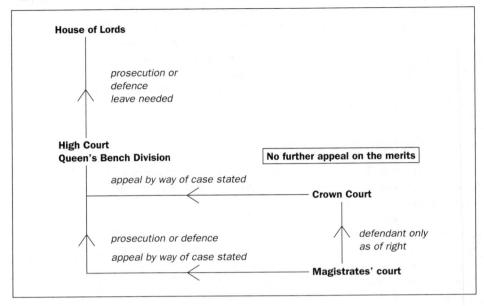

matters can still come before the Crown Court. There is an elaborate system of classification of offences for the purposes of determining where trial will take place.[12]

The system of appeals following trial in the magistrates' courts is a complex combination of appeal on the merits and supervisory jurisdiction. Appeal on the merits, that is, against conviction or sentence, lies to the Crown Court as of right, but there is no further appeal on the merits. Appeals in exercise of the supervisory jurisdiction lie by way of case stated from the magistrates' court or the Crown Court to the High Court and then direct to the House of Lords if a sufficiently important point of law is raised. This system is represented in the diagram at Figure 1.2.

Trial on indictment follows the committal of a person for trial generally by magistrates sitting as examining justices in committal proceedings. This is designed to act as a filter to weed out cases where the evidence is not sufficiently strong to justify an expensive trial in the Crown Court. Appeal following trial on indictment lies, generally with leave, to the Court of Appeal, Criminal Division, and thereafter to the House of Lords if a sufficiently important point of law is raised. This system is represented diagrammatically in Figure 1.3.

The other forum before which the ordinary citizen is likely to appear is a tribunal. This is a generic label for modern forms of court established to meet specific needs and to provide a system of adjudication which is less formal and more accessible than the system of courts with their rituals and complex rules of evidence. Two examples, which are considered in detail later in this book are those

---

[12] See Ch. 7.

Figure 1.3. **Trial on indictment**

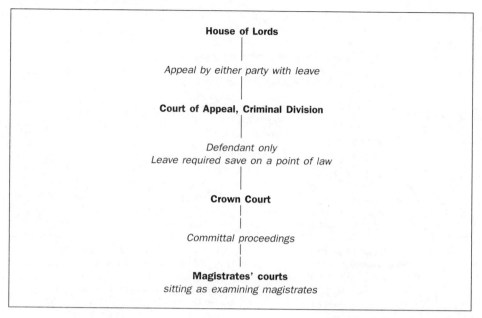

tribunals which hear appeals concerning entitlement to social security benefits from initial decisions of officers in the Department of Social Security and Department of Employment,[13] and employment tribunals[14] which have a wide jurisdiction concerning the relationship of employer and employee.[15]

Other major institutions involved in the administration of justice are the legislature, the police, the judiciary and the legal profession. For our purposes more need be said at this stage only about the legal profession. This is divided into two branches: solicitors and barristers. Each has different functions, though the tasks each performs are not exclusive to it, and changes introduced in the early 1980s have blurred the distinction even further. Though barristers are generally seen as the specialist trial advocates, they often draft documents and give advice, while solicitors often appear as advocates in court. Two points should, however, be noted about the impact of the current division of the profession. First, clients generally have direct access only to solicitors who alone can instruct barristers to act for clients. Secondly, barristers alone enjoy, by virtue of their standard qualifications, the right to appear as advocates (known as having a right of audience) in the higher courts. It is now, however, possible for solicitors to acquire as a result of further training rights of audience in the higher courts.[16] This will in due course open the door to the appointment of solicitor advocates to higher judicial office.[17]

---

[13] See Ch. 14.   [14] Formerly, industrial tribunals.   [15] See Ch. 15.   [16] See Ch. 17.
[17] Sachs J. was the first solicitor to be appointed to the High Court bench in 1993; in 1998 two solicitors were appointed as Deputy High Court judges.

Figure 1.4. **Courts, judges and jurisdiction**

House of Lords
Type: Superior court
Judges: Lords of Appeal in Ordinary (Law Lords)
Jurisdiction: appellate only; unlimited
Audience: higher advocacy rights

Court of Appeal
Type: Superior court
Part of Supreme Court of Judicature

Divided into:

Civil Division	*Criminal Division*
Judges: Master of the Rolls	Judges: Lord Chief Justice
Lords Justices of Appeal	Lords Justices of Appeal
Jurisdiction: appellate, unlimited, civil only	Jurisdiction: appellate, unlimited, criminal
Audience: higher advocacy rights	Audience: higher advocacy rights

High Court of Justice	**Crown Court**
Type: Superior court	Type: Superior court except when exercising
Part of Supreme Court of Judicature	appellate jurisdiction
divided into:	Part of Supreme Court of Judicature
Chancery Division	Judges: Puisne judges (High Court judges)
Family Division	Circuit Judges and Recorders
Queen's Bench Division	Jurisdiction: original and appellate
Judges: Puisne judges (High Court judges)	almost always criminal
Jurisdiction: appellate, supervisory and	unlimited
original civil and criminal	Audience: higher advocacy rights
unlimited	
Adience: higher advocacy rights	

County courts	**Magistrates' courts**
Type: Inferior courts	Type: Inferior courts
Judges: Circuit Judges and District Judges	Judges: justices of the peace,
JurisdictionL original, civil only	stipendiary magistrates
limited geographically and by value	Jurisdiction: original, civil and criminal
Audience: general advocacy rights	limited by function and seriousness of offence
	Audience: general advocacy rights

The institutional picture developed so far can be summarised in Figure 1.4. The hierarchy of courts is also portrayed by putting the highest court in the hierarchy at the top of the chart and ranking other courts beneath it. The principal judges to be found in each court are also noted.

Before moving on there are four courts which warrant mention because otherwise confusion might arise when reference to them is met. All are part of a wider legal system than the English legal system, though all have a major impact on the English system. The first three are the Court of First Instance and the Court of Justice of the European Communities in Luxembourg, and the European Court of Human

Rights in Strasbourg, whose influences are considered in the next chapter. The fourth is the Judicial Committee of the Privy Council.

The Judicial Committee of the Privy Council

The Privy Council is the body on whose advice and through which the sovereign exercises her statutory and a number of prerogative powers. The Judicial Committee of the Privy Council is an appellate court which derives its appellate jurisdiction from the right of all the Queen's subjects to appeal to the Crown for redress. The primary function of the Judicial Committee is to act as a final appeal court from the Channel Islands, the Isle of Man, the colonies, protectorates and associated states, and from those independent countries within the Commonwealth which have not abolished such appeals. Since the legal systems of many of these countries are closely modelled on the English system, many of the decisions of the Judicial Committee are of relevance to the English lawyer and English courts treat decisions of the Judicial Committee with great respect. Another reason is that there is some overlap of personnel, since the Law Lords are members of the Judicial Committee.

Processes

A description of institutions gives only a formal structural view of some public parts of the legal system. It also tends to suggest that the selected institutions are something which can legitimately be called a system. Though a minimum of factual knowledge about institutions is needed for any consideration of the administration of justice, the problem with focusing on institutions is that it tells us very little about how the system operates.

Much more interesting and exciting is the study of institutions in action. The study of processes tells us so much more about the functioning of institutions in the system: are they usable? are they accessible? are they fair to litigants? do they provide an appropriate means of dispute resolution? Without an appreciation of legal processes, it is all too easy to get a distorted picture of the operation of law in society. It will be little use knowing the substantive rules of negligence or of the criminal law, if there is no context in which to place that knowledge. In understanding the law of negligence, it is necessary to know how victims of accidents learn about their rights, of how a typical personal injuries action will proceed, and what factors influence participants in the process. In understanding the prosecution of a criminal offence, it is necessary to know how the offence came to the attention of the police, how the offence has been investigated, what pressures are placed on defendants, whether the legal advice defendants receive is effective, and whether the trial process operates fairly and effectively. How is 'effectiveness' to be measured? It is after all processes which ultimately determine the effectiveness of the substantive law.

In recent years there has been increasing emphasis on such a perspective on the administration of justice and much research has been carried out that is beginning to enable us to understand how the system operates in practice rather than in theory, or put another way, in the real world rather than in the books. In adopting this perspective greater emphasis is placed on the consumer, with attempts made to view the processes through the eyes of the individuals who are caught up in the system. The role of the lawyer is not quite as central, because from this perspective much happens both before and after the lawyer appears on the scene. Indeed in some cases, the lawyer never appears on the scene.

Some Theory

Many who write about the institutions and processes involved in the administration of justice talk of a legal system.[18] This suggests a planned, coherent, and complete set of structures following well-defined rules and producing predictable and desirable outcomes. The briefest acquaintance with the institutions which might be said to populate the legal system of England and Wales[19] shows that it is far from systematic, that many aspects of the system are the result of historical accretion rather than logical plan, and that the relationship between institutions is complex. This is nowhere clearer than the distinction made between courts and tribunals. This book argues that tribunals are simply more modern forms of court. It would follow that their role should be considered alongside other institutions administering civil justice. Yet they are frequently seen as, at best, some sort of public law adjunct to the system,[20] or even not to come with the ambit of civil litigation.[21]

One risk of the imposition of structure on the institutions and processes which make up the system in England and Wales for the administration of justice is that it reflects essentially arbitrary decisions on what to include and what to exclude that build into axioms about the content of the system. The focus taken in this book is on official institutions and processes. This refers to the formal public institutions rather than less formal private institutions. It also focuses on those areas where the volume of activity is greatest, and with which the ordinary citizen might have

---

[18] For a detailed discussion on the problems of defining the English legal system, see F. Cownie and A. Bradney, *English Legal System in Context* (London: Butterworths, 1996), ch. 1.

[19] The legal system of Scotland is entirely different, while that of Northern Ireland, though similar in many respects to that of England and Wales, has a number of marked differences.

[20] J. R. Spencer, *Jackson's Machinery of Justice* (Cambridge: Cambridge University Press, 1989), Part III, *passim*, and R. J. Walker and R. Ward, *Walker and Walker's English Legal System*, 7th edn. (London: Butterworths, 1994), pp. 175–80.

[21] J. O'Hare and R. N. Hill, *Civil Litigation*, 8th edn. (London: Longman, 1997) and D. Barnard and M. Houghton, *The New Civil Court in Action*, 3rd edn. (London: Butterworths, 1993). Both choose not to deal with tribunal procedure in these works because they are not defined as part of the civil justice system.

contact. This is not to deny the significance of private actors whose role is similar to the public counterpart. So, for example, there is a very significant volume of private policing, and even of privately managed prisons.[22] So, ultimately this book will reveal only one perspective on the administration of justice.

A number of theoretical bases inform the approach adopted in this book. The first has come to be characterized by contrasting law in action with law in the books, and has its origins in legal realism as espoused by a number of American scholars.[23] In its modern form it can be labelled sociological jurisprudence.[24] Law in the books refers to the formal rules of substance and procedure, while law in action refers to the manner in which those rules are applied in practice. Studies which have adopted this perspective have invariably shown that there is a gap between the law in the books and the law in action. A number will be the subject of comment later in this book.

The access to justice approach has also influenced the selection of material for discussion in this book. This approach focuses on the system for vindicating people's rights under the general auspices of the State and requires such a system of remedies to be both equally accessible to all and to lead to results that are individually and socially just.[25] Though most frequently applied to civil matters, the approach can inform discussion of the protections afforded to suspects in interactions with the police and to defendants before the criminal courts.

The approach adopted in this book in looking at the civil and criminal justice systems is broadly to follow the fate of a man or woman caught up in a civil or criminal case from the event which begins the process through to the disposition of a final appeal. As we go along, necessary institutional and procedural background is given so that by the end of each part of the book the reader should be able to construct an accurate basic account of the institutions and procedures involved, as well as having seen how some researchers have found that the system actually operates in the real world.

---

[22] See, for an introduction to a perspective which seeks to address the relationship of private policing to public policing, F. Cownie and A. Bradney, *English Legal System in Context* (London, Butterworths, 1996), ch. 11.

[23] See for a useful summary J. W. Harris, *Legal Philosophies*, 2nd edn. (London: Butterworths, 1997), ch. 8.

[24] Ibid., ch. 18. Some well-chosen extracts from key scholars can be found in M. Freeman, *Lloyd's Introduction to Jurisprudence*, 6th edn. (London: Sweet & Maxwell, 1994).

[25] See, especially, M. Cappelletti and B. Garth, 'Access to Justice: The Worldwide Movement to Make Rights Effective. A General Report' in M. Cappelletti and B. Garth (eds.), *A World Survey*, vol. 1, Book 1 of M. Cappelletti (ed.), *Access to Justice*, four vols. (Alphen aan den Rijn: Sitjhoff and Noordhoff, 1978), ch. 1.

2

EUROPEAN INFLUENCES

Introduction

The United Kingdom has been a member of the Council of Europe since 3 August 1949 and a Member State of the European Communities since 1 January 1973. Membership of the Council of Europe has carried with it an expectation of participation in the European Convention on Human Rights, and the United Kingdom has been a party to this Convention since its entry into force on 3 September 1953. In their own different ways, membership of the European Communities and participation in the regional system for the protection of human rights have had significant influences on the development of United Kingdom law and the operation of its legal system.

The standard setting of the European Convention human rights system continues to result in changes to the structure and procedure of English institutions, while exposure to a different style of legislative drafting has necessitated a broader approach to the reading of legal texts than the literal approach to statutory interpretation which has been the traditional starting point in any attempt to give meaning to a statutory provision. The European Union has generated a body of substantive law and important principles which must now be applied by English courts and tribunals.

The Nature of the European Union

The European Union has evolved from the three original European Communities: the European Economic Community governed by the EEC Treaty, the European Coal and Steel Community governed by the ECSC Treaty, and the European Atomic Energy Community governed by the Euratom Treaty. These three communities continue to exist, but the European Economic Community has been renamed the European Community, and is now governed by the EC Treaty, while the Treaty on European Union[1] created a tripartite Union consisting of the supranational

---

[1] Sometimes known as the Maastricht Treaty.

European Communities, and the essentially intergovernmental pillars known as the Common Foreign and Security Policy (CFSP) and Justice and Home Affairs (JHA), which are described in Article A of the Treaty on European Union as 'policies and forms of co-operation'. The structure of the Union is presented in diagrammatic form in Figure 2.1. When the Treaty of Amsterdam comes into force, areas currently within JHA will move over to the supranational European Community pillar, which will also acquire new competences under a revised version of the EC Treaty.[2] The remaining co-operative areas of JHA will be renamed police and judicial co-operation in criminal matters. There are currently fifteen Member States of the European Union,[3] but accession negotiations are under way with six further countries.[4]

There are traditionally said to be two types of international organisation: the intergovernmental organisation and the supranational organisation. Relations between the countries participating in an intergovernmental organisation operate on a country to country level. Typically, intergovernmental organisations cannot bind any participating country without its consent. Though participating countries can agree to extend certain rights to those within their jurisdiction, those rights generally only flow, in countries with constitutional traditions like those of the United Kingdom, from an explicit extension of rights to individuals by legislative act of the State. By contrast, supranational organisations are characterised by an ability to make decisions binding on participating countries by majority decision. So a country may be bound by a rule with which it disagrees. Furthermore, the supranational organisation can create rights and duties for those within the jurisdiction of the participating countries without the intervention of national law-making bodies. The European Community pillar of the European Union has its own legislative capacity and decisions are made in many areas by qualified majority voting.

The Court of Justice of the European Communities in Luxembourg[5] has played a major role in explaining the nature of Community law and has stressed the creation of rights and duties for individuals flowing from Community law. In one of its earliest cases, the Court described Community law in the following terms:

The objective of the EEC Treaty, which is to establish a Common Market, the functioning of which is of direct concern to interested parties in the Community, implies that this Treaty is more than an agreement which merely creates mutual obligations between the contracting states. This view is confirmed by the preamble to the Treaty which refers not only to governments but to peoples. It is also confirmed more specifically by the establishment of institutions endowed with sovereign rights, the exercise of which affects Member States and also their citizens.[6]

---

[2] Whose numbering is dramatically changed. This chapter retains reference to the existing EC Treaty articles, unless otherwise stated.

[3] Austria, Belgium, Denmark, Finland, France, Germany, Greece, Ireland, Italy, Luxembourg, Netherlands, Portugal, Spain, Sweden and the United Kingdom.

[4] Cyprus, Hungary, Poland, Estonia, the Czech Republic and Slovenia. A further five countries are involved in 'enhanced pre-accession strategies': Romania, Slovakia, Latvia, Lithuania and Bulgaria. Closer relations with Turkey, which has also applied for membership, are also planned.

[5] Referred to throughout this chapter as 'the Court of Justice'.

[6] Case 26/62 *Van Gend en Loos* [1963] ECR 1, 12.

Figure 2.1. **The structure of the European Union**

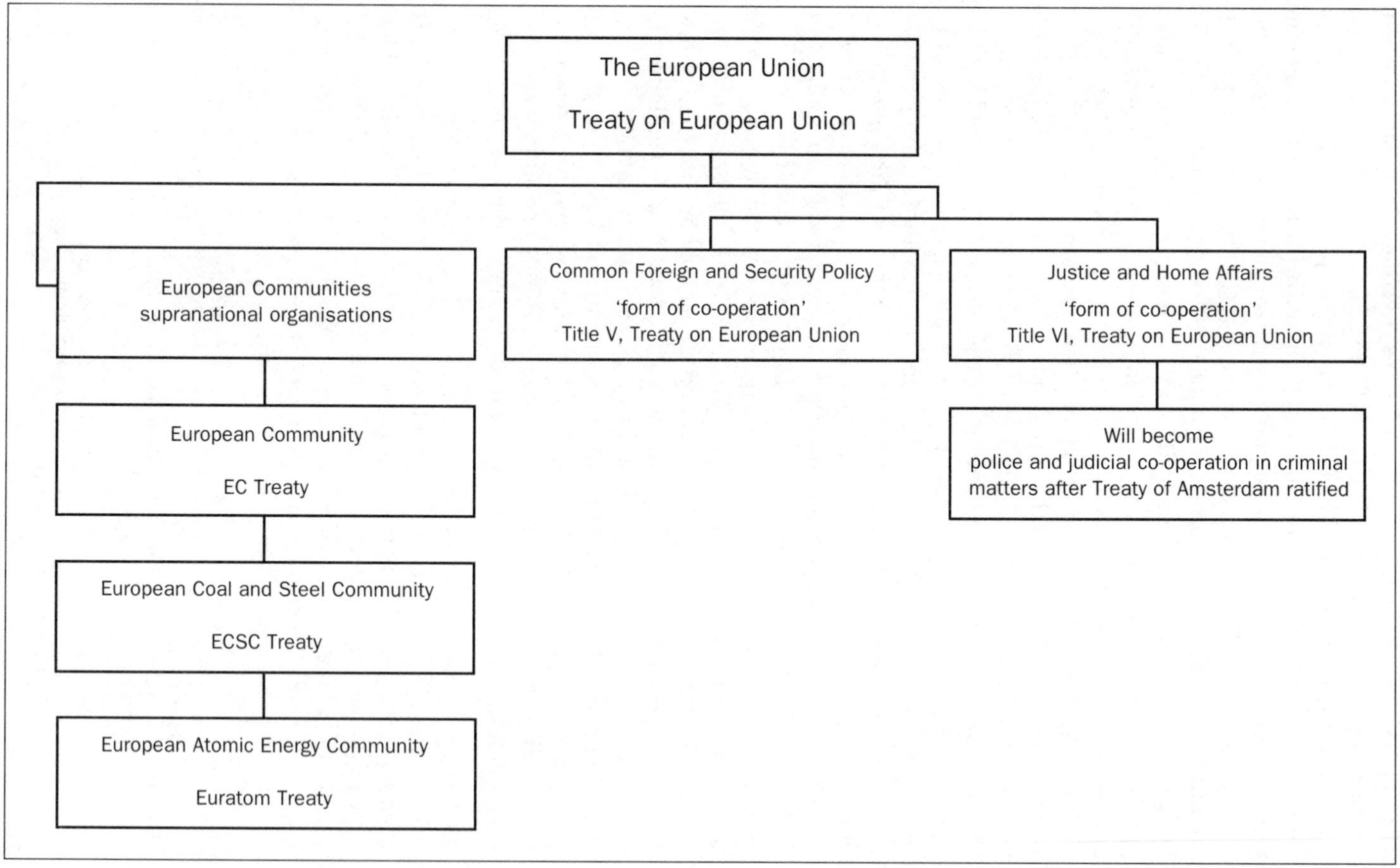

The European Union
Treaty on European Union

European Communities
supranational organisations

European Community
EC Treaty

European Coal and Steel Community
ECSC Treaty

European Atomic Energy Community
Euratom Treaty

Common Foreign and Security Policy
'form of co-operation'
Title V, Treaty on European Union

Justice and Home Affairs
'form of co-operation'
Title VI, Treaty on European Union

Will become
police and judicial co-operation in criminal
matters after Treaty of Amsterdam ratified

The Court went on to describe the nature of the legal order created by the EEC Treaty:

the Community constitutes a new legal order of international law for the benefit of which the states have limited their sovereign rights, albeit within limited fields, and the subjects of which comprise not only Member States but also their nationals. Independently of the legislation of Member States, Community law therefore not only imposes obligations on individuals but is also intended to confer upon them rights which become part of their legal heritage.[7]

Following this seminal case, the Court has developed key doctrines and fundamental principles which flow from Community law. That law consists not only of the Treaty provisions, but also of secondary legislation made under them, as well as of certain general principles of law. There are three types of Community secondary legislation. First, there are regulations, which have general application and are binding and directly applicable in all Member States. Regulations are the statutes of the Community, and any inconsistency between them and national law is resolved in favour of the Community regulation under the doctrine of the supremacy of Community law.[8] Secondly, there are directives. These are co-ordinating measures. They require implementation in each Member State in order to secure their objectives, but leave each Member State free to choose the form and method of implementation. They set a deadline for their implementation in the national legal order, and it is now well settled that, where they have not been implemented by the deadline, or have not been fully implemented, individuals may rely on their provisions in actions before the national courts against the State[9] where the rights given by the directive are sufficiently clear and precise.[10] Finally, there are decisions, which have more of an executive or administrative character; they are used frequently in the application of the Community competition rules. A good example of a decision is the grant of an exemption from the application of Community competition rules.

In addition to this secondary legislation, the Court of Justice has developed a 'common law' of the Community, building upon ideas to be found in the general scheme of the Treaties and in the national laws and traditions of the Member States. These general principles are used to assist in the interpretation of Community legislation and in determining the legality of acts of the Community institutions. The justification for the creation of general principles of law flows from the words of Article 164 EC: 'The Court of Justice shall ensure that in the interpretation and application of this Treaty the law is observed'.

---

[7] Ibid.

[8] See generally T. Hartley, *The Foundations of European Community Law*, 4th edn. (Oxford: Oxford University Press, 1998), ch. 7.

[9] Or an 'emanation of the State': see T. Hartley, *The Foundations of European Community Law*, 4th edn. (Oxford: Oxford University Press, 1998), pp. 208–11.

[10] Under the doctrine of direct effect. See generally T. Hartley, *The Foundations of European Community Law*, 4th edn. (Oxford: Oxford University Press, 1998), ch. 7.

The 'law' to which Article 164 refers is not defined, and it is argued that it means something more than simply the Treaty itself.[11] The Community general principles of law are among the significant influences of Community law in national law.[12]

The Luxembourg Courts

There are two courts serving the European Union: the Court of First Instance, and the Court of Justice. The Court of First Instance was added to the Court of Justice in 1989 as a means of reducing the pressure of work on the Court of Justice.[13] Both courts are located in Luxembourg.

The Court of First Instance

On the introduction of the Court of First Instance, those cases involving the personnel of the Community and those cases involving complex facts were transferred to the Court of First Instance in order to leave the Court of Justice with more time to deal with those cases raising matters of political or constitutional importance. The Court of First Instance now determines disputes between the Community and its staff;[14] it is a kind of Community employment tribunal. Its other jurisdictions are much more important. They include actions by private individuals and companies to seek the annulment of Community legislation,[15] actions by private individuals and companies for failure of an institution to act,[16] actions for damages for non-contractual liability of the Community institutions,[17] and actions by private individuals and companies for judgment pursuant to an arbitration clause contained in a contract.[18] The jurisdiction is of particular importance in relation to the Community's competition and trading rules. Appeals lie, on points of law only, from final decisions of the Court of First Instance to the Court of Justice.

The Court of Justice

The Court of Justice was first established by the Treaties establishing the European Economic Community, the European Coal and Steel Community and the European Atomic Energy Community as a separate court for each Community, but it now operates as a single court serving the interests of the European Union. The Court sits on a permanent basis in Luxembourg and consists of judges and

---

[11] See generally T. Hartley, *The Foundations of European Community Law*, 4th edn. (Oxford: Oxford University Press, 1998), ch. 5.   [12] See below.

[13] Council Decision 88/591 of 24 October 1988, [1988] OJ L319/1.

[14] Under Art. 179 EC and Art. 152 Euratom.

[15] Under Art. 173 EC, Art. 33 ECSC, and Art. 146 Euratom.

[16] Under Art. 175 EC, Art. 35 ECSC, and Art. 148 Euratom.

[17] Under Art. 178 EC, Art. 40 ECSC, and Art. 151 Euratom.

[18] Under Art. 181 EC, Art. 42 ECSC, and Art. 153 Euratom.

advocates general. Under the normal procedures, a single advocate general delivers an opinion in each case prior to the determination of the case by the Court of Justice. The purpose of the advocate general's opinion is to assist the Court. Hartley comments:

[The advocate general] represents neither the Community nor any Member State: he speaks only for the public interest. He works quite separately and independently from the judges; one could say that he gives a 'second opinion' which is in fact delivered first. This opinion shows the judges what a trained legal mind, equal in quality to their own, has concluded on the matter before them. It could be regarded as a point of reference, or starting point, from which they can begin their deliberations. In many cases they follow the advocate general fully; in others they deviate from his opinion either wholly or in part. But always his views will be of great value.[19]

The Court itself issues a single judgment and there are no dissenting opinions expressed. Sometimes this results in a decision in which the differences of views among the judges are accommodated by opaque language. In such cases, the opinion of the advocate general is particularly valuable since it will canvass the issues in much greater detail. The Court is a multi-lingual Court. Each advocate general and judge is assisted by legal secretaries.[20]

The jurisdiction of the Court of Justice is usually divided into direct actions[21] and indirect actions.[22] Direct actions refer to those jurisdictions where a party brings a dispute direct to the Court. A good example is an action under Article 169 EC by the Commission against a Member State arguing that the Member State has violated its obligations under the Treaty, for example, by failing to transpose a directive into national law within the time limit allowed by the directive. Another example is the judicial review jurisdiction of the Court under which the legality of Community legislation can be challenged.[23] Direct actions brought by private individuals or companies are now dealt with by the Court of First Instance, but the Court of Justice has jurisdiction where such actions are brought by a Community institution or by a Member State.

Indirect actions are preliminary references under Article 177 EC made by national courts seeking an authoritative statement from the Court of Justice on the interpretation of Community law (including provisions of the Treaties), on the direct effect of Community law, and on the validity of legislative acts of the Community institutions.[24] Under this jurisdiction, any court or tribunal in a Member

---

[19] T. Hartley, *The Foundations of European Community Law*, 4th edn. (Oxford: Oxford University Press, 1998), p. 55.

[20] Scholars from the Member States seconded to the Court; the French term *référendaires* sounds less clerical in nature. Most judges and advocates general seek to have more than one nationality among their staff (known by the French term *cabinet*); they are also assisted by a research and documentation division at the Court.   [21] Or contentious business.

[22] Or non-contentious business.

[23] All Community legislation must be based on a provision of the EC Treaty and may be challenged, *inter alia*, if it is outside the scope of the provision claimed to be its legal base.

[24] See A. Arnull, 'References to the European Court' (1990) 15 ELRev 375; and D. O'Keeffe, 'Is the Spirit of Article 177 under Attack? Preliminary References and Admissibility' *European Law Review*, forthcoming.

State, which finds itself faced with a point of Community law which is relevant to the determination it is called upon to make, is able to refer questions to the Court of Justice for its authoritative ruling. The decision to refer is for the court or tribunal in the Member State, and not for the parties to the litigation in the Member State. Of course, the parties can argue that a reference is needed (or not needed), but it is for the national court alone to decide whether to make the reference. Courts, other than final appeal courts, have a discretion as to whether or not a reference is made, but where a question of Community law is raised before a final appeal court which it is necessary to answer in order to determine the question before that court, there is an obligation to make a reference.[25]

Where a reference is made, it has the effect of adjourning[26] the case before the national court or tribunal until the decision of the Court of Justice is given. When the Court of Justice delivers its opinion, the national court or tribunal reconvenes and is obliged to follow the ruling of the Court of Justice on the content or validity of the Community law in issue in the case. The Court of Justice advises on the meaning of Community law, and the national court or tribunal applies that advice to the case before it.

The Court of Justice has emphasised that the objective of the preliminary ruling procedure is a partnership between national courts and tribunals and the Court of Justice.[27] The Court of Justice has indicated that any attempt by national authorities to restrict the discretion of national courts or tribunals in making references is contrary to Article 177 EC.[28] Five propositions emerge from consideration of the case law of the Court of Justice:[29]

(1) It is for the national court or tribunal to decide at what stage of the proceedings it is appropriate for a preliminary ruling to be requested.
(2) In order to assist the Court of Justice, it is essential for the national court or tribunal to define the legal context in which the reference is made.
(3) This suggests that in some cases it might well be appropriate for the facts in the case to be settled at the time of the reference.
(4) Attempts to fetter or limit the discretion of the national court or tribunal are inconsistent with Community law.
(5) The decision to refer is that of the court or tribunal and not that of the parties.

Practice in English courts and tribunals has been influence by guidelines expressed by Lord Denning in *Bulmer* v. *Bollinger*,[30] but these are not binding on any court or tribunal and aspects of them are inconsistent with statements made by the

---

[25] T. Hartley, *The Foundations of European Community Law*, 4th edn. (Oxford: Clarendon Press, 1998), p. 72.   [26] Suspending.
[27] Case 166/73 *Rheinmuhlen* [1974] ECR 33, 38.   [28] Ibid.
[29] See Case 166/73 *Rheinmuhlen* [1974] ECR 33; Joined Cases 36 and 71/80 *Irish Creamery Milk Suppliers Association* v. *Ireland* [1981] ECR 735; Case 72/83 *Campus Oil* v. *Minister for Industry and Energy* [1984] ECR 2727; and Case 14/86 *Pretore di Salo* v. *Persons Unknown* [1987] ECR 2545.   [30] [1974] Ch. 401.

Court of Justice, which in 1996 itself issued notes for guidance on references by national courts for preliminary rulings.[31] It is important that the question posed relates to Community law, and that the question is posed as a general question of interpretation or validity rather than as a request to the Court to tell the national court or tribunal the decision it should make. The Court of Justice is fastidious in only advising on the Community law issue raised, leaving it for the national court to apply this in the case before it. The question or questions posed should be self-contained and self-explanatory, since they will be notified to the Commission, Council and the Member States, who may choose within two months to submit written observations on the questions raised. Though the only formal requirement is the formulation of a question or questions for the Court of Justice, the Court finds it helpful to have the following information included in the reference:

- the facts of the case;
- the relevant provisions of United Kingdom law;
- the provisions of Community law thought to be relevant;
- a summary of the contentions of the parties on the question or questions referred; and
- if necessary, the reasons why the answers to the questions posed are considered necessary to decide the case.

The ambit of Community law is now vast; there are few areas of law untouched by the European influence. There are probably very few of the main English courts or tribunals which have not found the need to make references to the Court of Justice in Luxembourg.

Rules of interpretation

Article 5 EC embodies a principle of solidarity, which requires the Member States to 'take all appropriate measures . . . to ensure fulfilment of the obligations arising out of this Treaty or resulting from action taken by the institutions of the Community'. Furthermore, Member States are required to 'facilitate' the achievement of the Community's tasks, and to refrain from any measure which might jeopardise the attainment of the objectives of the Treaty.

The Court of Justice has fashioned from this principle a requirement that courts and public authorities in the Member States must interpret national legislation, so far as it is possible to do so, in a manner which meets the requirements of Community law.[32] This rule of interpretation was first enunciated in the *Von Colson* case,[33] where the issue arose in relation to national legislation passed to implement

---

[31] Reproduced in (1997) 22 ELRev 55.
[32] See J. Temple Lang, 'The Duties of National Courts under Community Constitutional Law' (1997) 22 ELRev 3; and J. Temple Lang, 'The Duties of National Authorities under Community Constitutional Law' (1998) 23 ELRev 109.
[33] Case 14/83 *Von Colson and Kamann* v. *Land Nordrhein-Westfalen* [1984] ECR 1891.

a particular directive. Such a position is entirely logical, since the national legislature clearly intended to implement the requirements of the directive in the legislation in issue. However, in *Marleasing*[34] the requirement was extended to legislation whenever passed. Again there is logic to this position. A Member State faced with a directive must determine the form and method of the implementation of its requirements. In some cases, a Member State will conclude that its law already provides the protection required by the directive and that no further action is necessary. Here again it can be argued that the Member State legislature intended the prior legislation to fulfil its obligations under Community law.

A question arose in the *Webb* case in the United Kingdom as to the circumstances in which the rule of interpretation must be applied. The issue arose in a difficult sex discrimination case. Ms Webb had been employed to replace a worker who had gone on maternity leave, but shortly after she started work, she discovered that she too was pregnant. The employer purported to dismiss her on the basis that she would be unavailable to provide the maternity leave cover for which she had been appointed. She argued that she had been dismissed by reason of pregnancy, which is unlawful. The case started in an industrial tribunal but went on appeal all the way to the House of Lords. That court looked at the relevant provisions[35] of the Sex Discrimination Act 1975 and did not find them ambiguous; they appeared to permit dismissal where a woman could not carry out her contract of employment. But interpretation in this way was inconsistent with the requirements of Directive 76/207/EEC[36] which did not appear to allow dismissal of a pregnant woman because she could not fulfil her contract. The House of Lords referred questions to the Court of Justice; underlying them was the question of whether the rule of interpretation required an interpretation of the national legislation in a manner consistent with Community law even if that was a forced interpretation of the words of the national legislation. The House of Lords appeared to be sympathetic to the argument that a consistent interpretation should be applied only where the national legislation was on its face open to an interpretation consistent with the Community directive. In others words the only obligation would be to apply an interpretation consistent with Community law where there was an ambiguity, and an interpretation consistent with Community law was one interpretation which could be applied. The Court of Justice does not answer this underlying question directly, but it is clear from the reasoning of the Court that it considered that the rule of interpretation requires an interpretation consistent with Community law save perhaps where the drafting of the national law is such as to indicate that an interpretation consistent with Community law is precluded.

Though most of the case law of the Court of Justice has arisen in relation to national law implementing directives, the rule of interpretation is not limited to such cases and applies whenever interpretation of national law is relevant to the attainments of the objectives of the Community.

---

[34] Case C-106/89 *Marleasing* [1990] ECR I-4135.
[35] i.e. ss. 1(1)(a) and 5(3) of the 1975 Act.   [36] [1976] OJ L39/76.

The Nature of the Council of Europe

The aim of the Council of Europe, which came into being on 3 August 1949, is 'to achieve a greater unity between its Members for the purpose of safeguarding and realising the ideals and principles which are their common heritage and facilitating their economic and social progress'.[37] This aim is to be pursued 'through the organs of the Council by discussion of questions of common concern and by agreements and common action in economic, social cultural, scientific, legal and administrative matters and in the maintenance and further realisation of human rights and fundamental freedoms'.[38] Under Article 3 of the Statute every Member State must 'accept the principles of the rule of law and of the enjoyment by all persons within its jurisdiction of human rights and fundamental freedoms'.

The Council of Europe sponsored the European Convention on Human Rights, which deals mainly, but not exclusively, with civil and political rights, and the European Social Charter which deals with economic and social questions. The Council of Europe is an international organisation with an intergovernmental character. It now has forty members.[39]

The European Convention on Human Rights

The European Convention[40] was a response to the horrors experienced in Europe in two world wars. This enabled issues which were traditionally considered to be matters within rather than beyond States to be regarded as matters of concern to other States. The Convention largely protects civil and political rights: the right to life, liberty and security; to freedom from torture, inhuman and degrading treatment, slavery, servitude, and forced labour; the right to a fair trial; and freedom of conscience, of speech and of assembly. But there are protections which go beyond traditional civil and political rights: the property rights contained in Article 1 of Protocol 1 and the right to education in Article 2 of that Protocol are good examples.

Under the Convention, Contracting Parties guarantee to all within their jurisdiction, regardless of nationality, the protection of the rights set out in the Convention and the Protocols to which they are a party. How that guarantee is achieved is a matter for each Contracting State. Nearly all States have secured the Convention rights by incorporating the Convention into national law. This means that the Convention has been given the force of national law, and can be pleaded before

---

[37] Statute of the Council of Europe, Art. 1(a).   [38] Statute of the Council of Europe, Art. 1(b).

[39] Albania, Andorra, Austria, Belgium, Bulgaria, Croatia, Cyprus, Czech Republic, Denmark, Estonia, Finland, France, Germany, Greece, Hungary, Iceland, Ireland, Italy, Latvia, Liechtenstein, Lithuania, Luxembourg, the former Yugoslav Republic of Macedonia, Malta, Moldova, Netherlands, Norway, Poland, Portugal, Romania, Russia, San Marino, Slovakia, Slovenia, Spain, Sweden, Switzerland, Turkey, Ukraine and the United Kingdom.

[40] See generally, D. Harris, M. O'Boyle, and C. Warbrick, *Law of the European Convention on Human Rights* (London: Butterworths, 1995); and F. Jacobs, and R. White, *The European Convention on Human Rights*, 2nd edn. (Oxford: Clarendon Press, 1996).

national courts and tribunals. But there is no obligation to incorporate the Convention, and until recently the United Kingdom argued that this was not necessary in order to secure the guarantee contained in Article 1 of the Convention. The Human Rights Act 1998 incorporates the Convention into United Kingdom law in a manner which accommodates strict adherence to the constitutional separation of the role of the judiciary from that of the legislature.[41] The former President of the Court has expressed the advantages of incorporation as follows:

It has in fact two advantages: it provides the national court with the possibility of taking account of the Convention and the Strasbourg case-law to resolve the dispute before it, and at the same time it gives the European organs an opportunity to discover the views of the national courts regarding the interpretation of the Convention and its application to a specific set of circumstances. The dialogue which thus develops between those who are called upon to apply the Convention on the domestic level and those who must do so on the European level is crucial for an effective protection of the rights guaranteed under the Convention.[42]

A unique contribution of the Convention is the system of international protection it offers to individuals. This has developed over the years and has recently been transformed into a wholly judicial procedure applicable to all forty Contracting Parties to the Convention. It is, however, necessary[43] to describe the system of protection both prior to 1 November 1998, and after that date when the amendments made by Protocol 11 came into effect.

The 'old' system of protection

The Convention created two organs 'to ensure the observance of the engagements undertaken by the High Contracting Parties':[44] the European Commission of Human Rights[45] and the European Court of Human Rights.[46] The main function of these two organs, sometimes collectively referred to as the Strasbourg organs,[47] is to deal with applications made by States and by individuals alleging violations of the Convention. Under Article 24, any State party to the Convention may refer to the Commission any alleged breach of the provisions of the Convention by another State party. Under Article 25, the Commission may receive applications from any person, non-governmental organisation, or group of individuals claiming to be the victim of a violation by one of the Member States of the rights set forth in the Convention and any relevant Protocols. Initially, acceptance of the jurisdiction of the Commission to receive individual petitions was optional, but in recent years it

---

[41] See below.

[42] R. Ryssdal, Speech at the ceremony for the 40th anniversary of the European Convention on Human Rights at Trieste, 18 December 1990 (Council of Europe document Cour (90) 318), p. 2.

[43] Because Commission decisions and reports will continue to have influence on the development of Convention rights after 1 November 1998.   [44] Art. 19 ECHR.

[45] Referred to in this chapter as 'the Commission'.

[46] Referred to in this chapter as 'the Court of Human Rights'.

[47] Together with the Committee of Ministers: see below.

has come to be an expected requirement of participation in the Convention system. The procedure differs depending on whether the application is made under Article 24 or 25; what follows describes the process in relation to individual applications under Article 25.

Once an application is registered,[48] the Commission first considers, and issues a decision on, whether the application meets the admissibility requirements.[49] If it does not, that is an end of the matter. If the application is declared admissible, the Commission goes on to conduct and investigation into the merits of the complaint and to consider whether there has been a violation of the Convention. The result is a report from the Commission expressing an opinion[50] as to whether or not there has been a violation. The report is communicated on a confidential basis to the applicant and to the State concerned and is delivered to the Committee of Ministers, the political organ of the Council of Europe. Throughout this time, attempts will have been made to secure a friendly settlement 'on the basis of respect for human rights'.[51]

Final decisions on cases on which the Commission has reported and which have not resulted in a friendly settlement are made by the Committee of Ministers, or the Court of Human Rights. Recognition of the jurisdiction of the Court is technically voluntary under Article 46 of the Convention, but in recent years there has been a clear expectation that Contracting Parties will recognise the competence of the Court.[52] Within three months of the transmission of the Commission report to the Committee of Ministers, the application can be referred to the Court for determination by the Commission, the defendant State, or the State whose national is alleged to be the victim.[53] The applicant has no standing to refer the application to the Court, unless the defendant State is a party to Protocol 9.[54] Where this is so, the applicant may refer the matter to the Court, but (unless it is also referred to the Court by the Commission or a State) it must first be submitted to a panel of three judges, who can decide unanimously that the application shall not be considered by the Court because it does not raise a serious question affecting the interpretation or application of the Convention.

If the case is referred to the Court and heard by it, there is a full judicial procedure, and even where Protocol 9 has not been ratified, some accommodations have been made which allow limited participation by the applicant. The Court sits in plenary session or in Chambers of nine.[55] Decisions are made by a majority of the judges present and voting, with the President enjoying a casting vote if this is necessary. Separate opinions may be attached to the judgment of the majority.

Those cases which are not referred to the Court within three months of transmission of the Commission's report to the Committee of Ministers are automatically referred to the Committee of Ministers for final decision. The practice of the

---

[48] About 400 applications a year have been made against the United Kingdom in recent years.
[49] See below.   [50] This is not legally binding.   [51] Art. 28 ECHR.
[52] And this has happened.   [53] Art. 48 ECHR.
[54] Twenty-four Contracting Parties (not including the United Kingdom) have ratified Protocol 9.
[55] Art. 43 ECHR.

Committee of Ministers in recent years has been to endorse the Commission report without any further investigation of the merits of the case.

The use of a political organ was a compromise to ensure that all applications resulted in a final determination. In the early years, there were States which had not recognised the competence of the Court, and there have always been cases which no one has referred to the Court.

The 'new' system of protection

Protocol 11 has amended the Convention to make provision for a new wholly judicial system of determination of applications. The Commission and the Court have been replaced from 1 November 1998 by a new permanent Court, which handles both the admissibility and merits phases of application. The Court is also charged with seeking to secure friendly settlement of matters before it.

Individual applications are made to the Court under Article 34[56] and individuals have full standing before the Court. There will, undoubtedly continue to be a filtering process by Court staff before applications are registered. In 1997 the Commission opened 12,469 provisional files, but only registered 4,749 applications.[57] The difference in the figures is explained by the practice of the Commission Secretariat of explaining in correspondence why certain applications are destined to fail—for example, because the complaint is made about a State which is not a party to the Convention or the violation alleged is not of a right protected by the Convention.[58] Complaints are initially considered by a three-judge committee which will consider whether the application meets the Convention's admissibility criteria,[59] but it can only rule an application to be inadmissible if it is unanimous.[60] These criteria have not changed and flow from the terms of Articles 34 and 35 and involve the consideration of nine questions:

(1) Can the applicant claim to be a victim?
(2) Is the defendant State a party to the Convention?
(3) Have domestic remedies been exhausted?
(4) Is the application filed within the six-month time limit?
(5) Is the application signed?
(6) Has the application been brought before?
(7) Is the application compatible with the Convention?
(8) Is the application manifestly ill-founded?
(9) Is there an abuse of the right of petition?

[56] All reference in this section are to provisions of the European Convention as amended by Protocol 11.
[57] Council of Europe, *European Commission of Human Rights: Survey of Activities and Statistics 1997*.
[58] See E. Fribergh, 'The Commission Secretariat's Handling of Provisional Files' in F. Matscher, and H. Petzold, (eds.), *Protecting Human Rights: The European Dimension. Essays in Honour of Gérard Wiarda*, (Köln: Carl Heymans Verlag KG, 1990), p. 181.
[59] Arts. 27–28 ECHR. For a discussion of the conditions of admissibility, see F. Jacobs and R. White, *The European Convention on Human Rights*, 2nd edn. (Oxford: Clarendon Press, 1996), pp. 346–68.
[60] Art. 28 ECHR.

In recent years somewhere around one in four to one in seven applications has been declared admissible, though over the life of the Convention fewer than one in ten applications has progressed beyond the admissibility phase.

Those cases which are not ruled inadmissible by the three judge committee are put before a seven judge chamber of the Court, which will include the judge sitting in respect of the defendant State. The chamber will consider the written arguments of the parties, investigate the material facts if these are in contention, and hear oral argument. This stage of the proceedings concludes with a decision whether the complaint is admissible and whether a friendly settlement is possible.[61] There follows a consideration of the merits. In some cases, no doubt the admissibility and merits phases will be joined.

Certain cases of special difficulty can be referred by a chamber to a Grand Chamber of seventeen judges.[62]

Incorporating the European Convention in the United Kingdom

The Human Rights Act 1998 which is expected to enter into force late in 1999 or early in 2000 has incorporated the European Convention into United Kingdom law. The Act is a clever and elegant piece of legislation which carefully accommodates the constitutional traditions of the United Kingdom. There are, however, some problematic provisions whose interpretation by the courts will be needed.

The United Kingdom has, of course, been a party to the Convention since its entry into force, and the Government would argue that the United Kingdom record of legislative compliance with its requirements is good. Despite that, there is an improved system of pre-legislative scrutiny. Under section 19, the minister responsible for any Bill put before Parliament must either make a statement of compatibility indicating that the provisions of the Bill are consistent with Convention rights, or decline to make a statement of compatibility but nevertheless indicate that the Government wishes to proceed with the Bill. Either statement must be in writing and must be published. Critics of the Bill would argue that without some form of Human Rights Commission[63] the level of scrutiny is unlikely to be as thorough as is necessary to secure compliance with the Convention in every case.

The substantive articles of the Convention and Protocols to which the United Kingdom is party are restated[64] as provisions of United Kingdom law with the exception of Article 13.[65] The rights listed in Schedule 1 are known as 'Convention

---

[61] Arts. 29 and 38 ECHR.   [62] Arts. 30–31 and 43 ECHR.
[63] An official and independent body composed of experts charged with advancing human rights in the United Kingdom.   [64] See the Human Rights Act 1998, s. 1, Sch. 1.
[65] Art. 13 provides: 'Everyone whose rights and freedoms as set forth in this Convention are violated shall have an effective remedy before a national authority notwithstanding that the violation has been committed by persons acting in an official capacity'. The significance of the omission of Art. 13 is discussed below.

rights'. Under section 6(1) of the Act, it is unlawful for any public authority to 'act in a way which is incompatible with a Convention right'. Public authorities include a court or tribunal, and 'any person certain of whose functions are functions of a public nature',[66] but does not include either House of Parliament. There remains considerable uncertainty as to the ambit of the term 'public authority', and clearly flesh will need to be given to this term by case law. Under section 7 any person who claims that a public authority has acted in a manner which is incompatible with a Convention right may bring proceedings against the authority in a court of tribunal as determined by rules to be made under the Act.[67] Equally any party to proceedings can rely on a Convention right in any legal proceedings. Applicants bringing judicial review proceedings will have standing if they are, or would be, considered a victim of a violation under Article 34 of the Convention.[68]

Whenever Convention rights are in issue, new rules of interpretation come into play. First, in determining whether there has been a violation of a Convention right, a court or tribunal must 'take into account'[69] case law of the Commission, Court of Human Rights and Committee of Ministers. Furthermore, in interpreting any primary or secondary legislation whenever enacted, the court or tribunal must 'so far as it is possible to do so, read and give effect to that legislation in a way which is compatible with the Convention rights'.[70]

If a court or tribunal concludes that there has been a violation of the Convention, 'it may grant such relief or remedy, or make such order, within its jurisdiction as it considers just and appropriate'.[71] This is an enabling provision giving courts and tribunals powers similar to those enjoyed by the Court of Human Rights under Article 41 of the Convention to afford just satisfaction to a victim of a violation. One problem is that Convention case law on the nature of just satisfaction is not well developed or entirely consistent.[72] However, damages can only be awarded by those courts or tribunals which have power to award damages, or to order the payment of compensation, in civil proceedings.[73]

The failure to incorporate Article 13, which guarantees a right to a remedy in national law, may be problematic here. The Government position in Parliamentary debates was that the whole Act meets the requirements of Article 13, and there was concern that its incorporation might give all courts and tribunal sweeping new powers to grant remedies which would be inappropriate. Much will be depend on the content of the rules to be made under the Act which will assign jurisdiction to particular courts and tribunals. An example might help to illustrate the possible lacuna. Suppose a claimant before a social security appeal tribunal succeeds in persuading the tribunal that there has been an excessive delay in giving judgment

---

[66] See s. 6(3) of the 1998 Act.

[67] Where the alleged violation is by a judicial act, the point can only be taken on appeal from that court or tribunal, or by way of judicial review: ibid., s. 9(1).

[68] See F. Jacobs and R. White, *The European Convention on Human Rights*, 2nd edn. (Oxford: Clarendon Press, 1996), pp. 349–52.   [69] See s. 2(1) of the 1998 Act.

[70] Ibid., s. 3(1).   [71] Ibid., s. 8(1).

[72] D. Harris, M. O'Boyle and C. Warbrick, *Law of the European Convention on Human Rights* (London: Butterworths, 1995), pp. 682–8.   [73] Ibid., s. 8(2).

on an appeal.[74] In this type of case, the Court of Human Rights has often awarded some compensation for the delay, but a social security appeal tribunal has no power to award compensation, or interest on late benefit. This would leave the individual without a remedy unless the mere statement that there was a violation was considered sufficient in the circumstances of the case. Any claim for compensation would have to be the subject of separate (and wholly novel) proceedings in a different forum. It is at least arguable that making a person in this position go to two judicial bodies for a remedy for the same violation is a failure to provide an effective remedy.

Where the new rules of interpretation do not enable a court or tribunal to read and give effect to primary legislation in a way which is compatible with the Convention rights, the declaration of incompatibility comes into play. Section 4(2) provides that a court which is satisfied that a provision of primary legislation is incompatible with a Convention right 'may make a declaration of incompatibility'. For England and Wales, the following courts have power to make such a declaration: the High Court, Court of Appeal, House of Lords, Judicial Committee of the Privy Council, and the Courts-Martial Appeal Court. Where a lesser court or a tribunal is faced with such an issue, it must apply the 'incompatible' legislation and the matter will have to be taken on appeal until a court with the power is reached. In employment and social security cases, that may mean taking two appeals, since neither the Employment Appeal Tribunal[75] nor the Social Security Commissioners[76] have this power.

The declaration of incompatibility is the solution to the dilemma of having judges declaring legislation invalid, which was seen to be an interference by judges in the role of the legislature. The declaration of incompatibility does not affect the validity, continuing operation or enforcement of the provision, and is not binding on the parties to the proceedings in which it is made.[77] Its effect is to prompt the legislature to consider making a remedial order under section 11. This is a fast track legislative procedure designed to remove the incompatibility at the heart of a court's declaration. Again critics of the Act argue that there is a role for a Human Rights Commission to assist in ensuring that any defect is fully corrected.

The incorporation of the Convention does not in any way deprive those who believe they are victims of violations of the Convention from making applications to the Court in Strasbourg. They would, of course, be required to show that they have used all domestic remedies available to them, including appeals, to seek a resolution in the national forum before such an application would be declared admissible.

The incorporation of the Convention will require many more lawyers to gain familiarity with the substance of Convention rights and with the Convention case law. The need for education in the law of the Convention is recognised by lawyers.[78]

---

[74] This would constitute a violation of Art. 6(1) ECHR.   [75] See Ch. 15.
[76] See Ch. 14.   [77] See s. 4(6) of the 1998 Act.
[78] G. Chambers, *Practising Human Rights: UK Lawyers and the European Convention on Human Rights*, the Law Society Research and Policy Planning Unit Research Study No. 28 (London: the Law Society, 1998).

At present there is a very small number of solicitors and barristers who would describe themselves as specialists in this area, and many who do so describe themselves have handled few applications to the Strasbourg organs. Despite this, human rights arguments based on the Convention have featured in British courts, though often under the guise of protecting fundamental rights under the common law.[79] One author has counted 472 English cases in which reference has been made to the European Convention with many more references being made to the Convention since 1990 than before that year.[80] So even the unincorporated Convention has generated judicial activity. Its incorporation is likely to lead to much more significant judicial consideration of human rights in our courts and tribunals.

Influences

Methods of interpretation

The traditional task of the judges in seeking to give meaning to the words of primary or secondary legislation has been said to be to give effect to the ordinary and natural meaning of those words taken in context, resolving any ambiguities in a way which avoids conflict with the purpose of the legislation.[81] In dealing with legislation concerning either the law of the European Union or of the European Convention on Human Rights, there is now a significantly different rule. The search is for a possible—and not necessarily the obvious—interpretation which is consistent either with Community law or with Convention rights. One judge has suggested that there is a 'rebuttable presumption in favour of an interpretation consistent with Convention rights'.[82] The same principle applies to legislation touching on issues of Community law.

Since both Community law and Convention law are so pervasive, it is realistic to predict that the application of methods of interpretation arising in this context are likely to affect the approach to interpretation in contexts where no such issues arise. In other words, there will be a much more marked shift from an emphasis on the ordinary and natural meaning of words to one which emphasises the purpose of the legislation.

A requirement to produce an interpretation of national law which is consistent either with Community law or with the requirements of the European Convention on Human Rights, as well as a more general move to purposive interpretation, will require decision-makers to develop skills in determining the underlying purpose of the legislation they are interpreting. In the case of Community law, there

---

[79] See M. Beloff and H. Mountfield, 'Unconventional Behaviour? Judicial Uses of the European Convention in England and Wales' [1996] EHRLR 467.

[80] M. Hunt, *Using Human Rights Law in English Courts* (Oxford: Hart Publishing, 1997), pp. 325–84.

[81] See R. Cross, *Statutory Interpretation*, 3rd edn. by J. Bell and G. Engle (London: Butterworths, 1995), ch. 3.

[82] Lord Steyn, 'Incorporation and Devolution—A Few Reflections on the Changing Scene' (1998) 2 EHRLR 153, 155.

is a considerable body of secondary legislation adding detail to the broad statements in the Treaty; there is a substantial case law from the Luxembourg courts to assist in interpreting Treaty provisions and secondary legislation. The task is rather harder in the case of Convention rights, since there is nothing equivalent to the secondary legislation of the European Union institutions. There are only the broadly drafted provisions of the Convention and the case law. This is substantial, but it is often not as specific or coherent as the case law emerging from the Luxembourg courts. What is clear is that both the Luxembourg courts and the Strasbourg organs adopt a highly purposive[83] approach to the interpretation respectively of provisions of European Union law, and the Convention, which sometimes offends those wedded to a much more literal approach to interpretation.

Effective enjoyment of rights

Both the European Union and the European Convention system place considerable stress on the importance of securing effective enjoyment of the rights granted by the founding treaties.

In European Union law, this principle finds its clearest expression in the development of use of Community law by individuals. So, individuals can use the provisions of regulations before national courts just as they use rights granted to them by national legislation. Individuals can also plead provisions of a directive against the State either if that directive has not been implemented or if the national implementation is in some way defective. The two key requirements are that the directive must contain a right for individuals which is spelled out in a sufficiently clear and precise manner and that the date set for the implementation of the directive has passed.

The ability only to be able to plead the provisions of directives against the State (or a body whose functions are equated to the State) leaves those who wish to assert their rights against others in a disadvantageous position. Where the directive has been implemented in some form, the rule of interpretation is particularly valuable, since the individual can argue for an interpretation of the national legislation in a manner consistent with Community law (even if that interpretation is not the most obvious interpretation of the words of the national law). Finally, through the application of what is generally known as the *Francovich* principle, Community law requires national law to provide a remedy for losses suffered by individuals as a result of a failure by a Member State to apply Community law to their situation.[84]

The doctrine of the supremacy of Community law requires national courts to 'disapply' even primary legislation which is inconsistent with the requirements of Community law.[85]

---

[83] Or teleological.
[84] T. Hartley, *The Foundations of European Community Law*, 4th edn. (Oxford: Oxford University Press, 1998), pp. 226–32.
[85] Ibid., pp. 224–6.

Similar principles can be found in the case law of the Strasbourg organs in relation to the European Convention on Human Rights. In a whole series of cases, the Court of Human Rights has stressed the need to provide remedies which are 'practical and effective' as distinct form being 'theoretical and illusory'.[86] Given the experience of United Kingdom courts in handling European Community law, it would be very surprising if a similar approach to Convention rights following the entry into force of the Human Rights Act 1998 were not followed.

Proportionality

The principle of proportionality is central to both European Union law and to the law of the European Convention. Both systems grant freedoms or guarantee rights subject to exceptions in limited circumstances. Both the Luxembourg courts and the Strasbourg organs have stressed that interferences with freedoms or rights must be the minimum necessary to secure a legitimate objective justifying the interference.

The Treaty of Amsterdam has added a Protocol on the application of the principles of subsidiarity[87] and proportionality, which refers to proportionality as the requirement that any action by the Community must not go beyond what is necessary to achieve the objectives of the Treaty. It is, however, clear from the case law of the Court of Justice that the principle also applies to the legitimacy of the burdens imposed by Community law, and in assessing action by Member States within the scope of the Treaty.[88] A good example in the latter context is the case concerning the United Kingdom rules on importing UHT milk.[89] The United Kingdom authorities required importers to have a licence arguing that this was necessary to police health requirements. They also required the milk to be packed in a dairy approved by the competent local authority, which had the effect of requiring the milk to be treated and packed in the United Kingdom. The requirements were clear exceptions to the rules relating to the free movement of goods, which could only be justified if it could be shown that the measures were strictly necessary for the protection of the health and life of humans. The Court ruled that such restrictive measures were not needed (and so were disproportionate to the harm sought to be avoided) to secure the protection of health and were unlawful. Consumers could be protected by requiring importers to produce certificates from the competent authorities in the Member State of export, and a sampling system could check the quality of the imported milk.

The issue of proportionality is deeply embedded in the European Convention. Many articles express a right in the first paragraph, but subject the enjoyment of

---

[86] F. Jacobs and R. White, *The European Convention on Human Rights*, 2nd edn. (Oxford: Clarendon Press, 1996), pp. 35–8, and authorities cited there.

[87] In areas not within the exclusive competence of the Community, it will only take action where the objectives of any proposed action cannot be sufficiently achieved by action of the Member States and where action by the Community is required: Art. 3b EC.

[88] See generally J. Usher, *General Principles of EC Law* (London: Longman, 1998), ch. 3.

[89] Case 124/81 *Commission* v. *United Kingdom* [1983] ECR 203.

the right to limitations expressed in a second paragraph. A typical example is Article 8 concerning the right to respect for private and family life:

1. Everyone has the right to respect for his private and family life, his home and his correspondence.

2. There shall be no interference by a public authority with the exercise of this right except such as is in accordance with the law and is necessary in a democratic society in the interests of national security, public safety or the economic well-being of the country, for the prevention of disorder or crime, for the protection of health or morals, or for the protection of the rights and freedoms of others.

In many claims of violations of this article (and other similar articles), the case turns on whether an interference with the right is justified under paragraph 2. This involves enquiry into the required legal basis for the interference, which must be 'in accordance with the law' and for a specified legitimate aim. In many cases these conditions can readily be satisfied, but the enquiry then moves on to consider whether the interference is 'necessary in a democratic society'. The Court has said that meeting this test requires the identification of a pressing social need demanding action, and asking whether that action is 'proportionate to the legitimate aim pursued'. This requires consideration of whether the interference with the Convention right is the minimum interference necessary to address the pressing social need.[90]

One result of the incorporation of the European Convention by the Human Rights Act 1998 will be that national courts will be asked to consider these question with much greater frequency than at present. A major jurisdiction will be judicial review.[91] Currently the Divisional Court will only interfere with decisions of Government where those decisions are '*Wednesbury* unreasonable' which means that the decisions are such that no body, fully informed on the relevant issue and acting with due appreciation of its responsibilities, could reasonably have come to the decision being challenged.[92] This is a very different test from that of proportionality. Yet the latter test is the one which the Divisional Court will need to apply where Convention rights are in issue. I would predict that this will result, over time, in a shift of emphasis in the judicial review jurisdiction away from *Wednesbury* unreasonableness towards proportionality as the test applied in all cases.

Due process and fair trial

Due process is in many ways at the heart of both European Union Law and the European Convention, but it receives its most explicit expression in the European Convention. One scholar has described it as being the unifying theme of the

---

[90] F. Jacobs and R. White, *The European Convention on Human Rights*, 2nd edn. (Oxford: Clarendon Press, 1996), ch. 19, and the authorities cited there.   [91] See Ch. 16.

[92] See A. Bradley and K. Ewing, *Constitution and Administrative Law*, 12th edn. (London: Longman, 1997), pp. 773–80.

European Convention and its interpretation by the Court of Human Rights.[93] Due process involves, according to Gearty's analysis, concern for procedural fairness at three different levels of generality.[94] First, there is technical due process which is embodied in the concept of a fair trial in Article 6 and in the procedures surrounding lawful deprivations of liberty under Article 5. Secondly, there are the procedural safeguards which the Convention requires before an interference with the rights of vulnerable groups will be lawful. Thirdly, argues Gearty, the Court decisions on freedom of expression, assembly and association can be seen as concerned with 'a kind of fair play for society'.[95]

Transparency of reasons for actions is inherent in this approach, since otherwise there may be difficulties in showing that interferences with rights protected by the Convention are 'necessary in a democratic society'. European Union law also requires legislative acts to be reasoned,[96] and has stated that national authorities must give reasons for decisions which impact upon Community rights so that they may be challenged in national courts if they are considered to breach the requirements of Community law. The *Heylens* case[97] concerned a Belgian national who was a football trainer. He held a Belgian diploma in football training. He was prosecuted in France for engaging in professional football training without the diploma required by French law or any qualification recognised as equivalent. Heylens had applied for recognition of his Belgian diploma, but this had been refused without any reasons being given. On a preliminary reference from the French court, the Court of Justice said that a decision refusing to recognise qualifications issued in another Member State must be reasoned and must be subject to judicial review in order that the legality of the decision under Community law could be considered.[98]

The concept of fair trial is to be found in Article 6 of the European Convention and is a central article in the scheme of protection provided by the European Convention. In one survey, half of all applications made against the United Kingdom were made under this article.[99] It is one of the best examples of detailed standard setting for the legal system of the Contracting States. The Strasbourg organs have indicated that Article 6(1) demands not only an overall requirement of a fair hearing but also the presence of specific features in order for there to be a fair trial. The overall requirement has been summarised as follows:

The effect of Article 6(1) is, *inter alia,* to place the 'tribunal' under a duty to conduct a proper examination of the submissions, arguments and evidence adduced by the parties, without prejudice to its assessment of whether they are relevant to its decision.[100]

---

[93] C. Gearty, 'The European Court of Human Rights and the Protection of Civil Liberties: An Overview' (1993) 52 CLJ 89.   [94] Ibid., 98.

[95] Ibid., 99.   [96] Art. 190 EC.   [97] Case 222/86 *Heylens* [1987] ECR 4097.

[98] See similarly Case C-340/89 *Vlassopoulou* [1991] ECR I-2379, which concerned a decision by German authorities concerning the legal qualifications of a Greek national.

[99] G. Chambers, *Practising Human Rights: UK Lawyers and the European Convention on Human Rights,* the Law Society Research and Policy Planning Unit Research Study No. 28 (London: the Law Society, 1998).

[100] *Kraska* v. *Switzerland*, judgment of 19 April 1993, Series A, No. 254-B; (1994) 18 EHRR 188, para. 30 of the judgment.

Four features inherent in the concept of a fair trial have flowed from this general notion of a fair trial.

The first and perhaps most important is the concept of *égalité des armes,* which translates inelegantly into English as 'equality of arms'. In English law, it is an aspect of the requirement of natural justice. It requires that each party has a broadly equal opportunity to present a case in circumstances which do not place one of the parties as a substantial disadvantage as regards the opposing party.[101]

Secondly, there must be a judicial process, which requires each side to have the opportunity to have knowledge of and comment on the observations filed or evidence adduced by the opposing party.[102] Non-disclosure of material by one side to the other is likely to give rise to violations of this feature of a fair trial, as might issues of the circumstances in which evidence was acquired.

Thirdly, there is a requirement for a reasoned decision, which is regarded as implicit in the notion of a fair trial. The level of reasoning need not be detailed. If a court gives reasons, then the requirement for a reasoned decision is *prima facie* met, but a decision which on its face shows that it was made on a basis not open to the judge cannot be said to be a reasoned decision.[103]

The final issue is whether a trial can be fair if there is no right of appearance in person. In general, entitlement to appear in person will be required in criminal cases. The law, however, remains in a state of development and the Court has yet to pronounce in detail on this in civil cases, but the Commission has held that in some cases a fair trial is only possible in the presence of the parties. An example would be a case where the personal character and manner of life of a person are directly relevant to the formation of the court's opinion on the point at issue.

There are four specific features of a fair trial to be found on the face of Article 6. First, trial must be before 'an independent and impartial tribunal established by law'. This requirement includes a subjective and an objective element. The subjective test involves an enquiry into whether the particular judge in the case was actually biased, or lacking in independence or impartiality. Propriety will be presumed in the absence of specific evidence of bias. The objective test involves determination of whether the court or tribunal offers guarantees sufficient to exclude any legitimate doubt about its impartiality or independence. This can include both specific difficulties caused by certain persons being involved in particular decisions, as well as what might be called structural problems with the forum for the resolution of the dispute.[104] A good example of structural problems can be found in the cases concerning English courts-martial, which have determined that the (then existing) role of the convening officer in the management of the prosecution case conflicted

---

[101] See *Dombo Beheer BV* v. *The Netherlands,* judgment of 27 October 1993, Series A, No. 274-A; (1994) 18 EHRR 213, para. 33 of the judgment.

[102] *Ruiz-Mateos* v. *Spain,* judgment of 23 June 1993, Series A, No. 262; (1993) 16 EHRR 505, para. 63 of the judgment.

[103] See *De Moor* v. *Belgium,* judgment of 23 June 1994, Series A, No. 292-A; (1994) 18 EHRR 372.

[104] See generally F. Jacobs and R. White, *The European Convention on Human Rights,* 2nd edn. (Oxford: Clarendon Press, 1996), pp. 137–40, and D. Harris, M. O'Boyle and C. Warbrick, *Law of the European Convention on Human Rights* (London: Butterworths, 1995), pp. 230–9.

with his role as convenor of the court-martial, in particular his appointment of its members (who were subordinate in rank to himself and fell within his chain of command).[105]

Secondly, publicity is seen as one of the guarantees of the fairness of a trial, but the requirement for hearings to be in public is surrounded by a substantial list of circumstances in which the presumption of public hearings is displaced. A written procedure may suffice provided that there are proper opportunities for requesting or ordering an oral hearing.

Thirdly, Article 6(1), on its face, requires that judgment is pronounced publicly, and this requirement is not expressed to be subject to the list of limitations which apply to a public trial. The leading case is *Pretto*.[106] The Court seems to have been very accommodating to a wide range of practice in this regard among the Contracting States, indicating that the form of publicity to be given to a judgment is to be assessed in the light of special features of particular proceedings. It certainly appears to be the case that nothing more than the formal disposition need be announced publicly, and it seems that the public availability of the outcome is as important as the matter being read out in open court. So in the *Pretto* case, the availability to the public of the disposition in the court registry was considered to meet the requirements for public pronouncement of the judgment.

Lastly, under Article 6(1), litigants are entitled to judgments in a reasonable time. Complaints of violations of this requirements have been the single most numerous sort of alleged violation of the Convention. Such cases have rarely involved the United Kingdom.[107] Though the case law is voluminous, the principles can be stated quite simply. The first task is to determine the period or periods in issue, before moving on to consider the reasonableness of the length of the proceedings. The period in issue will include any appellate proceedings. In forming judgments on the reasonableness of the length of the proceedings, the following factors are relevant: the complexity of the case, the behaviour of the applicant, the conduct of the judicial authorities, and what is at stake for the applicant. However, backlogs of judicial business are not a defence to unreasonable delays.

Article 6 does not require Contracting States to have a system of appeals from decisions at first instance but if the State does provide a system of appeals, it too must comply with the guarantees to be found in Article 6(1).[108] It follows that a defect at first instance might be corrected at the appellate stage of the proceedings. Where there is an appeal, the requirement to exhaust domestic remedies before a complaint can be made under the Convention means that it must be used, and it will then be the totality of the domestic proceedings which is considered by the Commission and Court.

---

[105] See *Findlay* v. *United Kingdom*, judgment of 25 February 1997; (1997) 24 EHRR 221; and *Coyne* v. *United Kingdom*, judgment of 24 September 1997.

[106] *Pretto and others* v. *Italy*, judgment of 8 December 1983, Series A, No. 71; (1984) 6 EHRR 182.

[107] But see *Robins* v. *United Kingdom*, judgment of 23 September 1997.

[108] *De Cubber* v. *Belgium*, judgment of 26 October 1984, Series A, No. 86; (1985) 7 EHRR 236, para. 32 of the judgment; and *Fedje* v. *Sweden*, judgment of 26 September 1991, Series A, No. 212-C; (1994) 17 EHRR 14, para. 32 of the judgment.

The Court has recognised that Article 6 must contain a right of access to a court for the determination of a particular issue. So the (then existing) prohibition in English Prison Rules on bringing a defamation action against a prison officer who had allegedly accused the prisoner wrongly of having assaulted him violated this right.[109] The right might even include a right to some sort of representation in order to make the right effective. In the *Airey* case[110] the applicant had been unable to find a lawyer to act for her because of her financial position and the absence of legal aid. She needed a separation order to protect her from her husband who was prone to violence towards her. The procedure was complex and not such as could be managed effectively by a litigant in person. The Court concluded that, in such circumstances, Article 6 requires the provision of legal assistance where 'such assistance proves indispensable for an effective access to court'.[111] The case is sometimes wrongly read too sweepingly as imposing an obligation on a State to have a legal aid scheme, at least for complex litigation. The judgment is rather more limited; it will be necessary to look at the nature of the right being protected by the litigation, what is at stake for the applicant, and the complexity of the procedure before the particular decision-making body in making a judgment as to whether Article 6 requires a State to provide legal assistance.

Concluding Comment

The nature of both European Union law and the incorporated European Convention on Human Rights is such that new rights for individuals have been developed which can be argued before English courts and tribunals. European Union law is in many ways more developed, because if a national court or tribunal requires an authoritative opinion on the interpretation or validity of Community law, it can adjourn the proceedings and make a reference to the Court of Justice in Luxembourg. By contrast, where a Convention right is raised, the national court or tribunal must come to a conclusion on the issue aided by past case law, but without the ability to raise questions of the Court of Human Rights as to the interpretation of Convention rights.[112] The range of issues which may be raised is very wide indeed; some examples have already been given in this chapter. Where they relate to Convention rights, those issues will, in future, be able to be argued before the English courts and tribunals.

There has been a tendency to insulate considerations of the operation of the legal system from the impact of European law, both in its European Union and

---

[109] *Golder* v. *United Kingdom*, judgment of 21 February 1975, Series A, No. 18; (1979–80) 1 EHRR 524.

[110] *Airey* v. *Ireland*, judgment of 9 October 1979, Series A, No. 32; (1979–80) 2 EHRR 305.

[111] Ibid., para. 26 of the judgment.

[112] There is an advisory opinion procedure but such opinions may only be sought by the Committee of Ministers and may not deal with questions relating to the content or scope of the rights and freedoms set out in section I of the Convention: Art. 47. Unsurprisingly the procedure has never been used.

European Convention on Human Rights identities. Many English courts and tribunals have become used to dealing with European Community law arguments, and are becoming increasingly skilled in handling them. The European content has increased dramatically as a result of the incorporation of the European Convention into United Kingdom law. There is considerable similarity between key principles of European Union law and European Convention law. One judge of the House of Lords, speaking in December 1997, has commented on the impact of the incorporation of the European Convention in the following terms:

Clearly these are great challenges for the courts. It will be necessary to teach judges new techniques of interpretation and adjudication. Academic lawyers and practitioners will have to educate the judges. The educational task will be incomplete unless it embraces the constitutional underpinning and theoretical foundations of their new tasks. In the House of Lords we are certainly in need of continuing education. After all, it is only a few weeks since we at last acquired a set of reports of the ECHR. You are entitled to wonder how some of those great cases would have been decided if the purchase had been made earlier.[113]

---

[113] Lord Steyn, 'Incorporation and Devolution—A Few Reflections on the Changing Scene' (1998) 2 EHRLR 153, 156.

PART 2

THE CRIMINAL PROCESS

3

UNDERSTANDING THE
CRIMINAL JUSTICE SYSTEM

Introduction

There is no single government department responsible for criminal justice policy. The responsibility is shared among a number of departments, though key departments are the Home Office and the Lord Chancellor's Department. Finding formal statements of government policy on criminal justice is not easy. Early in 1996 the Conservative Government stated that its strategy was:

to ensure that:
- everything possible is done to prevent crime;
- the police have the powers they need to apprehend the guilty;
- procedures are in place to ensure both that the innocent are acquitted and that the guilty are convicted; and
- those who are convicted are dealt with effectively and appropriately.[1]

In its final response to the recommendations of the Royal Commission on Criminal Justice,[2] the Conservative Government indicated that its most important priorities for the criminal justice system were:

maintaining law and order; protecting the public; ensuring that the innocent are acquitted but the guilty convicted; ensuring a proper balance between the interests of the prosecution and the defence; to make the process of justice more rational and less of a game played to arcane rules; improving the treatment of victims and other witnesses; achieving maximum efficiency in the use of available resources; and speeding up as far as possible the delivery of justice.[3]

---

[1] Home Office, *Protecting the Public: The Government's Strategy on Crime in England and Wales* (London: HMSO, 1996), p. 3. [2] See Ch. 5.
[3] Lord Chancellor's Department, Home Office, Law Officer's Department, *Royal Commission on Criminal Justice: Final Government Response, June 1996* (London: Home Office Communications Directorate, 1996), p. 1.

It does not seem that the underlying policies of the new Labour Government will be markedly different, though the tone is slightly different. Writing as Shadow Home Secretary, Jack Straw said:

We need a strategy which first tackles the underlying social and economic inequalities in which crime breeds; secondly, addresses the fear of crime, disorder and community breakdown; thirdly, aims in practical ways to prevent crime; and fourthly, deals more effectively with offenders, so that fewer of them reoffend.[4]

It is clear from these statements that the criminal justice system is seen to involve a variety of institutions and processes. These will encompass the police, lawyers and the courts, both of first instance and those hearing appeals, as well as prisons and the probation service. But are there any aspects of the system which exercise significant influences on the operation of the processes which are generally viewed as constituting the criminal justice system? I would argue that there are two such key influences. The first is a civil libertarian one; generally no one can be compelled to co-operate with the police in the construction of a case against them. The second is the adversarial nature of the criminal trial, which colours the preparation of cases at the pre-trial stages of the process.

Civil Liberties

The democratic traditions of the United Kingdom restrict public interference in private lives.[5] In the area of criminal justice, this means that generally there must be some positive rule entitling the police to require a person to answer questions or admit them to their property, or even to surrender their liberty. Legislation governing police powers sets the boundaries between what is private and what is not, and between the liberty the citizen enjoys and the control the police may exercise. The rule of law seeks to guarantee that the boundaries set by the law are honoured and the courts have a duty to protect the freedoms the citizen enjoys. Many of the freedoms are defined in the European Convention on Human Rights, which contains provisions against torture or inhuman and degrading treatment, against arbitrary arrest and detention, providing for a right to family and private life, to freedom of conscience and of expression.

Those freedoms may now be pleaded before national courts following the incorporation of the Convention into United Kingdom law. Some have predicted that criminal cases will account for almost half of all domestic Convention case law, as

---

[4] J. Straw, 'The Penal System in Crisis' in D. Bean (ed.), *Law Reform for All* (London: Blackstone Press, 1996), p. 34. These views were reflected in New Labour's 1997 Election Manifesto.

[5] See generally D. Feldman, *Civil Liberties and Human Rights in England and Wales*, (Oxford: Clarendon Press, 1993), ch. 1.

defendants argue that aspects of their treatment or of the criminal process itself do not meet up to the standards set out in the Convention.

An Adversarial Process

The second major influence on the shape of the English criminal justice system has been the use of adversarial processes.[6] The main characteristic of the adversarial system is that the presentation of any case is a matter for the prosecutor and the defendant. They prepare their cases with very little court intervention, and they select the evidence they are going to adduce and the witnesses who will establish that evidence. The role of the judge at trial is to act as an umpire to ensure that the rules of procedure and evidence are obeyed by the parties. Evidence is presented by one side and attacked by the other in order to seek to prove the prosecution case or to show that it is flawed. The adversarial nature of the trial impacts upon earlier stages in the criminal process.[7]

The adversarial system is frequently contrasted with the inquisitorial system, which typically involves much greater judicial involvement in the preparation and presentation of the evidence to be considered at the trial. The role of the judge is to build up the dossier which makes up the case to be considered at trial. The judge will take the lead in questioning witnesses who are called by the court rather than the parties, with the lawyers for the parties pursuing their lines of questioning after the initial questioning by the judge. Under the inquisitorial system there is nothing which corresponds exactly to the guilty plea, which in adversarial procedures obviates the need for any proof of guilt.

The Royal Commission on Criminal Justice considered whether there should be a move to more inquisitorial procedures, but rejected this idea.[8] Indeed the Royal Commission noted that the differences between the two systems can be overstated, and Ashworth has also noted that close examination of the criminal process in a number of European countries reveals some convergence between the two approaches.[9] However, the notion that establishing the truth and so securing the conviction of the guilty and the acquittal of the innocent is dependent upon adversarial procedures appears to be deeply rooted in the psyche of British policymakers and lawyers.

The requirements of Articles 5 and 6 of the European Convention on the protection of liberty and on the right to a fair trial apply equally to adversarial and inquisitorial processes, which re-inforces the view that the standards of the two

---

[6] Sometimes referred to as accusatorial processes.   [7] See Ch. 5.

[8] *Report of the Royal Commission on Criminal Justice (Runciman Commission)* (London: HMSO, 1993), ch. 1, paras. 11–15. See also L. H. Leigh and L. Zedner, *A Report on the Administration of Criminal Justice in France and Germany*, Royal Commission Research Study No. 1 (London, HMSO, 1993).

[9] A. Ashworth, *The Criminal Process: An Evaluative Study*, 2nd edn. (Oxford: Oxford University Press, 1998), p. 302.

systems are not so dissimilar. Both are subject to a single set of civil libertarian requirements.

The Rarity of the Contested Trial

The following chapters will guide the reader through the pre-trial, trial and appellate processes in criminal cases. That tour will reveal that few defendants are subjected to the process of trial and so proof of guilt by contested trial before magistrates or judge and jury is the exception rather than the rule. The system is structured to encourage guilty pleas in the lowest level of court possible. As a result something like ninety-seven per cent of criminal business is transacted in the magistrates' courts. It would appear that the initial interaction between the suspect and the police is a principal determinant of later processes. The private interactions of the suspect or defendant with the police, friends, lawyers and even judges seem more important for most defendants than the public process of adjudication seen by the public in the courtroom. With this basic appreciation of the inter-dependence of the various phases of the criminal justice system, we are equipped to consider the operation of the system as a whole. One of the most fruitful ways of looking at the system as a whole is to compare its performance against theoretical models. If a particular model appeals, then adherence to the philosophy behind that model may well justify acceptance of action which, when seen in isolation, would be unlikely to be acceptable.

The notion of central ideals in a criminal justice system is not just the creation of academic comment on the operation of the system. Even though concerned only with the criminal justice system up to the point of trial, the recommendations in the Report of the Royal Commission on Criminal Procedure are based upon the notion of a fundamental balance between the interests of the community in bringing offenders to justice and the rights and liberties of persons suspected of having committed criminal offences.[10] Much of the Report is concerned with constructing a package where new powers for the police in the investigation of offences are carefully balanced by safeguards against their abuse. The Report concludes:

Ultimately however society faces and will always have to face an ineluctable problem. The nature of the criminal justice process is such that there will continue to be areas in which pressures meet, where interests conflict, where checks and safe-guards may have been provided but prove inadequate to deal with a particular situation. The tensions that these pressures create cannot always be relieved by the application of good sense and reconciliation or by ad hoc and informal adjustments. The role of the police in society and their relationship with the public are, in our view, too important for that. If the fundamental balance in pre-trial procedures is to be held firmly and steadily within

---

[10] *Report of the Royal Commission on Criminal Procedure (Philips Commission)* (London: HMSO, 1981, Cmnd. 8092–1).

the limits of public understanding and tolerance, and if the best use is to be made of scarce resources, a critical responsibility falls on Parliament. Our proposal for regulating in a comprehensive statutory framework arrangements for the investigation of offences and the prosecution of offenders affirms that Parliament has the duty of striking the fundamental balance and of keeping it under regular review.[11]

This long quotation quite clearly indicates that there is a political choice as to where the fundamental balance lies, which in turn requires a clear understanding of the objectives of the criminal justice system. The notion of the fundamental balance can also be applied to the trial and appellate stages of the criminal process.

The 1993 Royal Commission on Criminal Justice was also concerned to secure a balance. This time it was between three competing values: the conviction of the guilty, the acquittal of the innocent, and the efficient use of resources. The Report has been subject to considerable criticism for taking a very pragmatic or utilitarian view of its terms of reference which resulted in seriously flawed conclusions.[12]

Modelling the criminal justice system in order to develop improved systems for handling the business of the system is also a concern of the Home Office. The passage of defendants through the police, magistrates' courts, Crown Court and prison systems can then be simulated through a series of stages over a number of years. This enables estimates of future resource needs to be made. More significantly, alternatives can be modelled to see whether the flow of defendants can be speeded up or resources used more efficiently.[13] Two areas of particular concern in recent years have been the effect of committal proceedings on the throughput of defendants and the use of custody on the remand population. Proposals for alternatives to mode of trial proceedings and committal proceedings owe something to the use of such models.

Research and writing in the United Kingdom on theoretical models of criminal justice is comparatively new, but is already leading to new perspectives on the operation of the criminal process.

Models of Criminal Justice

The work of Herbert Packer

Any discussion of models of criminal justice must begin with the work of the American scholar, Herbert Packer, who argued that systems of criminal justice

---

[11] *Report of the Royal Commission on Criminal Procedure (Philips Commission)* (London: HMSO, 1981, Cmnd. 8092–1), at para. 10.16.

[12] See M. McConville, 'An Error of Judgment' and N. Lacey, 'Missing the Wood . . . Pragmatism versus Theory in the Royal Commission' in M. McConville and L. Bridges, *Criminal Justice in Crisis* (Aldershot: Edward Elgar, 1994) at pp. 24 and 33.

[13] P. Morgan, *Modelling the Criminal Justice System*, Home Office Research and Planning Unit Paper 35 (London: HMSO, 1985), and H. Pullinger, *The Criminal Justice System: the Flow Model*, Home Office Research and Planning Unit Paper 36 (London: HMSO, 1986).

could usefully be examined to see to what extent they corresponded with two theoretical models: the due process model and the crime control model.[14]

The due process model is immediately recognisable to most readers as that which corresponds to the rhetoric of the English criminal justice system. The hallmarks of this model are the presumption of innocence and the requirement of proof of guilt beyond all reasonable doubt. At all stages of the process suspects and defendants enjoy safeguards against self-incrimination. There are obstacles in the face of the police and prosecutors which operate as a form of quality control ensuring that the criminal process constantly weeds out all those who appear to be innocent. At the centre of the due process model is the trial stage, which is again marked by restrictions on the introduction of prejudicial material not directly relevant to the offence or of doubtful probative value. Ultimately the due process model accepts that the price paid for the certainty that no innocent person is convicted will be the occasional acquittal of the guilty.

The contrasting crime control model replaces the judicial procedures with administrative procedures and formal processes with informal processes. Great trust is placed on informal fact-finding, that is, what the police know rather than what is admissible in a process of formal adjudication. The conclusions of the police as fact-finders are the principal determinants of guilt. Repression of criminal conduct is seen as the most important function of the criminal process. Criminal procedure becomes geared to the speedy processing of suspects and defendants. The obstacles of the due process model disappear to be replaced by low visibility administrative processing. Packer comments that: 'If there is confidence in the reliability of informal fact-finding activities that take place in the early stages of the criminal process, the remaining stages can be relatively perfunctory'.[15]

The presumption of innocence in the due process model is replaced by an implicit presumption of guilt, so that the police are relied upon by courts to weed out the innocent at the investigation stage.

The crime control model is usually rejected as inapplicable to the English criminal justice system. But the rejection seems premature when the evidence of routine violation of the rules governing the police powers of arrest, search and seizure, and interrogation are considered. Add to this evidence showing how rarely suspects relied on the right of silence[16] and the overwhelming number of guilty pleas, where no proof of guilt is required, where there is currently no independent assessment of the evidence and where there are no adversarial procedures, and the crime control model begins to look remarkably apposite. Perhaps the operation of the system only sometimes corresponds to the rhetoric of due process regarded as the proud heritage of every English citizen.

---

[14] H. Packer, *The Limits of the Criminal Sanction* (Stanford: Stanford University Press, 1968).

[15] Ibid., pp. 160–1.

[16] Prior to the introduction of rules allowing adverse inferences from silence in certain circumstances to be found in the Criminal Justice and Public Order Act 1994, ss. 34–38.

Other models

Packer's models have not gone unchallenged, and other writers have added further models to the two posited by Packer. In his study of the guilty plea in the magistrates' court, that most common phenomenon of the English criminal justice system, Michael King has trawled the literature and identified a further four process models.[17] When taken with the due process and crime control models, King argues that these will provide a multi-theoretical approach which will 'avoid the errors and distortions that may result from total subjectivity or from the use of one ideological viewpoint to the exclusion of all others'.[18] The various models need not be viewed as mutually exclusive; indeed there may be considerable overlap.

The third model identified by King is the medical model. This is based on the social function of rehabilitation. The committing of crimes is a symptom requiring social intervention. Rehabilitation will result in the offender refraining from conduct labelled as criminal. The processes seen in this model are the traditional medical processes of diagnosis, prognosis, treatment and cure. The role of the police and of the courts is to collect appropriate information for evaluation by decision-makers who act in an informed way on the basis of that information to determine the right treatment for the offender. Where custodial sentences are meted out by the courts, these are seen as having a rehabilitative function. This model, along with the due process and crime control models, is most likely to be seen as reflecting the attitudes of regular participants in the criminal process. As such, they are labelled 'participant approaches'. Probation officers and social workers are most likely to subscribe to the medical model. Any who favour this model to the exclusion of others will need to explain why major decisions are left to non-specialist decision-makers: lay justices in the magistrates' courts and juries in the Crown Court.

While the first three models reflect the general attitudes of regular participants in the process, the remaining three models reflect the different views of the process as perceived in the literature of sociology and may be labelled 'social models'. The fourth model is the bureaucratic model, which stresses management considerations. The hallmarks of such a model are the processing of suspects and defendants according to standard procedures by actors independent of political control by the government of the day. Because bureaucratic institutions tend to standardise and streamline procedures to encourage speed and efficiency, rewards are given for co-operation with the system and sanctions are imposed for time-wasting and unnecessary prolonging of procedures. Recording of decisions is seen as important. The role of the various actors—police, lawyers, court staff, probation officers, judges—are seen as complementary with little overlap of function.

The status passage model, the fifth model, relies upon the process of stigmatisation both to indicate the anti-social nature of the behaviour of a suspect or defendant and to strengthen 'cohesiveness among law-abiding members of society'. In

---

[17] M. King, *The Framework of Criminal Justice* (London: Croom Helm, 1981).   [18] Ibid., p. 11.

such a system the ritual aspects of the process involving degradation and isolation of the suspect or defendant have an important role to play. The stigmatisation is usually temporary and acts as a deterrent both to the offender and to others. It is not insignificant in this context that public appearance in court on a criminal charge with the possibility of a report of criminal conduct in a local newspaper is viewed by many defendants as the worst part of their brush with the law.[19]

The final model is the power model whose function is seen as the maintenance of class domination. King describes this model as follows:

This perspective sees the courts and the agents of criminal justice very much as part of the state machinery, a machinery which is dominated by the interests of the ruling class. This does not mean that policemen, lawyers, magistrates, clerks and probation officers are all conspirators in a plot to maintain and perpetuate the dominance of the ruling class, but rather that the state creates the conditions by which through the pursuit of their apparent self-interests each of these groups helps to advance the interests of the state and thus the dominant power elite.[20]

This process is cloaked in some legal rationality. This model is the hardest to visualise, but one feature which can be identified is the narrow range of individuals represented among the judiciary and an official version of the operation of the system which denies its capacity systematically to disadvantage any group or interests.

Michael King's approach is multi-theoretical because he advocates measuring the ideals contained in the three participant approaches against the operation of the criminal justice system to identify 'the gap between aspiration and performance'. The social models may then be deployed because their application may explain why certain ideals are chosen for the system and why there is a gap between aspiration and performance in a given case, particularly where the system appears to be pursuing multiple objectives.

Models as an Aid to Policy-Making

The thumbnail sketches offered above of six process models show just how complex the criminal process is. It is also possible to find evidence in the current system which fits each model, though no single model seems alone adequate to encapsulate the whole system. This is hardly surprising, for the system itself changes gear or mode depending upon such matters as the seriousness of the offence or the intended plea of the defendant. The same data is also subject to differential interpretations. Let us take for example the role of representation of defendants. Under the due process model, the function of representation is seen as a safeguard of the rights of defendants; the lawyer will probe and test the evidence adduced by the

[19] M. King, *The Framework of Criminal Justice* (London: Croom Helm, 1981), pp. 92–5.
[20] Ibid., p. 27.

prosecution against the defendant. Under the crime control model representation may be interpreted as a device for ensuring public confidence in the fairness of the system or in smoothing the way for a guilty plea. Under the medical model representation is part of the exercise of information gathering prior to the determination of the appropriate treatment for the defendant. The lawyer's role in the bureaucratic model is to contribute to the efficient functioning of the system by providing independent advice to defendants which will result in the minimum court time in the processing of defendants. The lawyer knows the rules of the process and can secure client compliance with them, thus contributing to the smooth running of the institution. In the status passage model, the defence lawyer may be called upon to join in the denunciation of the defendant in the kind of statements traditionally offered by way of plea in mitigation. The physical distance placed between defendant and lawyer, even where the defendant is not required to be in the dock, also contribute to the degradation of the defendant. The role of the law can also be fitted into the power model; it is clear that the lawyer has power over the defendant and can tell the defendant what action should be taken in certain situations in the defendant's own best interests. The oppressive conduct by some counsel in their advice to defendants discussed in the material on plea bargaining in Chapter 8 provides a good example of the exercise of power. The irresistibility of the power of expertise is summed up by one defendant in Baldwin and McConville's research:

I never made any decisions, they were all taken for me. I felt I wasn't controlling things with the solicitor and barrister; I was just being dragged along on the tide of what they said. I had to follow a set route all the way through. I couldn't say 'No, I don't want to go down that way', the way it was put there was only one route to follow. It's just like a blind-folded man being guided through a maze; I had to go but I wasn't sure where I was going.[21]

In the above examples the role of representation has been interpreted differently in fitting it into each model. Is one interpretation correct or are there elements of truth in each of the interpretations? What is certain is that interpretations at variance with the official rhetoric of a due process model are easy to sustain. Comparing the operation of the system against theoretical models broadens the conceptual framework for evaluation of the system and invites a broader analysis of the many interactions that go to make up the criminal justice system.

For the policy-maker who is contemplating some reform or change, the device of process models allows a more ready identification of personal value preferences for the system. Thus, if the ideals of the due process model are preferred, the type of reform likely to be seen would be further barriers to the prosecution such as the mandatory exclusion of improperly obtained evidence. The obstacles to the proof of guilt become tougher to protect the liberties of the individual. The ideals of the crime control model would reduce these obstacles and be likely to admit any material indicative of guilt however obtained. The system in England and Wales

---

[21] J. Baldwin and M. McConville, *Jury Trials* (Oxford: Clarendon Press, 1979), pp. 85–6.

is ambivalent on this issue, since it gives judges a broad discretion in-deciding whether to accept improperly obtained evidence.

An Alternative Analysis

The use of process models has provided an aid for measuring the gap between aspiration and performance. This suggests that once the ideals are chosen and the fundamental balance struck, the gap can be measured and changes made to bring aspiration and performance into congruence. This assumes that the gap is caused by aberrations which careful monitoring and tuning of the system can avoid. Doreen McBarnet has argued that this is a false dichotomy. There is a gap, but it is between the rhetoric of the law and its actual operation. In other words the system officially operates in one way while proclaiming that it operates in another way. The defects are therefore no longer aberrational, but become systemic.[22] Under this analysis, it is not the operation of the law which is problematic; it is the law itself. Dr McBarnet concludes:

Focusing . . . on the gap between the law in the books and the law in action, in effect whitewashes the law itself and those who make it. . . . Shifting the focus to the substance of the law places responsibility for the operation of criminal justice . . . squarely on the judicial and political elites who make it.[23]

Let us take a closer look at the arguments used to back up such claims. Even towards the more serious end of the trivial/serious spectrum of crimes, the overwhelming majority of prosecutions result in guilty pleas. Few cases are contested and even fewer are resolved using jury trial. The principal feature of guilty pleas is that the formal protection of due process is almost totally absent. There is no formal consideration or testing of the evidence; the mouthing of the word 'guilty' removes evidential obstacles and virtually forecloses the possibility of appeal. The processes which have resulted in conviction have taken place in the police station where all the evidence shows routine violations of the rules designed to protect the interests of suspects. The response is that the incidence of guilty pleas is justified and represents no more than the accommodation of the criminal justice system to a massive workload. Though there is little research in this area in the United Kingdom, there has been research in the USA on the incidence of plea bargaining by reference to the severity of workloads of courts. This showed that even where court resources were under-utilised, bargains were still struck with the same frequency as in heavily pressed courts.[24]

Does not all this suggest that all the actors in the criminal process—especially the police, lawyers and judges—develop working relationships which emphasise

---

[22] D. McBarnet, *Conviction, Law, The State and the Construction of Justice* (London: Macmillan, 1981).
[23] Ibid., p. 156.
[24] For example, P. Nardulli, 'The Caseload Controversy and the Study of Criminal Courts' (1979) J of Crim. Law and Criminology 89.

co-operation rather than confrontation, and that all work to eliminate the uncertainties and conflict inherent in the trial process? Due process becomes a matter of last resort rather than of first resort. Interaction with the police in the form of admissions and informal advice on plea are greater determinants of a guilty plea than the adversarial process. The police control information exclusively at the early stages of the criminal process and lawyers do not effectively challenge that monopoly on information which in the case of the guilty plea is never broken.

Apologists for the defects in the English criminal justice system will continue to assert that problems arise only as a result of aberrations from the ideal standards of due process, and that where the courts are faced with these aberrations, they are recognised as unlawful actions. The question is raised as to how this condemnation of unlawful action can be seen as consistent with systemic injustice. Adherents to the systemic theory would respond that judges are adept as dealing with such issues. Judges manage the ideological gap between official practice and rhetoric by the process of individualising cases and issues. When faced with a complaint based on a failure to meet the standards required by the rhetoric of the law, they are frequently able to find particular aspects of individual cases allowing the claim to be rejected while at the same time making general statements re-inforcing the rhetoric of the law.

McConville and Baldwin have also taken up the theme of systemic injustice in their examination of the prosecution process.[25] They see the need to change some central features of the system if its defects are to be remedied. The major change seen as necessary is the reduction in the numbers of guilty pleas, which in turn requires changes in the ability of the police 'to decide the fate of the suspect in conditions that they alone control'.[26] The protections demanded by due process must be entrenched so that judges cannot 'strip formal protections of any meaning'. Their conclusions are pessimistic and, of course, there must be real cause for concern if the defects of the criminal justice system are design faults rather than merely 'bugs' in the system. A later study of the role of the defence tended to show that even the defendants' representatives tended to assume their clients' guilt, and through inexperience or inadequate training contributed to re-inforcement of the case constructed against them by the police.[27]

A Principled Approach

An important contribution to the debate on underlying values was made in 1994,[28] and this has taken on added significance in the light of the Government's decision

---

[25] M. McConville and J. Baldwin, *Courts, Prosecution and Conviction* (Oxford: Clarendon Press, 1981).
[26] Ibid., p. 210.
[27] M. McConville and others, *Standing Accused: The Organisation and Practices of Criminal Defence Lawyers in Britain* (Oxford: Clarendon Press, 1994).
[28] A. Ashworth, *The Criminal Process: An Evaluative Study*, 2nd edn. (Oxford: Oxford University Press, 1998).

to incorporate the European Convention on Human Rights into United Kingdom law under the Human Rights Act 1998. Ashworth,[29] discussing the pre-trial stages of the criminal process, argues for a rights-based approach based on the values implicit in the protections to be found in the European Convention. He regards the search for a balance between objectives as misplaced and as giving no clue as to which objectives are to be accorded priority when conflicts arise. He labels this a utilitarian approach. The principled approach would identify key values and require any derogation from them to meet tests of necessity and proportionality. The test of necessity requires that the interference with the key value be explained, reasoned and shown to meet a significant community argument. Proportionality[30] requires that the interference with the key value be the least restrictive to secure the identified community argument which is used to justify the interference. In making the judgments inherent in this test, there would be a place for empirical studies. So Ashworth notes that empirical evidence (which tends to show that there are few ambush defences[31] and that the chances of acquittal in such cases are not greatly increased) would be significant in determining whether limitations should be placed on a suspect's right to decline to answer questions put by the police. In the face of this evidence, it is much harder to justify the introduction of limitations which interfere with the right of an innocent person not to be convicted,[32] than if a utilitarian balancing of values takes place. In his first edition,[33] Ashworth advocates including the leading principles in primary legislation; in his second edition, he notes that the Human Rights Act 1998 enacts key principles as part of English law.

The incorporation of the European Convention has gone some way to including leading principles in primary legislation, since among the Convention rights are those which set standards for the operation of the criminal process; these are now part of English law, and may be pleaded by parties to criminal proceedings.[34]

Concluding Comment

This chapter has tried to encapsulate the arguments of a number of books. The material is important because it sets an agenda for reform depending upon the theory or approach which is accepted and utilised.

The aberrational theory is optimistic because, as the failings of the law in action are recognised, steps can be taken to avoid them for the future. The criminal justice system is seen as essentially healthy and can improve by a process of evolutionary change. The depressing feature of systemic injustice is its official tolerance and

---

[29] A. Ashworth, *The Criminal Process: An Evaluative Study*, 2nd edn. (Oxford: Oxford University Press, 1998), pp. 306–8.   [30] See Ch. 2.

[31] That is, explanations which have not been previously disclosed to the prosecution and which take them by surprise at trial.   [32] The presumption of innocence.

[33] Ibid., p. 299.   [34] See Ch. 2.

acceptance of a system without due process. To cure systemic injustice revolutionary change is needed.

The use of models and theories highlights the central role of the police in our criminal justice system, a centrality found only in few other systems. To note this centrality is not to attack the police. Criticisms of their dominance is as much a criticism of the system as of the police. Indeed the proposals for the now implemented and independent prosecution service were designed to remove one source of conflict in their role.

Ultimately the main question is: are the defects of the English criminal justice system aberrational or systemic? If aberrational, they can be corrected by adjustments to the system; if systemic, the system itself needs to be designed afresh.

4

MAGISTRATES' COURTS AND THE CROWN COURT

Introduction

An appreciation of the distinction between magistrates' courts and the Crown Court is fundamental to an understanding of the criminal process. In essence the distinction is simple: magistrates' courts deal in bulk with less serious or routine crime, including most motoring offences, while the Crown Court deals with a comparatively small number of more serious criminal offences. But beneath this simple distinction is a far more complex difference: the processes by which each court fulfils its functions are dramatically different. It would be quite misleading to think of the process in magistrates' courts as simply a quicker and less formal process than that to be found in the Crown Court.

Magistrates and Magistrates' Courts

There are two types of magistrates: lay magistrates, or justices of the peace (JPs), and stipendiary magistrates. Lay magistrates are amateurs. They are unpaid, though there are allowances for travel, subsistence and loss of earnings. They receive only basic legal training for the exercise of their functions and rely upon a justices' clerk to advise them as to law and procedure and to undertake the administration of the courts. Stipendiaries are professional lawyers who exercise the functions both of lay magistrates and of their clerks. Stipendiary magistrates have a much shorter history than lay magistrates. They first came to be appointed in the eighteenth century as an alternative to corrupt lay magistrates in some urban areas.[1] There are currently ninety-one stipendiaries; most are to be found in London and the rest in large cities

---

[1] E. Moir, *The Justice of the Peace* (Harmondsworth: Penguin, 1969), pp. 127–8, 179, 196–7.

elsewhere.[2] Stipendiaries typically assist where case loads are very high or where court business will run into several days.[3] Though the use of stipendiaries has increased and is likely to continue to do so, their role is seen as supporting rather than superseding the work of the lay magistracy.[4] There are just over 30,000 lay magistrates[5] sitting in about 600 magistrates' courts, each having jurisdiction only in its own area, known as a petty sessional division. About 400 of these are located in rural areas. The bulk of criminal business is conducted in the magistrates' courts in the large towns and cities.

The lay magistracy dates back to the twelfth century and has survived many major reforms of the legal system. It is now seen as a central feature of the English legal system and as a great strength of the criminal process. There is undoubtedly a benefit in involving laymen in the administration of criminal justice. The main benefit is summed up neatly, if somewhat idealistically, by Sir Thomas Skyrme in his book on the magistracy:

The collective views of a cross-section of the population, representing different shades of opinion, can be more effective in dispensing justice acceptable to the public than the decision of a single individual necessarily drawn from a fairly narrow social class and whose experience of local problems may be limited . . . The system enables the citizen to see that the law is his law, administered by men and women like himself, and that it is not the esoteric preserve of lawyers.[6]

Official comment echoes these sentiments:

We consider that the administration of justice at a local level by members of the community may act as a bridge between the public and a court system which might otherwise seem remote.[7]

Magistrates sitting in benches of three (sometimes two)[8] exercise a wide variety of jurisdictions. They try less serious criminal cases; they consider the evidence against those charged with serious offences and determine whether it is sufficient to send them for trial in the Crown Court; they deal with applications for gaming and liquor licences; they exercise an important civil jurisdiction, principally

---

[2] As at 1 January 1998, 49 were London-based, and 42 sat in the provinces: figures from Lord Chancellor's Department Consultation Paper, *Creation of a Unified Stipendiary Bench* (March 1998). There is a statutory maximum of 60 in London and 50 elsewhere (though these figures may be changed by Order in Council): Justices of the Peace Act 1997, ss. 11 and 16.

[3] The use of stipendiaries is likely to increase but this is not likely to encroach significantly on the work of lay magistrates. Expenditure on the stipendiary magistrates is around £6 million per year, whereas allowances for all 30,000 magistrates amount to around £9.5 million per year. See speech by the Lord Chancellor to the Magistrates' Association on 24 July 1997.

[4] See *Report of the Home Affairs Committee on Judicial Appointments Procedures*, HCP 52-I, (1995–96), para. 196.

[5] As at 1 January 1997 there were 15,858 men and 14,516 women magistrates. Source: *Judicial Statistics 1996* (London: HMSO, 1997, Cm. 3716).

[6] T. Skyrme, *The Changing Image of the Magistracy*, 2nd edn. (London: Macmillan, 1983), p. 8.

[7] *Report of the Home Affairs Committee on Judicial Appointments Procedures*, HCP 52-I, para. 198, endorsed by the Government in its response, *Judicial Appointments* (London: HMSO, 1996, Cm. 3387), p. 10.

[8] The Crime and Disorder Act 1998 has extended the range of functions which can be undertaken by a single magistrate.

concerning family matters when sitting as family proceedings courts; and, finally, as youth courts, they deal with a wide range of cases involving the welfare of those under eighteen. Part Two of this book is concerned with the role of magistrates in the criminal process when dealing with persons aged eighteen or over. Special powers for dealing with threats of terrorist activity are not covered.

Until April 1992 the Home Office was responsible for certain aspects of the organisation of magistrates' courts, but since April 1992, the Lord Chancellor's Department has been the responsible government department. Local Magistrates Courts Committees have responsibility for aspects of managing the courts within their jurisdiction.[9] The magistrates' courts are subject to inspection by the Inspectorate of the Magistrates' Court Service, which is concerned to measure their efficiency in such things as fine enforcement.[10]

The new Labour Lord Chancellor has embarked on a process of rationalisation of magistrates' court provision by the abolition of some magistrates courts committees and the merging of others to create fewer and larger administrative units. The objective is the better distribution and use of public resources, and to secure a greater alignment between areas served by the Crown Prosecution Service and the police.[11] The proposals have been controversial because some see them as a threat to local justice; the Lord Chancellor has responded by offering re-assurance that the plan is not about 'losing local courts' and re-affirming his commitment to a lay magistracy. His argument was that justice delivered locally is not the same as justice organised locally.

Proposals have also been made for a unified stipendiary bench.[12] The idea is to form a single national judicial corps of stipendiary magistrates with a judicial head of the stipendiary bench. Again some concerns have been expressed that local knowledge might be lost by the creation of a national system, which would almost certainly result in a lessening of such local connection as currently exists between stipendiary magistrates and the areas in which they sit.

Choosing magistrates

A network of 105 local advisory committees advises the Lord Chancellor of the names of persons thought suitable for appointment as magistrates. In Greater Manchester, Merseyside and Lancashire appointments are made by the Chancellor of the Duchy of Lancaster. Considerable secrecy used to surround the selection and appointment of magistrates, but the process has become much more open since the end of 1992. The membership of the advisory committees is now made public, though the level of availability of this information apparently varies considerably.[13]

---

[9] See generally Justices of the Peace Act 1997.

[10] See, for example, *The Annual Report of her Majesty's Chief Inspector of the Magistrates' Courts Service 1995–1996*, HCP 15 1996–7, 29 October 1996 (London: The Stationery Office, 1996).

[11] Ministerial Statement to the House of Lords, 29 October 1997.

[12] Lord Chancellor's Department Consultation Paper, *Creation of a Unified Stipendiary Bench* (March 1998).

[13] *Report of the Home Affairs Committee on Judicial Appointments Procedures*, HCP 52-II, p. 240.

This is a laudable attempt to respond to criticisms that the former methods of selection lacked fairness and openness and served to perpetuate the middle class character of the magistracy.

Appointment as chairman of an advisory committee is made by the Lord Chancellor who regards the local knowledge the committees have as important in securing a magistracy that is a microcosm of society. Members are appointed by invitation of the chairman. In 1982 it seemed that only nine per cent of members of the committees were neither serving nor retired magistrates.[14] Membership remains predominantly serving magistrates.[15] The system has its roots in the recommendations of the Royal Commissions on Justices of the Peace in 1910[16] and in 1948.[17] It was designed primarily to avoid political influence in the appointment of magistrates. Despite increased openness in membership of advisory committees, the process of appointment to them was described by the Magistrates' Association in their evidence to the Home Affairs Committee as 'shrouded in mystery' resulting in 'self-perpetuating oligarchies'.[18] The Committee considered that there could be more open recruitment procedures for membership to the advisory committees, but did not accept that current arrangements made their membership exclusive.[19]

To be eligible for appointment to the magistracy, a person must live locally and not be over sixty years of age, or be in an occupation which might conflict with the role of magistrate. Compulsory retirement arrives at the age of seventy. Advisory committees must interview all potential magistrates and are expected to follow detailed guidelines laid down in a booklet prepared by the Lord Chancellor's Department, *Notes on Procedure for Advisory Committees*. The Lord Chancellor's Department also produce *Directions for Advisory Committees*.

A booklet prepared by the Lord Chancellor's Department says:

When new magistrates are needed, the committees seek nominations. They ask local organisations or business; they may put notices in the press or use another means to find candidates. It is part of the local advisory committee's job to make sure that magistrates are drawn from many walks of life and that the composition of the bench in this sense is broadly balanced.[20]

The *Directions for Advisory Committees* state that they must:

have due regard to obtaining a balance in benches in terms of age, gender, ethnic origin, occupation, place of residence, and political inclination in order that the bench may reflect the community it serves.[21]

---

[14] M. King and C. May, *Black Magistrates* (London: Cobden Trust, 1985), p. 26.

[15] At 80 per cent of their membership. See *Report of the Home Affairs Committee on Judicial Appointments Procedures*, HCP 52-I, paras. 185–6.   [16] 1910, Cd. 5250.

[17] 1948, Cmd. 7463.

[18] *Report of the Home Affairs Committee on Judicial Appointments Procedures*, HCP 52-II, p. 241.

[19] Ibid., HCP 52-I, para. 218.

[20] Lord Chancellor's Department, *Today's Magistrates* (London: Lord Chancellor's Department, 1992), p. 3.

[21] *Directions for Advisory Committees*, para. 4.10. The Government Response to the Home Affairs Committee's Report conceded that this balance is often not met: *Judicial Appointments* (London: HMSO, 1996, Cm. 3387).

Some wage earners may be put off by the commitment required. No figures are kept of the number of magistrates in employment, but evidence to the Home Affairs Committee reported a decline in the number of employed people in the magistracy.[22] A magistrate is expected to sit between thirty-five and forty half days each year. This commitment is quite considerable, and even though employers are required to allow persons time off to sit on the bench, they are not required to pay them. The loss of earnings allowance is not overly generous and for some this may present a disincentive to allowing their names to go forward for consideration for appointment. Job and promotion prospects may also be affected by the absences from work.[23]

Late in 1997 in a welcome move, seven advisory committees volunteered to take part in an experiment to seek suitable blind candidates for appointment to the bench. Currently a person whose sight or hearing is impaired cannot be appointed. Blind people currently serve on tribunals, and one is a Deputy Chancery Master.[24]

Training

It is remarkable that it was not until 1 January 1966 that there was a system of compulsory training for new magistrates;[25] native wit, a willingness to learn and the received wisdom of the bench the new magistrates were joining was previously thought sufficient.[26] Following the recommendations contained in a 1975 White Paper,[27] a new compulsory two stage system of training was introduced. The first stage consisted of basic training in law and procedure, criminology and penology. It also includes sitting in court as an observer. This stage should be completed before the new magistrate sits on the bench for the first time. The second stage covers the first twelve months of a magistrate's career and consists of further courses of instruction and visits to various types of penal establishment. Those appointed on or after 1 January 1980 are also required to attend approved continuing training totalling not less than twelve hours every three years. This must be regarded as the barest acceptable minimum of training, and bears no comparison with the years of training required of all other members of the judiciary. There have also been suggestions that the compulsory training is not always fully implemented.[28] In fairness, it should be added that many courts offer voluntary courses of training both as refresher courses and as guides to new developments relevant to the magistrates' functions to all magistrates, whenever appointed. Attendance at such courses will be expected of all magistrates. How well organised such courses are often depends on the initiatives of senior members of the bench and of justices' clerks.

---

[22] *Report of the Home Affairs Committee on Judicial Appointments Procedures*, HCP 52-I, para. 201.

[23] See *Report of the Home Affairs Committee on Judicial Appointments Procedures*, HCP 52-I, para. 226.

[24] A sort of junior judge in the High Court dealing with interlocutory matters.

[25] Statutory provision for training was made in 1949 but it was not a requirement for service as a magistrate. See Justices of the Peace Act 1949, s. 17.

[26] T. Skyrme, *The Changing Image of the Magistracy*, 2nd edn. (London: Macmillan, 1983).

[27] *The Training of Justices of the Peace in England and Wales* (London: HMSO, 1975, Cmnd. 2856).

[28] J. Baldwin, 'The Compulsory Training of Magistrates' [1975] Crim. LR 634.

Magistrates appointed after 1989 must also undertake special training in acting as chair of the bench before they can serve in this capacity. Such individuals are subject to appraisal. Since 1996 those new to chairing the bench must undertake refresher training in the task every six years.

The training given is basic, designed to equip magistrates to perform their functions rather than to convert lay people into legal experts. The legal expertise is provided by the clerks to the justices. One clerk to the justices has described the tenor of the training given in the following terms:

Training has to be very practical. You have exercises on sentencing and videos about procedure. You can't come on like a university professor giving a lecture on criminal law. It has to be practical. The whole point of the magistrates is that they are lay people coming in possibly once a fortnight and bringing with them their outside experience as citizens and the fresh approach which legal professionals can lack. A lot of training is to give them confidence, to say to them don't be overawed by lawyers; hold on to common sense; remember what the witness has said, and if you're worried about a legal point, ask the Clerk.[29]

The scope and type of training is in the process of change. The Judicial Studies Board has, following consultation with magistrates and others, accepted recommendations contained in a report prepared for them by the University of Birmingham for a more practical approach to training.[30] The focus of training is to change from a focus on a list of topics and a required number of hours to a system which is 'organised and delivered around magistrates being able to demonstrate that they have acquired the necessary areas of knowledge and skills required at different stages in their magisterial career'.[31] Though attendance at courses will still be a part of the programme of training, there will be much more experiential learning. This new system was inaugurated in September 1998.

A cross-section of the community?

As noted above, the intention is that magistrates are drawn from all walks of life, though the cardinal principle for selection is merit.[32] It seems that this may not be achieved, though progress on a number of fronts, such as the balance between men and women, has been impressive. The difficulties faced by wage earners has already been mentioned.

Evidence presented to the Home Affairs Committee suggested that the average age of magistrates is high with about three-quarters of all magistrates aged fifty or more. Among Kent Magistrates only three and a half per cent were aged forty

---

[29] Lord Chancellor's Department, *Today's Magistrates* (London: Lord Chancellor's Department, 1992), pp. 11–12.

[30] J. Tann, A. Platts, and C. Allison, *Training Needs Analysis for Magistrates in England and Wales* (Birmingham: University of Birmingham, 1996).

[31] See speech by the Lord Chancellor to the Magistrates' Association on 24 July 1997.

[32] *Report of the Home Affairs Committee on Judicial Appointments Procedures*, HCP 52-I, para. 182.

or less.[33] Officially available statistical information tends to be poor. No figures are kept on the number of serving magistrates in employment, nor is there data on the number who come from ethnic minority backgrounds. Data is, however, kept on appointments, and in 1994 five per cent of those appointed came from such backgrounds. The available information led the Home Affairs Committee to conclude: 'that the aim of balancing the bench to take account of age, employment background and political leanings of magistrates has not, as yet, been achieved'.[34]

From time to time attempts are made by researchers to produce a profile of the magistracy to determine whether it is representative of the community at large. From these attempts it is clear that among magistrates proportionately more members of political parties are likely to be found than among the public at large. There also seems to be an over-representation of the middle classes.[35] By contrast members of ethnic minorities are seriously under-represented.[36] It also seems that women and ethnic minorities are poorly represented on the advisory committees.[37]

Such evidence as is available points to a disproportionate social balance among the magistracy with comfortably-off, middle-aged, middle class magistrates sitting in judgment on the less-well-off working class members of society.

Of particular concern is the very low number of magistrates from the ethnic minority communities. An important study in 1985[38] showed that recruitment rates of black magistrates varied widely. In eight of twenty-five representative courts surveyed, the representation of black magistrates would at least need to double before the composition of the bench reflected the number of black people living in the area.

King and May's conclusion is that there was evidence of racial bias among members of the advisory committees. This takes the form of negative stereotyping of black people and the imposing of requirements on black candidates, which are not applied to white candidates. One example is the requirement of one committee that Asian candidates be 'acceptable to the whole Asian community' in the area. In general a serious criticism is expressed of the general fairness of the selection process for all candidates. In some areas secret enquiries are made and selection decisions are based on 'soft' information, that is second- or third-hand information which has not been verified or put to the candidate. No reasons are given to rejected candidates; indeed, in some cases unsuccessful candidates were not even informed that they have been unsuccessful. They simply heard nothing further about the matter.

The study does, however, recognise the difficulty of recruiting ethnic minority magistrates. It found a remarkably small number of black people prepared to be candidates for appointment. This reluctance to serve was, however, itself linked to perceptions of a discriminatory selection procedure and a view of the magistrates'

---

[33] *Report of the Home Affairs Committee on Judicial Appointments Procedures*, HCP 52-I, para. 199.
[34] Ibid., para. 205
[35] J. Baldwin, 'The Social Composition of the Magistracy' (1976) 16 Brit. J of Crim. 171.
[36] See T. Skyrme, *The Changing Image of the Magistracy*, 2nd edn. (London: Macmillan, 1983) and M. King and C. May, *Black Magistrates* (London: Cobden Trust, 1985).
[37] E. Burney, *Magistrate, Court and Community* (London: Hutchinson, 1969).
[38] M. King and C. May, *Black Magistrates* (London: Cobden Trust, 1985).

courts as part of the white establishment. The researchers also acknowledge the inherent tension between the concept of popular justice: justice administered, as Sir Thomas Skyrme put it, by men and women like the defendant; and professionalism, which emphasises the gravitas of the judicial function, the need for the magistrate to be a person whose judgment is valued in the community, and the need for efficiency in the despatch of heavy caseloads without undue delay.

The Clerk to the Justices

Magistrates are advised on law and procedure by a professionally-qualified clerk. The role of the clerk to the justices is vital to the work of the magistracy. Clerks to the Justices and their staff administer the courts[39] and act as legal advisers to each bench of magistrates when they are sitting. The Clerk to the Justices is often also the bench's training officer. The new Labour Lord Chancellor has announced a policy of requiring all court clerks in future to be professionally qualified as either a barrister or a solicitor, while at the same time separating the administrative functions of organising the courts from those of giving legal advice to magistrates. This will result in courts having chief executives with responsibility for administration and clerks to the justice responsibility for legal advice to the bench.

During hearings the clerk must take care not to overstep the purely advisory role. So a clerk can advise on the admissibility of a piece of evidence (an issue of law) but must not give any hint as to a view on the credibility of a witness (an issue of fact). The dividing line is not always easy to define. But guidance has been given by the Lord Chief Justice on both the matters on which magistrates may consult, and the manner of consultation.[40] These stress the need for it to be clear from the conduct of the clerk that it is the magistrates who are making the decisions. So the clerk should never routinely retire with the magistrates to their deliberation room. The clerk may be called in by the magistrates for further advice, but should return to the courtroom as soon as the advice has been given. The clerk to the justices also enjoys some limited quasi-judicial authority, such as the issuing of summonses and the granting of legal aid.

Given the centrality of the clerk in the work of magistrates, there are surprisingly few research studies of the role.[41] Such work as has been done tends to stress the centrality of the role of the clerk as the preserver of the legitimacy of the court,

---

[39] Though now the bulk of the administration and management of magistrates' courts complexes is undertaken by justices' chief executives.

[40] *Practice Note: Justices' Clerks* [1953] 1 WLR 1416, and *Practice Direction: Clerks to the Justices* [1981] 1 WLR 1163. Different considerations apply when the magistrates are sitting as family proceedings courts: see *Practice Note: Justices' Clerks* [1954] 1 WLR 213.

[41] See P. Darbyshire, *Magistrates' Clerks* (Chichester: Barry Rose, 1984); H. Astor, 'The Unrepresented Defendant Revisited: A Consideration of the Role of the Clerk in Magistrates' Courts' (1986) 13 J of Law and Soc. 225; and, in relation to their role in dealing with legal aid applications, R. Young, T. Moloney and A. Sanders, *In the Interests of Justice: The Determination of Criminal Legal Aid Applications by Magistrates' Courts in England and Wales*, Report to the Legal Aid Board (Birmingham: The Institute of Judicial Administration, 1992). See also O. Hansen, 'What a Difference a Clerk Makes' *LAG Bulletin*, March 1982, 11.

ensuring that rules of law, evidence and procedure are observed. In one study[42] an attempt was made to characterise the approach of clerks to the assistance of those appearing before the court without representation. Observations in nine courts ranging from a busy urban court to a rural court sitting only two days a week led to the conclusion that the approach of the clerks varied considerably, and that this variation was not part of a court culture but reflected the approach of the individual. In many cases, great care was taken to assist the unrepresented defendant, but in other cases judgements were made by clerks which appeared to influence the extent of their interventions to assist. A similar conclusion resulted from a study of clerks' approaches to legal aid applications, where the researchers concluded: 'in a sense, courts do not have policies other than those pursued in a rather idiosyncratic fashion by individual clerks'.[43]

The work of magistrates

Magistrates deal with around two million cases each year, though just over half of these will be motoring offences. Many of the other cases will be fairly minor matters; some, of course, will be trivial. But some of the cases dealt with by magistrates are sufficiently serious that each year magistrates sentence around 28,000 offenders to immediate custodial sentences. They will also consider the evidence against about 106,000 persons accused of serious crime to determine whether there is sufficient evidence for them to be sent for trial in the Crown Court.[44] This workload represents a staggering ninety-eight per cent of all criminal business. The magistrates could not cope if about eight out of every ten defendants did not plead guilty. In cases tried before them, magistrates determine both guilt and the sentence to be imposed, advised as to law and procedure by their clerk. The picture which begins to emerge is of an institution which processes large numbers of individuals, most of whom do not contest the evidence against them. It is sometimes asserted that magistrates' courts are guilty plea courts and that there is little point in contesting a case before them because they will invariably believe the prosecution evidence. In so far as it is possible to extract information from the criminal judicial statistics, it seems that magistrates find about half those who contest cases before them not guilty. This is roughly the same as the proportion acquitted in the Crown Court. Magistrates' courts are also said to be very cheap and economical; this is only true because of the high rate of guilty pleas before magistrates' courts. When the hourly cost of contested cases before magistrates' courts and in the Crown Court is compared, the resulting figures are remarkably similar.[45]

---

[42] H. Astor, 'The Unrepresented Defendant Revisited: A Consideration of the Role of the Clerk in Magistrates' Courts' (1986) 13 J of Law and Soc. 225.

[43] R. Young, T. Moloney and A. Sanders, *In the Interests of Justice: The Determination of Criminal Legal Aid Applications by Magistrates' Courts in England and Wales, Report to the Legal Aid Board* (Birmingham: The Institute of Judicial Administration, 1992), p. 104.

[44] *Criminal Statistics England and Wales 1996* (London: HMSO, 1997, Cm. 3764). But note the new procedure for sending those charged with offences triable only on indictment direct to the Crown Court in the Crime and Disorder Act 1998, s. 51: see Ch. 7.

[45] See *Report of the Interdepartmental Committee on the Distribution of Criminal Business between the Crown Court and Magistrates' Courts, (James Committee)* (London: HMSO, 1975, Cmnd 6323).

The Crown Court

Following the recommendations of the Beeching Report in 1969,[46] the old Courts of Assize and Quarter Sessions were replaced in 1972 by a single Crown Court as the forum for the trial of more serious criminal cases. Though a single court, the Crown Court may sit anywhere and a national network of trial centres has been established. When the Crown Court sits in the City of London it is known as the Central Criminal Court, or colloquially as the Old Bailey. Most large towns have a Crown Court. Contested trials in the Crown Court, where, of course, only two per cent of criminal business is conducted, are the epitome of the ordinary citizen's view of the criminal justice system. Lawyers represent both prosecution and defence, and, employing formidable forensic skills, seek to persuade a jury of twelve individuals chosen at random of the guilt or innocence of the accused. The judge is there to decide points of law and to sum up the evidence to assist the jury in its task of determining guilt or innocence.

The jury is perhaps the most sacred institution of the criminal justice system and has evoked over the years emotive labels from major public figures. In 1830 Blackstone commented that the 'liberties of England cannot but subsist so long as this palladium remains sacred and inviolate',[47] and in 1956 Lord Devlin described the jury as 'the lamp that shows that freedom lives'.[48] Equally florid comments vilifying the jury can be found, but the weight of comment is favourable, and public opinion is massively in favour of the jury.[49] Whether its popularity is deserved will be considered in Chapter 8.

Though the process of jury trial appears to be a model of fairness, it is wrong to isolate it from the processes which have gone before. There is evidence to suggest that the outcome of cases in the Crown Court is as much dependent upon what happens to an accused person in the police station, and in the magistrates' court, as upon the process of jury trial.[50] There have also been persistent complaints that too great a pressure is placed upon some defendants to plead guilty rather than to continue to fight the case.[51] Even in the Crown Court seven out of every ten defendants plead guilty.

As a generalisation the Crown Court deals with more serious crime, though it is still possible for a defendant to insist on being tried by a judge and jury for comparatively minor matters. For example, a person accused of shoplifting goods costing only a few pence has a right to elect jury trial. When the government of the day sought to introduce in the Criminal Law Bill in 1977 a minimum monetary value of the property stolen as a qualification for the right to elect trial by jury,

---

[46] *Report of the Royal Commission on Assizes and Quarter Sessions* (London: HMSO, 1969, Cmnd 4153).
[47] *Blackstone's Commentaries*, 17th edn., vol. iv (1830), p. 350.
[48] P. Devlin, *Trial by Jury* (London: Stevens, 1956), p. 164.
[49] J. Baldwin and M. McConville, *Jury Trials* (Oxford: Clarendon Press, 1979), ch. 1.
[50] See D. McBarnet, *Conviction, Law, The State and the Construction of Justice* (London: Macmillan, 1981); M. McConville and J. Baldwin, *Courts, Prosecution and Conviction* (Oxford: Clarendon Press, 1981), and M. McConville and others, *Standing Accused: The Organisation and Practices of Criminal Defence Lawyers in Britain* (Oxford: Clarendon Press, 1994).
[51] J. Baldwin and M. McConville, *Negotiated Justice* (Oxford: Martin Robertson, 1977).

public opinion was mobilised so strongly against the proposal that it had to be dropped from the Bill. There is also a principle that the more serious the crime the more senior and experienced the judge to try it.

The Crown Court is staffed by High Court judges, Circuit judges and part-time judges, called Recorders and Assistant Recorders. The bulk of the work is done by other than High Court judges, who try some of the most serious or complex cases. At the end of 1995 there were 517 Circuit judges,[52] 891 Recorders,[53] and 354 Assistant Recorders.[54] This body of judges will try nearly 90,000 defendants a year.[55]

In addition to its trial work, the Crown Court deals with around 5,600 persons sent to the Crown Court for sentence where the magistrates do not consider their limited sentencing powers sufficient to deal with a person convicted before them. Generally speaking, magistrates cannot sentence a defendant to a period of imprisonment exceeding six months for any one offence or exceeding twelve months for any two or more offences. Nor may they normally fine a defendant more than £5,000.[56]

Finally, the Crown Court acts as an appeal court against conviction or sentence, or both, in the magistrates' court. In this capacity Crown Court judges sit with magistrates and deal with around 26,000 cases a year.

Choosing judges

In making all full-time judicial appointments, the Lord Chancellor is guided by three principles: the merit of the candidate which includes a knowledge of the relevant area of law, the views of serving members of the judiciary, and service in a part-time capacity.[57] Appointment to initial judicial appointment will inevitably be in a part-time capacity, and the same principles are applied, though clearly with modifications since there will be no period of judicial office for assessment. Vacancies for appointments as a Circuit judge or a High Court judge are now advertised, though the Lord Chancellor reserves the right to appoint from among those he has invited to consider such an appointment.[58]

Any solicitor or barrister who has been qualified for at least ten years may apply for appointment as a Recorder or Assistant Recorder. The target age range for appointment as an Assistant Recorder is between thirty-five and fifty, for a Recorder is between thirty-eight and fifty, and for a Circuit Judge is forty-five to sixty, though the Lord

---

[52] Their average age was 57.8; 86 per cent were barristers and 14 per cent were solicitors. Women accounted for 5.6 per cent of their number and those from ethnic minority backgrounds one per cent.

[53] Their average age was 52; 91 per cent were barristers and 9 per cent were solicitors. Women accounted for 6.1 per cent of their number and those from ethnic minority backgrounds 1.3 per cent.

[54] Assistant Recorders sit less frequently than Recorders. Their average age was 45.7; 81 per cent were barristers and 19 per cent were solicitors. Women accounted for 14.7 per cent of their number and those from ethnic minority backgrounds 2.5 per cent.

[55] See *Judicial Statistics 1996* (London: HMSO, 1997, Cm. 3716).

[56] Unless the statutory provision expressly provides for a higher sum. See generally, Magistrates' Courts Act 1980, s. 32.

[57] Lord Chancellor's Department, *Judicial Appointments: The Lord Chancellor's Policies and Procedures* (London: Lord Chancellor's Department, 1995), pp. 5–6.

[58] The first advertisements for appointments to the High Court appeared in 1997.

Chancellor applies these ranges flexibly.[59] Any barrister of at least ten years call or any solicitor who has served as a Recorder for three years may apply for appointment as a Circuit judge. Applicants for these posts are selected and interviewed by members of the Judicial Appointments Group of the Lord Chancellor's Department in much the same manner as they would be for any civil service post. A panel of three consisting of a serving judge, a senior member of the Judicial Appointments Group in the Lord Chancellor's Department, and a lay member[60] interview candidates and make recommendations to the Lord Chancellor. Circuit judges are paid a minimum of £86,639.[61]

Appointment as a High Court judge is open only to barristers who have been qualified for at least ten years and those with relevant service as a Circuit judge.[62] Recommendations from judges, senior barristers and officials of the Lord Chancellor's Department appear to be particularly important in the selection of High Court judges; these will, in turn, be based upon the reputation acquired by advocates in court. Little dossiers build up on potential candidates over a number of years. The final decision to issue an invitation comes after the Lord Chancellor has met with his senior colleagues to draw up an informal short list. The final choice is that of the Lord Chancellor alone; technically appointments are made by the Queen, but by convention she always acts on the advice of the Lord Chancellor. Comparatively few High Court judges are recruited from among Circuit judges.

Some invitations are turned down. The minimum salary of £115,556 per year[63] is modest compared with the earnings of leading practitioners,[64] though the pension provision is generous. Once appointed, a judge is expected to continue in office until compulsory retirement age, which is now seventy with possible extension to the age of seventy-five. Indeed, when Sir Henry Fisher left the High Court bench in 1970 for better paid work, his fellow judges made little secret of their disapproval of his conduct.

The Home Affairs Committee considered the process of selection and pronounced itself broadly satisfied.[65] Considerable attention was given to the system for collecting opinions from serving members of the judiciary and the impact this had on recruitment. The Committee concluded that much of the subjectivity which had surrounded the taking of 'soundings' had been removed by a greater emphasis on recording comments and ensuring their accuracy. There was, however, scope for improvement in the transparency of the process.

[59] Lord Chancellor's Department, *Judicial Appointments: The Lord Chancellor's Policies and Procedures* (London: Lord Chancellor's Department, 1995), para. 165.

[60] A panel of ten lay members has been appointed for this purpose drawn from the Advisory Committees on Justices of the Peace. See *Report of the Home Affairs Committee on Judicial Appointments Procedures*, HCP 52-I.

[61] As at 1 April 1999. See *Review Body on Senior Salaries. Twentieth Report on Senior Salaries* (London: HMSO, 1998, Cm. 3837).   [62] There are 96 High Court judges, one of whom is a solicitor (Sachs J.).

[63] As from 1 April 1999.

[64] A survey of the pre-appointment earnings of those appointed as High Court judges since 1990 revealed average earnings of £338,700 per year, with the upper quartile earning £425,000. Even solicitors appointed to Circuit judgeships had average earnings of £113,600 per year: Appendix 6 to *Review Body on Senior Salaries. Twentieth Report on Senior Salaries* (London: HMSO, 1998, Cm. 3837).

[65] *Report of the Home Affairs Committee on Judicial Appointments Procedures*, HCP 52-I, para. 62.

The Home Affairs Committee also considered the proposals which had been made for a Judicial Appointments Commission as an independent body making recommendations for judicial appointment.[66] The conclusion, which appears well-founded in the light of the considerable developments in the procedures for appointment, was that such a body was not needed.[67]

A cloistered collegiate group

It is still the case that the overwhelming majority of judges are recruited from the small world of the Bar, and most of them are men. It will take many years for the overall profile to change. This invariably gives the judiciary a collegiate atmosphere. The social profile of the judiciary, even today, shows a predominance of middle and upper class origins and of education at public school and Oxbridge. This will have been followed by two decades or more of life at the Bar. It is impossible to argue that the world of the Inns of Court is not cloistered and full of ritual and tradition. The socialising influence of the life is powerful. While judges today live more ordinary lives than in the past, it is absurd to suggest that they are a microcosm of society. They are not. Pannick comments:

It is not surprising that a Bench composed almost entirely of former barristers should lack expertise and knowledge of many of the matters which are central to the lives of those people who come into court as litigants and witnesses.[68]

Senior members of the judiciary tend to over-emphasise the 'ordinariness' of judges; the dignity and traditions of judicial office alone prevent that. Widening the group eligible for higher judicial office will certainly break down some of the traditions which make it difficult to rebut the charge that judges inhabit a judicial ivory tower remote from the problems of the ordinary citizen. But it is unlikely to make a dramatic difference to the public perception of the majesty of the law embodied in our senior judges. Psychological profiling of those who choose law as a career tends to show a dominance of those with conservative instincts who have a natural liking for working within a clearly defined framework of rules.[69]

Despite all these criticisms, one commentator on judges, who is by no means a sycophantic supporter of every aspect of the judiciary, says:

What has changed markedly is the general standard of judicial performance. Today it is high, most probably higher than ever before in terms of ability, conduct and understanding of the needs of society.[70]

---

[66] *Report of the Home Affairs Committee on Judicial Appointments Procedures*, HCP 52-I, paras. 129–42. See also JUSTICE, *The Judiciary in England and Wales* (London: JUSTICE, 1992).

[67] See also, *Judicial Appointments Commissions: The European and North American Experience and the Possible Implications for the United Kingdom*, discussion papers by C. Thomas and K. Malleson, Lord Chancellor's Department Research Series No 6/97 (London: Lord Chancellor's Department, December 1997).

[68] D. Pannick, *Judges* (Oxford: Clarendon Press, 1988), p. 53.

[69] A. Sherr, and J. Webb, 'Law Students, the External Market and Socialization: Do we make them turn to the City?' (1989) 16 J of Law and Soc. 225.

[70] D. Pannick, *Judges* (Oxford: Clarendon Press, 1988), p. 15.

Training of judges

Training of judges has since 1978 been in the hands of the Judicial Studies Board which has a salaried director and holds regular training seminars in the criminal jurisdiction both for the newly appointed judge and refresher courses for experienced judges, particularly in matters of sentencing. Only in October 1985 was the task of the Judicial Studies Board extended to cover the civil and family jurisdictions. The pattern which has emerged is of seminars lasting three or four days.

No real attempt is made to convert from advocacy to judicial skills; it is assumed that those selected will have the 'judicial attitude' necessary to enable them to perform well in their new role. Snobbery and arrogance precludes the acceptance of the need for skills training in these important areas. The skills will be learned on the job at the expense of advocates, litigants and witnesses. Pannick argues: 'The amateur approach which the English legal system adopts in this context hinders the effective performance of the judicial function'.[71]

The Relationship Between Magistrates' Courts and the Crown Court

The nature and seriousness of the offence are the major factors in determining whether a case will be dealt with by a magistrates' court or the Crown Court. It is the system of classification of offences for the purpose of determining the mode of trial that assigns each crime to a particular category. There are now only three classes of offences:

- offences triable only on indictment, that is, in the Crown Court;
- offences triable only summarily, that is, in the magistrates' courts;
- offences triable either way, that is, either in the Crown Court or in a magistrates' court.

Obviously no problem arises concerning the mode of trial of offences triable only on indictment or only summarily; there is no choice. Offences triable only in the Crown Court include the most serious offences, such as murder, manslaughter, rape, robbery or arson, while offences triable only in the magistrates' court are much less serious; good examples are minor motoring offences. But there is a whole range of offences which are triable either way, of which the most significant are burglary and theft. Details of how the choice in such cases between magistrates' court and the Crown Court is made are to be found in Chapter 7. It is enough to note here that in all such cases the defendant has a right to insist on being tried by a jury in the Crown Court by refusing consent to trial in the magistrates' court, but in all such cases the magistrates initially consider, having regard to the seriousness of the case and all other relevant circumstances, which form of trial is more appropriate.

---

[71] D. Pannick, *Judges* (Oxford: Clarendon Press, 1988), p. 73.

5

POLICING: ON THE STREET

The Work of the Police

Constables and chief constables

The police play a central role in the criminal process. The investigation of an offence and the interactions between the police and persons identified as suspects are the core of the criminal process. For many accused of crime, the whole process will be determined by what happens in these pre-trial interactions.

In England and Wales, every police officer, with the exception of the Commissioner of Police for the Metropolis, holds the 'ancient and honourable office of constable' under the Crown.[1] The constable is not an employee, but an independent office holder.[2] Though the police service is run on rigid, quasi-military, hierarchical lines, there are areas where each constable is, at least theoretically, answerable only to the law and not to his or her superiors. In these areas no police officer of higher rank can interfere with the judgement exercised by the constable. But constitutional fiction has been replaced by modern reality. One commentator notes:

The police officer can no longer be seen as a self-directed decision maker answerable only to the law. Rather he is a person subject to organisational and occupational/professional rules and norms, like other employees.[3]

The Police Act 1964, responding to the Royal Commission on the Police of 1962,[4] established forty-three police areas for England and Wales (including the Metropolitan Police District and the City of London Police) each under the direction of a chief officer of police, known in almost every case as a chief constable.[5] Chief

---

[1] *The Royal Commission on Criminal Procedure, (Philips Commission), The Investigation and Prosecution of Criminal Offences in England and Wales: The Law and Procedure* (London: HMSO, 1981, Cmnd. 8092-I), para. 3.

[2] See *Fisher* v. *Oldham Corporation* [1930] 2 KB 364, and cogent critique of the case by L. Lustgarten, *The Governance of the Police* (London: Sweet & Maxwell, 1986), pp. 56–60.

[3] L. Lustgarten, *The Governance of the Police* (London: Sweet & Maxwell, 1986), p. 30.

[4] *Final Report of the Royal Commission on the Police (Willink Commission)* (London: HMSO, 1962, Cmnd. 1728).

[5] See, for current legislative framework, the Police Act 1996. For studies of the role of chief constables, see R. Reiner, *Chief Constables* (Oxford: Oxford University Press, 1991), and D. Wall, *The Chief Constables of England and Wales* (London: Ashgate, 1998).

officers of police are responsible (except in the case of the Metropolitan Police District[6] and City of London Police)[7] to police authorities and to the Home Secretary for the direction and control of their forces, but alone carry responsibility for the way in which they decide to investigate and prosecute offences. Police authorities[8] are local committees generally consisting of seventeen members charged with the duty to maintain an adequate police force for the area. Nine are members of the local authorities in the area, five are described as 'independent' members,[9] and three are magistrates.

There is often said to be a distinction between operational matters which are within the sole province of the chief constable and policy matters where the police authority has a role to play. Some doubt the ability to divide police activities into two such distinct areas.[10]

The Home Secretary's ministerial responsibility for the police extends to his approving the appointment by police authorities of chief constables and assistants.[11] The Home Office also produces regulations governing the appointment, discipline, and promotion of officers at superintendent level and below.[12] In practice no one becomes a senior police officer without the approval of Home Office civil servants.

Keeping the peace

A 1993 Government White Paper[13] stated:

The main purposes of the police service should be:
  • to fight and prevent crime;
  • to uphold the law;
  • to bring to justice those who break the law;
  • to protect, help and reassure the community;
  • in meeting those aims, to provide good value for money.
In fulfilling those aims the police must maintain their traditional role of policing by consent.[14]

Not so very long ago, preventing and detecting crime, and making the initial decision to put a case forward for prosecution were just three of eight functions of the police identified by the Willink Commission in 1962.[15] The first and paramount

---

[6] Where the Commissioner is directly responsible to the Home Secretary.
[7] Where the chief constable is responsible to the Common Council of the City of London.
[8] Police Act 1996, s. 2 and Sch. 2.
[9] Persons selected by panels for nomination as members; they are appointed by the Home Secretary: Police Act 1996, Sch. 3.
[10] G. Marshall, 'Police Accountability Revisited' in D. Butler and A. Halsey, *Policy and Politics* (London: Macmillan, 1978), and L. Lustgarten, *The Governance of Police* (London: Sweet & Maxwell, 1986), pp. 20–2.
[11] Police Act 1996, ss. 11 and 12.
[12] The statutory ranks are, in order of seniority, constable, sergeant, inspector, chief inspector, superintendent, assistant chief constable, and chief constable: Police Act 1996, s. 13.
[13] *Police Reform. A Police Service for the Twenty-First Century* (London: HMSO, 1993, Cm. 2281).
[14] Ibid., p. 2.
[15] *Final Report of the Royal Commission on the Police* (London: HMSO, 1962, Cmnd. 1728).

function was stated to be 'the duty to maintain law and order and to protect persons and property'.[16]

Under section 37 of the Police Act 1996, the Home Secretary can state objectives for all police forces. The latest set of objectives is as follows:[17]

(a) to deal speedily and effectively with young offenders and to work with other agencies to reduce re-offending;

(b) to target and reduce local problems of crime and disorder in partnership with local authorities, other local agencies and the public;

(c) to target drug-related crime in partnership with other local agencies;

(d) to maintain and, if possible, increase the number of detections of violent crime;

(e) to increase the number of detections for burglaries of people's homes; and

(f) to respond promptly to emergency calls from the public.

Many commentators stress the general peace-keeping and community-serving function of the police: 'The core mandate of policing, historically and in terms of concrete demands placed upon the police, is the more diffuse one of order maintenance'.[18]

So just as it is a misconception to assume that most lawyers spend most of their time in court or engaged in court work, so too it is a misconception to assume that crime fighting is the prime activity of the police.[19] One study of police encounters with the public describes police patrol as a 'quite mundane and undramatic activity' which is due largely to the 'mundane nature of the calls which the public make on the police'.[20] How then do the police use their time?

How do the police use their time?

A major report by the Policy Studies Institute into policing by the Metropolitan Police, commissioned by Sir David McNee when he was Commissioner of Police for the Metropolis, gives a rough but fascinating breakdown of the time spent by officers in the Metropolitan Police on various tasks.[21] The typical pattern which emerges for a uniformed police constable is that fifty-five per cent of time is spent outside the police station and forty-five per cent of time in it. Much of the time in the police station is spent on administrative tasks and around five per cent on training. Outside the police station ten per cent of time is spent on foot patrol and eighteen per cent on vehicle patrols. Other time outside the police station is spent attending court, or contacting and interviewing witnesses and informants. Overall it seems

---

[16] *Final Report of the Royal Commission on the Police* (London: HMSO, 1962, Cmnd. 1728).

[17] The Police (Secretary of State's Objectives) Order 1998, S.I. 1998 No. 216.

[18] R. Reiner, *The Politics of the Police* (Brighton: Wheatsheaf, 1985), p. 172.

[19] For an anthropological study of the police, see M. Young, *An Inside Job* (Oxford: Clarendon Press, 1991). See also D. Bayley, 'The Future of Policing' (1996) 30 Law and Soc. Rev. 585.

[20] P. Southgate, *Police-Public Encounters*, Home Office Research Study No. 90 (London: HMSO, 1986), p. 53.

[21] D. Smith and others, *Police and People in London*, 4 vols. (London: Policy Studies Institute, 1983), esp. vol. III.

that only one per cent of uniformed police time is spent interviewing suspects and witnesses at the police station. This proportion of time is very low; both activities are seen by the police as the most important sources of information leading to the apprehension of offenders.

The figures for detectives[22] show that they spend fifty-five per cent of their time on police premises and forty-five per cent off them. Outside the police station the largest single activity accounting for seventeen per cent of time is the contacting or interviewing of informants or witnesses. In the police station thirty-five per cent of time is spent on administration. Only eight per cent of time is occupied interviewing suspects or witnesses at the police station. So even detectives spend only a small amount of their time on what might popularly be regarded as classic detection work.[23] For all police only two per cent of police time is spent on this task.

The other significant aspect of the use of police time that emerges from the survey is that sergeants and inspectors had little time for direct supervision of constables.

How good are the police at detecting crime?

One of the early studies of the investigation of crime in this country was conducted by Michael Zander.[24] The results of an investigation into 150 cases tried at the Old Bailey in 1974 were analysed to see how the offender had been caught. In most cases establishing the identity of the offender required no skilled detective work. In nearly half the cases, the person reporting the crime had known the identity of the offender. In a further four in ten cases the offender had been caught at or near the scene of the crime almost immediately, and in one in six cases the police had a good description of the offender or knew the registration number of his car.

In a research study carried out for the Royal Commission on Criminal Procedure, David Steer broadly confirmed Zander's conclusions.[25] Three out of four offenders were caught because they were known to the victim of the crime, were caught red-handed at or near the scene of the crime, or were one of a small group of people who alone could have committed the offence. One in four cases required traditional skills of detection: fingerprinting, police questioning, tip-offs and local knowledge. Interrogation of suspects was seen as important in obtaining information about other criminal activity (the suspect's own or that of others) rather than in securing a confession to the crime under investigation. It also seems that an initial assessment is made of the information available about a crime by investigating officers. Those cases which appear to promise some success in detecting the

---

[22] Those generally referred to as working in the CID, that is, Criminal Investigation Departments.

[23] See P. Morris and K. Heal, *Crime Control and the Police*, Home Office Research Study No. 67 (London: HMSO, 1981).

[24] M. Zander, 'The Investigation of Crime: A Study of Cases Tried at the Old Bailey' [1979] Crim. LR 203.

[25] D. Steer, *Uncovering Crime—The Police Role*, Royal Commission on Criminal Procedure Research Study No. 7 (London: HMSO, 1980). See also W. Skogan, *Contacts between Police and Public: Findings from the 1992 British Crime Survey*, Home Office Research Study No. 134 (London: HMSO, 1994).

offender are investigated further, while those which do not are quietly shelved. Steer also reports unpublished research by a senior detective police officer which supports this: it found that the average time spent on the investigation of unde-tected crime was 2 hours 48 minutes and on the investigation of crimes that were cleared up was 4 hours 30 minutes.

In terms of overall success rate the Steer survey showed that the investigation of 959 crimes selected at random produced 373 suspects of whom thirty-four were cautioned and 289 prosecuted. The 289 prosecutions resulted in 261 convictions.

These figures show that the work of the police had changed from a proactive role to a reactive role. Proactive policing refers to the practice of preserving law and order and detecting crime by patrolling officers, often on foot. Reactive policing responds to reports from the public; it is sometimes called 'fire brigade policing' because much time is spent responding to emergency calls.

Measuring success in terms of the ratio of convictions to reported crimes suggests that the police secure convictions in only three out of every ten crimes reported. Fascinating though these figures are, they represent only 'crimes known to the police' and not the totality of criminal activity. In the Steer survey some 80 per cent of offences investigated by the police were reported to them by members of the pub-lic rather than discovered by the police. This figure is roughly in line with that produced by other studies.[26] There is a considerable body of research which sug-gests that crime reported to the police is only the tip of the iceberg. In a 1977 study it was suggested that only one in eleven criminal offences is reported to the police.[27] Many of the unreported offences would be trivial and the reasons for non-reporting perfectly valid: for example, a conclusion that the police would be unable to solve the crime. The success rate of the police in the apprehension of offenders noted above is measured against the level of offending the community regards as sufficiently serious to report to the police in the first place.[28]

Policing in an adversarial system

The Royal Commission on Criminal Procedure of 1981[29] pointed out that the adversarial nature of the criminal trial largely determines the nature of the pre-trial procedures. The essence of the adversarial system is that the trial takes the form of a contest between prosecution and defence which is governed by strict rules

---

[26] M. McConville, A. Sanders and R. Leng, *The Case for the Prosecution* (London: Routledge, 1991).

[27] R. Sparks, H. Genn and D. Dodd, *Surveying Victims: A Study of the Measurement of Criminal Victimisation, Perceptions of Crime and Attitudes to Criminal Justice* (Chichester: John Wiley, 1977).

[28] P. Mayhew, D. Elliott and L. Dowds, *The British Crime Survey 1988*, Home Office Research Study No. 111 (London: HMSO, 1988). See also P. Mayhew, N. Aye Maung and C. Mirrlees-Black, *The 1992 Brit-ish Crime Survey*, Home Office Research Study No. 132 (London: HMSO, 1993), and W. Skogan, *Contacts between Police and Public: Findings from the 1992 British Crime Survey*, Home Office Research Study No. 134 (London: HMSO, 1994). See also C. Mirrlees-Black, P. Mayhew, and A. Percy, *The 1996 British Crime Survey*, Home Office Statistical Bulletin 19/96 (London: HMSO, 1997).

[29] *Report of the Royal Commission on Criminal Procedure* (London: HMSO, 1981, Cmnd. 8092).

of evidence and which alone determines whether the accused committed the crime charged. The pre-trial stages merely represent the collection of evidence and preparation of cases of each side. Lustgarten also stressed the importance of the adversarial nature of the criminal trial for the style of policing and provides a useful contrast with criminal procedure in inquisitorial systems.[30]

The key point is that in an adversarial system convictions are secured in one of two ways. First, the prosecution may succeed in adducing admissible evidence which persuades the magistrates or jury beyond all reasonable doubt that the accused committed the act constituting the offence with the requisite intent. Secondly, the accused may plead guilty, bypassing completely the necessity for proof of commission of the offence. It is small wonder that the police go to considerable lengths to secure a criminal trial of the second type. There is no uncertainty as to outcome; and the result will be seen by the police to accord with what they know rather than what they can prove. The evidential burdens of the adversarial system invariably mean that the police will 'know' more than they can prove. The adversarial system also leaves the pre-trial stages of the process in the hands of the police, largely uncontrolled by outside interference until the point at which the police decide to put a case forward for consideration by the criminal courts.[31]

The 1993 Report of the Royal Commission on Criminal Justice[32] considered but did not recommend any change to the adversarial system and concluded that it was fundamental to the system that the prosecution should be obliged 'to establish the defendant's guilt on the basis of evidence which the defence is entitled to contest'.[33]

The Great Reform of Police Powers

The climate for reform

The 1950s had been the golden age of public acceptance of the police. Policing by consent was achieved to the greatest extent then. A survey conducted in 1960 for the Willink Commission revealed that eight out of every ten citizens had great respect for the police; the survey results represented a massive vote of confidence in the police.[34]

---

[30] L. Lustgarten, *The Governance of Police* (London: Sweet and Maxwell, 1986).

[31] See discussion of the distinction between adversarial and inquisitorial procedures in Ch. 3.

[32] *Report of the Royal Commission on Criminal Justice (Runciman Commission)* (London: HMSO, 1993, Cm. 2263). [33] Ibid., ch. 1, para. 15.

[34] *Final Report of the Royal Commission on the Police (Willink Commission)* (London: HMSO, 1962, Cmnd. 1728). Surveys have shown a consistently high regard for the police, but the level of satisfaction has also been consistently decreasing: see W. Skogan, *The Police and the Public in England and Wales: A British Crime Survey Report*, Home Office Research Study No. 117 (London: HMSO, 1990), p. 49, reporting a fall in the proportion giving the police the highest confidence ratings from 43 per cent to 25 per cent between 1982 and 1988.

The positive relationship between the community and the police came to be known as 'the British police advantage' and was envied by many other countries.[35] By the middle of the next decade, this advantage was slipping away. Some put this down to the dramatic increase in car ownership, which not only made the police more remote from the citizen, but also provided increased opportunities for negative contacts between the public and the police as they dealt with motoring and other traffic-related offences. The transformation of policing into a professional specialist activity also produced an alienating influence.

There was considerable debate on the style of policing with some emphasis placed on the need for the consent and general support of the community for police activity. By contrast others favoured 'hard' policing and saw the overriding model as being conflictual: tough measures were seen as essential in the fight against crime. There was also debate about the extent to which the police themselves unearth crime. Some argued that the police should be principally reactive, responding to reports of offences from victims or others affected by criminal conduct. Others saw a role for pro-active policing where the police actively seek out crime. This approach is particularly controversial in the context of the so-called 'victimless' crimes involving drugs or pornography.[36]

In their various roles, the police are given special powers to stop, detain and question persons suspected of having committed criminal offences. Often what results from this initial interaction between suspect and the police forms the basis of the case against the suspect. Because at this stage the suspect is deemed innocent, it is often said that there is a careful balance to be struck between the liberties of the individual and the protection of society.[37] In the mid-1970s there was serious concern that the balance had been lost. Some argued that the increasing incidence of serious crime was partly caused by the restraints of criminal procedure preventing the police from proceeding against persons known to have committed offences. Others argued that a serious gap had arisen between the formal protection provided for suspects by the rules of criminal procedure and the actual practice of those rules. The formal protection was, it was argued, illusory.

Matters were brought to a head by the wrongful conviction of three youths for the murder of Maxwell Confait. The subsequent enquiry into this case revealed improprieties in the police conduct of the investigation of the offence.[38] The response to these concerns was the establishment in June 1977 of the Royal Commission on

---

[35] J. Benyon, 'In the Limelight: the Changing Context of Policing' in C. Bourn and J. Benyon, *The Police: Powers, Procedures and Proprieties* (Oxford: Pergamon Press, 1986), p. 3.

[36] For a useful discussion of the literature see A. Sanders and R. Young, *Criminal Justice* (London: Butterworths, 1994), pp. 27–34.

[37] See generally *Report of the Royal Commission on Criminal Procedure (Philips Commission)* (London: HMSO, 1981, Cmnd. 8092), and *Report of the Royal Commission on Criminal Justice (Runciman Commission)* (London: HMSO, 1993, Cm. 2263).

[38] *Report of an Inquiry into the Circumstances leading to the Trial of Three Persons on Charges arising out of the Death of Maxwell Confait and the Fire at 27 Doggett Road, London SE6, (Fisher Report)*, HCP 90 (London: HMSO, 1977).

Criminal Procedure ('the Philips Commission') which reported in 1981 on the processes of investigation of crime and the prosecution of offenders.[39]

The Philips Commission's 'fundamental balance'

The Philips Commission was noteworthy for the volume of original research which it commissioned in order to provide a sound empirical basis on which its recommendations could be based. The research studies were published under the aegis of the Philips Commission and provide valuable information about the operation of the criminal process. The Report of the Philips Commission had as its philosophical base the concept of a fundamental balance between the interests of the community in bringing offenders to justice and the liberties of persons suspected of crime. The Report recognises the difficulty of identifying the central features of this fundamental balance. Ultimately the Report concludes that it is the responsibility of Parliament to load the scales in order to strike the fundamental balance, and to keep that balance under regular review. But throughout the Report it is clear that the Commission considered that individual rights and community interests should be carefully balanced and that this would provide the litmus test for determining the coherence and effectiveness of the pre-trial criminal process. The choices made should manifest qualities of fairness, openness and workability.

The Philips Commission considered that it had produced a carefully constructed package which clarified police powers, but in each case balanced them with safeguards designed to protect the citizen. It was a powerful and challenging report that generated discussion and debate on policing. It was the kind of report which cannot be shelved. The government's response was to base new legislation on its recommendations.

PACE and the Codes of Practice

The legislation was so controversial that the first attempt to secure a new statute was a casualty of the calling of the 1983 general election. During the Parliamentary session before the 1983 election, the major report on policing in London which had been commissioned by Sir David McNee, the Metropolitan Police Commissioner, into his force was published.[40] This provided further evidence of the failure of existing safeguards to protect the citizen. The study presents a picture of the police a world away from the cosy comfort of the 'Dixon of Dock Green' image of the 1950s. Following their return to power, the Conservative Government returned to Parliament with substantially the same bill. In due course this became

---

[39] *Report of the Royal Commission on Criminal Procedure (Philips Commission)* (London: HMSO, 1981, Cmnd. 8092).

[40] D. Smith and others, *Police and People in London*, 4 vols. (London: Policy Studies Institute, 1983).

the Police and Criminal Evidence Act 1984 ('PACE'). This Act and its counterpart, the Prosecution of Offences Act 1985, have been described by Lord Scarman as follows:

The two Acts will in due course work great changes in the way the criminal law is enforced. They will re-structure the whole criminal process from arrest or summons up to the moment at which the trial begins. Our police and prosecution services will be changed irreversibly; the old pattern will fade into history.[41]

PACE itself contains a core of rules dealing with the pre-trial criminal process from stop and search on the street to charge at the police station. It also makes changes to the rules of evidence and updates the police complaints procedure. PACE adopts the device of coupling rules in the primary legislation with detailed guidance contained in Codes of Practice, which the Home Secretary is required to prepare and submit to Parliament for approval under sections 66 and 67 of PACE. These Codes are of enormous significance. Though not technically subordinate legislation, they have much the same effect.

PACE and its Codes remain at the heart of the pre-trial criminal process, though a number of significant changes have been made to the rules it contains.

Continuing concerns

The Philips Commission had addressed the investigation of offences and the decision to prosecute, but a number of high-profile miscarriages of justice called into question the ability of the institutions of the criminal justice system to rectify mistakes. The eventual over-turning of the convictions of the Guildford Four[42] and the Birmingham Six[43] were the immediate catalysts for the establishment of the Runciman Commission. Further miscarriages of justice followed thick and fast: the Maguires,[44] Judith Ward,[45] Stefan Kiszko,[46] the Tottenham Three,[47] the Darvell Brothers,[48] the Cardiff Three,[49] the Taylor sisters,[50] Ivan Fergus,[51] together with a number of lesser profile cases where the conviction resulted from the misconduct of the West Midlands Serious Crimes Squad.[52] More recently, there has been the overturning of the conviction in the Bridgewater Four case.[53] Though some of the

[41] C. Bourn and J. Benyon, *The Police: Powers, Procedures and Proprieties* (Oxford: Pergamon Press, 1986), p. xix.
[42] Amstrong, Conlon, Hill and Richardson, released in October 1989 after serving 14 years in prison.
[43] *McIlkenny and others* (1991) 93 Cr. App. R 287.   [44] (1992) 94 Cr. App. R 133.
[45] *Judith Ward* (1993) 96 Cr. App. R 1.
[46] Released in February 1992 after serving 16 years for the murder of the schoolgirl, Lesley Molseed. See A. Sanders and R. Young, *Criminal Justice* (London: Butterworths, 1994), p. 185.
[47] *Raghip, Silcott and Braithwaite, The Times*, 9 December 1991.
[48] Released in July 1992 after serving six years for the murder of a Swansea sex shop manageress: see JUSTICE, *Annual Report 1989*, pp. 21–3 and *Annual Report 1993*, p. 16.
[49] *Paris, Abdullahi and Miller* (1993) 97 Cr. App. R 99.   [50] (1994) 98 Cr. App. R 361.
[51] (1994) 98 Cr. App. R 313.   [52] See, for background, *Edwards* [1991] 2 All ER 266.
[53] Released in February 1997 after spending 18 years in prison for the murder of Carl Bridgewater. The fourth defendant, Pat Molloy, had died in prison. The police force involved was the West Midlands Regional Crime Squad.

investigations and convictions pre-dated the provisions of PACE and its Codes, a number had arisen despite what were seen as new protections against miscarriages of justice embodied in the post-Philips Commission changes.

The response was the establishment of a further Royal Commission in March 1991, which reported in July 1993.[54] The political climate in which the Runciman Commission deliberated included not only concern that there had been a series of appalling miscarriages of justice, but also a feeling that it was sometimes too easy to avoid conviction. The result was that the terms of reference of the Royal Commission included re-consideration of the so-called 'right to silence' at various stages of the criminal process. As with the Philips Commission, the Runciman Commission had the benefit of specially commissioned research studies on a number of key aspects of their enquiries in formulating their conclusions.

Yet more legislation

The immediate response to the report of the Runciman Commission was the enactment of certain provisions of the Criminal Justice and Public Order Act 1994, together with a new Criminal Appeal Act 1995, and more recently the Criminal Procedure and Investigations Act 1996.

The current status of the Codes

Codes of Practice are now a feature of the criminal process. There are a series of Codes made under PACE, as well as a Code for Crown Prosecutors made under the Prosecution of Offences Act 1995 and a Code under Part II of the Criminal Procedure and Investigations Act 1996. The Codes are not statutory material, though they are required by statute, and have been described as having the full 'authority of Parliament'.[55] They are intended to be clear and helpful working guidelines for police, prosecutors, and lawyers.

The PACE Codes were originally incorporated as part of the internal police disciplinary provisions, so that it was a breach of internal discipline for a constable to fail to comply with the provisions of the Code.[56] But this provision has been repealed in what can only be seen as a deliberate weakening of their status. Section 67(10) of PACE provides that a failure to comply with the provisions of the Codes does not, of itself, render a constable liable to any criminal or civil proceedings. This means that a police officer ignoring the provisions of the Codes only commits a criminal offence if the conduct would otherwise amount to a crime. Beating up a suspect in a police cell is a breach of a number of provisions of Code C on the detention, treatment and questioning of suspects, but it will only be a crime by the constable because the constable's conduct will almost certainly amount to

[54] *Report of the Royal Commission on Criminal Justice (Runciman Commission)* (London: HMSO, 1993, Cm. 2263). For a series of essays on aspects of the Runciman Commission's Report, see M. McConville and L. Bridges (eds.), *Criminal Justice in Crisis* (Aldershot: Edward Elgar, 1994).

[55] *McCay* (1990) 91 Cr. App. R 84, 87–8, CA.   [56] PACE, s. 67(8).

an offence against the person under the criminal law. Equally, a failure to comply with Code A in stopping and searching a person will not, of itself, render the constable liable in damages for trespass to the person. The aggrieved individual will have to establish such a claim under the ordinary rules of the law of tort.

In each of the above examples, the person complaining about police conduct can adduce in evidence the requirements of the relevant Code's provisions. Section 67(11) of PACE provides that:

if any provision of such a code appears to the court or tribunal conducting the proceedings to be relevant to any question in the proceedings it shall be taken into account in determining that question.

Note that the provision is mandatory. The use of the word 'shall' makes clear that if a provision of a Code is relevant to a question before any court or tribunal, it must be taken into account.

The Court of Appeal has emphasised, however, that a common sense approach is needed to the interpretation of the PACE Codes:

It is plainly desirable that [the provisions of the PACE Codes] should not become so highly technical and sophisticated in their construction and application that no police officer, however well intentioned and diligent, could reasonably be expected to comply with them. There has to be a reasonable common-sense approach to the matter such that police officers, confronted with unexpected situations, and doing their best to be fair and to comply with the Codes, do not fall foul of some technicality of authority or construction.[57]

The European Convention on Human Rights

The incorporation of the European Convention on Human Rights into United Kingdom law by the Human Rights Act 1998[58] has introduced a further code to which the police as public authorities will need to have regard. There are many provisions of the European Convention which are relevant to the pre-trial stage of criminal proceedings. Of particular relevance are Article 3 on the prohibition on torture, inhuman and degrading treatment, Article 5 on protection of liberty, and Article 8 on the protection of family and private life, home and correspondence. There are also implications flowing from Article 6 on the right to a fair trial which impact upon the method of collecting evidence and upon the quality of evidence. For the first time, suspects will be able to raise their Convention rights in the criminal courts rather than pursuing their remedies elsewhere, possibly having no alternative but to submit an application to the Strasbourg organs.[59]

---

[57] *Marsh* [1991] Crim. LR 433, CA.   [58] See Ch. 2.

[59] See generally, L. Leigh, 'The Influence of the European Convention on Human Rights on English Criminal Law and Procedure' (1993) 1 *European Journal of Crime, Criminal Law and Criminal Justice* 3; S. Sharpe, 'The European Convention: A Suspect's Charter?' [1997] Crim. LR 848; and C. Ovey, 'The European Convention on Human Rights and the Criminal Lawyer' [1998] Crim. LR 4.

Discretion

The police have considerable discretion in the investigation and prosecution of criminal offences. Obviously with something in excess of 8,000 different criminal offences, the criminal justice system would soon grind to a halt if the police relentlessly and inexorably pursued to prosecution every infringement which came to their knowledge. There is insufficient staff in the police force, in the legal profession and in the courts for such action; nor is there a public demand for such intensive policing. Four distinct areas of police discretion can be identified: the chief constable's discretion in allocating the resources of his force; the allocation of resources to the solving of a particular crime; choice on the street; and choice over whether or not to charge an offender.

Allocating the resources of the force

The first area of discretion is that vested in each chief constable to determine the general allocation of resources to particular operational tasks.[60] The courts will not interfere with the judgment of chief constables in determining priorities for their forces. The classic statement of this discretion is by Lord Denning:

It is for . . . the chief constable . . . to decide in any particular case whether enquiries should be pursued, or whether an arrest should be made or a prosecution brought. It must be for him to decide on the disposition of his force and the concentration of his resources on any particular crime or area. No court can or should give him directions on such a matter. He can also make policy decisions and give effect to them . . . But there are some policy decisions with which, I think, the courts in a case can, if necessary, interfere. Suppose a chief constable were to issue a directive to his men that no person should be prosecuted for stealing any goods less than £100 in value. I should have thought that the courts could countermand it. He would be failing in his duty to enforce the law.[61]

This principle has been restated with approval.[62] In the *CEGB* case the Court of Appeal refused to interfere with a policy decision by John Alderson, the architect of community policing, not to use the police to remove objectors whose presence was interfering with a CEGB survey of a potential site for a nuclear power station. These cases make it clear that chief constables may not re-write the law by, for example, making a general policy decision not to prosecute cases of theft involving less than £100, but may make decisions on issues involving the allocation of police resources.

---

[60] *Fisher* v. *Oldham Corporation* [1930] 2 KB 364.

[61] *R* v. *Commissioner of Police for the Metropolis, ex parte Blackburn* [1968] 2 QB 118, 136.

[62] *R* v. *Commissioner of Police for the Metropolis, ex parte Blackburn (No. 2)* [1968] 2 QB 150, and in *R* v. *Chief Constable of Devon and Cornwall, ex parte Central Electricity Generating Board* [1982] QB 458.

Allocating resources to a particular crime

The second area of discretion involves a police officer's decision as to the resources to be devoted to the investigation of a particular crime. Again it is clear that the police are under no duty to investigate to the limit of their resources every complaint of an alleged offence which is reported to them. As noted above cases where the chances of apprehending the offender seem slim receive only minimal attention.

Where police-public encounters involved a request for some form of assistance, most dissatisfaction has arisen where the public regard the police as not putting in as much effort in responding to the issue as the public had expected.[63]

Choice on the street

The third area of discretion is that enjoyed by a police officer in deciding how to respond to some incident in which he or she becomes involved. The classic example is the minor motoring offence. A driver is observed by the police driving a car with a defective brake light. There has clearly been an offence, but the police may choose whether or not to stop the car and, if they do so, whether or not to press charges. If the driver is stopped, the police may simply advise the driver to have the light repaired as soon as possible. This is a fairly uncontentious example.

More contentious are the decisions made by police officers as to whether to stop, to stop and search, or to arrest individuals, all of which involve an exercise of discretion by the police. The exercise, and control, of discretion in these types of cases obviously has an impact on the style of policing. In this area research has suggested that stereotyping of individuals plays an important role.[64] One (now dated) guide for police officers even lists indications of suspiciousness, which suggests that young people, anyone unconventional in appearance, or people in old cars should be regarded as suspicious.[65] The Policy Studies Institute's Report found that Afro-Caribbean men between the ages of fifteen and twenty-four were likely to be stopped with considerable frequency, and with much greater frequency than white or Asian males in the same age group.[66] Other studies have produced similar findings.[67]

One justification put forward for the use of stereotypes is that they are the product of experience, but it should be noted that the use of stereotypes can lead to self-fulfilling prophecies. If more members of a particular group are stopped, then it is likely that offences by that group will take on a prominence quite independently of the accuracy of the stereotyping. Equally, even where statistical evidence provides some basis for the stereotype, it is inaccurate in relation to the majority

---

[63] W. Skogan, *The Police and the Public in England and Wales: A British Crime Survey Report*, Home Office Research Study No. 117 (London: HMSO, 1990), pp. 19–25.

[64] S. McCabe and F. Sutcliffe, *Defining Crime: A Study of Police Definitions* (Oxford: Basil Blackwell, 1978), and see D. Smith and others, *Policing and People in London*, 4 vols. (London: Policy Studies Institute, 1983).

[65] D. Powis, *The Signs of Crime: A Field Manual for Police* (Maidenhead: McGraw-Hill, 1977).

[66] See also D. Smith and others, *Policing and People in London*, (London: Policy Studies Institute, 1983), vol. I.

[67] W. Skogan, *The Police and the Public in England and Wales: A British Crime Survey Report*, Home Office Research Study No. 117 (London: HMSO, 1990), ch. 3.

of persons within that group. Stops of individuals in London result in the discovery of some offence in only about one in eight cases, which, of course, means that seven innocent individuals have been stopped. The solution to the problem of the appropriate exercise of discretion in this area would seem to depend on the existence of effective human awareness training as part of police training. Some efforts are made to do this, but there still seem real problems over the existence of a 'police culture' inside police stations where group norms operate very powerfully to ensure compliance with the prevailing culture which may be at variance with that put forward in training.[68]

Choice on the street is, however, not wholly personal. Police officers are subject to instructions contained in detailed standing orders. There will be force expectations about the appropriate response to particular incidents. A decision to stop and search, or to arrest an individual, is effectively subject to supervision by decisions taken by superior officers, who may require particular action consequent upon the constable's initial action. For example, a more senior police officer may require that a suspect be charged, where the arresting officer proposes only a caution. Where police discretion is greatest, because it is not susceptible to hierarchical decision-making, is where a constable chooses *not* to take action. In most cases, that will be the end of the matter.

Charging offenders

The final discretion residing with the police is whether or not to charge or summons when they have clear and credible evidence that the suspect has committed the alleged offence. The advent of the Crown Prosecution Service[69] has not altogether removed this area of discretion; it still remains for the police to start the ball rolling by charging a suspect or issuing a summons. The way the police exercise this discretion is considered below in Chapter 6.

The police remain in almost exclusive control of the pre-trial stages of the criminal process, from initial interaction on the street to the point of charge or the issuing of a summons. At many points they will exercise choices as to how they should tackle the issue facing them.

Stop and Search

The problem

The Philips Commission noted the confusing state of the law relating to the police's powers of stop and search, which formed a mosaic of local and national

---

[68] See D. Smith and others, *Policing and People in London* (London: Policy Studies Institute, 1983), vol. I, and M. Young, *An Inside Job: Policing and Police Culture in Britain* (Oxford: Clarendon Press, 1991), ch. 3.
[69] See Ch. 6.

provisions. The position was sufficiently complex that few could have any certainty that they knew the law applying in the place they were and consequently few were in a position to challenge action taken by the police. .

Some argued that the existence of stop and search powers was a source of friction between the police and the public. A minority of those giving evidence to the Philips Commission argued that specific powers were not needed, because a power of personal search existed on arrest; interference with an individual's civil liberties should not arise unless there was a level of suspicion sufficient to justify an arrest. The majority of submissions, however, merely called for rationalisation of the powers of stop and search, and improved remedies for those against whom such powers are used unlawfully.

The exercise of a power to stop and search has always been triggered by a requirement of reasonable suspicion that the constable will find on the person, or in the vehicle, searched a specific article evidencing the commission of an offence to which the power attaches. The courts have never required a high level of suspicion to justify a stop and search. Mere suspicion was enough. This led to stops being based on appearance and, it seems, racial group rather than satisfaction of some objective test. Empirical evidence bears this out.

The Policy Studies Institute's Report found that the requirement of reasonable suspicion was not an effective constraint on police officers in their decisions whether or not to stop and search. The Report also finds that the choice of person to stop is not random, but is based on stereotypes of persons thought likely to be offenders. The study estimated that the police in London stopped 1.5 million people or vehicles each year and that this resulted in the discovery of about 100,000 offences. Only one person in twenty was arrested as a result of the stop and search. In one-third of the cases observed the survey could see no good reason for the stop.[70] In giving evidence to the Philips Commission, a number of police forces admitted stopping and searching individuals where there was no authority to do so. The justification put forward was that the use of stop and search was a valuable tool in the fight against crime and that in almost all cases the person stopped 'consented' to the stop and search. This, of course, begs the question. There may have been no objection raised, but this absence of protest is likely to have been based on the assumption that the police had a power to stop and search. In such cases the consent is illusory because it is not informed. The survey notes that about four in five stops are fairly relaxed and amiable affairs, but nevertheless concludes that 'stops tend to have a poor effect on people's relations with the police even where . . . they are fairly relaxed and amiable encounters'.[71]

The Philips Commission recommended a consolidation and rationalisation of the powers of stop and search available to the police. Part I of PACE does not contain a comprehensive code on the powers of stop and search, because it does not re-enact specific powers given in other legislation. The most significant of these is

---

[70] D. Smith and others, *Policing and People in London* (London: Policy Studies Institute, 1983), vol. IV.
[71] Ibid., p. 323.

the power to stop and search persons suspected of being in possession of controlled drugs under the Misuse of Drugs Act 1971. There have been a number of amendments to Part I of PACE, and additional powers have been included in other legislation. The legal position is again beginning to resemble the mosaic of provisions which the Philips Commission found to be a source of confusion.

Powers of stop and search

A helpful methodology for considering police powers of stop and search is to consider what items have a power of stop and search attached to them, when the power may be exercised, and where and how it must be exercised.[72]

What for?

A complete (but not guaranteed to be exhaustive) list of powers of stop and search can be found in Appendix A to Code of Practice A on Stop and Search.[73] The powers most frequently exercised are (1) for stolen goods, prohibited articles, and items with points or blades under section 1 of PACE; and (2) for controlled drugs under the Misuse of Drugs Act 1971. In addition there is a power to search at random when violence is anticipated.[74]

Section 1 of PACE enables a police officer to stop and search any person or vehicle in a public place or a place to which the public has access, if the police officer has reasonable grounds for suspecting that the person is in possession of, or the vehicle contains, stolen goods or other prohibited articles, or 'any article to which subsection (8A) below applies'. Prohibited articles include offensive weapons (articles made, adapted, or intended to be used, for causing injury) or articles made or adapted for use in connection with a burglary, theft, taking of a motor car or the obtaining of property by deception. Subsection (8A) includes certain articles having a blade or point and cross-refers to section 139 of the Criminal Justice Act 1988.[75]

So the first question that constables must consider is what they are searching for. There is no power to search in the general hope of finding something possession of which is unlawful. The law requires a much more specific target item than that.

When?

In most cases, the crucial trigger justifying the stop and search remains reasonable suspicion of possession of stolen goods or prohibited articles, or some other article for which a power of stop and search exists. Reasonable suspicion was originally explained in Annex B of Code A, which applied to all stop and search powers whatever their authority. The test laid down in Annex B was much tougher than that applicable before the implementation of PACE. The level of suspicion required

---

[72] Unless otherwise stated, this chapter does not deal with special powers available for the prevention of terrorism.   [73] Revised edition, effective 15 May 1997 (London: HMSO, 1997).

[74] See Criminal Justice and Public Order Act 1994, s. 60, which is discussed below.

[75] But see *Deegan*, Court of Appeal, 4 February 1998, for the problems of interpreting the knives which fall within s. 139.

was the same as that required for arrest. The exercise of the lesser intrusion into a person's civil liberties of stop and search rather than arrest is preferred because it may obviate the need for an arrest. Mere suspicion, hunch or instinct would not be sufficient justification. The test required the existence of material susceptible to objective evaluation. A good way of looking at the test was to consider whether an impartial third party, presented with the specific observations of the constable in the face of a particular incident together with any other information known to the constable, would agree that there were reasonable grounds for suspecting possession of the specific article sought by the person in question. Reasonable suspicion must exist before a person is stopped. Questioning following a stop cannot provide reasonable suspicion, though naturally it may confirm or dispel it. Code A has now been substantially rewritten in the face of complaints from the police that the original version was difficult to follow and apply. The definition of reasonable suspicion has been changed by the removal of the requirement that the facts upon which the reasonable suspicion is based are particular to the individual to be searched. The test is no longer as tough as it was in the first version. The Code now reads:

1.6 Whether a reasonable ground for suspicion exists will depend on the circumstances in each case, but there must be some objective basis for it. An officer will need to consider the nature of the article suspected of being carried in the context of other factors such as the time and the place, and the behaviour of the person concerned or those with him. Reasonable suspicion may exist, for example, where information has been received such as a description of an article being carried or of a suspected offender; a person is seen acting covertly or warily or attempting to hide something; or a person is carrying a certain type of article at an unusual time or in a place where a number of burglaries or thefts are known to have taken place recently. But the decision to stop and search must be based on all the facts which bear on the likelihood that an article of a certain kind will be found.

1.6A For example, reasonable suspicion may be based upon reliable information or intelligence which indicates that members of a particular group or gang, or their associates, habitually carry knives unlawfully or weapons or controlled drugs.

1.7 Subject to the provision in paragraph 1.7AA below, reasonable suspicion can never be supported on the basis of personal factors alone without supporting intelligence or information. For example, a person's colour, age, hairstyle or manner of dress, or the fact that he is known to have a previous conviction for possession of an unlawful article, cannot be used alone or in combination with each other as the sole basis on which to search that person. Nor may it be founded on the basis of stereotyped images of certain persons or groups as more likely to be committing offences.

1.7AA However, where there is reliable information or intelligence that members of a group or gang who habitually carry knives unlawfully or weapons or controlled drugs, and wear a distinctive item of clothing or other means of identification to indicate membership of it, the members may be identified by means of that distinctive item of clothing or other means of identification.

The standard embodied in this guidance is not high.

Where?

The statutory provision giving the power to stop and search will often specify where the power may be exercised. For example, the power in the Misuse of Drugs Act 1971 enables the power to be exercised anywhere.[76] By contrast, the power in section 1 of PACE enables searches to be conducted:

(a) in any place to which at the time when he proposes to exercise the power the public or any section of the public has access, on payment or otherwise, as of right or by virtue of express or implied permission; or

(b) in any other place to which people have ready access at the time when he proposes to exercise the power but which is not a dwelling.

This rather complex provision covers such things as private car parks and shopping centres, garage forecourts, restaurants and cinemas when open to the public, open ground, and unlocked buildings which are not dwellings. There could be debate about the difference between the 'public', a 'section of the public', and 'people'.[77] A person can only be searched in the garden or yard of a dwelling house where the constable has reasonable grounds for believing that the person does not live there and is not in the garden or yard with the permission of the owner.

How?

PACE and Code A also contain rules on the conduct of the search, which include requirements before the search is conducted, rules on the conduct of the search, and action to be taken on completion of the search. Constables not in uniform are required to produce their warrant card, that is, documentary evidence that they are a constable.[78]

In all cases there are notification requirements, which are designed to ensure that constables have directed their minds to the statutory requirements governing the exercise of the powers. First, the constable should consider whether a stop *and* search is necessary. It may, for example, be that a few questions will remove the need to proceed to a search. Code A makes clear that questioning cannot provide the basis for reasonable suspicion where that is required; such suspicion must exist before the person is stopped.[79]

If the constable decides to proceed to a search, then he or she must notify the person to be searched of their name, the police station to which they are attached, what they are searching for, and the basis for the search.[80] In most cases, the person searched will also be entitled to a copy of the national search record, and notification of entitlement to this is also required.[81] Where reasonable suspicion is required, the notification might be in the following terms:

---

[76] See s. 23(2) of the 1971 Act, though this provision does not give a right of entry onto private property in order to conduct the search. The constable must be lawfully there in order to exercise the power.

[77] See H. Levenson, F. Fairweather and E. Cape, *Police Powers. A Practitioner's Guide*, 3rd edn. (London: Legal Action Group, 1996), pp. 21–2, and K. Lidstone and C. Palmer, *Bevan and Lidstone's The Investigation of Crime. A Guide to Police Powers*, 2nd edn. (London: Butterworths, 1996), pp. 65–8.

[78] PACE, s. 2(2)(b)(ii) and Code A, para. 2.5.

[79] Code A, para. 2.3. But see *Lodwick* v. *Sanders* [1985] 1 WLR 382.

[80] PACE, s. 2.   [81] PACE, s. 3.

My name is Police Constable Wendy Clive and I am stationed at Charles Street Police Station. I wish to search you for drugs, since I just saw you exchange money for a foil packet which I believe to be drugs. After the search, I will give you a record of it to keep.

In carrying out the search, embarrassment to the person must be kept to a minimum. Force may only be used as a matter of last resort, but section 117 of PACE authorises the use of reasonable force where necessary in exercise of powers given by PACE. Most searches should take no more than a few minutes.[82]

Where a search takes place in public, the person searched may not be required to remove more than an outer coat, jacket and gloves.[83] The omission of reference to headgear may be an oversight, though the Code suggests, rather confusingly, that removal of footwear and headgear may be required 'in a police van or a nearby police station if there is one'.[84] Since removal of the person under compulsion to a police station would constitute an arrest, it is difficult to see what the Code is envisaging here.

The omission of any reference to searching bags has also given rise to academic argument as to whether the power extends to such searches. It probably does, because section 2(9)(a) of PACE is concerned with the reduction of embarrassment and the search of a bag is not cognate with requirements that a person removes items of clothing. Any other interpretation would also result in an anomaly. If the bag was in or on a vehicle, it could be searched,[85] but if it is being carried by a person it could not.

The constable must as soon as is reasonably practicable after the completion of the search make a record of the search which states the name of the person searched, the object of, and grounds for, the search, the date and time of the search and the identity of the officer making the search. If a vehicle is searched, a note describing the vehicle must be made. This record is known as the national search record. The police officer need not make a record if it is impracticable to do so. An example would be where multiple searches are made of persons attending a football match where the need to make notes would interfere with the purpose of the searches. Within twelve months of the date of the search, the person searched is entitled on request to a copy of any record made of the search. In most cases a copy of the national search record is handed over on the spot.

The annual reports of police authorities must contain information about searches carried out within their areas. Though information about specific searches is not required, a monthly breakdown of searches for stolen goods, offensive weapons and for other prohibited articles and the total number of arrests each month resulting from such searches must be given.

Random searches under section 60 authorisation
The Criminal Justice and Public Order Act 1994[86] introduced a system of random searches limited in time and location where the requirement of reasonable

---

[82] Code A, para. 3.3.   [83] PACE, s. 2(9)(a).   [84] Code A, para. 3.5.
[85] PACE, s. 1(3).   [86] As amended by the Knives Act 1997.

suspicion of possession of the item for which the search is made would not apply. Such searches require authorisation from a police officer of at least the rank of inspector[87] who reasonably believes that incidents involving serious violence may take place in a locality, or that persons are carrying dangerous instruments or offensive weapons in any locality. The authorisation permits random searches in a defined locality for up to 24 hours, but the authorisation can be extended for a further six hours beyond 24 hours by an officer of at least the rank of superintendent.

Apart from the absence of any requirement of reasonable suspicion, the safeguards of notification and recording equally apply to searches under section 60. The power was exercised extensively during the Euro 96 football competition. Unfortunately the number of section 60 authorisations is not recorded, but in the financial year 1996/97[88] some 7,974 searches were conducted under such authorisations. These resulted in 177 persons being found in possession of offensive weapons and 129 arrested for this reason. Interestingly the random searches resulted in 392 arrests for other reasons.[89]

Has the new law made any difference?

The principal safeguard against abusive searches is the requirement of reasonable suspicion, which is supported by the notification and recording requirements. It is open to question whether these safeguards are effective. The powers given by legislation are sweeping and it seems that the requirement of reasonable suspicion is not an effective constraint. Much will therefore depend on the response to the monitoring of stops and searches. No specific sanctions are provided in the Act for failure to follow the required procedures. Some empirical evidence since the introduction of PACE suggests that factors other than those to which the legislation and Code directs the constable's mind are again taking over. Constables explained their reasons for stopping and searching individuals in the following terms: 'Just a matter of instinct . . . something undefinable'.[90] 'When you get to know an area, and see a villain about at 2.00 am . . . you always stop him to see what he's about'.[91]

Some statistical information on the incidence of stop and search since the implementation of PACE is now available. This showed an initial sharp reduction in the numbers of stops and searches, followed by a steady increase in their use. Figure 5.1 shows the overall position in chart form. In the corresponding period, the number of arrests resulting from searches as a proportion of the number of searches has declined from just over 17 per cent to just 10 per cent. There are also

---

[87] Formerly authorisation was required from an officer of at least the rank of superintendent: see Knives Act 1997, s. 8, for amendment lowering the rank.

[88] Figures are now kept by financial year rather than calendar year.

[89] G. Wilkins and C. Addicott, *Operation of Certain Police Powers under PACE, England and Wales 1996*, Home Office Statistical Bulletin Issue 27/97 (London: Home Office, December 1996).

[90] M. McConville, A. Sanders and R. Leng, *The Case for the Prosecution* (London: Routledge, 1991), p. 27.

[91] Ibid., p. 24.

Figure 5.1. **Searches and arrests resulting from searches***

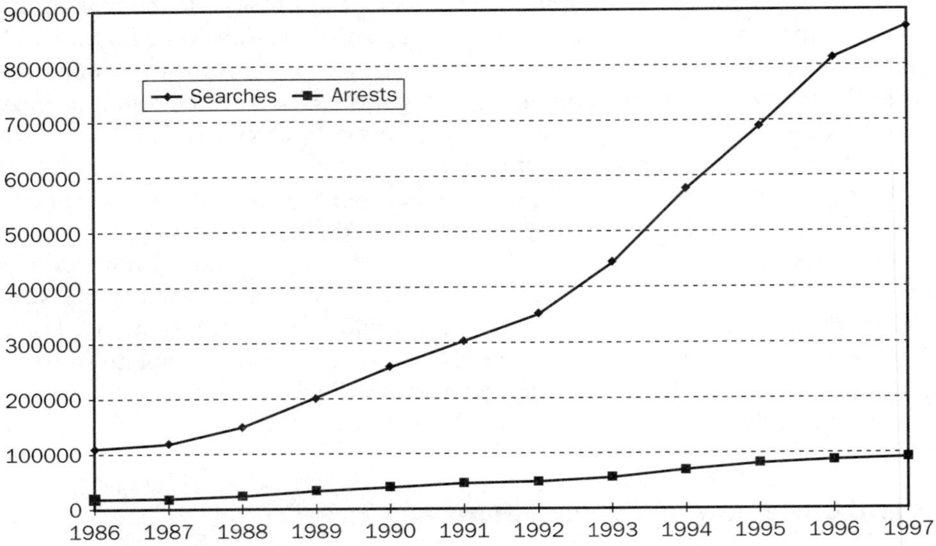

*Source of data: G. Wilkins and C. Addicott, *Operation of Certain Police Powers under PACE. England and Wales 1996*, Home Office Statistical Bulletin Issue 27/97 (London: Home Office, December 1996).

very significant regional variations; you are twice as likely to be stopped and searched in Leicestershire than in the neighbouring counties of Nottinghamshire and Staffordshire.

It can be argued that the old discredited 'sus' laws under which a person could be stopped on the vague grounds of behaving suspiciously[92] have been reintroduced in modern dress by the steady erosion of the protections which were initially contained in PACE and its accompanying Code A. The current definition of 'reasonable suspicion' is much less demanding that the original version, and now there is also the possibility of random searches under section 60 of the Criminal Justice and Public Order Act 1994. But much more worrying is the empirical evidence that those exercising the powers do not feel constrained by the strictures of the legislative requirements when taking decisions on the streets.

The troublesome issue of consent

During the debates and discussions leading to the enactment of PACE, the police had argued that there was little problem with the exercise of stop and search on an informal basis, since most stops and searches were amiable affairs in which most

---

[92] Technically 'being a suspected person loitering with intent to commit an arrestable offence' under the repealed Vagrancy Act 1824, s. 4. See also P. Boateng, '"Sus" Law' (1979) 3 *Rights!* (London: NCCL, 1979), 10.

reasonable people readily consented to being searched. The question is whether the consent search has survived the changes introduced by PACE.

Code A is now equivocal on this issue. Note 1B fairly points to the duty[93] of every citizen to assist the police. Equally Note 1D properly notes that the statutory provisions do not affect the routine searches of those entering sports grounds or other events as a condition of entry to them, but the note goes on to state that the Code does not affect 'the ability of an officer to search a person in the street with his consent where no search power exists'. The note does make it clear that such a search should only proceed where the person has been told that they need not consent and that without consent they will not be searched.

Note 1E is most odd: 'If an officer acts in an improper manner this will invalidate a voluntary search'.

Two questions can be posed. What does 'invalidation' of the search mean? Does it mean that any arrest based on what is found will be unlawful and will not be accepted by the custody officer? Secondly, why are voluntary searches needed? The answer is presumably to look for things for which Parliament has not given any power of stop and search, or to circumvent the safeguards which surround statutory searches.

Remedies

A person who is sure that a constable is acting without any lawful authority is entitled to resist any attempt at a search. The constable, believing he or she has power to do so, may well choose to use force, and will treat the person's resistance as an assault on a police officer in the execution of her or her duty.[94] The result will almost certainly be an uphill struggle in defending a prosecution for the assault on the constable. This self-help remedy is not therefore a remedy which is realistically available to any but the most knowledgeable and confident of individuals.

An alternative could be to object to the stop and search but not resist the constable, and later to sue in the civil courts for trespass to the person. There appear to be no reports of any cases where such an action has been taken. If it were, the damages would be likely to be very small since the interference is minor and of restricted duration.

The third possibility is a complaint against the police.[95]

There is also the possibility that an unlawful search might violate your rights under certain provisions of the European Convention, but the requirement to pursue domestic remedies will mean that one or more of the above strategies would need to be adopted before the matter could be raised in Strasbourg; in many cases the violation would be exceedingly minor, for example, being deprived of your liberty for a matter of minutes.

---

[93] Which is unenforceable since there is no sanction if a citizen declines to assist.
[94] An offence under the Police Act 1996, s. 89.   [95] See Ch. 6.

Entry, Search and Seizure

On occasion, the police will need to enter premises to search for evidence. The general rule is that, unless some affirmative justification exists, a constable may not enter premises without the consent of the occupier. There are, however, innumerable statutory rights of entry given to the police and various other officials.[96] We are here concerned only with those general powers available to the police for the purpose of the investigation of suspected criminal activity. The protection of the home and correspondence under Article 8 of the European Convention on Human Rights is likely to result in some development of the law in this area, since the development of the rights in this article remains to be completed by Strasbourg's Court of Human Rights.

Search with a warrant

PACE leaves unaffected most rules concerning the obtaining of search warrants. There are many statutes, such as the Theft Act 1968 and the Misuse of Drugs Act 1971, empowering magistrates to issue warrants authorising entry to and search of premises for specific purposes. Magistrates have a duty to satisfy themselves that it is right to issue a warrant and may question the person swearing the information requesting the warrant. Where the information is based on a tip-off from an informer, there is no obligation to disclose the identity of the informer, though the magistrate may ask questions to assess the likely truth of the tip-off. The Philips Commission noted the criticisms raised by some who gave evidence 'that magistrates may exercise insufficient care in ensuring that a warrant is necessary; and that too often they merely rubber stamp police requests'.[97]

Prior to PACE the police had no *general* power to seek warrants to search for evidence. Specific powers had to be exercised. The absence of a general power gave rise to anomalies. The Philips Commission noted that there was no power of entry to search the scene of a kidnap or murder. Section 8 of PACE remedies this, deficiency by allowing the issue of a warrant to search for evidence where there are reasonable grounds for believing that a *serious arrestable offence* has been committed. Section 116 of PACE contains a rather tortuous definition of serious arrestable offences. This is an important category of offences, because additional police powers are available where such offences are involved. In very broad terms serious arrestable offences include murder, manslaughter, rape, kidnapping, serious sexual offences, and offences involving the use of firearms or explosives. Also included are any offences whose *consequences* are likely to be serious as a threat to national security or public order, or because they involve a risk of death or serious injury or serious financial loss to any person. In *Samuel*[98] the Court of Appeal agreed that

---

[96] See R. Stone, *Entry, Search and Seizure. A Guide to Civil and Criminal Powers of Entry*, 3rd edn. (London: Sweet & Maxwell, 1997).

[97] *Report of the Royal Commission on Criminal Procedure* (London: HMSO, 1981, Cmnd. 8092), para. 3.37.

[98] [1988] 2 All ER 135.

a burglary involving theft of property worth £1,135 was elevated to the category of serious arrestable offences because of the serious financial loss caused to the householder. There is no consideration in the case of whether the householder was insured against such loss.

Once it is established that a serious arrestable offence is involved, it is necessary to show reasonable grounds for believing that there is admissible evidence relating to that offence on any premises and that at least one of the following conditions applies:

- it is not reasonably practicable to communicate with any person who would be entitled to grant permission to enter the premises;
- such a person has unreasonably refused access to the premises or to the evidence;
- the evidence is likely to be concealed, removed or destroyed if access is sought without a warrant.

Objections have been made to these provisions on two grounds. First they have the potential for authorising the police to go on 'fishing trips' for evidence, and, secondly, the stringent safeguards recommended by the Philips Commission have been largely ignored. The Philips Commission had recommended authorisation by a Circuit judge rather than by a magistrate; the fear was that magistrates might rubber stamp these types of warrant as they are alleged to do with other types of search warrant. There is case law to support this view. In one case,[99] the Divisional Court quashed an order given on an *ex parte* application in relation to the premises of reputable solicitors, because the magistrates could not have been satisfied that the material sought was not covered by legal professional privilege nor that the conditions set out above were satisfied. The Philips Commission had also recommended the adoption of similar safeguards to those applying to excluded or special procedure material discussed below.

Sections 9 to 14 of PACE contain special rules relating to material held in confidence, which is called 'excluded material' and 'special procedure material' in PACE. These special rules encompass privileged communications between solicitors and their clients, personal records as part of business or professional information held in confidence, body samples held in confidence for medical diagnostic or treatment purposes and journalistic material held in confidence or acquired or created for the purposes of journalism. To get at such material a warrant must be obtained from a Circuit judge and the holder of the evidence is entitled to be heard on the application for the warrant. To obtain a warrant the police must satisfy the Circuit judge that:

- there are reasonable grounds for believing that the evidence is on the premises and would be of substantial value in the investigation of a serious arrestable offence which has already been committed;

---

[99] *R v. Guildhall Magistrates, ex parte Primlaks* [1990] QB 261.

- other efforts to obtain the evidence have failed or have not been tried because they are certain to fail;
- it is in the public interest that the evidence is handed over.

If so satisfied, the Circuit judge will grant an order addressed to the holder of the evidence requiring its delivery to the police. Only on a failure to comply with such an order, or where the police can show that the issue of an order for delivery of the evidence would seriously prejudice the investigation, will the Circuit judge issue a warrant authorising entry to and search of the premises for the evidence.

The significant differences between the safeguards attaching to this material and those applicable in the case of the general warrant to search for evidence will now be obvious.

Search without a warrant, other than on arrest

Search on arrest is considered below. Section 17 of PACE lists the situations in which the police may enter premises without a warrant. These are limited to constables in uniform who are seeking to effect an arrest, or to recapture a person unlawfully at large and who is being pursued, or to save life and limb, or to prevent serious damage to property.

Entry to prevent a breach of the peace

Section 17 of PACE abolishes all common law powers of entry save that relating to a breach of the peace. The power of entry to deal with a breach of the peace was established in the early nineteenth century, though it was not until the case of *Thomas* v. *Sawkins*,[100] that it was made clear that the power extended to entry to prevent a breach of the peace. This power raises problems similar to those discussed below in relation to the common law power of arrest for breach of the peace.

Seizure of evidence

Section 19 of PACE replaces the rules on what may be seized in consequence of any lawful search previously laid down in the case of *Ghani* v. *Jones*.[101] Police officers may seize any items other than those to which legal privilege attaches which they reasonably believe to be evidence in relation to the offence under investigation, or to any other offence, or to have been obtained in consequence of the commission of an offence; it must also be necessary to seize the items to prevent their removal, concealment or destruction. The power is considerably broader than that proposed by the Philips Commission which would have limited the seizure of items not directly related to the offence under investigation to evidence in relation to some 'grave offence', a group of offences broadly similar to serious arrestable offences under PACE.

---

[100] [1935] 2 KB 249.   [101] [1970] 1 QB 693.

General safeguards

Searches are only lawful to the extent that they are required for the purpose for which the power to search arose. This is intended to preclude excessive vigour in the execution of searches; it will be unlawful to rip furniture apart on a warrant to look for stolen video recorders. There are also notification and recording safeguards. Warrants must contain information as to the name of the person applying for them, the date of issue, the authority under which they are sought, the articles sought and the premises to be searched. Occupiers of premises searched must be given a copy of the warrant and, on request, a list of items seized. Warrants must be endorsed with the results of the search and a list of items seized. Similar requirements for recording the outcome of searches apply to searches and seizures without warrants.

Arrest

Part III of PACE has not clarified matters as much as it might have done and the law on arrest remains a mixture of statute and common law. Arrest is essentially a deprivation of the liberty to go where one pleases. Lord Parker C.J. described arrest as follows:

There are a number of cases both ancient and modern as to what constitutes an arrest . . . There may be an arrest by mere words, by saying 'I arrest you' without any touching, provided of course that the defendant submits and goes with the police officer. Equally it is clear, as it seems to me, that an arrest is constituted when any form of words is used which in the circumstances of the case were calculated to bring to the defendant's notice, and did bring to the defendant's notice, that he was under compulsion and thereafter he submitted to that compulsion.[102]

The arrest may be lawful or unlawful. There are three kinds of lawful arrest: arrest under warrant; arrest without a warrant under statute; and arrest without warrant under common law. All arrests which do not meet the conditions for a lawful arrest are unlawful. There are unlikely to be many successful challenges to British law under the European Convention in this area, since the formal protections surrounding arrest under English law at least meet, and probably exceed, the protections offered by the Convention.

Helping the police with their enquiries

Individuals frequently attend at the police station at the request of the police 'to help them with their enquiries'. Such individuals sometimes find it harder to leave the police station, though as a matter of law they are free to leave at any time unless placed under arrest. Again ignorance of the legal position and equivocation by the

---

[102] *Alderson v. Booth* [1969] 2 QB 216, 220.

police about their status can operate to deny such persons the freedom to leave. Section 29 of PACE clarifies the position by specifying that persons attending voluntarily at a police station are entitled to leave unless arrested and by requiring them to be informed at once of the fact of their arrest if they are prevented from leaving. There is no specific sanction in the Act for failure to comply with these requirements.

Arrest under warrant

PACE leaves the power of arrest under warrant largely unaffected. The usual procedure is governed by section 125 of the Magistrates' Courts Act 1980 whereby the police present and swear an information to a magistrate that a particular person has, or is suspected of having, committed an offence and on the basis of that information the magistrate issues a warrant for the arrest of the person. Warrants for arrest are not normally available unless the offence is one triable either way or the address of the person is not sufficiently established for a summons to be used to secure attendance at court. The magistrate has an unreviewable discretion as to whether or not to issue a warrant. A police officer may use reasonable force to enter premises where the suspect is known to be to effect the arrest.

Arrest without warrant under statute

For arrestable offences

Except for the nineteen statutes listed in Schedule 2 to PACE, the rules contained in Part III of PACE replace the existing statutory powers of arrest without warrant. Under section 24 of PACE a police officer may arrest without warrant any person who is in the act of committing, or who is reasonably suspected to be committing or to have committed, an *arrestable offence*. A police officer may also arrest someone about to commit or reasonably suspected to be about to commit an arrestable offence. The power of arrest extends to persons conspiring or attempting, or inciting, aiding, abetting, counselling or procuring the commission of an arrestable offence. The definition of arrestable offence is very important because it delimits the scope of the power. Arrestable offences are (1) those for which the sentence is fixed by law (the best example is murder which carries a statutory penalty of life imprisonment); (2) those for which persons aged twenty-one or over may be sentenced to a term of imprisonment of five years and (3) those offences specifically listed in section 24(2), of which the most notable are official secrets offences and various sexual offences.

Whether a police officer has reasonable grounds for suspecting that a person is guilty of an offence before that person is arrested is to be determined objectively from the information available to the arresting officer. More than an honest belief founded on reasonable suspicion is required.[103] There are, accordingly two

---

[103] *Castorina* v. *Chief Constable of Surrey, New Law Journal*, 24 June 1988, 180.

key questions. First, did the constable suspect that the person who was arrested was guilty of an offence? Secondly, if so, was there evidence upon which the constable could reasonably have formed that conclusion? If both tests are satisfied, the constable enjoys a discretion to make an arrest.

For any offence

Section 25 of PACE lays down general grounds for arrest where one or more of what are called *general arrest conditions* is satisfied. The power applies where a police officer has reasonable grounds for suspecting that *any* offence has been committed or attempted if one of the following general arrest conditions is satisfied:

- the suspect's name and address are not known to and cannot be ascertained by the police officer;
- the police officer has reasonable grounds for believing that the name and address supplied by the suspect are false;
- arrest is reasonably thought necessary to prevent suspects from causing (1) physical harm to themselves or others, (2) loss of or damage to property, (3) an offence against public decency or (4) an unlawful obstruction of the highway;
- arrest is reasonably thought necessary for the protection of a child or other vulnerable person from the suspect.

The Philips Commission had by majority recommended the creation of the above powers but envisaged that their use would be 'a very rare occurrence'. The minority did not consider the problems covered by the section to be such as to justify the creation of a power of arrest, which they considered would be a source of friction between the police and members of the public.

For fingerprinting

On conviction for a *recordable offence*[104] and where fingerprints have not previously been taken, section 27 of PACE enables a police officer within one month of the date of conviction to arrest without warrant a convicted person to secure attendance at a police station for fingerprinting.

Arrest without warrant under common law

The common law power of arrest without a warrant was neatly summarised by Lord Diplock in *Albert* v. *Lavin*:

Every citizen in whose presence a breach of the peace is being, or reasonably appears to be, committed has the right to take reasonable steps to make the person who is breaking or threatening to break the peace refrain from doing so; and those reasonable steps in appropriate cases will include detaining him against his will. At common law this is

---

[104] Recordable offences are defined by the National Police Records (Recordable Offences) Regulations 1985, S.I. 1985 No. 1941, as amended.

not only the right of every citizen, it is also his duty, although, except in the case of a citizen who is a constable, it is a duty of imperfect obligation.[105]

The concept of a breach of the peace which triggers the power of arrest is notoriously difficult to define. As recently as 1981 the criminal division of the Court of Appeal confirmed that the presence or threat of violence was required,[106] but in the *CEGB* case,[107] the civil division of the Court of Appeal intimated that 'passive resistance' in the form of a non-violent campaign of obstruction which might provoke a violent response by a third party would amount to a breach of the peace even before any resort to force was imminent.

General Duties Following Arrest

Section 28 of PACE lays down certain general duties to be complied with on the arrest of a person whatever the basis of the power of arrest. Failure to comply with the requirements renders the arrest unlawful. Unless it is impracticable to do so because the suspect has escaped from custody and unless the suspect has been arrested by being informed that he or she is under arrest, the police officer must inform the suspect as soon as practicable that he or she is under arrest and of the grounds for the arrest, and must do so even though the fact of the arrest is obvious. This statutory formula replaces the narrower requirements formerly laid down in the famous case of *Christie* v. *Leachinsky*.[108]

A person arrested must also be cautioned.[109] The form of the caution is as follows, though minor deviations do not constitute a breach of the requirement, and if it appears to the officer that a person does not understand what the caution means, that officer should explain its significance in his or her own words:[110]

You do not have to say anything. But it may harm your defence if you do not mention when questioned something which you later rely on in court. Anything you do say may be given in evidence.

Though suspects can remain silent in the face of police questioning on arrest, any failure to explain the presence of any 'object, substance or mark' on their person, clothing, footwear or otherwise in their possession can be brought to the attention of a court which may draw such inferences as appear appropriate from that silence.[111] The person must have been warned by the constable that the presence of the object, substance or mark and the reasonable belief of the constable that its presence may be attributable to the commission of an offence specified by the constable. Similar provisions relate to questions about the suspect's presence at a

---

[105] [1982] AC 546, 565.   [106] *Howell* [1982] QB 416.
[107] *R* v. *Chief Constable of Devon and Cornwall, ex parte CEGB* [1982] QB 458.
[108] [1947] AC 573.   [109] Code C, para. 10.3.   [110] Code C, note 10C.
[111] Criminal Justice and Public Order Act 1994, s. 36.

particular place.[112] The statutory provisions are not limited to questioning in the police station, but Code C, paras. 11.1A and 11.1 are drafted on the assumption that such questioning will take place at a police station.

The Power of Search Following Arrest

Prior to PACE it was uncertain what powers of search arose on the arrest of a person, though it was common police practice both to search the person and his or her home immediately following arrest. There was authority allowing the room in which a person was arrested to be searched,[113] though a search of premises is unlawful where there is no connection between the search and the offence for which the arrest was made. Thus in *Jeffrey* v. *Black*,[114] it was held to be unlawful to have searched the flat of a suspect following his arrest by members of the drug squad for the theft of a sandwich from a public house. The search discovered cannabis in the flat. Though the search was unlawful, the evidence so obtained was nevertheless admitted at trial on a drugs charge. The law is now clarified in sections 18 and 32.

Section 32 of PACE deals with searches of persons and premises where the arrest took place or where the suspect was immediately prior to arrest. Under section 32 of PACE arrested persons may be searched if a police officer has reasonable grounds for believing that they may present a danger to themselves or others, or may be in possession of articles which might be used to escape from police custody, or might be evidence relating to an offence. The constable may enter and search any premises in which the arrested persons were immediately prior to the arrest. The power is limited to a search reasonably required for the purpose of discovery of such articles or evidence. In conducting all these searches the police may use such force as is reasonably necessary. The police may seize other articles found on a search of individuals or premises if the constable reasonably believes them to be evidence of any offence and that their seizure is necessary to prevent their concealment, loss or destruction.

Section 18 of PACE permits the search of any premises occupied or controlled by suspects *following their arrest for an arrestable offence* where the police have reasonable grounds for believing that they will find evidence relating either to the offence for which the suspect was arrested or to some other arrestable offence connected with, or similar to, that offence. The power may be exercised without authorisation if the search is made before the suspect is taken to the police station 'if the presence of that person at a place other than a police station is necessary for the effective investigation of the offence'. But after the suspect has been taken to the police station, the written authorisation of a senior police officer not below the rank of inspector is required.

---

[112] Criminal Justice and Public Order Act 1994, s. 37.
[113] *Dillon* v. *O'Brien* (1887) 16 Cox CC 245.   [114] [1978] 1 QB 490.

Searches without prior written authorisation must be notified as soon as reasonably practicable to a senior police officer not below the rank of inspector. In either case a record of the search must be kept including a note of the grounds for it and the nature of the evidence sought.

To the Police Station

Section 30 requires a person arrested elsewhere than at a police station to be taken to a police station as soon as practicable after the arrest unless a police officer is satisfied that there are no grounds for keeping the suspect under arrest. In this case a record of the release from arrest must be made. A delay in taking a suspect to the police station will be justified 'if the presence of that person elsewhere is necessary in order to carry out such investigations as it is reasonably necessary to carry out immediately'. If such a delay occurs, its existence and the reasons for it must be recorded.

The normal procedure on arrest (after making any searches deemed necessary) will be to take arrested persons to the police station where they will be subject to the standard procedure for the reception of arrested persons. It is likely that they will enter the police station from a rear yard through one or more locked doors. They will then be presented to the custody officer, normally a uniformed police sergeant, who will determine whether the person's detention for question is required. The process is humiliating; even where the police follow all the rules contained in PACE and the Codes, reception into custody at the police station is necessarily a degrading and oppressive experience.[115]

[115] B. Irving and L. Hilgendorf, *Police Interrogation: The Psychological Approach*, Royal Commission on Criminal Procedure Research Study No. 1 (London: HMSO, 1980); B. Irving, *Police Interrogation: A Case Study of Current Practice*, Royal Commission on Criminal Procedure Research Study No. 2 (London: HMSO, 1980); and B. Irving, 'The Interrogation Process' in C. Bourn and J. Benyon (eds.), *The Police: Powers, Procedures and Proprieties* (Oxford: Pergamon Press, 1986), p. 136.

6

POLICING: IN THE STATION AND INTO COURT

Detention and Questioning of Suspects

General principles

The explanation of the provisions of PACE which follows covers only the questioning of persons aged seventeen or over; there are special rules which apply to juveniles and other vulnerable people.[1] The general principle infusing the exercise of all police powers is that of minimum interference with the civil liberties of the citizen. PACE requires the duration of detention to be as short as is consistent with the proper exercise of police investigation of crime.[2]

The rules in Part IV of PACE and Code C on the detention treatment and questioning of persons by police officers govern the whole period a suspect will be in a police station, that is, from initial reception at the police station to charge or release (possibly on bail) by the police. There are three main concerns running through the Code: keeping the duration of detention as short as possible, ensuring that the questioning of suspects is fairly conducted, and caring properly for those in custody. Such controls are very necessary because the police have overwhelming powers over suspects in the station. They have absolute physical control over their movements and contacts with others at the initial stages of their enquiries. A number of provisions of the Code are designed to reduce the effects of isolation and disorientation which inevitably accompany incarceration in a police station, and which can lead to unreliable information being provided by suspects in their desire for release.[3]

The custody officer

General role

The custody officer in the police station is a police officer charged by statute with responsibility for the liberty and welfare interests of suspects. There is nothing in

---

[1] Such as those suffering from mental illness or with a poor command of English.

[2] PACE, s. 34(1) and (2).

[3] See generally, *Report of the Royal Commission on Criminal Justice (Runciman Commission)* (London: HMSO, 1993), ch. 3.

the legislation which requires custody officers to be a separate corps of police officers, nor that they perform these functions for a particular length of time. In some forces, officers are detailed to be a custody officer for a period of weeks or months so that they are carrying out these functions daily over a period. In other forces police officers may not know until they come on duty whether they are to act in this capacity. Probably in the majority of forces, custody officers perform dual functions.[4] The Runciman Commission discovered that performing the role was not a popular one among the police, nor was it always carried out in good working conditions.[5] The Commission recognised the inherent tension involved in the task. On the one hand the police are charged with investigating offences and bringing offenders before the courts. On the other hand, they are also charged with protecting the interests of those they are investigating, sometimes for brutal and heartless acts. The Commission, however, concluded that it would be wrong in principle to hand over the protective role to another agency, since they considered it important that the police took full responsibility for the integrity of the evidence they collected. The Royal Commission recommended some strengthening of the role and improvements in training,[6] but no legislative change.

Powers

On arrival at the police station, the suspect must be presented to the custody officer, who will normally be a sergeant.[7] The role of this officer is central to the scheme in the Code for the protection of those detained in the police station. Crucial decisions about the detention and treatment of the suspect are primarily in the hands of this quasi-independent officer who is charged with the care of suspects while at the station. The custody officer cannot be directly involved in the investigation of the offence and applies an element of impartial decision-making. The custody officer must keep a detailed chronicle of events while the suspect is in police custody; this chronicle is known as the custody record. Suspects and their legal advisers are entitled to a copy of the custody record. Any disagreement between the custody officer and the investigating officers must be referred for resolution to an officer of the rank of at least superintendent.[8]

The very first duty of the custody officer under section 37 of PACE is to determine whether there are sufficient grounds for keeping the suspect in custody at all. The custody officer must proceed immediately to charge if there is sufficient evidence for a charge to be preferred.[9] If the custody officer decides that there

---

[4] J. Burrows, P. Henderson and P. Morgan, *Improving Bail Decisions: The Bail Process Project, Phase 1*, Home Office Research and Planning Unit Paper No. 90 (London: Home Office, 1994), pp. 6–7.

[5] See *Report of the Royal Commission on Criminal Justice (Runciman Commission)* (London: HMSO, 1993), ch. 3, para. 24, and D. Brown, T. Ellis and K. Larcombe, *Changing the Code: Police Detention under the Revised PACE Codes of Practice*, Home Office Research Study No. 129 (London: HMSO, 1992).

[6] Currently two days of the training newly promoted sergeants receive is devoted to custody officer duties; the Runciman Commission thought it should be more.

[7] This will include a constable acting up as a sergeant: see *Vince and others* v. *Chief Constable of Dorset* [1993] 2 All ER 321. The Runciman Commission recommended that this should happen only very exceptionally.   [8] PACE, s. 39(6).

[9] *Ibid.*, s. 37(1) and (7).

is insufficient evidence for a charge to be preferred, the suspect must be released with or without bail unless there are reasonable grounds for believing that the suspect's detention is necessary either to secure or preserve evidence of, or relating to, the offence for which the arrest was made, or to obtain such evidence by questioning the suspect.[10] If the custody officer decides that there are grounds to keep the suspect in custody, the suspect must be told this and the grounds for detention.[11]

The custody officer must also tell suspects of the rights not to be held incommunicado, to free legal advice, to consult the Codes of Practice, and to receive a copy of the custody record.[12] The right to legal advice is a continuing one and suspects must be told they can exercise it at any time. Suspects must be given written notice setting out these rights and will be asked to sign the custody record to acknowledge receipt of this notice. The custody officer also gives suspects at this time written notice of the arrangements effective at the police station for obtaining legal advice there.[13] It seems that in most cases, custody officers communicate these rights effectively. A typical notification might be as follows:[14]

Now listen to what I've got to say to you. While you are at the police station you have certain rights. You have the right to have someone told that you're here. You have the right to consult an independent solicitor free of charge. If you don't have your own, we can get one for you. And you have the right to see a copy of our Codes of Practice, which is a book of rules and procedures that we have to follow while you're being held here. You don't have to do any of these things now, but you can change your mind at any time while you are here.

Suspects would then be asked whether they wished to exercise each of these rights in turn. In a minority of cases, the notification can be perfunctory. In one extreme case, the notification was: 'Here are your rights—you know what they are, sign here'.[15]

The next decision for the custody officer is whether to subject the suspect to a personal search. It is normal for suspects to hand over all their property to the custody officer for safe keeping. The custody officer has a statutory duty to ascertain all property in the suspect's possession and may search the suspect for this purpose under section 54 of PACE.[16] Even if no search is conducted at this time, it is possible to conduct such a search at any time while the suspect is in custody.[17]

---

[10] PACE, s. 37(2)–(4).   [11] Ibid., s. 37(5).   [12] Code C, para. 3.1.

[13] Code C, para. 3.2. The Runciman Commission recommended that work be undertaken on a simpler form of written notification. See also I. Clare and G. Gudjonsson, *Devising and piloting an experimental version of the 'Notice to Detained Persons'*, Royal Commission on Criminal Justice Research Study No. 7 (London: HMSO, 1993).

[14] D. Brown, T. Ellis and K. Larcombe, *Changing the Code: Police Detention under the Revised PACE Codes of Practice*, Home Office Research Study No. 129 (London: HMSO, 1992), p. 30.

[15] Ibid. See also M. Maguire, 'Effects of the PACE provisions on detention and questioning: some preliminary findings' (1988) 28 Brit. J. of Crim. 19, and A. Sanders and others, *Advice and Assistance at Police Stations and the 24-hour Duty Solicitor Scheme* (London: Lord Chancellor's Department, 1989).

[16] See also Code C, para. 4.   [17] PACE, s. 54(6A).

In rare instances, a strip search or an intimate search may be ordered.[18] Annex A of Code C summarises the grounds for these. Section 55 of PACE permits a superintendent to authorise an intimate search, that is, a physical search of the body orifices,[19] by a medical practitioner[20] or police officer[21] if there are reasonable grounds for believing that the suspect may have concealed an article which could be used to cause physical injury and might be so used while in custody. Such searches are rarely made in practice and are invariably unpleasant affairs. The medical profession has indicated that it will only carry out such searches with the informed consent of the suspect.

A modest number of intimate searches is conducted each year, mostly for drugs; few are successful. In 1996 there were 132 intimate searches conducted in England and Wales; all but a handful were under medical supervision. Drugs were the object of the search in 117 cases and drugs were found in 17 cases. The remaining searches were for other harmful articles and none was successful.[22]

Strip searches should be distinguished from intimate searches. A strip search involves the removal of more than outer clothing, and is governed by Part B of Annex A of Code C. Strip searches can only take place if it is considered necessary in order to find and remove an article which a person would not be allowed to keep. There is no requirement to keep statistics on such searches, which are simply a more thorough form of ordinary search; they may include a visual inspection of, though no contact with, the genital and anal areas. The procedure governing such searches is designed to minimise embarrassment.[23] The incidence of a strip search must be recorded in the custody record.[24] It has been argued that reasons must be given for a search under section 54 whether a strip search or not.[25] Some have argued that strip searches are used to humiliate, degrade and punish, and should be more formally controlled.[26] In one study of 5,519 arrests in 1988, there were 59 strip searches and seven intimate searches.[27]

Reception into custody takes about 15 minutes. Once completed, the suspect will be escorted to a single cell and left there to await the attentions of the investigating officers. Suspects may have been required to hand over any belt or braces if the custody officer believed that they might use them to cause injury to themselves or others, or to assist in an escape.[28] They will probably be required to leave their shoes outside the cell. A period of total isolation usually follows.

---

[18] PACE, s. 55.   [19] Ears, nose, anus and vagina, but not the mouth: PACE, s. 65.

[20] If the object of the search is drugs, the examination can only be undertaken by a nurse or a doctor.

[21] In all cases, such a search can only be conducted by a constable of the same sex as the suspect.

[22] G. Wilkins and C. Addicott, *Operation of Certain Police Powers under PACE: England and Wales 1996*, Home Office Statistical Bulletin Issue 27/97 (London: Home Office, December 1996).

[23] Code C, Annex A, para. 11.   [24] Code C, Annex A, para. 12.

[25] See H. Levenson, F. Fairweather and E. Cape, *Police Powers: A Practitioners' Guide*, 3rd edn. (London: Legal Action Group, 1996), p. 189, arguing the application of the pre-PACE case of *Brazil* v. *Chief Constable of Surrey* [1983] 3 All ER 587.

[26] See United Campaign against Strip Searches, *Strip searching: personal testimonies—an enquiry into the psychological effects of strip searching* (London: UCASS, 1990), noted in *Legal Action*, February 1990, 4–5.

[27] D. Brown, *Detention at the Police Station under the Police and Criminal Evidence Act 1984*, Home Office Research Study No. 93 (London: HMSO, 1989).   [28] Code C, para. 4.2.

The right not to be held incommunicado

Suspects detained at a police station have a right under section 56 of PACE to have a person known to them who is likely to take an interest in their welfare informed as soon as practicable and at the public expense of their whereabouts. Code C, para 5.1, provides that up to two alternatives may be chosen if the first person named cannot be contacted. The custody officer has a discretion to allow further attempts to contact someone to be made. The person contacted may visit or telephone the suspect at the custody officer's discretion. The suspect may also make one telephone call for a reasonable time. The police will listen to any such conversations. Friends or relatives telephoning to enquire about suspects should be told their whereabouts.

Annex B of Code C restates the rules in section 56 of PACE which permit delay in the exercise of this right. The right may only be denied or delayed in cases involving serious arrestable offences[29] and only on the authority of a police officer not below the rank of superintendent. There must be reasonable grounds for believing that the exercise of the right will interfere with the proper investigation of the offence. In no circumstances may access be delayed beyond thirty-six hours.

David Brown's two studies of the operation of the detention and treatment provisions of PACE showed that about one in five suspects exercise the section 56 right.[30] There is, however, wide variation in take-up rates between police stations. In some one in three exercise the right, while in others only one in twelve do so. The variation is largely unexplained, but one relevant factor suggested is the way in which custody officers outline the rights to suspects. In most cases contact was made with the person named within half an hour; only one in four cases took longer.

By contrast only about one in eight suspects elected to make a telephone call. One in twenty received a visit from a friend or relative, though no figures are available for refusals of visits.

The right to legal advice

The content of the right

The right of suspects to legal advice while in custody received formal recognition for the first time in section 58 of PACE. The right is additional to the right not to be held incommunicado in section 56 of PACE, and consists of the right *at any time* to consult and communicate privately, in person, in writing or by telephone, with a solicitor. The right extends to a solicitor's clerk authorised to provide advice on behalf of the solicitor unless an officer of the rank of at least inspector considers that such a visit will hinder the investigation. If the clerk is refused access,

---

[29] Defined in PACE, s. 116 and Sch. 5. See above Ch. 5.

[30] D. Brown, *Detention at the Police Station under the Police and Criminal Evidence Act 1984*, Home Office Research Study No. 93 (London: HMSO, 1989), and D. Brown, T. Ellis, and K. Larcombe, *Changing the Code: Police Detention under the Revised PACE Codes of Practice*, Home Office Research Study No. 129 (London: HMSO, 1992).

the solicitor must be notified immediately so that alternative arrangements can be made.[31]

The police can only delay access to legal advice under section 58 in cases involving serious arrestable offences; the rules are similar to those governing delay in notifying a person reasonably named of the suspect's whereabouts and are also covered by Annex B of Code C. In *Samuel* [32] the police were sharply criticised by the Court of Appeal for delaying access to a solicitor allegedly for fear that the solicitor would inadvertently warn others involved in the offence under investigation. Hodgson J. said of the test permitting delay in allowing access:

The task of satisfying a court that reasonable grounds existed at the time the decision was made, whether in respect of intentional or inadvertent conduct, will, we think, prove even more formidable. Any officer attempting to justify his decision to delay the exercise of this fundamental right will, in our judgment, be unable to do so save by reference to specific circumstances, including evidence as to the person detained or the actual solicitor sought to be consulted.

Though not dissenting from the conclusion in the case, a differently constituted Court of Appeal in *Alladice* [33] did not share the earlier Court's scepticism about solicitors being used as unwitting channels of communication between rogues.

Any scheme which establishes a right to legal advice will only be as good as the system for delivering that advice. One response to ensure the ready availability of legal advice has been the introduction of statutory 24-hour police station duty solicitor schemes.[34] Schemes now cover all but three police stations.[35] The Duty Solicitor Arrangements provide that duty solicitors must be persons vetted and approved by local committees on the basis that they are qualified solicitors with current practising certificates who regularly practise in criminal defence work and have comprehensive experience of the criminal process including advocacy in the magistrates' courts throughout the previous twelve months. Where a scheme is in operation, a suspect may request the services of the duty solicitor on call on that day or night. The service is provided as part of the legal aid scheme, but there is no means or merits test.

There are two sorts of on-call system operated: rota schemes which are used in connection with busier schemes, and panel schemes where business is less. There is a telephone call system operated by the Duty Solicitor Call Centre Service[36] covering the whole of England and Wales. Under rota schemes the task of the telephone service is to call the named solicitor on call who guarantees their availability,

---

[31] Code C, para. 6; see also *R v. Chief Constable of Avon and Somerset, ex parte Robinsons* [1989] 2 All ER 15.   [32] [1988] 2 All ER 135.

[33] (1988) 87 Cr. App. R 380.

[34] The operation of these schemes is now governed by the Legal Aid Board Duty Solicitor Arrangements 1994, as amended; see *Legal Aid Handbook 1996/97* (London: Sweet & Maxwell, 1996), p. 476. There is also now a formal system of accreditation for solicitor's representatives and trainee solicitors, and legal aid payments will only be made in respect of accredited persons or solicitors.

[35] *Legal Aid Board Annual Report 1996–97*, HCP 52 (1997–98) (London: HMSO, 1997).

[36] Currently operated by International Assistance Services.

subject, obviously, to the duty solicitor work in hand. Under panel schemes, the telephone service calls solicitors on the panel in turn until one is found who is available and willing to act.

It seems that about one in three suspects asks for legal advice.[37] As with the right not to be held incommunicado, there are significant regional variations with the greatest variations surprisingly clustering around the more serious offences. Nine out of ten requests results in some contact. A study in twenty-five police stations in ten force areas between August 1995 and February 1996[38] showed an increase in the number of requests for legal advice, though this appears to have been accounted for by an increase in the number of requests from juveniles. There was, however, considerable variation between police stations for which there was no obvious explanation.

In the 1990s a steady pattern has emerged of contact being with a solicitor of the suspect's choosing in two-thirds of cases and with the duty solicitor in one-third of cases. In three-quarters of cases, a solicitor or solicitor's representative attends at the police station, while in the remaining cases, advice is given by telephone.[39] In 1996, 720,094 suspects were assisted at a total cost of just under £90 million.[40]

The Legal Aid Board has targets for contacting a duty solicitor: in ninety-five per cent of cases, contact should be made with a duty solicitor.[41] In eighty per cent of rota cases, and seventy-five per cent of panel cases, the request should be processed by the Duty Solicitor Call Centre Service within half an hour,[42] and no more than half of all cases should involve only telephone advice.[43] In most cases a legal adviser attends the police station within about an hour of being requested to do so.

Relating outcome to receipt of legal advice in the police station shows that there is little difference between the treatment of those who have received legal advice and those who have not. There is certainly nothing in the figures to justify the howls of anguish once heard from the police that the presence of solicitors in the police station so hampers police enquiries that large proportions of those held at the police station would have to be released without charge. The level of penetration of advice in police stations is confirmed by the Birmingham University study,[44] which found that over one-third of all advice at the police station came from duty solicitors. Though there is no evidence of widespread denial of access to legal advice by the police, there was evidence of incomplete notification of the right to

---

[37] D. Brown, T. Ellis and K. Larcombe, *Changing the Code: Police Detention under the Revised PACE Codes of Practice*, Home Office Research Study No. 129 (London: HMSO, 1992), p. 59.

[38] T. Bucke and D. Brown, *In Police Custody: Police Powers and Suspects' Rights under the Revised PACE Codes of Practice*, Home Office Research Study No. 174 (London: Home Office, 1997), ch. 3

[39] *Legal Aid Board Annual Report 1996–97*, HCP 52 (1997–98) (London: HMSO, 1997).

[40] Ibid. The average cost per suspect was £124.92.

[41] 99 per cent of schemes met this target in 1996–97.

[42] 98 per cent and 88 per cent of schemes respectively met this target in 1996–97.

[43] 93 per cent of schemes met this target in 1996–97.

[44] A. Sanders and others, *Advice and Assistance at Police Stations and the 24-hour Duty Solicitor Scheme* (London: Lord Chancellor's Department, 1989).

legal advice and the use of ploys designed to discourage requests for legal advice. An example is the stressing of the delays that might be entailed if legal advice is requested. Half those requesting advice did not get to see a solicitor; they received telephone advice or no help at all. The study comments:

The police would have us believe that defence solicitors saw their main role in life as being to persuade suspects not to co-operate with them, and to defend suspects unreservedly—which is, after all, the theory of the adversary system. On closer questioning the police divide solicitors into two types, of which only one adheres to that model. And, indeed, some solicitors do, while others do not, adopt a combative adversarial stance. What is surprising is how many do not do so. And also that there is a third category which is either anti-suspect or uncaring about suspects, in that the advice they give is either perfunctory or doomed to being ineffective.[45]

How good is the advice given?

How good is the legal advice provided for the minority of suspects who actually receive advice at the police station? The empirical evidence suggests that it could be more effective; the main criticism is that it is too passive. Most consultations seem to last under fifteen minutes, with only one in a hundred lasting an hour or more.[46] One research study[47] which observed solicitors in interview rooms suggested that solicitors and their representatives made few interventions in interviews. In two-thirds of cases they said nothing. Only in one in eleven cases did they actively intervene on behalf of the suspected person. The study recognises that valuable advice might have been given in the private consultation between lawyer and client which was not the subject of observation. Another study[48] suggested that advisers had great difficulty finding out much about the case on arrival at the police station, though there is some hint that some did not work very hard in collecting information. Only one in six consulted the custody officer, and only one in ten asked for a copy of the custody record. In nearly half the cases observed, no attempt was made to obtain information from the investigating officers. As a result the principal source of information was the suspect, but even here there were failures to take full instructions which would have discovered important material known to the suspect. This study reports that three-quarters of solicitors or their representatives made no intervention during police interviews. The Runciman Commission called these findings 'disturbing' and called for better training and monitoring as well as improved remuneration for police station work.[49]

---

[45] A. Sanders and others, *Advice and Assistance at Police Stations and the 24–hour Duty Solicitor Scheme* (London: Lord Chancellor's Department, 1989), p. 191.

[46] T. Bucke and D. Brown, *In Police Custody: Police Powers and Suspects' Rights under the Revised PACE Codes of Practice*, Home Office Research Study No. 174 (London: Home Office, 1997), ch. 3.

[47] J. Baldwin, *The Role of Legal Representatives at the Police Station*, Royal Commission on Criminal Justice Research Study No. 3 (London: HMSO, 1993).

[48] M. McConville and J. Hodgson, *Custodial Legal Advice and the Right to Silence*, Royal Commission on Criminal Justice Research Study No. 16 (London: HMSO, 1993).

[49] *Report of the Royal Commission on Criminal Justice (Runciman Commission)* (London: HMSO, 1993), ch. 3, paras. 59–64.

Monitoring the length of detention

The law

PACE makes continuing detention at the police station subject to formal review after set periods of time.[50] The time limits specified in PACE are approximate;[51] this is designed to allow some flexibility and to avoid argument over legality if the police exceed the limits by a small margin. Each review of detention which takes place must be fully documented in the custody record. The overriding principle is that detention should end as soon as possible. Code C also contains detailed rules about the treatment of those in custody, which it is the responsibility of the custody officer to ensure are observed.[52]

The first formal review of detention is required not later than six hours after the detention was authorised, though postponement of the review is permittedwhere it is not practicable to carry out the review at that time and it is specifically stated that it may be postponed if it would mean interrupting the questioning of a suspect which would 'prejudice the investigation'. Thereafter reviews take place after a further nine hours and at subsequent intervals of not more than nine hours. The custody officer carries out the review in the case of suspects already charged,[53] while a police officer not below the rank of inspector, who is not directly involved in the investigation, reviews the cases of suspects who have not been charged. The purpose of the review is to establish whether continued detention is justified.

Twenty-four hours after arrest a special review by a police officer not below the rank of superintendent takes place. At this point the suspect may be detained further until thirty-six hours from the time of the arrest on the authority of the superintendent only:

- if the investigation is into a serious arrestable offence;
- if the investigation is proceeding with due diligence and expedition; and
- if the continued detention is necessary to secure or preserve evidence or to question the suspect further.

Detention beyond thirty-six hours may only be authorised by a magistrates' court (defined for this purpose as two magistrates sitting otherwise than in open court). The suspect is entitled to be heard on the application for further detention. Duty solicitor work at police stations includes free representation at such hearings.[54] Applying the same criteria as the police at the earlier review, the magistrates must decide whether further detention is justified and if so for what period up to a maximum of a further thirty-six hours ending not later than ninety-six hours after the time of the arrest or arrival at the police station whichever was earlier. Thus in order to detain a suspect for the full ninety-six hours, two applications to the magistrates are required, as well as a number of reviews at the police station by senior police officers.

---

[50] PACE, ss. 40–45.   [51] PACE, s. 45(2).   [52] PACE, s. 39.   [53] PACE, s. 46.
[54] Such work accounts for only 0.1 per cent of police station duty solicitor work: *Legal Aid Board Annual Report 1996–97*, HCP 52 (1997–98) (London: HMSO, 1997).

Practice

Under the PACE provisions, the mean period of detention in one survey[55] was just over five hours, while the median period of detention was three hours and nineteen minutes. By six hours just over three-quarters of suspects had been dealt with. It appears that the first review at six hours concentrates the minds of police officers and forces decisions to be made about the continued detention of suspects. By the end of twenty-four hours, when the limit of detention for ordinary offences arrives, ninety nine per cent of suspects have been dealt with, including half of the two per cent of those in custody in connection with serious arrestable offences. Warrants for detention beyond twenty-four hours were obtained in forty-six of the 5,519 cases in the sample, and beyond thirty-six hours were sought from magistrates in fourteen cases and obtained in eleven.

National figures for 1996 show that 550 defendants were detained for more than twenty-four hours and subsequently released without charge. There were 271 applications to magistrates for warrants of further detention; all but eight were successful. In 175 cases, the detainee was subsequently charged.[56]

The new provisions do not appear to have reduced dramatically the time suspects spend in the police station, but they are now better protected. Indeed the procedures required by PACE themselves account for some of the time spent in the police station. The time spent being questioned will only be part of the time spent in custody, which involves a considerable amount of time waiting in a cell.

Monitoring the questioning of suspects

The right to silence

It is, of course, the police's power to question suspects which is regarded as one of their most important powers. Suspects used to enjoy the right to silence; the suspect could refuse to answer any questions with impunity.[57] Under the adversarial system it was said to be for the police and prosecution to adduce admissible evidence of guilt unassisted by the suspect. The right applied both in the face of police questioning and in court, where a suspect could not be compelled to give evidence. Judges would remind juries that any person suspected of a criminal offence or charged with one is entitled to say nothing when asked questions about the offence, and that juries should not hold defendant's silence against them. Despite the right to

---

[55] D. Brown, *Detention at the Police Station under the Police and Criminal Evidence Act 1984*, Home Office Research Study No. 93 (London: HMSO, 1989). The later survey did not reveal any significant change in this pattern of detention: D. Brown, T. Ellis and K. Larcombe, *Changing the Code: Police Detention under the Revised PACE Codes of Practice*, Home Office Research Study No. 129 (London: HMSO, 1992).

[56] G. Wilkins and C. Addicott, *Operation of Certain Police Powers under PACE, England and Wales 1996*, Home Office Statistical Bulletin Issue 27/97 (London: Home Office, December 1996).

[57] See generally D. Morgan and G. Stephenson, *Suspicion and Silence: The Right to Silence in Criminal Investigations* (London: Blackstone Press, 1994).

silence, few suspects remained silent at the police station. Various research studies of questioning at the police station have shown that only about one in twenty-five suspects exercise the right to silence.[58]

Very many suspects make statements, admissions and confessions in the face of police questioning. The research studies carried out for the Royal Commission on Criminal Procedure had shown that the making of statements was common; anything between one in three and one in five suspects make incriminating statements to the police. It is therefore important that questioning is fair and that the statements made by suspects are reliable and freely given. A majority of the Runciman Commission recommended no change to the right to silence, but despite this recommendation, the Government introduced provisions in the Criminal Justice and Public Order Act 1994 which erode the right to silence, in that for the first time adverse inferences can be drawn from a failure to answer questions either at the point of arrest, in the police station, or in court.[59] On arrest and before being questioned every suspect must be cautioned. A new form of caution is introduced which warns suspects that their defence may be harmed if they do not mention something in questioning on which they later rely in court.[60]

The new provisions do not compel suspects and defendants to answer questions. They merely enable a court to draw adverse inferences from silence in the circumstances covered by sections 34 to 38 of the Criminal Justice and Public Order Act 1994. Sections 36 and 37 were considered in connection with the treatment of arrest.[61] They concerned the answering of questions about the presence of any object, substance or mark on the suspect or anything in his or her possession, and failure to provide an explanation for presence at a particular place. Section 34 is more broadly drafted and covers any matters which it would be reasonable to expect a person to mention, but which they do not mention.[62] An example would be circumstances which justify the action under investigation. Section 35 enables a court or jury to draw adverse inferences from the defendant's failure to give evidence in court. There is a safeguard in section 38 which provides that a person cannot be convicted solely on the inferences drawn from their silence; there must also be some other evidence pointing to their guilt.

Early indications are that these provisions have resulted in some reduction in refusals to answer some or all questions. Where special warnings are given under section 36 (concerning explanations for marks, objects or substances) or section 37 (explanation of presence at the scene), only one in ten gave a satisfactory explanation of the matter. Nearly seven out of ten offered no explanation.[63]

---

[58] R. Leng, *The Right to Silence in Police Interrogation: A Study of Some of the Issues Underlying the Debate*, Royal Commission on Criminal Justice Research Study No. 10 (London: HMSO, 1993). See also D. Brown, 'The incidence of right of silence in police interviews: the research evidence reviewed' (1994) 35 Home Office Research Bulletin No. 57.   [59] See ss. 34–38 of the 1994 Act.
[60] See Code C, paras. 10–12.   [61] See Ch. 5.
[62] See *Condron and Condron* (1997) 1 Cr. App. R 1.
[63] T. Bucke and D. Brown, *In Police Custody: Police Powers and Suspects' Rights under the Revised PACE Codes of Practice*, Home Office Research Study No. 174 (London: Home Office, 1997), ch. 4.

The use of adverse inferences in criminal trials is likely to raise issues under the European Convention. The *Condron* case[64] has already resulted in an application to the Commission of Human Rights. When the Condrons were interviewed by the police, their solicitor advised them to remain silent indicating his concern that they were suffering from withdrawal symptons after taking heroin. They remained silent, and despite the solicitor's explanation of the reasons for the advice given, the judge allowed the jury to consider making adverse inferences from their silence. The argument is that, in the particular circumstances of this case, that amounted to a breach of Article 6 and deprived the Condrons of a fair trial. The United Kingdom Government has been asked for its observations on the application.

Fair questioning

PACE and Code C contain detailed provisions for the recording of interviews with suspects. But it is first necessary to determine what constitutes an interview, since not all interactions between police and citizen constitute an interview. Code C[65] contains the following rather circular definition:

An interview is the questioning of a person regarding his involvement or suspected involvement in a criminal offence or offences which, by virtue of paragraph 10.1 of Code C, is required to be carried out under caution.

The law is in something of a muddle. The case of *Absolam* defined an interview as 'a series of questions directed by the police to a suspect with the view of obtaining admission on which proceeding could be founded'.[66] Another case, however, said that interviews did not include 'questioning a person only to obtain . . . his explanation of the facts'.[67] In *Cox* the Court of Appeal said:

The provisions of Code C, taken together, make clear that, other than in exceptional circumstances, the order of events contemplated by . . . the Code was: decision to arrest; arrest; arrival at the police station; notification of the right to free legal advice; free legal advice (if this is desired); interview (with a reminder of the right to free legal advice immediately before the start of the interview). It was against this framework that one had to ask, in any given set of circumstances, whether or not the questioning amounted to an interview.[68]

This is helpful and suggests that any questioning about a suspected offence will constitute an interview to which the protections of the Code attach. One question will suffice for an interview, and the exchange can be informal as well as formal.

Code C stresses the prohibition on interviews away from the police station save in exceptional circumstances.

---

[64] *Condron and Condron* (1997) 1 Cr. App. R 1.
[65] The three versions of Code C to date have each contained different definitions of what constitutes an interview. Some of the confusion results from earlier even less helpful definitions.
[66] (1989) 89 Cr. App. R 332.   [67] *Maguire* (1990) 90 Cr. App. R 115.
[68] (1993) 96 Cr. App. R 464.

The general expectation is that formal interviews in the police station will be tape-recorded.[69] Where they are not, there must be a contemporaneous written record.[70] Incidents occurring during the course of the interview must be fully documented.

The tape-recording of interviews is the main safeguard provided by PACE against oppressive interviewing in police stations. It has been a remarkable success after initial suspicion by the police that it would hinder investigations.[71] The next logical step which the Runciman Commission considered should be explored is to move to video-recording of interviews.[72]

Though audio-recording has removed the scope for argument over what was said and how it was said, there remain concerns about the objective and style of questioning. In many cases the interview is not an exercise in neutral fact-finding, but a confrontation in which the interviewers are seeking admissions or information about other criminal activity.[73] Many commentators point to the centrality of interrogation among police investigative techniques. It would appear that confessions and incriminating statements occur in six in ten cases where there is an interrogation, and in eight in ten cases resulting in guilty pleas.[74]

Interviews away from the police station

The increasing regulation of questioning at the police station has led to concerns that the police might seek to circumvent the protections available in the police station by questioning and interviewing suspects away from the police station. A survey for the Runciman Commission[75] sought to measure the incidence of questioning[76] and interviewing.[77] Just under one-third of suspects in the survey were questioned, mainly at the scene of the crime, but also at home or in the police station. Questioning in police cars was rare. Afro-Caribbean suspects seemed more likely to be subject to questioning.

One in twelve suspects was interviewed prior to arrival at the police station, two-thirds of whom had been questioned prior to the interview. Most interviews were initiated by the suspect,[78] while about forty per cent were initiated by the police.[79]

---

[69] PACE, s. 60 and Code E, *Code of Practice on Tape Recording of Interviews with Suspects*.
[70] Code C, para. 11.5.
[71] *Report of the Royal Commission on Criminal Justice (Runciman Commission)* (London: HMSO, 1993), ch. 3, para. 65. See also J. Baldwin, 'The Police and Tape Recorders' [1985] Crim. LR 695.
[72] See M. McConville, 'Video-taping interrogations: police behaviour on and off camera' [1992] Crim. LR 532.
[73] B. Irving, *Police Interrogation. A Study of Current Practice*, Royal Commission on Criminal Procedure Research Study No. 2 (London: HMSO, 1980); see also A. Sanders and R. Young *Criminal Justice* (London: Butterworths, 1994), pp. 147–91.
[74] See generally, M. McConville and J. Baldwin, *Courts, Prosecution and Conviction* (Oxford: Clarendon Press, 1981), chs. 6 and 7. See also M. Maguire and C. Norris, *The Conduct and Supervision of Criminal Investigations*, Royal Commission on Criminal Justice Research Study No. 5 (London: HMSO, 1992); and I. Bryan, 'Shifting Images: Police-Suspect Encounters during Custodial Interrogations' (1997) 17 *Legal Studies* 215.
[75] S. Moston and G. Stephenson, *The Questioning and Interviewing of Suspects outside the Police Station*, Royal Commission on Criminal Justice Research Study No. 22 (London: HMSO, 1993).
[76] Seeking information or an explanation in the ordinary course of an officer's duty.
[77] Questioning a person regarding his or her involvement or suspected involvement in a criminal offence.
[78] 29 of the 52 cases in this sample.   [79] 20 of the 52 cases in this sample.

Most interviews took place at the crime scene (forty-five per cent) while a quarter took place in a police car. In twenty-one of the fifty-two cases a full confession was obtained in the interview outside the police station, though a further seventeen suspect made damaging admissions short of full confessions. The Royal Commission clearly felt that interviews should only take place in the police station, but that it would be impossible to preclude confessions or interviews outside the police station completely. In these cases, the Commission considered that experiments in some forces in recording such interviews on portable tape recorders showed some promise. In cases of interviews away from the police station, the suspect should be asked to comment on the interview at the start of a taped interview in the police station.[80]

Charge or summons

At the end of questioning, a number of things may happen. To understand these, it is necessary to appreciate that there are two ways the police may put the matter in the hands of the criminal courts, which also triggers the transfer of the file to the Crown Prosecution Service. The first is by way of charge, which is a procedure which takes place at the police station. The suspect is brought before the custody office and the investigating officer proffers the charge which the custody officer accepts if satisfied that there is sufficient evidence to justify the charge. The case comes within the jurisdiction of the courts when the charge sheet is delivered to the magistrates' court.

The second method is to proceed by way of summons. To obtain a summons a constable must attend before a magistrate to swear an information. If the summons is granted, it must then be served on the defendant. This can be done personally or by using the postal system. Proceeding by way of summons involves more paperwork, but is frequently used for less serious offences. National figures show that around sixty per cent of defendants are brought before the courts by means of summons. Twenty-six per cent are arrested but subsequently bailed pending first appearance in court, while thirteen per cent (about 100,000 people a year) are arrested and held in custody pending first appearance.[81] For either way offences,[82] four out of every five defendants are arrested and charged, rather than summonsed to attend court.

At the end of detention, the suspect may be released without charge. This may mean an end of the matter, or the suspect may be advised that the question of prosecution will be considered. In the latter case, the police would normally bring the matter to court by means of information and summons. Alternatively, the suspect may be released without charge, but be bailed pending further enquiries. The final possibility is that the suspect may be charged and held in custody pending appearance before the magistrates.

[80] *Report of the Royal Commission on Criminal Justice (Runciman Commission)* (London: HMSO, 1993), ch. 3, paras. 7–15.
[81] *Criminal Statistics England and Wales 1996* (London: HMSO, 1997, Cm. 3764), ch. 8.
[82] Offences of middling seriousness. See Ch. 7.

Once persons are charged, the normal rule is that they may not be subjected to further questioning. It is therefore necessary to consider the police powers to grant bail and the decision to prosecute.

Police Bail

The police's powers to grant bail are separate from those enjoyed by magistrates, which are discussed in the next chapter. The refusal of bail by the police only triggers a detention in custody for a short time; the person must be brought before a magistrates' court as soon as practicable, and normally within twenty-four hours.

Bail pending further enquiries

When the custody officer decides that there is insufficient evidence to charge a person arrested and brought to the police station, that officer may release the suspect on bail.[83] This is bail pending further enquiries. The suspect is released but is under a duty to return to the police station when required to do so. Failure to attend is an offence under section 6 of the Bail Act 1976. A good example of this type of bail would be the arrest of a person on suspicion of possession of controlled drugs after a packet of what appears to be cocaine is found on him or her. Normally a charge cannot be brought until the substance has been analysed. Pending the outcome of the analysis, the suspect will be bailed. If the analysis confirms that the substance is a controlled drug, the suspect will be charged on return to the police station. A person so bailed need not return to the station if advised in writing by the police that there is no requirement to do so.

The power may also be used if the police want time to decide whether or not to proceed against the suspect,[84] though equally the suspect can be released without bail and the matter proceed by way of summons if the police decide to proceed.

Bail following arrest under a warrant

Where a person has been arrested on a warrant, the warrant will normally deal with the question of the detention of the suspect. In other words the magistrate makes the decision rather than the police. The decision is endorsed on the warrant and the police must comply with its terms on charging the suspect.

Bail following arrest without a warrant

Where a person is charged with an offence following arrest without a warrant, the custody officer determines whether the suspect is to be detained in custody or bailed under section 38 of PACE. Such a person may only be kept in police custody pending first appearance before a magistrates' court in the following circumstances:

---

[83] PACE, s. 37(2).   [84] PACE, s. 37(7) and (8).

- where the suspect's name and address cannot be ascertained or that proffered is believed to be false;
- where the custody officer believes that the arrested person may fail to attend at court;
- where the person is charged with an imprisonable offence,[85] the custody officer has reasonable grounds for believing that detention is necessary to prevent the arrested person from committing further offences;
- where the person is charged with an offence other than an imprisonable offence, the custody officer has reasonable grounds for believing that detention is necessary to prevent the person from causing physical injury to any other person or from causing loss of or damage to property;
- where the custody officer has reasonable grounds for believing that detention is necessary to prevent an interference with the administration of justice;
- where the custody officer has reasonable grounds for believing that detention is necessary for the protection of the arrested person.[86]

In making these decisions, the custody officer must take into account the same matters to which magistrates must address their minds in making bail decisions.[87] A record must also be made in the custody record of the grounds of detention.

The person charged and kept in custody must be brought before the magistrates' court as soon as is practicable.

The police can attach conditions to the grant of bail where the person has been charged in the same way as magistrates, except that the police cannot require a person to reside in a bail hostel or to co-operate in the preparing of a report.[88]

Application to vary bail conditions can be made either to another custody officer or to the magistrates' court.[89]

In one study covering the use of police bail[90] two-thirds of those charged were bailed unconditionally and one in five was kept in custody. Seventeen per cent were bailed subject to conditions. However, these were considered to be people who would previously have been granted bail unconditionally, and so it seems that the new powers have not resulted in any reduction in those kept in custody by the police. There were also significant variations of practice between police stations, suggesting that local cultures were developing around the legislative provisions.

The police decision to charge

Once the police have evidence that a person has committed an offence, there is no requirement that the suspect be charged and prosecuted; this is a matter initially

---

[85] One for which a sentence of imprisonment may be imposed in any circumstances.
[86] PACE, s. 38(1).   [87] See Ch. 7.
[88] Bail Act 1976, s. 3A. See J. Raine and M. Willson, 'Just Bail at the Police Station' (1995) 22 J of Law and Soc. 571.   [89] Bail Act 1976, s. 3A(4), and Magistrates' Courts Act 1980, s. 43B(3).
[90] T. Bucke and D. Brown, *In Police Custody: Police Powers and Suspects' Rights under the Revised PACE Codes of Practice*, Home Office Research Study No. 174 (London: Home Office, 1997), ch. 7.

for the discretion of the police. The police have a range of options even when they believe that they have enough evidence to secure a conviction. They can decide not to prosecute; they can issue the person with a caution if guilt is accepted, or they can charge the person with an offence.[91] So, the police are the gatekeepers of the criminal justice system; they determine which cases are passed to the Crown Prosecution Service. If they decide not to charge or summons a person, it is most unlikely that the case will come to court. There might be a private prosecution,[92] though these are difficult to mount and are rare occurrences.

The police now work to unpublished national guidelines on case disposal.[93] The first questions which the police will ask themselves is whether there is credible and admissible evidence to prove all the essential elements of the offence. If there is not, a charge or summons should not be sought. If there is, a further enquiry will take place to determine whether there are compelling reasons for not proceeding. Here the police will consider a number of specific gravity factors which relate to the offence, and general gravity factors which will relate to the offender and the victim of the crime. The result of weighing these factors will be one of five disposal options: a formal warning or simply not proceeding; the high probability of a caution; a pivotal case; high probability of prosecution; and prosecution save in the face of the most exceptional circumstances.

Cautions represent a non-statutory system of diversion of offenders away from the courts. There are national guidelines, but the Runciman Commission considered that the practice should be regulated by statute. They also wished to see the possibility of the Crown Prosecution Service being able to return a case to the police for a caution to be administered.[94]

Cautions will only be administered where the police have sufficient evidence of the suspect's guilt to give rise to a realistic prospect of conviction, where the suspect admits his or her guilt, and where the suspect consents to being cautioned.[95] The caution is noted in police files for the force concerned and will be taken into account in the event of any future decisions concerning the person cautioned. A caution does not count as a conviction for the offence, but it may be cited in court as an acknowledgement of guilt.[96]

---

[91] Or swear an information in order to secure a summons for them to appear before the magistrates' court.

[92] Used here to refer to a prosecution by an individual citizen. See generally K. Lidstone, R. Hogg and F. Sutcliffe, *Prosecutions by Private Individuals and Non-Police Agencies*, Royal Commission on Criminal Procedure Research Study No. 10 (London: HMSO, 1980).

[93] The Law Society, *Criminal Practitioners Newsletter*, October 1996, p. 1.

[94] *Report of the Royal Commission on Criminal Justice (Runciman Commission)* (London: HMSO, 1993), ch. 5, paras. 57–8. See also D. Dulai and M. Greenhorn, 'The criminal histories of those cautioned in 1985, 1988 and 1991' (1995) Home Office Research Bulletin No. 37, 71.

[95] Home Office Circular 18/1994. In 1996, 286,000 offenders were cautioned for all offences, excluding motoring offences: Home Office Statistical Bulletin, *Cautions, Court Proceedings and Sentencing, England and Wales 1996*, Issue 16/97.

[96] For a more extensive discussion of cautioning, see A. Sanders and R. Young, *Criminal Justice* (London: Butterworths, 1994), pp. 227–37. See also R. May, 'The Legal Effect of a Caution' [1997] Crim. LR 491.

Controlling Police Misconduct

There are four approaches that can be taken in the face of police misconduct. The first is self-help. Constables only enjoy special powers where the conditions for the exercise of those powers are met. If they are not, a citizen is not required to submit to the intrusion in his or her civil liberties. The second remedy is to challenge the admissibility of evidence obtained in breach of the provisions of PACE or the Codes. The third is to pursue a civil action against the police, who enjoy no immunity from civil suit if they overstep their powers. Finally, a complaint can be made about the constable's conduct which may result in internal disciplinary proceedings against the constable.

Self-help

A citizen is only required to submit to a search, or to arrest, where the conditions for the exercise of the power are met. So a person stopped on the mere whim of a constable need not submit to a search, and may lawfully resist any attempt by the constable to conduct the search using force. Equally, a person whose arrest is unlawful need not accompany the constable to the police station.

The difficulty, of course, is one of the balance of knowledge. Only the most knowledgeable and the most confident will feel able to stand up to a constable purporting to exercise statutory or common law powers. There is also the risk that the person resisting the exercise of the powers will be charged with obstructing the constable in the execution of his or her duty or assaulting a constable in the execution of his or her duty. Avoiding conviction for this offence will require success in persuading the criminal courts that the constable was acting unlawfully, and so was not acting in the execution of his duty.[97]

Self-help is a remedy only for the brave or the foolhardy.

Challenging the prosecution evidence

This is an important area. There are a number of provisions of PACE designed to ensure compliance with the provisions of the Act and the Codes by rendering evidence obtained other than wholly in compliance with the new rules liable to be excluded from any subsequent trial.[98] There are three principles which might apply in deciding to introduce rules which provide for the exclusion of evidence. First, there is the 'reliability principle': evidence of certain kinds is or may be so unreliable as to preclude its use in a criminal trial. Secondly, there is the 'disciplinary principle': exclusion of unfairly obtained evidence compels police compliance with rules on the collection of evidence. Thirdly, there is the 'protective principle': citizens have a right to protection against failure by the police to meet the standards

---

[97] See for example, *Lindley* v. *Rutter* [1981] QB 128, or *Yvonne Jones* [1978] 3 All ER 1098.

[98] For a detailed study, see S. Sharpe, *Judicial Discretion and Criminal Investigation* (London: Sweet & Maxwell, 1998).

required of them and, if they are not afforded that protection, they should not be put at risk, nor should the prosecutor gain an advantage. The courts have shown little favour towards the disciplinary principle; existing rules are based upon a combination of the reliability principle and the protective principle.

Confessions, including incriminating statements falling short of full confessions, are admissible against defendants without any corroborating evidence unless the defendant challenges the statement. When this happens, there must be a trial within a trial as to the admissibility of the evidence. Section 76 of PACE conditions the admissibility of confession on the concept of reliability. Where a confession is challenged, the prosecution must prove beyond reasonable doubt that the confession, notwithstanding that it may be true, was not obtained either by oppression of the person who made it; or in consequence of anything said or done which was likely in the circumstances existing at the time to render the confession unreliable.

Oppression *includes* torture, inhuman or degrading treatment and the use or threat of violence, whether or not it amounts to torture.[99]

Section 76 is concerned solely with confession evidence. Section 78 of PACE is wider. It is poorly drafted and the explanation for this is horse-trading during the Parliamentary stages of the legislation.[100] The section gives the courts a *discretion* to refuse to allow evidence to be admitted on which the prosecution proposes to rely, if it appears that, having regard to all the circumstances, including the circumstances in which the evidence was obtained, the admission of the evidence would have such an adverse effect on the fairness of the proceedings that it ought not to be admitted. Section 78 is a new rule and does not displace pre-existing common law powers to exclude evidence.[101] The burden of proof where challenges are raised under section 78 is with the defendant on the balance of probabilities.

In the pre-PACE case of *Sang*[102] which was concerned, in part, with evidence other than admissions, the House of Lords had held that, although the courts had a discretion to exclude evidence the prejudicial effect of which outweighed its probative value, they lacked any general discretion to refuse to admit relevant admissible evidence because it was obtained unfairly. As long ago as 1949 in *Noor Mohammed*[103] Lord du Parcq sitting in the Privy Council had given guidance on the application of the weighing of prejudicial effect against probative value:

The judge ought to consider whether the evidence is sufficiently substantial, having regard to the purpose to which it is professedly directed, to make it desirable in the interests of justice that it should be admitted. If, so far as that purpose is concerned, it can in the circumstances have only trifling weight, the judge will be right to exclude it. To say that is not to confuse weight with admissibility. The distinction is plain, but cases must occur in which it would be unjust to admit evidence of a character gravely prejudicial to the accused even though there may be some tenuous ground for holding it technically admissible.[104]

---

[99] PACE, s. 76(8).
[100] P. Sieghart, 'Reliable evidence, fairly obtained' in J. Benyon and C. Bourn, *The Police: Powers, Procedures and Proprieties* (Oxford: Pergamon Press, 1986).   [101] PACE, s. 82(3).
[102] [1980] AC 402.   [103] [1949] AC 182.   [104] Ibid., 192.

Section 78 has become one of the most important provisions in PACE and one of the most often referred to in practice.[105] The Court of Appeal has said that the provision is 'not an apt field for hard case law and well-founded distinctions between cases'.[106] It follows that each case should be decided on its own particular facts.

In *Mason*[107] a fabricated story by detectives which had induced the defendant to confess and which had been proffered to his lawyer as the truth resulted in the quashing of a conviction for arson. In so doing, Watkins L. J. repeated the point made frequently by the courts that criminal trials and appeals against criminal convictions are not the place to discipline the police.

In *Samuel*[108] the Court of Appeal quashed a conviction for robbery in circumstances where Samuel had been unlawfully denied access to a solicitor at the police station. The confession made by Samuel had to be excluded from the court's consideration. But in *Alladice*[109] a failure to comply with the suspect's right to legal advice under section 58 of PACE did not prejudice the defendant because it was clear that the defendant was aware of his right (at the time) to remain silent in the face of police questioning.

In *Hughes*[110] the Court of Appeal considered that the fairness at which section 78 aims is in the nature of a balance between the interests of the prosecution and the defence, and not simply the protection of the accused against the admission of prejudicial evidence. The Court of Appeal has also stressed that the effect of the evidence on the fairness of the trial is the governing consideration.[111] In *Keenan*[112] Hodgson J. sitting in the Court of Appeal considered that significant and substantial breaches of Code C relating to admissions and other incriminating statements were likely to lead to exclusion of the evidence, but he stressed the need for significant and substantial breaches of the provisions if they were not to amount simply to punishing the police for failure to observe the Codes.

Pronouncements of the Court of Appeal provide important guidance, but for defendants it will be the approach taken by the trial judge in the Crown Court which directly affects them. Few decisions at first instance are reported, and none officially. However, a research study of practice in thirty-four trials in the Leeds Crown Court[113] raised a number of hypotheses. Trial judges appeared to use the provision most frequently to exclude evidence where there had been a denial of access to legal advice, where there were other substantial breaches of Code C, and where there had been breaches of Code D on identification arrangements. Interviews with the judges revealed that few had any familiarity with the three principles referred to above, and most stressed that general notions of 'fairness' which came from the general 'feel' of the case guided their decision-making.

Section 78 of PACE has introduced an important new discretion to exclude evidence. The approach of the courts suggests that a blend of the reliability and

---

[105] *Archbold 1998*, para. 15.429 (London: Sweet & Maxwell, 1997).
[106] *Jelen and Katz* (1990) 90 Cr. App. R 456, 465.   [107] [1988] 3 All ER 481.
[108] [1988] 2 All ER 135.   [109] (1988) 87 Cr. App. R 380.   [110] [1988] Crim. LR 519.
[111] *O'Leary* (1988) 87 Cr. App. R 387.   [112] [1989] 3 WLR 1193.
[113] Hunter, 'Judicial Discretion in Practice' [1994] Crim. LR 558.

protective principle underlines the actions of judges in courts of first instance. In applying the test the interests of the prosecution and defence must be balanced, but the power will not be exercised merely to discipline the police for a failure to follow the requirements of PACE and the Codes. The Court of Appeal will not interfere with the trial judge's exercise of the discretion where the proper issues have been considered and the judge responded within the bounds of reason to the issues before him or her.

There is an area where section 78 does not appear to have changed the earlier position. This relates to the exclusion of real evidence[114] found as a result of an unlawful search. In the pre-PACE case of *Jeffrey* v. *Black*,[115] the Brighton Drugs Squad had been keeping Christopher Black under surveillance. They saw him steal a sandwich from a public house. They arrested him and subsequently took him to his flat where they found cannabis. The Divisional Court accepted that the search was unlawful, but refused to exclude the evidence of the cannabis found in the search. There is no known case in which section 78 has been used to exclude real evidence found as a result of an unlawful search.[116]

Though the existence of the discretion in section 78 would be regarded as contributing to the guarantee of a fair trial under Article 6 of the European Convention on Human Rights, there may well be arguments based upon practice in the application of the provision. For example, it would not be surprising if a defendant sought to argue that the practice of not excluding improperly obtained real evidence (as distinct from incriminating statements) affected the guarantee of a fair trial under Article 6.

Suing the police

There is a growing number of civil actions against the police.[117] This is partly because it is a remedy which delivers compensation and the case remains in the control of the complainant, and partly because of some disillusionment with the police complaints procedure. Of considerable significance is the difference in the burden of proof. In the civil courts the burden of proof is on the balance of probabilities; to sustain a complaint against the police the criminal standard of proof beyond reasonable doubt applies.[118]

A constable is susceptible to civil action because constables enjoy no immunity from suit where they overstep their powers. If the constable had no lawful justification for his or her actions at the time of their exercise, the constable will almost certainly commit a tortious act, which cannot be made lawful by subsequent

---

[114] Something tangible.   [115] [1978] 1 QB 490.

[116] Save for the decision in *Fennelley* at Acton Crown Court, which is generally regarded as wrongly decided: [1989] Crim. LR 142.

[117] See generally R. Clayton and H. Tomlinson, *Civil Actions against the Police*, 2nd edn. (London: Sweet & Maxwell, 1992), and J. Harrison and S. Cragg, *Police Misconduct: Legal Remedies*, 3rd edn. (London: Legal Action Group, 1995).   [118] See below for changes effective from April 1998.

events.[119] The torts most likely to be involved in police misconduct are assault and battery, where someone is hurt or searched; false imprisonment, where someone is stopped, detained or arrested; malicious prosecution, where a person is prosecuted even though the police know they did not commit the offence charged; trespass to property, where a constable enters premises without lawful authority; and trespass to goods, where the police take or damage property without lawful authority.

Where a civil action is being pursued, it is recommended that no complaint against the police be filed at the same time and that no co-operation is offered in connection with any police internal disciplinary enquiry.[120]

The total amount paid out by the Metropolitan Police has been increasing dramatically in recent years: in 1976 a mere £7,251 was paid out in damages and settlements; by 1986 this had increased to £377,169. The 1989 total was £479,000 and the 1996 figure was £2,489,000.[121] The upward trend is partly explained by the diminishing public confidence in the complaints machinery and a preference for civil action. Though more modest sums are involved, a similar pattern emerges in relation to provincial forces.[122]

Making a complaint

The procedure for making a complaint about the conduct of a constable is simple and cheap, but once made the matter is largely out of the hands of the complainant.[123] No compensation will be paid as a result of the complaint. In *ex parte Broome*,[124] the court said that where a complaint was made the 'overriding interest is the upholding of proper standards of police conduct'. A person can complain about any matter within the Police Discipline Code, which lists large numbers of matters of police discipline. The list extends far beyond the limited range of complaints which can be dealt with by the civil courts. Rudeness, racist comments or even conducting a search without good cause (a species of abuse of authority) are included. The downside is that there is still little confidence in the process;[125] the chances of success are slim at less than one in ten complaints upheld.[126]

---

[119] *Chic Fashions (West Wales)* v. *Jones* [1968] 2 QB 299, 313.

[120] J. Harrison and S. Cragg, *Police Misconduct: Legal Remedies*, 3rd edn. (London: Legal Action Group, 1995), pp. 200–3.

[121] *Report of the Commissioner of Police for the Metropolis 1996/97* (London: Metropolitan Police, 1997), p. 95.

[122] For indication as to the level of damages, see S. Cragg and J. Harrison, 'New Guidelines for Police Misconduct Damages' *Legal Action*, May 1997, 22. See also *Thompson* v. *Commissioner of Police for the Metropolis* and *Hsu* v. *Commissioner of Police for the Metropolis* [1997] 2 All ER 762.

[123] See generally Part IV of the Police Act 1996, and J. Harrison and S. Cragg, *Police Misconduct: Legal Remedies*, 3rd edn. (London: Legal Action Group, 1995), ch. 3.

[124] *R* v. *Police Complaints Authority, ex parte Broome*, Divisional Court, 6 December 1988, LEXIS transcript.

[125] See M. Maguire and C. Corbett, *A Study of the Police Complaints System* (London: HMSO, 1991).

[126] *The 1996/97 Annual Report of the Police Complaints Authority*, HCP 95 (1997–98) (London: HMSO, 1997).

The system for dealing with police complaints has long been a matter of concern. The Government was concerned to ensure that there was seen to be effective independent review of the process of investigation as well as of the results of investigations. There was also room for better matching of resources applied to the investigation of complaints depending on the seriousness of the allegation. Overall the Government's aim is to persuade the public that complaints are fully and properly dealt with and to assure police officers that they will be treated fairly in the investigation of complaints against them. The Police Complaints Authority, an independent body of at least eight members none of whom has been a police officer,[127] has power to supervise the investigation of complaints. Indeed the Authority is required to supervise the investigation of the most serious cases and has power to call in other investigations for supervision. In these cases the police investigation of the complaint is answerable to the Authority. Serious cases include those involving death or serious injury. Regulations have been made requiring the reference of all cases involving allegations of corruption, assaults occasioning actual bodily harm and other complaints adversely reflecting on the reputation of the police service so that the Authority can determine whether or not to supervise their investigation. On the conclusion of these investigations the Authority will have to certify that they are satisfied with the conduct of the investigation. In all cases the Authority retains the power to order or advise on particular disciplinary action, or on the referral of the case to the Director of Public Prosecutions for consideration of the prosecution of any police officer. The Authority also retains the Board's powers to sit with the chief constable on certain disciplinary hearings.

Apart from these serious cases, it is the responsibility of the chief constable, or his deputy, on receipt of a complaint to determine whether it should be resolved formally or informally.[128] Cases suitable for informal resolution are those complaints which, if true, are unlikely to result in criminal or formal disciplinary proceedings against the police officer concerned. Informal resolution requires the consent of the complainant. In such cases the investigating officer may direct that an apology is made to the complainant or may advise the complainant that he has 'had a word' with the officer against whom the complaint has been made. Independent oversight of such cases is left in the hands of the local police authority and HM Inspectorate of Constabulary.

Formal resolution of complaints requires investigation by an officer not below the rank of chief inspector and not connected with the case appointed by the chief constable from his own or some other force. On receipt of the report of an investigation the chief constable, or his deputy, must consider whether or not a criminal offence appears to have been committed, in which case the file must be referred to the Director of Public Prosecutions for consideration of prosecution. If no criminal offence appears to have been committed, the chief constable must consider whether disciplinary proceedings should be instituted. In both these matters, the

---

[127] Police Act 1996, s. 66 and Sch. 5. As at 31 March 1997, there were 13 members.
[128] Police Act 1996, ss. 68–69.

chief constable is subject to directions from the Authority. Minor matters are heard by the chief constable, or his deputy, alone, but more serious matters are heard by a disciplinary tribunal consisting of the chief constable, or his deputy, sitting with two members of the Authority. The police officer against whom such proceedings are taken is entitled to be legally represented and the penalties available are formidable, ranging from a caution to dismissal from the force and loss of pension rights. There is an appeal following a decision at first instance to the police appeals tribunals.

The Home Affairs Committee reported critically on police complaints in December 1997,[129] and the Home Secretary has announced an intention to implement many of the Committee's recommendations. In particular, there will be changes to the burden of proof. In the past the burden of proof required for a complaint to be upheld has been akin to that applicable in criminal proceedings, that is, proof beyond all reasonable doubt, but from April 1998, there will be a sliding scale. For minor matters, something akin to the balance of probabilities will suffice, whereas for more serious matters the burden will more closely resemble that in criminal proceedings. There is also to be a new fast track system to deal with dismissals from the force in serious cases, and the abuse of the system resulting from officers going sick in order to avoid facing disciplinary proceedings is to be tackled. However, there will be no move to a more transparent system and police officers will retain their right to legal representation in internal disciplinary proceedings; this is a right not extended to other employees in internal proceedings. The rejection of the Committee recommendation is based on the fact that police officers have no entitlement to raise their dismissal before industrial tribunals, and so fairness demands that they enjoy extra rights in the internal process.

The Crown Prosecution Service

Background

The Crown Prosecution Service (CPS) is a national agency created in 1985 and operational from October 1986, which provides the bridge between the police investigation of cases and the determination of guilt or innocence by the criminal courts. On charge or the obtaining of a summons, the police files passes into the hands of the CPS, who have the power to discontinue the matter if they are not satisfied that the case is strong enough to put before the courts. The CPS is also responsible for the presentation of cases before the magistrates' court and the Crown Court.[130]

---

[129] Home Affairs Committee, *Police Disciplinary and Complaints Procedures*, HCP 258 (1997–98) (London: HMSO, 1997).

[130] See Prosecution of Offences Act 1985. For background, see R. White, 'A Public Prosecution Service for England and Wales' in J. Benyon and C. Bourn, *The Police: Powers, Procedures and Proprieties* (Oxford: Pergamon Press, 1986), p. 193.

Part I of the Prosecution of Offences Act 1985 establishes a Crown Prosecution Service which consists of the Director of Public Prosecutions (DPP) as head of the service and of Chief Crown Prosecutors for areas based on existing police force areas, though some areas share a Chief Crown Prosecutor. The DPP is henceforth to be appointed by the Attorney General.

Section 3 of the Prosecution of Offences Act 1985 spells out the functions of the DPP:

- the conduct of all criminal proceedings other than proceedings specified by order made by the Attorney General instituted by or on behalf of a police force, including all binding over cases;
- to institute and have the conduct of criminal proceedings the importance or difficulty or other characteristics of which make it appropriate for the proceedings to be instituted by the DPP;
- to take over proceedings concerning the forfeiture of obscene articles under section 3 of the Obscene Publications Act 1959;
- to appear for the prosecution on all criminal appeals;
- to discharge such other functions assigned from time to time by the Attorney General.

Barristers and solicitors employed by the CPS are known as Crown Prosecutors and a Chief Crown Prosecutor has been appointed for each area. Without prejudice to the functions assigned to them in their capacity as members of the CPS, every Crown Prosecutor 'shall have all the powers of the Director as to the institution and conduct of proceedings but shall exercise those powers under the direction of the Director'.[131]

Accountability for decisions involves supervision of the operation of any system and may involve some system either for vetoing decisions inconsistent with established police guidelines or for providing an explanation of the basis of decisions. The only formal accountability of the CPS is the requirement that an annual report be presented to the Attorney General, which he is obliged to lay before Parliament. It will not be open to any Member of Parliament to raise any specific case in any debate on the report. It is difficult to see this system providing any real control of decision-making.

The CPS was in operation nationally by October 1986. In its early years the CPS experienced difficulties in recruiting enough lawyers.

CPS staff are available to advise the police if the police wish to receive advice. The Runciman Commission reported some tension between the police and the CPS, particularly when the CPS asked for further investigations when they received the file, for which the only sanction in the face of a police refusal is discontinuance of the case, which may not be appropriate.[132]

---

[131] Prosecution of Offences Act 1985, s. 1(6).
[132] *Report of the Royal Commission on Criminal Justice (Runciman Commission)* (London: HMSO, 1993), ch. 5, paras. 24–6.

The Glidewell Report[133] into the CPS was sufficiently damning about its management that the Director of Public Prosecutions proposed to the Attorney General that her successor be appointed early so as to be in post in time to be fully involved in the reorganisation of the service; in effect, she was forced to resign. Though the Report did not find examples of bad decision-making in relation to discontinuances[134] or decisions to reduce the charges laid by the police, the relationships between the CPS and both the police and the courts were seen to be in need of major improvement. The report considered that greater attention needed to be given to more serious cases, that there was a crying need for a new organisation, structure and style of management, and that the CPS needed to establish firmly its proper role in the criminal justice process. The overall assessment of the CPS was that it had not yet secured the hoped-for improvement in the effectiveness and efficiency of the prosecution process. The suggested purpose of the CPS was expressed thus in the report:

The vigorous, effective and efficient presentation of criminal cases instituted by the police in a manner which ensures fairness, timeliness and consistency.[135]

The operation of discretion

The DPP has issued a Code for Crown Prosecutors under section 10 of the Prosecution of Offences Act 1985. The purpose of the Code is to promote efficient and consistent decision-making in order to develop and maintain public confidence in the CPS. The Code has been revised on a number of occasions; the current version was issued in 1994 and was accompanied by an explanatory memorandum.

On receiving a file from the police, the first role of the CPS is to review the file to determine whether the prosecution should continue. The overriding purpose of the review is to ensure that only fit and proper cases are brought before the courts. Over the years the rate at which cases have been dropped by the CPS has varied, but seems to have settled at around 12 per cent.[136] Two sets of criteria are applied. First, there is the evidential test, under which the CPS must be satisfied that a jury or a bench of magistrates, properly directed in the law, would be more likely than not to convict the defendant of the charge alleged. Testing the evidence involves consideration both of its admissibility and its reliability. On admissibility, the Code directs the Crown Prosecutor to consider whether any challenges to the admissibility of the evidence might succeed.[137] On reliability, the Code draws attention to problems over the reliability of confessions on grounds other than admissibility.[138] If the evidential sufficiency criteria are met, the Crown Prosecutor should go on to

---

[133] *The Review of the Crown Prosecution Service (Glidewell Report)* (London: HMSO, 1998, Cm. 3960).

[134] See below.

[135] *The Review of the Crown Prosecution Service (Glidewell Report)* (London: HMSO, 1998, Cm. 3960), p. 122.

[136] *Crown Prosecution Service Annual Report 1996–97*, HCP 68 (1997–98) (London: HMSO, 1997). In 1996–97 154,391 cases were discontinued. See also D. Crisp, 'Standardising prosecutions' (1993) Home Office Research Bulletin No. 34, 13.

[137] Code for Crown Prosecutors, para. 5.3 (London: Crown Prosecution Service, 1994).   [138] Ibid.

consider the public interest criteria.[139] In weighing reasons why a prosecution might not be pursued, the Code says: 'In cases of any seriousness, a prosecution will usually take place unless there are public interest factors tending against prosecution which clearly outweigh those tending in favour.'[140]

The Code goes on to list factors tending in favour of prosecution, such as, the likelihood that conviction will result in a significant sentence, that the offence was premeditated or committed by a group, as well as those tending against prosecution, such as delay, an adverse effect on the victim's mental or physical health, and that the defendant has made reparation.[141] So it would follow that the lighter the likely penalty, the easier it will be to justify discontinuance. If by the trial date, the offence is likely to be more than three years old, there would need to be special reasons for proceeding. Prosecution should generally be avoided if a court is likely to view the old age of the offender is such as to warrant the imposition of only a nominal penalty. If the weighing of the factors leaves some doubt, the advice is to proceed and leave it to the court to be the final arbiter of the matter.[142]

Where a Crown Prosecutor decides not to proceed, then the proceedings will be discontinued under section 23 of the Prosecution of Offences Act 1985. Where a defendant has been charged after being taken into custody without a warrant but no magistrates' court has been informed of the charge, the notice of discontinuance ends the matter there and then. Once a court is seised of the matter, the procedure is more complex. Reasons for discontinuance must be given to the court, but need not be given to the defendant. The defendant on receiving a notice of discontinuance of proceedings in this instance may nevertheless elect to have the case proceed by serving a counter-notice. This requires the matter to be brought before the court, where, of course, the prosecution may be called to account for the decision and orders for costs can be made.

Service of a notice of discontinuance does not prevent the institution of fresh proceedings for the same offence, if further evidence against the defendant subsequently comes to light. Some commentators feel that the process of 'uncharging' is inappropriate, and that it would have been better to have the file passed to the CPS when the police felt there was enough evidence to charge. This would have placed the decision to prosecute solely in the hands of the CPS. Under the system adopted, the ball is firmly rolling by the time the Crown Prosecutor sees the file; this is too late to be an effective safeguard against weak and inadequate prosecutions.[143]

The private prosecution has not been abolished by the new legislation. It remains open to any citizen to bring a private prosecution, though such prosecutions are automatically referred to the CPS to determine whether they wish to take them over. There would seem to be nothing to prevent such a prosecution being taken over solely with a view to the discontinuance of the proceedings. A recent difficulty

---

[139] Code for Crown Prosecutors, para. 6.2 (London: Crown Prosecution Service, 1994).
[140] Ibid.   [141] Ibid., paras. 6.4 and 6.5.
[142] For an assessment of the impact of the revised Code, see A. Hoyana and others, 'A Study of the Impact of the Revised Code for Crown Prosecutors' [1997] Crim. LR 556.
[143] A. Sanders, 'Prosecution Decisions and the Attorney-General's Guidelines' [1985] Crim. LR 4; and A. Sanders, 'An Independent Crown Prosecution Service?' [1986] Crim. LR 16.

has arisen in connection with the seeming reluctance of the CPS to take proceedings against the police following deaths in police custody.[144] The result was the establishment of an independent enquiry in July 1997 to consider these matters.

The CPS is markedly different from the much praised Scottish system. Yet even there research has shown that there is a gap between the rhetoric of the system and the protection it affords to defendants.[145] The research study showed that there is almost a presumption of prosecution which is only rebutted in a small number of cases. Furthermore the existence of fiscals does not seem to have resulted in any clearer understanding of the basis of decision-making in the exercise of the discretion to prosecute. Most decisions not to proceed are based on an insufficiency of evidence or on the triviality of the offence. Decision-making is based on received wisdom learned in post rather than from the formulation and revision of prosecuting guidelines.

A significant aspect of the decision to prosecute is that it is an essentially private process seldom open to any kind of public scrutiny. Internal checks and monitoring are therefore the only means of ensuring that in every case full and thorough consideration is given to the circumstances of the case before a decision to proceed is taken.

The pressure of work in the CPS led to the introduction of case-screening by Executive Officer grades, who are not lawyers. Two days special training was given and a special manual prepared for their use. Case-screeners could decide that a case was to proceed, but any consideration of discontinuance had to be referred to a Crown Prosecutor. Case-screeners were also encouraged to refer to Crown Prosecutors any cases where they felt unsure as to the correct decision to make. The first annual report of the DPP states that the function of the case-screener is to act as a first filter under the supervision of a senior Crown Prosecutor to ensure the efficient and effective consideration of all files referred to the CPS. In May 1988 the Divisional Court declared this practice *ultra vires*.[146] Watkins L.J. declared that the DPP had acted unlawfully in setting up the scheme:

We do not regret arriving at such a conclusion seeing that one of the main purposes for which the Prosecution of Offences Act was enacted was to bring an independent legal mind to bear on each prosecution. If an executive officer can decide to allow a prosecution to continue with the result that because the accused pleads guilty the case never goes to a Crown Prosecutor, that, in our view, frustrates that very important purpose of the Act, and although in the context of the Crown Prosecution Service's workload that case may be insignificant, it is to the individual who is accused a matter of great concern.

The CPS will also determine whether the charge made by the police is the most appropriate. In considering this matter the CPS works to national Charging

---

[144]   In particular of Shiji Lapite and Richard O'Brien: *Legal Action*, September 1997, 28.

[145]   S. Moody and J. Toombs, *Prosecution in the Public Interest* (Edinburgh: Scottish Academic Press, 1982).

[146]   *R* v. *Director of Public Prosecutions, ex parte Association of First Division Civil Servants*, *The Times*, 24 May 1988.

Standards. Examples are the sets of guidelines for dealing with offences against the person,[147] and with driving offences.[148] Such guidelines increase the chances of national consistency in the conduct which results in a particular charge.

The Runciman Commission felt that the public interest criteria were generally working well, though they recommended further consideration of the use of Public Interest Case Assessments under which probation officers collected information from those charged in order to ensure that all the relevant information for the application of the public interest criteria can be put before Crown Prosecutors. Pilot schemes had proved to be a success in providing crucial information on this aspect of decision-making.[149]

The conduct of the prosecution

Where the decision of the CPS is to proceed with a prosecution, the CPS has the responsibility to arrange for a lawyer to present the case in court. All Crown Prosecutors have rights of audience in the magistrates' courts, and it will usually be one of them who deals with such cases. But the workload is such that the CPS still spends significant sums of money on the employment of solicitors in private practice to act as agents for them in court proceedings.

It is the work of the CPS in magistrates' courts which has caused greatest criticism. Delays, missing files, and confusion over who is to handle the case have all given rise to complaints about the service. In a number of cases, prosecutions have been dismissed by magistrates because the prosecution was in such a state of disarray.

Where the case is sent to the Crown Court for trial, the CPS must instruct a barrister to appear for them, since Crown Prosecutors have no rights of audience in the Crown Court. The Prosecution of Offences Act 1985 enables the Lord Chancellor to make a direction extending rights of audience to them, but this has not yet happened. It is certain to come in due course, because there is little beyond the Bar's self interest to justify the expense of instructing counsel, for example, for at the very least the many guilty pleas which take place in the Crown Court.

Barristers appearing in the Crown Court rather oddly enjoy a degree of independence from the CPS which instructs them. Despite the scrutiny to which the case has been put by the CPS, it remains open to a barrister to conclude on the day that the case is not strong enough to proceed and to offer no evidence, or to accept a plea of guilty to a lesser offence.[150]

Section 53 of the Crime and Disorder Act 1998 enables the Director of Public Prosecutions to designate staff who are not Crown Prosecutors[151] to undertake

---

[147] (1994) 144 *New Law Journal* 1168.   [148] (1996) 146 *New Law Journal* 414.

[149] *Report of the Royal Commission on Criminal Justice (Runciman Commission)* (London: HMSO, 1993), ch. 5, para. 61.

[150] D. Farquharson, 'The Role of Prosecution Counsel: Report by a Committee under the Chairmanship of the Hon. Mr Justice Farquharson' *Law Society's Gazette*, 26 November 1986, 3599.

[151] This will include those who are not professionally qualified as a barrister or solicitor.

certain tasks previously the exclusive responsibility of Crown Prosecutors. These include making continuance decisions, representation at bail hearings, and the conduct of proceedings in the magistrates' courts other than trials. Such desgnated persons are subject to instructions made by the DPP. This is a worrying trend in lowering the skill level required to make important decisions in the criminal process.

The Serious Fraud Office

In one area the investigation of offences and the decision to prosecute are integrated. This is in the area of serious fraud. There was growing concern about the ability of the police to investigate serious frauds efficiently and to secure convictions in such cases. The whole area was considered by the Roskill Committee on Fraud Trials.[152] The recommendations made in their Report were implemented in the Criminal Justice Act 1987. Now a staff of lawyers, accountants and police officers working together in the Serious Fraud Office is responsible for the investigation and prosecution of serious frauds. The Serious Fraud Office is responsible to the Attorney General. There is no right to silence in the face of an investigation by the Serious Fraud Office, though some protection is afforded to statements made in the course of an investigation.[153]

Concluding Comment

What happens to suspects and defendants in the stages of the criminal process described in this chapter will tend to be crucial to the outcome of the case. It is often interactions with the police from the point of arrest to charge which are as determinative of the result of the prosecution as what happens at later stages. Lawyer intervention is less at these stages, and may be less effective. There is also scope for errors in police practice and lawyer intervention which can be the root cause of a miscarriage of justice. Applying the due process and crime control models considered in Chapter 3, an argument can easily be made that crime control considerations take precedence over due process considerations at a number of points.

---

[152] *Report of the Fraud Trials Committee (Roskill Committee)* (London: HMSO, 1986).
[153] J. Wood, 'The Serious Fraud Office' [1989] Crim. LR 175.

7

THE DEFENDANT IN
THE MAGISTRATES' COURT

Protecting the Interests of Defendants

Every case concerning an adult charged with a criminal offence will pass through the magistrates' court. In dealing with defendants, magistrates exercise a variety of functions. As was noted in the previous chapters, much of the police investigation of offences is unregulated by the courts, though there are key areas where authorisation from magistrates is required. Examples are the obtaining of warrants for arrest or for search, or for further detention in police custody beyond thirty-six hours. In such cases magistrates are clearly exercising a supervisory function, designed to protect the liberty interests of defendants.

The protection of the liberty interests of defendants continues once magistrates have jurisdiction over the case, which occurs when the charge sheet is delivered to the court or where a summons is issued on the swearing of an information. In the time leading up to the trial and sentencing of the guilty, there are a number of important issues which come before magistrates. This chapter is as much concerned with these issues as with trial in the magistrates' courts. Magistrates determine, among other things, whether defendants are represented at the public expense; remain at liberty pending their trial; and are tried in the magistrates' court or the Crown Court.

In more serious cases, magistrates act as a filter to determine whether there is adequate evidence to justify sending the defendant for trial in the Crown Court, although in the case of offences triable only on indictment, they send defendants 'forthwith to the Crown Court for trial'.[1] Finally, magistrates sentence those found guilty before them. If they feel their sentencing powers are inadequate, they may, in either way cases, commit the defendant for sentence to the Crown Court. One in ten of those charged with, and tried for, an offence triable either way in the magistrates' courts is given an immediate custodial sentence.[2]

---

[1] Crime and Disorder Act 1998, ss. 51, 52 and Sch. 3.
[2] Home Office Statistical Bulletin, *Cautions, Court Proceedings and Sentencing, England and Wales 1996*, Issue 16/97.

The effective performance of this range of tasks involves a variety of skills. In making bail decisions, magistrates will be assessing the personality of defendants in order to make a prediction about their future conduct. In making decisions on legal aid, magistrates will be assessing the likely consequences of the prosecution for defendants and whether they will be able effectively to argue their own case. Inevitably, magistrates have broad discretionary powers, but these are increasingly being placed within a statutory framework for decision-making. The requirement of giving reasons for, and recording, decisions is often used to check that the formalities have been observed.

The material in this chapter should not be isolated from the processing of defendants by the police, nor should the textbook separation of the various tasks detract from the important interrelationship between every stage of the criminal process. Often what has gone before is the major determinant of later decisions.

Getting Legal Help

The problem

At a multitude of points in the pre-trial criminal process, the suspect or defendant will look to others for advice on how to act or respond. Those to whom suspects and defendants turn are the police, their families and friends, and lawyers. Once it is clear that the case is to proceed to court, defendants' needs for legal advice become compelling. In 1996–97 over £355 million was spent on publicly funded legal help for those at the police station and appearing before the magistrates' courts.[3] Yet the provision of help is neither systematic nor comprehensive; it is a mixture of basic emergency cover, some advice in the lawyer's office and representation on a significant scale only for those charged with the most serious offences.[4]

If the offence is very serious, then virtually all defendants will be represented. These cases will be tried in the Crown Court. For less serious offences dealt with in the magistrates' courts, the proportion of defendants who will be unrepresented remains substantial. No precise figures are available detailing those who appear unrepresented in the magistrates' courts, which is itself surprising. In one study of 909 cases triable either way where the sample was weighted in favour of cases committed to the Crown Court for trial, one in five defendants was unrepresented when their cases came to court.[5]

---

[3] *Legal Aid Board Annual Report 1996–97*, HCP 52 (1997–98) (London: HMSO, 1997). The figure excludes the cost of legal aid in the Crown Court, which is administered by the Lord Chancellor's Department rather than the Legal Aid Board. The net cost of legal aid in the Crown Court was £309 million: *Judicial Statistics 1996* (London: HMSO, 1997, Cm. 3716).

[4] See generally R. Young and D. Wall (eds.), *Access to Criminal Justice: Legal Aid, Lawyers and the Defence of Liberty* (London: Blackstone Press, 1996).

[5] D. Riley and J. Vennard, *Triable-either-Way cases: Crown Court or Magistrates' Court* Home Office Research Study No. 98 (London: HMSO, 1988).

A question which is often asked is why defendants need representation if they are pleading guilty. The assumption that such defendants can be dealt with unassisted by a representative fails to recognise the important role of the representative in guiding defendants through the complex and mysterious process in the criminal courts, which often leaves defendants confused. Even a guilty plea requires the skills of marshalling fact and argument, so that the magistrates are fully informed when they consider the sentence to be imposed. Advocates are the articulate spokespersons of often inarticulate clients; the client provides the script and the advocate ensures that everything that can be, and needs to be, said for the defendant is presented to the court in a manner which is efficient, effective and directed to the issues the magistrates will need to consider.

Assistance to defendants at the public expense may be provided on an emergency basis under the court duty solicitor scheme, or on a more planned basis under the Green Form scheme, or under legal aid for representation in criminal proceedings. The range of schemes is impressive, but remains haphazard in coverage. The duty solicitor scheme only provides limited help, while the tests for full representation at the public expense are tough and, in practice, help mainly those whose cases are tried in the Crown Court.

The Benson Commission[6] in 1979 argued for a massive extension of the criminal legal aid scheme. Under their proposals there would be a statutory right to legal aid for bail applications, committal proceedings, and trial of offences triable on indictment or triable either way. For offences triable only summarily there would be a statutory presumption in favour of the grant of legal aid which could only be rebutted if the court was satisfied both that there would be no likelihood of a custodial sentence or substantial damage to the defendant's reputation, and that adequate presentation of the defendant's case, including a plea in mitigation, did not require legal representation. It is clear from the recent legislation and from the official response to the Benson Commission's recommendations[7] that the Government has firmly rejected these recommendations.

The current concern is to cash limit expenditure on legal aid, and to this end certain aspects of criminal legal aid now attract fixed fees. Consideration is being given to securing coverage through the letting of block contracts.[8] It will be difficult to meet tough budgetary targets without limiting the coverage of the scheme in criminal cases.

Duty solicitor schemes

Police station duty solicitor schemes were discussed in the last chapter. Those who see a solicitor in the police station may well continue to use the services of that

---

[6] *Final Report of the Royal Commission on Legal Services (Benson Commission)* (London: HMSO, 1979, Cmnd. 7648).

[7] *The Government Response to the Report of the Royal Commission on Legal Services* (London: HMSO, 1983, Cmnd. 9077).

[8] *Legal Aid Board Annual Report 1996–97*, HCP 52 (1997–98) (London: HMSO, 1997), ch. 7.

solicitor at a later stage of the criminal process under another part of the legal aid scheme. The police duty solicitor scheme grew out of the voluntary court-based schemes, which were a response to the problem of defendants appearing in the magistrates' courts bewildered and with little understanding of what was happening to them. Duty solicitor schemes operating in magistrates' courts offer a safety net to catch those who appear without having obtained any legal advice.

The Benson Commission was impressed with duty solicitor schemes and recommended their extension to provide coverage in all the busy courts. As a result, duty solicitor schemes were placed on a statutory footing in 1982 and are currently governed by Part III of the Legal Aid Act 1988 and regulations made under the Act. The detailed organisation of the scheme is laid down in the non-statutory Legal Aid Board Duty Solicitor Arrangements 1994.

The administrative scheme established by the 1994 Arrangements provides for a three-tier committee structure. A national Duty Solicitor Committee is appointed by the Legal Aid Board to oversee the operation of the scheme nationally. Beneath this committee is a network of regional duty solicitor committees, which determine the needs for duty solicitor schemes in their regions. These committees must contain a majority of solicitor advocates, and must have a representative from each local duty solicitor committee in the region plus a magistrate, a justices' clerk and two lay members, as well as representatives of the police, the probation service and the Crown Prosecution Service, and a stipendiary magistrate. The regional committees decide in which courts schemes are to be set up and generally supervise the operation of schemes in their region, ensuring that they operate effectively. Beneath regional committees are local duty solicitor committees for each operational scheme. It is the local committee which is initially responsible for the selection of duty solicitors, but any solicitor who is excluded has an appeal to the appropriate regional committee. The scheme contains detailed rules on the experience required to qualify a solicitor for selection as a duty solicitor, designed to ensure that duty solicitors have sufficient experience of criminal advocacy to be able to take instructions from, and act effectively for, a number of defendants at short notice.

The Arrangements also set out the service to be offered by duty solicitor schemes. Duty solicitor schemes usually operate as follows.[9] The duty solicitor will be a local solicitor from private practice who has agreed to be 'on call' at the court on certain days on a rota basis. The duty solicitor is there to help any defendant who is without representation, and will see both defendants in custody and those arriving at court from their homes. The co-operation of court personnel and the police is also sought to ensure that the presence of the duty solicitor is widely known.

The duty solicitor obviously cannot do more than provide 'first aid'; he or she will, after all, not have seen the defendants until that morning. What the duty solicitor usually can do is to give general advice, to oppose any objections to bail where appropriate, and to make straightforward pleas in mitigation where the defendant is pleading guilty. If the defendant is intending to plead not guilty or if

---

[9] H. Johnston, 'Court Duty Solicitors' *Legal Action*, May 1992, 11.

the duty solicitor needs more time adequately to represent the defendant, the duty solicitor will apply for legal aid and seek an adjournment. If the defendant wishes, the solicitor will continue to act for the defendant, but representation on any future occasion will be on the traditional solicitor/client basis. There is an embargo on a duty solicitor acting, as duty solicitor, for a defendant who has previously been assisted by a duty solicitor, unless a failure to do so may lead to the defendant being at risk of imprisonment. This rule is designed to avoid repeated representation by a duty solicitor being used by courts as a substitute for the grant of criminal legal aid. It is also made clear that duty solicitors cannot act for defendants pleading not guilty or in committal proceedings.[10] Duty solicitors are only in exceptional circumstances to assist persons charged with non-imprisonable offences; this narrowed the scope of service offered by some existing duty solicitor schemes. The scheme makes provision for the remuneration of duty solicitors, who are paid a modest hourly rate for their attendance at court.

Research comparing a court with a duty solicitor scheme with a neighbouring court without such a scheme, but served by the same clerk and magistrates, showed that the duty solicitor scheme resulted in more defendants released on bail and more defendants being granted legal aid.[11] But other research has suggested that the presence of duty solicitors leads to a higher proportion of guilty pleas.[12] Duty solicitor schemes have only a limited potential in ensuring that defendants are treated fairly by the criminal justice system. This was recognised by the Benson Commission which coupled its recommendation for the continuation of duty solicitor schemes with a recommendation for a massive increase of spending on criminal legal aid.[13]

Solicitors' participation in the scheme is not wholly altruistic. It is a means of developing a criminal legal aid practice. The introduction of voluntary schemes coincided with a period when competition in the conveyancing sector of legal practice meant that solicitors were feeling the need to diversify. At that time criminal legal aid was seen to pay well if the work could be done on a sufficient scale. Now there is something of a crisis, because many solicitors are giving up poorly paid legal aid work in favour of other more remunerative work.

The Green Form scheme

Assistance from a duty solicitor, whether at the police station or in court is neither means tested nor merits tested. Those defendants who consult a lawyer *before* reaching court are likely to receive initial assistance under the advice and assistance scheme.[14] This has come to be known as the Green Form scheme from the original colour of the application form. Eligibility for advice under the Green Form scheme

[10] Legal Aid Board Duty Solicitor Arrangements 1994, para. 51.
[11] M. King, *The Effects of a Duty Solicitor Scheme: an Assessment of the Impact upon a Magistrates' Court* (London: Cobden Trust, 1977).
[12] L. Bridges, J. Carter and S. Gorbing, 'The Impact of Duty Solicitor Schemes in Six Magistrates' Courts' *LAG Bulletin*, July 1982, 12.
[13] In 1996 net expenditure on magistrates' courts duty solicitor schemes was £14 million, compared with £89 million for police station schemes.   [14] Legal Aid Act 1988, Part III.

is means tested but not merits tested. It is available for advice on any point of law except one arising in connection with conveyancing or the making of a will. It does not include representation in any court or tribunal. The initial limit is two hours of the solicitor's time, though this can be extended on obtaining authorisation from the legal aid area committee. £26 million was spent on advice and assistance in criminal cases in 1996–97.[15]

The means test is a simple one conducted by the solicitor providing the advice. It takes no more than a few minutes to determine whether applicants are eligible for free help, will have to pay a contribution, or have sufficient capital and income to take them outside the scope of the scheme. Although the scheme provides no help from a lawyer in court, there is much that can be done to assist a defendant outside the courtroom. It can cover the cost of taking a statement from the defendant and any potential defence witnesses, or applying for criminal legal aid for representation, and of obtaining advance disclosure of the prosecution case. Discussion and consideration of any choices open to the defendant on the mode of trial and on intended plea also take place in the solicitor's office rather than in court.

If representation is needed, defendants must either pay the solicitor from their own resources, or succeed in an application to the magistrates' court for criminal legal aid.

Consideration is being given by the Lord Chancellor to the removal of Green Form assistance for criminal matters. In order to provide data to assist in making this decision, a study of the use of Green Form assistance in criminal matters was commissioned. That survey[16] looked at the use of the scheme in 39 solicitors' firms drawn from London and eight provincial locations heavily involved in criminal legal aid work. The survey revealed considerable variation in the patterns of use of the scheme, which make it difficult to predict with a high degree of certainty the effect of its withdrawal. However, it did appear that there were both minor cases and more serious cases in which the only legal aid provided was under the Green Form scheme. On the withdrawal of the Green Form scheme, the cases would be likely to result in greater demands on court duty solicitors, while the more serious cases might result in full criminal legal aid applications. The survey also revealed that well over half of all criminal legal aid orders arose in cases where the Green Form scheme had not been utilised. Where it had, the most frequent use had been to fund the making of a full legal aid application, though the scheme had also been used for obtaining evidence and corresponding with the police and the Crown Prosecution Service.

Criminal legal aid

Criminal legal aid for representation before the criminal courts is both means tested and merits tested and is governed by Part V of the Legal Aid Act 1988. Merits

---

[15] *Legal Aid Board Annual Report 1996–97*, HCP 52 (1997–98) (London: HMSO, 1997).
[16] L. Bridges and C. Noble, *The Uses of the Green Form Scheme in Criminal Matters: Report of a Survey* (Warwick: Legal Research Institute, 1997).

testing requires the defendant to satisfy the 'competent authority' (in most cases, the magistrates' court) that there are features of the case which make representation necessary. There are statutory tests to be applied in determining the answer to this question. Applications are usually made by completing an application form and submitting it to the clerk to the justices, who will consider the application. The clerk may choose to refer difficult cases to the magistrates, but now decides most cases without reference to them. It is possible to apply for legal aid orally before the magistrates, but invariably the magistrates will require an application form to be completed.

In place of the old fairly flexible financial limits, there is now a formal assessment of the disposable income and capital of the defendant by staff in the magistrates' court. This is similar to that which has operated for many years for civil legal aid. Following the calculation of disposable income and capital, weekly contributions may be required and a lump sum payment of all disposable capital in excess of £3,000 by way of contribution towards the lawyer's fees. Any culpable failure to pay any weekly contribution may result in revocation of the legal aid order. The contribution system goes directly against the recommendation of the Benson Commission that contribution orders under criminal legal aid in the magistrates' courts should be abolished.

The following defendants *must* be granted legal aid if they apply and do not have the means to meet the likely costs of representation:

- those committed for trial on a charge of murder, for the trial;[17]
- those applying for bail after having been kept in custody following a remand hearing at which they were unrepresented, for the bail hearing;[18]
- those to be kept in custody after conviction but before sentence pending the obtaining of a report or pending an enquiry, for the sentencing hearing;[19]
- those about to be sentenced to a term of imprisonment provided that they have not been in prison before, for the sentencing hearing;[20]
- those about to be sentenced to a period of youth custody or to a sentence of custody for life, for the sentencing hearing;[21]
- where the prosecutor appeals or applies for leave to appeal to the House of Lords, for the proceedings on the appeal.[22]

For the rest it will be the application of the notoriously vague merits test that determines whether legal aid will be granted. The merits test provides that legal aid for trial proceedings should be granted when it is 'desirable to do so in the interests of justice'. Non-statutory criteria, widely known as the 'Widgery criteria', have since 1966 guided magistrates in determining when the grant of legal aid will be in the interests of justice. These were given statutory form in section 22 of the Legal Aid Act 1988 where they are described as follows:

---

[17] Legal Aid Act 1988, s. 21(3)(a).   [18] Ibid., s. 21(3)(c).   [19] Ibid., s. 21(3)(d).
[20] Powers of Criminal Courts Act 1973, s. 21(1).
[21] Criminal Justice Act 1982, s. 3; this provision relates to persons under 21.
[22] Legal Aid Act 1988, s. 21(3)(b).

- the offence is such that if proved it is likely that the court would impose a sentence which would deprive the accused of his liberty or lead to loss of his livelihood or serious damage to his reputation;
- the determination of the case may involve consideration of a substantial question of law;
- the accused may be unable to understand the proceedings or to state his own case because of his inadequate knowledge of English, mental illness or other mental or physical disability;
- the nature of the defence is such as to involve the tracing and interviewing of witnesses or expert cross-examination of a witness for the prosecution;
- it is in the interests of someone other than the accused that the accused should be represented.

The Widgery criteria gave as an example of the last head, the trial of a charge of sexual assault against young children where it is undesirable that the defendant should cross-examine the witness in person. The list in section 22 is not exhaustive,[23] but magistrates must consider each of the factors listed there. The Lord Chancellor has taken power to modify the factors either by amendment or addition of factors to be taken into account.[24]

Many of the questions on the application form are directed at obtaining information to show whether any of the criteria for the grant of representation for trial proceedings is met. Some can only properly be answered with advice from a solicitor and the form itself recommends consulting a solicitor. Green Form money can be used for this purpose. The broad effect of the application of the criteria is that virtually all those who are to be tried in the Crown Court will obtain legal aid, but for those who are to be tried in the magistrates' court, there is less chance.

One continuing concern about the operation of the criminal legal aid scheme has been the wide variations in the rates of refusals for criminal legal aid among the country's magistrates' courts.[25]

Appeal against a refusal of criminal legal aid

Those defendants who are refused legal aid by a magistrates' court may apply to the area committee for a review of the refusal. But they can only do so if the offence with which they are charged is one triable on indictment or either way.[26] There is still no appeal against a refusal of legal aid for representation in a case triable only summarily. The members of the area committee are solicitors and barristers

---

[23] *R* v. *Liverpool City Magistrates, ex parte McGhee*, Divisional Court, 3 March 1993, LEXIS transcript; [1993] Crim. LR 609.   [24] Legal Aid Act 1988, s. 22(3).

[25] *Final Report of the Royal Commission on Legal Services (Benson Commission)* (London: HMSO, 1979, Cmnd. 7648); H. Levenson, 'Uneven Justice—Refusal of Criminal Legal Aid', *LAG Bulletin*, March 1981, 106; R. Young, T. Moloney and A. Sanders, *In the Interests of Justice? The Determination of Criminal Legal Aid Applications by Magistrates' Courts in England and Wales* (London: Legal Aid Board, 1992).

[26] Legal Aid Act 1988, s. 21(1) and Legal Aid in Criminal and Care Proceedings (General) Regulations 1989, S.I. 1989 No. 344, as amended, regs. 15–17.

in private practice. Where a defendant applies for a review, the committee will consider the application in the light of the statutory test. Since area committees are based on legal aid areas, they will draw cases from a number of magistrates' courts and their influence should operate to secure greater uniformity in legal aid decisions by magistrates.

In 1996–97, some 5,706 refusals were referred to area committees; 59.1 per cent of these resulted in the grant of criminal legal aid.[27] Despite the introduction of these additional safeguards, some defendants are still denied representation for their criminal trial by accident of geography rather then the merits of their claim to legal aid.

Bail in the Magistrates' Court

The importance of bail

For those defendants remanded in custody by the police, the first appearance before the magistrates' court will concern the important question of whether they are to be kept in custody pending their trial. This is known as a *remand hearing*; a remand is technically continuing authorisation of the defendant's status as an arrested person. Even if released on bail, the defendant remains under arrest. Only very straightforward cases where the defendant is pleading guilty will be disposed of by magistrates' courts at the first appearance of the defendant.

A remand in custody is imprisonment without trial and flies in the face of the presumption of the criminal process that a person is innocent until proven guilty. At any given time, one in four of the prison population is a remand prisoner. A feature of recent years has been the sharp increase in the growth of the remand population despite the relative stability of the numbers passing through the magistrates' courts.[28] The growth has been so great that a number of remand prisoners have, since 1980, had to be accommodated at times in police cells, which are only designed for very short-term detention. They are quite inadequate for the longer term prisoner. In 1980 the average remand population, that is, the typical number of prisoners awaiting trial on any given day, was 6,600; by 1997 it had risen to an average of 12,100 out of an average prison population of 61,100.[29] Since June 1995 police cells have not been not used by the Prison Service to house some remand or convicted prisoners; this was the first time since 1980 that such accommodation had not been used to house remand prisoners.[30] The average length of remand in 1996 was fifty-three days, but thirty-five per cent of those remanded spend three

---

[27] *Legal Aid Board Annual Report 1996–97*, HCP 52 (1997–98) (London: HMSO, 1997).

[28] See generally P. Cavadino and B. Gibson, *Bail: The Law, Best Practice and the Debate* (Winchester: Waterside Press, 1993).

[29] P. White and J. Woodbridge, *The Prison Population in 1997*, Home Office Statistical Bulletin Issue 5/98 (London: Home Office, 1998).   [30] Ibid.

months or more in custody pending trial, and fifteen per cent spend more than six months in custody.[31]

The presumption of innocence until proof of guilt requires a clear justification for depriving a person of their liberty before conviction. There are generally seen to be three reasons which might justify so drastic a step:

- to protect the public from those considered dangerous or likely to commit further serious offences unless kept in custody;
- to secure the attendance at their trial of those who are considered likely to abscond;
- to prevent defendants from interfering with the administration of justice by, for example, threatening witnesses.

Those remanded in custody will have greater difficulty in preparing a defence. Apart from the obvious restriction on their freedom to come and go, access to their lawyers will be subject to the administrative arrangements made by the prison where they are held. The conditions of detention are a national disgrace. Remand prisoners may well be locked three to a cell built for one for twenty-three hours a day. A defendant is likely to spend between seven and sixteen weeks in prison awaiting trial. Yet between one-half and three-quarters of decisions to remand in custody are not contested.[32]

Prior to the Bail Act 1976, the grant of bail was a matter for the discretion of magistrates.[33] The Act controls this broad discretion and aims to secure the release of more defendants while awaiting trial. Section 4 of the Bail Act 1976 creates a right to bail, which can only be displaced if one of the statutory exception applies. The thrust of the legislation is that bail is to be granted unless there are compelling reasons for keeping a defendant in custody pending trial. What seems to have happened in practice is that defendants have an uphill struggle to establish reasons why they should be released when the Crown Prosecution Service raise objections to the right to bail.[34] In addition there has been some erosion of the broad rights given by the 1976 Act.

Before the establishment of the CPS, it was the police who put objections to bail before the courts. The process lacked uniformity since hundreds of police officers made objections to bail without any central supervision. There was little screening of police objections to bail even where police forces maintained their own prosecuting solicitors departments. The responsibility for making objections to bail now lies with the CPS; this has had the beneficial effect of providing a focal point for the screening of bail decision-making. Many CPS offices have reserved the handling

---

[31] *Prison Statistics, England and Wales 1996* (London: HMSO, 1997, Cm. 3742).

[32] B. Brink and C. Stone, 'Defendants who do not ask for bail' [1988] Crim. LR 152. There is also evidence that some defence solicitors do not fight hard for bail: see M. McConville and others, *Standing Accused: The Organisation and Practices of Criminal Defence Lawyers in Britain* (Oxford: Clarendon Press, 1994), pp. 173–81.

[33] See generally, M. King, *Bail or Custody*, 2nd edn. (London: Cobden Trust, 1973).

[34] J. Burrows, P. Henderson and P. Morgan, *Improving Bail Decisions: The Bail Process Project, Phase 1*, Home Office Research and Planning Unit Paper No. 90 (London: Home Office, 1994).

of custody cases on first appearance to a small number of in-house lawyers. This should, in turn, produce greater consistency in the formulation and presentation of objections to bail. It also makes it easier to operate bail information schemes because information is channelled to a single source.[35] More recent evidence suggests that there remain considerable variations in the approach to the initial bail decision in court by the CPS.[36] Like other areas of the criminal process, it can be argued that the formal decisions made in court merely reflect decisions that have effectively been made informally elsewhere.[37]

Exceptions to the right to bail

A person who has been charged or convicted with an offence of murder, attempted murder, manslaughter, rape or attempted rape who has previously been convicted of any of these offences must be remanded in custody.[38]

Other cases are governed by the provisions of the Bail Act 1976.[39] In spelling out the reasons which will justify a refusal of bail, the Act divides offences into two groups: imprisonable offences and non-imprisonable offences. For the purposes of the Bail Act any offence which carries the possibility of punishment by imprisonment is an imprisonable offence.[40] All restrictions on imposing custodial sentences arising as a matter of sentencing law and policy are to be ignored. This means that the category of non-imprisonable offences contains only the most trivial types of offence where magistrates would usually proceed by way of adjournment rather than remand in custody or on bail.

The very first question to which magistrates must address themselves will always be: is the offence charged an imprisonable offence or a non-imprisonable offence? Where the offence is non-imprisonable, the magistrates can only withhold bail from a defendant who has previously failed to surrender to custody and who, in the light of that failure, is believed to be likely to abscond.[41] If the defendant does not fall within this exception to the right to bail, bail can only be denied if one of the general, and rather limited, exceptions mentioned below is established.[42]

Where the offence is an imprisonable offence, as will usually be the case where there is a serious issue about entitlement to bail to be considered, a much more complicated enquiry must take place. The magistrates may, at their discretion, remand a defendant in custody if they are 'satisfied that there are substantial grounds for believing' that the defendant will, if released on bail abscond, or commit further

---

[35] C. Stone, *Bail Information for the Crown Prosecution Service* (Wakefield, Association of Chief Police Officers, 1988). See also A. Hucklesby, 'Bail or Jail? The Practical Operation of the Bail Act 1976' (1996) 23 J of Law & Soc. 213; and A. Hucklesby, 'Court Culture: An Explanation of Variations in the Use of Bail by Magistrates' Courts' (1997) 36 Howard J of Crim. Justice 129.

[36] J. Burrows, P. Henderson and P. Morgan, *Improving Bail Decisions: The Bail Process Project, Phase 1*, Home Office Research and Planning Unit Paper No. 90 (London: Home Office, 1994).

[37] A. Hucklesby, 'Remand Decision Makers' [1997] Crim. LR 269. The possibility of those without professional qualifications in the CPS being designated to do this work under the Crime and Disorder Act 1998, s. 53, is a worrying comment on the perceived importance of, and skills needed for, this work.

[38] Criminal Justice and Public Order Act 1994, s. 25.   [39] As amended.

[40] Bail Act 1976, Sch. 1, Part III, para. 1.   [41] Ibid., Sch. 1, Part II.   [42] Ibid.

offences, or interfere with witnesses or otherwise obstruct the course of justice.[43] In addition defendants need not be granted bail if the offence charged is triable either on indictment or either way and it appears to the court that they were on bail when the alleged offence was committed.

In determining whether a defendant is likely to abscond, commit further offences or interfere with the administration of justice, the magistrates are concerned to make a risk assessment. The magistrates' task is to predict the way the defendant will behave while awaiting trial. On what basis do they make this prediction? Schedule 1 to the Act requires magistrates to have regard to a number of matters, which seek to ensure that they obtain a good picture of the defendant. They must have regard to:

- the nature and seriousness of the offence;
- the defendant's character, previous convictions, employment record, associations and community ties;
- the defendant's previous record as regards past grants of bail;
- the strength of the case against the defendant; and
- any other factor which appears to be relevant.

The relevance of these factors is largely self-explanatory. The more serious the offence, the greater will be the incentive to abscond; the less serious the offence, the less likely it will be that the defendant will fail to appear for trial. The defendant's previous convictions will need to be considered with some care. Defendants with a long string of convictions for minor offences should not automatically be remanded in custody, especially if they have always turned up for trial in the past. The defendant's home circumstances and employment record are of very great significance. A defendant in employment with a stable home environment is likely to be regarded as a good bail risk even on a serious charge, while a defendant without employment and an established home is likely to be regarded as a poor bail risk. Where magistrates feel that bail could be granted if suitable accommodation were available for the defendant, the probation service should seek to ensure that the court is advised of the provision of places in bail hostels and other supported or supervised lodging arrangements.[44] Consideration of a defendant's having answered to bail on previous occasions includes grants of bail prior to the implementation of the Bail Act 1976. The strength of the evidence against the defendant is relevant, because a defendant likely to be convicted on a serious charge which will lead to the virtual certainty of a substantial custodial sentence is a defendant with a considerable incentive to avoid trial. An example of 'any other factor which appears to be relevant' is the practicality of obtaining a medical report on a person on remand on a charge of murder.[45]

---

[43] Ibid., Sch. 1, Part I, para. 2.

[44] The absence of a fixed address is a significant feature in many bail decisions: C. Lloyd, *Bail Information Schemes: Practice and Effect*, Home Office Research and Planning Unit Paper No. 69 (London: Home Office, 1992), chs. 4 and 7.   [45] *Vernege* [1982] 1 WLR 293.

None of the above considerations should operate as a bar to bail; they are merely matters to be considered in determining whether there are substantial grounds for believing that one of the three grounds for denying bail is established. Information about the defendant is central to the prediction about future behaviour. It is therefore somewhat surprising that the Act does not place any obligation on anyone in the criminal process to obtain relevant information about the defendant.[46]

There are two other limited grounds on which magistrates can withhold bail from a defendant charged with an imprisonable offence. First, where there is an adjournment for enquiries or a report, the magistrates can remand in custody if it appears impracticable for the enquiries or report to be completed without the defendant's being in custody.[47] This will usually be after a finding of guilt but where the magistrates need more information about defendants before sentencing them. Secondly, the magistrates can remand in custody where it has not been practicable to obtain sufficient information for want of time to enable a proper decision to be made.[48] This is an objectionable exception to the statutory right to bail. In such cases sufficient enquiry can be made of the defendant in person to enable a decision to be made. If it is felt necessary to verify information given by the defendant, this could be done by the court or a probation officer and will normally take no more than an hour or so. The court should not rise until decisions in such cases have been made. The incidence of the use of this ground for refusing bail is not known.

Finally, there are three general exceptions which apply regardless of whether the offence charged is imprisonable or non-imprisonable. First, the magistrates may withhold bail if satisfied that defendants need to be kept in custody for their own protection.[49] Secondly, defendants already in custody following sentence and before the court for some other offence will not be granted bail.[50] Thirdly, those who abscond lose the statutory right to bail.[51]

Conditions, security and sureties

Where after careful consideration the magistrates are left with some doubt as to the safety of releasing a defendant on bail, they may be able to resolve those doubts by attaching conditions to the grant of bail, by requiring security to be provided, or by requiring sureties.[52] These qualifications should only be added where strictly necessary. Conditions are straightforward: the most common condition of bail is a requirement to live at a particular address; other common conditions are to stay away from a particular person or place and to report to a police station at specified intervals.[53] During the 1984 miners' strike, a number of those charged with

---

[46] But see below on bail information schemes.   [47] Bail Act 1976, Sch. 1, Part I, para. 7.
[48] Ibid., Sch. 1, Part I, para. 5.   [49] Ibid., Sch. 1, Part I, para. 3 and Part II, para. 3.
[50] Ibid., Sch. 1, Part I, para. 4 and Part II, para. 4.
[51] Ibid., Sch. 1, Part I, para. 6 and Part II, para. 5.   [52] Ibid., s. 3.
[53] J. Burrows, P. Henderson and P. Morgan, *Improving Bail Decisions: The Bail Process Project, Phase 1*, Home Office Research and Planning Unit Paper No. 90 (London: Home Office, 1994), p. 40.

offences while picketing, were granted bail subject to the condition that they did not engage in further picketing. The legality of the condition was challenged by way of judicial review but was upheld as lawful.[54] The case confirmed that magistrates have a broad discretion in the attaching of condition to the grant of bail, but must consider that there is 'a real and not a fanciful risk' of a failure of bail without the condition being attached.

Originally, security could only be required by or on behalf of a defendant where it appears that he or she is likely to leave Great Britain before trial, but it is now generally available.[55] Security involves the actual deposit of something of value likely to ensure compliance with the terms of bail.

Sureties are persons acceptable to the court who know the defendant and are prepared to risk a sum of money, known as a *recognisance*, against default of the defendant. No money is actually deposited with the court. A surety is expected to do everything reasonably practicable to ensure the compliance of the defendant with the requirements of bail. If the defendant defaults, the surety will be brought before the court to determine whether the whole or a part of the recognisance should be forfeited.[56]

There have been criticisms of some conditions attached to the grant of bail by magistrates which are unenforceable[57] and that the use of conditions is used as an alternative to unconditional bail when it is designed to be an alternative to a remand in custody.[58]

Giving reasons for decisions

The principal device adopted to ensure compliance with the complex statutory code for making bail decisions is the requirement that decisions be recorded and reasons given for adverse decisions. There can be no doubt that this has increased the workload of magistrates' clerks upon whom this task falls. Whether the device achieves its purpose is another matter; it would be a poor clerk who could not formulate a reason falling within the terms of the Act and it would be a foolish magistrate who insisted on recording a personal prejudice as the reason for the decision.

One objective of the Bail Act 1976 was to move away from the notion that operated in some magistrates' courts that entitlement to bail depended on the offence charged. So it was common before the implementation of the Bail Act 1976 to find bail routinely refused if the offence charged was burglary. Given this objective,

---

[54] *R* v. *Mansfield Justices, ex parte Sharkey and others* [1985] QB 613.

[55] Crime and Disorder Act 1998, s. 54.

[56] See *R* v. *Central Criminal Court, ex parte Gurney* [1996] 2 All ER 705.

[57] For example, a condition that a defendant 'keep out of the city centre' or to have 'no dealings whatsoever with motor vehicles'.

[58] A. Hucklesby, 'The Use and Abuse of Conditional Bail' (1994) 33 Howard J of Crim. Justice, 258. See also J. Raine and M. Willson, 'The Imposition of Conditions in Bail Decisions: From Summary Punishment to Better Behaviour on Remand' (1996) 35 Howard J of Crim. Justice 256.

it is unfortunate (though perhaps understandable) that section 153 of the Criminal Justice Act 1988 has amended the Bail Act 1976 to require magistrates to give reasons for *granting* bail where the offence charged is murder, attempted murder, manslaughter, rape and attempted rape.[59]

Bail information schemes

The vital importance of information about the defendant was acknowledged in the Report of the Home Office Working Party in 1974 on *Bail Procedures in Magistrates' Courts,* whose recommendations were largely implemented in the Bail Act 1976.[60] Research prior to the Bail Act highlighted the speed with which bail decisions were made and the paucity of information available about defendants.[61] It has been suggested that the Bail Act is an example of 'lawyers' law' which would not result in any significant change of practice.[62]

Bail information schemes now exist in at least 179 magistrates' courts and thirty-one prisons.[63] They owe their origins to schemes developed in the USA, though the implementation of schemes in England and Wales differs markedly from the American experience in a number of respects.

The points system used in the Manhattan Bail Project run by the Vera Institute of Justice seems to offer an effective aid to making the bail decision and has had a profound influence on developments in this country. Under the scheme consenting defendants are asked by 'bail investigators' employed by the probation service to provide basic information about themselves which after verification is used to establish a points score which determines the type of bail risk the defendant presents. The information is available to judges on the defendant's first appearance, but is not binding on them. The scheme has worked well in the USA and has been widely adopted. Typically, on its introduction more persons have been released on bail and fewer have defaulted. The success of such schemes shows that bail decisions can be made objectively and that careful screening does seem to identify successfully those who can safely be released on bail.[64]

With Home Office approval, the Vera Institute advised the Inner London Probation Service on the introduction of a pilot scheme at Camberwell Green Magistrates' Court. This proved a considerable success. After some hiccoughs in the development of schemes because of resource constraints, the initiative appears to have gained ground, and further pilots resulted in the same positive response as

---

[59] Ibid., Sch. 1, Part I, para. 9A.

[60] In announcing a package of measures intended to tackled a perceived abuse of bail, the Home Secretary in February 1992 stressed the importance of courts having the fullest information on which to make bail decision so that they could pick out bad risks: see J. Burrows, P. Henderson and P. Morgan, *Improving Bail Decisions: The Bail Process Project, Phase 1*, Home Office Research and Planning Unit Paper No. 90 (London: Home Office, 1994), p. 1.   [61] M. King, *Bail or Custody*, 2nd edn. (London: Cobden Trust, 1973).

[62] R. White, 'The Bail Act—Will it make any difference?' [1977] Crim. LR 338.

[63] P. Cavadino and B. Gibson, *Bail: The Law, Best Practice and the Debate* (Winchester: Waterside Press, 1993), pp. 94 and 100.   [64] See M. King, *Bail or Custody*, 2nd edn. (London: Cobden Trust, 1973).

the earlier experiments.[65] Other similar experiments have enjoyed success, such as the bail action project run by the Inner London Probation Service at HM Prison Wormwood Scrubs.[66]

Typical schemes run on a shoe-string using a member of staff qualified in probation work alongside ancilliaries who are not qualified social workers.[67] Bail information officers would contact police stations in their catchment areas to establish which defendants had been held in custody overnight and the reasons for their having been kept in custody. Attempts would then be made to collect information and to verify it in order to pass any positive information to the CPS and to the defence lawyers. Information is not passed directly to the court.[68] Schemes appear to vary in their relationship to the CPS; some schemes are seen as only being helpful to defence lawyers, whereas others are seen as improving the decision-making of the CPS in deciding what approach to take to the issue of a remand in custody or on bail. One deficiency of scheme is that they only pass on 'positive' information and not 'negative' information resulting from their enquiries. The outcome is not reported to the CPS and defence lawyers in all cases where information is sought.

Some schemes are 'second appearance' schemes. The prison-based schemes are by definition such schemes. These schemes seek to check whether a continued remand in custody is justified where there has been a first remand in custody. In these cases, much work involves securing appropriate accommodation for the person remanded in custody since concerns about accommodation appeared to be the most frequently met reason for the remand in custody.[69]

Measuring the success of the schemes is difficult, but the general view is that they improve the quality of decision-making which is consequently more reliable. Such schemes are also claimed to be cost effective when assessments are made of the increased numbers remanded on bail and the costs of the schemes are measured against the costs of a remand in custody for those whose liberty might be said to result from the intervention of the schemes.

There does now seem to be general agreement that bail information schemes contribute effectively to bail decision-making, though greater uniformity of operation and greater understanding of their object and purpose by all actors in the criminal process are needed. The reasons given for the delivery of information to the prosecution and defence rather than to the court seem unconvincing. It has

---

[65] C. Stone, *Bail Information for the Crown Prosecution Service* (Wakefield, Association of Chief Police Officers, 1988).

[66] G. Mair, *Bail and Probation Work: the ILPS Temporary Bail Action Project*, Home Office Research and Planning Unit Paper No. 46 (London: Home Office, 1988).

[67] Current schemes are funded 80 per cent by the Home Office and 20 per cent by a local authority. Annual costs in 1992 were between £20,000 and £40,000: C. Lloyd, *Bail Information Schemes: Practice and Effect*, Home Office Research and Planning Unit Paper No. 69 (London: Home Office, 1992).

[68] See generally C. Fiddes and C. Lloyd, 'Assessing the impact of bail information schemes' (1990) 29 *Home Office Research Bulletin* 23; C. Lloyd, *Bail Information Schemes: Practice and Effect*, Home Office Research and Planning Unit Paper No. 69 (London: Home Office, 1992); and J. Burrows, P. Henderson and P. Morgan, *Improving Bail Decisions: The Bail Process Project, Phase 1*, Home Office Research and Planning Unit Paper No. 90 (London: Home Office, 1994).

[69] P. Morgan, 'Remands in Custody' (1990) 29 *Home Office Research Bulletin* 18.

been suggested that delivery direct to the magistrates might result in their confusing bail information reports with social enquiry reports,[70] and that a court scheme would require information to be provided in every case if magistrates were not to draw adverse inferences from the absence of a report. The first objection would be removed by training, while the second could be considered desirable. However, it is pointed out that only one per cent of those granted bail by the police are remanded in custody and to require reports in these cases would generate unnecessary work. The production of reports in these cases and in other cases where the CPS decides not to oppose the grant of bail is seen as otiose.

Bail failure

Bail failure can be said to arise when a bailed person fails to attend court, commits a further offence while on bail, or interferes with the course of justice. The extent of bail failure is a hotly contested issue.[71] How figures are kept can affect the results returned. Looking at a number of studies, it seems that about one in eight of those bailed will commit an offence while on remand.[72] About one in 15 fail to attend when required, that is, they abscond.[73] No information appears to be kept on the numbers who interfere with the administration of justice.[74] A number of observations should be made. There does not appear to have been any marked change in the pattern of bail failure over a number of years.[75] Though the level of failure may be regarded as unacceptable, it does not necessarily follow that the decision to grant bail was wrong. It will be important to determine whether the repeat offending is serious or trivial. It is equally true that a number of defendants are remanded in custody who are subsequently acquitted. That too is a bail failure. Here the figures may be even higher with one in five being acquitted, and four in ten not receiving a custodial sentence,[76] though this may be explained by the court's taking into account the period in custody on remand.

Challenging an adverse bail decision

The defendant
The normal effect of a remand pending trial in the magistrates' court or committal for trial in the Crown Court is to authorise the defendant's detention in

[70] Reports about the background of the defendant for the assistance of the court in determining sentence. See C. Lloyd, *Bail Information Schemes: Practice and Effect*, Home Office Research and Planning Unit Paper No. 69 (London: Home Office, 1992), and P. Jones and J. Goldkamp, 'Judicial Guidelines for Pretrial Release: Research and Policy Developments in the United States' (1991) 30 Howard J of Crim. Justice 140.

[71] R. Morgan and S. Jones, 'Bail or Jail?' in E. Stockdale and S. Casale (eds.), *Criminal Justice under Stress* (London: Blackstone, 1992).

[72] P. Morgan, *Offending while on Bail: A Survey of Recent Studies*, Home Office Research and Planning Unit Paper No. 65 (London: Home Office, 1992).

[73] *Criminal Statistics England and Wales 1995* (London: HMSO, 1996, Cm. 3421), p. 187. The figure has remained fairly constant over a number of years.

[74] J. Burrows, P. Henderson and P. Morgan, *Improving Bail Decisions: The Bail Process Project, Phase 1*, Home Office Research and Planning Unit Paper No. 90 (London: Home Office, 1994), p. 5.

[75] P. Henderson and T. Nichols, 'Offending while on Bail' (1992) 32 *Home Office Research Bulletin* 23.

[76] Ibid.

custody for eight clear days.[77] The requirement to return to court every eight days resulted in large numbers of prisoners being moved from prison to court for very short hearings. The normal rule is now frequently displaced and a remand can take place in the absence of the defendant if both the defendant and the prosecutor consent. Defendants cannot consent unless they have a solicitor acting for them. Remands in the absence of the defendant can only take place on three successive occasions, unless the court decides to exercise its discretion to remand in custody for a longer period not exceeding twenty-eight days.[78]

The repetition of remand hearings every eight days was once thought to be an effective way of having a decision to remand in custody reviewed. But this was foreclosed by the decision of the Divisional Court upholding the practice of the Nottingham justices. That bench had adopted a policy, the effect of which was that on a third or subsequent remand hearing, full argument on the question of granting bail would only be heard if there was a change of circumstances such as to justify a full hearing. Two full hearings were permitted, since, on a first appearance, the defendant may have been represented by a duty solicitor who would only have had a limited chance to take instructions. Full argument might only have been possible on a second hearing, when the defendant's solicitor would have had plenty of time to take detailed instructions. In *R v. Nottingham Justices, ex parte Davies*,[79] an order of mandamus was sought to compel the magistrates to hear full argument every time the defendant was remanded. Donaldson L. J. (as he then was) upheld the policy of the Nottingham justices characterising the finding of the magistrates that there were substantial grounds for believing that the defendant would default as a finding of fact that could only be overturned on appeal or if it could be shown that the facts underlying the decision had changed necessitating a reconsideration. He recommended the use of the following question on third and subsequent remands: 'Are there any new considerations which were not before the court when the accused was last remanded?' If there were none, there would be a further remand in custody; the hearing would be a mere formality. It was to deal with this type of case that the remand hearing in the absence of the defendant was introduced. Statutory effect has now been given to this practice.[80]

The standard avenue of appeal against a refusal of bail is the right of appeal to the Crown Court.[81] The appeal does not lie against a decision to impose a condition or to require surety.[82] Legal aid is readily available to cover such applications, because a criminal legal aid order granted for representation in the magistrates' court automatically extends to cover the costs of an appeal to the Crown Court against a refusal of bail.[83] The defendant is not entitled to be present at the hearing without the leave of the Crown Court. The decision will be made after hearing argument from counsel for each side; solicitors enjoy a right of audience for

---

[77] Magistrates' Courts Act 1980, s. 128.   [78] Magistrates' Courts Act 1980, s. 128A.
[79] [1981] QB 38.   [80] Bail Act 1976, s. 5(6A)–(6C) and Sch. 1, Part IIA.
[81] Criminal Justice Act 1982, s. 60.
[82] For which the remedy remains application to a judge in chambers under the Criminal Justice Act 1967, s. 22.   [83] Legal Aid Act 1988, s. 21(3)(c).

these appeals. For those denied legal aid, the Official Solicitor will act. The Official Solicitor is a government lawyer who has as one of his duties the safeguarding of the rights of prisoners.

There will need to be careful consideration given to when it will be appropriate to seek to persuade magistrates that there has been a change of circumstances justifying the grant of bail, and when it will be appropriate to exercise the right of appeal. The difficulty is that an unsuccessful appeal will render it extremely difficult to persuade the magistrates on any later remand hearing that there has been a change of circumstances. Practitioners often advise that, except in the most urgent or convincing cases, it is not wise to apply elsewhere until all possibility of reconsideration in the magistrates' court has been exhausted.[84]

The new remedy of appeal to the Crown Court has not entirely replaced the old remedy of application to a High Court judge in chambers under section 22 of the Criminal Justice Act 1967. Indeed this procedure is the only means of challenging at higher level the imposition of a condition or the requirement of surety. Under the procedure, defendants are not present at the hearing of their applications; their cases will be put by counsel who relies on an affidavit setting out the relevant facts which will have been prepared by defendants' solicitors.

The prosecution

Where new information is available, the prosecutor can apply to the magistrates for a bail decision to be reconsidered provided that the offence charged is one which is triable only on indictment or either way.[85]

A formal appeal by the prosecutor against a bail decision was introduced by the Bail (Amendment) Act 1993. The appeal is made on the spot and is only available if the defendant has been charged with an offence punishable by a term of imprisonment of five years or more, taking a motor vehicle without consent, or aggravated vehicle taking.[86] Pending the outcome of the appeal, the defendant is denied bail. The hearing of the appeal must take place within forty-eight hours of the application. It may be started and then adjourned to another time to meet the deadline. The effect of the oral application of appeal is to override the decision of the magistrates. It is most unusual for a decision of one of the parties to take precedence over a decision of the court.

Bail at committal

Where the magistrates' court commit a defendant for trial, consideration is given to whether the defendant should be kept in custody pending trial in the Crown Court.[87] Once remanded in custody on committal, there is no requirement of repetition of remand hearings every eight days. The decision lasts for the duration of the detention, subject to applications made by the defendant and the time limits

---

[84] A. Hall, 'Bail Appeals' [1984] *LAG Bulletin* 145.   [85] Bail Act 1976, s. 5B.
[86] Bail (Amendment) Act 1993, s. 1.   [87] Magistrates' Courts Act 1980, s. 6(3).

considered below. For defendants already granted bail, the decision is likely to be a formality with the magistrates renewing the grant of bail or any conditions applied at the earlier stage. If the defendant is in custody, the question arises as to whether the remand hearing should be an occasion on which to hear full argument. A full hearing should take place since the committal papers will enable the court for the first time to make a truly informed assessment of the strength of the evidence against the defendant.[88]

Appeal to the Crown Court is available if the magistrates refuse bail following committal, but it is also possible to make application to the Crown Court for bail after committal. Theoretically, this can be done even after an unsuccessful appeal against the magistrates' court's decision. This is because on committal, the Crown Court gains jurisdiction over the defendant, and the court with jurisdiction over the defendant always has power to grant bail.[89] The statutory framework for decision-making contained in the Bail Act 1976 applies to bail decision-making in the Crown Court.

Adjournment as an alternative to remand

An alternative to remand is simple adjournment. Some cases where attendance at court has been secured by charge are not at all serious and in these cases the magistrates may well not remand in custody or on bail, but will simply adjourn the case until a specified day and time or to a day to be fixed later, which is called adjournment *sine die*. Simple adjournments are used when it is not considered necessary to take any special precautions to ensure that the defendant attends court on some future occasion. The requirement to remand the defendant, either on bail or in custody, rather than to deal with the case by adjournment arises where the defendant is charged with an offence triable only on indictment[90] or where the defendant is charged with an offence triable either way and was initially arrested by the police.[91] Where the defendant is brought before the court by summons for an offence triable either way, the magistrates have a discretion as to whether or not to proceed by remand or simple adjournment. The same is true of offences triable only summarily, though there would usually need to be some special feature to the case before the magistrates would decide to proceed by way of remand.

Custody time limits

Scotland has long operated a system of time limits in criminal cases. In summary cases, if a defendant in custody is not brought to trial within forty days, the prosecution lapses and the defendant must be freed. Where committal for trial is involved, there is a similar custody time limit of 110 days between committal and

---

[88] R v. *Reading Crown Court, ex parte Malik* [1981] 2 WLR 473.   [89] Ibid.
[90] Magistrates' Courts Act 1980, s. 5.   [91] Magistrates' Courts Act 1980, s. 18(4).

the start of the trial. In rare cases having exceptional features, the extension of these time limits are available on application to the courts.[92]

A timid and excessively cautious system of custody time limits has been introduced in most of England and Wales by section 22 of the Prosecution of Offences Act 1985 to combat the grave injustice of long remands in custody pending trial. There is no absolute time limit; generous provision is made for courts to extend the time limits specified in the regulations.[93] There is no appeal against the extension of time limits. One or more extensions may be granted provided that the prosecution can show that there is good and sufficient cause for doing so and that the prosecution has acted with all due expedition. The legislation introduces two types of time limit: custody time limits and overall time limits.

A custody time limit restricts the period a defendant can be kept in custody:

- pending the start of summary trial;
- in cases of trial on indictment, between first appearance in court and committal for trial;
- in cases of trial on indictment, between committal for trial and the start of the trial.

All periods in custody for the same offence are aggregated. Expiry of a custody time limit triggers automatic right to bail. On the expiration of the limit, the person is in the custody of the court and is only entitled to release once the court has so ordered.[94] The case may, however, proceed to trial provided that it remains within any overall time limit.

The clock can be stopped by conduct of the defendant. Escape from custody and failure to surrender to custody stop all time limits. Arrest for breach of a condition of bail stops custody time limits. The initial custody time limit is seventy days between first appearance and summary trial or committal to the Crown Court for trial. But if the court determines within the first fifty-six days of detention that the defendant is to be tried summarily, the custody time limit becomes fifty-six days. The custody time limit between committal for trial and the start of trial in the Crown Court is 112 days.

The custody time limits arising before and after committal are independent custody limits. Once a custody time limit has expired and the prosecution, for whatever reason, has failed to obtain an extension under the Act, magistrates have no power to grant an extension of time and bail must be granted. However, when the defendant is committed for trial, the committing magistrates have power to remand

---

[92] Criminal Procedure (Scotland) Act 1975, s. 101; see also R. Renton and H. Brown, *Criminal Procedure According to the Law of Scotland*, 4th edn. by G. Gordon (Edinburgh: W. Green, 1972). See also A. Samuels, 'Custody Time Limits' [1997] Crim. LR 260.

[93] The seriousness of the offence alone will not justify an extension: *R* v. *Governor of Winchester Prison, ex parte Roddie* (1991) 93 Cr. App. R 190, but the complexity of the case alone might: *R* v. *Leeds Crown Court, ex parte Briggs*, Court of Appeal, 19 February 1998.

[94] *Olutu* v. *Home Office and another* [1997] 1 WLR 328, and so the failure to release does not result in a person being falsely imprisoned.

the defendant in custody pending the trial even though he or she has earlier been released on bail on the expiry of the first custody time limit.[95]

An overall time limit restricts the overall length of time, whether in custody or not:

- pending the start of summary trial;
- in cases of trial on indictment, between first appearance in court and committal for trial;
- in cases of trial on indictment, between committal for trial and the start of the trial.

Expiry of an overall time limit results in the release of the defendant, who is to be treated for all purposes as having been acquitted of the offence. Regulations have yet to be made specifying overall time limits.

Disclosure

Defendants and their advisers will be interested in knowing information of two types in preparing the defence. First, they will wish to know the case the prosecution proposes to mount against them so that they can prepare a response to it, and, secondly, they will wish to know whether the prosecution holds any information which may assist in the preparation of the defence case. Different considerations apply to disclosure of this information.

Tapes of interviews

Background
Those questioned at the police station will almost all have had their interviews taped. In many cases what was said in those interviews forms a significant part of the case against them. Unsurprisingly defence lawyers are interested in knowing the contents of those tapes. Surprisingly few listen to the tapes, choosing to rely instead on written summaries of the tapes, called records of interview. These are prepared by police officers present at the interview. In one study only sixty-nine requests for tapes were made by solicitors from a sample of 600 cases.[96] If so many cases rely on the written summary, the quality and accuracy of that summary will be vital. So, how good are they? The conclusions of one researcher are:

The results of this study, which closely parallel those of the author's earlier study in the West Midlands, indicate that there is about a fifty per cent. chance that any record of interview will be faulty or misleading—a proportion that increased with the length of interviews—even when imaginative approaches are examined, records of interview

---

[95] *R* v. *Sheffield Justices, ex parte Turner* [1991] 2 QB 472.
[96] J. Baldwin, *Preparing Records of Taped Interviews*, Royal Commission on Criminal Justice Research Study No. 2 (London: HMSO, 1992), p. 4, n. 4.

remain dangerously flawed in a high percentage of cases. There seem to be fundamental and inherent difficulties that undermine the usefulness of the records of interview prepared by police officers.[97]

Records of interviews are made in accordance with national guidelines issued by the Home Secretary.[98] But the skill of selecting and summarising key aspects of what may be a fairly lengthy interview is a high level skill which may not best be carried out by police officers. No easy—and cheap—solutions to the problem can be suggested in the light of the empirical work.

The only conclusion is that there is no substitute for lawyers listening to the tapes rather than relying on written summaries. The result would be that the record of interview could revert to being simply a written aide memoire for the prosecution file.

When the Runciman Commission considered the problem, it recognised both the difficulties and the absence of any obvious solutions, though it can be criticised for not stating more clearly that more defence lawyers should listen to the tapes.[99] Four possibilities were identified for further exploration. First, summaries might be dispensed with leaving both the CPS and defence lawyers to listen to the tapes; doubts are expressed about whether it is practicable or justifiable to listen to every tape. Secondly, the task remains with the police subject to investigation of the relative costs of their continuing the function and its being passed elsewhere. Thirdly, responsibility for preparing the summaries might pass to the CPS, but it is recognised that CPS staff might take longer to do the task than officers who had been present at the interview. Finally, the possibility of replacing summaries with transcripts should be explored; it is suggested that transcripts are easier and quicker to consult than an audio tape. Again the resource implication of preparing a transcript in every case is raised. That refers to what is seen as the unnecessary cost of preparing transcripts where there is a guilty plea.[100]

Advance disclosure of the prosecution case

A defendant charged with an either way offence is entitled on application to advance disclosure of the prosecution case.[101] Those charged with either way offences are given a notice by the prosecution advising them of their entitlement under the section. Disclosure of the prosecution case normally takes the form of copies of the written statements of witnesses whose evidence will be adduced against the defendant. If the prosecutor believes that disclosure of the information might lead to the intimidation of a witness or to any other interference with the course of justice, the information may be withheld. A notice must then be served on the defendant

[97] J. Baldwin, *Preparing Records of Taped Interviews*, Royal Commission on Criminal Justice Research Study No. 2 (London: HMSO, 1992), p. 21.   [98] Home Office Circular 21/1992.
[99] *Report of the Royal Commission on Criminal Justice (Runciman Commission)* (London: HMSO, 1993), ch. 3, para. 79, where the Report does say that, in principle 'the more the tapes themselves are listened to, the better'.   [100] Ibid., ch. 3, paras. 73–80.
[101] Criminal Law Act 1977, s. 48, and the Magistrates' Courts (Advance Information) Rules 1985, S.I. 1985 No. 601.

to alert him or her to the withholding of information. Before enquiring into issues relevant to the determination of the appropriate mode of trial, the magistrates' court must satisfy itself that the defendant has had the benefit of advance disclosure of the prosecution case.

Proper advice to defendants and preparation of their cases would suggest that solicitors who failed to seek advance disclosure are acting negligently.[102] Yet one survey showed that only around half the defence solicitors sought advance disclosure of the prosecution case, though the use (at the time) of summaries rather than copy statements, a clear intention to plead guilty before the magistrates, or an intention to fight the case in the Crown Court where full disclosure would be made on committal, may account for these figures.[103] Many solicitors will properly continue to seek advance disclosure in all cases; advice given following study of information provided by advance disclosure must be better informed that than which is given without such information.

Common law disclosure

Two decisions of the Court of Appeal have clarified the common law obligation on the prosecution to disclose material to the defence.[104] The prosecution has a duty to supply to the defence any witness statement from a person they elect not to call where that person's evidence may weaken the prosecution case or strengthen the defence case. Normally copies of the statement should be supplied, but if there is good reason for not doing so, the witness's name and address should be supplied. The duty extends to copies of statements recording relevant interviews. Furthermore disclosure should be made of all relevant experiments and tests; this includes those which may cast doubt on the opinion expressed by an expert. Where the prosecution believe that what is called public interest immunity[105] applies, an application must, wherever possible, be made to a court for a ruling and the defence must be told that such an application has been made.[106]

Statutory disclosure

Part I of the Criminal Procedure and Investigations Act 1996 has introduced a further system of disclosure by both prosecution and defence.[107] There is a duty on a

---

[102] Advice from the Law Society's Criminal Law Committee is that immediate steps should be taken to obtain advance information: see *The Magistrates' Court. A Guide to Good Practice in the Preparation of Cases* (London: The Law Society, 1993), p. 39.

[103] D. Riley and J. Vennard, *Triable-Either-Way cases: Crown Court or Magistrates' Court*, Home Office Research Study No. 98 (London: HMSO, 1988).

[104] *Attorney General's Guidelines: Disclosure of Information to the Defence* [1982] 1 All ER 734; *Ward (Judith)* [1993] 1 WLR 619, and *Davis, Johnson and Rowe* [1993] 1 WLR 613.

[105] That it is in the public interest that material should not be disclosed, which requires a balancing of the interests of the defendant with the public interest in keeping the information confidential.

[106] This is a simplified statement of complex obligations which are most likely to apply in the Crown Court; for the detail see *Davis, Johnson and Rowe* [1993] 1 WLR 613, and *Archbold 1998* (London: Sweet & Maxwell, 1998), paras. 12–45 to 12–131.

[107] See also the Code of Practice issued under s. 23(1), Criminal Procedure and Investigations Act 1996, s. 23(1).

police officer known as a disclosure officer to collate information for disclosure.[108] Primary prosecution disclosure[109] requires the prosecutor to disclose to the accused in contested cases any prosecution material which has not previously been disclosed and which, in the opinion of the prosecutor, might undermine the prosecution case. This information is to be provided within time limits which will be set in due course, but until then, the duty is to disclose as soon as is reasonably practicable after the accused indicates a plea of not guilty.[110] Disclosure will normally involve passing a copy of the relevant material to the defence.

In cases tried in the magistrates' court, the defence may elect to disclose the defence.[111] This involves delivering to the prosecutor a defence statement which sets out the nature of the defence, the matters on which the defence takes issue with the prosecution case, and the reasons for so doing. If the defence involves an alibi, details must be provided.

The delivery of a defence statement triggers the obligation on the prosecution to make secondary prosecution disclosure.[112] This requires the prosecutor to disclose any prosecution material not previously disclosed except that covered by public interest immunity. Nil returns are required if all relevant material has been included in the primary disclosure. The material to be disclosed here is all material and not just that which in the opinion of the prosecutor might undermine the prosecution case. There is also a continuing duty on the prosecutor to disclose.[113]

Why should defendants choose to disclose their defence? Clearly defendants will only be advised to do so if there is seen to be some advantage in doing so. The obvious motivation for defence disclosure would be a belief that the prosecutor holds material which will help the defence. But it has been argued that the prosecutor's common law obligations to disclose probably cover most such material. Section 21 of the Act purports to revoke the common law rules, but this is not an easy matter. Though particular rules of common law can be abolished, it is rather harder to remove completely the principles underlying those rules and this may result in resurrection of the rules.[114]

Determining which Court is to Try the Case

The classification of offences

The importance of the system of classification of offences for the purposes of determining the mode of trial in the relationship between the magistrates' courts and the Crown Court was referred to at the end of Chapter 4. There are only three classes of offence for this purpose. First, there are offences triable only on indictment, which must be tried in the Crown Court. Such offences are all common law

---

[108] Code of Practice, paras. 3.1–3.6.   [109] Criminal Procedure and Investigations Act 1996, s. 3.
[110] Ibid., ss. 12–13.   [111] Ibid., s. 6.   [112] Ibid., s. 7.   [113] Ibid., s. 9.
[114] See R. Leng and R. Taylor, *Blackstone's Guide to the Criminal Procedure and Investigations Act 1996* (London: Blackstone Press, 1996), pp. 18–19.

offences, such as murder and manslaughter, together with those offences created by statute which provide for a penalty to be imposed only on indictment. Examples are robbery, and wounding with intent contrary to section 18 of the Offences Against the Person Act 1861.

Secondly, there are offences triable only summarily, which can be tried only in the magistrates' courts. Such offences are those created by statute which provide for a penalty to be imposed only on summary conviction. Thirdly, there are offences triable either way, which may be tried either in the magistrates' courts or in the Crown Court depending on their seriousness. Such offences are those listed in Schedule 1 to the Magistrates' Courts Act 1980, and those offences created by statute which provide for a penalty to be imposed following conviction on indictment or summarily.

The choice of venue where an offence is triable either way is a matter for decision by the magistrates' court. It is for them to determine which mode of trial is more suitable having regard to all the circumstances of the case. Defendants always have a right to elect to be tried in the Crown Court, though they have no corresponding right to elect to be tried in the magistrates' courts. All they can do is to make representations and hope that the magistrates agree that trial in the lower court is appropriate.

The first task of magistrates is to determine the classification of the offence charged. This will be determined by looking at the statute creating the offence or at the Schedule to the Magistrates' Courts Act 1980.

The special case of criminal damage

There is one offence which has a hybrid character. The offence of criminal damage contrary to section 1 of the Criminal Damage Act 1971 is triable either way, but in some circumstances it is treated as an offence triable only summarily. Where the value of the property damaged or destroyed is clearly less than £5,000, the offence is triable only summarily. But if the value of the damage clearly exceeds £5,000, the offence retains its character as an offence triable either way. Where it is unclear whether the value of the damage is more or less than £5,000, the defendant can choose how the offence is to be classified.

There are therefore only three possibilities and the magistrates do not enter into lengthy considerations of the value of the damage caused. They will hear representations, but will not take evidence.[115] First, the value of the damage involved is clearly less than £5,000: the offence is triable only summarily and with the restricted sentencing powers.[116] Secondly, the value of the damage clearly exceeds £5,000: the offence is triable either way and the magistrates will proceed in exactly the same manner as for any such offence. Thirdly, it is unclear whether the value of the damage is more or less than £5,000. In these cases, the defendant can choose whether

---

[115] *R* v. *Canterbury Justices, ex parte Klisiak* [1982] QB 398. For an example of a case where there were difficulties determining the value of the damage, see *R* v. *Salisbury Magistrates' Court, ex parte Martin* (1986) 84 Cr. App. R 248.   [116] Magistrates' Courts Act 1980, ss. 22 and 23.

the offence is treated as triable only summarily or as triable either way, and the offence must be so treated.

Where the defendant has caused damage to two objects in the same spate of violent activity, he or she has committed two offences. The value of the damage for the purpose of classifying the offence is the aggregate of the damage caused.[117]

Indications as to plea

Indications as to plea are an innovation in the process by which the mode of trial is determined.[118] Its underlying purpose is to encourage trial in the magistrates' court rather than the more expensive Crown Court trial of offences which could easily be dealt with in the magistrates' courts. The Runciman Commission had drawn attention to the significant number of defendants who elect to be tried in the Crown Court on the basis that they intend to plead not guilty but who subsequently change their plea to guilty.[119] A Home Office Research Study[120] suggested that as many as 25,000 defendants are committed for trial in the Crown Court who might be willing to plead guilty at the magistrates' court.

Those brought before the magistrates' court charged with an offence triable either way are asked whether, if the offence were to proceed to trial, they would plead guilty or not guilty. Before being asked this question, defendants must have the significance of the question explained to them. The effect of an indication of a guilty plea is that the magistrates' court will proceed to deal with them for the offence charged as if the indication of plea were an actual plea of guilty. The magistrates' court could, of course, commit the person for sentence to the Crown Court if their sentencing powers were considered inadequate in all the circumstances of the case.

If a defendant asked the question indicates an intention to plead not guilty, the magistrates will proceed to the normal enquiry concerning the trial of the either way offence. There is no requirement that the defendant be represented before indicating a plea. An indication of an intention to plead not guilty can be converted into an actual plea of guilty at any time.

The effect of these provisions is that earlier pleas of guilty will be taken, that the mode of trial rules will not apply where an intention to plead guilty is indicated; and that there will be a decrease in the number of cases committed to the Crown Court for trial and in the number of cases dealt with by magistrates as guilty pleas, but that there will also be likely to be an increase in the number of cases committed to the Crown Court for sentence. The new rules also allow an element of choice in the court of *sentence,* as distinct from the court of *trial* although it should

---

[117] Magistrates' Courts Act 1980, s. 22(11).

[118] See ibid., ss. 17A–17C, inserted by the Criminal Procedure and Investigations Act 1996, s. 49.

[119] *Report of the Royal Commission on Criminal Justice (Runciman Commission)* (London: HMSO, 1993), ch. 6, paras. 4–19.

[120] C. Hedderman and D. Moxon, *Magistrates Court or Crown Court*, Home Office Research Study No. 125 (London: Home Office, 1992). See also D. Moxon, 'Crown Court or Magistrates' Court' (1992) 32 *Home Office Research Bulletin* 28.

be noted that the new rules do not change the entitlement to refuse consent to summary trial of an either way offence.[121]

Magistrates' courts have limited sentencing powers. They can only sentence a defendant to imprisonment for a maximum of six months for a single offence or twelve months for more than one offence. The maximum level of fine which can be imposed for a single offence is £5,000.[122]

Dealing with either way offences

Where the offence is triable either way and the defendant has not indicated an intention to plead guilty, the magistrates conduct an enquiry to decide which mode of trial is more suitable in the particular circumstances of the case before them. Sections 18–21 of the Magistrates' Courts Act 1980 lay down the procedure to be followed. In essence the magistrates' court has to decide whether it would be more appropriate to try the case summarily, and the defendant has to consent to the case being so tried. Before considering this issue the magistrates must satisfy themselves that the defendant knows of the right to advance disclosure of the prosecution case. If a request has been made to the prosecution which has not yet been complied with, the court must usually adjourn the hearing.[123]

The magistrates' court then turns its attention to the issue of the mode of trial. The prosecution and the defendant, in that order, are given the opportunity to make representations as to the appropriate mode of trial. It is rare for magistrates to dis-agree with the representations made by the prosecutor; in a study carried out in 1986 the magistrates disagreed with the prosecutor's proposal that the case was suit-able for trial summarily in only twenty-three out of 663 cases.[124] The preference expressed by the prosecutor is in no way binding on the court, unless the Attorney General, Solicitor General or Director of Public Prosecutions is prosecuting. In these cases the court is bound by an election that trial in the Crown Court is more suitable. These binding elections relate only to the decision to go to the higher court. Where no binding election is made, the magistrates must decide which court is more appropriate and the Act directs them to consider:

- the nature of the case;
- whether the circumstances make the offence one of a serious character;
- whether the magistrates' sentencing powers are adequate having regard to the nature of the offence, and disregarding at this point the defendant's previous record;
- any other circumstances relevant to determining the suitability of the offence for trial one way or the other, such as the complexity of issues of fact or law involved or the public importance of some issue raised by the case.

[121] See R. Leng and R. Taylor, *Blackstone's Guide to the Criminal Procedure and Investigations Act 1996* (London: Blackstone Press, 1996), pp. 66–72.   [122] Magistrates' Courts Act 1980, ss. 31–32.
[123] Magistrates' Courts (Advance Information) Rules 1985, S.I. 1985 No. 601, r. 7.
[124] D. Riley and J. Vennard, *Triable-Either-Way cases: Crown Court or Magistrates' Court*, Home Office Research Study No. 98 (London: HMSO, 1988).

The court has a clear duty to consider the mode of trial and to decide which will be more suitable, though there is no requirement here to give reasons for the decision.

If the magistrates think summary trial is more appropriate, they must tell the defendant so and also tell him of their power to commit him to the Crown Court for sentence if at the end of the case they decide that the more severe penalties available in the Crown Court should apply. The defendant is then asked whether he consents to summary trial. The defendant always has the right to elect to be tried in the Crown Court. Neither prosecution nor defendant can elect as of right to be tried in the magistrates' court. If the defendant consents, summary trial will follow there and then or at some later date. If the defendant does not, committal proceedings will follow there and then or at some later date.

If the magistrates decide that trial on indictment is more appropriate, they tell him of their decision which is conclusive. Committal proceedings will follow either immediately or at some later date.

Magistrates are now assisted in deciding which mode of trial is more appropriate by national guidelines.[125] These make a number of general points, and then address issues specific to particular offences. In general, magistrates should assume that the facts outlined by the prosecutor can be proved, should ignore the effect of any previous convictions and mitigation, should not make decisions on grounds of expedience or expedition, and should note the presence of complex points of law which would tend to favour a trial in the Crown Court.

The magistrates should then look at guidance on specific cases. For example, where the offence is criminal damage, it is suggested that high value damage, damage by groups, and deliberate fire-raising should go to the Crown Court for trial, but only if the presence of such factors means that the magistrates believe that their sentencing powers will not be adequate to deal with the offence if proved.

Before the introduction of the new procedures relating to indications of plea, six out of every ten defendants tried in the Crown Court had exercised their right to be tried there; the remaining four in ten had been committed there at the discretion of the magistrates. Four in every ten of those committed by decision of the magistrates would have consented to summary trial.

Electing trial in the Crown Court

This rather technical account of determination of the mode of trial conceals the very important influence the mode of trial has on the way in which the defendant will be treated. The reasons defendants choose to exercise their right to be tried by judge and jury in the Crown Court reveal much about perceptions of the different processes.

---

[125] 'Practice Note: Mode of Trial Guidelines' [1990] 3 All ER 979, as amended in January 1995. The revised guidelines have not been published, but are reproduced in *Blackstone's Criminal Practice* (London: Blackstone Press, 1998), pp. 1065–8. See also S. White, 'The Antecedents of the Mode of Trial Guidelines' [1996] Crim. LR 471.

Magistrates' courts deal with cases in bulk and so an element of routinisation inevitably exists in its processes. In the Crown Court, where trial is slower and consequently more expensive, a greater proportion of defendants contest cases. The Crown Court is a professional court dominated by lawyers, while the magistrates' courts are run by lay magistrates. There are significant differences in the number of defendants represented by lawyers: almost all defendants in the Crown Court are represented, whereas for offences triable either way in the magistrates' courts about six in every ten defendants are represented. There is also a widespread belief that trial in the Crown Court is a superior procedure.[126]

It is a truism to say that not every defendant views his or her involvement with the criminal courts in the same way. But research has identified four typical approaches to the process.[127] First, there are the 'rights-assertive' defendants, who are likely to have considerable experience of the criminal process. They are fully aware of their rights and typically exercise all available rights and privileges. They are not as clever as the 'strategists' who again will normally have considerable experience of the criminal process and be aware of all the rights and privileges available to them. But they elect only to exercise those rights which might result in some advantage. The third group are the 'remorse-dominated' who readily acknowledge their guilt and are typified by their wish to make expiation for their wrongdoing by co-operating fully with the criminal process which will bring them their just deserts. Finally, there is a group which comprises about one-third of all defendants: the 'passive'. These defendants take the easy option of letting the whole process happen around them. Such defendants plead guilty, do not opt for trial on indictment, do not apply for legal aid and do not seek any legal help. Some will be sent to prison. They will probably not understand much of what is happening to them.

It is against this categorisation of defendants that most can perhaps be gleaned from the two surveys which have been carried out into the views of defendants as to choice of venue.[128] In looking at the reasons discovered in each of these surveys, care should be taken to remember that the choice of venue can never be isolated from other aspects of the process, of which perhaps the most important are bail, representation and intended plea.

The two surveys agree that the major reasons for not electing to be tried in the Crown Court are the avoidance of delay, the better chance of a lighter sentence from the magistrates and the view that the case is too trivial for the Crown Court. When views as to the reasons for electing trial on indictment are compared, the principal reasons differ under each survey. Bottoms and McClean's findings show a belief that trial on indictment is fairer, the following of solicitors' advice and a belief that there is a better chance of acquittal as the principal reasons. Gregory

---

[126] *Report of the Interdepartmental Committee on the Distribution of Criminal Business between the Crown Court and Magistrates' Courts (James Committee)* (London: HMSO, 1975, Cmnd. 6323). The belief continues to persist: see A. Sanders and R. Young, *Criminal Justice* (London: Butterworths, 1994), pp. 299–304.

[127] A. Bottoms and J. McClean, *Defendants in the Criminal Process* (London: Routledge & Kegan Paul, 1976).

[128] A. Bottoms and J. McClean, *Defendants in the Criminal Process* (London: Routledge & Kegan Paul, 1976), and J. Gregory, *Crown Court or Magistrates' Court* (London: HMSO, 1976).

lists as principal factors the more thorough consideration of the case, the fact that the jury decides guilt or innocence, the following of solicitors' advice and a fear that magistrates' courts are biased in favour of the police. A more recent survey has broadly confirmed the findings of these surveys. Defendants who want to plead not guilty saw the Crown Court as offering a better prospect of acquittal and were not deterred by the longer waiting times or the chance of a heavier sentence if convicted.[129] The predominant factor determining whether a defendant elects to be tried in the Crown Court is intended plea.

Lurking behind all these reasons is the issue of 'routinisation', which is the hallmark of justice in the magistrates' courts, compared with the slower more careful examination of cases that takes place in the Crown Court. But it is certain that without a speedy and relatively cheap forum for processing large numbers of minor offences, the criminal justice system would soon grind to a halt. At present the concern is that the need for speed has routinised magistrates' justice too much. There would seem to be some justification for the view that magistrates' courts work best when dealing with guilty pleas and do not offer an adequate system for dealing with contested cases. There is indeed some research to suggest that magistrates tend too readily to accept prosecution evidence, though the same research also suggested that most convictions in contested trials in magistrates' courts were in accord with the weight of the evidence. One explanation for the ready acceptance of prosecution evidence may well be the reluctance of defence lawyers to challenge it sufficiently forcefully, for when prosecution evidence is challenged it seems that there is a far better chance of acquittal.[130]

The Riley and Vennard study[131] showed that just over half of cases committed for trial to the Crown Court are sent there by decision of the magistrates, that in one in three cases, the defendant elects trial in the Crown Court despite the magistrates considering that summary trial is appropriate to the case, but that in two out of three cases tried in the Crown Court, the sentence is within the sentencing powers of the magistrates.

Three main reasons for electing trial in the Crown Court seem to emerge from the research studies. First, defendants wish to put off the day of trial. If they believe they will be sent to prison, then time spent on remand in custody counts towards the final sentence and the conditions of remand prisoners are marginally better than those of convicted prisoners. Secondly, many defendants believe that there is a better chance of acquittal in the Crown Court. Finally, defendants seem to believe that they will receive a lighter sentence.

While the first ground is undoubtedly true, such considerations only apply to a minority of defendants. There is some evidence to show a basis for the second

---

[129] D. Riley and J. Vennard, *Triable-Either-Way Cases: Crown Court or Magistrates' Court*, Home Office Research Study No. 98 (London: HMSO, 1988).

[130] J. Vennard, *Contested Trials in Magistrates' Courts*, Home Office Research Study No. 71 (London: HMSO, 1982); see also M. McConville and others, *Standing Accused: The Organisation and Practices of Criminal Defence Lawyers in Britain* (Oxford: Clarendon Press, 1994), pp. 237–8.

[131] D. Riley and J. Vennard, *Triable-Either-Way Cases: Crown Court or Magistrates' Court*, Home Office Research Study No. 98 (London: HMSO, 1988).

belief, though the point needs to be set in the context of the very high rate of guilty pleas. In one study of either way offences, it appeared that fifty-seven per cent of cases tried in the Crown Court resulted in acquittal as against thirty per cent of cases tried before the magistrates.[132] But the third belief appears to be misplaced. Research by Hedderman and Moxon[133] matched cases across the two types of court. Judges in the Crown Court were three times as likely to impose an immediate custodial sentence and these were two and a half times as long as sentences imposed by magistrates. Overall judges in the Crown Court imposed seven times as much custody as magistrates.

Committal for trial

When dealing with a person charged with an offence triable only on indictment, the magistrates must send the defendant 'forthwith to the Crown Court for trial'.[134] There is no consideration of the evidence against the defendant. This is achieved by serving notice on the defendant and on the Crown Court to whom the defendant is sent. Once the documents containing the evidence against the defendant have been served on him or her, an application for dismissal may be made. Such applications are heard by the Crown Court judge who is required to dismiss the charge if satisfied that the evidence against the defendant would not be sufficient for a jury properly to convict. This is considered on the papers and representations made on behalf of the prosecutor and accused unless the judge gives permission for oral evidence also to be admitted in the interests of justice.

In dealing with either way cases which they consider should be tried in the Crown Court, the magistrates must examine the case against the defendant to determine whether there is sufficient evidence to put before a jury in the Crown Court.[135] This process is known as committal for trial. The purpose of committal proceedings is to act as a filter to ensure that only those against whom there is reasonable evidence are sent for trial. They also ensure that defendants know the case against them and enable an indictment to be drawn up. An indictment is the formal charge against defendants where they are to be tried in the Crown Court. It replaces any earlier charge against the defendant and will be drawn up only after committal.

There are basically two types of committal proceedings.[136] The most commonly met type of committal will be the uncontested committal. This will arise where a

---

[132] J. Vennard, 'The Outcome of Contested Trials' in D. Moxon (ed.), *Managing Criminal Justice* (London: HMSO, 1985).

[133] C. Hedderman and D. Moxon, *Magistrates Court or Crown Court*, Home Office Research Study No. 125 (London: Home Office, 1992).

[134] See the Crime and Disorder Act 1998, ss. 51–52, Sch. 3. There are special provisions for dealing with those charged with an offence triable only on indictment together with an offence triable either way or only summarily.

[135] For a brief history of the confused state of Government policy on committal proceedings, see M. Zander, *Cases and Materials on the English Legal System*, 7th edn. (London: Butterworths, 1996), pp. 261–5. See also I. Brownlee and C. Furniss, 'Committed to Committals' [1997] Crim. LR 3.

[136] Magistrates' Courts Act 1980, s. 6.

defendant is represented and the solicitor has read through the prosecution case. The written statements of the prosecution witnesses will be presented to the court but not read. The committal will take place without those statements being read.

A defendant's solicitor[137] can trigger a contested committal by making a submission that the written evidence does not disclose sufficient evidence on which the defendant should be sent for trial in the Crown Court. In such cases, the magistrates must read through the prosecution witness statements and listen to representations made by the prosecution and defence. They will then decide for themselves whether there is sufficient evidence to commit the defendant for trial in the Crown Court.

The effect is that there is almost a presumption that a person will be committed for trial unless that person's lawyer takes action to challenge the sufficiency of the prosecution evidence.

Committal proceedings have already been abolished in serious fraud cases handled by the Serious Fraud Office established under the Criminal Justice Act 1987. In such cases the matter is placed in the Crown Court's jurisdiction by the service of a notice by the Director of the Office transferring the case to the Crown Court.[138] Offences triable only on indictment are also now sent direct to the Crown Court, as noted above.

Trial

Attendance

In general, appearance by the defendant in person will be necessary,[139] but there are important exceptions. For example, few of those charged with minor motoring offences appear in person; many choose to plead guilty by post to the written statement of facts served with the summons, and will send to the court a written statement of any mitigating circumstances. This procedure can be used for any summary offence which does not carry the possibility of more than three months' imprisonment. It is the prosecutor who decides whether or not to use it. It is most frequently used for minor motoring offences and for trivial offences like failure to have a television licence. A person represented by a solicitor or barrister need not be present in court, though they usually will be present and will inevitably need to be present in defended cases. Finally, there are special rules for companies who may appear through a solicitor, though if the case is to be contested, there will need to be company witnesses present. But there is no requirement that a director be present.

---

[137] There is a special procedure where the defendant appears unrepresented.
[138] See also the little used voluntary bill procedure: 'Practice Direction: Crime: Voluntary Bills' [1990] 1 WLR 1635.
[139] For certain purposes attendance through a live television link will suffice: Crime and Disorder Act 1998, s. 57.

The experience of this process is extended under the Magistrates' Courts (Procedure) Act 1998, which amends the Magistrates' Courts Act 1980 to allow a witness statement to be served with the summons. In response to this, the defendant may plead guilty by post, but where there is no response and the defendant does not attend, the case can proceed in the absence of the defendant with the witness statement being admitted to prove the defendant's guilt.

Whenever the charge is for an offence triable only summarily, the magistrates can proceed in the absence of the defendant or his representative even where the defendant is absent and where no witness statement has been served. In such cases, the prosecution must prove both that the defendant has been served with the summons and that the defendant committed the offence charged. The case proceeds in much the same way as if the defendant had pleaded not guilty (see below), but, obviously, there will be no case for the defence put to the court. Often such cases required an adjournment when the defendant did not attend when first summonsed. The new procedures are designed to bypass such adjournments. Pilots in Leeds proved very successful, and reduced the average time from issue of summons to determination by the court from twenty-two weeks to just four weeks.

The guilty plea

The procedure will be determined by the plea. The charge is read out to the defendant who is asked how he pleads. Where the defendant pleads guilty, the representative of the Crown Prosecution Service outlines the facts of the case, and will give details of any previous convictions. At this point the defendant can ask for any other offences to be 'taken into consideration' in assessing sentence. These are offences the defendant has committed but for which he or she has not been tried. The prosecution usually raises no objection to such a request. Sentence is limited to the maximum for the offence for which the defendant has been tried. Although not technically convicted of offences taken into consideration, no prosecution for such offences will ever take place. The advantage for defendants is that they can put all previous wrongdoing behind them safe in the knowledge that it will not return to haunt them in the form of later prosecution.

The defendant is then given an opportunity to make a plea in mitigation, which is his explanation of any circumstances surrounding the offence which explain how it came to be committed and provide some excuse for its commission. Only mitigating factors relating to the offence should be included, but the court should also have attention drawn to the defendant's conduct after the offence which indicates contrition and any factor in the defendant's personal life that suggests the appropriateness of a lenient penalty. Mitigation is not usually backed up by formal evidence. But, occasionally, to add weight to the plea, defendants will go into the witness box and explain matters on oath. They may then be cross-examined by the prosecution. Pleas in mitigation are often no more than ritual incantations of contrition delivered on behalf of the defendant by his solicitor. The magistrates then determine what penalty is to be imposed.

The not guilty plea

When the defendant pleads not guilty, the prosecution must prove its case and the burden of proof is proof beyond all reasonable doubt. The prosecution may make an opening speech before calling witnesses who after answering the prosecutor's questions are cross-examined by the defendant or his lawyer. The prosecutor may re-examine to clarify any points raised in cross-examination. The purpose of re-examination is to defuse the effect of cross-examination. At the conclusion of the prosecution case, it is time for the defence case to be put. There is no obligation on the defence to put forward any case at all since the prosecution has the burden of proof. If the defendant's solicitor does not feel that the prosecution has made a case against the defendant, he or she can make a submission of no case to answer. If this is rejected, he or she can still go on to put the defence case, which may well swing matters in the defendant's favour. Often it will be the defendant's explanation which defeats the prosecution case. Once defence witnesses have given evidence, been cross-examined and re-examined, the defence solicitor may make a closing speech if he or she has not made an opening speech or if the magistrates have agreed to let each side speak twice. Normally only one speech is permitted. At this stage, the magistrates determine guilt or innocence.

If the finding is one of guilty, the prosecutor puts any previous convictions before the magistrates and the defendant is permitted to make a plea in mitigation before the decision on sentence is taken.

Surprisingly, a defendant who is found not guilty is not automatically entitled to costs from the prosecution. Under section 16 of the Prosecution of Offences Act 1985, it is a matter for the discretion of the magistrates' courts. Even if an award is made, it may be for a lesser sum than the full amount of the defendant's costs.

The adversarial system

Once again this technical description of the procedure disguises the realities of the processes in the magistrates' courts. Fewer than two in ten defendants before magistrates' courts contest their guilt, whereas in the Crown Court about one in three contest the issue of guilt. In both courts such information as can be gleaned from the official statistics suggests that about half of those contesting the cases will win. It is undoubtedly true that the criminal justice system encourages guilty pleas; some would argue that there is pressure to plead guilty. This encouragement takes a variety of forms. The principal encouragement is that the system co-operates with those who plead guilty. A plea of guilty will be rewarded by an early disposal of the case and a sentencing discount to the defendant pleading guilty.[140] The 'discount' may be as much as thirty per cent.[141] The reasoning is that the guilty plea is a sign of contrition and this justifies a lighter sentence than in the case of a defendant who

---

[140] Criminal Justice and Public Order Act 1994, s. 48.
[141] D. Thomas, *Principles of Sentencing*, 2nd edn. (London: Sweet & Maxwell, 1978), and D. Moxon, *Sentencing Practice in the Crown Court*, Home Office Research Study No. 103 (London: Home Office, 1988).

unsuccessfully fights the case and who, by inference, has wasted the court's valuable time.

In many cases defendants will have received advice from the police, family, friends and even lawyers, that a plea of guilty will get the matter over with speedily and with the minimum of publicity.[142] In more serious cases there may even be suggestions by the police that an indication of a guilty plea will smooth the way to release on bail. The availability of legal aid may also influence the decision to plead guilty. Finally the widely held view that magistrates' courts will believe the police anyway can lead to the feeling that there is little point in fighting the case in the face of an inevitable conviction.

For the minority of defendants who contest their guilt in the magistrates' court, the adversarial system is supposed to provide the most effective means of discovering the truth in what is often an argument about fact rather than law. But unless defendants are represented, they will be at a disadvantage. They are unlikely to be skilled in the advocacy techniques that are essential to the establishing of their case. It has also been argued that the adversarial system, far from being the best vehicle for establishing the truth, is inherently unreliable, since the 'suggestive' questions put in cross-examination to attack the credibility of the evidence cloud rather than clarify the issues. The amount of evidence increases, but its clarity decreases.[143] Research has also shown that recollections of an incident will vary considerably among witnesses who will honestly but inaccurately recall what they have witnessed. Physical features such as lighting, distance and duration of the incident witnessed may lead to differing perceptions of the same incident. Add psychological factors such as emotion, interest, expectation and individual prejudice and further distortion takes place.[144] Indeed some steps have been taken to prevent errors in identification evidence, once considered the surest indicator of guilt.

The anxiety of being subjected to the attack on one's credibility that is implicit in cross-examination leads many who have appeared as witnesses to describe the experience as an ordeal. When the scales are loaded, it seems that the prosecutor has an unfair advantage. Part of police training concerns the presentation of evidence and police witnesses are allowed to refresh their memories from their note books, which are supposed to be contemporaneous accounts of incidents, though the practice of collusive preparation of note book accounts of incidents is widely accepted. Police officers also gain experience by repeating the operation of giving evidence. A research study[145] into prosecution evidence in contested cases in magistrates' courts showed that there was direct evidence, often in the form of witnesses

---

[142] M. King, *The Framework of Criminal Justice* (London: Croom Helm, 1981).

[143] D. Greer, 'Anything but the Truth: the Reliability of Testimony in Criminal Trials' (1971) 11 Brit. J of Crim. 131; see also M. McConville and others, *Standing Accused: The Organisation and Practices of Criminal Defence Lawyers in Britain* (Oxford: Clarendon Press, 1994), ch. 9.

[144] D. Greer, 'Anything but the Truth: the Reliability of Testimony in Criminal Trials' (1971) 11 Brit. J of Crim. 131.

[145] J. Vennard, *Contested Trials in Magistrates' Courts*, Royal Commission on Criminal Procedure Research Study No. 6 (London: HMSO, 1980).

to the crime, in three-quarters of the 394 cases in the sample. In these cases conviction is highly likely. But in about thirty per cent of the cases there were admissions varying from a full written confession to 'verbals', like the alleged statement to the police, 'It's a fair cop, Guv'. In a significant number of these cases, there was an attempt to have the statements excluded as 'involuntary', that is, given in the face of unreasonable pressure from the police and so making them unreliable, or, in the case of 'verbals', as not having been made at all. It seems that magistrates are reluctant to exclude such evidence and the research study suggests that existing safeguards may not be adequate for the verification of incriminating statements.

Further research suggests that magistrates have a tendency to assume police reliability in giving evidence and are ignorant of the increasing body of evidence suggesting the fallibility of eyewitness accounts. Some of this empirical research shows that the police are likely to be susceptible to the misinterpretation of certain conduct and are more likely than civilians to be prone to errors of recall after a period of time. All this tends to suggest a willingness to convict and a reluctance to require as clear a discharge of the burden of proof as juries seem to require. But the same research also suggests that, broadly speaking, convictions following contested trials in the magistrates' courts follow the weight of the evidence.[146]

Defendants will be unfamiliar with the processes; they may not be represented; they may have been advised that they are foolish to try to fight the case. Ultimately it is easy to see why some argue that the process systematically disadvantages them. Some social scientists have even suggested that trial before the magistrates, far from being the impartial weighing of each side's case and of information about the defendant, is no more than an elaborate 'game' in which those regularly participating in the game (police, lawyers, magistrates, probation officers and court officials) know the rules while the defendant stands as a 'dummy player' absorbing the gains and losses of the regular players.[147] Other commentators draw attention to the penitence ritual aspects of the process, which are so much to the forefront that magistrates' courts deal badly with the contested case which is a manifestation of no penitence at all.[148]

The challenge is to develop processes which deal with minor offences speedily, cheaply and uniformly and separate out offences of violence and dishonesty of sufficient seriousness to warrant a less routinised process in the magistrates' court to trial in the Crown Court. Fixed penalties for parking offences and minor motoring offences are an example of acceptable routinisation. There have also been proposals to create separate traffic courts to deal with most motoring offences. These changes would relieve pressure on court time and allow a more measured treatment of more serious matters. But time alone may not be enough and there is a case for a more radical reorganisation of processes for dealing with criminal offences.

[146] J. Vennard, *Contested Trials in Magistrates' Courts*, Home Office Research Study No. 71 (London: HMSO, 1982).   [147] P. Carlen, *Magistrates' Justice* (Oxford: Martin Robertson, 1976).
[148] Z. Bankowski and G. Mungham, *Images of Law* (London: Routledge & Kegan Paul, 1976); and M. King, 'Roles and Relationships in Magistrates' Courts' [1976] *LAG Bulletin* 7.

Committal for sentence

There will be some cases where the magistrates discover that their restricted sentencing powers are inadequate to deal with the defendant. There are two classes of case where the magistrates may conclude their deliberations on sentence by deciding that the defendant should be sent to the Crown Court for sentence. The first class of cases are those where the magistrates consider the appropriate sentence on conviction for an offence triable either way to be greater than that they can impose. There are three types of such case. First, the magistrates may commit for sentence where they decide that their sentencing powers are inadequate as a result of hearing about the defendant's previous convictions, character and antecedents (school and employment record and background). Secondly, they may commit an offender between fifteen and twenty years of age with a recommendation for youth custody (formerly Borstal Training). Thirdly, they may commit where they believe a hospital order with an order restricting the circumstances in which the defendant should be released is the appropriate method of dealing with the defendant.

The second class of cases covers situations where the defendant needs to be dealt with further by the Crown Court for earlier offences. This will arise where the magistrates convict a defendant who is subject to a conditional discharge or a probation order imposed by the Crown Court or where the defendant is convicted by the magistrates of an offence during a period of suspension of a sentence imposed by the Crown Court.

8

THE DEFENDANT IN THE CROWN COURT

A Professional Court

The Crown Court is the forum for the trial of serious criminal cases, and occupies centre stage in the public's image of the criminal justice system. It is a professional court and its processes are generally regarded as a model of due process.[1] The defendant is almost always represented by solicitor and counsel, and the judge is a professional judge. The lay element remains important. It is the jury who determine the guilt or innocence of the accused.[2] The jury hear the evidence of witnesses which is subjected to cross-examination to test its credibility, and listen to prosecution and defence counsel's submissions and to the judge's summing up. The members of the jury then retire and deliberate in strict secrecy. They return to open court in due course to announce their verdict. They do not explain how they arrived at their decision, and attempts by judges to elicit reasons for a particular verdict have met with sharp rebukes from the Court of Appeal.

If the verdict is an acquittal, it cannot be overturned. Even a conviction carries a degree of finality to it. The process of appeals following trial on indictment does not readily allow a jury's decision to be impugned. It is not easy to adduce fresh evidence on appeal and the ordering of a re-trial is a rare event. Most successful appeals are based on some error in the judge's summing up or on the existence of some irregularity in the course of the trial, which will again be the judge's responsibility.

The Indictment

Trial in the Crown Court is called trial on indictment because on committal, a formal document called an *indictment* is prepared. This replaces the original charge

---

[1] At least when dealing with not guilty pleas, but empirical evidence and the incidence of miscarriages of justice should cause this assumption to be questioned.

[2] For a broadly-based study of the role of the jury, see J. Gobert, *Justice, Democracy and the Jury* (Aldershot: Dartmouth, 1997).

Figure 8.1. **Specimen single count indictment**

THE CENTRAL CRIMINAL COURT

THE QUEEN -v- ABEL BAKER

ABEL BAKER is charged as follows:

Statement of Offence

Theft, contrary to section 1 of the Theft Act 1968

Particulars of Offence

Abel Baker, on the third day of March, 1998, in the City of London stole £1,345 in money, the property of Sterling Limited.

---

or charges and the defendant is tried on the basis of the accusations made in the indictment. The indictment should be drawn up and preferred within 28 days of committal unless a judge grants an extension. The time limit is directory and not mandatory; failure to comply with it will not be a ground for seeking to have any conviction based on it quashed.[3] Preferring the indictment merely involves delivery to, and signature by, an officer of the Crown Court. Indictments are prepared by officers of the Crown Court, or in complex cases by counsel, on the basis of the committal documents. Indictments may contain accusations of more than one offence; each separate offence is called a 'count' on the indictment and is recited in a separate paragraph. Indictments must contain three parts: the commencement, the statement of offence and the particulars of the offence. A simple single count indictment would look as shown in Figure 8.1.

Distributing Work among Crown Court Centres

There is a national network of Crown Court trial centres. Distributing work among them is based on the principle that the more senior and experienced judges try the more serious cases.[4] The distribution of the business of the Crown Court in order to ensure that time spent awaiting trial is kept to a minimum is an important aspect of the criminal process. The organisation of the Crown Court into tiers helps. There are three tiers and the tier of the court indicates its importance as a trial centre. First tier centres, like all Crown Court centres, are staffed by Circuit judges, but are also regularly visited by High Court judges. They will be the centres most likely to deal with very serious cases. Second tier centres will be visited less often by High Court judges. Consequently there will be fewer very serious cases tried at second tier centres. Third tier centres will only rarely be visited by High

---

[3] *Sheerin* (1977) 64 Cr. App. R 68; and *Soffee* (1982) 75 Cr. App. R 133.
[4] Supreme Court Act 1981, s. 75.

Court judges; the mundane work of the Crown Court goes on at such centres. Magistrates commit defendants to the most convenient appropriate trial centre, having regard to the classification of offences for this purpose.

Offences are classified into four categories for the purpose of allocation both among Crown Court centres and among the judiciary of the Crown Court.[5] Class 1 offences (examples: murder and treason) must be tried by a High Court judge unless released for trial before a Circuit judge. Class 2 offences (examples: manslaughter and rape) must normally be tried by a High Court judge unless the judge presiding over the circuit assigns the case to a Circuit judge or Recorder. Rape and other serious sexual assault cases may only be released for trial before a judge approved by the Lord Chief Justice to try such offences. Class 3 offences (examples: arson and robbery) may be tried by either a High Court judge, Circuit judge, or Recorder, and Class 4 offences (example: burglary) will normally be tried by a Circuit judge or Recorder. Nearly nine out of every ten offences falls into this classification of offence. The system appears to work well in ensuring that the most experienced judges hear the most serious and most complex cases.

Legal Representation in the Crown Court

Legal aid

The process of applying for criminal legal aid was explained in the last chapter. Virtually all defendants in the Crown Court are represented under the criminal legal aid scheme. This involves representation by a solicitor and barrister.[6] It is an essential element of the legal aid schemes that assisted persons have a free choice of solicitor. Once the solicitor has been chosen, it will normally be the solicitor who chooses the barrister who will act in the case. Most barristers do both prosecution and defence work in their careers. For the most serious cases a legal aid order will pay for the services of two barristers, a senior barrister, known as a 'silk' or Queen's Counsel, assisted by another barrister, known as a 'junior', who may, despite the appellation, be a very experienced barrister. A barrister receiving instructions (known as a 'brief') from solicitors is required to accept the instructions at a proper professional fee unless the barrister is already engaged in another case on the day of trial or there are other 'special circumstances' which justify a refusal of a particular brief. This is known as the 'cab-rank' rule. It ensures that representation is readily available for all defendants, especially those charged with crimes to which considerable notoriety attaches. The limited freedom to refuse instructions protects members of the Bar from general unpopularity because they have, for

[5] *Practice Direction: Allocation of Crown Court Business* [1995] 1 WLR 1083.
[6] Solicitors can now acquire rights of audience in the Crown Court by taking an additional qualification. As at 25 July 1996, 236 solicitors had acquired higher criminal court advocacy rights. The term 'advocate' is used in this section to refer both to barristers and solicitors with rights of audience in the higher courts.

example, defended those charged with offences arousing a general sense of revulsion. But in practice it is not difficult for a barrister to decline to act in a case. The fee for any brief will be determined either by negotiation with the barrister's clerk, or in the case of a defendant with criminal legal aid in accordance with the legal aid regulations.

Duties to the court

Solicitors and barristers are officers of the court and consequently owe duties to the court as well as to their clients. For this reason a solicitor or barrister must refuse to continue to act for a defendant who has admitted his guilt but nevertheless still wishes to enter a plea of not guilty. So long as the lawyer does not know that the defendant is guilty, it does not matter that the lawyer may believe him to be guilty. For this reason trainee solicitors and pupil barristers are trained never to ask the direct question to the defendant, 'Are you guilty?' Provided that guilt has not been admitted, the lawyer is supposed to set aside all personal impressions and to act in the best interests of the client. The role of prosecuting counsel is not, as is sometimes supposed, to secure a conviction at all costs. The duty to the court requires prosecuting counsel to prosecute fairly.[7] This means that prosecuting counsel must be ready to acknowledge any weaknesses in the prosecution case and must not seek to hide evidence tending to contradict that put to the court. Indeed prosecuting counsel should disclose to defence counsel evidence known to the prosecution which might be helpful to the defence. Whether it will be depends entirely upon the discretion of counsel, always, of course, assuming that the evidence in question has been included in the instructions. There have been well documented cases in which such evidence has not been disclosed where miscarriages of justice have resulted.[8]

The dangers of annoying the judge

The concerns which have been expressed about the system of representation often centre on the increased expense of having a solicitor do the paperwork preparation of the case while the barrister does the advising and advocacy. But there is also a concern that there is a possibility of divided loyalties for advocates, and to some extent solicitors which explains their observed conduct. Because the higher judiciary is generally chosen from among the ranks of advocates and because judges pass on comments about particular barristers to the Lord Chancellor who refers to this information when judicial vacancies occur, ambitious advocates may have too much of an eye to ensuring a good record with the Lord Chancellor. This may sometimes conflict with the need to present a defendant's case with all the vigour

---

[7] D. Farquharson, 'The Role of Prosecution Counsel: Report by a Committee under the Chairmanship of the Hon. Mr Justice Farquharson' *Law Society's Gazette*, 26 November 1986, 3599.

[8] *Report of an Inquiry into the Circumstances leading to the Trial of Three Persons on Charges arising out of the Death of Maxwell Confait and the Fire at 27 Doggett Road, London SE6 (Fisher Report)*, HCP 90 (London: HMSO, 1977). See also the new disclosure provisions described and discussed below.

it requires, particularly when the line of defence is one known to be unpopular with the judge in a case. An advocate may wish to avoid getting a reputation for 'throwing mud at the police' or of clashing too frequently with trial judges. It is also said among advocates that for those with an ambition to become a judge it is wise to do a balance of prosecution and defence work. It is axiomatic that those with a reputation for hostility towards the police are unlikely to be briefed by the Crown Prosecution Service. All this may tend to inhibit the advocate and result in too great a deference to the smooth functioning of the system at the expense of the interests of the defendant. The collegiate atmosphere at the Bar, and its relatively small size, encourage conformity and the perpetuation of particular practices.[9]

Case Preparation

The separation of the preparation of the case and its presentation in court places a considerable premium on the effectiveness of the case preparation. However, for many solicitors firms the work is downgraded and much preparatory work is done by non-qualified staff with little supervision.[10] Considerable reliance is therefore placed on the conference which can take place with the barrister,[11] although sometimes this takes place too close to the date of trial to allow time for remedial work to be done. Barristers in general seemed to be more interested in seeking disclosures from defendants, which could form the basis of a guilty plea, than in carefully weighing the evidence against their client. Barristers trade on their inside knowledge to manage the case:

When barristers introduce into discussions sentencing and charge propensities of particular judges and dark suggestions of backstairs' dealings, the contingent nature of the outcome is beyond measure and can only be stated.[12]

A number of aspects of the preparation of cases for trial in the Crown Court were explored in a research study conducted for the Runciman Commission.[13] The focus of part of the study was on contacts with the barristers who would argue the case in court. There was a conference between the CPS and the prosecuting barrister in around half the contested cases in the sample.[14] Of these one in six was by telephone. Nearly nine out of every ten barristers said more consultation would have been useful. Half of prosecuting barristers only got the brief the day before the trial, though ninety-five per cent said this allowed adequate time for preparation. Attendance at trial by the CPS was normally by an unadmitted law clerk.

[9] R. Hazell (ed.), *The Bar on Trial* (London: Quartet Books, 1978).
[10] See generally M. McConville and others, *Standing Accused: The Organisation and Practices of Criminal Defence Lawyers in Britain* (Oxford: Clarendon Press, 1994), ch. 8.
[11] Ibid. This research was conducted at a time when solicitors had not yet acquired rights of audience in the Crown Court.   [12] Ibid., p. 269.
[13] M. Zander and P. Henderson, *Crown Court Study*, Royal Commission on Criminal Justice Research Study No. 19 (London: HMSO, 1993), cited in this chapter as 'the Crown Court Study'.   [14] N=600.

Whereas the CPS rated the preparation and performance of barristers as uniformly high, the police were less fulsome in their praise, rating them as adequate or worse in a third of cases.

The picture is similar on the defence side. There was no conference in three in ten contested cases. In only one in four conferences was a qualified solicitor present, and in one in three the solicitor's firm sent an unqualified person to the conference, though barristers generally considered the person attending had a sufficient knowledge of the case. Solicitors were equally happy with the performance of barristers, and believed their clients were as well. Only five per cent of defendants rated their barrister's work as less than adequate, and eighty-five per cent rated it good or very good.[15] Defendants first met their barrister on the day of the trial in sixty per cent of cases in the sample. Only one in three met their barrister two weeks or more before the trial. Most conferences on the day of the trial lasted between half an hour and an hour. One third of defendants thought there was insufficient time for consultation with the barrister. Barristers overall views of defence solicitors' work rated it good or very good in three-quarters of cases, adequate in twenty-one per cent, poor in four per cent and very poor in one per cent of cases in the sample.[16]

The incidence and timing of conferences with counsel place a premium on the brief delivered by the CPS or the defence solicitor. One in four prosecuting and defence barristers said that the brief was not adequate. Missing documents and missing crucial points were the most frequently cited inadequacies, but half defence barristers said the brief was 'too skimpy'. The defect was remediable in around three-quarters of these cases, but where it was not it was said to matter 'a great deal' in a significant number of cases.[17]

Disclosure

The defendant will obtain considerable detail of the prosecution case at the committal proceedings. Copies of witness statements tendered to secure the committal for trial will have been supplied and read. This represents disclosure of the evidence on which the prosecution propose to rely rather than an indication of how that evidence will be used to seek to prove all the matters necessary to secure a conviction for the offence charged. However, the prosecution duty to disclose does not stop there. Under the Criminal Procedure and Investigations Act 1996,[18] a duty of primary prosecution disclosure arises under which the prosecutor must disclose any prosecution material which has not already been disclosed and which

---

[15] Defendants rating of the performance of their solicitors was similar.
[16] N=702; there were 14 failures to reply.   [17] Constituting about one in twenty briefs.
[18] See generally R. Leng and R. Taylor, *Blackstone's Guide to the Criminal Procedure and Investigations Act 1996* (London: Blackstone Press, 1996), ch. 1 and J. Niblett, *Disclosure in Criminal Proceedings* (London: Blackstone Press, 1997). These disclosure procedures came into effect in April 1997.

in the opinion of the prosecutor might undermine the case for the prosecution.[19] Such material should be collated by a disclosure officer designated under the Code of Practice.[20] The test for disclosure is at this stage a subjective one based on the prosecutor's opinion.

Primary prosecution disclosure triggers a duty on the defendant to provide a defence statement in writing, which sets out in general terms the nature of the defendant's defence, indicates the reasons why issue is taken with the prosecution case, and gives further particulars of the defence if it involves an alibi.[21] This provision is seen as controversial[22] since it requires the defence to define its position at a relatively early stage in a criminal process where the burden of proof falls squarely on the prosecution. Any defect or inconsistency in the defence statement can result in comment at trial, and the jury can draw such inferences as appear proper from the failure.[23]

Defence disclosure triggers secondary prosecution disclosure[24] which requires the prosecutor to disclose any material not already disclosed which might reasonably be expected to assist the defence case as disclosed in the defence statement. This is determined by applying an objective test, and, of course, requires attention to be addressed to what has been disclosed in the defence statement. The prosecutor will rely on the advice received from the disclosure officer who should review the file in the light of the defence statement.[25] If the defence believes there is material which has not been disclosed, application can be made under section 8 for disclosure of the material. The duty to disclose by the prosecutor does not stop there, since section 9 of the Act imposes a continuing duty to disclose. As noted in the last chapter, disclosure of certain material may be avoided where public interest immunity applies.[26]

Pre-trial and Preparatory Hearings

The Criminal Procedure and Investigations Act 1996 also made statutory provision for pre-trial and preparatory hearings. Until then there had only been a discretionary statutory procedure for fraud trials, though informal pre-trial hearings had taken place at some Crown Courts for many years and were officially recognised in a practice rules in use in the Central Criminal Court in 1977.[27] The 1980s were a decade of considerable experimentation in the use of pre-trial

---

[19] Criminal Procedure and Investigations Act 1996, s. 3.
[20] Issued under ibid., s. 23(1).   [21] Ibid., s. 5.
[22] See J. Sprack, 'The Criminal Procedure and Investigations Act 1996: (1) The Duty of Disclosure' [1997] Crim. LR 308, and A. Edwards, 'The Criminal Procedure and Investigations Act 1996: (2) The Procedural Aspects' [1997] Crim. LR 321. See also J. Wadham, 'Prosecution Disclosure, Crime and Human Rights' *New Law Journal*, 9 May 1997, 697.   [23] Criminal Procedure and Investigations Act 1996, s. 11.
[24] Ibid., s. 7.   [25] Code of Practice, para. 8.2.   [26] *Archbold 1998*, paras. 12–65 to 12–71.
[27] *Report of the Royal Commission on Criminal Justice (Runciman Commission)* (London: HMSO, 1993), ch. 7, para. 8.

hearings. In the Crown Court Study, one in four cases involved a pre-trial hearing with a greater concentration of hearings in contested cases. In most cases there was only one such hearing which lasted less than half a day. The main objective of the hearings appears to have been a discussion about plea. About half the defendants in these cases ended up pleading guilty. Other purposes, which are some distance behind discussion on plea in volume, were the clarification of factual issues and the resolution of legal issues.

The Runciman Commission did not think that pre-trial hearings were needed in every case, though they did recommend that they should take place for all trials expected to last for more than five days and that provision should be made for them in other circumstances where such a hearing might be warranted.[28] The scheme in the 1996 Act is somewhat different.[29] The Crown Court judge is given a discretion to order a preparatory hearing by reason of the complexity of the case or its likely length for the purpose of identifying issues likely to be material to the verdict of the jury, assisting the jurors' comprehension of such issues, expediting the proceedings before the jury and assisting the judge's management of the trial.[30] The trigger for making such an order is a belief that substantial benefits will be likely to accrue from such a hearing.

Plea Bargaining

An essential component of the administration of justice?

Pressures on defendants to plead guilty do not disappear in the Crown Court. The criminal judicial statistics show that two-thirds of all defendants in the Crown Court plead guilty. There is no doubt that the majority of these pleas are properly entered by defendants who have been carefully advised by their lawyers but have no defence to the charges made against them. But some of the pleas will have been entered with some reluctance, and in some cases the pressure to plead guilty will have been the result of what is known as plea bargaining. That some of these pleas are regretted is evidenced by the number of appeals to the Court of Appeal seeking to have the convictions based on them quashed on the basis that the plea was not voluntary. The defendant may have resisted considerable pressures in deciding to go to the Crown Court for trial, and yet as a result of this process finally joins the many who plead guilty. As we shall see, there are positive and negative aspects to the process. Pioneering, and controversial, research by Baldwin and McConville of the Institute of Judicial Administration at Birmingham

---

[28] *Report of the Royal Commission on Criminal Justice (Runciman Commission)* (London: HMSO, 1993), paras. 4–36.

[29] Criminal Procedure and Investigations Act 1996, Part III, and 'Practice Direction: Plea and Directions Hearings' [1995] 1 WLR 1318.

[30] s. 29, Criminal Procedure and Investigations Act 1996. Separate rules continue to apply to serious fraud cases.

University is the main source of information about plea bargaining in England and Wales.[31]

The process of plea bargaining seems to have developed in the USA, and a word about its use there will help to understand plea bargaining in England. In the USA bargains between prosecution and defence have become an integral part of the criminal process. But two aspects of the American criminal justice system, which do not have counterparts in the English system, have encouraged its development. The first is the existence in many states of very severe mandatory penalties for specific offences. The second is the ability of prosecution counsel to recommend particular sentences. So defendants have much to gain by being able to bargain for either a guilty plea to a lesser offence which does not carry the harsh mandatory penalty, or for a recommendation from the prosecutor of a lenient sentence. The United States Supreme Court has endorsed and encouraged the process. In a decision which has been cited with approval on many subsequent occasions, Chief Justice Burger described the process as 'an essential component of the administration of justice', and went on to outline its benefits as follows:

Disposition of charges after plea discussions is not only an essential part of the process but a highly desirable part for many reasons. It leads to prompt and largely final disposition of most criminal cases; it avoids much of the corrosive impact of enforced idleness during pre-trial confinement for those who are denied release pending trial; it protects the public from those accused persons who are prone to continue criminal conduct even while on pre-trial release; and by shortening the time between charge and disposition, it enhances whatever may be the rehabilitative prospects of the guilty when they are ultimately imprisoned.[32]

In *Roberts* v. *US*[33] the Supreme Court explained that the process was approved because there was a relative equality of bargaining power between the prosecutor and defendant which prevented the process from being 'fundamentally unfair'. In the USA the vast majority of guilty pleas follow some negotiation or deal between prosecution and defence. The commonly obtained benefits are: sentence concessions, concurrent charging of multiple charges, the charging of a lesser offence, and the dropping of one or more charges altogether. The essence of the bargain is a guilty plea in exchange for some lessening of the sentence.

No place in the English criminal process

The comments of the Supreme Court stand in marked contrast to judicial comments in England. In *Atkinson*[34] Lord Scarman said:

Plea-bargaining has no place in the English criminal law. It is found in some systems of law in which the prosecution are entitled to make submissions as to the character

[31] J. Baldwin and M. McConville, *Negotiated Justice* (Oxford: Martin Robertson, 1977) and J. Baldwin and M. McConville, 'Plea Bargaining and the Court of Appeal' (1979) 6 Brit. J of Law and Soc. 200.
[32] *Santobello* v. *New York* (1971) 404 US 257, 261.   [33] (1980) 445 US 552.
[34] [1978] 1 WLR 425.

or length of sentence. In such systems of law it is possible for a bargain to be driven between the defence and the prosecution, but never, so far as my researches have gone, with the court itself. In our law the prosecution is not heard on sentence. That is a matter for the court, after considering what has to be said on behalf of an accused man. Our law having no room for any bargain about sentence between court and defendant, if events arise which give the appearance of such a bargain, then one must be very careful to see that the appearance is corrected.

Again in *Wise*[35] Lord Widgery C.J. said:

If the facts were successfully established and the plea bargain thereby sustained, it would be regarded as a very serious matter, and it would be open to question whether anyone who so blatantly indulged in plea bargaining could sit on the criminal law bench.

It would seem that the judicial denunciations of plea bargaining relate principally to bargaining involving the judge, particularly where the obvious conclusion to draw from the judge's comments is that he or she has presumed the guilt of the defendant. But bargains are struck in the English criminal justice system. It is clear that the ability of the prosecution to offer no evidence on certain counts on the indictment and to accept a plea of guilty to the lesser of alternative charges enables discussions about plea to take place between prosecution and defence that are really bargains. This ability to bargain is somewhat more fettered than in the USA, but few would deny that such practices are common aspects of the English criminal process. There is also the tacit bargain offered to all defendants in the form of the sentencing discount with which a guilty plea will be rewarded.[36] In *Boyd*,[37] Cumming-Bruce L.J. said:

The policy of the courts is that where a man does plead guilty, which does give rise to public advantage and avoids the expense and nuisance of a trial, which may sometimes be a long one, the court encourages pleas of guilty by knocking something off the sentence which would otherwise have been imposed if there had not been a plea of guilty.

Counsel who does not draw the attention of a client with a weak defence to this aspect of the sentencing process is not acting in the best interests of the client. On the other hand, it is virtually impossible for prosecution and defence counsel to bargain over specific sentences, because sentence is at the discretion of the court in all cases except murder, which carries a mandatory sentence of life imprisonment. Nor is it considered proper, as Lord Scarman noted in the quotation cited above, for prosecuting counsel to make recommendations about sentence.

More contentious are discussions involving the judge immediately prior to, or during the course of, the trial in which the matter of sentence is raised. The Court of Appeal has laid down strict guidelines governing such exchanges. The leading

---

[35] [1979] RTR 57.

[36] Judicially approved in, for example, *de Haan* [1968] 2 QB 108, and *Cain* [1976] Crim. LR 464, and set in statute in the Criminal Justice and Public Order Act 1994, s. 48, which provides that account must be taken of the stage in the proceedings at which the indication of a guilty plea was made and the circumstances in which the indication was given.   [37] (1980) 2 Cr. App. R (S) 234, 235.

case is *Turner*.[38] Turner, a defendant with previous convictions, was on trial on a charge of theft. He had pleaded not guilty and the basis of his defence was an attack on the credibility of a police witness. During the course of the trial, his counsel advised him in strong terms to change his plea to one of guilty, indicating his view that a guilty plea would probably result in a non-custodial sentence, whereas if he persisted in his defence, he was likely to be sent to prison. Turner refused to change his plea. A little later counsel had a discussion with the judge in private. On his return, counsel repeated his advice, which was accepted. Turner changed his plea and was fined. Turner subsequently regretted his change of plea and appealed against his conviction, claiming that the change of plea was not voluntary, because he believed that counsel was expressing the views of the judge. The Court of Appeal allowed the appeal, treating the guilty plea as a nullity. A proper trial was ordered, known as *venire de novo*, to replace the trial regarded as a nullity because of the nullity of the plea. The Court of Appeal felt that in the circumstances, though counsel had not behaved in any way improperly, Turner had reasonable grounds for his belief that counsel had been expressing the views of the judge.

The Court went on to lay down guidelines on judicial involvement in discussions about a defendant's plea. Five points were made, between some of which there is an inherent tension:

(1) Counsel must be free to advise a guilty plea and to indicate that this is likely to affect sentence. Counsel should always ensure that the defendant does not plead guilty unless he has committed the acts constituting the offence charged with the requisite intent.

(2) The defendant must retain at all times complete freedom as to choice of plea.

(3) There must be free access between counsel and the judge. As far as possible discussions between counsel and the judge should take place in open court. But occasionally the need will arise for discussions in private where matters can be raised that it would be inappropriate to raise in open court. In such cases the discussion should be in the presence of both counsel and of the defendant's solicitor if he so wishes. Examples given in the judgment are discussions concerning a defendant with a terminal illness of which he had been kept in ignorance, and concerning the acceptability of a guilty plea to a lesser offence.

(4) The judge must never indicate the type or length of sentence he or she has in mind unless able to indicate the form of sentence regardless of the defendant's plea.

(5) Where any discussion has taken place in private, counsel must disclose the essence of the discussion to the accused.

The obvious purpose of the guidelines is to limit as far as possible any hint of pressure by the judge on a defendant to plead guilty, while preserving the ability of counsel to advise a defendant in strong terms to plead guilty where such advice

---

[38] [1970] 2 QB 321.

seems appropriate. Nevertheless, since *Turner* there are still said to be occasions where bargaining involving the judge takes place. But, despite the covert nature of the process which makes establishing what actually transpired particularly difficult, there has been a steady flow of cases in which defendants have appealed against conviction on the grounds that unreasonable pressure has been placed upon them.

The opportunities for bargaining

The opportunities for bargaining are not difficult to find. At the pre-trial review, the judge learns from counsel the intended plea, number of witnesses, evidence agreed and the probable length of the trial. It is an informal process which has been described as in the nature of a supervised conference between the parties. Though counsel are trained to avoid plea bargaining at such reviews, the Crown Court Study showed that discussions about plea are the most frequent matter raised at such reviews. The hinted bargain or unspoken understanding may be far more widespread than is commonly supposed.

The results of empirical research into 121 cases tried in the Birmingham Crown Court where there was a late change of plea to one of guilty showed that only thirty-five defendants (28.9 per cent) could clearly be categorised as not involved in any deal or subjected to any pressure. The pleas of twenty-two defendants (18.2 per cent) were the direct result of an offer made and accepted by the defendant who gained some benefit from the deal. Of these cases, thirteen fell within the *Turner* guidelines and nine outside them. A further sixteen defendants (13.2 per cent) assumed that a bargain had been made, though no explicit bargain had. A very worrying figure is that some forty-eight defendants (39.7 per cent) claimed to have changed their pleas as a result of pressure from their own barristers even though unaccompanied by any offer.[39] The Birmingham research indicated that some barristers involved in cases in their sample behaved improperly in acting oppressively in their advice to defendants to change their pleas. The advice went beyond advising defendants to weigh up the risks in an informed way and amounted to such pressure that the defendant could no longer be said to have a free choice of plea.

To check the strength of the case against the defendants in the sample Baldwin and McConville had the committal papers assessed independently by a retired chief constable and a retired clerk to the justices. This assessment resulted in a prediction of acquittal in one in five of the cases. In these cases the disposition of the case on a guilty plea may not have been in accordance with the evidence. At best these assessments show that there may have been serious errors of judgment by counsel in some of the cases in the sample.

The Crown Court Study showed that nine out of ten defence barristers, eight out of ten prosecution barristers, and two out of three judges thought that the *Turner*

---

[39] There is also some evidence that defence solicitors can deny clients real choice over the matter of plea: see M. McConville and others, *Standing Accused: The Organisation and Practices of Criminal Defence Lawyers in Britain* (Oxford: Clarendon Press, 1994), pp. 68–71.

guidelines should be revised to permit 'realistic discussions' of plea and sentence.[40] The Runciman Commission responded by recommending that counsel should be able to ask at any time what the sentence would be if the defendant pleaded guilty at that stage. The judge would be free to refuse such an indication if insufficient information to do so were available.[41] No amendment to the *Turner* guidelines has yet been set in place, but section 48 of the Criminal Justice and Public Order Act 1994 gives statutory recognition to the sentence discount and recognises that it is a sliding scale.

Evaluation

In evaluating the process of plea bargaining it is worth noting some of the factors which persuaded the United States Supreme Court to endorse the process. Key factors are the relative openness of the deal and the equality of bargaining power between prosecution and defence. The latter presumably refers to the existence of public sector lawyers acting for both prosecution and defence in many cases: District Attorney for the prosecution and public defender for the defence. But in the English system both safeguards are missing. The deal is done very much behind the scenes, and the nature of the deal is nowhere recorded. The open adjudication of criminal cases is replaced by 'nod and wink' understandings. Administrative convenience replaces due process. The issue of equality of bargaining is also very different. In the English criminal justice system barristers may be called upon to prosecute or defend. There is nothing corresponding to District Attorney and public defender, though there is now the Crown Prosecutions Service, and there are firms of private practitioners specialising in criminal defence work. There are also some barristers whose work is predominantly criminal prosecution or defence, but they lack the coherence and organisation of the American counterparts. The arrangements in England have led Baldwin and McConville to suggest that it is arguable that 'counsel's primary interests inevitably lie with the court system and not with the defendant'. This results in counsel quietly conspiring to ensure a smooth flow of cases in the Crown Court. Counsel may not want to get a reputation for being 'difficult'. At the end of the day appointment to the bench may depend on this co-operative attitude. The lack of openness also presents prosecutors with the temptation to 'over-charge' so that there will be something to bargain away for the guilty plea. The Birmingham research into this practice happily showed that there is no evidence of systematic over-charging of defendants.

The criminal justice system relies heavily on the guilty pleaders to avoid a colossal backlog of trials. The negotiated or bargained guilty plea clearly contributes to court efficiency. Where the guilty plea is the result of a pragmatic approach to the realities of the situation by all participants in the process, it has a useful purpose to serve. Equally it is easy to understand the sentencing discount for those

---

[40] Crown Court Study, para. 4.13.1.

[41] *Report of the Royal Commission on Criminal Justice (Runciman Commission)* (London: HMSO, 1993), ch. 7, paras. 41–58.

pleading guilty. Its removal would undoubtedly be likely to encourage many more 'no-hopers' to contest their guilt. The key issues are the presence of some notion of due process in plea discussions, and equality of bargaining position. The former should now be achieved by the notes which are required to be kept of any discussion with the judge. The issue of equality of bargaining power is much more problematic, since it requires a change of attitude, and possibly a change of structures, within the legal profession. But it may be that the regulation of the process rather than a denial of its existence would itself lead to better judgments and fewer mistakes by all involved. So long as sentence remains discretionary, and it remains improper for prosecuting counsel to make recommendations on sentence, there is no reason to suppose that official recognition and regulation of the process would lead to an explosion of plea bargaining. Finally, more openness about the sentencing discount, perhaps even the development of guidelines, would enable counsel to advise defendants with greater uniformity and certainty about the impact on sentence of a guilty plea.

The Jury

Selection of the jury

The principle underlying the selection of the English jury is that of randomness. The theory is that a jury chosen at random will be representative of the community. Any prejudices held by particular members of the jury are likely to be counteracted by the good sense of the other members of the jury. No attempt is made to enquire about these prejudices. In marked contrast the principle underlying the selection of the jury in the USA is that of securing a 'neutral' jury which will try the case dispassionately according to the evidence. This desire to secure a jury of twelve persons free of prejudices which might possibly affect a juror's ability to be strictly neutral as between prosecution and defence has resulted in complex jury selection procedures, known as *voire dire*. Potential jurors are subjected to detailed questioning either by counsel or by the judge to reveal any prejudices and to confirm neutrality. The significance of the principle of random selection which is deeply rooted in the English system will soon become apparent.

The basic qualification for jury service is a simple age and residence qualification. *Prima facie* all persons aged between eighteen and seventy registered as Parliamentary or local government electors who have been resident in the United Kingdom for at least five years since attaining the age of thirteen are eligible for jury service.[42] The current practice is for summoning officers to choose a number of wards in the catchment area of the Crown Court, from which jurors are randomly chosen by computer programme.

---

[42] Juries Act 1974, s. 1.

Certain groups of individuals are removed from this pool of eligible jurors.[43] Some, like lawyers, judges and the police, are ineligible because they might have an undue influence on the jury, while others like the mentally ill are ineligible because they are deemed not competent. The reasons for the ineligibility of the clergy are less obvious. The Morris Committee[44] noted that they might be in a pastoral relationship with the defendant. The Report also notes that clergyman may be too inclined to compassion and 'might find it difficult to consider the claims of justice alone'. Finally monks and nuns are considered to lack the necessary experience of the world to qualify as jurors. It might have been preferable to leave the clergy to determine these issues for themselves and to have included them in the groups of persons with a right to be excused.[45]

Persons with certain criminal convictions are disqualified either for life or for ten years depending on the seriousness of the offence.[46]

There is a group in the population who have a right to be excused if summoned; for them, service as jurors is optional. These include those over sixty-five, members and officers of Parliament, the military and the medical profession including veterinary practitioners. Surprisingly teachers are not included in this group.[47]

There are two general grounds on which a juror has a right to claim to be excused jury service. These arise, first, where the juror has attended court for jury service within the previous two years or where the juror has been excused jury service for a longer period which has not expired.[48] It is not uncommon for judges to grant lifetime exemptions from further jury service to those who have served in long and complex trials. Secondly, a juror who shows, or about whom it becomes apparent, that he or she cannot act effectively as a juror because of a physical disability or insufficient understanding of English, must be discharged.[49]

There is also a general discretion to excuse persons from jury service where they can show good reason for being excused.[50] Practice varies widely on what amounts to a good reason. Some Crown Court centres are generous, others are demanding. The generosity may vary from time to time depending on the number of jurors summoned and the expected number of trials where juries will be needed. As an alternative to excusal, attendance for jury service may now be deferred to more convenient days.[51]

Where a person seeks to be excused from jury service, the application is initially made to an officer of the Crown Court. The decision of that officer may be appealed to a Crown Court judge, who has the final say in the matter though the person appealing has a right to make oral representations to the judge.[52] That right does not extend to a right to be legally represented on the appeal, though the judge

---

[43] Juries Act 1974, Sch. 1.

[44] *Report of the Departmental Committee on Jury Service (Morris Committee)* (London: HMSO, 1965, Cmnd. 2627).

[45] The Runciman Commission thought clergymen should be removed from the category of those ineligible to serve as jurors: *Report of the Royal Commission on Criminal Justice (Runciman Commission)* (London: HMSO, 1993), ch. 8, para. 57.   [46] Juries Act 1974, Sch. 1, Part II.

[47] Ibid., Sch. 1, Part III.   [48] Ibid., s. 8.   [49] Ibid., ss. 9B and 10.   [50] Ibid., s. 9.

[51] Ibid., s. 9A.   [52] Crown Court Rules 1982, S.I. 1982 No 1109, s. 25, as amended.

has a discretion to permit this.[53] Each case must be decided on its merits; excusal is a personal matter.[54]

It has occasionally been suggested that all these provisions result in some of those most competent to try criminal cases being excluded. Much of this must, of course, be pure supposition. The Crown Court Study showed that in eighty per cent of cases in the sample the ratio of men to women was 5:7, 6:6, 7:5 or 8:4, and that overall men were slightly over-represented.[55] There was a good age spread of jurors, nine out of ten of whom were in full-time or part-time work. These figures showed that the jurors were a broad cross-section of those eligible.

Jury vetting

In certain cases the principle of random selection is modified because it is felt that random selection might result in bias.[56] Where the offence is a terrorist case or a case involving national security in which some of the evidence will be heard *in camera*,[57] certain pre-trial checks known as authorised checks may be permitted of the panel of jurors. In December 1988, honouring a promise made in Parliament during the passage of the Criminal Justice Act 1988, the Attorney General issued a revised set of guidelines on jury checks.[58] Authorised checks require the personal authority of the Attorney General, who will act on a recommendation of the Director of Public Prosecutions.

The guidelines begin by affirming three principles. First, juries are selected at random. Secondly, the Juries Act 1974 alone identifies those who are ineligible to serve, or are disqualified from serving, as jurors. Thirdly, the correct way to seek to exclude a member of the panel from sitting as a juror is by the exercise in open court of the right to request a stand by or, if necessary, to challenge for cause. Despite these provisions, the guidelines say there are 'certain exceptional types of case of public importance for which the provisions as to majority verdicts and the disqualification of jurors may not be sufficient to ensure the proper administration of justice'. In these cases, further safeguards against the possibility of bias 'may be necessary'. In national security cases, the justification for further safeguards is said to be the danger that a juror, either voluntarily or under pressure, may make improper use of evidence heard in the case. In both national security and terrorist cases, it is asserted that there is a danger that a juror's political beliefs may be so biased as to go 'beyond normally reflecting the broad spectrum of views and interest in the community' such as might lead the juror to 'exert improper pressure on his fellow jurors'.

---

[53] *R* v. *Guildford Crown Court, ex parte Siderfin* [1989] 3 All ER 73.

[54] 'Practice Direction: Jury Service: Excusal' [1988] 1 WLR 1162.

[55] Crown Court Study, para. 8.13. Men constituted 53 per cent of jurors whereas their distribution in the general population is 48 per cent.

[56] For the historical development of jury vetting, see R. White, *The Administration of Justice*, 2nd edn. (Oxford: Blackwell, 1991), pp. 117–19, or A. Sanders and R. Young, *Criminal Justice* (London: Butterworths, 1994), pp. 355–7.   [57] That is, in the absence of the public, including the press.

[58] Attorney General's Guidelines: Jury Checks [1988] 3 All ER 1086.

In such cases a limited investigation of the background of the jurors on the panel may be justified. This will involve enquiries of the police Special Branches and of the security services (MI5 and MI6).

The result of an authorised check is sent to the DPP, who decides what, if any, information should be brought to the attention of prosecution counsel in the case. The DPP may alone authorise counsel to exercise the right of stand by on the basis of information so obtained. Counsel is, however, given a discretion as to the information to be disclosed to defence counsel in the case. Upward reporting of the use made of any information disclosed to counsel is required so that the Attorney General can monitor the operation of the guidelines. The incidence of vetted juries is not routinely reported, but there will be few cases each year attracting this special procedure. When the Attorney General first made the guidelines public in 1978, he stated that he had been notified of twenty-five cases where vetting had been authorised since August 1975 when guidelines were first introduced. These consisted of twelve terrorist cases involving the IRA, two Official Secrets cases and eleven serious gang cases. Since the revised guidelines are narrower, the numbers are likely to be less.

In addition to authorised checks, there will be many more cases in which a criminal records office check is run against those called for jury service. The Attorney General has annexed to the guidelines on authorised checks, the recommendations of the Association of Chief Police Officers on criminal records office checks.[59] The guidelines note that 'any search of criminal records for the purpose of ascertaining whether or not a jury panel includes any disqualified person is a matter for the police as the only authority able to carry out such a search and as part of their usual function of preventing the commission of offences'. The recommendations are broadly drafted and reserve considerable discretion to individual chief constables. In *any* case where the chief constable or the DPP considers that it would be 'in the interests of justice' to carry out a criminal records office check of jurors on the panel, such a check may be carried out. The recommendations state that it will normally be in the interest of justice to make a check where:

- there is reason to believe that a particular juror is disqualified or that 'attempts are being made to circumvent the statutory provisions excluding disqualified persons from service on a jury;
- in a previous related abortive trial, an attempt was made to interfere with a juror;
- the DPP or chief constable thinks it is particularly important to ensure that no disqualified juror serves on the jury.

Checks on behalf of the defence will only be conducted on the authority of the DPP. Information resulting from such a check will be passed to prosecuting counsel who will decide what use to make of it. The current incidence of such checks is not routinely reported.

---

[59] Attorney General's Guidelines: Jury Check [1988] 3 All ER 1086.

In the case of both authorised checks and criminal records office checks, the procedure for dispensing with the services of an 'unsuitable' juror is the exercise of the right of stand by for the Crown which does not require any reason to be given.[60]

It is alarming to see the requirements of due process so obviously eroded. One consequence of vetting where selected information is passed initially only to prosecuting counsel is that the court's determination of the suitability of a juror is being subordinated to the discretion of counsel for one of the parties.[61] But the major point is that practices labelled by senior judges as unconstitutional are now governed by administrative directions and recommendations of senior police officers. Adherence to the principles of due process demands that the practice should either be abandoned or regulated by statute. If it is not, it will be difficult to counter charges that the jury is being subverted.[62] It is certainly impossible to reconcile the practice of vetting with the principle of random selection of jurors, which has formed the basis of Parliamentary policy in the legislation on juries and of much judicial comment on the jury system.

Affecting the composition of the jury in the courtroom

The procedures described above involve enquiries made outside the courtroom, the result of which are seen in the courtroom when counsel object to a juror as he or she comes forward to swear the juror's oath at the start of the trial. There are a number of procedures that can be used in the courtroom to affect the composition of a particular jury that is to try a case. The law in this area is a mixture of common law and statutory powers.[63]

It is possible for either prosecution or defence counsel to issue a challenge to the array. This is an objection to the whole panel of jurors summoned to attend at the Crown Court on the grounds of bias or other impropriety by the summoning officer.[64] Though there may be some life yet left in the procedure, it is so rarely used that it need concern us no further here.

The prosecution has the ancient common law right to ask jurors to stand by for the Crown without showing cause. There is no limit to the number who may be stood by in this way, save that if the number of jurors available to complete the jury from the panel is exhausted, then those stood by may be called to serve and may then only be challenged for cause. Under the system of pre-trial checks discussed above, the prosecution has used this right of stand by on the basis of information obtained in the vetting process.

---

[60] See further below.

[61] In *R v. Crown Court at Sheffield, ex parte Brownlow* [1980] QB 530, two of the judges thought the practice was 'unconstitutional'; *contra: McCann and others* (1991) 92 Cr. App. R 239. In *Mason* [1981] QB 881, Lawton L. J. considered criminal records office checks a matter of common sense.

[62] H. Harman and J. Griffith, *Justice Deserted: The Subversion of the Jury* (London: NCCL, 1979); P. Duff and M. Findlay, 'Jury Vetting—The Jury under Attack' (1983) 3 *Legal Studies* 159; and R. East, 'Jury Packing: A Thing of the Past' (1985) 48 MLR 518.

[63] R. Buxton, 'Challenging and Discharging Jurors' [1988] Crim. LR 152.

[64] See *Danvers* [1982] Crim. LR 680.

Though the defence has no right of stand by, it has been held that the judge may in exceptional circumstances allow the defence to stand by jurors.[65]

In November 1988 the Attorney General issued guidelines on the exercise by the Crown of the right of stand by.[66] The guidelines remind counsel that the right should not be used 'in order to influence the overall composition of a jury or with a view to tactical advantage'. The right is to be used very sparingly 'on the basis of clearly defined and restrictive criteria'. The guidelines set out the circumstances in which the exercise of the right will be appropriate:

- where an authorised check reveals information about a juror which results in the Attorney General personally authorising counsel to stand by a particular juror;
- where a person about to be sworn in as a juror is 'manifestly unsuitable' and defence counsel agrees that the exercise of the right of stand by is the most appropriate way to remove the juror from the panel.

Either side may challenge any number of jurors for cause, that is, some reason why the particular juror should not sit in the case. Counsel will have very little information about jurors on which to base the challenge. All that is generally available is a list of names and addresses. It used to be the case that occupations were included, but a directive from the Lord Chancellor in 1973 required these to be excluded. Nor will counsel be able to ask questions to establish the existence of good cause. Following the so-called *Angry Brigade* trial in 1972[67] in which the trial judge acceded to a request to put certain questions to jurors so that they might be excluded for cause, Lord Widgery C. J. banned such questioning of jurors[68] and restated the basic principle of jury selection as follows:

A jury consists of 12 individuals chosen at random for the appropriate panel. A juror should be excused if he is personally concerned in the facts of the particular case, or closely connected with a party to the proceedings or with a prospective witness. He may also be excused at the discretion of the judge on grounds of personal hardship or conscientious objection to jury service. It is contrary to established practice for jurors to be excused on more general grounds such as race, religion, or political beliefs or occupation.

In September 1988 the Lord Chief Justice revoked the 1973 directions and issued revised guidance.[69] The salient paragraphs read:

There will . . . be circumstances where a juror should be excused, for instance where he or she is personally concerned in the facts of the case or is closely connected with a party or prospective witness. He or she may also be excused on grounds of personal

---

[65] *Chandler* [1964] 2 QB 322; see also A. Dashwood, 'Juries in a Multi-Racial Society' [1972] Crim. LR 85.

[66] Attorney General's Guidelines on the Exercise by the Crown of its Right of Stand By [1988] 3 All ER 1086.

[67] See A. Dashwood, 'The Jury and the Angry Brigade' (1974) 11 *Western Australia Law Review* 245.

[68] Practice Note: Jury Service: Excusal [1973] 1 WLR 134.

[69] Practice Direction: Jury Service: Excusal [1988] 1 WLR 1162.

hardship or conscientious objection to jury service. Each such application should be dealt with sensitively and sympathetically. Any person who appeals to the court against a refusal by the appropriate officer to excuse him or her from jury service must be given an opportunity to make representations in support of his or her appeal.

Though on the face of it primarily concerned with excusals, such directions have always been seen as indicating the bases on which a challenge for cause might be appropriate. It will usually only be where defendants identify jurors to counsel as known to them that a challenge for cause will arise. In other cases it will be the juror who takes the initiative if known to the defendant or a witness. The only other possibility is that counsel will have some information as a result of pre-trial checks. The limited basis for challenges is perfectly consistent with the underlying principle of random selection.

There used to be a right of *peremptory challenge* of up to three jurors, which belonged exclusively to the defence. No reason whatever needed to be given for the challenge and in cases where there was more than one defendant each could challenge up to three jurors. The peremptory challenge gave defendants a limited opportunity to secure a jury believed to be as sympathetic as possible to the defendant. Defendants, of course, had no real information to go on, but they could at least remove those whose demeanour they believe would make them hostile to their cause. Peremptory challenges were used most by counsel to influence the composition of the jury in accordance with supposed notions that certain types of juries are more lenient than others. Typical jury lore suggested that women are less likely to convict than men, except in cases involving sexual offences, and that younger juries are more sympathetic than older juries.[70] But the results of Baldwin and McConville's research into the correlation between jury composition and outcome showed that views popularly held among lawyers are no more than legal mythology. They concluded that:

We can confidently state that no single social factor (nor, as far as we could detect, any group of factors operating in combination) produced any significant variation in the verdicts returned across the board.[71]

Peremptory challenges have also been used to secure representation by members of ethnic minorities on juries. They are abolished completely by section 118(1) of the Criminal Justice Act 1988.

Securing ethnic minority representation on the jury

The results of Baldwin and McConville's research in Birmingham revealed a serious under-representation of members of ethnic minorities on juries.[72] But the Crown Court Study revealed a close approximation between the sample mix and

---

[70] J. Vennard and D. Riley, 'The Use of Peremptory Challenge and Stand By of Jurors and their Relationship to Trial Outcomes' [1988] Crim. LR 731.

[71] J. Baldwin and M. McConville, *Jury Trials* (Oxford: Clarendon Press, 1979), p. 104.

[72] Ibid., pp. 97–9.

that in the general population.[73] Despite this, in two-thirds of cases, there was no non-white juror, and in only one in five juries in the sample had three or more non-white jurors.

In cases involving members of ethnic minorities, there has been some small evidence of judicial sympathy for the proposition that the jury should contain a proportion of jurors from that ethnic minority.[74] It has long been accepted that there is a residual common law discretion in a trial judge to discharge a particular juror who ought not to be serving on the jury.[75] This is part of the judge's duty to ensure that there is a fair trial. In *Binns* Judge Stocker was not prepared to go as far as authorising the summoning of a new panel to achieve a racially balanced jury. It was not necessary in *Binns* because the jury sworn after the use of the peremptory challenge contained three jurors from ethnic minorities.

The example given above in *Binns* may be an example of exceptional circumstances justifying allowing the defence an opportunity to exercise a right of stand by, and certainly offers a convenient way to secure racial balance in a jury where this is appropriate.[76] In *Bansal*[77] the trial judge gave directions that the jury panel should be selected from a geographic area known to contain members of the Asian community. More recently it was accepted that a discretion vested in the trial judge to use the power of discretionary discharge to alter the composition of the particular jury to try a case in order to achieve what was felt to be an appropriate racial representation.[78]

But in *Ford*,[79] the Court of Appeal in a judgment handed down by the Lord Chief Justice held that the trial judge enjoyed no discretion to interfere with the composition of a jury to secure a multi-racial jury for particular trials. Earlier decisions suggesting otherwise were wrongly decided. In a statement which stands in marked contrast to the views taken by the judiciary on pre-trial jury checks, the Lord Chief Justice said: 'If it should ever become desirable that the principle of random selection should be altered, that would have to be done by way of statute. It could not be done by any judicial decision'.

The Runciman Commission was aware of the arguments about racial balance in juries, as well as the ruling in *Ford*. It recommended that *Ford* be reversed to permit a judge to secure a racially mixed jury on application on behalf of the defendant but only in cases presenting unusual and special features. Such situations would not arise merely because the defendant was black, but specially composed juries might be appropriate where 'black people [are] accused of violence against a member of an extremist organisation who they said had been making racial taunts against them and their friends'.[80]

The requirement that trial be before an independent and impartial tribunal under Article 6 of the European Convention on Human Rights has been applied

---

[73] Crown Court Study, para. 8.13.6.   [74] *Binns* [1982] Crim. LR 522 and 823.
[75] *Mansell* (1857) 8 E & B 37.   [76] See *Chandler (No. 2)* [1964] 2 QB 322.
[77] [1985] Crim. LR 151.   [78] *Thomas* (1989) 89 Cr. App. R 370.   [79] [1989] QB 868.
[80] *Report of the Royal Commission on Criminal Justice (Runciman Commission)* (London: HMSO, 1993), ch. 8, para. 63.

to juries in a number of cases. The *Pullar* case[81] concerned a jury trial in Scotland, where a member of the jury was an employee of one of the two key prosecution witnesses. It was argued that this prevented the trial from being impartial and independent. The Court accepted that the composition of the jury could, in certain circumstances, affect the fairness of the trial by reason of bias, but, contrary to the unanimous opinion which had been expressed by the Commission, concluded by five votes to four that there had been no violation of Article 6(1).

The role of judge and jury

The judge deals with questions of law and the jury deals with questions of fact. The distinction between questions of law and questions of fact is a subtle one. Most people would recognise that the issue of whether the defendant was at a particular place at a particular time as a question of fact. Indeed lawyers would call this a question of primary fact. But in a criminal trial where intention is relevant, that too is a question of fact, though it will require an evaluation of all the surrounding circumstances in coming to a conclusion about the defendant's state of mind. For example, in a case of shoplifting (the offence of theft) a jury might be called upon to determine whether the defendant took the goods while in a state of confusion resulting from the side effects of medication and so had no intent to steal. In complex cases of fraud or deception, these issues are often more important than the primary facts. By contrast, defining the constituent elements of the offence of theft is a question of law for the judge.

The judge controls the trial and directs the jury. At all stages, the role of the jury is passive. The trial may last as little as a few hours to as long as a month or more; the average length of contested cases is around nine hours, which is under two days of court time.[82] The judge may exclude the jury while points of law, often involving the admissibility of evidence, are argued and decided, but otherwise the jury listen and form opinions about the veracity of witnesses. Most jury deliberations seem to take no more than a couple of hours.[83]

The judge may direct the jury to return a verdict of not guilty. Once the jury has been empanelled, the trial can normally only end following a decision of the jury on guilt or innocence. If during the course of the trial it becomes clear that a conviction cannot, as a matter of law, be sustained in the case, the judge is required to direct the jury to return a verdict of not guilty. This is a direction which the jury cannot ignore. The resulting verdict is called a *directed acquittal.*[84] A significant number of cases end in ordered and directed acquittals.[85] These figures suggest that more than half of all acquittals result from a judge's direction rather than a substantive

---

[81] *Pullar* v. *United Kingdom*, Judgment of 10 June 1996 (1996) 22 EHRR 391.

[82] *Judicial Statistics 1996* (London: HMSO, 1997, Cm. 3716), ch. 6; see also Crown Court Study, para. 8.9.

[83] Crown Court Study, para. 8.10.

[84] As distinct from an *ordered acquittal*, which arises when no prosecution evidence is presented; the case never gets off the ground. The judge discharges the defendant before the jury is empanelled.

[85] *Judicial Statistics 1996* (London: HMSO, 1997, Cm. 3716), ch. 6; see also Crown Court Study, para. 6.3–6.4.

decision of the jury. Apart from the power to order or direct an acquittal, judges cannot instruct juries as to the verdict they must return. They certainly cannot direct them to convict.[86]

The Runciman Commission expressed concern at the number of ordered and directed acquittals.[87] A research study had noted that ordered acquittals had increased while directed acquittals had decreased since the introduction of the CPS.[88] This study examined seventy-one CPS case files which had ended in an ordered acquittal and twenty-eight which had ended in a directed acquittal in order to determine whether the ordered or directed acquittal was foreseeable. They concluded that about a quarter were foreseeable and a further quarter possibly foreseeable.

The judge has the last word before the jury retires to consider a verdict when he sums up the case for the jury. The summing up is very important. In it the judge, from an independent and impartial standpoint, summarises the case, explains the legal issues in contention and may comment on factors which lend weight to, or cast doubt on, certain evidence. Lord Hailsham described it as follows:

The purpose of a direction to the jury is not best achieved by a disquisition on jurisprudence or philosophy or a universally applicable circular tour round the area of law affected by the case . . . A direction to a jury should be custom-built to make the jury understand their task in relation to a particular case. Of course it must contain references to the burden of proof and the respective roles of jury and judge. But it should also include a succinct but accurate summary of the issues of fact as to which a decision is required, a correct but concise summary of the evidence and arguments on both sides and a correct statement of the inferences which a jury are entitled to draw from their particular conclusions about the primary facts.[89]

Verdicts are called perverse either when the jury must have ignored the judge's explanation of the law in coming to its decision or when the jury returns a verdict with which neutral observers would disagree on the basis that it goes against the weight of the evidence.

All issues of fact are for the jury. They must debate in their secret deliberations whom they believe and disbelieve. They must form a view collectively as to what happened many months before, constructing a single reality from the evidence before them. They alone determine whether the defendant's actions constitute the offence charged. Once the jury has retired, all must await the outcome of their deliberations. None may interfere. The jury will be kept isolated from outside contacts, for days if need be, until a decision is reached. Sometimes juries cannot agree and if every effort at coming to a decision fails, they will be discharged and a re-trial will be necessary. Such a jury is known as a 'hung' jury.

---

[86] *Gent* (1989) 89 Cr. App. R 247.

[87] *Report of the Royal Commission on Criminal Justice (Runciman Commission)* (London: HMSO, 1993), ch. 5, para. 8.

[88] B. Block, C. Corbett and J. Peay, *Ordered and Directed Acquittals in the Crown Court*, Royal Commission on Criminal Justice Research Study No. 15 (London: HMSO, 1993). See also B. Block, C. Corbett and J. Peay, 'Ordered and Directed Acquittals in the Crown Court: A Time for Change' [1993] Crim. LR 95. This research is supported by J. Baldwin, 'Understanding Judge Ordered and Directed Acquittals in the Crown Court' [1997] Crim. LR 536. [89] *Lawrence* [1982] AC 510, 519.

A jury can acquit or convict if ten jurors agree where the jury consists of eleven or twelve members, or if nine agree where the jury consists of ten jurors.[90] Juries sometimes fall below twelve members if one or more dies, or falls ill, during the course of the trial. Provided that the number does not fall below ten, the trial will continue.

Before a majority verdict can be returned, the jury must have retired for at least two hours in an attempt to come to a unanimous decision. In practice, if after two hours and twenty minutes they have not done so, the judge will recall them and give them a direction permitting the return of a majority verdict.[91] Majority verdicts have occasionally been linked with the issues of vetting and of selection of jurors as evidence of subversion of the jury,[92] but the arguments are overstated. Given respect for the random selection of jurors, majority verdicts merely enable extreme views to be discounted by the jury in its deliberations. For example, in a trial on a charge of incitement to racial hatred, it would enable the racist views of a member of an extreme right-wing political party to be discounted in the jury's decision-making.

Where a judge suspects that one or more jurors is being unnecessarily difficult, there has been controversy over the extent to which the jury should be encouraged to work together to reach a conclusion. In *Watson*,[93] a five judge Court of Appeal stressed the need to ensure that a jury must be free to deliberate without any form of pressure being imposed upon them. But a model direction for use in such cases either in the principal summing up or when the majority direction is given was recommended in the following terms:

Each of you has taken an oath to return a true verdict according to the evidence. No one must be false to that oath, but you have a duty not only as individuals but collectively. That is the strength of the jury system. Each of you takes into the jury box with you your individual experience and wisdom. Your task is to pool that experience and wisdom. You can do that by giving your views and listening to the views of others. there must necessarily be discussion, argument and give and take within the scope of your oath. That is the way in which agreement is reached. If unhappily, [ten of] you cannot reach agreement you must say so.

Once the judge has summed up, the jury is put in the charge of the jury bailiff and retires to the jury room in order to conduct its deliberations. In earlier times, a jury which was unable to reach its decision before early evening could not go home until its task was complete, but would be accommodated in a local hotel under strict instructions not to discuss the case, or to have contact with members of the public. However, this is now a matter of discretion.[94]

The need to keep the role of judge and jury quite distinct is illustrated by the case of *Larkin*,[95] where the judge's curiosity as to the basis for a jury's verdict led

---

[90] Juries Act 1974, s. 17.
[91] Practice Direction: Majority Verdicts [1967] 3 All ER 137; Practice Direction: Majority Verdicts [1970] 1 All ER 215.
[92] H. Harman and J. Griffith, *Justice Deserted: The Subversion of the Jury* (London: NCCL, 1979).
[93] [1988] 1 All ER 897.   [94] Juries Act 1974, s. 13.   [95] [1943] 1 All ER 217.

to his raising questions of the foreman which placed on record a serious confusion in their minds about the basis for the verdict they had returned. This resulted in the conviction being quashed. Equally, a judge must not place pressure on the jury to return its verdict, or even be seen possibly to have hinted at pressure.[96]

Control of jury's decisions

Acquittal by a jury is sacred; there is no appeal available to the prosecution against an acquittal. Even convictions carry some finality. The basic rule is that the Court of Appeal will not re-open or re-consider a jury's decision unless there has been an open and material defect of procedure taking place outside the confines of the jury room. Where this occurs, it is really a failure by the trial judge to conduct the trial properly. The Court of Appeal will certainly never enquire into the deliberations of the jury.[97]

An illustration of the application of this rule is *Thompson*,[98] in which it was discovered that the jury had been in favour of acquittal until the foreman of the jury had produced a list of the defendant's previous convictions. Such information is deliberately kept from juries to avoid the possibility of prejudice to the defendant. The Court of Appeal would not interfere with the conviction. They refused to enquire into the jury's deliberations.

By contrast an appeal was allowed in *Dubarry*.[99] In this case the jury had retired and were deliberating when the need arose to send a question to the judge. A member of the jury took a note to the door of the retiring room and handed it to the jury bailiff. The door of the jury room opened on to the courtroom and the juror saw the defendant obviously on trial for other offences. The jury bailiff advised the judge, who simply asked the shorthand writer to note the event. The Court of Appeal said that he should have considered the issue of prejudice to the defendant. Having failed to do so, the defendant must be given the benefit of the doubt that his trial had been prejudiced and the conviction was quashed. Modern courtroom design avoids having jury rooms opening directly on to the court. In an extraordinary case, a retrial was ordered when it came to light that some jurors had consulted a ouija board while spending a night in a hotel to assist them in making their decision.[100]

Jury decision-making

Perhaps more ill-informed words have been written on the matters that influence juries and whether they acquit too readily than on any other aspect of the criminal justice system. The reason is clear: much of it is based on pure supposition. Even scholarly research presents great difficulties. Research has never been allowed into the deliberations of 'live' juries; most has involved the use of simulations using volunteers. It is not difficult to appreciate the caveats that must, and do, surround

---

[96] See *McKenna* [1960] 1 QB 411; and *Rose* [1982] AC 822.　　[97] *Ellis* v. *Deheer* [1922] 2 KB 113.
[98] [1962] 1 All ER 65.　　[99] (1976) 64 Cr. App. R 7.　　[100] *Young, Stephen* [1995] 2 WLR 430.

the results of such research. Even the research of Baldwin and McConville, generally acknowledged as the most authoritative yet produced, is based on *post hoc* analysis of real cases, and does not include discussions with the actual jurors.[101]

For many years convention alone required jurors not to disclose their deliberations. But the increasing frequency of disclosure, culminating in the publication of the views of jurors in the Jeremy Thorpe trial in the New Statesman,[102] led to the passing of section 8 of the Contempt of Court Act 1981. This makes it an offence to obtain, disclose or solicit any particulars of the deliberations of a jury except in the course of criminal proceedings. The section not only catches the objectionable aspects of cheque book journalism but also effectively closes the door firmly on research into jury decision-making based on the experiences of actual jurors. The Runciman Commission recommended that the provision be amended to allow research into jury decision-making.[103]

Work with simulated juries both at the London School of Economics[104] and at the Oxford University Penal Research Unit[105] suggests that jurors approach the task of determining guilt as a serious responsibility. They listen carefully to directions from the judge. The LSE Jury Project's findings suggest that the jury's knowledge of a defendant's previous convictions do increase the probability of a guilty verdict somewhat but, contrary to popular supposition, jurors generally complied with a direction by the judge to disregard these convictions. It also showed that the form of words used to describe to the jury the standard of proof laid on the prosecution had little impact on the outcome of cases, despite lawyers beliefs that this aspect of the summing up is crucial to outcome. The results of both research studies strongly suggested that jurors do indeed try cases according to the evidence and not on personal whims or hunches.

The Oxford University Penal Research Unit analysed the reasons for acquittals in 173 cases in their sample into six groups.[106] In only fifteen cases (nine per cent) could the verdicts be described as wayward, in that interviews with other participants in the process described them as unjustified in the light of the evidence. But in a number of these it was possible to suggest that 'feelings of fair play' accounted for the verdict. Having regard to all the surrounding circumstances and in the face of evidence strong enough to convict, the jury nevertheless chose to acquit. This is sometimes labelled jury equity. The largest group of acquittals (thirty-four per cent) were those directed by the judge where the prosecution case clearly failed at an early stage. Some of these failures were the result of technical flaws in the prosecution evidence or were identifiable as policy prosecutions with little hope of success. Indeed a number of acquittals by the jury (twenty-five per cent) were considered to be attributable to policy prosecutions, particularly in a

---

[101] J. Baldwin and M. McConville, *Jury Trials* (Oxford: Clarendon Press, 1979).

[102] *Attorney General* v. *New Statesman and Nation Publishing Co. Ltd* [1980] QB 1.

[103] *Report of the Royal Commission on Criminal Justice (Runciman Commission)* (London: HMSO, 1993), ch. 1, para. 8.   [104] L. Sealy and W. Cornish, 'Juries and the Rules of Evidence' [1973] Crim. LR 208.

[105] S. McCabe and R. Purves, *The Shadow Jury at Work* (Oxford: Blackwell, 1974).

[106] S. McCabe and R. Purves, *The Jury at Work* (Oxford: Blackwell, 1972).

number of shoplifting cases in the sample. It was noted that the failed prosecution may nevertheless serve a purpose in gaining publicity for a police drive against particular types of offence. In twenty-eight cases (sixteen per cent) it was the defendant's explanation which was considered to have accounted for the acquittal, while in eight cases (five per cent) it was the failure of prosecution witnesses to 'come up to proof'. This phrase is lawyers' jargon for the situation where a witness provides a good written statement of evidence (called a 'proof' of evidence) prior to the trial, but when giving evidence and subjected to cross-examination fails to be as convincing as the written statement given earlier. The remaining twenty cases in the sample (eleven per cent) were simply weak prosecution cases. In these cases the prosecution was just about strong enough to put to the jury but was not strong enough to secure a conviction.

Other research has concentrated on whether jurors acquit too many defendants. Such research became very topical following the assertions made by Sir Robert Mark, a former Metropolitan Police Commissioner, in the 1973 Dimbleby Lecture that 'the proportion of . . . acquittals relating to those whom experienced police officers believe to be guilty is too high to be acceptable . . .' and that there was a cadre of 'lawyers producing, off the peg, the same kind of defence, for different clients'. The defences were described as 'concocted far beyond the intellectual capacity of the accused'.[107]

Following the Dimbleby Lecture, much attention was focused on the allegations made by Sir Robert Mark. It was noted that seven out of ten defendants plead guilty in the Crown Court to the charges against them and that a significant proportion of acquittals result from a judge's direction to acquit. A major plank in Sir Robert's cases was the argument that 'professional' criminals were able to manipulate various features of the criminal process to their own advantage. Both Zander[108] and Baldwin and McConville[109] concluded that there was no significant difference in the probability of acquittals of those who might be described as 'professional' criminals when compared with all defendants. Only the research of Mack[110] has shown any success at avoiding conviction by 'professional' criminals when compared with others. The success cannot be described as more than marginal, and his results have not gone unchallenged.[111] Sir Robert Mark also suggested that a significant number of acquittals resulted from concocted defences by crooked lawyers. These allegations have never been substantiated despite requests from the Law Society for details of cases known to Sir Robert Mark. Baldwin and McConville have also shown that there would be appear to be no evidence to back up Sir Robert's assertions.[112]

---

[107] R. Mark, *Minority Verdict*, the 1973 Dimbleby Lecture (London: BBC, 1973).

[108] M. Zander, 'Are too many Professional Criminals Avoiding Conviction—A Study of Britain's Two Busiest Courts' (1974) 37 MLR 28; J. Baldwin and M. McConville, 'The Acquittal Rate of Professional Criminals: A Critical Note' (1974) 37 MLR 439; and M. Zander, 'The Acquittal Rate of Professional Criminals: A Reply' (1974) 37 MLR 444.

[109] J. Baldwin and M. McConville, *Jury Trials* (Oxford: Clarendon Press, 1979), ch. 7.

[110] D. Mack, 'Full-time Major Criminals and the Courts' (1976) 39 MLR 241.

[111] A. Sanders, 'Does Professional Crime Pay? A Critical Comment on Mack' (1977) 40 MLR 553.

[112] J. Baldwin and M. McConville, 'Allegations against Lawyers' [1978] Crim. LR 744.

Baldwin and McConville's major research on jury trials[113] focused on 370 defendants tried by juries out of a total of 2,406 defendants passing through the Birmingham Crown Court in the study period. There is also some comparison with cases tried in London. The opinions of judges, of prosecution and defence lawyers, of defendants and of the police were sought on a wide range of aspects of the cases. The researchers examined the incidence of agreement and disagreement with the verdicts of the juries. There was a higher incidence of disagreements with both acquittals and convictions than had been indicated by earlier research studies. In all cases of acquittal, participants were generally agreed on the most important reason for the acquittal. The most commonly mentioned factors were the strength of the defence case, the weakness of the prosecution case, and the jury's being swayed by sympathy for the defendant or antipathy to the victim of the crime. This latter category was described as part of 'jury equity' in which juries are prepared to allow extra-legal considerations to influence their decision-making. This factor was identified as the most important factor in about a quarter of the cases resulting in acquittal.

Baldwin and McConville went on to examine more closely the incidence both of questionable acquittals and of doubtful convictions. They preferred the label 'questionable' to wayward or perverse to indicate that this group reflected the questions and doubts raised by other participants in the process. An acquittal was regarded as questionable if the judge and one other respondent voiced doubts about it. This produced forty-one cases of questionable acquittal out of 114 acquittals (thirty-six per cent). Though one might have expected some correlation between these cases and those where respondents had mentioned factors involving jury equity, this was generally not the case. Indeed Baldwin and McConville could discern no common characteristics of the group of questionable acquittals. They concluded:

The number of defendants who seem to us to have been acquitted in questionable circumstances, without any apparent equitable justification save in a handful of cases, suggests that trial by jury is a relatively crude instrument for establishing the truth.[114]

When they applied the same sort of analysis to convictions, there was no disagreement with the juries' verdicts in nearly nine out of every ten cases. But in the minority of cases where doubts were expressed, these amounted to serious concerns about the correctness of the conviction. In considering the possible reasons for doubtful convictions, Baldwin and McConville identified two factors as important: first, that the juries appeared to have been too easily satisfied of the guilt of the defendants and did not demand proof beyond reasonable doubt, and, secondly, that the juries seemed to have failed to comprehend the issues involved. There is also a hint that racial prejudice might be involved: black defendants were over-represented in the group of doubtful convictions. This evidence must, of course, add weight to the arguments of those who claim that trial by jury is not an appropriate form of criminal trial in the twentieth century. This simplified summary of

---

[113] J. Baldwin and M. McConville, *Jury Trials* (Oxford: Clarendon Press, 1979).   [114] Ibid., p. 67.

some of the findings of the research does little justice to the wealth of information and comment in the researchers' book, *Jury Trials*, which should be read by all those interested in the issues involved in consideration of the merits of trial by jury.

Evaluation

The jury continues to attract strong public support. Juries receive high marks for their work from those involved in the process, though some surprise was expressed at a significant number of acquittals.[115] Juries seem able to cope with the issues raised in most of the cases they hear.[116] All the evidence shows that jurors approach the task of determining the guilt or innocence of the defendant in a most diligent manner. The jury seems to be good at achieving the objective of securing the acquittal of the innocent, though some have suggested that this is at the price of also acquitting some who are guilty. This may be no more than a clash between due process and crime control philosophies.

From time to time alternatives to the jury are suggested, such as lay assessors sitting with judges or trial by a bench of judges, and examples are given of such systems of criminal trial in other jurisdictions. But it is virtually inconceivable that trial by jury will disappear in the English criminal process; public opinion regards it as a vital part of the trial of serious criminal offences. Though the jury is far from perfect,[117] the alternatives seem even less attractive.[118] It should, however, be remembered that contested trials remain a minority activity of the Crown Court, constituting about one-third of its trial business.

Trial

The guilty plea

The order of events in a trial on indictment is not markedly different from that in a summary trial. Briefly the main stages of the trial are as follows. First comes the arraignment. The clerk of the court calls upon the defendant by name, reads out the indictment and asks him how he pleads. Ignoring the rare cases in which the defendant remains silent for which there are special procedures, the defendant will then plead either guilty or not guilty. Following a plea of guilty, the proceedings are virtually identical to summary trial, though the prosecution will be represented by counsel. In most cases there will be a social enquiry report available to assist in the sentencing process. The prosecution will also indicate whether the defendant

---

[115] Crown Court Study, ch. 8.

[116] Doubts have only really been expressed in relation to lengthy and complex fraud trials: for a useful summary of developments, see M. Zander, *Cases and Materials on the English Legal System*, 7th edn. (London: Butterworths, 1996), pp. 394–6

[117] M. Findlay and P. Duff, *The Jury under Attack* (London: Butterworths, 1988).

[118] E. Knittel and D. Seiler, 'The Merits of Trial by Jury' [1972] CLJ 316; and M. Freeman, 'The Jury on Trial' [1981] CLP 65. See also S. Doran and J. Jackson, 'The Case for Jury Waiver' [1997] Crim. LR 155.

has asked for other offences, not on the indictment, to be taken into consideration in assessing sentence. If there are, a schedule of offences agreed by the defendant and his counsel is presented to the court. These offences are known colloquially by their initial letters as 'tics'. Though technically not convicted of these offences, the defendant can 'wipe the slate clean' and will in practice never be prosecuted for them. Following presentation of this information, the defence may make a plea in mitigation before the court proceeds to sentence.

The not guilty plea

The defendant is brought before the court and the substance of the indictment is put to him. If the plea is one of not guilty, then a jury must be empanelled. The clerk announces to the group of potential jurors who will usually be waiting at the back of the court: 'Members of the jury in waiting, please answer to your names and step into the jury box as you are called'.

The twelve chosen are then named. The clerk then addresses the defendant: 'Prisoner at the bar, the names you are about to hear called are the names of the jurors who are to try you. If therefore you wish to object to them or to any of them, you must do so as they come to the book to be sworn, and your objections shall be heard'.

Each juror is then required to swear, or affirm, in the following terms: 'I swear by Almighty God that I will faithfully try the defendant and give a true verdict according to the evidence'.

The clerk will then read the indictment to the jury and tell them that the defendant has pleaded not guilty, for example:

Members of the jury, are you all sworn? The prisoner stands indicted for that he on the third day of May 1998 did steal £1,345 in money, the property of Sterling Limited. To this indictment he has pleaded not guilty and it is your charge to say, having heard the evidence, whether he be guilty or not.

Battle can now commence. Prosecuting counsel then makes an opening speech outlining the case to be made against the defendant. The prosecution witnesses then give evidence and are cross-examined by defence counsel and, if necessary, re-examined by prosecuting counsel.

At the end of the prosecution case, defence counsel may make a submission that there is no case for the defendant to answer if he or she considers that the prosecution has not adduced sufficient evidence to prove its case or if cross-examination has cast such doubt on the evidence that it cannot be regarded as sufficient to ground a conviction and renders it unnecessary for a defence case to be put. Such a submission is made in the absence of the jury. Following the submission, the judge should direct the jury to return a verdict of not guilty if there is no evidence on which, if it were accepted, a reasonable jury, properly directed, could convict. But if the doubts relate to the weight of the evidence or the credibility of witnesses, the question should be left to the jury. The judge will direct the jury on this issue and the jury will retire consider the issue.[119] Of course, if the jury think there is a case to answer, they will simply decline to return a verdict of not guilty at this stage.

The case for the defence may then be put. Defence counsel is only permitted to make an opening speech if the defendant and other witnesses are to be called to give evidence on the facts, as distinct from evidence as to the character of the defendant. The defence case is then put. At the end of the defence case, prosecuting counsel and defence counsel, in that order, make their closing speeches to the jury. These are followed by the judge's summing up. Immediately this is ended, the jury must retire to consider their verdict. Following the return of a verdict of guilty, the prosecution puts any previous convictions and the defendant's antecedents to the court and the defendant is permitted to make a plea in mitigation before the court proceeds to sentence. If no social enquiry report is available and a prison sentence is contemplated, there will need to be an adjournment for one to be prepared.

Evaluation of the Crown Court

The public image of the Crown Court is at variance with practice. There are twice as many guilty pleas as there are contested cases.[120] Efficient management and effective case disposal are at work in this court just as they are in the magistrates' courts. Though not guilty pleas may be viewed as the epitome of due process, even here there is more at work than the determination of the truth. There is an interplay between many actors, with different roles assigned to each.[121] Defences may not have been as well prepared as they should, and while the jury clearly does its best, it does not seem to be a particularly effective determiner of the truth, though it does seem to keep faith with the due process objective of only convicting those whose guilt has been proved beyond reasonable doubt.

Consideration of trial on indictment has drawn attention to certain areas where, at the very least, there is some concern about the process. There is no doubt that this is the weight of the State being marshalled against an individual. Two views are possible of the process in the Crown Court. The first is that it is indeed a model of due process, and that the defects that have been identified in this chapter occur in only a small number of cases. They are the result of aberrations which can be avoided by fine tuning of the process. The opposing view is that the defects are symptoms of fundamental faults in the system. There are design faults which will not be removed by tinkering. Any injustice which results is not merely an aberration, it is systemic. The system needs radical change.[122]

---

[119] *Galbraith* [1981] 1 WLR 1039.

[120] See P. Robertshaw, *Judge and Jury: The Crown Court in Action* (Aldershot: Dartmouth, 1995), who argues that there are many more similarities between trial in the magistrates' courts and in the Crown Court than is often suggested.

[121] See P. Rock, *The Social World of an English Crown Court* (Oxford: Clarendon Press, 1993), an anthropological study of a particular Crown Court.

[122] D. McBarnet, *Conviction, Law, The State and the Construction of Justice* (London: Macmillan, 1981).

9

CHALLENGING THE DECISION OF THE TRIAL COURT

The Reasons for Having an Appeal System

Just as summary trial and trial on indictment are two very distinct forms of criminal trial, so too the systems for challenging the decisions of the trial courts are very different. Both systems of appeal, however, have three main purposes. The first is to ensure that the defendant's trial was fair and that there was no material irregularity in the proceedings. The second is to allow for the development of rules of criminal procedure and of the substantive criminal law. The third is to ensure some degree of consistency in the administration of criminal justice and in the sentencing of convicted offenders. There is no overriding principle that the purpose of appeals is to avoid miscarriages of justice. One reason for this is the traditional reluctance to interfere with the jury's findings of fact, which also has had some impact on criminal appeals following summary trial. The appeal is not regarded as a second trial, even where the procedure allows a complete re-hearing of the evidence.[1]

The Royal Commission on Criminal Justice was established in the wake of major miscarriages of justice[2] but only concerned itself with appeal following trial on indictment. An opportunity was missed to compare the processes of appeal operating following trial in the magistrates' courts and in the Crown Court.

Appeals may be against conviction or against sentence, or against both. It is important to grasp the distinction between appeal against conviction and appeal against sentence. Defendants appealing against conviction are claiming that they have been improperly convicted. The reasons may be that the trial judge or magistrates erred in the application of the law, or that there was a prejudicial procedural error, or that the defendant maintains his or her innocence of the offence. By contrast an appeal against sentence is a disagreement only with the harshness of the penalty

---

[1] See generally, R. Pattenden, *English Criminal Appeals 1844–1994* (Oxford: Clarendon Press, 1996).

[2] *Report of the Royal Commission on Criminal Justice (Runciman Commission)* (London: HMSO, 1993); see for background J. Rozenberg, 'Miscarriages of Justice' in E. Stockdale and S. Casale, *Criminal Justice under Stress* (London: Blackstone Press, 1992), p. 91.

imposed by the trial court. It is, therefore, possible to appeal against sentence even after a plea of guilty before the trial court, whereas it is not possible to appeal against conviction after a properly entered plea of guilty. The defendant who has pleaded not guilty may, of course, appeal against both conviction and sentence. As a general rule only defendants may appeal, though there are important exceptions and qualifications to this general rule described later in this chapter.

Appeal Following Summary Trial

Three types of challenge

A decision of a magistrates' court may be challenged in one of three ways: appeal on the merits to the Crown Court;[3] appeal by way of case stated to the High Court;[4] and application to the High Court for judicial review.[5] Appeals on the merits against conviction or sentence lie to the Crown Court, but applications for judicial review and appeals by way of case stated lie to the Queen's Bench Division of the High Court.

Appeal to the Crown Court lies as of right and is concerned with the merits of the conviction or sentence. This appeal is available only to the defendant. Both prosecution and defence can appeal by way of case stated and the purpose of this special type of appeal is solely to correct an error of law or an act in excess of jurisdiction. Applications for judicial review are available to either prosecution or defence in order to cure some illegality in the trial proceedings or in appellate proceedings of the Crown Court. The primary purpose of the appeal and the party wishing to appeal will be the principal determinants of the procedure chosen.

Appeal to the Crown Court

Persons convicted in a magistrates' court may appeal as of right to the Crown Court against sentence if they pleaded guilty, or against conviction and/or sentence if they did not. These appeals will be heard without a jury by a Circuit judge or Recorder sitting with between two and four justices. There are a number of unusual features of these appeals, which are the result of historical accident and piecemeal reform of the appellate system following summary trial. Originally justices met in quarterly meeting to exercise their judicial functions, but as early as the seventeenth century, the justices were authorised to exercise their judicial functions 'out of sessions', that is, other than in the quarterly meetings. But a person aggrieved by a decision made out of sessions could have the case heard again in quarter sessions. In time the out of sessions or summary jurisdiction became the norm and the

---

[3] Magistrates' Courts Act 1980, s. 108.   [4] Ibid., s. 111.
[5] Supreme Court Act 1981, ss. 29–31, and RSC Ord. 53.

quarterly meetings or 'quarter sessions' increasingly dealt with more serious crime and with the re-hearing of cases heard in petty sessions. In the nineteenth century borough courts of quarter sessions consisting of a professional judge, known as a Recorder, sitting with lay justices began to become commonplace. Both petty sessions and quarter sessions were inferior courts. Even with the advent of the ability of quarter sessions to try certain cases on indictment, their status as inferior courts remained.

The reforms contained in the Courts Act 1971 did not affect the system of criminal appeals which had developed; the new Crown Court simply inherited the appellate jurisdiction of quarter sessions. The result is somewhat curious. The Crown Court is a hybrid. For certain purposes it is a superior court of record of equal status to the High Court, while for others it is an inferior court susceptible to the supervisory jurisdiction of the High Court. For all purposes connected with trial on indictment, the Crown Court is a superior court[6] but in the exercise of its appellate jurisdiction, it is deemed to be an inferior court.[7] Sometimes the Divisional Court, perhaps understandably, overlooks this distinction and exercises judicial review of the Crown Court in its indictable jurisdiction.[8]

Aggrieved defendants wishing to appeal to the Crown Court must file a notice of appeal within twenty-one days of the decision of the magistrates' court with which they take issue. It is not necessary to state the grounds of appeal, though it is sensible to indicate in general terms the nature of the defendant's grievance with the decision at first instance. Most appeals against conviction assert simply that the conviction was 'against the weight of the evidence' while appeals against sentence are usually against custodial sentences which are considered 'excessive or wrong in principle'.[9]

The appeal adopts the unusual form of a complete rehearing. The historical development of the remedy described above, coupled with the absence of written records in the magistrates' courts, accounts for this. The practical effect of the appeal by way of re-hearing is that the case must be re-created before the Crown Court. Proceedings on an appeal against conviction will look just like a trial in the magistrates' court, while an appeal against sentence will look just like proceedings on a guilty plea at first instance. But case law affirms the appellate nature of the proceedings[10] and, of course, the judge and justices hearing the appeal will know that there has been a conviction in the magistrates' court. Nevertheless the function of the proceedings is not to decide whether the magistrates decided correctly, but is to make a fresh decision on conviction or sentence in the light of the evidence adduced in the Crown Court. The result of an appeal against conviction will be

---

[6] Supreme Court Act 1981, s. 45; *ex parte Brownlow* [1980] QB 530.

[7] Supreme Court Act 1981, ss. 28 and 29.

[8] This happened in *R* v. *Central Criminal Court, ex parte Crook* (1984) 82 *Law Society's Gazette* 1408. It is also arguable that the Divisional Court lacked jurisdiction to deal with the problem of conscientious objection to jury service which arose in *R* v. *Guildford Crown Court, ex parte Siderfin* [1989] 3 All ER 73.

[9] I. Scott, 'Appeals to the Crown Court following Summary Conviction', paper delivered to SPTL Criminal Law Group, September 1977.   [10] *Drover* v. *Rugman* [1951] 1 KB 380.

expressed in terms of a confirmation or quashing of the conviction. The Crown Court has wide powers and may in addition vary the decision appealed, remit the matter back to the magistrates with their opinion, or make such other order as the court thinks just.[11]

When considering sentence, another unusual feature is present. It is open to the Crown Court to impose any sentence available to the magistrates even if it is more severe than that actually imposed by the magistrates.[12] This is one of only two occasions on which an appeal court can increase the sentence imposed by the court below. The Crown Court only rarely increases sentence.

Around 20,000 appeals against conviction and/or sentence are made to the Crown Court each year, making it the main focus of appeals against decisions of magistrates. About half are successful.[13] This may seem a large number of appeals, but measured against more than two million cases dealt with by magistrates each year, it represents an appeal in less than one in 100 cases. It seems that there are very few appeals in respect of offences triable only summarily and motoring offences. It also seems that there are very few appeals against sentence other than custodial sentences. Since less than two per cent of those defendants convicted on summary trial receive immediate custodial sentences, these figures are perhaps not so surprising.[14] Nevertheless it appears that the appeal to the Crown Court is under-utilised. The James Committee was wisely cautious about assuming that the reason for the paucity of appeals was general satisfaction with summary trial and noted that delay, expense, the avoidance of further anxiety, a wish for finality, and the possibility that the Crown Court might increase sentence were all disincentives to appealing.[15]

Expense is a major factor. If legal aid has been available for the proceedings in the magistrates' court, that will include the provision of advice as to any grounds of appeal.[16] But legal aid is not readily available in magistrates' courts, and it is unlikely that an unassisted litigant at first instance will obtain legal aid for an appeal. In all cases a separate consideration of the merits is required before the grant of legal aid for appellate proceedings.

There is no appeal following a decision of the Crown Court in the exercise of its appellate jurisdiction other than to the Divisional Court. The only subsequent appeals available after appeal to the Crown Court are the exercise of supervisory jurisdiction by the High Court. Either prosecution or defence may seek judicial review to cure some illegality or appeal by way of case stated, but no further appeals on the merits are available.

---

[11] Supreme Court Act 1981, s. 48.   [12] Ibid., s. 48(4).

[13] *Judicial Statistics 1996* (London: HMSO, 1997, Cm. 3716). The typical distribution of appeals is that one-third are against conviction and two-thirds against sentence.

[14] I. Scott, 'Appeals to the Crown Court following Summary Conviction', paper delivered to SPTL Criminal Law Group, September 1977.

[15] *Report of the Interdepartmental Committee on the Distribution of Criminal Business between the Crown Court and Magistrates' Courts (James Committee)* (London: HMSO, 1975, Cmnd. 6323), paras. 38 and 251.

[16] Legal Aid Act 1988, s. 19(2).

Appeal by way of case stated

Either prosecution or defence may apply for a case to be stated by the magistrates' court, or Crown Court, where they believe that the decision of that court is wrong in law or in excess of its jurisdiction. Such appeals, when taken successfully by the prosecution, can operate to reverse an acquittal, and are an exception to the general rule that acquittals are final. There are few appeals by way of case stated each year, though they often include important points of law and practice.

In 1996 there were only 197 such appeals, 166 from magistrates' courts and thirty-one from the Crown Court. About one in three such appeals is successful.[17]

The grounds of appeal are limited to complaints that the magistrates' court acted in excess of jurisdiction or in error of law. The reason for the former ground is historical and today duplicates the remedy of certiorari available on application for judicial review.[18] Most appeals by way of case stated are for this reason based on errors of law, and most go to the merits of the conviction rather than to issues of sentence. The time limit for entering such an appeal is again twenty-one days from the date of the decision. Procedure on application for a case to be stated by a magistrates' court is as follows, though where the application relates to a decision of the Crown Court, there are some differences. The application for a case to be stated is sent to the clerk to the justices, who is principally responsible for drafting the case to be sent to the High Court. The case consists of a statement of the charge, the facts as found by the magistrates, the arguments adduced on the law and the justices' decisions on the law, the outcome of the case, and the question upon which the opinion of the High Court is sought. The only circumstances in which the evidence before the court is summarised is where the ground of the appeal is that the justices erred in law by making a finding of fact for which there was no evidence, or where the justices made findings of fact which no reasonable justices could have made on the evidence before them. In drafting the case, the clerk will consult the justices and the parties and will take account of representations made by them. In applications relating to decisions of the Crown Court, the appellant's solicitors will be responsible for the initial drafting of the case for signature by the Circuit judge or Recorder. The final version of the case is sent to the appellant's solicitors who are responsible for lodging it in the Crown Office at the Royal Courts of Justice within ten days of its receipt.

The appeal is heard by a Divisional Court of the Queen's Bench Division, that is, by at least two judges of the High Court, and usually by three. It is common practice for these appeals to be heard by the Lord Chief Justice and two puisne judges. If a two judge court is evenly split, it seems that the decision of the court below stands.[19] The Divisional Court hears only legal argument and no evidence. In disposing of the case, the Divisional Court has wide powers similar to those of the Crown Court when exercising its appellate function.

---

[17] *Judicial Statistics 1996* (London: HMSO, 1997, Cm. 3716). The numbers have remained fairly constant for at least a decade.   [18] See below.
[19] *Flannagan* v. *Shaw* [1920] 3 KB 96.

This type of appeal may well become important once the Human Rights Act 1998 enters into force, since the High Court is the lowest level of court able to make a 'declaration of incompatibility'.[20] If the defendant is arguing that the legislation under which he or she has been convicted breaches the European Convention, they will need to get before the High Court in order to secure a declaration.[21]

Appeal following a decision of the Divisional Court lies direct to the House of Lords.[22] Following summary trial, the Court of Appeal, Criminal Division, has no role whatsoever to play in the appellate process.

Before an appeal from the Divisional Court to the House of Lords is possible, two conditions must be satisfied. First, the Divisional Court must grant a certificate that a point of law of general public importance is involved. If no certificate is granted, no appeal is possible; there is no appeal against a refusal of a certificate. Secondly, either the Divisional Court or the House of Lords must grant leave to appeal. It is sometimes seen as curious that a court refuses leave to appeal in the face of a certificate that a point of law of general public importance is involved in the case. The reason for this curiosity is once again to be found by delving into history. But the issue is so closely bound up with the creation of a system of appeals following trial on indictment, where an identical rule governs appeal from the Court of Appeal, Criminal Division, to the House of Lords, that it is best to offer the explanation in that context.

Application for judicial review

If there has been some illegality in the proceedings, either prosecution or defence may seek to correct that illegality by way of application to the High Court for judicial review. Leave to seek judicial review is always required and forms part of the application. There are three orders available. Certiorari quashes an unlawful decision in the course of proceedings of an inferior court, for example, the imposition of a sentence in excess of that allowed in magistrates' courts. Mandamus compels an inferior court to carry out its functions, for example, to secure consideration of the appropriate legal criteria for the grant of legal aid or bail. Finally, prohibition orders an inferior court to cease acting unlawfully.[23] This jurisdiction will be of particular importance where issues arise under the Human Rights Act 1998.

Appeals lie to the Court of Appeal, Civil Division and onwards to the House of Lords.

Applications for judicial review of criminal proceedings are not numerous. In 1996 there were 297 applications for leave to seek judicial review determined by the High Court. In the same year fifty-eight applications resulted in the grant of an order.[24]

---

[20] See Ch. 2.

[21] Even though this has limited application on the parties to the case: Human Rights Act 1998, s. 4(6).

[22] Administration of Justice Act 1960, s. 1.

[23] For an example see the case of *R* v. *Hatfield Justices, ex parte Castle* [1981] 1 WLR 217.

[24] *Judicial Statistics 1996* (London: HMSO, 1997, Cm. 3746).

Interrelationship of the appeal procedures

Overlap exists between the three different types of challenge to decisions of magistrates' courts. An application for a case to be stated on the grounds of an excess of jurisdiction overlaps with an application for an order of certiorari; and there is a choice of appeal to be made where a defendant believes the magistrates erred in their interpretation of the law, where appeal to the Crown Court and appeal by way of case stated on the grounds of error of law overlap. An appeal by way of case stated precludes appeal to the Crown Court,[25] whereas there is always the possibility of an appeal by way of case stated following the re-hearing of the case by the Crown Court, if the defendant believes there is still an error of law in the decision. Where application for judicial review and the appeal by way of case stated coincide, the Divisional Court has made it clear that judicial review should only be used for straightforward applications.[26] Where detailed information from the justices is likely to be an important part of the appeal, the case stated procedure is considered the only convenient and proper way to bring the case before the High Court.[27]

The confusing overlap of procedures and the piecemeal development of appeals following summary trial result in a system of appeals that lacks coherence. There is clearly a case for removing the hybrid status of the Crown Court and for transferring to it the jurisdiction currently vested in the High Court to entertain appeals by way of case stated and applications for judicial review.[28] Such cases ought be listed before a High Court judge sitting in the Crown Court. All that would be lost would be the supervisory jurisdiction of the High Court over the Crown Court, which is exercised in very few cases each year. The Crown Court would then become the forum for all appeals from criminal proceedings in magistrates' courts. This could relieve the over-burdened High Court of a small body of cases without swamping the Crown Court, whose status as the equal of the High Court would be recognised in its exercise of appellate jurisdiction.

The benefits of the appeal taking the form of a complete re-hearing may well be one reason for the lack of serious criticism of the appeal system following trial on indictment. One reason why a re-hearing is required is the absence of transcripts of summary trials, but the absence of research comparing the two processes is surprising given the focus of attention of the efficacy of the appeal process in avoiding miscarriages of justice. This is not say that the appeal system following summary trial avoids miscarriages of justice; between a quarter and a third of appeals against conviction in the magistrates' courts is successful. This certainly shows that magistrates' courts are capable of generating a significant number of miscarriages of justice and raises questions for enquiry about the reasons for them.

---

[25] Magistrates' Courts Act 1980, s. 111(4).

[26] *R* v. *Crown Court at Ipswich, ex parte Baldwin* [1981] 1 All ER 596.

[27] On the relationship between appeal to the Crown Court and judicial review, see *R* v. *Peterborough Magistrates' Court, ex parte Dowler* [1997] 2 WLR 843, and *R* v. *Hereford Magistrates' Court, ex parte Rowlands* [1997] 2 WLR 854.

[28] Though this would have implications in relation to declarations of incompatibility under the Human Rights Act 1998.

Appeal Following Trial on Indictment

A heavily circumscribed system

Compared with the generous, but under-used, provision for appeal following summary trial, appeals following trial on indictment are hedged about with conditions and the powers of the Court of Appeal, Criminal Division, are heavily circumscribed. The reason for this is the sanctity of the jury verdict, which has meant that it is extremely difficult to re-open the findings of fact upon which the jury will have based its decision to convict. This tradition has meant that the Court of Appeal failed to prevent a whole series of miscarriages of justice. Underlying many of them were irregularities in the police investigation of the case coupled with a signal reluctance of the Court of Appeal to consider fresh evidence tending to show that those convicted had not committed the horrendous crimes for which they were serving long prison sentences.[29]

An appreciation of the historical development of criminal appeals following trial on indictment helps to explain some of the anomalies of the present system. Until 1848 decisions resulting from trial on indictment were final. At best a trial judge could refer a question of law following a conviction informally to his fellow judges before delivering judgment or before the sentence was put into effect. If the judges considered that the conviction was mistaken, a recommendation would be made that a pardon be granted. This informal procedure was institutionalised in 1848 with the creation of the Court for Crown Cases Reserved, but the reserving of cases was at the absolute discretion of the judges.[30] This unsatisfactory state of affairs continued until the enactment of the Criminal Appeal Act 1907, which established the Court of Criminal Appeal. There had been thirty-five previous attempts to secure legislation on criminal appeals and it is generally accepted that it was the imprisonment for seven years of Adolf Beck on mistaken identification evidence which finally stirred consciences sufficiently to establish a formal system of appeals following trial on indictment. But the Court of Criminal Appeal was an odd hybrid court at the periphery of the court system; it built on the experience of the Court for Crown Cases Reserved more than it represented a radical innovation in the criminal justice system. The Court of Criminal Appeal was presided over by the Lord Chief Justice who usually sat with two High Court judges to hear appeals. It was therefore a court without its own judiciary, which consisted of trial judges sitting by rotation to review the work of their colleagues.

Criminal appeals did not take on their modern form until the reforms of the Criminal Appeal Act 1966, which followed the study of criminal appeals by the Interdepartmental Committee on the Court of Criminal Appeal known as the Donovan

---

[29] Some of these are chronicled in J. Rozenberg, 'Miscarriages of Justice' in E. Stockdale and S. Casale, *Criminal Justice under Stress* (London: Blackstone Press, 1992), p. 91.

[30] W. Holdsworth, *A History of English Law*, 7th edn. by A. Goodhart and H. Hanbury (London: Methuen, 1956).

Committee.[31] Under the Criminal Appeal Act 1966 the Court of Criminal Appeal was abolished and re-constituted as a division of the Court of Appeal. The new division is headed by the Lord Chief Justice and all the Lords Justices of Appeal are judges of the Court, though High Court judges retain their eligibility to sit in the criminal division of the Court of Appeal. It remains common for a court to be composed of a Lord Justice of Appeal and two High Court judges. Indeed courts consisting of two judges may now dispose of appeals against sentence.[32] Most of the law relating to criminal appeals following trial on indictment has been consolidated in the Criminal Appeal Act 1968, as amended.

Getting advice on appealing

Virtually all defendants tried in the Crown Court have the benefit of representation under a criminal legal aid order. It has long been the case that legal aid for such purposes includes the giving of advice on any grounds for appealing against either conviction or sentence, or both, and, if such grounds exist, to meet the cost of preparing and filing the application for leave to appeal.[33] This right was first introduced in the Criminal Justice Act 1967, but it never seems to have worked effectively. A survey in 1970 based on interviews with prisoners showed a significant failure to provide such advice with the result that the Court of Appeal was inundated with hopeless hand-written applications for leave to appeal.[34] The response was new court directions[35] and an accompanying pamphlet, which required solicitors and counsel to ensure that defendants convicted at the Crown Court were automatically advised whether there were any grounds of appeal, and that provisional oral advice should be confirmed by letter. The procedure was amended in 1976, and a new edition of the pamphlet, approved by the Lord Chief Justice, was produced in 1983.[36] Even those new procedures did not operate as intended. The Benson Commission considered that the rules governing advice on appeal should be made more formal.[37]

Lord Widgery C. J. expressed his frustration by announcing in 1980 that time spent awaiting appeal would not normally count as part of the sentence if the recommended procedures had not been followed.[38] The current Guide requires solicitors to instruct counsel to give advice and assistance on appeal following conviction and sentence in the Crown Court. Solicitors and counsel should see defendants

[31] *Report of the Interdepartmental Committee on the Court of Criminal Appeal (Donovan Committee)* (London: HMSO, 1965, Cmnd. 2755).   [32] Supreme Court Act 1981, s. 55.
[33] By reason of the definition of 'representation' in the Legal Aid Act 1988, s. 2(4).
[34] M. Zander, 'Legal Advice and Criminal Appeals: A Survey of Prisoners, Prisons and Lawyers' [1972] Crim. LR 132.   [35] Practice Note: Crime: Appeal Preparation [1974] 1 WLR 774.
[36] D. Thompson, *A Guide to Proceedings in the Court of Appeal, Criminal Division*, reproduced at (1983) 77 Cr. App. R 138; an amended version was issued in 1990, but significantly it is not reproduced either in *Archbold 1998* (London: Sweet & Maxwell, 1998), or in *Blackstone's Criminal Practice 1998* (London: Blackstone Press, 1998); see also M. Zander, 'Legal Advice on Appeal: The New Machinery' [1975] Crim. LR 364.
[37] *Final Report of the Royal Commission on Legal Services (Benson Commission)* (London: HMSO, 1979, Cmnd. 7648), paras. 14.16–14.17.
[38] Practice Direction: Crime: Leave to Appeal [1980] 1 All ER 555.

immediately following conviction and sentence, and counsel should express a provisional view on the existence of any grounds of appeal. Within fourteen days counsel must send written advice on appeal to the solicitors accompanied, where appropriate, by signed grounds of appeal. These documents are then sent to defendants to reach them within twenty-one days of conviction and sentence. If counsel has advised an appeal, the solicitors should forthwith complete and lodge application for leave to appeal to reach the Registrar of Criminal Appeals within twenty-eight days of conviction and sentence.[39] In addition to exhortations to lawyers, a system of legal aid officers was set up in prisons. These officers are not lawyers but have some knowledge of the criminal justice system and are charged with advising prisoners of their rights.

Despite all this effort to secure proper advice to those convicted in the Crown Court, it seems that the system for providing legal advice following conviction is failing. A scathing research study for the Runciman Commission[40] revealed significant departures from the requirements of the Court of Appeal's guidance. Two-thirds of cell visits by solicitors' firms were by unadmitted staff. Many prisoners reported that they had not received advice on appeal when visited in cells, and in nine out of ten cases, the advice was not stated in writing as required. The reason for following up oral advice in writing is that many defendants are in shock following conviction and need a record of the advice to consult when they are in a calmer frame of mind. Indeed it seems that in one in ten cases, convicted defendants did not receive a visit from their lawyers in their cells. Time limits are widely breached. Only four in ten prisoners reported the receipt of advice in prison, though nearly all solicitors had promised this. The one in three prisoners who reported having received no advice on appeal in court cells immediately following their conviction included one in four who also said they had received no advice in prison. This means that one in four convicted prisoners received no advice at all from their lawyers. The performance of legal aid officers in prisons was found to be very variable. Where prison visits were made by lawyers, difficulties were frequently experienced, and in many cases several days notice of the visit was required despite the running of the twenty-eight-day time limit for appealing. The Runciman Commission viewed these defects as 'serious matters',[41] and urged immediate improvements in the system.

Some, though little, sympathy may be expressed for the profession. No doubt it is difficult to explain to defendants who believe that they have just been victims of miscarriages of justice that the grounds of appeal against conviction and sentence are narrow and technical, and that appeal against conviction is not a general means of obtaining a review of the correctness of the conviction. But that is no excuse

---

[39] If counsel advises that there are no grounds of appeal but the solicitor disagrees, the solicitor may draft the grounds of appeal under a criminal legal aid order.

[40] J. Plotnikoff and R. Woolfson, *Information and Advice for Prisoners about Grounds for Appeal and the Appeals Process*, Royal Commission on Criminal Justice Research Study No. 22 (London: HMSO, 1993).

[41] *Report of the Royal Commission on Criminal Justice (Runciman Commission)* (London: HMSO, 1993), ch. 10, para. 14.

for what appears to be a widespread failure to comply with mandatory guidelines, albeit guidelines for breach of which there are few effective sanctions.[42]

Appeals against conviction: the need for leave

The Registrar of Criminal Appeals has stated that the Court of Appeal is essentially concerned with two questions in considering appeals against conviction: was the result right? and was the trial conducted in an acceptable manner?[43]

Few would argue with these purposes. The two questions relate to different aspects of the trial process. The first considers whether there has been a miscarriage of justice, despite all the safeguards built into the system, which has resulted in the conviction of an innocent defendant. The second goes to issues of due process: regardless of the outcome of the case, did the trial meet the required standards of fairness and impartiality? There is, perhaps, a third group where the development of the law is in issue, as, for example, in the case of *Kelly and Lindsay*[44] where the Court of Appeal had to consider whether parts of a corpse constituted property which could be stolen despite the common law principle that there was no property in a corpse or parts of a corpse.

An aggrieved defendant may appeal as of right where the trial judge has granted a certificate that the case is fit for appeal.[45] Such appeals are very rare.

Virtually all appeals require leave for the appeal which is obtained from the Court of Appeal. Within twenty-eight days of the conviction and sentence, notice of application for leave to appeal and the grounds of appeal must be lodged with the Registrar of Criminal Appeals. These may be accompanied by a transcript of the judge's summing up or of part of the evidence if that is relevant to the appeal. These are then considered by one of the judges eligible to sit in the Court of Appeal, criminal division, known as 'the single judge'.

Consideration of the application by the single judge is on the papers alone. Refusal of leave at this stage is not final, but there are risks for a defendant in pursuing the matter further. Defendants refused leave by the single judge may give notice within fourteen days that they wish to renew the application before the full court. At this stage no legal aid is made available to the applicant and the full court will consider the application on the papers alone. The decision on the renewed application is given in open court, at which time the court may, if the application is refused, make directions that time spent in custody since the filing of the application is not to count as part of any custodial sentence imposed on the defendant.[46] This loss of time, which may also be ordered by the single judge in cases deemed to be unarguable, operates as a powerful disincentive to the pursuit of appeals.

---

[42] For a very good description of the appeal process see JUSTICE, *How to Appeal: A Guide to the Criminal Appeal System* (London: JUSTICE, 1996), which is supplied free to prisoners on request.

[43] D. Meador, *Criminal Appeals—English Practice and American Reforms* (Charlottesville: University Press of Virginia, 1973), p. 97.

[44] Court of Appeal, judgment of 14 May 1998, *The Times*, 21 May 1998.

[45] Criminal Appeal Act 1968, s. 1(2)(b).

[46] Practice Direction: Crime: Leave to Appeal [1980] 1 All ER 555.

Nearly three-quarters of all applications for leave to appeal against conviction fall by the wayside at this stage. The Runciman Commission saw no reason to depart from the loss of time provisions.[47] In practice very few seeking to appeal suffer this sanction.

If leave is granted, legal aid will normally be granted for the arguing of the appeal, but unless the collection of new evidence is needed, this will be limited to counsel only. To obtain an extension to include legal aid for a solicitor, counsel must apply in writing to the Registrar showing that there is work to be done which can only be done by solicitors. This rule operates in practice to isolate defendants from their legal advisers; counsel will normally argue the case on the basis of the papers prepared in connection with the advice on appeal and the filing of the notice for leave, plus perhaps a brief conference with the defendant on the day of the appeal.

Appeal against conviction: the grounds of appeal

The sole ground of appeal referred to in the legislation is that the court thinks that 'the conviction is unsafe'.[48] This encompasses all three grounds previously stated in the legislation, namely, that the conviction is unsafe or unsatisfactory; that the trial judge made a wrong decision on a question of law; or that there was a material irregularity in the course of the trial. The intention of the amended wording is to widen the scope for allowing appeals, though the Runciman Commission suggested that the wording ought to be that 'the conviction is or may be unsafe'.[49]

One difficulty which appears to be experienced by the Court of Appeal is the legacy of tradition. Prior to the introduction of the unsafe or unsatisfactory test,[50] the test had been even more strict; to be quashed the verdict had to be one which was 'unreasonable or could not be supported having regard to the evidence'. The Court of Criminal Appeal had construed the provision very narrowly refusing to intervene except in cases where there was literally no evidence against the defendant to support to conviction.

The unsafe or unsatisfactory test is subjective. Lord Justice Widgery (as he then was) explained it as follows:

In cases of this kind the court must in the end ask itself a subjective question, whether we are content to let the matter stand as it is, or whether there is not some lurking doubt in our minds which makes us wonder whether an injustice has been done. This is a reaction which may not be based strictly on the evidence as such; it is a reaction which can be produced by the general feel of the case as the court experiences it.[51]

---

[47] *Report of the Royal Commission on Criminal Justice (Runciman Commission)* (London: HMSO, 1993), ch. 10, para. 26. [48] Criminal Appeal Act 1968, s. 2(1)(a).

[49] *Report of the Royal Commission on Criminal Justice (Runciman Commission)* (London: HMSO, 1993), ch. 10, para. 32, though a minority did not like the use of the word 'unsafe' at all.

[50] Which is the only ground which enables a defendant to appeal on the grounds that the conviction was against the weight of the evidence, or that new evidence is available.

[51] *Cooper* [1969] 1 QB 267, 271.

This broad interpretation of the power was prefaced by a reminder of the sanctity of jury decision-making, and represents a considerable qualification of the test:

It has been said over and over again throughout the years that this court must recognise the advantage which a jury has in seeing and hearing the witnesses, and if all the material was before the jury and the summing up was impeccable, this court should not lightly interfere.[52]

Despite the more generous wording of the amended legislation, criticism continued to be expressed that the Court of Appeal was reluctant to quash convictions on the ground that they were unsafe or unsatisfactory. An analysis of the case law since 1966 suggests that of those cases where leave to appeal is granted which are argued on this ground, about four in ten succeed.[53] However, it is the presence of a procedural irregularity or a series of small problems in the conduct of the trial which appear to provide the basis for many of these decisions. There are very few cases which can be said to be a review of the merits of the conviction. It does not seem that appeals often succeed on this ground where no fault can be found with the trial. JUSTICE could identify only six cases since 1968 where convictions were quashed because of doubts about the correctness of the jury's verdict. The 'lurking doubt' test laid down in *Cooper* will usually only be satisfied by pointing to some defect in the trial. Because of this the Court of Appeal is still able effectively to wash its hands of the issue of guilt, and to restrict its determinations to whether there was sufficient evidence upon which a reasonable jury could convict or whether there was some error of law or procedure made by the trial judge. The search for error is clear from the other two grounds of appeal, which are largely self-explanatory.

The 1989 JUSTICE Report estimates that there are at least fifteen people a year wrongly convicted after trial by jury.[54] Five common themes are identified in such cases: incorrect identification; false confession; perjury by a co-defendant or witness; police misconduct; and poor tactics by defence lawyers. The Court of Appeal is criticised for its restrictive attitude to quashing convictions on the basis that they are unsafe or satisfactory. Only six cases since 1968 could be identified where convictions had been quashed because the Court was in doubt as to the correctness of the jury's verdict. The charge is made that the establishment is too concerned with maintaining the correctness of convictions.

Particular problem areas have included cases involving the receipt of fresh evidence and appeals based on errors by lawyers. Frequently defendants will wish to adduce fresh evidence to support their appeal. Either new information will be available, or perhaps a witness now admits to having committed perjury in giving evidence at the trial. The Court's approach to fresh evidence cases is restrictive. The House of Lords had indicated that the proper approach was for the Court of Appeal only to admit fresh evidence where the Court believes the outcome would have been affected by the evidence rather than to do so where it considered that the jury

---

[52] Cooper [1969] 1 QB 267, 271.
[53] JUSTICE, *Miscarriages of Justice* (London: Justice, 1989).   [54] Ibid.

might have been affected by it.[55] Lawyers' errors do not constitute valid grounds of appeal,[56] unless there was 'flagrantly incompetent advocacy'.[57]

Research for the Runciman Commission[58] into decisions of the Court of Appeal in 1990 and 1992 showed that fresh evidence was admitted only in very rare cases and suggested that the Court is concerned to control the flow of appeals. Malleson concludes;

Only in very limited circumstances will such evidence be admitted and if admitted, form the basis of a successful appeal. Moreover, the Court rarely sets out the reasoning behind its decisions about fresh evidence so that it is hard to discern in detail what the Court's approach is to this category of appeal.[59]

Malleson's research also suggested a marked reluctance by the Court of Appeal to consider lawyer's incompetence as a ground of appeal. No case was granted leave on this basis and the nine cases in the sample all involved unrepresented renewed applications.

If the Court of Appeal thinks that the conviction is unsafe, it is required to allow the appeal. This will result in the quashing of the conviction. In certain circumstances, the Court of Appeal can order a retrial.[60]

There are around 2,300 appeals against conviction each year, of which one in four secures leave to appeal. In 1996 the Court of Appeal disposed of 719 appeals against conviction, allowing 250 and refusing 469.[61]

Appeal against conviction: the powers of the Court of Appeal

The Court of Appeal has powers to quash a conviction, to admit fresh evidence, to order a retrial and to convict in the alternative.

The hearing of appeals normally involves only legal argument and not any rehearing of evidence. Where evidence given at the trial is relevant to the appeal reliance will be placed on a transcript of the trial proceedings. But it may be that an appellant wishes to adduce evidence not put at the trial in support of the appeal.

The Court of Appeal always has a discretion to receive evidence, and in deciding whether to exercise that discretion must now consider whether the evidence appears to the Court to be capable of belief, whether it may afford any ground for allowing the appeal, whether the evidence would have been admissible at the trial, and whether there is a reasonable explanation for the failure to adduce the evidence at trial.[62]

---

[55] *Stafford and Luvaglio* v. *Director of Public Prosecutions* [1974] AC 878. But amendments to Criminal Appeal Act 1968, s. 23 are intended to make it easier for fresh evidence to be admitted. See below.

[56] *Irwin* (1987) 85 Cr. App. R 294, and *Gautam* [1988] Crim. LR 109.

[57] *Ensor* (1989) 89 Cr. App. R 139, though JUSTICE does not believe any conviction has been quashed on this ground.

[58] K. Malleson, *Review of the Appeal Process*, Royal Commission on Criminal Justice Research Study No. 17 (London: HMSO, 1993).   [59] Ibid., p. 11.

[60] See below.   [61] *Judicial Statistics 1996* (London: HMSO, 1997, Cm. 3716).

[62] Criminal Appeal Act 1968, s. 23.

The explanation for some of these matters is that the legislature does not wish defendants to have an opportunity to argue their defence in a different way on appeal. The role of the appellate proceedings is not 'to give a second bite of the cherry'. So a wrong choice of defence witnesses at trial cannot be remedied on appeal. It remains to be seen whether the more generous formula in the new wording of the statutory text results in a change of approach by the Court of Appeal.

Whether the incidence of miscarriages of justice could and would be reduced by giving the Court of Appeal a general power to order retrials has long been a highly contentious issue. The Tucker Committee, whose report prefaced the introduction of the power to order a retrial in fresh evidence cases, were divided on this issue. A majority of five to three rejected the idea.[63] The JUSTICE Committee which considered the issue was also divided but by a majority of nine to four came down in favour of granting the court such a power.[64] Those opposed to a general power see basic values embedded in the criminal justice system as being at stake. It is argued that to allow retrials would be to erode not only the finality of jury verdicts but also the finality of the trial process itself. There was also concern expressed that the floodgates would be opened and that there would be too many retrials at huge public expense. Finally it was considered that defendants tried for a second time might be prejudiced since the jury would almost certainly learn that it was a second trial and might infer that the Court of Appeal had ordered a retrial because they felt that the defendant was guilty.

The arguments in favour of a general power maintain that the power is needed to provide a further safeguard against miscarriages of justice. Ordering a retrial would avoid the conviction of the innocent and, given the difficulty the Court of Appeal has over the application of the proviso, would avoid the quashing of convictions in favour of unmeritorious appellants on technicalities. Such defendants could be re-tried in conformity with the rules of due process. Finally, it is argued that the experience of other jurisdictions does not bear out the fears expressed by those opposed to the court's having such a power.

The arguments in favour of such a power certainly seem more compelling than those against. Parliament has at long last agreed; section 43 of the Criminal Justice Act 1988 has swept away the restriction on the Court of Appeal's power to order a retrial only in fresh evidence cases.[65] The effect is to allow the Court of Appeal a discretion to order a retrial whenever it allows an appeal against conviction if it appears in the interests of justice to do so. The new power is likely to be used to avoid those unsatisfactory appeals where a conviction is quashed on a technicality. In such cases the defendant can be sent back for a trial at which the rules of due process are followed. The result has been a significant increase in retrials. Whereas there was only one in 1989, there were fifty-three in 1996. [66]

Amendments to the procedural rules governing retrials are designed to mitigate the disadvantages of delay and a lack of finality introduced by the wider power.

---

[63] *Report of the Departmental Committee on New Trials in Criminal Cases (Tucker Committee)* (London: HMSO, 1954, Cmd. 9150).   [64] JUSTICE, *Criminal Appeals* (London: JUSTICE, 1964).
[65] See Criminal Appeal Act 1968, ss. 8 and 9, as amended.
[66] *Judicial Statistics 1996* (London: HMSO, 1997, Cm. 3716).

Where a retrial is ordered, the defendant must be brought to trial within two months, unless leave of the Court of Appeal has been obtained. The defendant is entitled to make representations on any application for an extension of the time limit. Provision is made for limiting extensions to cases where the prosecution has acted 'with all due expedition' and there remains 'good and sufficient cause for a retrial in spite of the lapse of time'.

Finally, the Court of Appeal has the power to substitute an alternative verdict provided that it was open to the jury to have convicted on an alternative charge, that the jury did not expressly acquit on that charge, and that the court is satisfied that the jury could on the evidence before it have convicted on that charge.[67] An example makes this easier to understand. A defendant is tried on a two count indictment charging theft and handling, and is convicted of theft, but expressly acquitted of the handling charge. In this case, the Court of Appeal has no power to substitute a verdict of guilty of handling for that of theft, even if it thinks that it is the correct verdict, since the jury acquitted on the handling charge. But if in such a case the trial judge on receiving the verdict of guilty on the theft charge had discharged the jury in respect of the handling charge, the Court of Appeal could substitute a verdict of guilty on the handling count for the theft conviction.

The role of the Court of Appeal will be central where issues involving possible declarations of incompatibility under the Human Rights Act 1998 are raised following trial on indictment. The Crown Court has no jurisdiction to make such declarations, and where such a declaration is sought, the defendant will need to pursue an appeal before the Court of Appeal.

Venire de novo

The Court of Appeal's power to order a retrial is often confused with the power to order a new trial by issuing the old common law writ of venire de novo. This is the power to order a fresh trial where the first trial was a nullity because of some fundamental defect. A good example is a trial before a judge not qualified to sit as a judge.[68] Another is a conviction based on a wrongful pleas of guilty induced by oppression. In *Rose*,[69] the House of Lords confirmed that venire de novo is only appropriate where the defect renders the proceedings a nullity from beginning to end and is not available to secure a retrial where a serious irregularity will necessitate quashing a conviction on a technicality. These cases are now accommodated because a retrial can now be ordered; this may be the sort of case for which the wider power to order a retrial was designed.

Appeals against sentence

Appeals against sentence are separate appeals from those against conviction.[70] If a defendant appeals against conviction, but not against sentence, and is unsuccessful,

---

[67] Criminal Appeal Act 1968, s. 3.   [68] *Cronin* [1940] 1 All ER 618.
[69] [1982] AC 822.   [70] Criminal Appeal Act 1968, s. 9.

the Court of Appeal has no power to vary the sentence imposed by the Crown Court. There is no right of appeal against sentence following trial on indictment unless the trial judge grants a certificate that the case is suitable for appeal.[71] This is very rare. For the offence of murder there is no appeal against sentence at all, since the penalty of life imprisonment is required by statute. In all other cases leave of the Court of Appeal is required.

Leave to appeal against sentence is obtained in exactly the same way as leave to appeal against conviction. Appeals against sentence are far more numerous than those against conviction. About one in four appellants succeeds in obtaining leave.[72] The risk of losing time applies equally to appeals against sentence.

Section 11 of the Criminal Appeal Act 1968 does not spell out the grounds upon which such appeals are based. The basic ground will, of course, be that the defendant regards the sentence as too severe having regard to all the circumstances of the case. The abundant case law of the Court of Appeal, which is now sufficient to justify its own set of law reports[73] makes clear that the grounds of complaint must be that the sentence imposed by the Crown Court was excessive or wrong in principle.

If the Court of Appeal allow an appeal against sentence, they may vary the sentence by substituting any sentence which was available to the Crown Court, but they may not, taking the case as a whole, deal with the defendant more severely than the Crown Court. The proviso that allows the court to take the case as a whole means that where there is an appeal against conviction and sentence on two counts and the conviction on one of them is quashed, the court can increase sentence on the other provided that the substituted sentence is no more severe than the total sentence of the Crown Court. Somewhat alarmingly, it seems that not all advisers are aware that the Court of Appeal cannot increase sentence, and appear to confuse the rules on loss of time in connection with seeking leave to appeal with a power to increase sentence.[74]

There are about 6,500 appeals against sentence each year; around 1,800 result in the grant of leave to appeal and around seventy per cent of these result in some reduction of the sentence imposed by the Crown Court.[75]

The Criminal Cases Review Commission

Aggrieved defendants have twenty-eight days in which to apply for leave to appeal against conviction. If there was no other possibility of seeking a review by the Court of Appeal of the conviction other than within this time, considerable injustice could

---

[71] Ibid., s. 11.   [72] *Judicial Statistics 1996* (London: HMSO, 1997, Cm. 3716).
[73] Criminal Appeal Reports (Sentencing).
[74] J. Plotnikoff and R. Woolfson, *Information and Advice for Prisoners about Grounds for Appeal and the Appeals Process*, Royal Commission on Criminal Justice Research Study No. 22 (London: HMSO, 1993), p. 82.   [75] *Judicial Statistics 1996* (London: HMSO, 1997, Cm. 3716).

be caused where fresh evidence comes to light only at a later date. It would be possible to leave all such matters to be dealt with by the prerogative powers discussed later in this chapter, but section 17 of the Criminal Appeal Act 1968 allowed any person convicted on indictment to make application at any time to the Home Secretary, who could refer the whole or part of the case to the Court of Appeal. The Home Secretary could make such a reference even though there has already been an appeal to the Court of Appeal and even though the Home Secretary has previously referred the same case to the Court of Appeal. When the Home Secretary referred the whole of a case to the Court of Appeal, it was treated in effect as an appeal against conviction by the defendant who may bring up and argue matters additional to those which have led the Home Secretary to make the reference.[76] Though petitions to the Home Secretary were numerous, averaging around 2,650 each year,[77] many were unsubstantiated complaints and grievances. By 1992 the number of petitions had reduced to 790. Between 1981 and 1992, sixty-four cases were referred to the Court of Appeal under the procedure.[78]

The experience of this process as a means of avoiding miscarriages of justice was not a happy one. For example, the Home Secretary initially refused to refer back to the Court of Appeal the cases of the Maguire family and the Guildford Four, whose convictions were subsequently referred to the Court and quashed.[79]

Recommendations made by the Runciman Commission have been implemented and the Home Secretary's powers have been transferred to a newly created Criminal Cases Review Commission (CCRC)[80] which started work in April 1997.

The CCRC is an independent body with fourteen members supported by case workers and support staff with responsibility for reviewing convictions and sentences of both magistrates' courts and the Crown Court. Save in exceptional circumstances, the Commission cannot become involved unless there was an application for leave to appeal in the normal way. Reviews of convictions are to identify whether the conviction may have been unsafe, while reviews of sentence seek to identify whether a point of law was not raised in the court proceedings or new information is now available which has a bearing on sentence. In both cases the CCRC has to decide whether there is a real possibility of success. Where there is, the CCRC will refer the case back to the appropriate appeal court.[81] The Commission has no power of its own to overturn a conviction or alter a sentence.

In addition to its functions of reviewing cases, the CCRC can be asked by the Court of Appeal to investigate matters for them which will assist them to resolve a case before them.[82] Where the Home Secretary is considering advice to the Queen

---

[76] *Chard* [1984] AC 279.

[77] *Miscarriages of Justice*, Sixth Report of the Home Affairs Committee, HCP 421 (1981–82) (London: HMSO, 1982).

[78] *Report of the Royal Commission on Criminal Justice (Runciman Commission)* (London: HMSO, 1993), ch. 11, para. 5.

[79] See J. Rozenberg, 'Miscarriages of Justice' in E. Stockdale and S. Casale, *Criminal Justice under Stress* (London: Blackstone Press, 1992), p. 91.   [80] See Part II of the Criminal Appeal Act 1995.

[81] Crown Court if the original trial took place in the magistrates' court, or Court of Appeal where the original trial took place in the Crown Court.   [82] Criminal Appeal Act 1995, s. 15.

on the exercise of the Royal Prerogative of Mercy, he can seek assistance from the CCRC.[83] The CCRC can also refer cases to the Home Secretary which they consider appropriate for the exercise of the Royal Prerogative.[84]

The CCRC has no investigative staff of its own, but can appoint a police officer to conduct enquiries on its behalf.[85]

The CCRC has produced a helpful information pack which includes an application form. Green Form legal aid is available to help someone to complete the form and supply relevant information to the Commission. It is, however, likely to remain the case that those cases which attract public attention, and the interest of organisations like Liberty or JUSTICE, are most likely to succeed. In recent years television has proved to be a powerful vehicle for drawing public attention to miscarriages of justice. Only time will tell whether the CCRC can succeed where the Home Secretary failed in providing a means for identifying cases which should be referred back to the Court of Appeal. The Court of Appeal will also have to show greater willingness to overturn appeals than it has in the past.

Attorney General's References

Following an acquittal

There is one situation in which a point of law arising on an acquittal can be referred to the Court of Appeal, but the sanctity of the jury's acquittal is preserved because the proceedings in no way affect the decision to acquit. Section 36 of the Criminal Justice Act 1972 allows the Attorney General to refer a point of law arising in a trial in which the defendant was acquitted to the Court of Appeal for its opinion. The power is used sparingly and there have seldom been more than a handful of references in any one year. Even though the procedure does not prejudice acquitted defendants, they are entitled to have counsel present argument on their behalf at the public expense.

Reference on sentence

Sections 35 and 36 of the Criminal Justice Act 1988 introduced an Attorney General's reference on sentence. It is in effect a limited prosecution appeal against an unduly lenient sentence. Only the Attorney General can refer a case to the Court of Appeal for review of a sentence imposed in the Crown Court. The power is only available where the offence is triable only on indictment, or is an either way offence specified in an order made by the Home Secretary. The Home Secretary has specified certain offences against the person for this purpose,[86] as well as serious fraud

---

[83] Criminal Appeal Act 1995, s. 16(1).   [84] Ibid., s. 16(2).   [85] Ibid., ss. 19–20.
[86] Criminal Justice Act 1988 (Reviews of Sentencing) Order 1994, S.I. 1994 No. 119.

cases.[87] Where such a reference is made the Court of Appeal may quash the sentence imposed by the Crown Court and replace it with any sentence they consider appropriate up to the maximum available to the Crown Court.

Following the review by the Court of Appeal, either party may, subject to obtaining a certificate from the Court of Appeal, and with leave of either the Court of Appeal or House of Lords, further refer the case to the House of Lords for their opinion on any point of law of general public importance.

The decision to seek a referral lies with the Crown Prosecution Service, which introduces the spectre of prosecution concerning itself, at least after sentence has been imposed, with its propriety.[88] This may be more of an imaginary than real problem, since the types of sentence referred will be those where something has obviously gone wrong with the sentencing in the Crown Court. If this is the case, then the requirement of obtaining leave is unlikely to be a contentious issue. But the wider the range of cases, the more difficult this issue will be. No guidance is given in the statutory provisions as to the test to be applied by the Court of Appeal in permitting a reference to proceed.

There remains no power of review of magistrates' court sentencing. Magistrates' courts sentence those offenders charged with either way offences whose offence is of insufficient gravity to warrant trial on indictment. Yet, presumably, magistrates' courts are no less likely than Crown Court judges to pass 'rogue' sentences.

Appeal to the House of Lords from the Court of Appeal

Following a decision of the Court of Appeal, either party may appeal to the House of Lords. The pattern is similar to that for appeals following summary trial from the Divisional Court.[89] There are two preconditions for such an appeal. First, the Court of Appeal must grant a certificate that a point of law of general public importance is involved and, secondly, the Court of Appeal or House of Lords must grant leave on the basis that the appeal is one which the court ought to hear.

History tells us the reasons for these twin tests and provides the explanation for the seemingly curious situation in which it is accepted that a point of law of general public importance is involved but no leave is granted by either court. Appeal to the House of Lords in criminal cases grew out of the unsatisfactory procedure of the writ of error on the fiat of the Attorney General. The procedure was replaced by the Criminal Appeal Act 1907 which allowed the Attorney General on the application of either the defendant or the DPP to grant a certificate that the decision of the Court of Criminal Appeal involved a point of law of *exceptional* public importance and that it was desirable that a further appeal should be brought.

---

[87] Criminal Justice Act 1988 (Reviews of Sentencing) Order 1995, S.I. 1995 No. 10.

[88] See J. Fionda, *Public Prosecutors and Discretion: A Comparative Study* (Oxford: Clarendon Press, 1995).

[89] See above.

This would allow the House of Lords to consider an appeal. It seems to have been accepted that cases referred to the House should raise questions of general importance involving either statutory interpretation or the solution of particularly difficult problems of the common law. Such considerations were the basis of the grant of certificates by the Attorney General. The requirement that the point be of public importance indicates that wider considerations than the justice of the case in which the point arises are relevant. Doubts have also been expressed at the propriety of leaving the grant of such certificates in the hands of the senior law officer of the Crown.

The system was changed to its present form in 1960.[90] The test to be applied by the Court of Criminal Appeal, and subsequently by the Court of Appeal (or Divisional Court following summary trial), was made more generous; the requirement is that a point of law of *general* public importance is involved. In the course of the Parliamentary debates on the two limbs of the leave requirements, it was contemplated that, in the face of a certificate, leave of the lower court or the House of Lords might nevertheless be refused for one of three reasons: that the point is obscure and unlikely to arise again; that the point is so clear as to require no further argument; or that the point is so long established that it ought not to be disturbed. These reasons do not seem very convincing,[91] and it is difficult not to conclude that the real reason is simply to keep the conditions for a second appeal as restrictive as possible in order to avoid cases reaching the House of Lords, while retaining some flexibility about the cases that are actually heard.

Since case law seldom discusses the criteria for the grant or refusal of a certificate or leave, any suggestions as to these criteria must be speculative. It seems that it is proper for the Court of Appeal or Divisional Court to grant a certificate but to refuse leave where they accept that a point of law of general public importance is involved, but where the Court of Appeal believes that there is only one possible answer to that point, which is to be found in its judgment.[92] In such cases it will always be open to the aggrieved party to seek leave from the House itself. The Divisional Court and Court of Appeal often appear to take the view that it is for the House of Lords itself to exercise the gate-keeping function. Under the modern system it has been suggested that the case law indicates that the following criteria are relevant in considering whether the House ought to hear the appeal:[93]

- are there likely to be other cases whose outcome may be affected by the resolution of the point of law?
- does the point have considerable social implications, as in the consideration of intoxication as a defence in *DPP* v. *Majewski*?[94]
- is the law in the area unclear either because of conflicting cases or because of a dearth of cases?

---

[90] Administration of Justice Act 1960, s. 1.
[91] B. Downey, 'Administration of Justice Act 1960' (1961) 24 MLR 261.
[92] See *Henn and Darby* [1980] 2 WLR 507.
[93] A. Smith, 'Criminal Appeals in the House of Lords' (1984) 47 MLR 133.   [94] [1977] AC 443.

- does the point offer an opportunity to modify a decision of the House which has worked injustice?

It was stressed in the analysis that the House does not seem to be concerned with the notion of doing justice to the individual appellant; that is seen as the role of the first appeal.

The procedure following an Attorney General's reference following an acquittal is different; no certificate is required. The Court of Appeal merely states that the point is one which ought to be considered by the House. If it does not, the matter may be referred to the appeals committee of the House of Lords. The Court of Appeal may also of its own motion refer the point to the House of Lords. Appeals following Attorney General's sentencing references follow the normal rules.

It has been said that the purpose of criminal appeals to the House of Lords is the attainment of certainty in the criminal law.[95] The system has been criticised as not being appropriate to this purpose: 'The House of Lords does not introduce certainty into the law, and it does not treat its task of deciding questions of general importance as being part of the law reform exercise'.[96]

In a modest proposal for reform, Smith goes on to suggest that appeals from the Divisional Court should go to the Court of Appeal, but no further, and that the ability of the Crown to appeal to the House of Lords should be replaced by an extension of the Attorney General's reference to decisions of the Court of Appeal with which the prosecution took issue. Because the Attorney General would be extracting a point of principle, the House should receive *amicus curiae* argument from others concerned in the development of the law, such as the Law Commission, so that a better contribution could be made to the development of the criminal law.

The Royal Prerogative of Mercy

This quaint title refers to the Crown's prerogative powers to grant pardons and remissions of sentence.[97] There is a clear theoretical distinction between the exercise of mercy and the operation of justice. Justice is achieved through the judicial process, but there may be a variety of reasons why justice should be tempered with mercy. Grounds of compassion may demand that a convicted prisoner be granted a pardon or remission of sentence. It is also clear that the criminal justice system is not infallible and produces miscarriages of justice. A succession of *causes célèbres* has shown that miscarriages of justice have occurred with an unacceptable frequency. For these cases the prerogative of mercy provides the last safety net. It is with such cases that we are concerned here.

In appropriate cases the Home Secretary can recommend the grant of a free pardon or the remission of the whole or part of a sentence. The use of free pardons

---

[95] See A. Patterson, *The Law Lords* (London: Macmillan, 1982).
[96] A. Smith, 'Criminal Appeals in the House of Lords' (1984) 47 MLR 133, 147.
[97] A. Smith, 'The Prerogative of Mercy, The Power to Pardon and Criminal Justice' [1983] PL 398.

has been criticised as inappropriate where its purpose is to provide redress for a miscarriage of justice. The notion of a pardon suggests that there is some wrong-doing to be forgiven.[98] The Home Affairs Committee[99] recommended some change of nomenclature and in its reply the Government did accept the point and will con-sider an amendment to legislation to introduce a new label for the process when the opportunity arises. The opportunity to do this has not yet been taken despite the passing of a number of statutes dealing with criminal justice. The number of pardons granted each year is around seventy-five, of which around ten will involve those wrongfully imprisoned.

There are two possibilities of securing compensation for a wrongful convic-tion. Section 133 of the Criminal Justice Act 1988 introduces a statutory right to compensation where a person has been convicted and sentenced for a crime he or she did not commit. The circumstances in which compensation will be paid are drafted extraordinarily narrowly. The aggrieved person must apply for compensa-tion; it is not automatic. That person must:

• have been pardoned on the ground that a new or newly discovered fact shows beyond reasonable doubt that there has been a miscarriage of justice; or
• have had a conviction quashed on an appeal made out of time; or
• have had a conviction quashed following a Home Secretary's reference under section 17 of the Criminal Appeal Act 1968; and
• not have been wholly or partly responsible for the non-disclosure of the unknown fact which now establishes innocence.

The Home Secretary determines entitlement to compensation and there is no appeal on this, though the decision may be challenged by judicial review. Straight-forward cases where a conviction is quashed on initial appeal to the Court of Appeal are excluded, even though such persons may have spent considerable periods in custody awaiting trial and the outcome of their appeal. The number of cases meet-ing these very strict criteria will be very few indeed.

The earlier discretionary scheme remains in force in so far as it is not super-seded by the statutory scheme. This scheme covers those outside the statutory scheme who have spent a period in custody following a wrongful conviction or charge where the Home Secretary is satisfied that it has been caused by serious default on the part of a police officer or some other public authority, and other exceptional cases.

There remains concern over the system for awarding compensation, and earlier calls for this to be determined by an independent review body are certain to be renewed.[100]

Article 5(5) of the European Convention provides for an enforceable right to compensation for those arrested or detained in breach of the other provisions of

---

[98] For the legal effect of a pardon, see *Foster* [1984] 3 WLR 401.

[99] *Miscarriages of Justice*, Sixth Report of the Home Affairs Committee, HCP 421 (1981–82) (London: HMSO, 1982).

[100] 'Call for compensation rethink' *The Lawyer*, 30 April 1996. See also JUSTICE, *Compensation for Wrongful Imprisonment* (London: JUSTICE, 1982).

Article 5. This is one of the least developed provisions of the Convention, and so any attempt to determine whether the English provisions on compensation meet its requirements must be purely speculative. Now that the point can be taken in domestic proceedings, it may be that there will be some further development of the content of this provision of the Convention.

Concluding Comment

This chapter has covered such a diverse range of procedures that the drawing of coherent conclusions on criminal appeals is very difficult. The most striking features of the system are the great difference between the procedures following summary trial, where the appeal by way of re-hearing has been accepted and causes few problems, and those following trial on indictment, which are narrow and technical. At present the procedures are least satisfactory where they need to be most satisfactory, that is, where the offences are more serious and consequently the penalties are more severe. The Court of Appeal does not achieve success either in producing certainty in the criminal law, nor does it ensure that convictions are based on accepted principles of due process and that doubtful convictions are properly reviewed. The pressing need for further development of the appellate process in criminal cases was recognised by the Runciman Commission and legislative changes have been made, but they are in the nature of tinkering and do not produce a more coherent system. More radical reform may be needed to ensure that the objectives of justice, due process and consistency of decision-making are better achieved.

PART 3

THE CIVIL PROCESS

10

UNDERSTANDING THE CIVIL PROCESS

The Context of Litigation

The object of civil proceedings will usually be the determination of the rights and duties of individuals or companies as between each other. Examples are the determination of rights arising under contracts, of obligations to pay damages for torts, of rights of property and succession and of questions of status, such as divorce, adoption and custody of children. Most of these rights are of a private nature, but there is also a body of civil law of a public nature, such as, for example, questions concerning taxation, immigration and compulsory purchase orders. In most civil proceedings the person instituting the proceedings will be the plaintiff who sues, or brings an action against, a defendant. The plaintiff will usually be seeking damages (monetary compensation) but may also ask for an injunction (an order prohibiting the defendant from committing or continuing to commit some wrongful act). The plaintiff usually has the burden of proof which is said to be on the balance of probabilities; this means that the plaintiff must show that it is more probable than not that what is alleged is true.

The focus of much of the material written in the area of civil procedure conceals an important aspect of the resolution of civil claims: most are settled even before the start of proceedings. This aspect of the negotiation of settlements by the parties either without recourse to the courts at all or without the resolution of the dispute by the trial process means that the various steps in civil procedure need to be assessed not only to determine their effectiveness in ensuring a full and fair trial, but also to determine whether they give one party an unfair advantage in the process of negotiation that so frequently leads to a pre-trial settlement.

Civil Justice Policy and Dispute Resolution

Just as there is no single government department responsible for criminal justice policy,[1] so too there is no single government department responsible for civil

---

[1] See Ch. 3.

justice policy, though the role of the Lord Chancellor's Department dominates to a greater extent than in the case of criminal justice policy. Since early 1998 a Civil Justice Council, composed of judges, practitioners, academics and consumer interests, has existed which has responsibility for promoting the needs of civil justice and of keeping under review the extent to which the system serves the needs of all users.

Civil justice policy has for many years been viewed from a court-centred perspective. This book, in focusing upon the public institutions of the legal system, in one sense, continues that tradition. However, it is worth stepping back to look at the wider picture in seeking to understand the civil process. Law can be said to have twin objectives: to solve conflicts and to encourage conformity to legal rules.[2] The civil process consists not only of the substantive rules but also of the procedural rules by which those rules become a reality in social interaction. This book is essentially concerned with the mechanisms by which substantive rules are given effect.

Comparatively little is known about what people want of a system for resolving disputes: what are their priorities for the system. A large-scale survey conducted by the National Consumer Council gives some clues to this.[3] Despite surveying 8,358 members of the public aged sixteen and over, some of the groups who had experienced certain aspects of the system were small and care should be taken in drawing too sweeping conclusions from their experiences. The survey concluded that around five million people had been involved in a civil dispute in the three years prior to the date of the interview. Damage to cars was the highest single category followed by divorce, personal injury, and unpaid debt. Other significant categories were faulty goods, neighbour disputes, disputes relating to work, and dealing with public authorities. Four out of every five people had sought some outside help in dealing with the dispute. Fear of cost did not feature highly as a reason for a person handling a dispute without specialist help. Experiences of disputes were accompanied by feelings of inequality between the parties, with most parties taking the view that the other side was better equipped to handle the dispute. Interestingly, those who had resolved their disputes after a full hearing felt less disadvantage than those whose disputes had settled after the start of legal proceedings but before trial. The civil justice system was seen as dated, capable of manipulation, slow and complex. Many who had raised a dispute claimed not to have done so for financial reasons, but to prevent the same thing happening again to themselves or others. Only one in five said that money compensation was the prime motivation. Resolution of disputes away from the courts was seen as a popular option. Three in four who had used the courts would have preferred some form of alternative dispute resolution. Over half selected mediation as their preferred option. One in four preferred arbitration. The clear message from these respondents was that being listened to in an informal setting was more important than an adversarial trial leading to a formal adjudication.

---

[2] W. Aubert, 'Courts and Conflict Resolution' (1967) 11 *Journal of Conflict Resolution* 40.

[3] National Consumer Council, *Seeking Civil Justice: A Survey of People's Needs and Experiences* (London: National Consumer Council, 1995).

The nearest the English system comes to a formal statement of the objectives of the civil process is the statement of objectives set out by Lord Woolf in his reports to the Lord Chancellor on the civil justice system in England and Wales.[4] Lord Woolf took access to justice as his guiding aim and defined a number of principles which he regarded as essential to this aim; he said that the system should:

(a) be *just* in the results it delivers;
(b) be *fair* in the way it treats litigants;
(c) offer appropriate procedures at a reasonable *cost*;
(d) deal with cases with reasonable *speed*;
(e) be *understandable* to those who use it;
(f) be *responsive* to the needs of those who use it;
(g) provide as much *certainty* as the nature of particular cases allows; and
(h) be *effective*: adequately resourced and organised.[5]

Such principles are helpful but we need first to explore further the values inherent in the underlying aim of securing access to justice.

Access to Justice

Though the notion of access to the courts for the redress of grievances has been a feature of the English legal system at least since Magna Carta, it is probably only this century that attention has moved from the existence of a formal right to use the courts in order to secure claimed rights to questioning whether that formal right was for many a real right. The distinction between the formal existence of the right and its reality focused on the availability of lawyers to assist the poor and those of modest means. This led in turn to questioning other aspects of the performance of the courts and other institutions involved in the redress of grievances. More recently the distinction between the substance of the right and the means for securing it have been challenged. Much of this thinking is summarised in a four volume report of a research study into access to justice.[6] The objectives of access to justice are to examine the system by which people seek 'to vindicate their rights and/or resolve their disputes under the general auspices of the state'. The system should 'be equally accessible to all' and 'lead to results that are individually and socially just'.[7] The concerns summarised by the phrase 'access to justice' appeared to be a worldwide phenomenon.

---

[4] Lord Woolf M. R., *Interim Report to the Lord Chancellor on the Civil Justice System in England and Wales* (London: HMSO, 1995) (cited in this chapter as 'Interim Report'); and Lord Woolf M. R., *Final Report to the Lord Chancellor on the Civil Justice System in England and Wales* (London: HMSO, 1996) (cited in this chapter as 'Final Report'). [5] Final Report, p. 1.
[6] M. Cappelletti (ed.), *Access to Justice*, 4 vols. (Alphen aan den Rijn: Sijthoff and Noordhoff, 1978).
[7] M. Cappelletti and B. Garth (eds.), *Access to Justice. Volume I: A World Survey* (Alphen aan den Rijn: Sijthoff and Noordhoff, 1978), Book I, p. 6.

Another source for some basic values in the civil process may be found in Article 6 of the European Convention on Human Rights, which provides for a right to a fair trial. The relevant words of the Article are:

In the determination of his civil rights and obligations . . . everyone is entitled to a fair and public hearing within a reasonable time by an independent and impartial tribunal established by law. Judgment shall be pronounced publicly.

From these words the European Commission of Human Rights and the European Court of Human Rights have fashioned a number of qualities required for a fair hearing.[8] There must be a proper examination of the submissions, arguments and evidence adduced by the parties,[9] which must take place in a process under which each side is presented with a reasonable opportunity to present their case on broadly equal terms to their opponent.[10] The process of consideration must be judicial which requires a degree of adversarial process.[11] The outcome must be a reasoned decision.[12] Appearance in person may not always be required, but there are certain types of case where the requirements of a fair trial could not be met without an entitlement to appear in person. The Court has extended the words of Article 6 to embrace a right of access to a court for a fair trial, which will include a right to assistance where the procedure is such that effective use of the procedure cannot otherwise be made.[13] The European Convention standards apply only to public authorities or to activities which the Government regulates. It follows that private processes adopted by parties to disputes to settle their differences do not need to display the characteristics required by Article 6 of the Convention.

Using these standards, it is easy to identify a number of potential barriers to access to justice: cost, delay, complexity, inequality between the parties, and a lack of certainty as to outcome and cost.

Experiences of the Civil Justice System

In 1995 the National Consumer Council sought to measure the volume of civil disputes and people's responses to them.[14] Some 8,358 members of the public over the age of sixteen were chosen at random from the electoral registers; the selection

---

[8] See also Ch. 2.

[9] *Kraska* v. *Switzerland*, judgment of 19 April 1993, Series A, No. 254-B; (1994) 18 EHRR 188, para. 30 of judgment.

[10] There is said to be a requirement of 'equality of arms', the nearest English translation of the French concept of *egalité des armes*. See *Dombo Beheer BV* v. *The Netherlands*, judgment of 27 October 1993, Series A, No. 274-A; (1994) 18 EHRR 213, para. 33 of the judgment.

[11] *Ruiz-Mateos* v. *Spain*, judgment of 23 June 1993, Series A, No. 262; (1993) 16 EHRR 505, para. 63 of the judgment. Note that the reference to adversarial processes does not require an adversarial process as distinct from an inquisitorial process.

[12] *Van de Hurk* v. *The Netherlands*, judgment of 19 April 1994, Series A, No. 288, para. 61 of the judgment.

[13] See *Golder* v. *United Kingdom*, judgment of 21 February 1975, Series A, No. 18; (1979–80) 1 EHRR 524; and *Airey* v. *Ireland*, judgment of 9 October 1979, Series A, No. 32; (1979–80) 2 EHRR 305.

[14] National Consumer Council, *Seeking Civil Justice: A Survey of People's Needs and Experiences* (London: National Consumer Council, 1995).

adjusted by a rolling multi-stage probability sampling technique in order to ensure that the profile represented the adult population of England and Wales. These individuals were then asked about their involvement in civil disputes in the previous three years.

Some thirteen different types of dispute were put to them: damage to a vehicle, divorce, personal injury, unpaid debt, faulty goods, neighbour problems, problems at work, problems with local or central government, faulty services, custody of and access to children, landlord and tenant problems, wills and estates, and repossession of home. It is perhaps unfortunate that social security benefits was not a category; whether respondents with problems with their benefits would view this as a dispute with a government agency might be doubted. Some 1,019 respondents had experience of such a problem: three quarters of them as the person initiating the complaint and one quarter of them as the person against whom the complaint was made. Extrapolating this figure to the population as whole suggest that around five million people would have been involved in a civil dispute within the previous three years.

The rest of the enquiry focused on the views of the 1,109 respondents with experience of a civil dispute. In some cases, the numbers reporting particular experiences were so small that care should be taken in forming conclusions based on their experiences.

Overall, it did not appear that age, gender, income or region affected the likelihood of being involved in a dispute. The most commonly met disputes initiated by respondents concerned damage to a vehicle, personal injury, divorce and debt. The most commonly met disputes initiated against respondents were repossession of their home, debt, custody or access to children, divorce, and neighbour disputes. Three-quarters of those in the sample had taken some sort of expert advice in connection with the dispute. A wide range of advisers was used, but one in five used a solicitor under legal aid, one in five a solicitor on a fee-paying basis, and one in five used a Citizens Advice Bureau. One in eight sought advice from an insurance company, most often in relation to a road traffic accident. The position is summarised in more detail in Figure 10.1. These figures show the importance both of legal advice from solicitors and of more general advice from Citizens Advice Bureaux. The incidence of problems in which no advice was sought also shows significant variations which may reflect the general perception both of the ability of advisers to assist and of the ability of individuals to deal with problems without expert advice. The most commonly expressed views for not seeking advice were a perception that the problem could be handled without expert advice and the dispute was not important enough to warrant such advice.

Where disputes had been resolved by the time of the survey, just over half had been resolved within five months, one-fifth in about a year; about one in four took more than a year. Problems involving faulty goods or services and unpaid debt settled quickest, while personal injury claims were the slowest to settle.

Two out of every three disputes were resolved without court or tribunal proceedings proving to be necessary. One in four were resolved following a court or

Figure 10.1. **Where people went for help, by type of dispute**＊

Problem	Legal aid	Solicitor (fees)	CAB	Insurance co.	None
Custody/access to children	62%	20%	25%	3%	8%
Divorce	51%	39%	18%	2%	10%
Repossession of home	40%	9%	35%	—	13%
Personal injury	37%	26%	14%	4%	4%
Will/estate	34%	44%	24%	3%	7%
Landlord/tenant	18%	30%	42%	—	15%
Unpaid debt	17%	17%	35%	10%	31%
Problem at work	15%	19%	26%	—	19%
Local/central government	14%	9%	23%	1%	34%
Faulty services	12%	13%	12%	4%	50%
Neighbour disputes	8%	18%	15%	—	27%
Damage to vehicle	6%	18%	10%	55%	13%
Faulty goods	4%	5%	16%	2%	44%

＊Source: National Consumer Council, *Seeking Civil Justice: A Survey of People's Needs and Experiences* (London: National Consumer Council, 1995). Some respondents used more than one type of advice.

tribunal decision, and a further one in eight were resolved after proceedings had been started but before any formal decision; in other words they settled before a hearing. Divorce, custody of and access to children, and home repossession cases were most likely to be settled by court decision, but this is unsurprising, since a court decision is necessary to obtain a divorce, and if children are involved the court will normally make decisions on custody and access even where this simply reflects an existing agreement between the parents. Disputes about faulty goods and services hardly ever needed court proceedings for their resolution. Around half personal injury cases were resolved without the need for court proceedings to have begun.

A series of questions addressed perceptions of the process of dispute settlement. Under a half thought there was a balance of advantage between the parties; most people thought the other side was in a stronger position than them. The dominant purpose in pursuing the dispute in court was to secure financial compensation.[15] However, one in four said that their objective was to prevent the incident which had triggered the dispute happening again.

Concerns were expressed about the legal help provided; only four in ten were quite or very satisfied, and one in five was dissatisfied with this. One in three respondents would have preferred their dispute to have been settled in some other way than it was, but one in two was satisfied with the settlement method. Of those expressing a preference for an alternative, one in two elected for mediation,[16] one in four chose arbitration,[17] and one in twelve chose full trial.

[15] Except in divorce or custody and access disputes; this question was not asked of those identifying this type of civil dispute as the one in which they were involved.

[16] Described in the questionnaire as sitting round the table with an expert to help them reach agreement themselves.

[17] Described in the questionnaire as sitting round a table with an expert to decide the dispute for them.

A final section sought people's views on the legal system. The results show that confidence in the legal system as a method of dispute resolution is not high. Three in four thought the legal system was too slow, easy to twist if you know the rules, too complicated, out-dated, and off-putting to ordinary people. Only one in four expressed positive views about the civil justice system, and only one in eight found it easy to understand. Interestingly, those who had sought to resolve their legal disputes without expert help were not only most keen on alternative dispute resolution which dispensed with the need for lawyers, but were also most likely to have a positive view of the civil justice system.

Too much can be made of surveys such as this. But the overall message is clear: the civil justice system is perceived as slow, complex and overwhelming. In many areas the citizen turns to the Citizens Advice Bureau for help rather than to lawyers, and in many cases a significant number do not seek any expert advice in seeking to resolve a problem. Yet twice as many disputes settle without the intervention of the courts or a tribunal than are processed through the formal institutions.

The Characteristics of English Civil Procedure

Rules of civil procedure

The English system of civil procedure is based upon the adversary principle: a series of statements of fact are put forward by one party to be attacked by the opposing party.[18] The judge acts principally as umpire or referee and leaves it to the parties to put the case before him. The rules of civil procedure which govern the handling of cases are technical, complex and detailed. They are designed to regulate the conduct of the parties and their advocates in an adversary trial. They can be found in the large volumes entitled *The Supreme Court Practice* (known among lawyers as 'the White Book') and *The County Court Practice* (known among lawyers as 'the Green Book'). This mass of rules really has three objectives. The first objective is to ensure that the facts on which a claim is based are accurately found and appropriately arranged so that the issues between the parties can be identified. The second is to ensure that the correct and appropriate rule of law is found and applied, and the third objective is to ensure that the remedy or remedies prescribed by that rule of law can be adequately enforced. It is not necessary to dwell on the detail of the rules of procedure, since a broad outline of the process in actions in personal injuries cases will serve for our enquiry. Whether the rules actually achieve their objectives remains to be assessed, but there has been a succession of calls over the last thirty years for the redrafting of the rules in order to make High Court practice and procedure quicker, simpler and cheaper.[19] Few of the recommendations

---

[18] See J. Jacob, *The Fabric of English Civil Justice* (London: Stevens, 1987).

[19] *Final Report of the Committee on Supreme Court Practice and Procedure (Evershed Committee)* (London: HMSO, 1953, Cmd. 8878); *Report of the Committee on Personal Injuries Litigation (Winn Committee)*

made by the early working parties and committees have been implemented, but the recommendations of the Civil Justice Review heralded a shift of emphasis and those of Lord Woolf will transform the culture of civil litigation by shifting the focus of case management from the parties to the courts. Changing cultures is, of course, one of the hardest objectives to achieve, and it remains to be seen whether the Woolf reforms can be converted into new practice and procedure in the handling of civil claims.

Discouraging litigation

In England and Wales, use of the courts to resolve disputes is seen very much as a matter of last resort. Even when proceedings have been started, there are usually procedures which encourage the parties to settle without the need for a court hearing. So under the rules governing litigation in the county courts and the High Court, it is possible to conduct correspondence without this being seen as an admission of liability. Any correspondence marked 'without prejudice' cannot be presented in evidence in court without the privilege attaching to such communications being lifted. This enables parties to discuss in a full and frank manner how the case might be settled by negotiation. Other devices such as payment into court encourage the settlement of cases without formal adjudication. Under this procedure, a defendant can pay a sum of money into court in full and final settlement of the claim. The defendant then has to decide whether to accept that sum or to continue to fight the case. Defendants who refuse the money paid in run the risk that, if the judge at trial awards a lesser sum,[20] the defendant will recover no costs from the date of the payment into court and will instead be liable for the other side's costs from that point. Since costs escalate dramatically nearer the trial, this can be a significant additional burden for defendants.

Except in the case of minors, the court does not normally concern itself with the fairness of any settlement.

The position in tribunals is similar. In the employment tribunals the filing of an originating application triggers a formal process of conciliation in order to seek to secure a conciliated settlement of the dispute.[21] In social security claims, the filing of an appeal triggers a formal review of the adjudication officer's decision in order to determine whether the decision appealed against is correct.[22]

(London: HMSO, 1968, Cmnd. 369); JUSTICE, *Going to Law: A Critique of English Civil Procedure* (London: JUSTICE, 1974); *Report of the Royal Commission on Civil Liability and Compensation for Personal Injury (Pearson Commission)* (London: HMSO, 1978, Cmnd. 7054); *Report of the Personal Injuries Litigation Procedure Working Party (Cantley Working Party)* (London: HMSO, 1979, Cmnd. 7476); *Civil Justice Review: Report of the Review Body on Civil Justice* (London: HMSO, 1988, Cm. 394); Lord Woolf M. R., *Interim Report to the Lord Chancellor on the Civil Justice System in England and Wales* (London: HMSO, 1995); and Lord Woolf M. R., *Final Report to the Lord Chancellor on the Civil Justice System in England and Wales* (London: HMSO, 1996).

[20] The trial judge will not know of the payment into court.   [21] See Ch. 15.   [22] See Ch. 14.

An adversarial procedure

Litigation has largely been run by the parties, with minimal supervision and direction from the courts. It will be for each side to determine how it is to run its case and which witnesses and evidence will be presented at any trial. This places a premium on the expertise of the parties' lawyers. The use of procedure can be a matter of seeking to secure a tactical or strategic advantage rather than of ensuring equality of arms and the presentation of all relevant matter to the court. The process of pleadings[23] has been described in one report by the use of a colourful military analogy:

Pleading therefore resembles nothing so much as naval warfare before the advent of radar, when each side made blind forays into the sea area of the other, while giving away as little as possible about the disposition of his own forces.[24]

Adversarial procedures place the onus on plaintiffs to establish the substance of their claims on the balance of probabilities. Though procedures and orders are available to plaintiffs to secure evidence and to gain access to certain types of information, the starting point is that they are alone responsible for the construction of their cases. Even in tribunals where the formal burden of proof does not lie so heavily on the person initiating the procedure, it frequently remains for that party to put together their claim. So applicants in the employment tribunals claiming to have been unfairly dismissed file an originating application in an unfair dismissal claim,[25] which has similarities to pleadings in the county courts or the High Court, and have to meet a certain threshold of complaint before the burden shifts to the respondent to show the reason for dismissal. Similarly in social security claims, the person appealing must state the grounds of the appeal, show their entitlement to any benefit claimed, and must bring some evidence and argument to support that claim. The tribunal will seldom initiate enquiries of its own.[26]

The role of the judge in a court is largely to act as umpire between the two sides in the presentation of evidence ensuring that the rules of procedure are observed. In the tribunals, a more interventionist role may be adopted than in the courts. In the latter, excessive judicial intervention could be a ground of appeal.[27] When the law is discussed, there is greater interchange between judge and lawyers, but the judges seldom conduct their own research and rely on the legal arguments presented by the parties. Decision-makers in tribunals will, however, frequently seek to elicit evidence from those appealing and rely upon their knowledge of the law when hearing cases where the parties are unrepresented, and so cannot be expected to present legal argument.

---

[23] The exchange between the parties of a formal statement of its case by each side.
[24] JUSTICE, *Going to Law. A Critique of English Civil Procedure* (London: JUSTICE, 1974), para. 50.
[25] See Ch. 15.   [26] See Ch. 14.   [27] As in *Jones* v. *National Coal Board* [1957] 2 QB 55.

Oral hearings

The typical trial or hearing in English law is the culminating event in a process in which there will be a set of papers defining the essential issue between the parties. In the county courts and the High Court, this will be the pleadings in the case. In employment tribunals, it will be the originating application and notice of response. In the social security tribunals, it will be the letter of appeal and adjudication officer's written submission. But in most cases,[28] it is the trial or hearing which is crucial. That will be an oral hearing, which is generally open to the public. Despite the age of the photocopier, the oral presentation of the evidence and argument are essential features of most procedures. It has been described as a 'deeply ingrained habit of the English legal process'.[29] The result is that much written material is read out in court. The purpose is to ensure that the trial is a single culminating event; the material which is read out is immediately available to all parties.[30] Jacob says:

> The advantage of orality is that it fosters the 'principle of immediacy', and together orality and immediacy have the effect of enabling the Court to conduct the kind of direct, immediate and dialectical investigation into the relevant facts and the applicable law and by this process of 'cross-fertilisation', they promote the ascertainment of the truth and the production of the correct decision.[31]

The disadvantage is that reading aloud written documents slows the trial, and there has in recent years been an increase in the use of written summaries of, for example, arguments in appeals. And, of course, the more written material, the more time which must be allowed for judicial preparation in readiness for trial.

Special jurisdictions and judges

The civil process is populated by a multiplicity of courts and tribunals. The English system has no 'general' civil court; it will be for the person bringing proceedings to bring them before the correct court or tribunal. Failure to do so can be costly both in financial terms and in delay. If a time limit has passed, it may be fatal to the claim. The purpose of narrowing the range of work done by particular institutions is to foster expert knowledge of subject matter and to enable procedure to reflect the nature of the claim. It is trite to say that litigation between two major corporations over a complex commercial matter should not be the same process as an individual citizen making a claim about a defective car or home computer system. Different processes can go some way to redressing the imbalance between the parties. Social security tribunals seek to accommodate the unrepresented appellant by their informal procedures, though it is still the case that the represented do better than the unrepresented.[32]

---

[28] Paper hearings have been introduced in the social security tribunals if the appellant does not ask for an oral hearing: see Ch. 14.

[29] J. Jacob, *The Fabric of English Civil Justice* (London: Stevens, 1987), p. 19.

[30] And to the public.   [31] Jacob, *supra* n. 29, p. 20.   [32] See Ch. 14.

Specialisation also impacts upon the judiciary of the civil justice system. The county court is served by Circuit judges, assisted by district judges, while the High Court is served by puisne judges. The process of selection and appointment is very similar to that for judges in criminal courts described in Chapter 4. The tribunal judiciary is selected in a similar manner. Applications are sought, initially for a part-time appointment, and interviews take place in the Lord Chancellor's Department. Appointment to a full-time tribunal post is normally only made from among those who have sat on a part-time basis for two years or more. Tribunal personnel tend to become specialists because of the relatively narrow range of the jurisdiction of the tribunal on which they sit.

The absence of contested cases

Just as the not guilty plea constitutes a small part of the operation of the criminal process, so too the contested civil case is very much a minority among civil cases. The fact that most cases settle affects the way in which they are prepared, the expectations of the parties and the demarcation between pre-trial and trial processes.

Though fewer cases settle as a proportion of total caseloads, the situation is similar in tribunals. Conciliation in employment tribunals and review of initial decisions in the social security jurisdiction reduce the number of cases which require adjudication.

Barriers to the Civil Process

Costs and legal assistance

Though there are no fees charged for bringing cases before tribunals, there are fees for bringing cases before the courts. However, these fees are predictable and fixed; they are paid at the start of the process. A current debate is the extent to which they should reflect the full cost of using the civil courts.[33] The Lord Chancellor announced in July 1997 that the underlying principle was to recover the full cost of providing the civil courts less the amount of any exemptions and remissions. Those in receipt of income support, family credit, disability working allowance, and income-based jobseeker's allowance are exempt from payment of court fees. Note that being in receipt of legal aid does not automatically exempt a litigant from the payment of fees. Over the years, more and more of the costs of running the courts in the civil justice system have been included in the running costs which it is sought to cover by the charging of fees. The Discussion Paper states that a fee of £900 in

---

[33] See Lord Chancellor's Department, *Access to Justice—Civil Fees*, A Discussion Paper (London: Lord Chancellor's Department, 1998).

the county courts and £1,800 in the High Court would be needed to reflect the true cost of a court hearing. Since many cases do not result in a hearing, the question arises whether the fee should be charged in one fell swoop on the initiation of the process, or whether a pay-as-you-go system should be introduced depending upon the actual services of the courts the litigation involves. For the future, the court fee or fees payable are likely to increase and so become a more significant factor in determining whether the courts are used.

Of much greater significance at present is the issue of paying for the help of a lawyer, and a potential liability in some cases to pay the other side's costs if you lose. In some cases, it is virtually impossible to proceed without some sort of legal assistance. In other cases, attempts have been made to modify the procedure to accommodate those arguing their own cases. None of these attempts has been wholly successful. Though the social security tribunals rightly pride themselves on their informality and thousands of unrepresented appellants successfully present their own appeals, the figures show that those who attend hearings with a skilled representative have a significantly greater chance of success.[34]

Very few would contemplate litigation in the county courts or the High Court (other than in the small claims jurisdiction)[35] without the assistance of a lawyer. It is simply too complex and too daunting; few have the confidence and forensic skills to tackle the task with any hope of success. However, lawyers are expensive and not every litigant is wealthy enough to pursue the case from their own resources. For those who cannot afford a lawyer, the legal aid scheme has been of huge importance, though for most litigants with money claims that is now likely to be replaced by conditional fee arrangements.[36]

The system of costs also acts as a disincentive to embarking upon action in court. Under the English rules on costs, the losing party is normally required to pay the legal costs of the winning party. So someone embarking on litigation takes a huge risk. If they win, they can recover most of their legal costs from the other side, but if they lose, they are likely to have to pay both their own legal costs and the legal costs of their opponent. It is virtually impossible to contain costs in litigation, since so much will depend on the response of the other side, on how your own legal advisers run the case, and whether there is an appeal.

There is much less risk in tribunals. Indeed there is none in the social security tribunals, though no legal aid is available for representation in these tribunals and so the barrier here is getting access to a representative willing to take on the case if the appellant does not feel confident enough to argue the case without a representative. In the employment tribunals, applicants can be put at risk over costs if they persist with their case after a tribunal has concluded that the claim has no reasonable prospect of success.[37] So the impact of costs pervades the civil process.

---

[34] H. Genn and Y. Genn, *The Effectiveness of Representation at Tribunals* (London: Lord Chancellor's Department, 1989).   [35] See Ch. 13.
[36] See Ch. 17.   [37] See Ch. 15.

Delay

The European Convention on Human Rights entitles litigants to judgment 'within a reasonable time'. English courts rarely fall foul of this provision,[38] but cases can take many years to be resolved and for those who have not been involved in litigation or been close to it, it is hard to imagine the anxiety that it can generate. Delay can have an insidious effect on litigation; the memories of witnesses invariably become less clear as time passes. Indeed some witnesses might have disappeared and cannot be traced. Controls through time limits in procedural rules of the courts are said to be widely ignored.[39] Above all, delay can keep a litigant who desperately needs compensation, for example, for a personal injury, away from that compensation for an unreasonable period.

Delay seems to affect both the work of the courts and of tribunals.[40]

Complexity

Complexity arises both from procedure and substance. The Woolf Report concludes that both give rise to difficulties.[41] Court structure can also be complex, with uncertainties arising as to the correct forum for the litigation. The remaining distinctions between county court procedure and High Court procedure are seen to be unhelpful.

An access to justice approach requires that the procedures are as simple as is consistent with the nature of the dispute placed before the court or tribunal. Procedure should be the servant of substance and not in command of it. Those rules should be effective and not be capable of being used strategically by one side against the other.

The Woolf Report

The Woolf Report is the latest of many attempts to tackle the perceived problems of the civil process. Criticisms of the civil process had been voiced by the Royal Commission on Legal Services in 1979.[42] In response, the Government of the day announced that the Lord Chancellor would undertake 'a complete and systematic review of civil procedure' in order to identify causes of delay and inconvenience and to restructure the system so as to 'achieve the most expeditious and convenient

---

[38] But see *Robins* v. *United Kingdom*, judgment of 23 September 1997, in which the United Kingdom was held to be in violation of Article 6 when it took the county court and Court of Appeal over four years to resolve a straightforward question of costs.   [39] Interim Report, *supra* n. 4, ch. 3, paras. 6–7.

[40] See Chs. 14 and 15.   [41] Interim Report, *supra* n. 4, ch. 3, para. 44.

[42] *Final Report of the Royal Commission on Legal Services (Benson Commission)* (London: HMSO, 1979, Cmnd. 7648), para. 43.3.

disposal of business'.[43] In February 1985 the Review Body on Civil Justice was established with the objectives of improving the machinery of civil justice in England and Wales by means of reforms in jurisdiction, procedure and court administration and, in particular, of reducing delay, cost and complexity. The Review Body on Civil Justice reported in June 1988.[44] But Lord Woolf's Interim and Final Reports make clear that its remedies have not been effective, though the Civil Justice Review did pave the way for greater integration of county court and High Court procedures.

The implementation of the recommendations of the Woolf Report will generate a fundamentally different landscape of civil litigation.[45] A new procedural code will ensure that cases are dealt with justly. Lord Woolf defines ten key features for the new world of civil litigation.[46]

(1) Litigation will be avoided wherever possible. This will be achieved by encouraging the use of alternative dispute resolution (ADR)[47] and by the use of protocols in particular types of cases designed to promote settlement. Costs will continue to be used to encourage settlement.

(2) Litigation will be less adversarial and more co-operative by the introduction of a requirement for greater openness and co-operation between the parties in pre-litigation protocols. The courts will adopt a more hands-on approach to case management. Failure to co-operate might result in the use of costs sanctions. A new approach will be adopted to expert evidence.

(3) Litigation will be less complex with a single set of court rules for the county courts and the High Court. Special rules for particular types of case will be avoided wherever possible. A single method of starting proceedings will be introduced, and there will be less focus on the technical nature of documents prepared by the parties. Court intervention will ensure that cases settle more quickly. There is to be a unified code of appeals.

(4) The time scale will be shorter and more certain. This will be achieved by insistence on keeping to a timetable set and monitored by the court. A fast track procedure is to be established for some cases.

(5) The cost of litigation will be more affordable, more predictable, and more proportionate to the value and complexity of individual cases. For fast-track cases, fixed costs will be introduced. A more rigorous approach will be adopted to the determination of costs to be awarded designed to bring down costs in all cases.

(6) Parties of limited financial means will be able to conduct litigation on a more equal footing. More help will be available from advice agencies and the courts. Court intervention will make it harder for the wealthier party to use procedure to gain an advantage. This provision has been overtaken

---

[43] *The Government Response to the Report of the Royal Commission on Legal Services* (London: HMSO, 1983, Cmnd. 9077).

[44] *Civil Justice Review: Report of the Review Body on Civil Justice* (London: HMSO, 1988, Cm. 394).

[45] Final Report, *supra* n. 4, p. 4.

[46] See generally Final Report, *supra* n. 4. The features are summarised in Section I of the Final Report.

[47] See below.

somewhat by the reduction in the scope of the legal aid scheme effective from some time in 1999.

(7) There will be clear lines of judicial and administrative responsibility for the civil justice system. A Head of Civil Justice for England and Wales will have responsibilities in this area.

(8) The structure of the courts and the deployment of judges will be designed to meet the needs of litigants.

(9) Judges will be deployed effectively so that they can manage litigation in accordance with the new rules and protocols.

(10) The civil justice system will be responsive to the needs of litigants. More advice and assistance will be provided through court-based or duty advice and assistance schemes. Better leaflets will be available and information technology will be used. Ongoing monitoring and research on litigants' needs is promised.

The Woolf Report also recommended the establishment of a Civil Justice Council. This has already been implemented.[48] This advisory body consists of judges, lawyers, civil servants connected with the administration of the courts, those with experience in and knowledge of consumer affairs, people from the lay advice sector, and 'persons able to represent the interests of particular kinds of litigants (for example, businesses or employees)'.[49] The Civil Justice Council is charged with keeping the civil justice system under review, considering how to make it more accessible, fair and efficient, advising the Lord Chancellor and the judiciary on the development of the civil justice system, making proposals for change in the civil justice system, and making proposals for research. A Head of Civil Justice has also been appointed.[50]

Alternative Dispute Resolution

Much is made of the contribution of ADR to improving the operation of the civil process. But what constitutes ADR is not well defined. Lord Woolf does not provide a generic definition of ADR in his reports. In the Interim Report, he includes a chapter entitled 'Alternative Approaches to Dispensing Justice'[51] which lists a number of forms of ADR. These include traditional arbitration, the work of tribunals, mini-trials, ombudsmen and mediation. The Lord Chancellor's Department has also provided a booklet for the public entitled *Resolving Disputes without Going to Court.*

It seems that there is no standard definition of what constitutes ADR. Many commentators note that ADR seems to be a phenomenon of the 1980s as a response

---

[48] Civil Procedure Act 1997, s. 6.   [49] Ibid., s. 6(2)(f).
[50] Sir Richard Scott, Vice-Chancellor.   [51] Interim Report, *supra* n. 4, ch. 18.

to an increase in litigation which has threatened to overwhelm legal systems.[52] Two American writers offer a helpful working definition of ADR as:

a set of practices and techniques that aim (1) to permit legal disputes to be resolved outside the courts for the benefit of all disputants; (2) to reduce the cost of conventional litigation and the delays to which it is ordinarily subject; or (3) to prevent legal disputes that would otherwise likely be brought to the courts.[53]

Viewed in this way, it is clear that ADR is not an entirely novel concept; it is generally a process which sits alongside 'official' methods of dispute resolution and relies upon this relationship for its effectiveness. So in its most traditional form, arbitration has been a favoured alternative to litigation because it avoids a consequence of adjudication that the parties perceive to be a disadvantage to them. Perhaps they do not wish to air their dispute in public, or perhaps they wish to resolve the matter giving priority to possible future relationships over a formal legal position. Perhaps they simply want to have greater control over the process than adjudication ultimately permits. There remain risks in ADR. It may substitute convenience for judgment; in other words is may 'delegalise' dispute settlement. There can be a benefit in having an official court-sanctioned result to a dispute. Fiss certainly argues that negotiated settlements may be more susceptible to differences in the bargaining position of the parties than a process of adjudication.[54] Measuring the success—even defining the criteria by which success is measured—of ADR is not easy. The general message of research in the USA suggests that ADR tends to be popular, that costs can be reduced but not by much, and that decisions can be made more speedily. Very significantly, compliance with the outcome seems high.[55] Because of this, ADR seldom has to worry about appellate procedures, since the essence of the selected process is often the consent of both parties.

An important issue is resourcing: who should pay for ADR? If it is a private alternative to the 'official system', then there is clearly an argument that those who choose to use ADR should meet its costs. On the other hand, it is clear that Lord Woolf includes among his examples of ADR, 'official' alternatives to the 'ordinary' courts, such as administrative tribunals, though he concedes that they deal with issues over which courts do not have jurisdiction and so are not alternatives in the true sense. Where the institutions are public and not optional, there is less of a case for passing on the full costs of using them to their users. It also remains the case that for certain matters, resort to the courts is compulsory. Examples are securing a divorce or obtaining authority for the administration of the estate of someone who has died.

---

[52] See M. Freeman (ed.), *Alternative Dispute Resolution* (Aldershot, Dartmouth, 1995). See also H. Brown and A. Marriott, *ADR: Principles and Practice* (London: Sweet & Maxwell, 1993).

[53] J. Lieberman and J. Henry, 'Lessons from the Alternative Dispute Resolution Movement' (1986) 53 Univ. of Chicago L Rev. 424, 425.

[54] O. Fiss, 'Against Settlement' (1984) 93 Yale LJ 1073.

[55] T. Tyler, 'The Quality of Dispute Resolution Procedure and Outcomes: Measurement Problems and Possibilities' (1989) 66 Denver UL Rev. 419.

Lord Woolf does not favour compulsory diversion into ADR, but sees a role for ADR as an adjunct to court processes.[56] Among favoured methods of dispute resolution are the use of ombudsmen, both in the public and private sectors,[57] and mediation, which Lord Woolf would like to see offered funding for their work. Court procedures should encourage consideration of the use of ADR and he recommends that a court questionnaire be amended so that reasons will have to be given why ADR has not been chosen in addition to the current confirmation that it has been considered by the parties.

One review of the literature on the use of out-of-court schemes as an alternative to litigation in the consumer field notes the need for vigilance in the quality of decision-making and in maintaining public confidence in the fairness and impartiality of some schemes.[58]

Official encouragement of the use of ADR, which may be provided by the private sector, raises questions concerning the due process standards of Article 6 of the European Convention. The case law on Article 6 has exclusively concerned State-provided courts and tribunals. The assumption presumably is that private dispute settlement arrangements are mutually agreed by the parties, and so do not need the protection afforded by Article 6. However, State encouragement and sponsorship of these procedures could result in the Strasbourg organs taking the view that the Government had a responsibility to ensure that their procedures met the standards set out in Article 6.

Comment

The civil process is much more diffuse than the criminal process, and though there are discussions of dispute resolution and the role of courts and other institutions within that framework, overarching theories of civil justice have not yet been developed. Due process is clearly a key value, as is the matching of the process of dispute resolution to the nature of the dispute. As with the criminal process, the absence of contested cases is a dominant feature, and we shall see that the gap identified between the rhetoric of the system and its delivery also exists in relation to many aspects of the civil process.

This part of the book selects the work of a number of courts and tribunals of first instance for detailed consideration. It cannot hope to be comprehensive. The determining factors have been volume of business, involvement of the ordinary citizen, and the existence of a developing literature on law in action in their contexts. Personal injuries litigation has been a mainstream activity of solicitors and barristers, and reflects the broad public perception of the work of courts in the civil

---

[56] Interim Report, *supra* n. 4, ch. 18.   [57] Especially in the private retail sectors.
[58] T. Goriely and T. Williams, *Resolving Civil Disputes: Choosing between Out-of-Court Schemes and Litigation: A Review of the Literature*, Lord Chancellor's Department Research Series, No. 3/97 (London: Lord Chancellor's Department, 1997).

context. The same may be true of debt cases, but here close scrutiny shows that the adjudication of claims has been supplanted by a largely administrative system. An acid test of a civil justice system is how it handles small claims: can it offer a procedure which is cheap and simple to use which provides a remedy where the values at stake are low? Two sets of tribunals[59] are then examined to determine how different their procedures are from those of the courts, and whether the handling of specialist claims allows a closer matching of process to circumstances than the more generic jurisdictions of the courts. The final chapter in this part examines the procedures by which errors at first instance are corrected and the civil law is developed through an appeal system.

The civil process provides the vehicle by which grievances are defined in terms of causes of action, which refers to recognised bases for making a claim against another. In most of these cases, it then provides merely the backdrop for the settlement of that claim. The civil process also deals with matters of status, such as the dissolution of marriages or the winding up of companies. Many of these cases too are routine; in many of them there is no dispute: both parties to the marriage wish it to be dissolved and the shareholders in a company are agreed that it should be wound up. Often the courts are involved as a safeguard for others who might be affected by the decision; for example, in family cases, there may be important decisions to be made about children of the marriage.

Where the courts are merely the backdrop to settlement, it can be argued that there should be more checks on the fairness of settlements, or, as Lord Woolf argues, greater control over the conduct of the dispute by the parties. But this approach does not tell us why certain cases are brought and others not, nor how the system might better identify cases which offer the opportunity to clarify or make law. The civil process currently appears content that most disputes are individual matters and does not seek to separate out cases which might have a wider impact. The result is that the development of the law is haphazard, dependent upon a case reaching the courts or tribunals, and probably the appeal courts, which then have an opportunity to analyse the current law and see whether it is adequate or needs interpretation or adaptation. One commentator has said:

Concentrating on trouble or hard cases misses much of the process of the civil courts. In many respects, the courts are functioning as administrative agencies or as facilitators of compromises rather than directly resolving contested issues of law and fact.[60]

---

[59] Those dealing with employment questions and those dealing with social security appeals.
[60] R. Cranston, 'What Do Courts Do?' (1986) 5 CJQ 123.

11

DEALING WITH PERSONAL INJURIES CLAIMS

Introduction

The civil claims with which this chapter is concerned are claims in tort for compensation for personal injury as a result of negligence or breach of statutory duty, which exceed the small claims limit in the county courts.[1] The majority of these claims will settle without the need even for court proceedings to begin. One factor which accounts for the settlement of so many personal injuries claims is the presence of insurance. It is a requirement of law that insurance for potential liability to accident victims is carried by motorists and employers. Accidents on the road and at work are, of course, common phenomena. While the legal system resolutely ignores the taking over of a claim against an insured party by the insurers,[2] requiring everything to be done in the name of the insured, the actuality is that the efficient routines of insurance companies in processing accident claims swing into action as soon as an accident is reported. Where the injuries sustained are not too serious and the question of liability is reasonably arguable, many insurers seek to settle, since, in the long term, this is far cheaper than fighting every claim. Whether all these settlements are fair to victims is another question and will often depend on whether victims receive legal advice as to the amount of damages (called '**quantum**' by lawyers) appropriate to their injuries and loss. It is probably true to say that most insurance companies do not behave unscrupulously, but all try to settle claims for the lowest sum possible, thus maximising profits and keeping premiums down.

The way the legal system deals with personal injuries claims is in the process of great change. The Labour Government has embarked on a programme which it has labelled the 'modernisation of justice', which will transform not only the way most personal injuries claims are funded, but also the course they will follow to final determination by a court where that proves to be necessary.

---

[1] Of £1,000 for personal injury claims; see Ch. 13.
[2] But see Supreme Court Act 1981, s. 51, and *TGA Chapman Ltd and another* v. *Christopher and another* [1998] 1 WLR 12.

Accidents and Claims

It has been estimated that there are over three million accidents involving personal injuries each year.[3] Of these about 215,000 occur on the road, 350,000 at work and the remainder elsewhere, mainly in the home. Almost 750,000 of those suffering accidents believe some other person was wholly or partly to blame for the accident. Accidents causing personal injuries result in about 300,000 compensation claims each year. Because liability is fault-based, these must be based on the principle that the person causing the injury was in some way at fault. In nine out of every ten claims insurance covers liability. Settlements are reached in eighty-six per cent of cases without the need to begin court proceedings. A further thirteen per cent are settled after issue of proceedings but before trial. Only about one per cent actually result in a contested trial. In 1996 1,543 personal injuries claims were started, and some 840 judgments were delivered, in the Queen's Bench Division; this represented six out of every ten judgments in that Division. It is not known how many of the 2.1 million default summonses issued in the county courts related to personal injury claims, but in 1996 there were 8,020 judgments in personal injury claims, making the county courts the dominant forum for personal injury cases if the volume of cases is used to determine this.[4]

One of the most alarming statistics is that two-thirds of those suffering injuries, which they feel to have been caused by the act or omission of another person, take no steps towards making a claim for compensation in tort. Among reasons given are absence of serious injury, ignorance of how to go about making a claim, fear of costs, too many practical difficulties and a feeling of inability to prove the claim.[5] The National Compensation Survey showed that only twelve per cent of all seriously injured accident victims claimed damages through the tort system.

Despite the significant number of cases which settle, court decisions have a considerable impact on the processing of accident claims. Case law lays down the criteria for determining the fault upon which liability is based. One decision of the Court of Appeal may lead to the settling of many thousands of cases by insurance companies. Case law also gives important guidance on the matter of quantum of compensation for particular injuries.[6]

No consideration of accident compensation claims would be complete without noting that there is an elaborate mosaic of State benefits which may provide some compensation for accident victims regardless of any determination of fault. These include free medical treatment within the National Health Service, industrial injuries benefits, incapacity benefit, disability living allowance and, as a matter of last resort, income support and other means-tested benefits which are not

---

[3] *Report of the Royal Commission on Civil Liability and Compensation for Personal Injury (Pearson Commission)* (London: HMSO, 1978, Cmnd. 7054).

[4] *Judicial Statistics 1996* (London: HMSO, 1997, Cm. 3716).

[5] Ibid. See also D. Harris and others, *Compensation and Support for Injury and Illness* (Oxford: Clarendon Press, 1984) (cited in this chapter as the 'National Compensation Survey').

[6] See generally P. Atiyah, *Atiyah's Accidents, Compensation and the Law*, 5th edn. by P. Cane (London: Butterworths, 1993).

conditional upon contributions to the National Insurance scheme. Broadly speaking the state benefits are based upon *need* whereas compensation in tort is based upon *actual loss* and will almost always give rise to higher levels of compensation. This system of mixed and overlapping State benefits must inevitably account for a fair number of those cases where accident victims do not pursue tort claims. The welfare state always provides some financial provision to cushion the losses arising following an accident.

Relevant Tort Principles

Liability

Most personal injuries actions will be pleaded in **negligence**. Basically, the plaintiff will have to show, on the balance of probabilities, the existence of a duty of care by the defendant to the plaintiff and a breach of that duty causing the plaintiff damage which is not too remote. The system is based on fault. Sometimes the law will presume a breach of duty by the application of the Latin maxim *res ipsa loquitur* (the matter speaks for itself) if the accident was caused by something under the defendant's control which would not normally happen without a lack of care: for example, a car being driven into a tree. In some cases, notably accidents at work, the plaintiff may also plead breach of statutory duty alleging that the employer has failed to provide a safe system of work.

Road accidents produce the greatest number of claims as a proportion of claims to accidents. One in three victims of road accidents brings a personal injuries claim. Fault is often a major issue in such cases with arguments from each side that the other driver failed to take proper care. If there has been a conviction for a relevant driving offence, the burden of proof is effectively reversed, because section 11 of the Civil Evidence Act 1968 renders the conviction admissible in civil proceedings as proof of fault. The defendant can only avoid this where it is possible to show that the conviction was wrong or irrelevant.

The occurrence of claims in road traffic accident cases is a consequence of the system of compulsory insurance required of drivers covering their liability to third parties. Claims can even be made against uninsured drivers because the Motor Insurers' Bureau operates an Uninsured Drivers Agreement under which it accepts responsibility for the liabilities of uninsured drivers, from whom the Bureau in turn seeks to recover any damages paid to victims of road accidents caused by such drivers.[7]

Accidents at work raise issues of breach of statutory duty as well as negligence and other common law principles. The most important will be the rules governing vicarious liability, where the employer can be held liable for the negligence of employees acting in the course of their employment. The employer is the favoured

---

[7] P. Atiyah, *Atiyah's Accidents, Compensation and the Law*, 5th edn. by P. Cane (London: Butterworths, 1993), pp. 212–16.

defendant since there is a statutory requirement that employers carry insurance against liability to injured employees. One in four of those injured at work claims against the employer.

The Law Reform (Miscellaneous Provisions) Act 1934 provides that existing causes of action survive against or for the benefit of the estate of the deceased party. The claim does not die when one of the parties does. An action brought by the estate of a deceased plaintiff is dealt with on the same basis as if the plaintiff were alive and the measure of damages is generally the same. The Fatal Accidents Act 1976 gives the dependants of a deceased accident victim a cause of action for the loss of their dependency if the deceased would have had an action if he or she had lived. The action is usually brought by the personal representatives of the deceased in conjunction with a 1934 Act claim, but if no action is started within six months of the deceased's death, any dependant can sue on behalf of all the dependants.

One of the big growth areas in accident compensation claims is actions by victims of medical negligence. Such cases can be very complex, raising novel issues concerning the standard of care required and of causation. They can also involve very large sums in damages, especially where plaintiffs are young and will need high levels of care for the rest of their lives.

Apart from a defence based on a denial of any lack of care, the main defence that is met is that the plaintiff was also negligent and such negligence was a contributory cause of the injuries suffered. Such a plea is known as a plea of contributory negligence. Where contributory negligence is pleaded, the courts have power to apportion the blame for the accident by reducing the damages payable. The reduction can be 100 per cent in extreme cases. The defence most often arises where the cause of action pleaded is negligence, but it is not limited to such cases and may be pleaded in other cases, such as, for example, cases of breach of statutory duty.

Another defence that may be pleaded is consent to the risk, known by the Latin phrase *volenti non fit injuria*.[8] In such pleas, the defendant must show that the plaintiff agreed to take the risk of injury resulting from the lack of reasonable care involved, knowing the nature and extent of the risk. The standard of consent to the risk is high and the plea is not often successful.

Damages

The objective of personal injuries claims is compensation, which goes some way to placing the plaintiff in the same financial position after the accident as before it. The law of damages is a complex topic, but the broad division is into general damages and special damages. General damages cover compensation for a number of heads: past, present and future physical and mental pain and suffering resulting from the injuries and the treatment for them; loss of amenity, which refers to the extent to which the injuries prevent the plaintiff from taking part in pre-accident

---

[8] That to which a person consents cannot be considered an injurious wrong.

activities; future loss of earnings; and loss of earning capacity. Damages for pain and suffering for particular types of injury are calculated by reference to a sort of tariff established by the case law. Special damages are the actual financial losses flowing from the accident, covering past loss of earnings and expenses incurred as a result of the accident.

Interest must now be awarded on all damages in excess of £200 unless there are special reasons for not doing so.[9] The purpose of interest is the obvious need to compensate the plaintiff for the delay in receiving the compensation for the accident. Where large damages are expected, but there is dispute as to the amount, interim damages may be appropriate. Such damages are payments on account of damages usually by insurance companies, which put the plaintiff in receipt of some funds and avoid the lengthy wait for the final amount of damages to be fixed by the court.

Formerly, only one award of damages could be made. If subsequent events showed that the damages were too generous or too niggardly, nothing could be done. The accident compensation system simply accepted that there are plaintiffs who are under-compensated and over-compensated. Cases in which the plaintiff's injuries were such that there was a chance of the plaintiff developing some serious disease or serious deterioration in his or her physical or mental condition presented very great problems, since damages in such cases require a figure to be placed on the risk of the onset of the further condition. The device of provisional damages has now been introduced to cope with such cases.[10] The effect of asking the court to consider provisional damages is that the court is given the opportunity to make two awards of damages. The first award is of damages at the appropriate level for the injuries ignoring the possibility that the serious disease or deterioration of health will occur. If within a period specified by the court (which may be for life) the serious disease or deterioration occurs, the plaintiff can return to the court for a second award of damages for the condition which has occurred. Provisional damages have not been used often;[11] it seems that plaintiffs and insurers like to close the files with a once and for all settlement. The cases in which provisional damages have been pleaded to date have generally involved head injuries carrying the risk of the onset of epilepsy, spinal injuries which carry the risk of future paralysis, and respiratory disorders resulting from exposure to substances such as asbestos, which can result in lung cancer. Provisional damages are an option for the plaintiff and will only be considered where the plaintiff asks for consideration of them.

Where very large sums in damages (in excess of £500,000) are involved, consideration is often given to what are known as structured settlements under which a regular income linked to the retail price index is awarded for a fixed term, which may be the remainder of the plaintiff's life.[12]

There is a question mark over whether the damages system effectively compensates victims of personal injury. A study carried out for the Law Commission of

---

[9] Supreme Court Act 1981, s. 35A(2).   [10] Ibid., s. 32A.

[11] J. Pritchard and N. Solomon, *Personal Injury Litigation*, 8th edn. (London: FT Law and Tax, 1995), p. 102.   [12] See generally Damages Act 1996.

accident victims who had received compensation produced some startling results.[13] A high proportion of accident victims regardless of the amount of their compensation did not return to work. This led to a shortfall in the damages awarded since the award for future losses was not always based on such an outcome. It appears that many accident victims are impressed with the size of the award when it is made, but as time goes by come to realise that the sum is not sufficient to meet the consequences of their accident. It also seems that there is a need for independent financial advice on how to preserve the value of the compensation for as long as possible. A key element which is not fully reflected in compensation awards, but is a significant factor in many cases, is the cost of care. The research found ample evidence of past and future unpaid care by relatives and friends of accident victims.

Recommendations of Review Bodies

The Civil Justice Review

In its official response to the Report of the Royal Commission on Legal Services, the Government indicated that the Lord Chancellor would undertake 'a complete and systematic review of civil procedure' in order to identify causes of delay and inconvenience and to re-structure the system so as 'to achieve the most expeditious and convenient disposal of business'.[14] Lord Chancellor Hailsham set up the Review Body on Civil Justice in February 1985 with the objective of improving the machinery of civil justice in England and Wales by means of reforms in jurisdiction, procedure and court administration and, in particular, to reduce delay, cost and complexity. Factual studies based on specification documents prepared by the Review were commissioned to inform the recommendations of the Civil Justice Review.

Inbucon Management Consultants investigated personal injuries litigation. The factual study resulting from this enquiry then formed the basis of a consultation document and the Report of the Review Body on Civil Justice followed in June 1988.[15] Primary legislation was needed to implement some of its recommendations and this was contained in the Courts and Legal Services Act 1990.

The Inbucon Management Consultants factual study examined a sample of 433 cases (234 in the High Court and 199 in the county courts) started in 1980–82, 251 cases tried in 1984, ninety-two cases set down for trial in District Registries

---

[13] Law Commission, *Personal Injury Compensation: How Much is Enough? A Study of the Compensation Experiences of Victims of Personal Injury*, Law Com. No. 225 (London: HMSO, 1994). Note that the survey is of those who received compensation, estimated to be one in eight of all accident victims.

[14] *The Government Response to the Report of the Royal Commission on Legal Services* (London: HMSO, 1983, Cmnd. 9077).

[15] *Civil Justice Review: Report of the Review Body on Civil Justice* (London: HMSO, 1988, Cm. 394).

(High Court centres in the provinces) and twenty cases drawn from insurers' files. In 721 cases the nature of the accident could be identified: 320 concerned injuries suffered on the road and 304 at work. The conclusion drawn from detailed consideration of the cases was that the accident compensation system is inefficient, dilatory and disproportionately expensive. It can take between three and six years for cases to be resolved. Three important points of delay are highlighted. First, it can take three years after the accident to get a case started. The limitation period in most cases before the claim is time-barred by statute is three years. Secondly, it can take two years from the start of a case in the High Court for a defendant to be given full details of the plaintiff's case. Finally, even when both sides are ready for trial, they will often have to wait up to a year for a date to be set in the High Court for a trial.

The expense of the system is also a matter of great concern. In county courts, for every £100 paid in damages, £125 or £175 (depending on the method of calculation) is spent on costs. Because awards of damages are higher in the High Court, the ratio is better: for every £100 in damages, £50 or £70 (depending on the method of calculation) is spent on costs.[16]

Delay means injustice in the form of unnecessary stress and anxiety to plaintiffs and their families as well as financial hardship resulting from the absence of early payment of much needed compensation. It is not in the public interest to have so slow and cumbersome a system of dispute resolution.

A central feature of the changes made in the handling of civil cases following the Civil Justice Review was that all civil cases should be dealt with at the lowest level appropriate to the case and this involved a dramatic shift for most cases from the High Court to the county courts.[17] Whereas the county courts have traditionally been seen as a local forum for the resolution of smaller disputes, they have become the focal point for most litigation. The High Court is reserved for judicial review cases, for specialist cases, and for other cases of unusual complexity or importance. County courts now have no formal upper limit on their jurisdiction. The amount of damages expected is, however, a factor in determining whether the case is more suitable for trial in the county court or the High Court. Cases involving less than £50,000 should be started by county court summons, while those expected to involve in excess of this sum may be started in the High Court. Cases of unusual complexity or difficulty can be transferred for trial in the High Court, while cases started in the High Court can be transferred to the county courts for trial if they are not considered to justify consideration by the High Court.

The Civil Justice Review also made a number of recommendations concerning the progress of cases through the courts designed to secure greater openness and court control in the processing of personal injuries claims.

---

[16] See also Annex III, 'Survey of Litigation Costs: Summary of Main Findings' in Lord Woolf M. R., *Final Report to the Lord Chancellor on the Civil Justice System in England and Wales* (London: HMSO, 1996).

[17] In 1996 the county courts handed down nearly ten times as many personal injuries judgments as the High Court (excluding those personal injuries cases within the small claims limit of £1,000 for such cases): *Judicial Statistics 1996* (London: HMSO, 1997, Cm. 3716).

The Woolf Report

Despite the changes made as a result of the Civil Justice Review, serious concerns remained about the operation of the civil process. Less than five years after the Civil Justice Review reported, the General Council of the Bar and The Law Society had set up a joint independent working party to 'undertake a radical review of the business of the civil courts'. Their conclusion was that the civil justice system remained in urgent need of 'further fundamental reform and modernisation'.[18] The response was for the Lord Chancellor in March 1994 to ask Lord Woolf to review the current rules and procedures of the civil courts in England and Wales. The issues of costs, complexity and delay were again identified. The answer this time was seen to be a much more proactive approach to the management of cases by the court once proceedings were begun. But it was also hoped that many cases would settle without resort to the courts, and new encouragement should be given to alternative dispute resolution. Both timetables and costs should be pre-determined as far as possible.[19]

A new fast-track and multi-track procedure is to be introduced.[20] The fast-track is designed for straightforward cases where the damages are not expected to exceed £15,000.[21] In these cases, there is to be a strictly time-tabled procedure designed to get cases to trial speedily under a system involving fixed costs. The length of any hearing will be strictly limited. These cases will be managed by district judges in the county courts.

For cases expected to involve more than £15,000, a new multi-track procedure which will operate in both the county courts and the High Court is to be introduced. The new procedure will 'provide appropriate and proportionate case management'.[22] There will be some standardisation for commonly met cases, but those requiring it will receive individual hands-on case management. Case management will flow from two key milestones in the procedure: first, at a case management conference early in the case, and, secondly, at a pre-trial review shortly before trial.

Cases will be allocated to a judge known as 'the procedural judge' who will conduct an initial scrutiny of cases in order to allocate them to the appropriate track and issue a notice of allocation. In multi-track cases, the procedural judge will fix a date for the case management conference, and will conduct that conference unless it is more appropriate for the trial judge to do so. The progress of cases and action

---

[18] Lord Woolf M. R., *Interim Report to the Lord Chancellor on the Civil Justice System in England and Wales* (London: HMSO, 1995) (cited in this chapter as 'Interim Report'), ch. 2, paras. 5–8.

[19] See discussion of the Interim Report in Ch. 10.

[20] Interim Report, *supra* n. 18, Section II, and Lord Woolf M. R., *Final Report to the Lord Chancellor on the Civil Justice System in England and Wales* (London: HMSO, 1996) (cited in this chapter as 'Final Report'). See also Lord Chancellor's Department, *An Access to Justice Working Paper: Judicial Case Management* (London: Lord Chancellor's Department, 1997).

[21] The limit proposed in the Woolf Report of £10,000 has been increased to £15,000.

[22] Interim Report, *supra* n. 18, ch. 4, para. 9. See also Final Report, *supra* n. 20, ch. 5, and Lord Chancellor's Department, *An Access to Justice Working Paper: Judicial Case Management* (London: Lord Chancellor's Department, 1997).

in them will be monitored by the procedural judge with appropriate sanctions for failure to comply.[23] The trial judge will normally conduct any pre-trial review.

In order to accommodate these changes, the High Court and county court rules of procedure are to be brought together. It is hoped that the new procedures might be implemented some time in 1999.[24]

Claims Consciousness

If accident victims are to benefit from the tort system, they must become aware of the possibility of claiming compensation. Many do not take any action. Legal advice will usually be needed. Research surveys have shown a marked failure by accident victims to seek out legal advice.[25] Significant factors accounting for failure to take legal advice are fear of cost and ignorance of the legal aid scheme. This is unfortunate because the legal aid scheme and related schemes can provide speedy and cheap advice.[26]

Between 1976 and 1977 the Oxford Centre for Socio-Legal research carried out a large scale study of accident victims, which has come to be known as the National Compensation Survey.[27] The study involved interviewing just over 1,000 people who had suffered injuries which had stopped them from carrying out their normal activities for over two weeks at some time in the preceding five years. The study sought to identify reasons why claims were not made as well as the outcomes of those that were made. Almost three out of every four accident victims did not even consider making a claim. Of the quarter who did, only about half actually took any further steps. The six main reasons for not making a claim were:

- ignorance of the procedure for claiming;
- problems in collecting evidence;
- fear of cost;
- accident was their own fault;
- ignorance or confusion;
- injuries not regarded as sufficiently serious to warrant claiming.

Some respondents did not know they had to make a claim. A man knocked down by a bus said, 'The police came to see me and I thought I would hear from

---

[23] On sanctions, see Final Report, *supra* n. 20, ch. 6.

[24] 'Modernising Civil Justice,' Speech by Geoff Hoon, M. P., at Nottingham Trent University on 1 May 1998.

[25] R. Abel-Smith, M. Zander and R. Brooke, *Legal Problems and the Citizen* (London: Heinemann, 1973); Adamsdown Community Trust, *Community Need and Law Centre Practice* (Cardiff: Adamsdown Community Trust, 1978); D. Harris and others, *Compensation and Support for Injury and Illness* (Oxford: Clarendon Press, 1984); and H. Genn, *Hard Bargaining: Out of Court Settlement in Personal Injury Actions* (Oxford: Clarendon Press, 1987).

[26] But note the exclusion of most personal injuries cases from the scope of civil legal aid mentioned below.

[27] D. Harris and others, *Compensation and Support for Injury and Illness* (Oxford: Clarendon Press, 1984).

the company, but never did'. Another said, 'I felt so poorly after the accident, I couldn't face doing anything'. A man injured at work said, 'I was grateful that the firm employed me at my age of 62 and I didn't want to cause any bother'. Among those who said someone else was to blame for the accident, four in ten did not make a claim. Paradoxically, two in ten of those who did claim said they did not blame anyone else for the accident. It seems that the factor most likely to lead people to claim is advice to claim by a third party. Three in four of those claiming said the idea of claiming had been suggested by someone else. The researchers conclude:

The accident victims who do succeed in obtaining damages for their injuries are a strange group. They are not necessarily the most seriously injured, nor those who have suffered the most prevalent types of accident, nor are they necessarily those who blamed some third party for the accident. They are not the people with most wealth and influence. But they do appear to have an important advantage in that they have access to advice about claiming and often receive this advice without soliciting it.[28]

Once the threshold of actually making the claim is overcome, the chances of obtaining some compensation are good, though the survey showed that the longer a claimant delays in instructing a lawyer the less the chance of recovering damages. Four out of every five claimants received something, though many of the amounts paid were very modest.

A scheme run by the Greater Manchester Legal Services Committee to raise claims consciousness proved very successful. A leaflet giving simple information about personal injuries claims and explaining how and where legal advice might be obtained was made readily available in hospitals and advice agencies. A free diagnostic interview was offered by participating solicitors. It uncovered some serious cases where individuals would not otherwise have taken any action.[29]

The success of the Manchester scheme persuaded the Law Society that the idea was a good one. The scheme has been introduced nationally as the Accident Legal Advice Service (ALAS) and is administered by local law societies. As a result coverage is patchy since not all local law societies are willing to act as co-ordinators for such a scheme. Levels of efficiency are also variable. The underlying concept of the scheme was to provide the free diagnostic interview in order to 'capture' clients by offering the initial service without charge.

These principles are embedded in the current Accident Line scheme, which is described both in a leaflet and on the Law Society's Internet pages. A freephone number is provided for accident victims, who will be referred to a local solicitors' firm which is a member of Accident Line. These firms are specialists in handling personal injury claims and have been vetted by the Law Society. They offer a free initial consultation. At that consultation, the prospects of success and the methods of funding any claim will be discussed without any obligation on the accident

[28] D. Harris and others, *Compensation and Support for Injury and Illness* (Oxford: Clarendon Press, 1984), p. 76.

[29] H. Genn, *Meeting Legal Needs?* (Oxford: Centre for Socio-Legal Studies, 1982).

victim to take matters forward. There is no doubt that the scheme is a helpful one in putting accident victims in contact with specialist personal injury lawyers.

Financing the Claim

Paying the lawyer

Becoming claims conscious, finding a lawyer and financing the claim are crucial stages on the route to accident compensation. Personal injuries claims are one of the main areas of litigation where many solicitors have considerable expertise. Getting good legal advice is crucial to success and is vital in obtaining a good settlement. Once claimants have found a lawyer, they are almost wholly dependent on the lawyer's knowledge and expertise. Finding the right lawyer is very important, but accident victims can be in a poor position to measure the expertise of their lawyers. All solicitors tend to hold themselves out as doing accident compensation work, but many do only a very small amount of the work and even fewer will have followed a contested case through to judgment in court.

Finding the right lawyer certainly used to be something of a lottery because claimants had very little information on which to base their choice. Hazel Genn, in her study of negotiated settlements[30] catalogues the dangers of having an inexperienced lawyer handling your accident compensation claim:

- it is difficult for non-specialists to keep up to date with court procedure;
- they may be reluctant to go to court to fight the case and so will settle at any price;
- they tend to delay the issue of court proceedings and so build unnecessary delays into the process;
- the delay leads to problems in the collection of evidence which may have gone stale;
- defendants' insurance companies will take advantage of the inexperienced plaintiff's solicitor;
- if negotiations break down, it may be too late to prepare the case adequately for a trial;
- they might advise the plaintiff to accept a low settlement in the knowledge that this advice is unlikely to be challenged.

Michael Joseph in his book *Lawyers Can Seriously Damage Your Health* makes similar points,[31] though based on anecdotal evidence and polemic rather than the skilled research methods used by Hazel Genn.

---

[30] H. Genn, *Hard Bargaining: Out of Court Settlement in Personal Injury Actions* (Oxford: Clarendon Press, 1987).
[31] M. Joseph, *Lawyers Can Seriously Damage your Health* (London: Michael Joseph, 1984).

The Law Society has responded to these criticisms by developing specialist panels of solicitors experienced in personal injury work. This has now grown into Accident Line.[32]

Civil legal aid has in the past offered considerable assistance for plaintiffs in accident compensation claims, but the dominant form of funding personal injury claims is now the **conditional fee agreement**.[33] For those within the Green Form financial limits, assistance remains available[34] and typical work the solicitor can do is to begin to collect evidence, and write preliminary letters. But in practice many clients already move directly from a free initial consultation to a conditional fee basis of payment.

The conditional fee is a sort of contingent fee arrangement, whereby a solicitor agrees to take no fee if the claim fails but will take a percentage of any compensation gained if the plaintiff wins. Contingent fees have been suggested as a way of helping those outside the legal aid financial limits for some time,[35] but initially they did not find favour with the legal profession. The Lord Chancellor's Green Paper on Contingent Fees in January 1989[36] resurrected interest in such schemes. The Courts and Legal Services Act 1990 empowered the Lord Chancellor to make regulations permitting lawyers to be instructed on a conditional fee basis, that is, that the lawyer will receive a fee only in the event of the action proving successful. The need for an uplift in the normal fee levels to compensate the lawyer for the risk of receiving nothing was accepted, but the maximum amount of the uplift would be controlled by the Lord Chancellor. The scheme was modelled on the speculative fee of the Scottish legal system.

A serious defect could have been the lack of protection against having to meet the other side's costs if the case were to be unsuccessful. Those put off taking a case because they cannot meet their own costs are unlikely to be willing to risk having to pay a like sum to the other side's lawyers. But the Law Society has succeeded in negotiating after-the-event legal expenses insurance to cover this risk.

A typical conditional fee arrangement works as follows.[37] An accident victim has a free consultation with a solicitor on the Accident Line panel. If the case looks promising, the solicitor will take the case details before the firm's risk assessment panel, which will decide whether the firm is willing to take on the case on a conditional fee basis. If so, a conditional fee agreement coupled with an Accident Line Protect insurance policy will be offered, which provides insurance against having to pay the other side's costs if the claim is unsuccessful. The insurance policy requires a one-off premium.[38] The conditional fee agreement will commit the firm

---

[32] Described above.

[33] Following the withdrawal of civil legal aid for most personal injuries claims sometime in 1999.

[34] For the time being. Significant changes to this aspect of legal aid are expected late in 1999.

[35] M. Zander, *Lawyers and the Public Interest* (London: Weidenfeld & Nicolson, 1968); M. Zander, *Legal Services for the Community* (London: Temple Smith, 1978); and R. White, 'Contingent Fees—A Supplement to Legal Aid' (1978) 41 MLR 286.   [36] London: HMSO, 1989, Cm. 571.

[37] See generally M. Napier and F. Bawdon, *Conditional Fees: A Survival Guide* (London: The Law Society, 1995). See also A. Unger (ed.), *Know-How for Personal Injury Lawyers and Conditional Fees* (London: FT Law & Tax, 1997).   [38] For road traffic accident cases, this was £96.25 as at January 1998.

to charging no legal costs if the claim fails. But if the case is won, then the solicitors are entitled to the legal costs they would have received had the accident victim been paying[39] plus an additional amount (known as the 'uplift') for the risk of getting nothing if the claim is unsuccessful. The maximum amount of the uplift is regulated.[40] This additional sum comes out of the accident victim's damages. In addition, there is a cap on the amount of damages that can be eaten up by the uplift; the Law Society's model agreement fixes this at twenty-five per cent of the amount of damages recovered. In addition, it is common for the accident victim to agree to pay for fees the solicitors have to pay, such as a fee for starting the claim in court or a fee to a doctor for a medical report, as the case goes along.[41] The overall effect of a conditional fee agreement is that accident victims will pay the uplift element of the legal costs out of the damages awarded, and will also have to meet the premium for the after-the-event insurance policy from their own resources.

At face value, conditional fees look to be a helpful way forward for accident victims, and appear to answer completely criticisms that the legal aid scheme only supported the poor, leaving middle income groups in a gap. They were too rich for legal aid, yet too poor to take on all the risks of embarking on litigation at their own expense. The absence of legal aid for personal injury claims, however, now leaves a gap for those who do not have the income to meet the Accident Line Protect insurance premium, and possibly disbursements as the case proceeds. The response of the Government has been to propose the introduction of an interim fund which would assist in high value claims, but this requires primary legislation. Where the injury is the result of an accident at work, accident victims who are members may be supported by their trades unions. It is also likely that firms will only be willing to take on cases which they regard as having a higher chance of success than those previously funded through legal aid.[42]

Some litigants will have legal expenses insurance,[43] which has in recent years been marketed with some vigour and with the support of the Law Society but with comparatively little market penetration. Such policies invariably provide cover for this type of litigation.[44]

As indicated above most defendants will be protected by insurance and the insurance company will pay the legal costs arising in the defence of any claim.

The system of costs

As the discussion above indicates, anyone embarking on litigation needs to know the rules on costs. Costs are the fees paid to the lawyers involved in the case plus

---

[39] And these will normally be recoverable from the defendant.
[40] The maximum uplift is 100 per cent. A straightforward claim is likely to be subject to an uplift of around 40 per cent.   [41] The lawyer's jargon for these is 'disbursements'.
[42] The Government has indicated that legislation will be brought forward which will require the likelihood of success under legal aid to be higher than the current requirement of a reasonable prospect of success.
[43] Sometimes now called 'before-the-event' insurance to distinguish it from the Accident Line Protect policies.
[44] J. Levin, 'Legal Insurance' *LAG Bulletin*, August 1982, 13; and R. White, 'Legal Expenses Insurance' (1984) 3 CJQ 245.

their out of pocket expenses in connection with the case. An award of costs is a matter for the discretion of the court, but the court usually exercises its discretion in favour of the winning party. The loser will be ordered to pay most of the winner's costs. It is important to realise that this is a very real discretion and not a rule. Lord Lloyd of Berwick commented:

As in all questions to do with costs, the fundamental rule is that there are no rules. Costs are always at the discretion of the court, and practice, however widespread and long standing, must never be allowed to harden into a rule.[45]

The law and practice on costs is considered to be difficult and time-consuming, and one of the most arcane, cold and dense areas of English law.[46] For our purposes, it is sufficient to know that the broad basis for calculating costs is the **indemnity principle**. This does not mean that the winner is entitled to everything his or her solicitor charges for the work done, but in many cases the bulk of those costs will be recovered in successful litigation. The most significant point is the principle that costs follow the event, since this means that unsuccessful litigants must not only cover their own legal costs, they must also meet the legal costs of the winning party. This practice has a profound effect on the conduct of civil litigation, and, as we shall see, can be used strategically by parties to litigation.

Collecting Evidence

The next hurdle faced by the plaintiff will be the collection of evidence in support of the claim. Here the plaintiff will often be at a disadvantage. Usually the accident will have been reported to the insurance company by the insured party. The insurance company will commonly, and very wisely, advise that no statements be made without the insurers' knowledge. The insurers will collect statements and conduct a general enquiry for their own use in determining whether to settle any claim, but these statements will not be made available to the plaintiff. In many cases plaintiffs, or their lawyers, will only consult witnesses after the insurers have seen them and may well find them unco-operative. Plaintiffs suffer the twin disadvantages of not being in a position immediately after the accident to collect evidence and of being dependent on their solicitors for the early collection of evidence. In addition to the inevitable disadvantage which arises for plaintiffs of instructing lawyers later than defendants, plaintiffs suffer the further disadvantage that lawyers often seek no evidence apart from the plaintiff's own statement.[47] Solicitors, it seems, take an office-bound approach to the collection of evidence; they rarely make site visits, take photographs or instruct engineers to make investigations on behalf of

---

[45] *Bolton MDC* v. *Secretary of State for the Environment* [1996] 1 All ER 184, 186.
[46] See generally J. O'Hare and R. Hill, *Civil Litigation*, 8th edn. (London: FT Law and Tax, 1997), ch. 23.
[47] H. Genn, *Hard Bargaining: Out of Court Settlement in Personal Injury Actions* (Oxford: Clarendon Press, 1987), pp. 69–70.

the plaintiff. It is not even universal practice to obtain a copy of the police report of a road traffic accident. Hazel Genn's study of settlement concludes that the failure of solicitors to obtain information at an early stage of the case will trail an effect across the whole case, since the absence of detailed information affects not only the solicitor's ability to make a sound judgment on the claim, but also counsel's ability to give advice.[48] It is clear that the collection of good, relevant evidence is crucial to the plaintiff's claim.

If there has been a motoring accident upon which a police report has been made, that report, including any witness statements, will be made available to the plaintiff on payment of the prescribed fee, though where criminal proceedings are pending some police forces will not disclose the report until the criminal proceedings are concluded. The Civil Justice Review recommended a change of this practice so that such reports could be made available to accident victims at the earliest opportunity. This has not yet been implemented, but for a reduced fee an abstract of the accident report may be made available together with copies of the police notebooks made up at the scene. The police normally keep reports only for three years, and so it may be important to request that they are kept longer in cases where reliance needs to be placed on such reports after that time.[49]

In cases of accidents at work, there may have been an investigation by the Health and Safety Executive (HSE), or a visit coupled with recommendations related to the provision of a safe working environment. Reports from the HSE are not often considered particularly helpful because of their brevity and blandness. A bare factual statement can normally be obtained together with copies of any photographs taken. The HSE does not normally release formal reports containing opinions, facts and statements unless served with an order for their production, but such an order can only be obtained after proceedings have started.[50]

Normally the courts will not intervene to assist a party to obtain information in order to bring a claim. Sections 33 and 35 of the Supreme Court Act 1981 are of assistance to a plaintiff seeking to establish whether there are grounds for beginning proceedings by allowing certain orders to be made *before* proceedings are started. Both the High Court and county courts can in personal injuries and fatal accident claims order the production of relevant documents from a party who might become a defendant. This provision covers such things as hospital notes or engineer's reports, but will not extend to witness statements. Secondly, under section 33(1) of the Supreme Court Act 1981, the High Court or a county court can in any action make orders for:

(a) the inspection, photographing, preservation, custody and detention of property which appears to the court to be property which may become the subject matter of subsequent proceedings . . . , or as to which any question may arise in any such proceedings, and

---

[48] H. Genn, *Hard Bargaining: Out of Court Settlement in Personal Injury Actions* (Oxford: Clarendon Press, 1987), pp. 81–2.

[49] See J. Hendy and others, *Personal Injury Practice*, 2nd edn. (London: Legal Action Group, 1994), pp. 39–40.   [50] Ibid., p. 43.

(b) the taking of samples of any such property as is mentioned in paragraph (a) and the carrying out of any experiment on or with any such property.

The section could cover inspection of such things as a machine in a factory or a car involved in a motoring accident.[51]

Negotiated Settlements

The civil justice system encourages settlement and provides incentives for this to occur. The principal encouragement is the protection against the use in court of 'without prejudice' communications in which each party can bargain freely without fear that admissions or concessions will be used against them if negotiations break down. The high incidence of settlement in personal injuries litigation may be seen to be a credit to the system. However, those settlements must be fair to the parties and not be the result of an unequal bargain. The National Compensation Survey concluded:

in practice, the damages system produces relatively low sums of money, which can seldom achieve the goal of the system, viz. to put the plaintiff, so far as money can do so, back into the position he would have been in had the accident not occurred . . . the precision of the rules on assessing damages which aim to give the plaintiff 'full recompense' for his injuries and losses, gives way in out-of-court settlements to many practical pressures towards lower amounts. The full amount which a court would be likely to award if 'full' liability were established against the defendant, is heavily discounted in an out-of-court settlement in order to take account of all the uncertainties facing the plaintiff.[52]

The major study of negotiated settlements is Hazel Genn's book *Hard Bargaining*, which shows that the process is not one of equal bargaining, but of a one-sided exercise disguised as a co-operative process for assisting victims of accidents.[53] An American commentator, Owen Fiss, has argued that negotiated settlements are not desirable.[54] He argues that processes of settlement out of court assume an equality of bargaining position between the parties. Settlement is such circumstances is the anticipation of the outcome of a trial and assumes that the terms of the settlement are the product of the parties' predictions of that outcome. Since the rough equality needed for a fair settlement is seldom present, Fiss does not approve the process, regarding it as a highly problematic technique for reducing the number of cases which come to trial and as the 'civil analogue of plea bargaining'. Justice may not be done. He concludes:

---

[51] See also Civil Procedure Act 1997, ss. 7, 8.   [52] National Compensation Survey, pp. 88–9.
[53] H. Genn, *Hard Bargaining: Out of Court Settlement in Personal Injury Actions* (Oxford: Clarendon Press, 1987).   [54] O. Fiss, 'Against Settlement' (1984) 93 Yale LJ 1073.

There is, moreover, a critical difference between a process of settlement, which is based on bargaining and accepts inequalities of wealth as an integral and legitimate component of the process, and a process like judgment, which knowingly struggles against those inequalities. Judgment aspires to an autonomy from distributional inequalities and it gathers much of its appeal from this aspiration.[55]

Hazel Genn carried out in-depth interviews with thirty solicitors, twenty barristers and twelve insurance companies involved in the bargaining process, and analysed the results of 131 questionnaires sent to solicitors' offices. The results show that claiming compensation is a highly adversarial activity. Insurance companies owe their primary obligation to their policy-holders and strive to keep costs to a minimum. They do not offer a 'fair' amount but the least that they believe the plaintiff will accept. Even where the plaintiff is legally represented, insurance companies feel that it is legitimate to take advantage of any weaknesses in the way the case has been prepared. Many plaintiff's solicitors believe they are acting in the best interests of their clients in seeking settlements, but proceed on the basis that nearly all cases will settle. Defendants' insurers take advantage of the generally half-hearted pursuit of the claim by plaintiff's solicitors by making low offers. Once negotiations break down, they know that the plaintiff's solicitors will be in a very weak position with little evidence to take to trial and little chance of constructing a convincing case at this stage. Waiting until the eleventh hour can still result in a low settlement, which the plaintiff's solicitor recommends the plaintiff to accept secure in the knowledge that the advice is unlikely to be challenged.

Hazel Genn's overall conclusion is that there are both structural and situational inequalities between the parties in personal injuries litigation which have a profound impact on the processes of negotiation and settlement. She notes that the specialist plaintiffs' solicitors do not talk of a co-operative approach, but recognise the adversarial nature of the process and adopt a confrontational approach to negotiating settlements, which seizes the advantage from the insurers' solicitors. By contrast the non-specialists speak of the importance of keeping on good terms with insurers in the interests of reaching speedy settlements. Hazel Genn concludes:

If there is, indeed, a public interest in seeing that injured plaintiffs obtain 'fair' compensation for their injuries, then the analysis of out of court settlement processes contained in this study suggests that there is a strong argument for attempting to reduce some of the imbalance between the parties by improving the access of unknowledgeable plaintiffs to solicitors who genuinely specialize in personal injury litigation; for speeding-up personal injury litigation procedure, particularly the low-value claims; for providing incentives to defendants to settle claims quickly; and for providing a means by which out of court settlements become more visible or subject to scrutiny.[56]

[55] O. Fiss, 'Against Settlement' (1984) 93 Yale LJ, 1078.
[56] H. Genn, *Hard Bargaining: Out of Court Settlement in Personal Injury Actions* (Oxford: Clarendon Press, 1987), p. 169.

Basic Practice and Procedure

Preliminary

What follows is a brief description of practice and procedure prior to the implementation of the recommendations contained in the Woolf Report, which are expected to come into effect in 1999. An outline of the proposed new procedures is set out later in this chapter.

The concerns expressed by Lord Woolf about delays in the system have already led to the courts taking a stricter view of time limits. The Court of Appeal explained the more rigorous approach to time limits in *Mortgage Corporation Ltd v. Sandoes*.[57] Lord Justice Millett said:

What I say now . . . is intended to be of general import. The Master of the Rolls and the Vice Chancellor, as Head of Civil Justice, have approved the following guidance as to the future approach which litigants can expect the court to adopt to the failure to adhere to time limits contained in the rules or directions of the court:

1. Time requirements laid down by the rules and directions given by the court are not merely targets to be attempted; they are rules to be observed.
2. At the same time the overriding principle is that justice must be done.
3. Litigants are entitled to have their cases resolved with reasonable expedition. Non-compliance with time limits can cause prejudice to one or more parties to the litigation.
4. In addition the vacation or adjournment of the date of trial prejudices other litigants and disrupts the administration of justice.
5. Extensions of time which involve vacation or adjournment of the date of trial should therefore be granted only as a last resort.
6. Where time limits have not been complied with the parties should co-operate in reaching an agreement as to new time limits which will not involve the date of trial being postponed.
7. If they reach such an agreement they can ordinarily expect the court to give effect to that agreement at the trial and it is not necessary to make separate application solely for this purpose.
8. The court will not look with favour on a party who seeks only to take tactical advantage from the failure of another party to comply with time limits.
9. In the absence of an agreement as to a new timetable, an application should be made promptly to the court for directions.
10. In considering whether to grant an extension of time to a party who is in default, the court will look at all the circumstances of the case including the considerations identified above.

One way in which this new approach to time has been implemented is the increasing use of what are called 'unless orders'. Such an order states precisely the time within which certain action must be taken and states the adverse consequences

---

[57] [1997] PNLR 263; *The Times*, 27 December 1996.

which will flow automatically from a failure to meet the time limit. This can include the striking out of an action.[58]

'Without prejudice' negotiations and the letter before action

At this stage the plaintiff will be in a position to begin serious negotiations with the insurance company. The first step, if it has not already been taken, will be the sending of a letter making a formal claim for compensation. It is at this stage, where there is a dispute which might result in litigation, that privilege can attach to correspondence between the parties. Such correspondence will be headed 'without prejudice' and all communications properly so headed cannot be used in evidence in any subsequent proceedings. What this means is that as part of the negotiating process, each party can make admissions and compromise suggestions which will not be held against them if the case proceeds to trial. Lord Griffiths confirmed the purpose of the rule in *Rush & Tompkins Ltd* v. *GLC*:

The 'without prejudice rule' is a rule governing the admissibility of evidence and is founded on the public policy of encouraging litigants to settle their differences rather than litigate to the finish.[59]

Lord Griffiths cited with approval Oliver L. J. in *Cutts* v. *Head* who had stated that parties should not be discouraged from entering into negotiations for settlement by any fear of what was said or not said in correspondence or other communications being used to their prejudice in the course of the proceedings.[60]

The privilege seems to work well in practice because such negotiations usually take place between lawyers and insurers (or their lawyers). It provides a useful and effective incentive to early settlement since admissions can be made and the strengths and weaknesses of cases aired without prejudice to what might later be argued in court. Its effectiveness probably depends upon the parties negotiating being familiar with the process and skills of negotiation; litigants in person may well lack these skills. A typical subject of without prejudice exchanges would be discussion as to the amount by which damages might be reduced because the victim was partly to blame for the accident. A privileged admission that there was a degree of contributory negligence would not preclude a complete denial of contributory negligence in any trial of the action.

If no settlement is achieved, it will be necessary to send a formal 'letter before action' threatening the issue of proceedings within seven or fourteen days if the claim is not admitted. The purpose of such a letter is to make clear the plaintiff's intention to pursue the claim before the courts; it will preclude any claim by the defendant to have been taken by surprise by the litigation. It has already been noted that some eighty-six per cent of claims are settled at or before this stage.

For those cases that do not settle, proceedings will need to be issued. This must usually be done within three years of the date of the accident failing which the

---

[58] See generally J. O'Hare and R. N. Hill, *Civil Litigation*, 8th edn. (London: Longman, 1997), pp. 123–4.
[59] *Rush & Tompkins Ltd* v. *GLC* [1989] AC 1280, 1299.   [60] *Cutts* v. *Head* [1984] Ch. 290, 306–7.

Limitation Acts may bar the action.[61] What follows is a description of the main procedural steps in a typical county court action, since (as noted above) these are now
the dominant forum for personal injury claims.

The procedural steps in the High Court and county courts are becoming increasingly similar, and the Woolf Report recognised the need for them to be unified.

Issuing proceedings

The plaintiff's solicitor will prepare a **default summons** together with particulars
of claim. The particulars must specify the cause of action, the remedy that is being
sought and will contain a brief statement of the material facts. A medical report
and a statement of the special damages must also be filed. If they are not available,
the claim may be filed, but a time limit will be set for their delivery. Sufficient
copies of the filed documents must be provided for the defendant(s) with a file
copy for the court. The documents may be filed in any county court. The appropriate court fee must be paid. The summons is then stamped with the court stamp
and a plaint note is prepared which records the court's unique number for the case.

There are three forms of service in the county courts: by post, by the court, or
personally. If service is to be by post, a stamped and addressed envelope must be
provided. If service is by the court, this will, in the first instance, also be by post.
In either case service is deemed to have been completed on the seventh day after
the county court summons was sent to the defendant. Service by a bailiff is only
available where postal service has been tried and failed. In many cases, the defendant's solicitors will have agreed to accept service of the summons in advance.

The issue and service of the summons will trigger a further round of negotiated
settlements. Nothing concentrates the minds of insurers who feel that a claim might
wither on the vine more than receipt of a summons which shows that the plaintiff
means to persist with the claim.

The defendant will be served a standard form for admitting or defending the claim,
or for making a counterclaim.

Pleadings

The **particulars of claim** are the first document in a series of documents which are
collectively known as pleadings. The particulars of claim are a brief account of the
material facts upon which the plaintiff relies for the claim. They do not set out the
evidence to be adduced in support of the allegations and contain no argument on
the law. In practice the statement will be drafted by reference to a standard form
precedent for such claims; the person drafting the particulars will seek to leave
open every avenue of attack against the defendant. Typical personal injuries statements are in four parts. First, there is a statement of the date, time and place of

---

[61] See J. O'Hare and R. N. Hill, *Civil Litigation*, 8th edn. (London: Longman, 1997), ch. 5, and M. Jones,
Limitation Periods in Personal Injuries Cases (London: Blackstone Press, 1993).

the accident and of the persons involved. Secondly, there is an allegation of negligence against the defendant following a ritual formula. Thirdly, there are details of the injuries suffered by the plaintiff and of any damage to the property of the plaintiff and of his actual loss of earnings. Finally, there will be a formal claim for damages. Plaintiffs claiming personal injuries must also provide a medical report setting out the nature of the injuries together with a schedule of special damages to date and an estimate of any future expenses and losses including earnings and pension rights, unless the court has given leave for these to be filed at a later date. If there is any change in the plaintiff's medical condition requiring an additional medical report, a copy of that report must be served on the defendant together with an up-dated schedule of special damages.

Statements in pleadings tend to give very little away because part of the skill of drafting statements of claim is in keeping open as many issues as possible to permit later room for manoeuvre. This is really only possible because the plaintiff is not required to give any indication of the evidence available to support the allegations made. Given that so few cases come to trial, the only point at which evidence is considered in detail, allegations may be made in pleadings for which there is little or no evidence available.

On receiving the statement the defendant must formulate a strategy for response. If some part of the statement of claim is unclear, further and better particulars of the claim can be requested. Indeed if a defendant wishes to be obstructive, this is sometimes regarded as quite a good ploy, because it increases the other side's costs (as well, of course, as the defendant's own) and may throw the other side into disarray. But the usual response is the filing of a defence.

The County Court Rules and the Rules of the Supreme Court provide that any allegation of fact is deemed to be admitted unless it is specifically denied. This means that defendants cannot file blanket defences to the effect, 'I didn't do it'. They must, where they deny facts alleged, put forward their own allegations of the true position. What happens in practice is that the defendant will admit the fact of the accident's having occurred and the persons involved. This means that there is no need for the plaintiff to adduce evidence as to these facts. But the defendant will go on to deny the allegation of negligence. Often there will be an allegation that the accident was caused wholly or partly by the negligence of the plaintiff and there will be detailed allegations of how the plaintiff was negligent. The details of the injuries and loss will be not admitted; this is different from a denial and means that the plaintiff must adduce evidence to prove the injuries and loss. The defendant is not denying that the plaintiff was injured, but is simply requiring the plaintiff to prove the injuries and loss. This is known as 'putting the plaintiff to proof'. Finally, the defendant will usually put in a blanket denial of all other matters. If the defendant does not file a defence then the plaintiff can obtain judgment by default.

In motor accident claims defendants will often counterclaim from plaintiffs for their own injuries and loss. Though often genuine, there is scope here for obstructionist tactics. The ball is now back in the plaintiff's court. The plaintiff may, if there is a need, seek further and better particulars of matters raised by the defendant, but, sooner or later, must file a defence to any counterclaim. Normally, pleadings are closed fourteen days after delivery of the defence or defence to the counterclaim. Even practitioner commentators acknowledge the limited scope of particulars and draw attention to the duty of the draftsman of pleadings to leave open as much room for manoeuvre as possible.[62] One Report uses a colourful analogy:

Pleading therefore resembles nothing so much as naval warfare before the advent of radar, when each side made blind forays into the sea area of the other, while giving away as little as possible about the disposition of his own forces.[63]

Pleadings close fourteen days after the last pleading has been filed. In a straightforward case, this will be the filing of the defence.

Preparation for trial

After close of pleadings comes the stage of **directions for trial**. In personal injuries cases (except medical negligence claims) a system of automatic directions applies. There is no need for formal application to be made. The following directions apply automatically:

- discovery of documents must take place within twenty-eight days of close of pleadings with inspection seven days later;
- where a party wants to call expert evidence at the trial, the substance of that evidence must be disclosed within ten weeks and agreed with the other side if possible, and the number of expert witnesses is limited to two medical experts and one expert of another kind on each side;
- any party wishing to rely on oral evidence must within ten weeks serve written statements of all such evidence which it is intended to adduce;
- photographs, sketch plans and any police report are receivable without calling the person who made them and should be agreed if possible;
- the plaintiff is to request a date for a hearing within six months where no trial date has been fixed;[64]
- setting down for trial should take place within six months and the court notified on setting down of the expected length of the trial.

In order to ensure that litigators do not delay matters, the automatic directions provide that failure to seek a trial date within fifteen months will result in the action being automatically struck out unless an extension is granted. This provision has, however, led to a mountain of 'satellite' litigation resulting from the poor drafting of the provision.[65] It has shown how foolish it is to address problems of delay with draconian sanctions which have not been fully thought through.

[62] See criticisms of current pleadings in Interim Report, *supra* n. 18, ch. 20.
[63] JUSTICE, *Going to Law: A Critique of English Civil Procedure* (London: JUSTICE, 1974), para. 50.
[64] CCR, Ord. 17 r. 11.
[65] On this issue, see *Bannister* v. *SGB plc and others, and 19 other appeals* [1997] 4 All ER 129, CA.

Another group of cases will settle at this stage of the pre-trial proceedings, because the next step is a tedious labour intensive exercise. It is known as discovery. Each side must compile a list of all documents relevant to the dispute and exchange it with the other side. This may sound a simple task, but it is not. Often there will have been no attempt prior to this stage of the proceedings to collect together all possible documentation; only the most relevant will have been used. Once all the documents have been collected they must be separated into three categories:

- those the party has and is prepared to disclose;
- those the party has but is not prepared to disclose because privilege attaches to them; and
- those the party has had but no longer has, stating the reason the party no long has them.

Examples in the last category would be originals of copy letters listed in the first category or an accident report book sent to the Factory Inspectorate. Documents to which privilege attaches are principally 'without prejudice' letters, solicitor/client communications, witness statements and documents prepared for the purposes of litigation. The reason for privilege attaching to solicitor/client communications is obvious; there must be no inhibition to free and frank disclosure even of pre-judicial matters between solicitor and client. Arguments may and often do arise over whether privilege attaches to a particular document, especially where the claim to privilege is based on a claim that it is a document prepared for the purposes of litigation. Under the rule in *Waugh* v. *British Railways Board* the test is whether the dominant purpose of the author in preparing the document was the submission of advice or assistance to a legal adviser in the conduct of contemplated litigation.[66] The above rules on discovery apply unless the claim is one in which liability is admitted or is a motor accident claim. In these cases the plaintiff need only disclose documents relating to special damages claims.[67]

Obviously the lists exchanged on discovery tell the other side very little. The process of inspection follows, whereby each party arranges for the other side to see all documents, other than those to which privilege attaches, and to photocopy such as the other party selects. It is an important step because it is the only opportunity before trial to make any assessment of the true strength of the documentary basis of the other side's case.[68] If there is some specific document one side believes the other side has but is not disclosing, application can be made to the court for an order of specific discovery requiring the production of the document. Application can also be made for discovery from those who are not parties to the proceedings, such as the Health and Safety Executive.

The final preparations for trial are again time-consuming and labour intensive; they will involve a review of the evidence, of the merits of the case, and a careful consideration of quantum. Since a trial now seems likely, a barrister may well be

---

[66] *Waugh* v. *British Railways Board* [1980] AC 521.
[67] Such as wage slips, medical bills, letters from the Department of Social Security.
[68] This tends to be less important in personal injuries cases than in other civil litigation

asked for detailed advice on evidence. This may involve further interviews with witnesses. There will also be the work of preparation of bundles of documents and of service of notices requiring the other side to produce specific documents at the trial. As with discovery and inspection, this labour intensive, and hence expensive, exercise induces a further round of settlements. Another factor inducing settlement will be the knowledge that the trial itself is the most expensive part of the whole process. It seems that costs are virtually doubled where the case goes to trial.[69]

Trials can now be split with the issue of liability and the issue of quantum being decided at separate trials. The logic is that in many cases where liability is determined, agreement on quantum may well follow. In personal injuries litigation, courts should consider whether a split trial should be ordered even where neither side makes application for this to happen.

Trial

Up to six years after the date of the accident, that rare case which 'goes all the way' will be tried.[70] This is the moment where evidence is produced and tested by the procedures of examination and cross-examination of witnesses. It is a dramatic ritual event. The judge will know very little about the case; at best he or she will have read the pleadings, while at worst nothing will have been read. The trial proceeds on the basis of orality; almost every document and every piece of evidence, even though agreed by the parties, is read out. Every word spoken is recorded either by mechanical means or by a shorthand writer and may be used later if there is an appeal. In the county courts, which are not courts where verbatim records are kept, the same principle of orality applies but the only formal record of the proceedings will be the judge's notes. By and large the judge plays very little role in the proceedings, leaving it to counsel to call witnesses and pursue lines of enquiry in their questioning of their own choice. Much of what was said about the unreliability both of human testimony and of the adversary process as a means of eliciting the truth in the criminal trial applies equally to the civil trial. At the end of the presentation of the case for the plaintiff and for the defendant (and much of the dispute is likely to be about facts and not about the law that applies), the judge gives a reasoned judgment in which the judge will determine both liability and quantum either immediately or at some later time. The latter is called a reserved judgment. In some cases there will have been no dispute about liability and the sole issue will be that of quantum.

The effect of a payment into court

The discussion of the system of costs made clear that the prospect of perhaps losing after an expensive trial, in which case losing defendants will have to pay not

---

[69] M. Zander, 'Cost of Litigation: A Study of the Queen's Bench Division,' *Law Society's Gazette*, 25 June 1975.

[70] In 1996 the average time between issue of proceedings and the start of the trial in personal injury cases was 92 weeks in the county courts and 185 weeks in the High Court (209 weeks in London): *Judicial Statistics 1996* (London: HMSO, 1997, Cm. 3716).

only damages but also their own and the plaintiffs' costs, is in itself a powerful incentive to settle early before costs have begun to pile up dramatically. Equally a party for whom costs do not represent any inhibition to litigation can seek to escalate costs at every opportunity and to 'scare off' the opposing party. Rules of court themselves use costs as an incentive both to early settlement and to the proper conduct of the case.

The device of payment into court places considerable pressure on a plaintiff to settle. At any point after service of a summons, the defendant can pay a sum into court. This frequently occurs where there is an allegation of contributory negligence, which reduces damages payable to the plaintiff. The plaintiff is notified of the sum paid into court, and must either accept or reject it. If he or she accepts it, that effectively ends the proceedings, though the plaintiff will be entitled to costs up to settlement. If the plaintiff rejects the sum paid in, serious costs consequences ensue. At trial the judge is not told of the payment into court. Provided the plaintiff wins damages at trial in excess of the amount paid into court, the usual costs rules apply. But if the plaintiff wins less, the judge will usually award the plaintiff costs up to the date of the payment into court and the defendant costs from that point onwards. Since we have seen that costs escalate the further the case progresses, costs awarded against the plaintiff will be far more than those awarded in the plaintiff's favour. Plaintiffs who reject payments into court are effectively gambling to 'beat' the payment into court. If the defendant assesses the damages skilfully, and assessment of damages is not an exact science, the plaintiff has a real dilemma in deciding how to respond. More than one payment into court may be made. Defendants' lawyers often advise that the best strategy is to make a reasonable but not too generous payment into court at the earliest opportunity after issue of the writ. If the plaintiff does not accept this, a higher payment into court should be made at a later date. But more than two payments into court may be counter-productive because it may be seen as a sign of weakness. Payments into court will be replaced by written offers of settlement under the Woolf reforms.

Post-Woolf Practice and Procedure

What follows is a brief description of practice and procedure as it is expected to operate on the implementation of the recommendations in Lord Woolf's Final Report coupled with changes to the availability of legal aid.[71]

A fast-track procedure will be available for claims in excess of the relevant small claims limit[72] but not in excess of £15,000, while cases involving in excess of £15,000 will follow the multi-track procedure.

A protocol for personal injury cases has been developed and piloted. This includes pre-action matters. The protocol is designed to ensure proper progress of the case and to shape the behaviour of the parties from the earliest stages. It contains

---

[71] It is based largely on Lord Chancellor's Department, *An Access to Justice Working Paper: Judicial Case Management* (London: Lord Chancellor's Department, 1997).

[72] £5,000, but £1,000 in personal injuries claims.

standard letters, encourages the use of alternatives to litigation, and, most importantly, sets timetables to be followed. Early settlement should be promoted, and the use of delaying tactics penalised. Failure to comply with the requirements of the protocol can be penalised by costs sanctions.

All claims will be issued using a single Claim Form which will gave basic details of the claim. In personal injuries cases this will be accompanied by a Details of Claim Form containing much the same information as is currently required for county court particulars in such cases. These documents will be served as soon as practicable on the defendant by first class post together with a form which will provide for filing an admission, a defence or a counterclaim. Part admissionscan also be made. The court will send the plaintiff a Notice of Issue giving the date the Claim Form is issued and its presumed date of service. The court will also notify any failure to secure service. If the person claiming elects to serve the Claim Form, there will be a one-month time limit which can be extended on application.

The defendant will be allowed fourteen days in which to file a defence or a notice of intention to defend; the latter will include an obligation to file the defence within twenty-eight days.

On receipt of a defence, the case will be automatically transferred to the county court nearest the defendant's address. At this point an Allocation Questionnaire will be issued to the claimant and defendant for return within fourteen days of its presumed date of receipt. One of the questions in the Allocation Questionnaire asks for details of any attempt to settle the claim by mediation. If no effort has been made and if the parties wish to attempt mediation, the proceedings are automatically stayed for three months for this purpose. The main purpose of the Allocation Questionnaire is to enable the procedural judge to be informed of those matters which will determine how the case is to be managed by the court. The initial decision will be whether the case is allocated to the fast-track or multi-track procedure. Once a decision has been made a Notice of Allocation will be issued, the parties will have fourteen days in which to make representations opposing the allocation decision.

Where the fast-track has been selected, the Notice of Allocation will include a detailed timetable which will set out specific dates for each stage of preparation of the case. The standard timetable is set out in Figure 11.1. The key to ensuring progress once a defence has been filed is judicial case management. One way in which effect will be given to management by judges is the use of 'unless orders' which will state the sanction to be imposed automatically if a party fails to comply with a requirement by the judge managing the case.

A Listing Hearing may be called if there are issues which cannot be resolved from the questionnaire returns, or if the questionnaires are not returned. At least eight weeks notice of a trial date will be provided to the parties. This means that the fastest fast-track cases could come to trial within twenty weeks of the Notice of Allocation.

Multi-track cases are, unsurprisingly rather more complex. On allocation, the procedural judge can issue written directions, and set a timetable to fix the Case

Figure 11.1. **Standard timetable: fast-track procedure***

Time limit	Procedure	Elapsed time
Day 1	Notice of Allocation	
28 days later	Disclosure of documents	4 weeks
21 days later	Exchange of witness statements	7 weeks
21 days later	Exchange of expert reports	10 weeks
Day 70	Court sends out listing questionnaire	10 weeks
14 days later	Listing questionnaire returned	12 weeks
No later than day 211	Hearing	maximum 30 weeks

*Source of data: Lord Chancellor's Department, *An Access to Justice Working Paper: Judicial Case Management* (London: Lord Chancellor's Department, 1997), para. 3.3.

Management Conference, a date for filing a completed Listing Questionnaire, a date for a Pre-Trial Review and a trial date or period within which trial is likely to take place. The purpose of the Case Management Conference is 'to set the agenda for the case at the earliest possible stage to ensure that the procedures followed and costs incurred are proportionate to the case'.[73] The normal expectation is that the parties will attend in person with their lawyers at the Case Management Conference and the Pre-Trial Review

No-Fault Schemes

Respondents to the Civil Justice Review argued strongly that for some claims a system of no-fault compensation was the solution to the difficulties encountered by the system of adjudicating such claims. Considerable thought has been given to the establishment of a system of compensation without fault. Following the thalidomide tragedy, the Government established the Pearson Royal Commission on Civil Liability and Compensation for Personal Injury in 1975. The Report was published in 1978[74] and recommended the introduction of a no-fault scheme for road accidents modelled on the industrial injuries benefit scheme. The proposals did not attract much support and were quietly shelved. Yet the idea of no-fault schemes will not go away.[75] Recommendation 62 of the Civil Justice Review is that the Lord Chancellor consider, in consultation with the insurance industry, the feasibility of a no-fault scheme restricted to less serious road accidents and financed by private insurance. The advantages of reduction in uncertainty for claimants, the avoidance of delay and costs associated with litigation and the saving in court time would have to be off-set against the inevitable increase in motor insurance premiums.

[73] Lord Chancellor's Department, *An Access to Justice Working Paper: Judicial Case Management* (London: Lord Chancellor's Department, 1997), para. 4.7.

[74] *Report of the Royal Commission on Civil Liability and Compensation for Personal Injury (Pearson Commission)* (London: HMSO, 1978, Cmnd. 7054).

[75] See generally P. Atiyah, *Atiyah's Accidents, Compensation and the Law*, 5th edn. by P. Cane (London: Butterworths, 1993), ch. 19.

A number of these issues have been considered before. The Pearson Commission reported in 1978 on a number of issues related to accident compensation and its interaction with the social security system.[76] Among its many recommendations was the introduction of a no-fault scheme for road accident victims. The scheme would cover all accidents involving motor vehicles in places to which the public has access. The recommendation proposed that the scheme should be funded by a levy on petrol, since this would relate the costs approximately to the degree of risk created by each motorist in terms of mileage driven. The Report calculated that a levy of one penny per gallon would raise £64 million after five years.

Concluding Comment

Great changes are beginning to take effect in both the financing and the running of personal injuries cases. The changes are being introduced incrementally. To some this change will appear fragmentary. For example, legal aid is being withdrawn for personal injury claims before changes to the legal aid scheme and costs rules which will make certain payments made by plaintiffs under conditional fee agreements recoverable from a defendant. Changes which require primary legislation are to be included in a splendidly titled Modernisation of Justice Bill, but there have been suggestions that time may not be available for such a Bill in the 1999/2000 Parliamentary session. This is not a satisfactory method of introducing change.

Whether those changes improve access to justice and achieve a proportionate approach to justice will have to await the next edition of this work. However, more than at any other time this century (save perhaps through the introduction of legal aid) there could be a major change in the approach of both litigants and lawyers to this area of the civil process. There are likely to be fewer claims reaching courts because of the requirement to reach a higher likelihood of success that funding through conditional fees brings, but those cases in which proceedings are started should move much more speedily to judgment. The problem is that there may be a group of citizens for whom the investment needed on their part to run a case on a conditional fee basis will be prohibitive. Such proposals as exist for meeting what could become their unmet need for legal help remain undeveloped and consequently unconvincing.

---

[76] C. Bourn, 'The Pearson Proposals in Outline' in D. Allen, C. Bourn and J. Holyoak, *Accident Compensation after Pearson* (London: Sweet & Maxwell, 1979), p. 9.

12

DEALING WITH DEBT CASES

Introduction

Nearly nine out of every ten cases started in the Queen's Bench Division of the High Court and in the county courts concerns debt—that is over two million cases. In the majority of these cases, the plaintiff is a business or institution suing a private individual for unpaid debts arising from the supply of goods, services or credit. Many will relate to rent or to fuel debt owed to a gas or electricity supplier. A phenomenon of recent decades has been the growth in the availability of credit. This has led to an increase in debt cases, though the availability of credit has increased at a much faster rate than the incidence of debt claims.[1] One explanation why so many cases involve institutional plaintiffs and individual defendants is that litigation among those likely to have a continuing business relationship is seen as inconsistent with the maintenance of goodwill between the parties. Where disputes arise, negotiation is seen as a far more satisfactory solution. Bad debts tend to be litigated because the likelihood of a continuing relationship in the face of serious bad debt is negligible.[2]

Very few debt cases are contested. The Payne Committee in 1969 reported:

Actions for the recovery of debts engage the legal machinery at its least point of strain. The recovery of debts is very largely an administrative process and the handling of uncontested claims forms such a large part of the work of the courts that one cannot overemphasise the need to make machinery for obtaining judgments in the High Court and in the county courts as simple as possible.[3]

In 1996 there appear to have been no more than 5,000 trials in the High Court or county courts concerning debt despite over 2 million claims in debt having

---

[1] See K. Rowlingson and E. Kempson, *Paying with Plastic: A Study of Credit Card Debt* (London: Policy Studies Institute, 1994).

[2] S. Macaulay, 'Non-Contractual Relations in Business: A Preliminary Study' (1963) 28 Am. Soc. Rev. 55; and H. Beale and A. Dugdale, 'Contracts between Businessmen: Planning and the Use of Contractual Remedies' (1975) 2 Brit. J of Law and Soc. 45.

[3] *Report of the Committee on the Enforcement of Judgment Debts (Payne Committee)* (London: HMSO, 1969, Cmnd. 3909), para. 64.

been started in the courts.[4] Over ninety-five per cent of all claims were for £5,000 or less.

The Civil Justice Review recognised the importance of the debt enforcement work as the largest component of the work of the civil courts, accounting for a substantial proportion of their resources, but also drew attention to the two long-standing concerns about the system of debt enforcement:

From the point of view of the debtor there are complaints that the system allowed creditors to proceed to enforcement without obtaining adequate information about the debtor's ability to pay; while from the point of view of the creditor there are complaints about the ineffectiveness of the enforcement procedures.[5]

The Woolf Report has little to say about debt cases and explicitly does not concern itself with enforcement procedures.[6] The new fast-track procedures[7] will apply to nearly all debt cases which are beyond the small claims limit. The increase in the small claims limit to £3,000 in January 1996, and to £5,000 in April 1999, will have taken very many debt cases into the small claims jurisdiction.[8]

The Causes of Debt

Research studies into the causes of debt have been consistent in concluding that the overwhelming majority of debtors fall into the 'can't pay' category rather than the 'won't pay' group. The Consumer Councils all agree that there are three broad categories of debt:[9]

- people who have suffered an unexpected drop in income, perhaps brought about by unemployment, sickness or marriage breakdown; simply meeting normal household bills to maintain lifestyles becomes difficult and often money is borrowed at high interest rates;
- people in long-term poverty, who typically generate housing and fuel debts, but may also get into difficulties repaying loans to buy essential household goods, such as a cooker or a washing machine;
- relatively affluent people seduced by easily available credit facilities who commit their income very fully; any fluctuation in income or outgoings, as when mortgage interest rates rise, results in an inability to service the loans obtained.

---

[4] *Judicial Statistics 1996* (London: HMSO, 1997, Cm. 3716).

[5] *Civil Justice Review: Report of the Review Body on Civil Justice* (London: HMSO, 1988, Cm. 394), para. 534.

[6] Lord Woolf M. R., *Interim Report to the Lord Chancellor on the Civil Justice System in England and Wales* (London: HMSO, 1995), para. 12.5.   [7] Described as they apply to personal injuries cases in Ch. 11.

[8] See Ch. 13.

[9] National Consumer Council and Welsh Consumer Council, *Consumers and Debt* (London: National Consumer Council and Welsh Consumer Council, 1983); Scottish Consumer Council, *Debt Advice in Scotland* (Edinburgh: Scottish Consumer Council, 1988); and R. Berthoud and E. Kempson, *Credit and Debt: The PSI Report* (London: Policy Studies Institute, 1992). See also M. Hope, *Household Indebtedness, Voluntary and Involuntary: A Study of Court Summonses*, Lord Chancellor's Department Research Series No. 8/97 (London: Lord Chancellor's Department, 1997).

Despite the high profile sometimes given in the media to the third group, it remains a minority of total debt problems, though in some cases the scale of debt accrued in a short time can be startlingly high.

The Touche Ross Management Consultants factual study in 1986 for the Civil Justice Review[10] tends to confirm these earlier findings. Most defendants in the sample were male, over thirty and married with dependants. Their average income was only £105 per week. Over a third were unemployed at the start of the proceedings.

The Amount Claimed

The most recent detailed analysis of the amounts claimed in debt actions is the Touche Ross study. In the county courts, three-quarters of claims were for less than £500 and one in three was for less than £100. Such claims would, of course, be dealt with as small claims. Only one in nine was for more than £1,000. The average claim in the county courts was for £230. By contrast the average amount claimed in the High Court was £5,000, though just over half of all claims were for less than £5,000. Two-thirds of debtors sued in the High Court were businesses, compared with only three in every ten defendants in the county courts. It is therefore fair to note that the character of High Court and county court debt work is different. The High Court tends to deal with business debt, while the county courts deal with personal debt.

Some twenty-three enterprises were identified by the Touche Ross study as 'bulk creditors', that is, those, broadly speaking, issuing 1,000 or more summonses a year. These included mail order businesses, the utility companies (gas, electricity and water boards) and banks. Five of these indicated that they had a definite policy of pursuing smaller debts in the High Court because the chances of success were improved. But the thresholds varied. One set the threshold at over £2,000, three at over £600 and one at over £300. Bulk creditors account for about sixty per cent of the two million debts cases begun each year. One study has suggested that bulk creditors can be divided into two groups: those who had information suggesting that the debtor could pay and those which did not. The Inland Revenue and the banks tended only to sue if they had reason to believe that the debtor had the resources to pay the debt. Other bulk creditors, however, brought cases to court as a matter of routine. If enough debts were processed, then the debt recovery department would show an overall profit. Such creditors would typically send a series of demands before taking court action, but would not visit the debtor and seldom had any information as to the reasons for non-payment of the debt.[11] The Touche Ross study seems to suggest that the majority of creditors use the courts in this way.

---

[10] Touche Ross Management Consultants, *Study of Debt Enforcement Procedures produced for the Lord Chancellor's Civil Justice Review* (London: Touche Ross, 1986).

[11] M. Cain, 'Who Loses out in Paradise Island' in I. Ramsay (ed.), *Debtors and Creditors* (London: Professional Books, 1986).

Basic Practice and Procedure

Venue

The county court has concurrent jurisdiction with the High Court for all claims in contract, and all debt cases will be based in contract. The value of the action will largely determine whether the action is brought in a county court or the High Court. Where the value is less than £25,000 there is a presumption in favour of the county courts and where the value is £50,000 or more, there is a presumption in favour of the High Court. For cases involving £25,000 to £49,999, complexity and importance will be relevant factors in determining where to start the action. The result is that the county courts are the dominant forum for actions in debt. In 1996, they issued over 2 million default summons[12] as against the 19,582 writs issued in the High Court for debt.[13] For this reason, and because actions in the High Court are often concerned with business debt, what follows focuses mainly on practice and procedure in the county courts.

Default actions

Debt actions in the county courts are begun by using the **default summons** procedure. The plaintiff files a request for summons together with the particulars of claim at the appropriate county court. The particulars of claim frequently consist simply of a copy of the plaintiff's unpaid bill or account. On payment of the court fee, which is determined by reference to the amount claimed, the court will prepare the summons to the plaintiff. Two copies of the particulars of claim must be filed: one for the court to keep and one for service on the defendant. The request for summons is a simple form giving the addresses of the plaintiff and defendant. Bulk creditors are able to use the services of the Summons Production Centre, a special facility for the preparation of court documents for creditors issuing more than 1,000 claims each year. In 1996 the Summons Production Centre issued nearly half of all default summonses issued in the county courts.[14] If the request and particulars are in order, the county court will, on receipt of the court fee, issue a plaint note giving the court's unique number for the case and will prepare a default summons for service on the defendant.

Service of the summons on the defendant in debt actions is usually achieved by first class post. If the summons is returned undelivered, the court will tell the plaintiff who has the opportunity to provide a new address. The court will then try to serve the summons again.

Default actions require defendants to deliver an admission with an offer of payment, or a defence, within fourteen days after service of the summons. Failure to

---

[12] That is, claims for a liquidated sum. This will include actions other than debt, but the bulk of these actions is for debt.   [13] *Judicial Statistics 1996* (London: HMSO, 1997, Cm. 3716).

[14] That is, 1,019,431 summonses: *Judicial Statistics 1996* (London: HMSO, 1997, Cm. 3716).

take such action entitles plaintiffs to enter judgment by default, usually on terms that the full amount is payable forthwith. This is done by administrative action. There is no judicial consideration of the merits of the claim, nor any requirement to prove the facts upon which the claim is based. Two-thirds of all debt actions result in judgment by default. The case only proceeds to trial if the defendant lodges a defence to the claim. Very few defendants obtain legal advice in debt actions and very few actions are defended. Only seventy-four of the 1,002 cases in the sample used by the Touche Ross study were defended. The study does not indicate the nature of the defence nor whether those cases resulted in contested trials. The role of legal aid is minimal; no more than around 6,000 defendants receive legal aid each year to defend debt actions.[15] Three-quarters of individual debtors in the Touche Ross study had received no advice at all about the case against them.

Once again the system has responded to its bulk users, who can use the County Court Bulk Centre for entering judgment and seeking warrants of execution[16] to enforce those judgments.

If the plaintiff admits all or part of the claim coupled with an offer to pay by instalments, the defendant may accept this. If the plaintiff wishes to find out more about the defendant's means, an oral examination can be requested for which a further fee is payable. The defendant (or a director of a company if a company is the defendant) is required to attend at court where a court officer will conduct an enquiry on oath into the defendant's means. The process can be a means of showing a recalcitrant defendant that the judgment creditor means to enforce the judgment, and for that reason can result in payment being made which would not otherwise have been paid. But it is important to realise that an oral examination is not a method of enforcing the judgment. In some courts, the defendant is asked to file a statement or affidavit[17] which may be accepted by the district judge without an oral examination.

In some cases defendants write back admitting part of the claim but denying liability for the higher sum claimed. Plaintiffs can, in such cases, choose to accept the lesser amount in full satisfaction of the whole claim or elect to have the case treated as a defended claim.

Most claims in which a defence is filed will be subject to automatic directions specifying the steps each party must then take. Some cases[18] will require a Pre-Trial Review, which has two purposes. The first is to determine whether there is a reasonable case in law to be tried. If there is not, then judgment for either plaintiff or defendant, as appropriate, can be entered there and then. In the case of judgment for the plaintiff, this will only occur if the plaintiff is present and ready to prove the claim. The second purpose is to give directions for the proper preparation of

---

[15] 6,154 defendants received legal aid in actions in contract; this figure will include contractual disputes other than debt claims: *Legal Aid Board Annual Report 1996–97*, HCP 52 (1997–98) (London: HMSO, 1997). [16] See below.

[17] Sworn statement.

[18] For example, actions arising out of a regulated consumer credit agreement within the meaning of the Consumer Credit Act 1974.

the case for trial. The District Judge has a discretion to enter judgment for either party at the Pre-Trial Review.

Summary judgment

In some cases, the defendant will file a defence which has little or no merit merely to put off the day of reckoning when judgment will be entered against him or her. The **summary judgment** procedure is designed to enable the plaintiff to obtain judgment at the earliest opportunity.

In any case where the plaintiff has claimed more than £3,000 and where the defendant files a defence, the plaintiff can apply for summary judgment on the ground that, notwithstanding the filing of a defence, the defendant has no real defence to the claim. The plaintiff must serve on the defendant, not less than seven days before the date fixed for the hearing of the application, a notice of the application together with a copy of the affidavit verifying the claim and asserting a belief that there is no defence to the claim. The hearing will usually also be the Pre-Trial review, at which the spurious nature of any defence can, in any event, be raised.

The Enforcement Process

The choices

Obtaining judgment in debt cases is merely the tip of the iceberg, because obtaining judgment and enforcing it are entirely separate processes. Many litigants breathe a huge sigh of relief when they obtain judgment in their favour, believing the long battle is over. Judgment is, however, merely a declaration of their success and enforcing a money judgment is a separate and sometimes lengthy and complex process. It is for the plaintiff to make strategic decisions about which of a range of enforcement measures will be sought. There are a host of these, but the four main methods of enforcing a judgment are execution against the debtor's goods, attachment of earnings, charging orders and garnishee orders.

There remain different systems of enforcement in the High Court and in the county courts. County court enforcement is carried out by bailiffs who are employees of the court service answerable to a supervising bailiff. Plaintiffs pay fixed fees for enforcement measures in the county courts. In the High Court the system has been privatised; sheriff's officers working for private companies do the work of enforcement. These companies are accountable to Under Sheriffs who are usually solicitors in private practice appointed by the High Sheriff of each county. The area for which each Under Sheriff is responsible is known as the 'bailiwick'. The private companies make their money from the fees paid on the valuation of goods in connection with the process of execution. The Under Sheriffs make their money from a percentage of the debt recovered, a sort of performance-related pay. Though empirical evidence suggest that there is little difference in the effectiveness of the

Figure 12.1. **Enforcement action in 1996***

	County courts	High Court
Warrants of execution/writs of fi.fa	707,014	52,309
Garnishee orders	9,890	529
Charging orders	16,181	1,253
Attachment of earnings	73,973	n/a
Administration orders	10,357	n/a
Bankruptcy petitions	19,626	12,331

*Source of data: *Judicial Statistics 1996* (London: HMSO, 1997, Cm. 3716).

enforcement systems,[19] practitioner's wisdom is that High Court enforcement processes are much more effective than the county court system. Transfer between the county court and the High Court is expected to become easier, which reflects these concerns.[20]

Where plaintiffs know little about the financial position of defendants, they can request an oral examination of the defendant. This procedure compels debtors to attend court in order to be questioned about their financial position. Most of these inquisitions, which occur only in a small number of cases, take place before executive rather than judicial staff of the court. Around 80,000 oral examinations take place each year.[21] Where a debtor persistently fails to attend for an oral examination, a warrant for his or her arrest may be issued. Imprisonment following such arrest can be avoided by the completion on the spot of a questionnaire about his or her means. The following section describes the four main enforcement measures in the county courts with some comment on the corresponding High Court measure.

Because of the differences in the enforcement methods, cases may be transferred from the county court to the High Court for enforcement of the judgment against the debtor's goods. Where the judgment debt is less than £1,000, it can only be enforced in the county court, but where it is £1,000 or higher, it may be transferred to the High Court. Where a judgment debt is for £5,000 or more, it can only be enforced against goods in the High Court.

Figure 12.1 shows the volume of enforcement action in both the county courts and the High Court in 1996.

Warrants of execution

The fearsomely titled **warrant of execution** is a direction to the county court bailiff to seize and sell goods belonging to the defendant to the value of the warrant. The only goods which are exempt from seizure are clothing, bedding, furniture and household equipment necessary for satisfying the basic domestic needs of the debtor and

[19] See below.

[20] See Lord Chancellor's Department Consultation Paper, *Simplification of the Transfer Procedure from the County Court to the High Court for Enforcement by Execution against Goods*, 1998.

[21] *Judicial Statistics 1996* (London: HMSO, 1997, Cm. 3716).

his or her family, and the tools of the debtor's trade. All other goods may be seized provided that they belong to the debtor. Goods on hire purchase do not become the property of the hirer until all instalments under the agreement are paid. The High Court counterpart to the warrant of execution is the writ of *fieri facias*, commonly known as the 'writ of fi. fa'. Creditors may seek warrants for the full amount of the debt or for a lesser sum, and may seek as many warrants as are needed to recover the full judgment debt. One advantage of seeking a part warrant is that the fee is lower and the exercise can be used to discover whether the debtor has goods of sufficient value to make further warrants cost effective.

In practice very few warrants actually result in the sale of the debtor's property. Only one in two hundred warrants actually results in seizure and sale. Debtors are often keen to retain their possessions. Sometimes they pay the amount of the warrant to the bailiff. Sometimes the bailiff will allow a reasonable time to find the money to meet the warrant. In such cases the debtor is required to acknowledge that the bailiff has taken notional possession of goods belonging to the debtor and agrees not to dispose of the goods. This is called agreement to 'walking possession'. Where such an agreement is signed, the bailiff is entitled to break into the home if the debtor subsequently refuses to open the door when the bailiff calls. Many debtors borrow money in order to keep the bailiff away, often compounding their financial difficulties.

Attachment of earnings

An **attachment of earnings order** is an order only available in the county courts[22] and is directed to the debtor's employer authorising deductions from the debtor's wages which are sent to the court in settlement of the judgment debt. Attachment of earnings orders are only available against debtors in employment; income from self-employment cannot be attached. Once an application is made and details of the debtor's earnings have been established, the court will fix the 'protected earnings level' and the 'normal deduction rate'. The protected earnings level is the amount below which the court thinks that the debtor's income should not be reduced; it is calculated by reference to income support rates under the government scheme of means-tested social security benefits. The normal deduction rate is the amount the court considers it reasonable for the debtor to have deducted from wages each week or month in satisfaction of the judgment debt. The procedure for obtaining an order can be quite lengthy, but for a debtor in stable employment, the order is an effective method of enforcement.

Charging orders

Charging orders provide a means of treating land and securities as security for the judgment debt by imposing a charge on the asset for the amount of the judgment

---

[22] Though High Court judgments can be transferred to the county court to enable this form of enforcement to be used.

debt. The charge has the same effect as a mortgage on a house. This means that the land or securities cannot be sold without part of the proceeds being used to meet the judgment debt. Once a charging order has been obtained, the creditor may apply to the court for an order compelling its sale and for the discharge from the proceeds of sale of the judgment debt. The court has a discretion as to whether it is appropriate to order sale.

The creditor initially obtains the order nisi (the Latin word for 'unless') which becomes an order absolute unless the debtor shows cause why the order should not be granted, for example, by paying the judgment debt. The order nisi operates to freeze the debtor's assets.

Garnishee orders

The **garnishee order** is another quaintly named remedy. The order requires a bank, building society, or other person who owes money to the debtor to pay that money direct to the creditor in satisfaction of the outstanding judgment. The order is first granted on a nisi basis, which freezes the assets in the hands of the bank, building society, or other party owing money to the debtor. Many orders are not made absolute because the debtor pays the amount being sought.

Administration orders

Generally there is no system of priority applicable to judgment debts. The plaintiff who is the first to seek an enforcement order will be the first to get paid. The administration order may, however, be sought by debtors and offers some protection against enforcement measures from a variety of creditors. The order is available to a debtor with multiple debts of up to £5,000 in total, of which at least one is a judgment debt. The applicant asks the court for an order that allows the debtor to discharge all the debts by making regular payments under the order which are then distributed among the creditors on a *pro rata* basis. Where an administration order is in force, all other enforcement measures are barred. Such orders are only available in the county courts, but the judgment on which the order is based may have been obtained in the High Court. The Touche Ross study found that one-third of the ninety-eight administration orders they examined were scheduled to last for five years, one-third for between five and ten years, and one-third for more than ten years. The longest order would take seventy years before the debts were fully paid!

The Civil Justice Review recommended that administration orders be subject to reform, including the removal of the £5,000 limit. The advantage of the administration order over all other remedies is that it considers the overall debt position of the debtor and seeks to satisfy the interests of all creditors. Changes to primary legislation were introduced by section 13 of the Courts and Legal Services Act 1990 to enable the recommendations to be implemented, but these have not yet been brought into force.

The dominance of warrants of execution

Warrants of execution (and their High Court counterpart) are the dominant form of enforcement. The Touche Ross study is confirmed by the findings of the Queen Mary College project on the enforcement of county court judgments for debt, cited in this chapter as the QMC study.[23] Warrants of execution are issued in two-thirds of judgments and in one-third of all cases two or more warrants are issued. Since 1984 the minimum figure for a warrant seeking to enforce part of a judgment has been £50 plus costs. Both the Touche Ross study and the QMC study report that between eight and nine full or part warrants out of every twenty issued will be paid in full. The main cause of warrants failing to produce payment is that the debtor has no goods worth seizing for sale. One in three warrants fails on this count. One in five fails because the debtor cannot be traced; either the address given is incorrect or the debtor has left that address. Most warrants are finalised on two visits and within three months. The conclusion drawn by the QMC study is that where the debtor has goods worth seizing and where the correct address is supplied to the court, most warrants will be successful.

The QMC study notes that there are a number of bulk creditors who use the county courts as part of their own debt enforcement machinery. Cost effectiveness and the need to streamline procedures become the principal determinants of action. A quarter of judgments for debt will not require any enforcement action; the debtor will pay, or make satisfactory arrangements to pay by instalments, on receipt of the judgment. In around half the warrants issued, full payment of the debt will ultimately be achieved, often without any further information being obtained about the debtor. Oral examinations are unpopular because the procedure is time consuming and so expensive. Any action which requires a court hearing is expensive and unpopular among creditors. Equally, other enforcement action requires information and cannot so readily be built into streamlined office procedures. Even if successful they will not necessarily provide a quick and substantial payment.

The QMC study points out that each enforcement measure carries a qualifying condition. For the warrant of execution, it is the ownership of goods worth seizing; for the attachment of earnings order, it is the receipt of sufficient wages from employment; for the charging order, it is property to which the charge can attach; and for the garnishee order, it is the existence of a debt owed to the debtor. In all cases except the warrant of execution, it is for the judgment creditor to establish the qualifying condition as part of the process of obtaining the remedy. But for the warrant of execution, it is the bailiff who establishes the qualifying condition *after* the order has been granted. The QMC study concludes:

The most cost-effective way to use the existing system when the defendant goes into default is to set judgment terms according to a formula, and instruct the bailiff to collect the payments by way of part-warrants. This strategy provides an experience on which perceptions are based that most debtors are able but unwilling to pay, and, therefore,

---

[23] J. Phipps, 'Warrants of Execution in the Recovery of Consumer Debts in the County Court. A Lost Opportunity for Change' (1990) 9 CJQ 234.

when warrants fail, it is perceived to be because either the bailiff is not acting correctly or the procedure is ineffective.[24]

Who handles the cash?

County courts have since their establishment in 1846 handled the cash payments resulting from judgments made by the court. This is known as **suitors' cash**, another term within the county court system which now has a quaint archaic ring to it. The requirement that all payments under a judgment must be paid into court by the debtor for payment out to the creditor has outlived its usefulness. Money is moved around by other means and the system merely duplicated administrative effort. It is, of course, particularly inappropriate for bulk creditors; many have been receiving payments direct under a system known as 'pass throughs' for some time. In such cases the creditor simply advised the court of money received direct from the debtor. From 1 April 1990, the county courts have only handled those cash payments that are necessary for the coherent and effective operation of the system or where to do otherwise would impose a burden on a third party not directly connected with the proceedings. The main payments that still pass through the court are payments under warrants and attachment of earnings orders, and payments into court in part satisfaction before judgment. All other payments pass directly between the parties who are responsible for keeping their own records. In practice, this probably means the creditor's records will be accepted in the case of dispute, since they are likely to be viewed as 'more official'. It would be remarkable if debtors whose financial management has been called into question by the existence of the judgment debt suddenly developed the skills of setting up and maintaining a scrupulously accurate recording system for payments made to a creditor. A leaflet written in plain English advising the debtor on such things as payment and record-keeping is available to them.

Register of county court judgments

Some debtors will be concerned that a judgment against them could adversely affect their credit-rating. Judgment creditors may also be interested in discovering whether a debtor already has other judgments against them. One means of finding whether there are other judgments against a debtor is the use of the Register of Judgments. Before the change in the handling of debtors' money, where at least £10 was outstanding on a county court judgment debt one month after judgment, the debt was recorded in a public register. Outstanding judgments remained on the register for six years, at which time they are automatically deleted. The register has been privatised, though responsibility for the register remains with the Lord Chancellor, and is operated by Registry Trust Limited, a non-profit-making organisation set up by the credit industry.

---

[24] J. Phipps, 'Warrants of Execution in the Recovery of Consumer Debts in the County Court. A Lost Opportunity for Change' (1990) 9 CJQ, at 251.

From 1 April 1990 the system of registration has changed. Nearly all judgments for more than £1 are registered at the time judgment is entered in the action. The exception is defended cases which proceed to a hearing and where the losing party does not ask to pay by instalments. The presumption is that such cases will result in payment forthwith. It is open to a judgment creditor in such cases to obtain registration on application. A debtor who pays within one month may apply for a certificate of cancellation which removes the entry. Debtors who keep up instalment payments and duly pay off their debts may apply for a certificate of satisfaction which entitles them to have the entry in the register marked as satisfied. One and a quarter million entries were made in the register in 1996.[25]

The Northern Ireland Enforcement of Judgments Office

The *laissez-faire* 'first come first served' approach to the enforcement of judgment debts adopted in England and Wales is sometimes contrasted with the different system which operates in Northern Ireland. There the Enforcement of Judgments Office (EJO) was established in 1969,[26] though it does not change the 'first come first served' basis of enforcement. The Hunter Committee has, however, recommended a change to an asset-sharing basis of enforcement, like that operating under an administration order.

In Northern Ireland, if a judgment is not satisfied within seven days, the plaintiff may apply to the EJO for enforcement. The EJO then interview the debtor either at home or at the EJO premises. A creditor's report is then prepared, often following a number of interviews with the debtor and verification of the information given. The EJO's enquiries determine which measures of enforcement are appropriate. If it seems that the debtor has no realisable assets or income, a certificate of unenforceability is issued. No measures of enforcement can be taken while such a certificate is in force.

Criticisms of the EJO are that the process is slower and more expensive than its creditor-driven counterpart in England and Wales. Defenders of the EJO argue that the EJO is considering the whole case of the debtor rather than merely the enforcement of the particular judgment debt. After examining the record of the EJO, the National Consumer Council concluded:

We are wary about setting up a new bureaucracy that may prove slow and unwieldy. We do not suggest a completely new administrative structure. There are elements of the enforcement office idea, however, which could usefully be incorporated within the

---

[25] *Judicial Statistics 1996* (London: HMSO, 1997, Cm. 3716).

[26] *Report of the Joint Working Party on the Enforcement of Judgments, Orders and Decrees of the Courts of Northern Ireland (Anderson Committee)* (Belfast: HMSO, 1965); and *Report of the Enforcement of Judgments Review Committee (Northern Ireland) (Hunter Committee)* (Belfast: HMSO, 1988).

existing system. These include the emphasis on collecting information about debtors and dealing with all debts together. We wish to see the courts have the power to issue certificates of unenforceability where enforcement procedures would serve no useful function.[27]

The Payne Committee

The most important result of the deliberations of the Payne Committee[28] in 1969 was the Government's acceptance of the recommendation of the minority that imprisonment as a method of enforcing ordinary civil debt should be abolished. The remaining exceptions to this exemption from committal to prison for non-payment of debts are maintenance debts and statutory debts in respect of fuel consumption (gas and electricity), water consumption, tax and non-payment of council tax. The recommendations of the Committee also resulted in the introduction in 1971 of attachment of earnings orders.

Many other recommendations of the Payne Committee have not been implemented. A major criticism in the Report was the overlapping jurisdictions of the courts in debt cases, which presented the lay person with a 'bewildering multiplicity and choice of courts and procedures'.[29] Enforcement was described as 'unduly cumbersome, inefficient and expensive'. The Committee continues:

One would have thought it self-evident that there was every possible objection to proceeding with the enforcement of a money judgment against a debtor without first ascertaining what property, assets, earnings and means he has at his disposal and what are his financial commitments and his circumstances; the size of his family, the nature of his business, the ownership or tenancy of his dwelling-house and so forth. And yet steps in enforcement are frequently taken before this information has been obtained and often as a means of obtaining the information itself.[30]

The Payne Committee recommended the creation of a new enforcement office in the county courts which would collect information about debtors and select the appropriate means of enforcement. In short, the Payne Committee recommended for England and Wales what the Anderson Committee had recommended for Northern Ireland in the form of the EJO. The Payne Committee's enforcement office would also co-ordinate all enforcement activity, over-riding the 'first come first served' basis of enforcement. The Payne Committee also recommended that there should be a single system of enforcement operated through the county courts, but the Law Society fought a successful campaign to prevent implementation of the recommendation. Cynics accuse the Law Society of merely protecting the interests of

---

[27] National Consumer Council, *Ordinary Justice* (London: National Consumer Council, 1989), p. 368.
[28] *Report of the Committee on the Enforcement of Judgment Debts (Payne Committee)* (London: HMSO, 1969, Cmnd. 3909).   [29] Ibid., para. 290.
[30] Ibid., para. 296.

those solicitors holding office as Under Sheriffs; others have commented that High Court enforcement is far more effective, though more expensive. The latter reason would seem to be supported by the number of cases brought in the High Court each year which are within the jurisdictional limits of the county courts, though it is not supported by the findings of the Touche Ross and QMC studies.

The Civil Justice Review Proposals

Reference has already been made to the factual study carried out by Touche Ross Management Consultants for the Civil Justice Review. Touche Ross established as their criteria for judging debt enforcement procedures the creditors' interest in getting the debt paid reasonably quickly at reasonable cost and using a fair procedure coupled with the debtors' interest in being treated fairly and sympathetically. Overall Touche Ross did not believe that root and branch reform was needed, preferring the strategy of making improvements to the current system.

In addition to the findings reported earlier in this chapter, the Touche Ross study showed that, contrary to popular wisdom, there was little difference between the recovery rate of county court bailiffs and High Court bailiffs. Within fifteen to eighteen months of the start of proceedings, over half the judgment debts remained unsatisfied in whole or in part. The majority of creditors who had used enforcement procedures considered that enforcement had not helped them to recover payment. But three-quarters of all creditors had taken no steps to obtain information about the debtor's circumstances. Indeed, two-thirds of business creditors in the county courts had made no credit checks at the time of the original transaction which had given rise to the debt claim. One in three defendants in the county courts said they had not filed a defence, but nevertheless disputed the claim.

The recommendations in the Report of the Civil Justice Review accept that fine tuning is what is needed rather than radical reform. Six objectives are set for debt recovery through the courts:

- the system should aim to recover as much as possible of the debt quickly, cheaply and simply;
- creditors should be able to obtain adequate information about debtor's circumstances;
- maximum information should be available about debtors on public files;
- there should be machinery for bringing together multiple debts;
- the period for repayment should not last indefinitely and a debtor should be restored to full economic status as soon as possible;
- debtors and their families should not be subjected to unwarranted hardship, fear or humiliation.

The Civil Justice Review's recommendations focus on six areas: terminology, the distribution of business and representation, responsibility for enforcement, the functions of bailiffs and Sheriffs, administration orders, and extending the goods exempt from seizure under a warrant. There is welcome recognition that the terminology used in describing enforcement measures is quaint and old-fashioned and will mean little to debtors, though no suggestions are offered for the new generation of names for enforcement measures.

The recommendations on the distribution of business presented the Civil Justice Review with a dilemma. There is a general acceptance that there is merit in having a single point of entry into the court system for the most common actions and that this should be the county court. Opposition to this for debt cases in the responses to the consultation paper drew attention to the different nature of the debts the subject of actions in the county courts and the High Court. County court debt is mostly consumer debt, while High Court debt is mostly business debt. There remained the conviction (which we have seen is not supported by the empirical evidence) that High Court enforcement is more effective. Finally, the transfer of business to the county courts might overwhelm them. Those arguments won the day and the Report recommended no change for the time being in the distribution of debt business between the High Court and the county courts. However, subsequently, the Government determined that the jurisdiction of the High Court and the county courts in debt cases should be concurrent.

The Review recognises the valuable work done by lay advice and assistance and accept that it is appropriate to permit lay representatives to appear in debt cases in the county courts. The formal recommendation on this appears in the chapter of the Review on access to justice and proposes a statutory right for a litigant in a debt case in the county court to be assisted or represented by a lay representative of their choice, subject to the discretion of the court 'to restrict the involvement of corrupt or unruly representatives, and, where necessary, to exclude them entirely'.[31]

The debate over the machinery for enforcement is one of long standing. Despite the findings of the factual study that there is comparatively little difference between the success rates of county court bailiffs and Sheriffs, the recommendation is again largely for no change. The different character of the nature and value of the business conducted by the two systems is seen to justify the maintenance of two systems. The recommendation of the Civil Justice Review seeks to reserve business debt for the High Court enforcement system and consumer debt for the county court bailiffs, but does not wholly erode the principal that the place where the action takes place determines the enforcement machinery available. The recommendation (which has largely been implemented) was that all judgments below £5,000 and all judgments arising out of the various credit arrangements regulated by the Consumer Credit Act 1974 will be enforced by county court bailiffs, whereas judgments above £5,000 should automatically be transferred, and county court judgments above £2,000 and of a commercial nature may be transferred, to Sheriffs for enforcement.

---

[31] *Civil Justice Review: Report of the Review Body on Civil Justice* (London: HMSO, 1988, Cm. 394), para. 254 and Recommendation 48. See now Courts and Legal Services Act 1990, s. 11.

The criticisms of the bailiff service in the county court are noted and recommendations are made for improving the management structure within the county court service to integrate the bailiff service more fully into the court service. The conduct of bailiffs should be more controlled and there should be greater recognition of their role as information gatherers. Local variations in practice demand the production of a complete, and publicly available, manual setting out the bailiff's duties. The recommendation relating to the High Court enforcement machinery is feeble, simply stating that the law governing the execution by Under Sheriffs and Sheriff's Officers should be the subject of detailed reform, though there is an agenda of largely technical matters for consideration by whichever body is to be charged with this task.

The Civil Justice Review again rather feebly recommends that the administration order should be the subject of detailed reforms. The recommendation for reform follows the recommendation made in 1982 that the procedure should operate as a 'poor man's bankruptcy'.[32] This is the one enforcement remedy available to either debtor or creditor which looks at the overall debt position of the debtor and seeks to satisfy the interests of all creditors. It is described as a sort of 'mini-bankruptcy'. Specific proposals are that the current £5,000 limit should be removed, that the qualifying condition of the existence of a judgment debt should be dropped, and that a time limit of three years should be placed on the duration of the order. If the debtor cannot reasonably be expected to meet all his or her liabilities in that period, then a composition order should be made reducing the overall indebtedness to a level which can reasonably be met and paying creditors rateably. The same recommendation also proposes the introduction of a certificate of unenforceability similar to that operating in Northern Ireland.

The Civil Justice Review recommends that the goods exempt from seizure under a warrant should be extended so that the protection afforded by section 283 of the Insolvency Act 1986 applies to warrants of execution. Section 283 excludes two groups of possessions: tools of a trade and essential household equipment. The former are such tools, books, vehicles and other items of equipment as are necessary for the debtor for use personally in employment, trade or business. The latter are such clothing, bedding, furniture, and household equipment as are necessary for satisfying the basic domestic needs of the debtor and his or her family. The need for guidance on what is 'necessary' is noted. It has not yet been provided and remains a matter of judgment.

The most significant omission from the recommendations of the Civil Justice Review is the summary rejection of the idea of an enforcement office, which had been canvassed in the consultation paper: 'The concept of an enforcement office has been rejected, mainly because of the extra cost and delay which this would introduce'.[33]

---

[32] *Report of the Review Committee on Insolvency Law and Practice (Cork Committee)* (London: HMSO, 1982, Cmnd. 8558).

[33] *Civil Justice Review: Report of the Review Body on Civil Justice* (London: HMSO, 1988, Cm. 394), para. 645.

The key function of the enforcement office is to investigate the means of the debtor and to select and process appropriate enforcement action. It is therefore unfair to suggest that the fees charged by an enforcement office should properly be compared with fees for execution against goods. The enforcement office is doing rather more. The fees only look expensive because at present creditors, and bulk creditors in particular, can get away without investigating the circumstances of the debtor. Little weight is given to the stark contrast between the position in England and Wales and Northern Ireland. In England and Wales four out of five judgments necessitate some enforcement activity, whereas in Northern Ireland three-quarters of applications to the EJO for enforcement were settled without the need for an enforcement order. The Hunter Committee which reviewed the work of the EJO concluded: 'Most debtors who can pay will do so when they are confronted with enforcement proceedings and . . . it is only in the minority of cases that actual enforcement measures have to be taken'.[34]

The Civil Justice Review did not examine the debt recovery jurisdictions that vest in the magistrates' courts concerning tax, council tax, 'distress' for rent, and disconnection for unpaid fuel debts. There is evidence of regional variations by magistrates' courts in their approach to debt similar to those found in the exercise of their criminal jurisdiction.

Ultimately the complaint that can be levied at the Civil Justice Review is that, though one of its aims appears to be to focus more on debtors than individual debt, the recommendations it makes will make few inroads into the practice of most creditors of focusing on individual debt rather than the overall circumstances of the debtor.

That this is a twilight area for reform is also evidenced by its omission from the matters considered by Lord Woolf in his recommendations for improving access to justice in civil litigation. However, the Lord Chancellor announced a comprehensive review of enforcement methods including the question of the administrative body which should carry responsibility for them in May 1998 with consultation running until September 1998.[35] Any changes that result are expected to take effect in 2001.

The National Consumer Council Proposals

The National Consumer Council's response[36] to the issues raised by the Report of the Civil Justice Review felt that it was important that the system of debt recovery sought to distinguish between those who cannot pay their debts and those who will

---

[34] *Report of the Enforcement of Judgments Review Committee (Northern Ireland) (Hunter Committee)* (Belfast: HMSO, 1988), para. 3.35.

[35] Lord Chancellor's Department Consultation Paper, *Enforcement of Civil Court Judgments*, 1998.

[36] National Consumer Council, *Ordinary Justice* (London: National Consumer Council, 1989). See also National Consumer Council, *Credit and Debt: The Consumer Interest* (London: National Consumer Council, 1990).

not pay them. The focus of the system on debts rather debtors is highlighted. Many debtors have two or three other debts in addition to the judgment debt and there may be judgments in respect of the other debts. Yet the present filing arrangements within the county courts do not allow courts to discover if debtors are being pursued for other debts. This results in a situation where, unless the debtor makes use of the administration order, debt enforcement becomes 'a case of every creditor for himself'. The National Consumer Council's response is to propose a ten point plan for reform of debt recovery systems in the county courts:[37]

- all consumer debts should be dealt with in the county courts;
- debtors should be protected against harassment and should have access to advice in negotiating informal settlements;
- defendants should be encouraged to put defences before the court by the use of well designed forms, information and advice;
- court staff should review all documents carefully to ensure that all valid defences are referred for adjudication;
- courts should keep information about debtors, rather than individual debts, and this information should be used to inform decisions about enforcement orders to be used;
- the threat to seize goods and sell them should be used as a last rather than the first choice of enforcement activity;
- the administration order should be reformed and expanded, and it should be made more readily available through the provision of money advice;
- debtors who show the courts that they have made their best efforts to pay and also show that they were not fraudulent or reckless in incurring debt should be given relief from liabilities after three years;
- creditors who are individuals rather than institutions should be given greater help and advice by court staff.

The National Consumer Council believes that the best forum for debt enforcement actions against individuals is the county court. The Council wishes to see all debt jurisdiction concentrated there. This would transfer the civil jurisdiction of magistrates' courts to the county court. All individual debts not exceeding £25,000 should start in the county court. There would be a procedure whereby the plaintiff could show that a debt for a lesser sum was incurred in the course of a business and seek transfer to the High Court.

The National Consumer Council welcomes the recommendations on the functions of bailiffs, but hopes that there will be a separation of the investigative role from that of the threat to seize goods. The authority to seize goods for sale should not be available until the existence of goods worth selling is established and an exploration has taken place of alternative methods of settlement of the debt.

The reform of administration orders is also welcomed by the National Consumer Council, but it expresses the view that 'specialist debt counselling is crucial

---

[37] National Consumer Council, *Ordinary Justice* (London: National Consumer Council, 1989), pp. 369–70.

to the success of administration orders'. A study in Birmingham showed that administration orders are much more likely to be used where the debtor has access to debt counselling. The Birmingham Money Advice Centre was involved in nineteen out of the thirty-one administration orders made by the Birmingham County Court in 1978. By 1982, two-thirds of the orders handled by the Money Advice Centre were up to date, whereas only one-third of orders handled elsewhere met this target. The success of the Money Advice Centre approach is attributed to their dealing with the whole financial situation of the debtor, a willingness to deal with debtors within and outside the order and the provision of continuing encouragement and support.[38]

The centrality of advice and assistance is stressed time and again in the National Consumer Council's response. One experiment which seems to have been a great success is the provision of a welfare officer at the Birmingham County Court to assist debtors. The National Consumer Council reports:

The welfare officer is able to take referrals directly from the registrar during the course of the hearing and can negotiate directly with creditors and put the defendant's side for the case before the court. She approaches people coming out of court where they appear to be confused about the order made. She also ensures good liaison with other advice agencies in the city. One registrar commented 'the present system is worth to me up to half a Registrar in the saving of judicial time'.[39]

With exemplary regard for fairness, the National Consumer Council also call for court provided advice and assistance for the individual creditor for whom the county court debt enforcement machinery will be as much unknown territory as for the debtor. This should extend to advice on enforcement of any judgment obtained.

Conclusion

Debt claims, more than any other claims, are handled as administrative matters, both at the merits stage and at the enforcement stage. The county courts, which were designed in 1846 to be the local forum for the ordinary person as plaintiff, have become the forum in which the ordinary person is sued and part of the machinery of debt collection.[40] Many procedures in this area are designed with the interests of bulk creditors in mind rather than the interests of the individual debtor. On balance, the changes resulting from the Civil Justice Review give more to creditors than to debtors, but interestingly not all the recommendations have been implemented. For the second time in twenty years, the opportunity has been missed to substitute a system based on informed choices about debtor's circumstances for a system of routinised justice which fails to be fair to debtors and is often perceived by creditors as being inefficient in securing payment of debts.

[38] J. Davies, 'Delegalisation of Debt Recovery Procedures: A Socio-Legal Study of Money Advice Centres and Administration Orders' in I. Ramsay (ed.), *Debtors and Creditors* (London: Professional Books, 1986).
[39] National Consumer Council, *Ordinary Justice* (London: National Consumer Council, 1989), p. 377.
[40] Consumer Council, *Justice out of Reach* (London: Consumer Council, 1970).

13

DEALING WITH SMALL CLAIMS

The Context

In 1986 the Office of Fair Trading, a statutory agency, conducted a large-scale survey into consumer dissatisfaction with goods and services.[1] This revealed that 18 million people have about 30 million consumer complaints a year. Around 12 million complaints related to six categories where the average purchase price of the goods or services exceeded £100: furniture, household appliances, cars, car servicing, building, and holidays. In these areas four out of five consumers took some action to redress their grievances. The most common action was to complain to the supplier. Persistence pays off, because those who refused to take no for an answer frequently achieved some success with their complaints. The survey, however, quantified the residual group of unresolved complaints at 4.5 million.[2]

For many, going to court appeared not to be an option. Less than one in fifty complainants threatened court action. Ignorance of the role of the county courts in providing a forum for the resolution of consumer complaints was one factor thought to account for this.[3] Even where the existence of this forum was known, many consumers were reluctant to use the county courts for fear of cost, publicity, formality and the worry generated by going to court.[4]

The Challenge

Access to the courts for persons wronged is, as we have seen in Chapter 10, viewed as a fundamental aspect of the English legal system. This proposition is as applicable to the machinery for processing minor disputes as it is to the processes for

---

[1] Office of Fair Trading, *Consumer Dissatisfaction: a Report on Surveys Undertaken by the Office of Fair Trading* (London: HMSO, 1986).

[2] These conclusions are largely confirmed by the ongoing consumer dissatisfaction surveys conducted by the OFT: see generally the OFT magazine, *Fair Trading*.

[3] National Consumer Council, *Simple Justice* (London: National Consumer Council, 1979).

[4] A. Smith and Y. McGivern, 'Data from CA: Taking Legal Action' (1994) 4 *Consumer Policy Review* 47.

determining liability in serious accident cases and contractual disputes. But litigation is an expensive business and the cost of taking action even in a small case can soon exceed several hundred pounds. One survey conducted for Lord Woolf revealed that 217 personal injury cases had resulted in an average of £694 in damages with average legal costs of £836.[5] The process costs (meaning not only legal and court costs but also loss of earnings in attending court and a money figure for the stress and the risks of litigation) involved in pursuing a small claim can easily exceed the amount in dispute. This can make it uneconomic to pursue the claim which may consequently be abandoned. If the claim was justified in the first place, then justice will not have been done. This chapter is concerned with the accommodations the English legal system has made to try to avoid such denials of justice.

Defining small claims is not easy. It is possible to define such claims either by monetary limits or by type of dispute. Since much of the focus of the debate in this area is on consumer complaints, then one approach would be to define a small claim as any complaint concerning the quality of goods or services regardless of the cost of the goods or services. After all the essential factual and legal questions involved in a dispute concerning the quality of a hi-fi system costing £600 or £6,000 will be the same. Though such an approach might be fruitful, it has not been adopted. The essential approach has been to define a small claim by the money value of the claim. Successive official reports have recommended an increase in the amount which will be regarded under the rules of civil procedure as a small claim. The county courts small claims procedure was introduced in 1973 with a money value of £75, which was subsequently raised to £200, then £500. The Lord Chancellor's Civil Justice Review, which reported in June 1988, recommended an increase to £1,000, and this was implemented.[6] The Woolf Report recommended an increase to £3,000 save in personal injury cases, where the limit should remain at £1,000.[7] This recommendation was implemented in January 1996;[8] the limit was further increased to £5,000 in April 1999. The result is that very large numbers of claims are now within the small claims limits; the small claims procedure is now the dominant trial process in the county courts.

Discussions of small claims invariably centre on the role of the locally-based county courts. The present system of county courts was set up in 1846 in what was then a radically new model for dispensing civil justice on a local basis. The establishment of the new courts was opposed by barristers who feared that their livelihoods would be lost to solicitors who were given rights of audience before county courts.[9] The main purpose of county courts in 1846 was to provide for the speedy

[5] Lord Woolf M. R., *Interim Report to the Lord Chancellor on the Civil Justice System in England and Wales* (London: HMSO, 1995), ch. 3, para. 20 (cited in this chapter as 'Interim Report').

[6] *Civil Justice Review: Report of the Review Body on Civil Justice* (London: HMSO, 1988, Cm. 394).

[7] Interim Report, *supra* n. 5, ch. 16, paras. 48–65.

[8] For a discussion of some likely effects of this change, see J. Baldwin, 'Raising the Small Claims Limit' in A. Zuckerman and R. Cranston (eds), *Reform of Civil Procedure: Essays on 'Access to Justice'* (Oxford: Clarendon Press, 1995), p. 185. For a discussion of the actual impact of the increase to £3,000, see J. Baldwin, *Monitoring the Rise of the Small Claims Limit: Litigants' Experiences of Different Forms of Adjudication*, Lord Chancellor's Department Research Series 1/97 (London: Lord Chancellor's Department, 1997).

[9] R. Cocks, *Foundations of the Modern Bar* (London: Sweet & Maxwell, 1983), pp. 86–8.

and easy recovery of small debts, but the courts were so successful that they soon became courts enjoying a wide civil jurisdiction.[10] Today practice and procedure in the county courts and in the High Court are being increasingly brought together with monetary limits on claims determining the distribution of business between them, though the jurisdiction of the county courts remains local and wholly regulated by statute.

The current wave of concern about the processing of small claims can be traced back to the 1970 report *Justice Out of Reach* in which the Consumer Council showed that the county courts were then an inadequate forum for the processing of consumer complaints. Far from being the court for the ordinary person, it was the court in which the ordinary person was sued for debt. The county courts had become part of the machinery of debt collection.[11] The Consumer Council recommended changes in county court practice and procedure in order to make the courts a more attractive forum in which consumers could pursue their claims. The official response to the report was that more use was made of the provision in the county courts legislation allowing arbitration of disputes. Small claims were to be diverted away from the formal adversarial system of dispute settlement by means of trial in open court to a less formal private resolution of the dispute before a registrar[12] or judge. Some have called this 'court-annexed arbitration', though the current Master of the Rolls has warned against viewing the process simply as arbitration.[13] Amendments and refinements over the years have led to this procedure coming to be known as the 'small claims procedure' in the county courts. It currently operates automatically in all cases involving £5,000 or less for most cases but with a lower limit of £1,000 for personal injury claims. With the agreement of the parties (and under the Woolf proposals with the encouragement of the court), the procedure can be used for disputes involving larger sums.

County courts deal with over 2.5 million cases each year. In 1993 about six out of ten of the 2.7 million default summonses issued were within the small claims limit.[14] Most of these cases settle without the need for a court hearing. The number of hearings rose from 43,000 in 1984 to 106,000 in 1993.[15] In 1996, 94,050 cases were disposed of by arbitration.[16] These included 73,411 debt cases and 5,217 personal injury cases. 47,250 plaintiffs and 61,000 defendants were individuals. In both cases the category of individuals includes those in business. The average waiting time for the hearing was twenty-one weeks and the average length of the hearing was forty-seven minutes.[17]

[10] W. Holdsworth, *A History of English Law*, 7th edn. by A. Goodhart and H. Hanbury (London: Methuen, 1956).

[11] Consumer Council, *Justice Out of Reach* (London: Consumer Council, 1970); and National Consumer Council, *Ordinary Justice* (London: National Consumer Council, 1989). See also Welsh Consumer Council, *Courting the Consumer* (Cardiff: Welsh Consumer Council, 1988).   [12] Now known as a district judge.

[13] See *Joyce* v. *Liverpool City Council; Wynne* v. *Liverpool City Council* [1996] QB 252, 265.

[14] National Audit Office, *Handling Small Claims in the County Court*, HCP 271 (1995–96) (London: HMSO, 1996), p. 1.   [15] Ibid.

[16] This will have included the first cases under the latest increase in small claims limits, but will also include a large number of cases started before the increase in those limits.

[17] *Judicial Statistics 1996* (London: HMSO, 1997, Cm. 3716).

Despite these developments in the county courts, other independent initiatives have been tried. Some have failed; others continue. A significant modern phenomenon is the development of alternative dispute resolution mechanisms for a broad class of what might be thought of as customer complaints. Their contribution to providing the means of settling small claims will also be considered in this chapter.

Practice and Procedure in the County Courts

Introduction

This section describes practice and procedure in small claims.[18] The procedures are now well established and there has been some fine tuning as a result of the implementation of recommendations made by Lord Woolf in his Interim Report. Much of the research that is reported in this section predates the two very significant increases in the small claims limits implemented following Lord Woolf's recommendations. Those changes could have an impact on the way in which the system operates, but it will be some time before research results on the operation of the raised limits is available.[19] What is now clear, as noted above, is that the small claims procedure is the most frequently used method for resolving contested cases in the county courts.

Discouraging the use of lawyers

The procedure described in this section applies to all money claims in the county courts where the damages or loss are expected to be £5,000 or less, or £1,000 or less for personal injury claims. For these claims the system is designed to be accessible to the litigant without the need to have representation in court by lawyers. Indeed the use of lawyers for this purpose is discouraged by two rules. First, the costs of representation are not normally recoverable by a successful party, and, secondly, civil legal aid will not normally be granted where value of the claim falls within the small claims limits. Of course, advice and assistance under the Green Form Scheme will be available, but this does not cover representation in court. To encourage use of the county courts without solicitors, the Lord Chancellor's Department has issued a series of seven leaflets, which have been awarded the Plain English Campaign's crystal mark for clarity. They replace a booklet *Small Claims in the County Court—How to sue and defend actions without a solicitor*. That booklet ran to seventy-two pages and required a fair degree of literacy to be used

---

[18] See generally G. Applebey, *A Practical Guide to the Small Claims Court* (Croydon: Tolley, 1994).

[19] But see J. Baldwin, *Monitoring the Rise of the Small Claims Limit: Litigants' Experiences of Different Forms of Adjudication*, Lord Chancellor's Department Research Series 1/97 (London: Lord Chancellor's Department, 1997), who concludes that the increase from £1,000 to £3,000 has, from the perception of litigants, been achieved 'without serious difficulty or disruption'.

effectively. Research for the Civil Justice Review found that two-thirds of plaintiffs had seen the booklet and four of five of this group found it useful.[20] The new
leaflets are simple and straightforward, but are not as readily available as might
be wished. One survey reports a third of litigants not having seen them and that
county court staff 'frequently struggle to find a complete set'.[21] It seems that many
litigants do not get to see the leaflets.[22] For those who do and are determined to
press their claims, the leaflets give helpful guidance, which is necessary because
the system remains adversarial. Court staff will assist with the completion of forms
but will not advise on the merits of the claim or on the likelihood of success.[23]
The documentation is directed towards plaintiffs, which can leave defendants at a
disadvantage. The criticisms which can be levelled both at the booklet and the
shorter leaflets highlight the complexity of the issues surrounding the delivery of
information to litigants.

Starting the action

The plaintiff is expected to have sent a 'letter before action' threatening proceedings
if the grievance is not settled forthwith. The relevant leaflet provides a precedent;
a letter before action is simply a letter advising the other party that legal proceedings will follow if the matter is not settled. In beginning proceedings destined
ultimately for the small claims procedure, a plaintiff uses the ordinary means of
beginning any action in the county court. The plaintiff must choose which of the
two types of summons to request: **a fixed date summons** or **a default summons**.
Default summonses are used for all money claims, whether debt or damages to be
assessed by the court, and fixed date summonses for seeking a remedy other than
money.[24] Most small claims will be begun by default summons.

   The form of request for a summons is a straightforward document, but it
may well seek information the plaintiff does not have. The plaintiff is required to
provide the name and address of the defendant. This may sound straightforward,
but there may be hidden difficulties. Many claims will be against businesses. The
plaintiff will need to determine whether the business is a partnership, a sole trader
trading under his or her own name or another name, or a limited company. If the
plaintiff is suing a limited company, the registered office address is the best address
for service, though an address where the company trades will suffice. A company

---

[20] Touche Ross Management Consultants, *Study of Small Claims Procedure, produced for the Lord
Chancellor's Civil Justice Review* (London: Touche Ross, 1986).

[21] J. Baldwin, *Small Claims in the County Courts in England and Wales* (Oxford: Clarendon Press, 1997),
p. 7; see also pp. 110–11. The author of this book failed to secure a complete set despite many requests to
the Court Service.   [22] Ibid.

[23] The Interim Report, *supra* n. 5, stresses the need for court staff to be willing to give advice on remedies, procedure and the completion of forms, but recognises that court staff cannot give advice on whether
a person 'has a sound case in law': ch. 17, para. 16.

[24] District judges may grant the same remedies under the arbitration procedure as judges at trial, including specific performance, injunctions and declarations: *Joyce* v. *Liverpool City Council*; *Wynne* v. *Liverpool
City Council* [1996] QB 252.

search may be needed to establish the registered office address if it is not clearly stated on any document from the trader. For a lawyer it is a simple task to find this out, and could easily be done over the telephone in a few minutes within the scope of advice and assistance. But for litigants in person it may seem an unnecessary difficulty placed by the system in their path. If the defendant is a person trading in partnership under a partnership name, then it will be necessary to find the name and address of at least one partner. This may be problematic; it is not uncommon for disreputable traders deliberately to disguise their identities by failing to comply with the requirements that note paper shows the names of partners in a business and that these names are displayed at business premises. It is always the plaintiff's responsibility to provide the correct name and address of any defendant.

The plaintiff can start the proceedings at any county court, though a contested case may need to be transferred to another court at a later stage in the process.

Having completed the request for a default summons, the plaintiff must also prepare **particulars of claim**. These are no more than a simple factual statement of the basis of the claim. The county court will provide appropriate blank forms. The general standard of particulars of claim in the county courts is poor. For example, it is common practice for businesses simply to use a copy of their invoices to customers as particulars in their debt claims. But the better drafted the particulars, the better the chance of early settlement of the claim. Again the relevant leaflet contains a helpful precedent, but even first year law students often find the task of preparing particulars daunting and so it would be wrong to assume that this is never problematic for litigants in person. It is a pity that more use is not made of advice and assistance for drafting particulars.

The request for summons and enough copies of the particulars of claim for each defendant plus one for the court and one for the plaintiff's own file should be presented at court together with the fee for filing a claim; fees are charged on a sliding scale starting at £10 for a claim of up to £100. The fee then rises in £10 units for each additional £100 or part until the claim reaches sums in excess of £500. For claims exceeding £500 but not £1,000 the fee is £60, and for claims in excess of £1,000 up to £5,000 the fee is £80.[25] For those on income support and certain other social security benefits, fees can be remitted, but it seems that hardly any requests for fee remissions are made.[26] Once issued the summons must be served on the defendant. This is normally done by post. The plaintiff will be given a notice of issue which acts as a receipt for the court fee and states the case reference number, a unique number used by the court to identify the case in its own records. Once the summons and particulars have been served on the defendant, a note to that effect is sent to the plaintiff, called the *notice of service*. The plaintiff will also be told if the summons could not be served; it is then the responsibility of the plaintiff to 'find out the correct address and let the court know'.[27]

[25] As at 1 January 1998.

[26] National Audit Office, *Handling Small Claims in the County Court*, HCP 271 (1995–96) (London: HMSO, 1996), p. 24.

[27] Leaflet 2, *How do I make a small claim in the county court?* (London: Lord Chancellor's Department).

Responding to the claim

With the summons and particulars, the defendant will have received a **form of admission, defence and counterclaim**. Defendants who wish to avoid having judgment entered against them in default must complete and return this form within fourteen days of service. If the defendant does nothing, the plaintiff can enter judgment against the defendant without the need for any hearing and can then proceed to enforce the judgment.[28] The Form of Admission, Defence and Counterclaim is set out in questionnaire form and enables the defendant to respond to the claim as follows:

- to admit the claim in full and to make proposals as to payment, either in full by a set date or by instalments, in which case details of means must be provided; or
- to admit part of the claim and dispute the rest, and to make proposals as to payment of the admitted amount; or
- to deny the whole of the claim and file a defence to it; and, if appropriate, to add a counterclaim against the plaintiff to any of the above.

A copy of any response by the defendant will be sent to the plaintiff. If the defendant has admitted the whole claim and made proposals on payment, the only matter in issue will be the manner of payment of the debt. Unless the plaintiff considers the defendant's proposals inappropriate, judgment will be entered in the terms of the offer. Otherwise there must be a determination, and possibly a hearing, to fix the manner of payment; such hearings are called 'disposals'. If the defendant has admitted part of the claim and contested part, the plaintiff may abandon the contested amount and settle on the terms of the offer. But if the plaintiff takes issue with the partial defence, or if the defendant has filed a defence to the whole claim, then at this stage the proceedings are automatically referred to arbitration by the district judge.

The reference to arbitration

Cases where the defendant does not admit the claim are automatically referred to arbitration. Arbitration is much less formal than trial in open court. A senior judge has described it as follows:

Court-based small claims arbitration is intended to be a greatly simplified procedure for determining claims. The district judge remains an adjudicator and the process adversarial but, as the [rules of procedure] make clear, the aim of the procedure is to get away from the rigid rituals which characterize ordinary litigation.[29]

At this stage either party may make application to vary the reference to arbitration by the district judge.[30] Either party may apply to have the dispute referred to

---

[28] See below.
[29] per Beldam L. J. in *Afzal and others* v. *Ford Motor Co. Ltd and other appeals* [1994] 4 All ER 720, 733–4.
[30] Formerly known as the registrar.

arbitration by the judge or by an outside arbitrator rather than the district judge. Such applications are very rare. More importantly either party may apply to the district judge to have the reference to arbitration rescinded, which will have the effect of bringing into play the normal trial rules in the county court. The district judge can also decide that the case is not suitable for arbitration. Order 19, rule 4 of the County Court Rules 1981 (CCR) specifies four grounds on which the district judge may rescind the reference:

- a difficult question of law or a question of fact of complexity is involved;[31] or
- a charge of fraud is in issue; or
- the parties are agreed that the dispute should be tried in court; or
- it would be unreasonable for the claim to proceed to arbitration having regard to its subject matter, the circumstances of the parties or the interests of any other person likely to be affected by the award.

No figures are available for the number of cases in which the reference is rescinded, and so the practical significance of the rule is unknown. In *Pepper v. Healey*,[32] the Court of Appeal upheld the decision of a registrar, affirmed on appeal by the judge, that inequality in the positions of the parties justified rescission under CCR Order 19, rule 4(d). In the case, the defendant had representation in court and was contesting liability in a motor accident case relying in part on expert evidence, but the plaintiff was a litigant in person. The reference was rescinded in order to enable the plaintiff to obtain representation and, if successful, to recover the costs of instructing the solicitor.

Similar issues arose in the *Afzal* case but with a rather different result.[33] The appeal was a consolidation of twenty-two appeals, which was really about the costs which might be recovered by those acting for plaintiffs. Where the case is within the small claims limits, the only legal costs which can normally be recovered are a small sum which is stated on the summons. In many cases of workplace injury, trades unions instructed solicitors to act for their members. The solicitors negotiated with the employers' insurers to secure both compensation and the recovery of their costs. Insurers began to refuse to include costs since the claims were within the small claims limits and if they were determined in court, no costs[34] would be recoverable. This made the work uneconomic for the union. The union solicitors began to ask for the reference to arbitration to be rescinded arguing that compulsory arbitration was unsuitable for personal injury claims involving employers' liability, which were by their nature exceptionally complex matters. They were successful, but the defendant companies appealed arguing that the rescinding of the reference did not come within the criteria set out above. An alternative strategy that was adopted was to claim personal injury damages limited to £3,000,[35] even though there was no reasonable prospect of recovering a sum in excess of the small claims limit.

---

[31] Prior to 8 January 1996 the requirement was for 'exceptional complexity'.   [32] [1982] RTR 411.
[33] *Afzal and others* v. *Ford Motor Co. Ltd and other appeals* [1994] 4 All ER 720.
[34] Other than those shown on the summons.
[35] And so taking the claim outside the small claims limit at the time.

The Court of Appeal allowed the appeals. The rescinding of references to arbitration was available (at that time) where difficult questions of law or fact of exceptional complexity were in issue, and that was not the case in relation to these claims. The alternative route was also foreclosed since the Court ruled that deliberate inflation of the sum claimed in the particulars of claim amounted to a 'misuse of process'[36] and could constitute 'unreasonable conduct' rendering them liable in costs.[37]

It remains to be seen whether it will be easier in future to have a reference to arbitration rescinded in the context of the significantly extended small claims limits, and now that the rules require only 'complexity' rather than 'exceptional complexity' to trigger rescission of the reference. The lower limit for personal injury cases reflects *per se* the more complex issues that can arise in such cases.

The reference to arbitration used to be followed by a preliminary consideration to enable the district judge and the parties to discuss the dispute and to consider how the action can best be dealt with. But such hearings rarely took matters forward, and they are no longer a normal part of the process. It remains possible for there to be a preliminary appointment,[38] but their use is intended to be exceptional.

Arbitration

Unless any special directions are needed, such as orders for the production of particular documents, the reference to arbitration will be in the standard terms laid down in CCR Order 19.[39] The arbitration may proceed on the basis of documents and written submissions presented by the parties, but it is advisable to attend. Most parties are not represented. In one survey three in four plaintiffs and just over half of defendants represented themselves.[40] Since 1992, lay representatives have had formal rights to act as representatives in small claims proceedings, but the take up has been very low.[41]

The hearing should be as informal as is consistent with making a fair decision and the formal rules of evidence do not apply. Evidence is not normally given on oath. The role of the district judge in putting the parties at ease and enabling them to feel comfortable about putting their case effectively is an essential ingredient to the success of the process. Unfortunately the one ingredient necessary to ensure this is in short supply: time. Official figures for 1996 show that the average length of arbitrations was forty-seven minutes.[42] Baldwin's survey reports that eighty per cent of observed cases lasted at least thirty minutes and twenty-five per cent lasted

---

[36] *Afzal and others* v. *Ford Motor Co. Ltd and other appeals* [1994] 4 All ER 720, 737.
[37] Ibid., at 739. See also *Newland* v. *Boardwell; MacDonald* v. *Platt* [1983] 3 All ER 179.
[38] CCR Ord. 19, r. 6.   [39] CCR Ord. 19, r. 7.
[40] National Audit Office, *Handling Small Claims in the County Court*, HCP 271 (1995–96) (London: HMSO, 1996), p. 20.
[41] Reported as occurring in 6 per cent of cases in National Audit Office, *Handling Small Claims in the County Court*, HCP 271 (1995–96) (London: HMSO, 1996), p. 20. Baldwin reports that lay representative appeared in five hearings of the 109 observed: J. Baldwin, *Small Claims in the County Courts in England and Wales* (Oxford: Clarendon Press, 1997), p. 78.
[42] *Judicial Statistics 1996* (London: HMSO, 1997, Cm. 3716).

over an hour.[43] Having heard the parties or considered their representations, the district judge will give judgment.

The adversarial nature of the proceedings was illustrated by the case of *Chilton v. Saga Holidays plc*[44] which was a small claim for £184 arising out of a holiday provided by Saga Holidays plc for the plaintiffs, Mr and Mrs Chilton. The plaintiffs were unrepresented, while Saga Holidays plc was represented by a solicitor. The defendant's solicitor wished to cross-examine Mr Chilton on certain evidence he had put to the registrar who was sitting as arbitrator. The registrar refused to allow this and insisted that any questions for Mr Chilton be directed through him. The plaintiffs secured judgment against the defendant company, who then applied to have the award set aside. The judge refused and Saga Holidays plc appealed to the Court of Appeal, where they were successful. In the course of his judgment, Sir John Donaldson M. R. said:

Both courts and arbitrators in this country operate on an adversarial system of achieving justice. It is a system which can be modified by rules of court; it is a system which can be modified by contract between the parties; but in the absence of one or the other, it is basically an adversarial system, and it is fundamental to that that the other party shall be entitled to ask questions designed to probe the accuracy or otherwise, or the completeness or otherwise, of the evidence which has been given.[45]

The decision has been criticised[46] as being out of sympathy with the objectives of small claims arbitration and as failing to tackle the issue of how rules of natural justice should operate in the context of the inequality of the positions of the parties where one is represented and the other is not. The Judicial Studies Board has issued a Protocol for District Judges on Small Claims Arbitration which stresses the need to permit an opportunity for direct questioning of the other side and citing the *Chilton* case as authority. Despite a change to the rule-making power which would have enabled the effect of the *Chilton* case to be overruled,[47] dangers are clearly perceived in excluding what is seen as a key feature of the adversarial process.

As part of the judgment successful plaintiffs will be able to recover most of their out of pocket expenses. This includes reasonable travel and subsistence costs for the plaintiff or a witness, up to £50 for loss of earnings of the plaintiff or a witness arising from attendance at the hearing, and up to £200 for an expert's report.[48]

It has already been stated that the costs rules which apply to small claims are designed to encourage direct access by litigants to the county courts and to discourage representation by solicitors in small claims. But it is only solicitor's taxed costs which are not recoverable; the successful plaintiff who has used a solicitor will be able to recover in respect of the solicitor's charges the fixed sum for such costs entered on the summons. This is a small sum which varies according to the money

---

[43] J. Baldwin, *Small Claims in the County Courts in England and Wales* (Oxford: Clarendon Press, 1997), p. 52.   [44] [1986] 1 All ER 841.

[45] Ibid., at 844.

[46] P. Smith, 'Small Claims: Back to an Adversarial Approach' (1986) 5 Civil JQ 292.

[47] Courts and Legal Services Act 1990, s. 6.   [48] CCR Ord. 19, r. 4(3).

sum claimed and bears no relationship to solicitor's costs actually incurred. If a party has acted unreasonably in the proceedings and the arbitrator so certifies, solicitor's taxed costs will be allowed as an exception to the normal rule. It is clear that attempts to manipulate the arbitration procedure to gain a costs advantage will be unreasonable conduct.[49] The Civil Justice Review found that the practice of registrars in the award of expenses varied so much that like cases were not treated alike. The award of expenses appears to be have been based in the past on individual discretion of district judges rather than on any uniform principles. In one survey, it appeared that expenses were awarded only in one in four cases.[50]

Challenging the decision

The party who loses has only very limited rights to challenge the decision of the district judge. There is no right of appeal against the decision. There are only very limited grounds on which the decision of the arbitrator can be set aside on application to a judge. Until 1992, these were very restrictive and their application was unclear in the small claims context. But a change in the County Court Rules in 1992 has considerably simplified matters. Order 19, rule 8 provides that decisions in small claims arbitrations are final and provide only three grounds for setting the decision aside. First, if a party has been absent from the hearing and can show good reason for that absence, the decision will be set aside and the case will be reheard. If the district judge can be shown to have erred in law in making the decision, it can be set aside. Finally, the decision can be set aside where there has been misconduct by the district judge. The Court of Appeal has said that the burden of showing that there has been misconduct on the part of an arbitrator in small claims proceedings 'is a very difficult one to discharge' and requires more than an assertion that the arbitrator was partial.[51]

Baldwin found that in the 1,800 case files examined in his survey, there had been 118 judgments set aside.[52]

Enforcing the judgment

If the award of the arbitrator is for the payment of a sum of money, this has the same effect as a county court judgment and there remains the need to enforce the judgment if payment is not forthcoming. This is a separate exercise, but this is seldom appreciated by successful plaintiffs.[53] Further fees have to be paid for enforcement procedures. To assist, the Lord Chancellor's Department has produced a series of leaflets,[54] but its impact has been small. Commenting on follow-up interviews

---

[49] CCR Ord. 19, r. 4(2)(c).
[50] National Audit Office, *Handling Small Claims in the County Court*, HCP 271 (1995–96) (London: HMSO, 1996), p. 26.   [51] *Starmer* v. *Bradley*, Court of Appeal, 16 March 1994, LEXIS transcript.
[52] J. Baldwin, *Small Claims in the County Courts in England and Wales* (Oxford: Clarendon Press, 1997), p. 43.   [53] See generally ibid., ch. 5.
[54] Replacing an earlier substantial booklet.

with successful litigants about enforcement of the decision, Baldwin says: 'Many plaintiffs had such bad experiences at this stage that it causes them to re-appraise the value of pursuing small claims in the first place'.[55]

The overall result is that even when enforcement methods are used, they do not work well and in many instances are described as 'wholly ineffectual'.[56] In one-third of cases in the sample, less than ten per cent of the amount of the award had been recovered six months later, and in one in six cases the successful plaintiff had abandoned all hope of recovering the money. This sad saga was not a new finding. The Civil Justice Review had found that while two-thirds of successful plaintiffs were paid the award in full, only one-third reported prompt payment. One in four failed to obtain payment of the award at all. The National Audit Office reported in 1996 that fewer than half the successful plaintiffs in their sample recovered the full amount of the award, while one in three recovered nothing.[57]

The lack of effective enforcement and the expectation of litigants that the court will take a proactive role in enforcing its own decisions undermines the value of the process for many litigants. Baldwin puts it strongly:

The sensitive playing of the judicial role counts for little if it does not produce a final result that the parties seek. If courts are to take seriously the needs and wishes of litigants, as they increasingly claim to do, then they have an obligation, in this writer's view, to assume a much more prominent role in the enforcement of judgments.[58]

How Effective is the County Court's Small Claims Procedure?

Who uses the procedure?

The statistics show that plaintiffs overwhelmingly succeed with their claims. The National Audit Office reported that most claims settle without a court hearing. Of the hearings covered by their survey, ninety-four per cent resulted in judgment for the plaintiff.[59] But there is some evidence to suggest that there is an increasing use of the procedure for debt collection by businesses.[60]

The Touche Ross study for the Civil Justice Review[61] suggested that three-quarters of litigants using the small claims procedure were 'small litigants' and one-quarter

---

[55] Baldwin, *supra* n. 53, p. 128.   [56] Ibid., p. 133.

[57] National Audit Office, *Handling Small Claims in the County Court*, HCP 271 (1995–96) (London: HMSO, 1996), p. 38. See also Office of Fair Trading, *Consumer Redress Mechanisms* (London: OFT, 1991), p. 50.

[58] J. Baldwin, *Small Claims in the County Courts in England and Wales* (Oxford: Clarendon Press, 1997), p. 149.

[59] National Audit Office, *Handling Small Claims in the County Court*, HCP 271 (1995–96) (London: HMSO, 1996), p. 38.

[60] G. Applebey, *Small Claims in England and Wales* (Birmingham: Institute of Judicial Administration, 1978).

[61] Touche Ross Management Consultants, *Study of Small Claims Procedure, produced for the Lord Chancellor's Civil Justice Review* (London: Touche Ross, 1986).

were 'large litigants'. Small litigants were defined as small businesses, local professional firms and private citizens, while large litigants were defined as large companies, banks, credit institutions and public utilities. These figures may be unreliable as an indicator of the overall use of the procedure,[62] since the consultants were asked to ensure that at least three-quarters of the sample were cases brought by individuals and small businesses! But even on the Touche Ross figures only thirty-eight per cent of plaintiffs were private citizens, whereas fifty-eight per cent of defendants were private citizens. Only one in ten claims involved faulty goods or services. In the Touche Ross survey sixty-seven per cent of cases were decided in favour of the plaintiff, nineteen per cent in favour of the defendant. In the remaining fourteen per cent of cases no judgment was recorded; these cases were settled or withdrawn at a late stage.

The National Audit Office reported that seventy per cent of plaintiffs were businesses (including self-employed individuals) as against thirty-eight per cent of defendants. Only twenty per cent of plaintiffs were individuals, while sixty per cent of defendants were individuals.[63] That report also stated that sixty per cent of the default summonses issued by the Summons Production Centre were within the small claims limits. This centre processes applications by plaintiffs who issue more than 1,000 summonses a year; they are by definition businesses involved in debt recovery on a massive scale.

Despite these figures which suggest that the small claims procedure has been colonised by big business for the recovery of debt, Baldwin suggests that a more sophisticated analysis of the figures is needed. His research focused on hearings, that is, those cases which are contested. His analysis of 1,800 case files produced the picture illustrated in Figure 13.1. Baldwin rightly notes that his sample shows that when it comes to hearings small businesses and individuals dominate. It is wrong to assume that meeting the needs of the small business is not an appropriate use of the small claims procedure. He concludes that 'considerable use is still being made of small claims procedures in England by those for whom it was originally intended'.[64]

Though the volume of default summonses issued that are within the small claims limits is enormous and is dominated by large business, it is the filing of a defence which triggers the transfer to the small claims procedure. Even where the action begins as a debt claim by business against an individual, the filing of a defence, argues Baldwin, transforms the claim into something different from a straightforward debt claim since the defence often involves adjudication on an issue other than merely that of non-payment of a debt. Yet he finds that only one in five cases in his sample can be categorised as consumer claims; one in three is categorised

---

[62] C. Whelan, 'The role of research in civil justice reform: small claims in the county court' (1987) 6 CJQ 237, and C. Whelan, 'Small Claims in England and Wales: Redefining Justice' in C. Whelan, *Small Claims Courts: A Comparative Study* (Oxford: Clarendon Press, 1990), p. 99.

[63] National Audit Office, *Handling Small Claims in the County Court*, HCP 271 (1995–96) (London: HMSO, 1996), p. 12.

[64] J. Baldwin, *Small Claims in the County Courts in England and Wales* (Oxford: Clarendon Press, 1997), p. 27.

Figure 13.1. **Analysis of parties to hearings***

Small firm or trader v. individual	440	24.4%
Small firm or trader v. small firm or trader	429	23.8%
Individual v. individual	362	20.1%
Individual v. small firm or trader	238	13.2%
Large business v. individual	188	10.4%
Large business v. small firm or trader	70	3.9%
Individual v. large business	48	2.7%
Small firm or trader v. large business	10	0.6%
Large business v. large business	5	0.3%
Other	10	0.6%
Totals	**1800**	**100.0%**

*Source: J. Baldwin, Small Claims in the County Courts in England and Wales (Oxford: Clarendon Press, 1997), p. 26.

as 'quasi-debt recovery' with a further one in ten characterised as 'straight debt recovery'; the other significant category arises from road traffic accidents and accounted for one in six cases.

Baldwin's analysis of the outcome of cases revealed no clear pattern of outcomes. The results did not support the thesis that business interests familiar with the procedure could exploit a process to their procedural advantage. Baldwin's success figures are, however, lower than the ninety-four per cent figure reported by the National Audit Office. Baldwin's survey showed that about two in three plaintiffs obtains an award for the whole or large part of their claim, with a further one in ten obtaining an award for less than half their claim.

The National Consumer Council survey showed some confusion in the minds of consumers about the procedures and recommended the creation of an entirely separate small claims division in each county court with its own self-contained code of procedure and the abandonment of the current principle of diversion to arbitration when a defence is filed. A model code of procedure has also been produced.[65] The Civil Justice Review recommended that greater emphasis should be placed on giving the small claims procedure a separate identity from ordinary county court work. Though there was no recommendation to establish a separate division of the county courts for small claims, it was recommended that greater use should be made of the terms 'small claims' and 'small claims court' in descriptions of the procedure.

An enabling role

A system which is designed to be used without representation places a heavy premium on court staff and decision-makers adopted an enabling role. Currently, there are limits to the advice which court staff may give in assisting litigants in person.

[65] National Consumer Council, *Model Code of Procedure for Small Claims Divisions of County Courts* (London: National Consumer Council, 1980); and see R. Thomas, 'A Code of Procedure for Small Claims. A response to the demand for do-it-yourself litigation' (1982) 1 CJQ 52.

They can advise on form filling and procedures, but cannot indicate likely success or warn of possible difficulties of enforcement. This severely limits their usefulness to litigants in person. Lord Woolf in his Interim Report[66] recommends a completely new approach to advice to litigants in person, but a number of his recommendations[67] will require a re-direction of legal aid spending.

Baldwin observed settlement discussions prompted by court ushers when litigants attended for their arbitration hearings. This seemed to be so established at one court that the district judge said the usher 'operated in effect as the preliminary hearing'![68]

Any attempt to consider the experience of litigants in person must recognise that no matter how approachable the court and its processes seeks to be, there is evidence that many find presence in the court building and the prospect of a court appearance a terrifying experience.[69] It will, however, at the end of the day be the performance of the district judge which will have the greatest impact on such litigants.

The National Consumer Council survey uncovered different approaches among courts to litigants in person; some were models of helpfulness, others regarded such litigants as nuisances.[70] There also appeared to be wide variations of approach by district judges to the task of acting as arbitrator. It is argued that it is difficult for district judges trained in and working for much of their time with adversarial procedures to adopt a sympathetic inquisitorial or investigative approach in arbitrations. There is also the problem that the small claims procedure is not genuinely inquisitorial; it still leaves the conduct of the case to the parties. It is important to remember that the ordinary civil burden of proof applies and it is therefore seen as improper for district judges to descend too willingly into the arena, particularly if one party is represented.[71]

The findings of the Civil Justice Review underlined this variation of practice among registrars sitting as arbitrators. Some adopt an overtly investigative approach to the determination of small claims, whereas others operate arbitration as mini-courts relying on rules of evidence, requiring evidence to be given on oath, and remaining largely passive while the plaintiff attempts to establish the claim with little assistance from the arbitrator. Of those unrepresented parties surveyed in the Touche Ross study, forty-five per cent thought that the registrar did not help them to put their case. The Civil Justice Review recommended that district judges should adopt an interventionist role recognising that the legal context in which the dispute would be played out would not be known to litigants in person.

Subsequent training through the Judicial Studies Board appears to have resulted in significant improvement in the performance of district judges, though there

---

[66] Interim Report, *supra* n. 5, ch. 17.   [67] For example, for court-based advice centres.

[68] J. Baldwin, *Small Claims in the County Courts in England and Wales* (Oxford: Clarendon Press, 1997), p. 65.

[69] See, for example, S. Merry, *Getting Justice and Getting Even: Legal Consciousness among Working-Class Americans* (Chicago: University of Chicago Press, 1990), p. 142, and J. Baldwin, *Small Claims in the County Courts in England and Wales* (Oxford: Clarendon Press, 1997), pp. 105–6.

[70] National Consumer Council, *Simple Justice* (London: National Consumer Council, 1979).

[71] See G. Appleby, *Small Claims in England and Wales* (Birmingham: Institute of Judicial Administration, 1978); National Consumer Council, *Simple Justice* (London: National Consumer Council, 1979); G. Appleby, 'Small Claims in England and Wales' in M. Cappelletti, *Access to Justice* (Alphen aan den Rijn: Sithoff & Noordhoff, 1979), vol. II, p. 683.

remains a tension between the district judges' need to manage court business and to define the dispute in legal terms and litigants-in person's wishes to have their day in court and to say what they planned to say in preparing for the hearing. Dissatisfaction can arise if the district judge redefines the issue in a way with which one or both the parties disagrees. District judges are required to view the disputes in a legal context, while unrepresented litigants cannot reasonably be expected to do so.

Baldwin's observations of hearings, however, showed that there remained considerable room for improvement.[72] In two-thirds of the observed hearings, the initial explanation was inadequate preparation for parties who would have little idea of what would happen in the hearing. Despite this Baldwin concludes that district judges were generally good at putting parties at their ease, and there was evidence in interviews with them of their having given considerable thought to what is meant by adopting an interventionist approach. Baldwin identified four broad approaches to the task. The first is described as 'going for the jugular'; this involved the district judge being firmly in the driving seat and keeping the parties strictly to the central legal issues in the case as perceived by the district judge. Though this resulted in good case management, it does put the litigants at a disadvantage. They will not appreciate the significance of legal points and may be forced to redefine their case on their feet. Few can be expected to do this well. The second group tended to adopt a much more open approach by giving the parties much more leeway to develop their arguments, even if this appeared somewhat tangential to the central legal issues apparently presented by the dispute. The third group adopted a passive role with the result that their hearings were mundane and prosaic in character.[73] The result was regarded as an unsatisfying experience for litigants. The final group are described as mediatory, favouring finding a compromise solution in preference to the judicially imposed decision in the dispute. This not only enabled extralegal considerations to be taken into account, but was also felt by its proponents to lead to greater satisfaction by litigants with the process. This is contradicted by one survey in which 'those who settled before a formal court decision appeared less satisfied than those who settled after legal proceedings began but before a formal decision'.[74]

Levels of satisfaction

Both the National Audit Office[75] and Baldwin[76] report high levels of satisfaction by users with the small claims process to the point of an award being made by the

---

[72] J. Baldwin, *Small Claims in the County Courts in England and Wales* (Oxford: Clarendon Press, 1997), ch. 3.   [73] Ibid., p. 62.

[74] National Consumer Council, *Seeking Civil Justice: A Survey of People's Needs and Experiences* (London: National Consumer Council, 1995), p. 7.

[75] National Audit Office, *Handling Small Claims in the County Court*, HCP 271 (1995–96) (London: HMSO, 1996).

[76] J. Baldwin, *Small Claims in the County Courts in England and Wales* (Oxford: Clarendon Press, 1997). See also J. Baldwin, *Monitoring the Rise of the Small Claims Limit: Litigants' Experiences of Different Forms of Adjudication*, Lord Chancellor's Department Research Series 1/97 (London: Lord Chancellor's Department, 1997), ch. 3.

district judge. Though there is room for improving the quality of information and the simplicity of the forms, no major problems are revealed by these two studies. There was a high level of dissatisfaction expressed about the procedures for enforcing the judgment.

The county court procedures are really an attempt to combine processes of conciliation, arbitration and adjudication in one system. It is now accepted, at least by judges in the Court of Appeal, that the small claims system offers a 'less sophisticated form of justice'[77] and is 'necessarily somewhat brisk and informal'.[78] There is a policy of seeking to achieve a settlement acceptable to the parties,[79] coupled with a process of adjudicating between competing claims in an informal atmosphere. But the requirement of party presentation of claims and the level of formality required in particular in starting the proceedings is too great to be universally attractive. If the do-it-yourself approach is to work for everyone, and not just for the articulate person of above average intelligence, then the processes need further simplification by transferring some of the responsibilities away from the parties and onto the decision-maker. A research study into fifteen American small claims courts supports this view. It revealed the substantial need for court-provided assistance to litigants, if they were to develop their cases to their full potential.[80]

It was some of these problems and issues which led to two important experiments in alternative methods of dispute resolution for small claims: the voluntary small claims arbitration schemes in London and Manchester.

The Voluntary Small Claims Schemes

Two major independent voluntary schemes have been established outside the official court structure to offer alternative methods for settling small claims. Both have ceased to operate through shortage of funds. The first was the Manchester Arbitration Scheme which operated between 1971 and 1980.[81] The second operated in London; between 1973 and 1977 it was known as the Westminster Small Claims Court and between 1977 and 1979 as the London Small Claims Court.[82] A third scheme in Lewisham closed after one year having heard only one case. Though there were

---

[77] per Simon Brown L. J. in *O'Grady* v. *Motor Cycle Services*, Court of Appeal, 20 June 1997, LEXIS transcript.

[78] per Simon Brown L. J. in *Starmer* v. *Bradley*, Court of Appeal, 16 March 1994, LEXIS transcript.

[79] Though there is little encouragement to do this in advance of the hearing. Previously this was one of the functions of the preliminary hearing.

[80] S. Weller, J. Martin and J. Ruhnka, 'In-court assistance to small claims litigants' (1984) 3 CJQ 62.

[81] See K. Foster, 'The Manchester Arbitration Scheme—an Interim Report' [1973] *LAG Bulletin* 190; National Consumer Council, *Simple Justice* (London: National Consumer Council, 1979); and G. Applebey, 'Small Claims in England and Wales' in M. Cappelletti, *Access to Justice* (Alphen aan den Rijn: Sithoff & Noordhoff, 1979), vol. II, p. 683.

[82] See M. Sherwin, 'The Westminster Small Claims Court' [1975] *LAG Bulletin* 65; National Consumer Council, *Simple Justice* (London: National Consumer Council, 1979); and G. Applebey, 'Small Claims in England and Wales' in M. Cappelletti, *Access to Justice* (Alphen aan den Rijn: Sithoff & Noordhoff, 1979), vol. II, p. 683; and A. Conway, 'The London Small Claims Court' [1980] *LAG Bulletin* 231.

detailed differences in the ways in which the Manchester and London schemes operated, there were sufficient similarities to justify a conflation of the two schemes for the purposes of our consideration of their contribution to our knowledge of processes for settling small claims.

The schemes were genuinely inquisitorial. The claimant indicated the nature of the dispute and the onus was then on the scheme to elicit all the relevant information from the parties and, if necessary, to obtain an expert report. Representation was banned. Use of the two schemes was restricted to claims in contract or tort by private individuals not in business, though small businesses could use the schemes other than for the recovery of business debts. In Manchester the financial limit on claims was £500, and in London £350; at the time these figures were well in excess of the small claims limit in the county court. Proceedings were begun by contacting the scheme and by completing a simple form which outlined the complaint and contained the agreement to arbitration. Very low registration fees were payable: £1 in Manchester, and in London a £2 registration fee plus a court fee of £3 for claims under £100 and £8 for claims in excess of £100. The next step was for the staff of the schemes to try to secure the consent of the defendant to arbitration under the scheme. If that consent was not forthcoming the scheme could not be used. This was because the schemes were arbitrations within the meaning of the Arbitration Acts 1950 to 1979 and in order to displace the jurisdiction of the county courts there must be a valid agreement to arbitrate concluded by the parties to the dispute. Despite broad support for the schemes from local trade and business organisations, it seems that refusals of consent were significant. Complete figures for all the years of operation are not available, but reported figures show refusal rates varying from twenty per cent to fifty-one per cent of claims registered.[83]

At the time that the agreement of the defendant was sought, the defendant's views on the complaint were also sought. All the facts and documents needed to consider the claim were collected in a file, following which a hearing was fixed, which could be 'on site' if that would be useful. Arbitrators under both schemes were appointed by the presidents of the local Law Societies from a list of volunteers. A fair number of arbitrators in Manchester were not lawyers; expert adjudicators included engineers, architects and surveyors. In London most arbitrators were lawyers. In London arbitrators were unpaid, but in Manchester a nominal fee of £25 for a session of three or more arbitrations, or £10 for a session of less than three arbitrations, was paid. A documents-only arbitration was possible, as were hearings outside normal office hours. Though legal or other professional representation was disallowed, both schemes allowed a friend to accompany the parties to the dispute. The arbitrator was not bound by the rules on evidence and would consult an expert of his or her own motion. The gradual building up of a case file without the single culminating equivalent of a trial is very reminiscent of civil law inquisitorial procedures. The administrator of the London Small Claims Court commented:

---

[83] G. Applebey, 'Small Claims in England and Wales' in M. Cappelletti, *Access to Justice* (Alphen aan den Rijn: Sithoff & Noordhoff, 1979), vol. II, p. 683; and National Consumer Council, *Simple Justice* (London: National Consumer Council, 1979).

The Court attempted to create, by the method it used to conduct hearings, an atmosphere which was friendly and unintimidating and where the parties involved fully understood what was going on. I believe the Court was successful in this respect.[84]

The costs rules operating under the schemes were simple. In Manchester the £1 registration fee was never recoverable, whereas under the London scheme the arbitrator had a discretion to order re-imbursement of the claimant's court fee. Under both schemes the arbitrator could as part of the award order one party to pay a sum towards the schemes' expenses, such as experts' fees, up to a maximum of £10, though in London advance agreement on meeting the expert's fees was often sought between the parties.

The awards of the arbitrators were usually met without difficulty, and this is unsurprising since both parties had agreed to the process of settlement. In any event as a valid arbitration, the enforcement procedures of the county court were available on registration of the award with the county court. In order to do this a plaint fee would of course have to be paid to the county court.

The schemes themselves argued that they were speedier, cheaper, simpler and more 'user-friendly' than the county court schemes. The claims to simplicity and a sympathetic approach to litigants in person can certainly be sustained. Empirical research in Manchester where the independent scheme operated in competition with the small claims procedures in the county courts showed the preference of litigants for the informal procedure. A survey was conducted to see what further steps were taken by persons who had begun proceedings under the Manchester Arbitration Scheme, but where the defendant had not agreed to submit the case to arbitration. Some 65 per cent decided not to proceed. Within this sample, 25 per cent abandoned the claim because they felt they could not cope with the county court procedures, 12.5 per cent because they thought it would be too expensive or that an expert report would be needed, and 8 per cent because they considered it would be too time-consuming. Though a small sample, and though county court procedures have been somewhat simplified by subsequent rule changes, the survey does suggest some misunderstandings and fear of the procedures available in the county courts among a group which had been sufficiently motivated to try to get a claim off the ground under the Manchester Arbitration Scheme.[85]

More doubt surrounds the claims to speed and cheapness. Given the small scale of the two schemes, comparisons of the time lags between filing a claim and decision between these schemes and the county courts are meaningless. Costs are disguised; there is clearly a transfer of some process costs from claimant to the scheme. But again problems of comparing like with like make comparisons with the county courts of doubtful validity. What the schemes did show was that it was possible to set up genuinely inquisitorial procedures for small claims which were readily accessible to claimants and, even on a voluntary basis, largely acceptable to defendants.

---

[84] A. Conway, 'The London Small Claims Court' [1980] *LAG Bulletin* 231.

[85] G. Applebey, 'Small Claims in England and Wales' in M. Cappelletti, *Access to Justice* (Alphen aan den Rijn: Sithoff & Noordhoff, 1979), vol. II, p. 683.

Trade Association Arbitration Schemes under OFT Codes

Under the provisions of the Fair Trading Act 1973,[86] the Director General of Fair Trading has a duty to promote codes of practice among trade associations laying down standards of conduct designed to remove abuse, promote higher standards and provide machinery for the proper handling of complaints. A significant number of codes have now been approved, many of which contain procedures for arbitration of disputes.[87] Adherence to the codes is usually voluntary. There are also a number of schemes operated by trade associations where there is as yet no code of practice approved by the Office of Fair Trading (OFT). Obviously since each code is tailor-made to a particular trade or product, there are significant variations in the schemes set up under them. But it is common to find a three-stage process. Consumers are first expected to raise the matter directly with suppliers, who commit themselves to seeking to resolve problems with their customers. If that does not resolve the problem, a free conciliation procedure involving the trade association comes into play, whereby consumer and retailer or contractor seek to agree a riendly settlement of the dispute. If this fails, independent arbitration may follow.[88]

A further example is to be found in the Association of British Travel Agents (ABTA) Tour Operators' Code of Conduct which provides that in the event of a dispute between a tour operator and a consumer, ABTA is prepared to offer help and impartial guidance with a view to the conciliation of the dispute. This scheme is the most frequently used of the trade association arbitration schemes.[89] If conciliation fails, the dispute may be referred to arbitration under the special scheme devised for the travel industry by the Institute of Arbitrators by arrangement with ABTA by joint application of the customer and the tour operator or travel agent. There is a nine-month time limit from the completion of the return journey for making the application. Under the arbitration scheme an independent arbitrator is appointed by the President of the Institute of Arbitrators. The scheme offers a documents-only procedure, and the claims limits are £1,500 per person and £7,500 per booking. There is a sliding fee scale: for claims of £1 to £1,500 for holidays taken by up to six people, the fee is £64.63; for claims between £1,501 and £3,000 the fee is £88.13; and for claims between £3,001 and £7,500 the fee is £111.63. The arbitrator has a discretion to direct the reimbursement of the registration fee. If for any reason the matter cannot be resolved on a documents-only basis, the application for arbitration is rescinded and the matter must be pursued through the courts. No detailed statistics on outcomes are currently kept, and there are no plans to keep

---

[86] See s. 124 of the 1973 Act.

[87] See Lord Chancellor's Department, *Resolving Disputes without Going to Court* (London: Lord Chancellor's Department, 1997), ch. 5. See also Office of Fair Trading, *Voluntary Codes of Practice: A Consultation Paper* (London: HMSO, 1996).

[88] R. Thomas, 'Alternative Dispute Resolution—Consumer Disputes' (1988) 7 CJQ 206; and R. Thomas, 'Consumer protection: strategies for dispute resolution' in K. Mackie (ed.), *A Handbook of Dispute Resolution. ADR in Action* (Routledge and Sweet & Maxwell, 1991), p. 157.

[89] Office of Fair Trading, *Consumer Redress Mechanisms* (London: OFT, 1991).

any.[90] This is regrettable, and is a clear deficiency in private systems. It means that users of the scheme have no way of knowing whether and to what extent claimants succeed. In 1996/97, ABTA dealt with 15,933 complaints and there were 1,472 arbitrations. In four out of five arbitrations, the claimant recovered compensation.[91]

An interesting and useful provision of independent expert testing is to be found in the Voluntary Code of Practice for Footwear, one of whose sponsors is the British Footwear Association. It is also of some importance because complaints about footwear are estimated to account for some one in twenty consumer complaints.[92] It is made clear in the code that retailers are responsible for providing redress, but if there is a disagreement about the cause of a fault, then an expert opinion may be sought from the independent Footwear Testing Centre in Kettering. The parties file a Test Application Form outlining the dispute. The test fee is £23.25;[93] the retailer pays £15.50 and the Consumer £7.75, which will be refunded by the retailer if the report is favourable to the consumer. All documents and the test report are seen by both retailer and consumer. The system seems to work well for those who use it; it seems to be cheap, quick and involves little paperwork. Not all codes have such satisfactory procedures.

In 1995/96, 380 complaints were referred to the Footwear Testing Centre, which was a twelve per cent reduction on the previous year's figures. Forty-one per cent of complaints were completely justified and forty-three per cent completely unjustified, with the remaining sixteen per cent being shared between consumer and retailer.[94] The small number of complaints suggests that details of the scheme are not widely known.[95]

The main drawback of the schemes in the codes is their diversity and a general ignorance about their existence.[96] A Report by the OFT in 1991 concluded that many consumers have complaints and that a high proportion take the matter up with suppliers. In two-thirds of these cases, a satisfactory solution is reached, though success rates vary considerably by sector. Despite a significant volume of dissatisfaction remaining after matters had been taken up with suppliers, only a relatively small number of consumers make use of the redress mechanisms which are then available.[97] Use of the schemes varies dramatically.[98] There are few other than consumer advisers who could claim to be certain about how many products and services are covered by codes.[99] The lack of consumer awareness of the codes

[90] Information supplied by the Public Relations Manager of ABTA to the author.

[91] Association of British Travel Agents, *Annual Report and Financial Statements for the Year ending 30 June 1997* (London: ABTA, 1997).

[92] See Office of Fair Trading, *Consumer Dissatisfaction: a Report on Surveys Undertaken by the Office of Fair Trading* (London: HMSO, 1986), and subsequent consumer dissatisfaction survey reported in *Fair Trading*.

[93] As at 1 January 1996.

[94] Footwear Testing Centre, *Twentieth Annual Report on the Footwear Testing Centre* (Kettering: Footwear Testing Centre, 1996).   [95] The current version of the OFT leaflet is dated January 1994.

[96] See generally National Consumer Council, *Out of Court* (London: National Consumer Council, 1991).

[97] Office of Fair Trading, *Consumer Redress Mechanisms* (London: OFT, 1991).

[98] R. Thomas, 'Alternative Dispute Resolution—Consumer Disputes' (1988) 7 CJQ 206.

[99] A fifth of referrals to the Footwear Testing Centre originated from advice centres; the remainder appears to have been referred at the suggestion of the retailer in response to a consumer complaint.

means that the advantage to the retailer of being a member of the code is lost if consumers do not choose where they shop on the basis of adherence to a code. The ignorance of the codes exists not only among consumers, but also among lawyers and even at shops which are parties to the codes. Among those who are aware of the schemes under the codes, there is some concern about the impartiality with which complaints are considered. Some are very slow.[100]

In 1981 the OFT reviewed the redress procedures under codes of practice. The review concluded that the arbitration schemes were useful alternatives to the county court procedures, but that improvements were needed. All arbitrations should be on a documents-only basis and the speed of decision-making should be improved. Arbitrators should always give a reasoned decision.[101] Unfortunately none of the proposals do anything to improve the lack of awareness of the provisions of the codes. They will normally only be used if a complaint is initially made to a Consumer Advice Centre or Trading Standards Department, who are among the few agencies likely to link a complaint to the availability of a remedy under a code of practice. Finally, given the strength of the substantive law protecting the consumer, there is an argument that the proliferation of codes with individual systems for redressing grievances tends to super-impose a veneer of 'pseudo-law' and to detract from the enforcement of legal rights and duties using the small claims procedure in the county courts.

The 1991 OFT Report[102] commented specifically on the arbitration schemes offered under trade association codes of practice. Trade association arrangements are seen to have a number of advantages and disadvantages.[103] Advantages are seen to be low cost, procedural flexibility, and expertise by the arbitrator which reduces, if not eliminates, the need for expert evidence, particularly where quality issues arise. Furthermore, the trade association accepts some responsibility for the enforceability of awards through the application of pressure. But failure of such pressure leaves the consumer with enforcement through the county court as the only remedy. Disadvantages are a lack of awareness by many consumers. The conciliation stage is perceived by some consumers as being biased in favour of the retailer.[104] There can be significant delays. Two areas are seen both as advantages and disadvantages. The first is the paper-only hearings, which are a common feature of many schemes. This is seen by some as an advantage in that attendance at a hearing is not required, but others feel that a hearing would be to their benefit since they believe that oral explanations in addition to the paper argument would lend greater weight to their case. The OFT Report is not in favour of the increased use of hearings, since it would increase the costs and delay in the process. The private nature of the arbitration process can reassure the consumer, but the lack of publicity means that 'there is a

[100] National Consumer Council, *Simple Justice* (London: National Consumer Council, 1979).

[101] Office of Fair Trading, *Redress Procedures under Codes of Practice* (London: Office of Fair Trading, 1981).

[102] Office of Fair Trading, *Consumer Redress Mechanisms* (London: OFT, 1991). See also National Consumer Council, *Out of Court* (London: National Consumer Council, 1991).   [103] Ibid., ch. 6.

[104] There is no readily accessible research on the operation of conciliation under trade association agreements. See National Consumer Council, *Out of Court* (London: National Consumer Council, 1991), pp. 59–60.

lack of knowledge and even information about the sort of cases that schemes deal with and the principles applied in deciding them'.[105]

The OFT Report recommends that traders should do more to bring the schemes to the attention of consumers, including information on the range of options available to them if conciliation fails. The increase in the county court small claims limit means that few trade association schemes now cover sums in excess of that limit, which was formerly the case. The introduction of a degree of independence in the personnel dealing with the conciliation phase would increase public confidence in its impartiality. Greater use could be made of annual reports to comment on performance in the sector.

Ombudsmen

The rise in the sale of services has been accompanied by a phenomenon of the 1990s: the use of ombudsmen to resolve consumer disputes.[106] The OFT Report says:

In essence the ombudsman is an independent person whose function is to settle a dispute between a company and its customer, ideally through mediation or conciliation, but ultimately by making a decision on the merits of the case.[107]

Ombudsmen have now been joined by the regulators of the privatised utilities.[108] Some schemes are statutory and some are voluntary. Their services are free. They are available to consumers who have not been able to resolve their complaints through the internal complaints machinery which service providers are now expected to have in place. In many cases their jurisdiction extends beyond the financial limits of the county court small claims procedure. The role of the ombudsmen is largely to determine whether the complaint has been properly handled internally. The Lord Chancellor's leaflet says:

Usually the Ombudsman or Regulator's job is to consider whether something has been badly or unfairly handled and to what extent you have experienced unreasonable delay, neglect, inaction, inefficiency, failure to follow policy or proper procedures, unfair discrimination, discourtesy, inconsistency, mistakes of law and inaccurate information or advice.

[105] Office of Fair Trading, *Consumer Redress Mechanisms* (London: OFT, 1991), p. 53.

[106] See generally P. Birkinshaw, 'Complaints mechanisms in administrative law: recent developments' in K. Mackie (ed.), *A Handbook of Dispute Resolution: ADR in Action* (Routledge and Sweet and Maxwell, 1991), p. 43; and J. Birds and C. Graham, 'Alternative dispute resolution: financial services' in K. Mackie (ed.), *A Handbook of Dispute Resolution: ADR in Action* (Routledge and Sweet and Maxwell, 1991), p. 121. See also T. Goriely and T. Williams, *Resolving Civil Disputes: Choosing between Out-of-Court Schemes and Litigation. A Review of the Literature*, Lord Chancellor's Department Research Series, No. 3/97 (London: Lord Chancellor's Department, 1997). [107] Ibid., p. 37.

[108] See Lord Chancellor's Department, *Resolving Disputes without Going to Court* (London: Lord Chancellor's Department, 1997), section 7. See also Office of Fair Trading, *Consumer Redress Mechanisms* (London: OFT, 1991), paras. 4.64–4.95 and ch. 7. See also Office of Fair Trading, *Draft Redress Directory for Consultation* (London: HMSO, 1997).

The ombudsman or regulator conducts an investigation in response to a written complaint and will usually issue a confidential written report setting out the findings. The process is entirely inquisitorial, since once accepted, the relevant ombudsman service undertakes the necessary fact-finding. The supplier of the service can be required to provide a remedy which may include an apology, publicity for the final decision, provision of a service, correcting an error or money compensation. An annual report summarising the performance of the sector is usually published.

Little research has been carried out on the operation of these schemes, but all seem to have experienced significant growth in the number of complaints referred to them, which slows down the speed of decision-making.[109] As with all schemes in which the complainant loses control after making the complaint, the quality of the initial complaint can be crucial. A poorly-drafted complaint may not equip the investigating ombudsmen to seek the relevant information. A well-drafted complaint with supporting documentation will serve to set out the complaint in the detail necessary to put the service provider on their mettle in responding to enquiries from the ombudsman.

In making decisions ombudsmen can take account not only of legal points, but also of good practice in the sector and of any relevant codes of practice. As with trade association schemes, the OFT Report showed that there was little public awareness of the schemes. Despite this the number of complaints has increased under all schemes.

The OFT Report expressed some concern that the increasing use of the term 'ombudsman' might result in its being debased and canvassed the issue of setting minimum standards for the use of the title in a regulatory scheme.

Strategies for Reform of Small Claims

The trends and experimentation in the processing of small claims have highlighted the need to achieve a delicate balance. That balance is between the need for individuals to be able to enforce by process of law rights given to them by the common law and statute as consumers and the requirement that disputes are judged fully and impartially by decision-makers. To put it another way: can we afford to meet the cost of providing justice for small claims? These themes have over the last decade been played against a backcloth of a general movement away from formality and procedural complexity and towards informal, simple and accessible procedures in the administration of justice.[110] The Woolf Report has described this as providing procedures that are proportionate to the value and complexity of

---

[109] But see M. Seneviratne, R. James and C. Graham, 'The Banks, The Ombudsman and Complaints Procedures' (1994) 13 CJQ 253.

[110] K. Economides, 'Small Claims and Procedural Justice' (1980) 7 Brit. J of Law and Soc. 111.

individual cases. It is only possible to have a simple informal system of processing disputes if there is a simple informal body of legal rules governing those disputes. One charge levelled at arbitration schemes under trade associations' codes of practice, and indeed at the voluntary schemes, is that they substitute for the relevant legal rules some general concept of fairness between the parties.[111]

Reactions based on concerns that some of the simpler and cheaper alternatives do not pay sufficient regard to the framework of applicable legal rules have caused many to see the long-term solution as lying with changes in the official court system. But in recent years that has been tempered by the development and encouragement of ADR methods. To some extent the court system remains the benchmark by which other processes are tested. In many cases, they are alternatives to the use of the small claims system, but in some they offer the only realistic solution for a grievance.

It now appears that the county court small claims system has come of age. The difficulty remains, however, that the experience of the Manchester and London schemes has been to show that inquisitorial procedures are appropriate for these claims and can work effectively. The National Consumer Council was right to call for a new national system of small claims divisions in county courts. Implementation of the recommendations of the Civil Justice Review and the Woolf Report has, in effect, established such a system. But it remains essentially adversarial in nature despite the adoption by district judges of various styles of intervention in arbitration hearings.

The issue of representation in any small claims procedure is a difficult one. The independent schemes were able to dispense with representation because they adopted a full inquisitorial model, placing a duty upon the arbitrator to find the facts needed to determine the claim. Though there is an important role for lawyers in inquisitorial procedures, their banning in small claims can be justified on economic grounds and in order to ensure some equality between the positions of the parties.

The National Consumer Council has changed its view on the banning of representation in county court procedure. In 1970 the Consumer Council in *Justice Out of Reach* argued strongly for a ban on legal representation, even though only a minority of jurisdictions operate such a ban in small claims cases. In 1979 the National Consumer Council took the view that legal representation should not be necessary in small claims proceedings and that it should not be permitted. Despite features designed to discourage representation, one party was legally represented in forty-eight per cent of cases in the Touche Ross study, though this appears to have little impact on outcome. One in ten cases involved legal representation of both parties. The National Audit Office Report suggested that those who represented themselves against represented parties tended to do less well.[112] The dilemma over

---

[111] National Consumer Council, *Simple Justice* (London: National Consumer Council, 1979); and K. Economides, 'Small Claims and Procedural Justice' (1980) 7 Brit. J of Law and Soc. 111.

[112] National Audit Office, *Handling Small Claims in the County Court*, HCP 271 (1995–96) (London: HMSO, 1996), p. 21.

the issue of whether or not to ban legal representation is that a ban restricts individual freedom without necessarily securing the objective of improving the informal conduct of the proceedings so that the need for representation disappears. The National Consumer Council has recently modified its position:

We concluded that although the procedure should aim to make representation un-necessary, litigants should have the right to be accompanied or represented by the person of their choice. Legal costs should not be allowed.[113]

This is in line with the recommendations of the Civil Justice Review. It acknow-ledges the difficulty of providing a do-it-yourself litigation scheme capable of being used effectively by all members of the public.

The arguments concerning the banning of representation are often clouded by pointing out that there might still be inequality between the parties. This is undoubtedly true. Companies or businesses sued under a system which did not permit representation would undoubtedly send along to any hearing a competent articulate representative. It is also possible that companies and businesses might be sued more than once and so their representatives would become experienced in small claims procedures. As 'repeat-players' they would have considerable advant-ages over 'one-shotters'; this has been shown to be a general problem in the use of litigation.[114] This relative advantage for 'repeat-players' is accentuated in an adver-sarial system, but within an inquisitorial procedure the decision-maker can ensure that it does not operate to the disadvantage of the 'one-shotter'.

The use of full inquisitorial procedures in small claims in the county courts would present a problem: that of numbers. A feature of inquisitorial procedures is early court intervention. Over 1.5 million default summonses are issued each year in the county courts for money claims within the small claims limits. Something in the order of fourteen out of every fifteen such cases resolve themselves. Either judg-ment is obtained by default, or the exchange of particulars and the form of admis-sion, defence and counterclaim results in settlement of the dispute. Obviously, there would be considerable resistance to any procedure which required examination of these cases. There is a case to suggest that they should be examined, because many are debt claims settled in favour of the plaintiff even where the defendant has a full or partial defence.[115] However, it is perfectly possible to have an inquisitorial system whose intervention takes effect after the initial stage of processing. If no settlement is reached, then the arbitrator must enquire fully into the case. Such a system might encourage the raising of defences at an early stage.

In examining the issue of small claims there is a tendency to consider that the choice is between formal procedures involving adversarial trial processes with detailed rules of evidence, representation and full rehearsal by each side of the

---

[113] National Consumer Council, *Ordinary Justice* (London: National Consumer Council, 1989), p. 294.

[114] M. Galanter, 'Why the "haves" come out ahead: speculation on the limits of legal change' (1974) 9 Law and Soc. Rev. 95.

[115] *Report of the Committee on the Enforcement of Judgment Debts (Payne Committee)* (London: HMSO, 1969, Cmnd. 3909); and T. Ison, 'Small Claims' (1972) 53 MLR 18.

legal arguments in the case, and informal processes involving much simpler more general inquiries in friendly surroundings where the facts are laid by the parties before an arbitrator who applies a compromise judgment based on his own enquiries and knowledge of the law. The loss of the safeguards of the formal process is seen as the price to be paid for general accessibility without lawyers to a system of redress. Economides has suggested that there is a third route, which he labels 'post-formal' justice, which represents a synthesis of both formal and informal justice.[116] The National Consumer Council's model code of procedure is a good basis for such a system, though it fails fully to address the issue of a move from adversarial to genuinely inquisitorial procedures. In commenting on the rules, Thomas stresses the need for a consumer-orientation in the services offered by the courts, for the role of the court to change fundamentally so that it does not remain 'aloof from the arena of battle', for judicial activism and for a style of judicial decision-making appropriate to the nature of the dispute.[117] But the model code does not introduce dramatic new procedures and new duties on the court likely to secure these objectives.

A belief that evolutionary change will never succeed has led Ison to argue that radical changes are needed.[118] Writing in 1972, before the major developments in county court procedure to accommodate litigants in person with small claims, Ison described the handling of small claims as 'probably the most deplorable feature of the administration of civil justice'. But Ison's proposals have not been overtaken by the new small claims procedure because he maintains that improvements in procedure have only a marginal impact. Arguing that the county courts have become merely collecting agencies for business in their handling of debt claims with enquiry into the merits of claims being almost wholly absent, Ison proposes the abolition of the debt action. This would result in greater care being taken by credit-granters in their predictions of the capacity of the credit-receiver to repay the loan. The ease with which debts can currently be collected through the county courts is, Ison argues, inconsistent with government policy to increase protection of the consumer, particularly where consumer credit transactions are involved. To encourage consumers to pursue claims, Ison proposes a system of well-paid, young (under thirty-three on appointment with compulsory retirement at forty-five) highly mobile judges fearlessly and vigorously investigating complaints by consumers. Ison comments: 'It may be hard to imagine a judge moving around the community, resolving disputes on the spot, and keeping in touch with his office by two-way radio; but why not?'[119]

The proposals are as imaginative as they are unrealistic, but they are backed by considerable argument and represent one of the few more radical proposals to resolve what is generally acknowledged as a problem for the legal system. As such they deserve consideration.

---

[116] K. Economides, 'Small Claims and Procedural Justice' (1980) 7 Brit. J of Law and Soc. 111.

[117] R. Thomas, 'A Code of Procedure for Small Claims. A response to the demand for do-it-yourself litigation' (1982) 1 CJQ 52.　　　　　　　　　　　　　　[118] T. Ison, 'Small Claims' (1972) 53 MLR 18.

[119] Ibid., at 30.

Most proposals for reform have argued that the small claim is the context in which most members of the community are likely to come into contact with the civil justice system and that the absence of a fair accessible system for resolving such disputes is likely to bring the whole of the civil justice system rapidly into disrepute. Such proposals often go on to suggest two key objectives in designing a small claims system: reducing the costs of litigation and making procedures simpler. The tension between these two objectives is not always fully explored. Reducing the cost to the litigant and making the procedures simple for the litigant probably increase the costs of operating the system. Costs are transferred from the parties to the dispute to the system. In a climate of expenditure cuts and a general reduction of public spending, such proposals are likely to be unattractive to government.

The OFT has helpfully provided a set of principles by which the effectiveness of redress mechanisms can be tested:

To be effective and win the support of the public, redress mechanisms should:
- be inexpensive
- be impartial
- take full account of the lack of experience of consumers
- be the consumers own choice
- work speedily
- result in enforceable findings
- be well publicised.[120]

That is a useful checklist against which to test any small claims procedure. That many now get close to meeting these criteria indicates the progress which has been made in this area of dealing with civil claims.

Reform of the effective legal protection of the consumer is likely to continue on three fronts, seeking to provide both new substantive rights and new procedural machinery for the settlement of disputes.[121] The first approach is to seek new and better substantive rights for consumers, like a general direct liability of manufacturers to consumers for defective goods. Certainly one commentator has suggested that the focus on procedural reform is misplaced.[122] The second approach is to improve public enforcement of consumer rights by extending the role of the OFT and local Trading Standards Departments.[123] This technique is known as surrogate advocacy. Its effectiveness depends upon the aggressiveness of the agency charged with the protection of the public interest. There is a danger of tokenism or purely symbolic protection.[124] The third approach is pressing for procedural reform. This can take the form of simplification or structural changes in court procedures and ADR as discussed in this chapter or the development of new remedies,

---

[120] *Fair Trading*, Spring 1996, p. 14.

[121] G. Applebey, 'Justice within Reach?—A Review of Progress in Reforming Small Claims' (1987) 6 CJQ 214.   [122] K. Foster, 'Problems with Small Claims' (1975) 2 Brit. J of Law and Soc. 75.

[123] R. Thomas, 'Alternative Dispute Resolution—Consumer Disputes' (1988) 7 CJQ 206.

[124] M. Cappelletti (ed.), *Access to Justice*, four vols. (Alphen aan den Rijn: Sitjhoff and Noordhoff, 1978), vol. III.

like the class action allowing the collective obtaining of remedies against manufacturers or suppliers by all consumers of particular products.[125]

Ultimately optimists will argue that evolutionary change on a broad front will in time produce a fair and balanced system, while pessimists will argue that only revolutionary change can succeed in providing effective access to adjudication for litigants with small claims.

---

[125] Van Bueren, 'Statutory Class Action' *LAG Bulletin*, August 1983, 7.

14

DEALING WITH SOCIAL SECURITY BENEFIT CLAIMS

Introduction

Many disputes are dealt with by bodies other than courts. These include tribunals, which are now a formal part of the system of adjudication. In 1957, they were recognised as such,[1] and in 1968 they were described as a 'more modern form of court'.[2] Three factors have tended to make classification of tribunals difficult. The first has been the link between the work of some tribunals and the development of a fully-fledged system of administrative law in England and Wales. The second has been the sheer number of institutions calling themselves tribunals. The third was the unfortunate linking of the work of tribunals and enquiries in the Report of the Franks Committee, which has led many writers to feel obliged to discuss tribunals and enquiries together.

There are three principal functions of tribunals and enquiries: adjudication, regulation and advice. The function of adjudication is the determination of the rights and duties of the parties presenting their dispute to the tribunal. The claimant takes issue with a decision made by a decision-maker, for example, with an adjudication officer concerning entitlement to a social security benefit, or with an employer concerning a dismissal. The issue is then referred to an independent tribunal for a binding decision as to whether the claimant is entitled to the benefit or has been unfairly dismissed.

The second function of tribunals is regulation. Here the tribunal is the decision-making instrument chosen by government for the implementation of some scheme of government regulation. A good example is the Civil Aviation Authority

---

[1] *Report of the Committee on Administrative Tribunals and Enquiries (Franks Committee)* (London: HMSO, 1957, Cmnd. 218).

[2] B. Abel-Smith and R. Stevens, *In Search of Justice* (Penguin: Harmondsworth, 1968), 228. See also discussion in H. Genn, 'Tribunal Review of Administrative Decision-Making' in G. Richardson and H. Genn (eds.), *Administrative Law and Government Action: The Courts and Alternative Mechanisms of Review* (Oxford: Clarendon Press, 1994), p. 249, esp. pp. 258–62.

determining entitlement to an air transport licence in accordance with the general objectives laid down in the legislation. The distinction between adjudicatory and regulatory tribunals is that the former are making a binding decision following a reference by a person aggrieved by a decision which has already been made, whereas the latter are directly applying a system of government regulation rather than supervising or reviewing the proper application of the system of government regulation. It is a characteristic of both adjudicatory and regulatory bodies that they produce a binding determination of the issue before them. Binding does not necessarily mean final, because the determination may be subject to re-consideration by an appellate body. But, unless and until the determination is successfully challenged, it will be binding.

The third function, which belongs principally to ministerial and public enquiries, is advice. One example from a multitude of possible examples is the compulsory purchase order enquiry. Local authorities have for many years enjoyed a power to purchase land compulsorily in order to carry out their statutory functions relating to highways or general development. If agreement to purchase land needed for particular projects cannot be secured and a compulsory purchase order is made, persons affected may object. If those objections are substantial, the relevant minister will order an enquiry into the proposals and the objections to them. This will be conducted locally by an inspector appointed by the minister who will hear evidence and argument both from the local authority and the objectors. The inspector will also visit the site. Following the hearing and site visit, the inspector will prepare a report for the minister, who will then decide whether to affirm the compulsory purchase order which he may do with or without variations, or whether to decline to make the order. The inspector's report is not binding on the minister; it is merely advisory. The report will be sent to the parties together with the minister's letter of decision, which will set out the factors which have influenced the minister. The exercise is principally an informational one: it ensures not only that the minister is informed of local views for and against a proposal but also that those views are tested in the inspector's enquiry, and fully considered in the subsequent report by the inspector to the minister.

Other types of enquiry are also advisory, but are more investigative in nature. An example would be an ad hoc public enquiry into a serious railway accident. The functions of such an enquiry would be to appraise ministers of the full facts surrounding the accident following an investigation of the causes of the accident. Whereas the compulsory purchase order enquiry is fairly passive, relying on party initiative to inform the minister, the investigative enquiry is more active in that it is seeks out information. The characteristic of both informational and investigative enquiries is that the results are advisory and may be accepted or rejected by the minister, though they will be used as part of the process of ministerial decision-making. This and the following chapter describe the work of two of the main court-substitute or adjudicatory tribunals: the social security appeal tribunals and the industrial tribunals.

The Franks Committee

No discussion of tribunals can ignore the impact of the Report of the Franks Committee, which is still viewed as laying down the ground rules for the operation of tribunals. Tribunals might well have continued to develop without any critical analysis of their impact on the administration of justice, had it not been for one of those incidents of poor administration whose wider implications cannot be ignored. The catalyst was the Crichel Down Enquiry in 1954 by the Minister of Agriculture into the sale and subsequent choosing of a tenant for Crichel Down in Dorset which had been purchased during the war as a bombing range.[3] This incident, despite having nothing to do with the operation of tribunals led to the establishment in 1955 of the Committee on Administrative Tribunals and Enquiries under the chairmanship of Sir Oliver Franks (as he then was). The Committee came to be known as the Franks Committee, and reported in 1957. The Franks Report has had a major impact on critical analysis of tribunals. The terms of reference were:

To consider and make recommendations on:
  (a) The constitution and working of tribunals other than the ordinary courts of law, constituted under any Act of Parliament by a minister of the Crown or for the purposes of a minister's functions.
  (b) The working of such administrative procedures as include the holding of an inquiry or hearing by or on behalf of a minister on an appeal or as a result of objections or representations, and in particular the procedure for the compulsory purchase of land.

The coupling of tribunals with ministerial enquiries has dominated the treatment of tribunals since the report of the Franks Committee. The report also began the dangerous process of generalisation about tribunals and enquiries by identifying 'general and closely linked characteristics which should mark these special procedures'. This general approach rather clouded the other important conclusion that tribunals are a new method for the independent adjudication of disputes. The Committee distinguished tribunals from 'ordinary courts' but went on to say: 'We consider that tribunals should properly be regarded as machinery provided by Parliament for adjudication rather than as part of the machinery for administration'.[4]

Key recommendations made by the Franks Committee concern the impartiality of tribunals and their supervision. Membership of tribunals should not be within the patronage of the minister, the decisions of whose officials are under review. The Committee suggested that the Lord Chancellor should appoint chairmen and clearly favoured an increase in the use of lawyer chairmen principally because lawyers were considered to have a good grasp of principles of procedural fairness. As a general principle it was recommended that hearings should be in public and that reasons should be given for decisions. Legal representation was not viewed as

---

[3] J. Griffith, 'The Crichel Down Affair' (1955) 18 MLR 557.
[4] *Report of the Committee on Administrative Tribunals and Enquiries (Franks Committee)* (London: HMSO, 1957, Cmnd. 218), para. 40.

necessary, but rules prohibiting legal representation were considered undesirable.[5] A proper system of appeals from decisions of tribunals should also be introduced.

Finally the Committee proposed the creation of two Councils on Tribunals (one for England and Wales, and one for Scotland) to exercise general supervisory powers over the operation of tribunals. Most of the Committee's recommendations were speedily implemented in the Tribunals and Inquiries Act 1958, which was amended by the Tribunals and Inquiries Act 1966. The legislation has been consolidated and the law can now be found in the Tribunals and Inquiries Act 1992.

The declared characteristics of tribunals specified in the Franks Report were 'cheapness, accessibility and freedom from technicality, expedition and expert knowledge of the particular subject' and it was stated that the objectives of tribunal procedure are 'openness, fairness and impartiality'. Little need be said of the declared hallmarks of the proper procedures of tribunals of 'openness, fairness and impartiality'. These are the hallmarks of any system of decision-making under any scheme of government regulation in a democratic society.[6] How far can the characteristics suggested for tribunals be said to be true of tribunals to the exclusion of other forms of dispute resolution? The answer is that they cannot. Tribunals are only cheap in the sense that no fees are payable on filing claims and that allowances are generally paid for out of pocket expenses in attending the tribunal. This is simply a transfer of spending from litigant to the State. Indeed effective use of tribunals may be more expensive to a claimant. There is little possibility of any recovery of the costs of using a lawyer from the losing party and legal aid will not finance representation.

Accessibility and freedom from technicality may be taken together. In this respect post-Franks developments of tribunals have overtaken the Franks Report. Tribunals tend to be geographically accessible, because they sit locally, like both magistrates' courts and the county courts. On the other hand, the problems of direct access without assistance or representation have continued to be a subject of considerable debate. The problem of accessibility is linked to the technical nature of the legal rules applied by many tribunals. The substantive law applied in many tribunals has become more complex since 1957, while procedural rules have developed which need to be fully understood and carefully observed to make the most effective use of the tribunal decision-making process. By contrast, rules operating in some courts, particularly in the small claims jurisdiction of the county courts, have become less complex. Even with the remaining difficulties, arbitration in the county court is certainly as accessible and free from technicality as pursuing an unfair dismissal claim before an industrial tribunal. It has become clear over the years that a level of formality is required for fair and impartial decision-making, though it is equally clear that proper decision-making does not always require ritual conduct or observance of the formal rules of evidence.

---

[5] See, more recently, Council on Tribunals, *Tribunals: their Organisation and Independence* (London: HMSO, 1997, Cm. 3744).

[6] And reflect the thrust of the requirements of Art. 6 of the European Convention on Human Rights; see generally F. Jacobs and R. White, *The European Convention on Human Rights* (Oxford: Clarendon Press, 1996), ch. 8.

The issue of delay depends upon a comparison of like with like. The speed of decision-making of some tribunals is broadly comparable with that of magistrates' courts and the county courts. If compulsory purchase order enquiries were contrasted with inferior courts, the courts would be speedier. Looking at the time lag between the filing of a claim and final disposition is in any event a crude measure. What is more important is to discover the causes of delay, without which general conclusions are likely to be unhelpful.

To suggest that tribunals have greater expert knowledge of the subject matter of disputes before them than judges is rather insulting to the judges. It is sitting as chairman or lay member of a tribunal which gives tribunals expertise, just as the lawyer appointed to judicial office in the courts will soon acquire expertise in those areas of law which did not form part of his or her practice before appointment. The general qualities of those appointed as judges, chairmen or lay members of tribunals, are considered more important than a detailed knowledge of the law relating to the particular types of dispute likely to be considered by those persons. The increasing incidence of the full-time lawyer chairman has narrowed the gap between judicial appointment as a judge and as a tribunal chairman. It is probably fair to say that full-time tribunal chairman are considered of roughly equal status to district judges, with Presidents, regional chairmen and lawyer members of appellate tribunals roughly equal to Circuit judges.

The thrust of this argument is that tribunals which resolve disputes have matured beyond the framework envisaged by the Franks Report. The aims of the modern tribunal are:

- to reach the right decision in law;
- to give the parties an impartial, fair and sufficient hearing;
- to use the advantages of tribunal procedure to enable claimants to have greater participation in the resolution of their dispute.

This and the following chapter look at two sets of tribunals which have a heavy caseload: the social security tribunals, and the employment tribunals. Whereas social security tribunals deal with disputes between citizens and the State and have stressed informality in their processes, employment tribunals deal with disputes between citizen and employer, and have been criticised for their 'legalism'. The structure of the social security tribunals will change when the Social Security Act 1998 is fully implemented; these impending changes are discussed at the end of this chapter.

The Independent Tribunal Service

Though it is possible to trace a system of remedies outside the court structure back a thousand years,[7] it is unnecessary to go back beyond the National Insurance Act 1911 for an historical background to modern tribunals. Following the scheme set

[7] R. Wraith and P. Hutchesson, *Administrative Tribunals* (London: George Allen and Unwin, 1973).

up in Germany, Lloyd George introduced a new system for the settlement of disputes arising out of claims to the new unemployment benefit provided by the Act
and administered by the Board of Trade. Initial decisions on entitlement were made
by employees of the Board of Trade known as insurance officers. A claimant dissatisfied with the decision of the insurance officer could have the decision reviewed
by a local Court of Referees consisting of a chairman appointed by the Minister of
Trade, one member chosen from an employers' panel and one member chosen from
a workmen's panel. There was a further final appeal to a national appellate authority known as the Umpire, a lawyer appointed by the Crown. The adoption of this
system of dispute resolution was in part a borrowing of the German experience,
but was also a reaction to the unsatisfactory operation of the resolution of disputes
in the county courts concerning workmen's compensation for injuries suffered
at work. This had not been intended to be legalistic, but in practice the claimant
had been put in the position of an ordinary plaintiff in a civil case arguing a case
against a powerful insurance company or mutual insurance society.[8] The new idea
introduced by local Courts of Referees was the free local non-legal forum for the
settlement of particular disputes. They were very successful and provided a model
for review procedures connected with a variety of benefits under the burgeoning
national insurance scheme.

Not everyone welcomed this new development. Some judges and lawyers saw
in the development a serious threat to the independent impartial adjudication of
disputes by the courts. The concern culminated in the publication in 1929 by the
Lord Chief Justice, Lord Hewart, of his book *The New Despotism* in which these
arguments and the theme that arbitrary power was being concentrated in the hands
of the bureaucracy were elaborated. By way of response the Government established
the Committee on Minister's Powers which reported in 1932 and has come to be
known as the Donoughmore Committee.[9] The terms of reference were narrowly
drawn and the Committee's report did not include any grand plan for the future
development of a tribunal system. Nor did it agree with the fear expressed by Lord
Hewart. Effectively the seal of approval was given to the type of tribunal established
under the National Insurance Act 1911.

The modern social security tribunal system has grown from these beginnings.[10]
The social security system has a multitude of benefits, but can still be related to
the post-war Beveridge Plan which settled the framework of the welfare state after
the Second World War.[11] Having received official blessing from the Donoughmore
Committee, tribunals mushroomed, particularly in connection with the social
security legislation introduced after the Second World War. The Beveridge Plan
was to raise the level of insurance benefits from survival level to subsistence level
and to protect adults against loss of income through a comprehensive system of

[8] D. Potter and D. Stansfield, *The National Insurance (Industrial Injury) Act 1946*, 2nd edn. (London:
Butterworths, 1950).

[9] *Report of the Committee on Minister's Powers (Donoughmore Committee)* (London: HMSO, 1932,
Cmd. 4060).

[10] For more detail on the history, see R. White, *The Administration of Justice*, 2nd edn. (Oxford: Basil Blackwell,
1991), pp. 231–7; and J. Farmer, *Tribunals and Government* (London: Weidenfeld and Nicolson, 1974), ch. 4.

[11] *Report on Social Insurance and Allied Services (Beveridge Report)* (London: HMSO, 1942, Cmd. 6404).

social insurance benefits to which legal entitlement would arise on payment of the requisite contributions. This system of social insurance was coupled with a proposal for a system of non-contributory family allowances to meet the needs of families. But the Beveridge Plan accepted the need for a safety net of means-tested benefits for those outside insurance, which it was envisaged would play very much a minor role in the new welfare state. The Beveridge Plan inspired the post-war burst of legislation establishing the welfare state. Under the National Insurance Act 1946 provision was made for tribunals to be established to consider questions of entitlement to, and amount of, contributory benefits, thus establishing the national insurance local tribunals. Under the National Assistance Act 1948, a National Assistance Board and national assistance tribunals replaced the Unemployment Assistance Board and the unemployment appeal tribunals, and became the parents of supplementary benefits appeal tribunals.

A major shift of emphasis took place in 1980 when the discretionary nature of the means-tested supplementary benefit was translated into a rights-based system. Shortly afterwards the respected national insurance local tribunals and the much-derided supplementary benefit appeal tribunals were merged to form the social security appeal tribunals.[12]

On 23 April 1984, the Health and Social Services and Social Security Adjudication Act 1983 amalgamated national insurance local tribunals and supplementary benefit appeal tribunals to form social security appeal tribunals (SSATs). The Department of Health and Social Security handed over all its responsibilities for the new tribunals to a newly created statutory authority known as the Office of the President of Social Security Appeal Tribunals (OPSSAT). The new central authority was headed by a Circuit judge assisted by seven regional chairmen, who were in turn assisted by a full-time chairmen. All are appointed by the Lord Chancellor. OPSSAT subsequently became the Independent Tribunal Service, but still receives its funding resources from the Department of Social Security with whom it negotiates a finance budget and a staff allocation. Staff of the Independent Tribunal Service act to the instructions and priorities set by the President. The tribunals sit at nearly 150 venues throughout England and Wales, and Scotland. The Independent Tribunal Service runs five sets of tribunals:

- social security appeal tribunals (SSATs) which hear appeals relating to most social security benefits;
- disability appeal tribunals which hear appeals relating to the disablement aspect inherent in claims for disability living allowance, attendance allowance, and disability working allowance;
- medical appeal tribunals which hear appeals dealing with the medical aspects relating to the level of disablement and diagnosis questions linked to a person's employment;

---

[12] See generally K. Bell et al., 'National Insurance Local Tribunals—A Research Study' [1974] 3 J Soc. Policy 289 and [1975] 4 J Soc. Policy 1; K. Bell, *Research Study on Supplementary Benefit Appeal Tribunals. Review of Main Findings: Conclusions; Recommendations* (London: HMSO, 1975); and R. Lister, 'SBATs—an Urgent Case for Reform' in M. Adler and A. Bradley, *Justice, Discretion and Poverty—Supplementary Benefit Appeal Tribunals in Britain* (London: Professional Books, 1975).

- vaccine damage tribunals, which review awards of the Benefits Agency to those who have suffered severe physical or mental impairment as a result of a vaccination against certain specified diseases; and
- child support appeal tribunals which decide appeals arising from assessment of child support maintenance payable by a parent.

Today, the tribunals belonging to the Independent Tribunal Service have the heaviest caseload of any tribunal. They currently expect to receive some 334,000 appeals a year.[13] In 1996/97 SSAT business accounted for 219,000 of the 290,000 cases taken in by the Independent Tribunal Service. As the dominant area of business, its work is the primary focus of this chapter.

SSATs consist of a lawyer chairman sitting with two lay members. Most cases are heard by part-time chairmen who must be solicitors, barristers or advocates of five years standing. They are appointed by the Lord Chancellor for renewable three year terms of office. Members are appointed by the President from those considered to 'have knowledge or experience of conditions in the area and to be representative of persons living or working in the area'.[14] The President has the responsibility of supervising the overall operation of SSATs, as well as of organising meetings, training courses and of preparing material for the guidance of SSATs. The system of adjudication of social security benefits is now integrated, but the price has been the judicialisation of the tribunal system without sweeping reforms in the provision of assistance and representation for persons wishing to claim. The main arguments which have led to the creation of the new tribunals with their own appellate tribunal have centred around the complexity of social security law, and yet there is no increased provision of funding for assistance either through legal aid, law centres or welfare rights services.

The Independent Tribunal Service has worked hard to increase the proportion of women and members of ethnic minorities who serve on the tribunals, and publishes details in its annual report. Around three in ten part-time chairmen are women and nearly four per cent are from ethnic minorities. Over four in ten members are women and over six per cent are from ethnic minorities. There is a provision in the legislation which says that, as far as practicable, at least one member[15] of the tribunal must be of the same sex as the claimant.[16]

Claiming Social Security Benefits

Initial adjudication of claims to social security benefits will generally take place in a local office of the Department of Social Security or Department of Employment

---

[13] Independent Tribunal Service, *Annual Report 1996–1997* (London: Independent Tribunal Service, 1997), p. 4.   [14] Social Security Administration Act 1992, s. 40(2).

[15] For this purpose, the chairman counts as a member of the tribunal.

[16] Social Security Administration Act 1992, s. 41(6).

depending on the benefit claimed. Claims to some benefits are, however, dealt with by centrally located benefit offices. All claims will require investigation of entitlement. Decision-making is split between adjudication officers and officers known as Secretary of State's representatives. Adjudication officers are employees in the relevant Department but exercise independent judgment on claims in making decisions within their province. They alone have authority to award benefit. Certain decisions are taken by officers designated as Secretary of State's representatives. Such decisions relate primarily to satisfaction of the contribution conditions,[17] but the legislation gives them competence on specific questions at many points. Where medical questions are involved, specific decision-making powers are given to medical adjudicating authorities. SSATs only have jurisdiction to consider an appeal against a decision of an adjudication officer. The proper remedy for dissatisfaction with a Secretary of State's decision is appeal on the question of law to the High Court. The scale of decision-making within the Department of Social Security and Department of Employment is vast; adjudication officers make decisions in more than 25 million claims each year. They are expected so far as practicable to make decisions on benefit entitlement within fourteen days, but this time limit is frequently exceeded. In *R* v. *Secretary of State for Social Services, ex parte CPAG*,[18] the Court of Appeal affirmed a decision of the High Court in which the trial judge had said that the practicability of such speedy decision-making was not such that the Secretary of State was required to appoint sufficient adjudication officers to enable claims to be decided within fourteen days, and recognised that workloads may lead to delays beyond the time limit expressed in the Social Security Act 1975.[19]

Once a decision is made it must be communicated in writing to the claimant, who then has three months in which to appeal against it to the tribunal. The document communicating the decision advises the claimant of the right of appeal. Fewer than one in five hundred decisions are appealed.

In reality the relationship between claimant and the Benefits Agency[20] is a good deal more complex than this description might suggest. A recent study[21] showed that claimants' descriptions of their responsibilities in presenting information when making a claim did not always match up with their practice. It seems that claimants generally recognised that they had a responsibility to provide all the information the Benefits Agency needed to determine a claim for benefit, but this was frequently not how they behaved. Indeed it seems that the language of roles and responsibilities had not occurred to many claimants until the issue was raised with them by the researchers. Nevertheless, claimants generally had a clear agenda of how the administration of their benefits could be improved. The study concluded that simply encouraging claimants to take more responsibility for their claims might

---

[17] Whether a person has paid or been credited with contributions to the National Insurance Fund, which is a condition of entitlement to certain benefits.   [18] [1989] 1 All ER 1047.

[19] The controlling legislation today is the Social Security Administration Act 1992; the Social Security Contributions and Benefits Act 1992; the Social Security (Incapacity for Work) Act 1994; and the Jobseeker's Act 1995.   [20] A 'Next Steps' agency of the Department of Social Security which handles claims.

[21] See J. Ritchie and M. Chetwynd, *Claimants' Perceptions of the Claim Process* (London: The Stationery Office, 1997).

not be the most effective way forward in a climate where such concepts had not occurred to many claimants.

Claimants generally find the task of completing a claim form difficult. Though many described themselves as careful to complete forms fully, they also stressed personal factors, such as stress, illness, literacy deficiencies and a lack of confidence as influencing the completion of the task. The forms themselves were not always clear in layout or content, and many claimants were irritated and bewildered by the need to provide the same information repeatedly in claim forms.

The clear message of the research is that claiming a benefit is not a simple task; it is not undertaken lightly by claimants, and there is a need for more assistance for some in the completion of the task. Clearly a benefit system is designed to get financial help quickly to those who need it. It is important that as many decisions as possible are right first time. The challenge is to balance speed and accuracy of decision-making.

The adjudication officer is central to the process of initial determinations of entitlement to benefit; the function is quasi-judicial, but research has shown that this is not achieved in the hectic environment of the local office.[22] Speed of decision-making has overtaken the need for accuracy. The exercise of independent judgment is all too often subordinated to administrative routine. One major study concludes that 'hurried decisions are not merely tolerated but expected'.[23]

This gloomy picture is confirmed by successive annual reports of the Chief Adjudication Officer. The latest annual report[24] reveals that one in three decisions on family credit was incomplete in some way;[25] nearly half of income support decisions were subject to comment and one in eight involved incorrect payments; and three-quarters of social fund payment decisions were the subject of comment. On decisions to recover overpaid income support, the picture was even more alarming with the comment rate varying from a low of sixteen per cent in one area to a high of ninety-three per cent in another area. Clearly an appeal system is vital in the face of such poor initial decision-making.

The Appeal Process

The nature of tribunal adjudication

The three members of the tribunal share the responsibility for decision-making on appeals; the lawyer and the lay members have an equal say on all issues whether of law or fact. The main role is the adjudication of the dispute between the claimant

---

[22] See J. Baldwin, N. Wikeley and R. Young, *Judging Social Security: The Adjudication of Claims for Benefit in Britain* (Oxford: Clarendon Press, 1992) (cited in this chapter as '*Judging Social Security*'), ch. 2.

[23] Ibid., p. 64.

[24] *Annual Report of the Chief Adjudication Officer 1996–97* (London: Central Adjudication Services, 1997).

[25] Not necessarily always resulting in detriment to the claimant.

and the relevant Department on entitlement to benefit. The process of judging in SSATs involves five tasks:

- reading the case papers;
- identifying the legal test relevant to the appeal;
- considering the evidence and making findings of fact relevant to the legal test;
- applying the legal test to the facts as decided by the tribunal and making a fair decision on the law;
- properly recording the evidence heard and considered, the facts found, the decision of the tribunal and the reasons for it.

The Foreword by the first President of the SSATs to *The Guide to Procedure* stresses the enabling functions of the tribunals:

Most claimants at the time of their appeal will be too troubled and hassled by the more practical day to day problems of their plight ever to have the emotional energy to study the nuts and bolts of the machinery by which their appeal will be processed. For them, any meaningful guide of one hundred pages is one hundred pages too long, no matter the style in which it is written. For people in the latter category my message is short: 'Comply with the instructions set out in the forms which bring your case before the tribunal. Once there, let others whose job it is to look after procedure do so. Don't worry about it yourself'.[26]

Tribunals should adopt a flexible procedure which facilitates the presentation of evidence and argument by claimants and representatives with a range of communication skills, some outstanding, some very limited. Within the requirements laid down by the Franks Report of the need for openness, fairness and impartiality, the objective is to achieve a formal procedure with an informal atmosphere. The Social Security Commissioners too have stressed the investigative or inquisitorial role of the tribunals. In *R(S)1/87*, Commissioner Hallett said:

The jurisdiction of . . . the social security appeal tribunal . . . is investigative or inquisitorial. A social security appeal tribunal is exercising quasi-judicial functions and forms part of the statutory machinery for investigating claims in order to ascertain whether the claimant satisfies the statutory requirements which entitle him to be paid benefit. It is not restricted, as in ordinary litigation which are proceedings between parties, to accepting or rejecting the respective contentions of the claimant on the one hand and the adjudication . . . officer on the other . . . Its investigatory function has as its object the ascertainment of the facts and the determination of the truth.[27]

A Tribunal of Commissioners echoes these sentiments in *R(S)4/82*, where they described the judicial process in tribunals as 'fair play in action'.[28]

One research study, which included observation of tribunals, showed that tribunal chairmen in the tribunals believed in the investigative approach to the determination of appeals:

---

[26] See *Guide to Procedure*, p. vii.   [27] *R(S)1/87*, para. 14(3).   [28] *R(S)4/82*, para. 26.

During observations of social security appeal tribunal hearings the vast majority of chairs were found to be courteous, sensitive and at pains to be helpful to appellants, reflecting, presumably, the 'enabling' role that has been stressed under the new regime and the belief expressed by all chairs that hearings were fundamentally 'inquisitorial'. In this context, the term inquisitorial seems to mean that chairs feel they have the freedom to investigate cases and elicit the information they think they need in order to get to the truth of the situation, rather than to choose between competing arguments.[29]

These findings are supported by other research.[30] The task of running a judicial process in an informal atmosphere is clearly not easy. Focusing exclusively on the legal framework with which claimants cannot be expected to be familiar is likely to result in their feeling that they have not had a fair hearing, while too much informality can result in the proceedings becoming disordered and sight being lost of the need to make a decision on entitlement on the legal criteria contained in the social security legislation. One chairman summarised the dilemma as follows:

I see my role as bringing in the members as much as possible and generally making sure than everybody has their say. It's my role too to explain the law to the members when we come to make our decision. And making sure that the proceeding doesn't become too untidy, that it's informal enough to be relaxing; formal enough to be tidy. You can't let it degenerate into a chat, but it has to be a fairly relaxed atmosphere. That's quite a tight line to keep but I do try to do that.[31]

However, as we shall see, the enabling role of tribunals does not appear to be able to remove the disadvantage which appears to exist for the unrepresented claimant, whose chances of succeeding in the appeal are lower than those of the represented claimant.

Making the appeal

Making an appeal to an SSAT is a very simple task. The appeal should be made by completing the form provided for this purpose by the Department, but an appeal made by writing a letter can be accepted if it contains the required information. This is the date of notification of the decision against which the appeal is made and a 'summary of the arguments relied on . . . to support his contention that the decision was wrong'.[32] Nothing very sophisticated is expected of the summary of the arguments relied on in making the appeal. No fee is payable on filing an appeal.

The time limit of three months from notification of the adjudication officer's decision is important. Appeals can only be accepted outside the time limit if there are special reasons of an exceptional nature explaining why the appeal could not have been made in time. Though the appeal need only state the reasons why the

---

[29] H. Genn and Y. Genn, *The Effectiveness of Representation at Tribunals* (London: Lord Chancellor's Department, 1989), p. 159.   [30] *Judging Social Security, supra* n. 22, ch. 4.
[31] Ibid., pp. 122–3.
[32] Social Security (Adjudication) Regulations 1995, S.I. 1995 No. 1801, r. 2(5), as amended, cited in this chapters as 'the Adjudication Regulations'.

appeal is being made in broad terms, there are two reasons why it is advisable to set out in some detail the reasons and facts upon which the appeal is based. The first is that, as we shall see, the letter of appeal will be included in documents made available to the tribunal in advance of the hearing and a good clear account will ensure that the chairman and members are clear about the claimant's grievance.

The second reason is that an appeal triggers a reconsideration of the case by an adjudication officer, who may revise the decision in the claimant's favour forthwith. Around one in four decisions will be changed in the claimant's favour at this stage.[33] The more information the adjudication officer has the more likely will be a revision in the claimant's favour. In order to make the best of a case at this stage most claimants will need advice and assistance because preparing a case for appeal involves three tasks: establishing the facts of the case, understanding the applicable legal rules and integrating facts and law in a well-constructed argument which includes meeting the reasons put forward by the adjudication officer for denying the claim. This issue of getting help is considered in more detail below. But the claimant who has received no help should not despair, because there is a significant element of inquisitorial procedures in the tribunal's decision-making process.

Judging Social Security[34] reports that review following the filing of an appeal can result in priority being given to accuracy over speed in decision-making. Those whose work involved the conduct of such reviews frequently stressed the reduction in pressure on them to process cases fast. Practice in conducting the review varies according to the benefit. Yet despite the obvious focusing of attention on detail which an appeal triggers, there remained a tendency for some adjudication officers to view the tribunal as the safety net for claimants and to leave any possible defects for correction through the appeal process.

The adjudication officer's written submission

The adjudication officer in all cases prepares a documentary case for submission to the tribunal in advance of the hearing. This is also sent to the claimant. It will contain details of the claim and of the adjudication officer's decision, together with a note of the statutory provisions and decisions of the Commissioners upon which the adjudication officer is relying. The claimant's letter of appeal will be included and there will be a full written submission by the adjudication officer setting out the facts and law as they have been determined and applied to the claimant's case. For the unrepresented claimant, these papers are undoubtedly daunting.[35] Their quality varies considerably; there is a tendency to make appeal fit specimen submissions.[36] Something between one-third and one-half of them are likely to be deficient in some significant measure.[37] The adjudication officer's submission will be accompanied by informational literature about the tribunal, but success at the

---

[33] *Judging Social Security, supra* n. 22, p. 68.   [34] Ibid., pp. 71–89.
[35] Ibid., pp. 157–60.   [36] Ibid., p. 91.
[37] For detailed figures, see *Annual Report of the Chief Adjudication Officer 1996–97* (London: Central Adjudication Services, 1997).

hearing will be determined in part by the use made of the information provided in the written submission. It seems that a curtain of gloom falls over some claimants at this stage who abandon their fate to their own written statement of appeal. Bell's research on national insurance local tribunals concluded that a major cause of non-attendance at the hearing results from 'a combination of pessimism about the outcome and practical difficulties'.[38]

The claimant will be asked whether they wish to have an oral hearing or not. Where a claimant either does not request an oral hearing or simply ignores the invitation to ask for an oral hearing, the appeal will be forwarded for a paper determination.[39] Early indications were that paper determinations occurred in four per cent of total hearings.[40]

Where there is a hearing, the parties are entitled to seven clear days notice of the hearing, unless they agree to shorter notice.

The hearing

The tribunal hearing itself is in an informal setting. All participants sit around a large table. Typically the tribunal members will sit along one side of the table, the clerk at one end and the adjudication officer and claimant opposite the tribunal members. Normally between four and six cases will be listed for a half day, which would allow about thirty to forty-five minutes per case if all the claimants attended, but some do not even though they have requested an oral hearing. This can allow more time for attended cases, since non-attended cases can tend to be dealt with very speedily. The tribunal clerk will have some idea of the numbers likely to attend and to be represented from the replies to the short questionnaire sent to claimants with the adjudication officer's submission. Standard practice is now for the chairman to welcome the parties and offer a brief explanation of the role of the tribunal. The quality of these introductions, which are very important in putting unrepresented claimants at their ease and enabling them to contribute effectively to a procedure which is very strange to them and generates considerable anxiety, vary considerably. Some are excellent, while others are rather perfunctory.

The hearing is technically in public, though it is very rare for anyone other than those immediately involved to be present. The claimant can request a private hearing. The procedure is for the chairman to decide. It is usual for the claimant to be asked to outline the reasons for the appeal following which the presenting adjudication officer may ask questions of the claimant and of any witnesses brought along by the claimant.[41] The tribunal chairman and members will also ask questions as the case proceeds. Witnesses do not give evidence on oath. The formal rules of evidence that apply in courts do not apply in tribunals. Any material which

---

[38] K. Bell et al., 'National Insurance Local Tribunals—A Research Study' [1974] 3 J Soc. Policy 289 and [1975] 4 J Soc. Policy 1.   [39] See below.

[40] Independent Tribunal Service, *Annual Report 1996–1997* (London: Independent Tribunal Service, 1997), p. 23.

[41] On the role of the presenting adjudication officer, see *Judging Social Security, supra* n. 22, ch. 7.

is relevant and helpful may be considered, though the weight to be attached to different types of evidence will vary. Tribunals will generally regard first-hand evidence as more likely to be correct than second-hand evidence, but there is no general requirement that what the claimant says must be corroborated by another person's evidence. Nor is there any requirement that evidence must be in writing to be persuasive.

The adjudication officer, who will not normally be the one who made the initial decision, will then put forward any submissions he or she may wish. It is clear that the role of the adjudication officer at the tribunal is not be an adversary of the claimant defending the Department's original decision. On more than one occasion the courts have stated that the procedure is investigatory and that the role of the adjudication officer is to act as amicus curiae (friend of the court) assisting the tribunal in its investigation of the claim.[42] Given this role, the increasing practice of the Department in not providing an adjudication officer for a hearing is to be deprecated and has led to adverse comment from the Social Security Commissioners. In *CS/096/1996*, Commissioner Goodman said:

In my view it is important that someone from the Department should attend hearings before social security appeal tribunals. The adjudication officer is the respondent to such an appeal and should be represented. Moreover the presence of a presenting officer is essential, to inform the tribunal of the relevant facts and regulations and to answer any questions. It is a serious matter if no one attends from the local office.[43]

Though the onus of proving entitlement to the benefit claimed is normally on the claimant, in a number of cases the burden of proof is placed on the adjudication officer to satisfy the tribunal on the balance of probabilities of particular facts. One example is disqualification from receiving jobseeker's allowance following the termination of employment as a result of misconduct.[44]

Attendance at the tribunal need not result in a claimant being out of pocket because the cost of transport to the tribunal and of any loss of earnings is re-imbursed by the tribunal. Similar costs incurred by witnesses reasonably called to support the claimant's case will also be met out of public funds.

Though chairmen generally perceive that they are operating a formal procedure in an informal setting, most claimants describe their attendance as an 'ordeal'.[45] Yet only one in twenty said they would prefer to have been spared a hearing and had their case dealt with on the papers alone. Eight out of ten claimants claimed to have understood what was going on in the hearing, thought they had been given a full opportunity to make their case, and considered that the tribunal had done all it could to put them at their ease. Nine out of every ten attending claimants expressed no serious criticism of the tribunals.[46]

---

[42] *R v. Deputy Industrial Injuries Commissioner, ex parte Moore* [1956] 1 QB 456; *R v. National Insurance Commissioner, ex parte Viscusi* [1974] 1 WLR 646.   [43] *CS/096/1996*, para. 7.

[44] *R(U)2/60*, dealing with a similar earlier provision relating to unemployment benefit, the predecessor of contribution-based jobseeker's allowance.   [45] *Judging Social Security, supra* n. 22, p. 179.

[46] Ibid., p. 170.

The decision

Once the tribunal has heard the submissions of the parties, everyone except the tribunal members leaves the room while the tribunal deliberates. It is presidential policy that, wherever practicable, claimants should be told the outcome of their appeals on the day, and given a short form written decision there and then. In some cases, it may be necessary for the decision to be reserved, that is, deferred pending further research and the circulation of a draft decision, but this is rare.

In all cases the claimant and adjudication officer can, within twenty-one days, request a written record of the decision which includes a statement of the tribunal's findings of fact and of the reasons for the decision. The grounds for any dissenting opinion must also be stated. Even full written decisions can usually be relatively brief, though it must be sufficiently full and complete that the claimant can tell what facts have been accepted and rejected, the reasons for the rejection of any evidence and how the law has been applied to the facts as found. Commissioner Watson said in *R(SB)5/81*:

Findings and reasons need not be lengthy; indeed brevity clearly indicating them is often to be preferred to a lengthy and possibly ambiguous record. It is not possible to lay down a general rule for recording findings and reasons since that depends on the nature of the evidence and of the case.[47]

If the decision is so brief as to be inadequate, this may provide grounds for an appeal to the Commissioners, since it will amount to an error of law. Where the decision is adverse to the claimant, information about the right of appeal to the Commissioners must be given.

In deciding appeals before them, SSATs are bound by decisions of the Commissioners. Their decisions form a self-contained body of rules of precedent value both for adjudication officers and for tribunals. It follows that it is important for relevant decisions to be considered in deciding cases.

Paper determinations

Paper determinations where a claimant does not request an oral hearing are a new innovation designed to assist in the clearance of appeals. The limited information on the operation of paper determinations is to be found in the Independent Tribunal Service's *Annual Report*.[48] There are some unsatisfactory features to current arrangements. Most importantly, it seems that the papers for such determinations are circulated in advance only to the chairman of the tribunal and not to the members with whom he or she sits. Since the only material on which the tribunal can determine such an appeal is that contained in the papers, advance reading of those papers would seem to be an essential requirement for a proper hearing. There does not yet appear to be a proper system in place within the Independent

[47]   *R(SB)5/81*, para. 10.
[48]   *Annual Report of the Chief Adjudication Officer 1996–97* (London: Central Adjudication Services, 1997).

Tribunal Service for monitoring this development, or for providing the necessary safeguards to ensure that the determination is of the best possible quality in the absence of the parties. It is, of course, true that prior to the introduction of paper determinations, the figures showed that about three in ten appellants did not attend their hearing. However, it is not known in how many of those cases there was also no presenting adjudication officer, effectively making the appeal a paper determination. Anecdotal evidence from tribunal members suggests that in some areas there were significant numbers of such cases.

Setting aside, reviews and appeals

There are three ways in which the decision of the tribunal can be changed. The first is where it is **set aside**, in which case it is treated as if it had never existed. There are three gateways to the setting aside of a decision:

- a document connected with the appeal was not received in time by one of the parties or their representative;
- a party to the appeal or their representative was not present;
- there has been a procedural mishap.

Once one of these grounds has been established, the party seeking the setting aside, which can be the adjudication officer or the claimant, must show that it is just to set the decision aside. The tribunal which decided the case considers the application, but, if it is allowed, the case must be listed for a tribunal composed of different people to be heard afresh.

Review is only available to adjudication officers, who can revise the decision where it is shown that it was given in ignorance of, or mistake as to, a material fact, or there has been a relevant change of circumstances. Again, once the ground for review has been established, the adjudication officer must consider whether it is right to revise the decision in the light of the circumstances now revealed. Any decision given on review attracts a further right of appeal just like the original decision.

The final way in which the decision might be varied is on **appeal**. Decisions of tribunals may be appealed to the Social Security Commissioners on a point of law. Leave must be obtained from the chairman of the tribunal which decided the case, but if it is refused, then leave can be sought from the Commissioners. The time limit for appeals is three months. Appeals are only available where a tribunal has been requested to provide full reasons for its decision. A chairman's discretion on the grant of leave is unfettered, provided that he or she acts judicially.[49] The Commissioner's guidance on the exercise of the discretion is as follows:

If the conduct of the proceedings before the local tribunal is seriously in question, leave should be given. Where, however, the local tribunal is attacked in general terms, without any particulars of the detailed conduct complained of . . . the chairman should refuse.

[49] *R(S)4/82(T)*, para. 30.

Such a refusal does not shut the claimant out, because he can seek leave to appeal, as of right, from a Commissioner.[50]

A refusal of leave by a Commissioner can be challenged by judicial review,[51] but no appeal lies to the Court of Appeal against a refusal of leave.[52]

The Social Security Commissioners

Appeals from decisions of SSATs lie, with leave, to the Social Security Commissioners, who are all lawyers. They normally deal with appeals individually, but the Chief Commissioner may decide to convene a Tribunal of three Commissioners to hear appeals involving questions of law of particular difficulty.[53] The Commissioners describe themselves as discharging the functions of a public law appellate court, which are 'directly comparable with those of the judges of the Chancery and Queen's Bench Divisions of the High Court who hear appeals on questions of law from tax tribunals'.[54]

The main procedure is a written one. Legal aid is not available for representation, though advice and assistance under the Green Form scheme will provide assistance. A former Chief National Insurance Commissioner has described the procedure on appeal as a good example of a procedure which is informal and yet under which an appellant's case is considered fully and fairly. He suggested that, in the vast majority of cases, the procedure was accessible to unrepresented appellants (though he did concede that they should receive assistance) and that it would be undesirable to extend legal aid generally to cover such appeals.[55] It is difficult to see how unrepresented claimants who fare so badly in tribunals of first instance could expect to fare better at the appellate level; indeed representation has increased considerably over the past few years.

The claimant sets out the grounds of appeal, though these need not be very detailed. But the clearer the grounds of appeal, the better the chances of success. The adjudication officer is then asked to respond and the claimant is given an opportunity to comment on those responses. The construction of a written case demands perhaps even greater skills than the preparation of oral argument. It is vital to cover all the ground and to be clear and accurate since there is no immediate opportunity to clarify matters by the process of question and answer. At this stage the parties can request an oral hearing which will be granted unless the appeal is an obvious winner or loser. The vast majority of appeals are decided on the papers alone. The paperwork is put into some sort of good order by legally qualified officers

---

[50] *R(S)4/82(T)*, para. 30.   [51] *R(SB)52/83*. On judicial review, see Ch. 16.
[52] *Bland* v. *Chief Supplementary Benefit Officer*, reported as Appendix to *R(SB)12/83*; and *R* v. *Social Security Commissioners, ex parte Morris*, reported as Appendix to Commissioner's Decision *R(A) 5/83*.
[53] Social Security Administration Act 1992, s. 57.
[54] See the Commissioners' website at http://www.hywels.demon.co.uk/commrs/work.htm.
[55] R. Micklethwait, *The National Insurance Commissioners* (London: Stevens, 1976).

known as 'nominated officers'. The Commissioners take considerable trouble to ensure that all relevant arguments are canvassed in the written case, and will invite observations on issues which appear to be relevant and which have not been raised in the written case. Following the decision of the Commissioner, a full written record of the decision is sent to the claimant and to the adjudication officer.

Decisions of the Commissioners are binding on adjudication officers and on tribunals, but not all decisions of the Commissioners are reported. It is the task of the Chief Commissioner to decide which decisions are to be reported and he is assisted by the Commissioners starring decisions they consider worthy of reporting. Parties and their legal advisers, as well as welfare organisations, may also make representations that a decision should be reported. The criteria for selection for reporting are that the case involves an issue of legal principle and contributes to the orderly development of the law. The Chief Commissioner seeks to ensure that all reported decisions have the assent of a majority of Commissioners. It remains open to claimants and the adjudication officer to cite unreported cases, but advance notice of their intention to do so is required. Adjudication officers are expected to rely on reported decisions as far as possible. The existence of this body of appellate decisions in social security matters has the obvious effect of contributing to consistency of decision-making not only by adjudication officers in their initial decisions on claims, but also by SSATs. About one in four appeals is successful.

Though appeals are available from the Commissioners to the Court of Appeal, these are comparatively rare. One reason for this has been the deference shown by the Court of Appeal to the expertise of the Commissioners, a deference which appears to be justified by the thoroughness of the re-examination of the cases by the Commissioners. The effective by-passing of the High Court (judicial review remains theoretically available) also reflects an increasing recognition of the Commissioners' specialist expertise.[56] Attempts have been made to use judicial review to challenge a refusal of leave, but these have found little favour with the High Court.[57] Overall little criticism can be levelled at the Commissioners' decision-making, though there is a problem over help for appellants to the Commissioners.

Attendance and Representation

Research in 1970 on national insurance local tribunals showed that about half of claimants do not attend the hearing and that representation was present only in one in five cases.[58] In so far as later information is available, no dramatic improvement

---

[56] A. Ogus and N. Wikeley, *Ogus, Barendt and Wikeley's The Law of Social Security*, 4th edn. (London: Butterworths, 1995), pp. 685–7.

[57] *Bland* v. *Chief Supplementary Benefit Officer*, reported as Appendix to *R(SB)12/83*; and *R* v. *Social Security Commissioners, ex parte Morris*, reported as Appendix to Commissioner's Decision *R(A) 5/83*.

[58] K. Bell et al., 'National Insurance Local Tribunals—A Research Study' [1974] 3 J Soc. Policy 289 and [1975] 4 J Soc. Policy 1.

of these figures is indicated.[59] One study showed that trades union representation was the major type of representation followed by relatives and friends, with lawyers representing only three per cent of those represented, about the same number as social workers.[60] But this is a fairly old study. Though the overall level of representation does not appear to have improved dramatically, it seems that the numbers represented by specialist lay advisers have increased so that now the most common representative is the trades union representative or the specialist lay adviser.

There is a significant variation in success rates depending on representation. The overall success rate has remained fairly constant over the years at about one in five cases. But if the claimant is not represented and does not attend, the success rate falls to one in twelve, while unrepresented attenders win in about one in six cases. Represented claimants are successful in two out of every five cases.[61] A similar sort of pattern emerged in supplementary benefit appeal tribunals. These marked differences between represented and unrepresented cases must place some question marks after the claim that the tribunals are genuinely inquisitorial and that their processes are accessible to claimants appearing in person.

Concern over the reported variations in success rates of represented and unrepresented applicants to tribunals led the Lord Chancellor in 1987 to commission a two-year research project to investigate the effectiveness of representation at tribunals.[62] The research would inform planning and decision-making over the use of legal aid in tribunals. The project was designed to establish whether representation affected the outcome of tribunal hearings, and to analyse the contribution of representation both to pre-hearing processes and to the hearings themselves.

This research showed that the level of advice and representation in SSATs is lower than in the other tribunals investigated. One in five appellants had made some attempt to obtain advice prior to the hearing, but only one in eight appellants is represented by an expert, as distinct from being accompanied by another member of the family or a friend without expert knowledge. About a third of the help came from advisers in Citizens Advice Bureaux. The presence of specialist representation increases the chances of success from one in three to one in two. Specialist lay representation tended to be more successful than representation by solicitors and barristers. The research also showed that attending the hearing, especially if a witness was brought along, also significantly improved the chances of success. Even the identity of the chairman could affect the likelihood of success. The study reported that one by-product of representation is that the tribunal tends to scrutinise other cases more carefully. So success rates in urban areas, where representation is more likely to be present, were higher than in outlying areas.

---

[59] A. Frost and C. Howard, *Representation and Administrative Tribunals* (London: Routledge and Kegan Paul, 1977), and H. Genn and Y. Genn, *The Effectiveness of Representation at Tribunals* (London: Lord Chancellor's Department, 1989).

[60] K. Bell et al., 'National Insurance Local Tribunals—A Research Study' [1974] 3 J Soc. Policy 289 and [1975] 4 J Soc. Policy 1.   [61] Ibid.

[62] H. Genn and Y. Genn, *The Effectiveness of Representation at Tribunals* (London: Lord Chancellor's Department, 1989).

In commenting on the enabling function of the tribunal, the research study speaks of the heavy burden placed on the tribunal of eliciting all the relevant information about the case and applying the law to the facts in an impartial and objective manner. Compensating for the absence of representation could be time-consuming and difficult when appellants are confused or inarticulate.

Social security appeal tribunals are categorised as the least formal of the tribunals investigated, but it is reported that appellants nevertheless found attendance before them a nerve-wracking ordeal. Many appellants reported extreme anxiety and bewilderment and confessed to having had difficulty expressing themselves.

The study concludes:

It has been persistently asserted by policy-makers, some administrative law scholars, and those concerned with the administration of tribunals, that the informality of tribunals, their simplicity, and their accessibility, have rendered representation both unnecessary and undesirable. The evidence of this study indicates that while simplicity in initiating proceedings, informality in surroundings, and procedural flexibility are valuable qualities worthy of preservation, they should not be used as a justification for denying the contribution that representation makes to tribunal decision-making processes, nor the need of appellants to have cases advocated on their behalf.[63]

Judging Social Security also addressed the problems of non-attendance and representation. The study found that nearly half of those who had appealed did not attend the hearing.[64] It did not appear that delay in listing the appeal caused appellants to lose interest, and the study hypothesises that a lack of understanding of the appeal system and a sense of powerlessness in the face of the procedure are the cause of many failures to attend at the tribunals. Like the Genn Study, *Judging Social Security* concludes that the inquisitorial procedures of the tribunal, even when operated at their most effective, do not compensate for the lack of expert representation.

The Social Security Act 1998

The Social Security Act 1998, which received the Royal Assent on 21 May 1998, will make major changes to decision-making in social security. Whether the changes operate as a rationalisation of the tribunal system which offers proportionality (in the Woolf sense) by offering greater flexibility in the composition of the tribunal, or as a way of de-skilling the process and controlling the number of appeals, remains to be seen.

The Act abolishes both the office of adjudication officer and the Independent Tribunal Service. In future, all initial decisions will be made by Secretary of State's representatives, who will presumably be subject to instruction in a way in which —at least formally—adjudication officers were not. The social security appeal tribunals, medical appeal tribunals, disability appeal tribunals, child support appeal

---

[63] H. Genn and Y. Genn, *The Effectiveness of Representation at Tribunals* (London: Lord Chancellor's Department, 1989), p. 248.   [64] *Judging Social Security, supra* n. 22, pp. 162–6.

tribunals, and vaccine damage tribunals disappear to be replaced by 'appeal tribunals' constituted under the Act. Though the Lord Chancellor will constitute panels to sit on the tribunals, they are directly answerable to the Secretary of State. Tribunals may consist of one, two or three persons, one of whom must be legally qualified, though that person will not necessarily be the chairman of the tribunal. Provision is made for the appointment of a President of the appeal tribunals.

The Council on Tribunals has expressed its concern over the new structure of the tribunals, which it describes as resembling the unsatisfactory system which was abandoned in the early 1980s.[65] It is also arguable that the new structure displays less independence from the minister, the decisions of whose officials are the subject of the appeals, than the Independent Tribunal Service. It must be at least arguable, having regard to the replaced Independent Tribunal Service structure, that the new structure is open to challenge under Article 6 of the European Convention on Human Rights as not being 'impartial and independent'. Such a view is reinforced when the provisions of section 26 are considered. This section allows the Secretary of State, in particular circumstances, to direct both the tribunals and the Commissioners not to determine an appeal, but to refer the appeal to him. Other provisions of the section permit other objectionable directions to be provided by the Secretary of State, who is in effect one of the parties to the appeal before the tribunals or the Commissioners.

Conclusion

Social security appeal tribunals under the Independent Tribunal Service have generally been regarded as the least formal system of adjudication. Social security legislation by contrast is a complex web of primary and secondary legislation. It is a tribute to the tribunals that the technicality at the heart of the appellate process in these tribunals can and does co-exist with the relative informality in atmosphere and with procedural flexibility. These are qualities which both the Genn Study and *Judging Social Security* argued should be preserved. Yet both studies show that no amount of enabling by the tribunal can compensate for the difficulties claimants face in attending the tribunal and arguing their cases.[66] It is unknown territory leading to confusion and bewilderment.

The challenge to the Lord Chancellor's Department is to preserve the best features of the tribunal system while providing the necessary advice and support needed by claimants to ensure that all of them put their cases at their best. When these tribunals operate at their best, they offer a consumer orientation sadly absent from other areas of adjudication. Whether the gains made over fifteen years by the Independent Tribunal Service are lost under the changes heralded by the 1998 Act remains to be seen. It would be a tragedy if they were.

---

[65] *Annual Report of the Council on Tribunals 1996/97*, HCP 376 (1997–98) (London: HMSO, 1997).
[66] See also H. Genn, 'Tribunals and Informal Justice' (1993) 56 MLR 393.

15

DEALING WITH UNFAIR
DISMISSAL CLAIMS

Introduction

Many tribunals are concerned with disputes between the citizen and authority in some form. The social security appeal tribunals are a typical example. They are concerned with grievances held by individuals against government officials who make initial decisions on entitlement to social security benefits. By contrast, employment tribunals in the exercise of the unfair dismissal jurisdiction are concerned with disputes between employee and employer. Such disputes are often disputes between citizen and citizen, though the employer will often be a partnership or business. Much of the jurisdiction of employment tribunals is concerned with rights given to individuals to be exercised against their employers. The unfair dismissal jurisdiction accounts for about half of the business of the tribunals. This represents around 40,000 cases a year.[1] Much of the jurisdiction of the employment tribunals, particularly in the areas of discrimination and equal pay, is shaped by European Community law.

The major study of the operation of the unfair dismissal jurisdiction of the employment tribunals remains that conducted by a team of researchers from the University of Warwick which involved large-scale interviewing of those involved in the tribunal processes in three regions of England and Wales.[2] The interviews sought information on 'the nature of the parties; what happened to them; their expectations, experience, perceptions and assessments of the employment tribunal system'.

Employment Tribunals

Industrial tribunals were established under section 12 of the Industrial Training Act 1964 with a narrow jurisdiction to consider appeals against the levy on employers

---

[1] See generally *Resolving Employment Rights Disputes. Options for Reform* (London: HMSO, 1994, Cm. 2707).
[2] L. Dickens et al., *Dismissed: A Study of Unfair Dismissal and the Industrial Tribunal System* (Oxford: Basil Blackwell, 1985), cited in this chapter as 'the Dickens Study'.

to finance the industrial training boards set up under that Act. In the following year they were given a new jurisdiction concerning redundancy payments, and concerning statutory rights to information about particulars of contracts of employment. Even with this fairly technical jurisdiction, some commentators saw the tribunals as providing the nucleus of a system of 'labour courts'.[3] The boost to their growing jurisdiction came when the Royal Commission on Trades Unions and Employers' Associations of 1968 approved the extension of tribunal jurisdiction.[4] The Donovan Commission had approved tribunals as 'an easily accessible, speedy, informal and inexpensive procedure' for the settlement of disputes between employers and employees. The unfair dismissal procedures first introduced in the ill-fated Industrial Relations Act 1971 survived the repeal of that Act by the Trades Union and Labour Relations Act 1974. There have been further new jurisdictions, including a very significant sex discrimination jurisdiction heavily influenced by European Community law.[5] In 1998 they were renamed employment tribunals.[6]

The structure of employment tribunals has long been settled. Tribunals normally consist of a lawyer chairman,[7] many of whom are full-time appointments, sitting with two lay members, one nominated by employer organisations and one nominated by employee organisations, often trades unions. The lay members bring industrial experience and practical knowledge to bear on the issues coming before the tribunal. They are of equal standing to the chairman. One commentator says of lay members:

Lay members, experienced in industrial relations, know what an employer should or should not put up with, equally they know what an employee can expect. They know the unwritten custom and practice which form such an important part of industrial relations. Thus they have a most valuable part to play in reaching a just decision.[8]

A presidential system has been adopted. A President is appointed who is responsible for the overall operation of the system. He is assisted by a network of regional chairmen. Since April 1997, the tribunals have been supported administratively by the Employment Tribunals Service agency. Each tribunal has a clerk who deals with the administration of the tribunal. Clerks are also expected to assist unrepresented parties with advice on the procedure adopted in the tribunals. Today the employment tribunals enjoy a wide jurisdiction over statutory employment rights. The most important, at least numerically, of these jurisdictions has been the unfair dismissal jurisdiction, but other employment disputes within their jurisdiction include

---

[3] K. Whitesides and G. Hawker, *Industrial Tribunals* (London: Sweet & Maxwell, 1975).

[4] *Report of the Royal Commission on Trades Unions and Employers' Associations (Donovan Commission)* (London: HMSO, 1968, Cmnd. 3623).

[5] The law relating to the constitution and jurisdiction of the tribunals can now be found largely in the Employment Tribunals Act 1996, formerly called the Industrial Tribunals Act 1996.

[6] Employment Rights (Dispute Resolution) Act 1998, s. 1. The term 'employment tribunals' is used throughout this chapter except where reference is made expressly to the tribunals as they existed or operated in earlier years. Unless the context otherwise requires, the term includes the industrial tribunals.

[7] Though increasing use is being made of a chairman sitting alone for some aspects of decision-making.

[8] M. Jukes, 'Reply: Tribunals—Justice for All?' *Industrial Society*, September/October 1978, 5.

discrimination and equal pay claims,[9] redundancy payments claims, and claims concerning particulars of contracts of employment. The jurisdiction upon which attention will be focused in this chapter is unfair dismissal claims.[10]

A former President of the Industrial Tribunals has said that:

The tribunals are meant to provide simple informal justice in an atmosphere in which the ordinary man feels he is at home . . . an atmosphere which does not shut out the ordinary man so that he is prepared to conduct his own case before them with a reasonable prospect of success.[11]

As this chapter will show, this goal has not been achieved because the tribunals have adopted an accusatorial or adversarial model of hearings, and operate within a context of complex legal concepts. The procedure is very like that operating in the county courts despite the provisions of the rules of procedure which state that tribunals 'shall so far as appears . . . appropriate seek to avoid formality in its proceedings'[12] and the absence of formal rules relating to the admissibility of evidence.

Protection against Unfair Dismissal

Before examining the practice and procedure of employment tribunals, an outline of the law relating to unfair dismissal will be offered. This is, of necessity, an incomplete and oversimplified account which reflects a typical claim before the tribunals. The employment protection legislation has created for certain employees a proprietary right in their jobs. Before this proprietary right was granted, the relationship between employer and employee was regulated solely by the contractual terms agreed between employer and employee and embodied in the contract of employment. Thus, provided that an employer gave the notice required by the contract, the employer was free to terminate an employee's contract. The employment protection legislation operates to restrict the grounds on which an employer can terminate the contract of employment with impunity. The protection is acquired once an employee has been in a particular employment for two years,[13] though there are special rules concerning part-time employees and for calculating the date up

---

[9] See A. Leonard, *Judging Inequality* (London: Cobden Trust, 1987) on the work of the tribunals in sex discrimination and equal pay cases.

[10] The current law is to be found in Part X of the Employment Rights Act 1996.

[11] D. Conroy, 'Do Applicants Need Advice or Representation?', edited transcript of proceedings of a conference held at the Institute of Judicial Administration, University of Birmingham, April 1971 (Birmingham: Institute of Judicial Administration, 1971), pp. 4–5.

[12] Industrial Tribunals (Constitution and Rules of Procedure) Regulations 1993, S.I. 1993 No. 2687, Sch. 1, para. 9(1), cited in this chapter as 'Rules of Procedure'.

[13] The Government is proposing to reduce this to one year: see DTI, *Fairness at Work*, White Paper (London: HMSO, 1998, Cm. 3968), para. 3.10.

to which the continuous employment is measured. No protection exists for those over sixty-five years of age or for persons over normal retiring age in a particular employment where that retiring age is less than sixty-five. Once the protection is acquired, the employee can make a claim that he or she has been unfairly dismissed.[14] The employer must then establish before a tribunal the reason, or if there is more than one, the principal reason, for the dismissal, and must show that it was one of the following reasons:

- a reason relating to the capability or qualifications of the employee for the particular employment; or
- a reason relating to the conduct of the employee; or
- that the employee was redundant;[15] or
- that some legislation precluded the continuance of the employment; or
- some other substantial reason justifying dismissal.

These general grounds have been elaborated by decisions of the Employment Appeal Tribunal on appeal from decisions of employment tribunals. Establishing the existence of a reason for dismissal falling within the legislation is only the first hurdle, upon which the employer has the burden of proof. But there is also a reasonableness test, where there is no burden of proof placed on either party. The reasonableness test is for the tribunal to consider, though both parties will normally submit evidence and make representations to the tribunal on this issue. The tribunal is required to determine whether the employer acted reasonably or unreasonably in treating the established reason for dismissal as sufficient reason for dismissing the employee having regard to equity and the substantial merits of the case and to the size and administrative resources of the employer's undertaking.[16]

Three remedies are available for persons found to have been unfairly dismissed: re-instatement, re-engagement or compensation. Re-instatement involves treating employees as if they had never been dismissed. So they must be paid all arrears of wages, granted full pension rights accruing through continuity of employment, and given any pay increases that would have been their due if they had not been dismissed. Re-engagement involves offering the employee a fresh contract of employment. Significantly, the employee will have to serve in that employment for two years before again gaining the protection of the unfair dismissal legislation. Compensation is calculated by a complex formula which includes a basic award related to gross earnings and length of service, and a compensatory award which seeks to meet the employee's actual and future losses arising as a consequence of the dismissal. Interest is payable on all sums due to applicants following employment tribunal awards. The most common remedy is compensation.

---

[14] Some dismissals are automatically unfair and can be the subject of complaint regardless of the age or length of service of the employee: Employment Rights Act 1996, ss. 99–104.

[15] That is, that the employer no longer had any need or had a lesser need for employees to do certain work.   [16] Employment Rights Act 1996, s. 98(4).

Practice and Procedure in Unfair Dismissal Claims

Pre-action procedures

In the consideration of the plight of litigants in the civil courts, reference was made to the difficulty of collecting evidence to support a claim. In some cases, notably personal injuries cases, rules of court have provided special machinery to assist a plaintiff. In employment law, three rules provide substantial assistance to an employee. The first is the requirement that not later than two months after the beginning of the employment, an employee is entitled to a written statement containing particulars of the terms of the employment, which must include details of disciplinary and grievance procedures available to the employee, unless the employer employs fewer than twenty people.[17] An employee denied such a statement may refer the matter to a tribunal which will determine the particulars which should have been included and referred to in such a statement.[18] In this way, all employees are able to ascertain the main terms of their employment. Many employees do not worry about such matters until a dispute arises, but the provisions do enable employees and their advisers to obtain details of the main terms of the contract of employment without too much difficulty.

The second rule assisting employees is the provision contained in the legislation entitling any employee of at least two years' standing to request a written statement of reasons for dismissal, which must be supplied within fourteen days of the request.[19] Not only is this statement admissible in tribunal proceedings, but unreasonable refusal to provide such a statement renders the employer, on the application of the employee to a tribunal, liable to a penalty payable to the employee of a sum equal to two weeks' gross pay.[20] This is an extremely useful provision which requires early disclosure by the employer of the case against the employee.

The third rule is that an application to a tribunal claiming unfair dismissal casts the burden of proving a reason for the dismissal falling within the Act on the employer. This is in marked contrast to the position of most other applicants or plaintiffs who will have the burden of proving the facts on which their claim is based. The justification for the reversal of the burden of proof in unfair dismissal cases is that employers will be in the best position to explain what reasons they had for terminating the employment.

The originating application

Armed with the written statement of reasons for the dismissal, an employee is in a position to begin proceedings before the employment tribunal. Commentators still tend to remark on the informality of employment tribunal procedure,[21] but

---

[17] Employment Rights Act 1996, ss. 1–3. [18] Ibid., s. 11. [19] Ibid., s. 92.
[20] Employment Rights Act 1996, s. 93.
[21] R. Walker and R. Ward, *Walker and Walker's English Legal System*, 7th edn. (London: Butterworths, 1994), pp. 175–7.

the employment tribunal's rules of procedure are no longer informal, and it has become an adversarial forum.[22] There are detailed rules contained in regulations, which can be used strategically by representatives, and the documents used to outline the grounds of claims are increasingly being regarded as pleadings, so that inconsistencies or changes of tack revealed later may prejudice the parties. Great care therefore needs to be taken over the completion of documents.

The employee opens the proceedings by completing an originating application (also known as Form IT1); this is accompanied by some notes for guidance, and the employee will usually have the Department of Trade and Industry booklet on unfair dismissal claims. The originating application requests the names of the parties, details of the employment and remuneration, of the date of dismissal, a statement of the grounds of the claim and a non-binding intimation of the remedy sought. The completed form is sent to the relevant Office of the Industrial Tribunals (OIT).[23] It must arrive within three months of the 'effective date of termination' of the employment; this is basically the date of dismissal or some later date deemed by statute to be the date the employment ended. No fee is payable on filing a claim.

The notice of appearance

On receipt of the originating application, the OIT acknowledges receipt of the application and sends a copy to the employer[24] with a Notice of Appearance (Form IT3), which the employer must complete and return within twenty-one days, showing whether the claim will be resisted and, if so, on what grounds. Failure to respond has draconian consequences. The employer ceases to be entitled to take any part in the proceedings.[25] Since the employer has the burden of proof, this will usually be fatal to the employer's case. For this reason failure to respond is rare and late responses setting out reasons for the later submission are deemed to include an application for an extension of time, which is frequently allowed. On receipt of the Notice of Appearance, the OIT sends a copy to the applicant and sends the papers to ACAS.[26] Either party, or the tribunal of its own motion, may request further and better particulars of the grounds on which the claim or reply is based.

The Dickens Study tells us that not every dismissed employee eligible to claim unfair dismissal does so. Only about one in ten of those eligible to claim actually does so. Among those who apply there is a greater tendency to bring unfair dismissal proceedings where the employer is a small single establishment employer with below average unionisation. Nearly half of all applications are against employers with fewer than twenty employees. The larger the employer, the less likely it is that there will be an unfair dismissal claim. There are a number of possible explanations for this pattern of application. First, larger employers are likely to

[22] The Dickens Study, *supra* n. 2; and H. Genn and Y. Genn, *The Effectiveness of Representation at Tribunals* (London: Lord Chancellor's Department, 1989), cited in this chapter as 'the Genn Study'.
[23] This is determined by the post-code of the applicant; the form matches post-codes to OITs.
[24] Form IT2: Notice of Originating Application.   [25] Rules of Procedure, *supra* n. 12, r. 3(2).
[26] See below.

have internal appeals procedures and failure there, where union representation may have been provided, is the point at which the employee draws the line. Secondly, employees may feel a sense of powerlessness in taking on a large organisation. Thirdly, it may be that advisers are more reluctant to take on large organisations.

The typical applicant to the tribunal is a male, middle-aged, white, non-union manual worker dismissed after a relatively short period of service. The study found that access to advice was an important factor, tending to be haphazard. Even where applicants had some access to advice and representation, that service itself adopted procedures for selecting the cases in which representation before the tribunal would be provided. The Genn Study confirms this profile of applicants.[27]

Seven out of ten applicants sought advice and half of these approached solicitors.[28] A real difficulty here is that legal aid does not extend to representation in the tribunal. The Green Form scheme is the only relevant part of the legal aid scheme and will provide advice only. Respondent employers also sought advice frequently, almost always from solicitors or in-house employment law experts.

ACAS conciliation

While the parties are sorting out any issues over the grounds of the claim, a formal statutory process of conciliation is brought into play. Conciliation officers from the Advisory Conciliation and Arbitration Service (ACAS) will have been sent copies of the Originating Application and Notice of Appearance. Figure 15.1 shows the incidence of ACAS conciliation in unfair dismissal cases.[29] They will intervene to try to secure a settlement of the claim without its being determined by an employment tribunal, and in doing so they are required to seek to promote the re-instatement or re-engagement of the employee. In practice conciliation officers tend to view the achievement of a settlement as their principal function, with the actual remedy a secondary consideration. Most settlements are for compensation.

Typically the conciliation officer will contact each party or their representatives to discuss the case. It is important for the parties to realise that the conciliation officer will tell the other side what each has said about the claim. Conciliation officers are often reluctant to express an opinion about the likelihood of success before the tribunal, but will make clear an opinion whether the case appears to them one which is strong or weak and so ought to settle. In particularly weak cases the conciliation officer will go so far as to advise the applicant to withdraw the claim. About one in three claims which do not go to a hearing are dropped by applicants. The process can be a useful one to get the other side talking about settling. Conciliation officers are very useful for advising employers of the tasks before them

---

[27] See also N. Tremlett and N. Banerji, *The 1992 Survey of Industrial Tribunal Applications*, Department of Employment Research Series No. 22 (London: Department of Employment, 1994), ch. 2.

[28] The Genn Study, *supra* n. 22, p. 41.

[29] For a general description of the role of ACAS, see ACAS, 'Industrial disputes: the ACAS role' in K. Mackie (ed.), *A Handbook of Dispute Resolution: ADR in Action* (Routledge and Sweet & Maxwell, 1991), p. 100.

Figure 15.1. **ACAS conciliation in unfair dismissal cases***

	1996	1995	Five year average
Cases received	46,566	40,815	44,819
Cases settled	19,376	18,405	18,157
Cases withdrawn	13,064	11,993	11,753
To adjudication	13,207	12,352	12,791
Total cases completed	45,647	42,849	42,702

* Source of data: *ACAS Annual Report 1996* (London: ACAS, 1997).

at a tribunal hearing. Many years after the introduction of employment protection, there are still some employers who do not appreciate its impact on managerial decision-making. The negotiations are conducted on a without prejudice basis and information communicated through conciliation officers is by statute not admissible at tribunal hearings unless the person who gave the information to the conciliation officer consents. The success of conciliation can be measured by the volume of withdrawals or conciliated settlements. Around two-thirds of all cases result in withdrawals or conciliated settlements. Agreements resulting from conciliation are normally registered with the tribunal as a form of consent decision.

Though a formal part of the processes which operate when an unfair dismissal application is made, conciliation is a separate process from adjudication by the tribunal. This is emphasised by conciliation being the province of ACAS and by the confidentiality which surrounds the process. Conciliation and adjudication are alternative methods of dispute settlement. There is a long history of the use of conciliation in employment relations, justified because one objective is to secure the continuance of the relationship between the parties in dispute. The process of conciliation in unfair dismissal cases serves two purposes. The first is to facilitate agreement between the parties on the settlement of the dispute on terms selected and agreed between them. The second is to act as a filter to ensure that only those cases which for some reason need to proceed to a formal process of adjudication do so. The conciliation process is very effective as a filter disposing of two out of every three applications without the need for adjudication.

The Dickens Study showed that the parties generally viewed the involvement of ACAS favourably, though opportunities for complaint about their involvement were limited in the interviews conducted by the researchers. Other writers have complained, particularly in discrimination cases, that conciliation officers are too willing to encourage settlement at any price and fail to provide the support an unrepresented applicant may need against the relatively advantaged position of the employer.[30]

Four out of every five settlements achieved by conciliation officers are for compensation and only one in ten for re-instatement or re-employment. The Dickens study concludes:

[30] J. Gregory, *Sex, Race and the Law* (London: Sage, 1987).

Very few offers of settlement conveyed by the conciliation officer are refused by applicants. The inequality in the employer/employee relationship and the relative disadvantage of an unfair dismissal applicant within the employment tribunal system is perpetuated, not ameliorated, by the neutral stance required of ACAS in concilia-tion. In the context of a tribunal system used by unaided and unrepresented applicants the description of conciliated settlements as voluntary agreed outcomes of an assisted bargaining process, qualitatively superior to tribunal imposed awards, is inappropri-ate. The description might have more applicability if there were rights enforcement officers to aid unrepresented applicants. Inherent in some of the criticism made of ACAS conciliators . . . is the assumption that they should take a more positive, rights-enforcing, stance.[31]

The Tremlett and Banerji study[32] of applications to the tribunals made between April 1990 and March 1991 reports similar activity by conciliation officers, though without the critical edge of the Dickens Study. This study,[33] however, found that only one in four cases were concluded at the conciliation stage. Where cases were settled in the unfair dismissal jurisdiction, the median amount of compensation was £999.

Interlocutory applications

The process of conciliation runs alongside other pre-hearing procedures. These include power to strike out an application because the applicant is not taking the proper steps to further the claim, or because it is 'scandalous, frivolous or vexa-tious'.[34] Because the formal rules of evidence do not apply, there is no automatic procedure equivalent to discovery and inspection, but documentary evidence is often important in unfair dismissal claims and there are powers to order the pro-duction of key documents on the application of one of the parties.[35] There are also powers to compel the attendance of witnesses by obtaining a witness order.

Pre-hearing reviews

At this stage either party can invoke a procedure first introduced in 1980 but modified in 1990, which can place pressure on the other side to withdraw or settle at an early stage. This is the pre-hearing review. The tribunal may also direct of its own motion that there be a pre-hearing review. Though available to either party it is in reality a procedure designed to enable employers faced with weak cases to apply a potential costs sanction to encourage the early demise of weak cases. The purpose of the pre-hearing review is to sift out those applications which are unlikely to succeed.

---

[31] The Dickens Study, *supra* n. 2, p. 180.
[32] N. Tremlett and N. Banerji, *The 1992 Survey of Industrial Tribunal Applications*, Department of Employment Research Series No. 22 (London: Department of Employment, 1994), ch. 5.
[33] Which covered all jurisdictions of the tribunals.   [34] Rules of Procedure, *supra* n. 12, r. 13(2)(d).
[35] See J. McMullen and J. Eady, *Employment Tribunal Procedure* (London: Legal Action Group, 1996), ch. 9.

Application for a pre-hearing review can be made by letter, and the obvious time for an employer to request such a hearing is when returning the Notice of Appearance. The material available for consideration is strictly limited by the Rules of Procedure to the originating application and notice of appearance, together with the written representations of the parties and any oral argument advanced on the issue.

Initially, the chairman alone will consider the paper claims and decide whether to allow the application. If it is allowed, both parties are invited to make written submissions and to attend a hearing before a full tribunal of three members. At this hearing no evidence is called, but the tribunal does like to have a full account of the claims of each party and of the evidence to be called to support them. The tribunal then decide whether the complaint or defence of it has any reasonable prospect of success. If it is determined that such is the case, the tribunal can order the party to pay a deposit of up to £150 as a condition of being able to proceed with the case.[36] The requiring of a deposit also increases the likelihood that the tribunal will award costs if the case is pursued unsuccessfully. The full hearing of the claim must be before a differently constituted tribunal who will not know until the end of the case of the requirement to have paid a deposit.

Pre-hearing assessments[37] initially appeared to be an effective means of scaring off applicants. In 1982, they were requested in six per cent of cases filed, about half by the tribunal of its own motion. Some 78 per cent of cases in which pre-hearing assessments were requested did not proceed to a full hearing. Of course, what is not revealed by these bald figures is anything qualitative about the claims. Without research into the merits of the claims, it is impossible to say with authority whether most claims terminated in this way had no hope of success or whether applicants are forced to withdraw by the fear of costs.

The use of the procedure then appeared to decline. In 1987 it was used only in one case in 400.[38] It also seems that applications to the tribunal selected for a pre-hearing assessment were more likely to proceed to a hearing than other cases, while at the same time the success rate for those who proceeded in the face of an unlikely to succeed warning was not very different from other cases.[39] No data is yet available on the impact of the newer pre-hearing reviews.

The hearing

If the applicant has survived this far and avoided a pre-hearing assessment, the case will be listed for hearing. Most tribunal accommodation is purpose built

---

[36] Before making such an order, the tribunal is required to consider the ability of the party to make such a payment: Rules of Procedure, *supra* n. 12, r. 7(5).

[37] Predecessors of pre-hearing reviews designed to serve the same purpose. The result could be the issuing of an 'unlikely to succeed' warning which exposed that party to the risk of costs if they persisted with the case.

[38] Department of Employment, *Consultation Paper on Industrial Tribunals* (London: Department of Employment, 1988).

[39] Ibid. See also on pre-hearing assessments, N. Tremlett and N. Banerji, *The 1992 Survey of Industrial Tribunal Applications*, Department of Employment Research Series No. 22 (London: Department of Employment, 1994), ch. 6.

and is reasonably comfortably equipped. The physical distance between the parties and the tribunal members is minimised. The tribunals sit in public and, for this reason, the members may sit on a slightly raised dais. Otherwise there is little of the ritual of the courts, though everyone is expected to stand when the tribunal members enter or leave. When questioning witnesses and addressing the tribunal, parties and their representatives do not stand. It is for the parties, and not for the tribunal, to see that all relevant evidence and legal argument is adduced. The procedure at the hearing is determined by the tribunal within the framework of the statutory rules which provide that the tribunal shall 'so far as appears to it appropriate seek to avoid formality'.[40] The formal rules of evidence do not apply.

The usual order of events in unfair dismissal cases is for the employer to open the proceedings by making a short opening address. Then witnesses are called. Evidence is given on oath and witnesses are subject to cross-examination. If the parties are not represented, it is usual for the chairman and members to ask many questions. Where the parties are represented, interventions from the tribunal are less frequent. The employee then puts his or her case in a similar manner. Once all the evidence has been given, each side may address the tribunal by way of summary and legal argument. One chairman has commented that tribunals operate a sliding scale of formality. Where representation is present and the 'stakes are high', the proceedings will be very formal, but where there is no representation, the proceedings are much less formal.[41] In practice the procedure is one which is best coped with by those with appropriate forensic skills in the questioning and cross-examination of witnesses, and the marshalling of evidence and argument, coupled with a sound knowledge of the legal framework within which such cases are determined.

The tribunal members retire and deliberate once both sides have presented their cases. The lay members have the same say as the chairman. Majority decisions are rare. The tribunal returns and the chairman announces their decision. This may be a brief summary of reasons or a full decision dictated by the chairman. In coming to a decision the tribunal is bound by decisions of the Employment Appeal Tribunal and must ensure that its decisions take full account of the cases presented to them and any others that are relevant. In general tribunal chairmen are well informed and familiar with most authorities. Having said that, most cases turn on their facts and not on points of legal principle. The parties are later sent by post either a summary decision or a full written decision as soon as it has been typed up and signed by the chairman, which is accompanied by information about applying for a review of the decision and of appealing to the Employment Appeal Tribunal. Since March 1985 a full written decision has only been provided at the request of either party. The purpose of the change was to save time and money, but the change is not wholly welcome, because in practice it will draw an even sharper distinction between represented and unrepresented parties. Representatives ask for a full written decision as a matter of course, whereas unrepresented parties are less likely to exercise the right to a full written decision.

---

[40] Rules of Procedure, *supra* n. 12, r. 9(1).
[41] J. Macmillan, 'Industrial Tribunals—A Defence and Some Proposals for Reform', *Law Society's Gazette*, 30 November 1983, 3901.

Contested cases where there is representation can easily last a full day, or even longer if the facts are at all complicated, and the written decisions are lengthy, often running to six or seven pages of single spaced typescript. Employees are successful in about one in three cases.[42]

Representation at the hearing

It appears that around one half of applicants are represented at employment tribunals. About thirty-three per cent. of applicants are legally represented, as compared with sixty-three per cent of respondents.[43] The Dickens Study reported that fifty-five per cent of applicants and sixty-seven per cent of respondents were represented, though in the remaining cases the company representative's status could not be readily identified. The Genn Study reported that thirty-eight per cent of applicants were represented either at a hearing or during settlement negotiations, though seventy per cent had sought advice about their application. Employers had expert representation at hearings in seventy-four per cent of the cases in the sample, compared with fifty-seven per cent of applicants. Both parties were represented in forty-eight per cent of cases and neither party in only seventeen per cent of hearings. In twelve per cent of cases an unrepresented applicant faced an employer represented by a lawyer, while an unrepresented employer faced an employee represented by a lawyer in only five per cent of the cases. The overall picture is represented in Figure 15.2.

In response to a question in Parliament in 1984, figures based on a ten per cent sample were given of the comparative success rates of different types of representation. The success rate of lawyers was consistently better than that of trades union representatives and of individuals representing themselves over the four years from 1979 to 1982 covered.[44] The success rate of lawyers in 1982 was 36.9 per cent whereas that for trades union representatives and for individuals representing themselves was 25.1 per cent. The Department of Employment review of representation concludes that the initial views that employment tribunals should be bodies where representation was not necessary must now be re-evaluated in the light of an increasing trend not just towards representation, but towards legal representation.[45]

The Genn Study is the most recent on the effect of representation and concluded:

As far as representation is concerned, applicants can only improve their chances of success through representation when the respondent is not represented. Where the applicant is legally represented and the respondent is not represented, the probability

---

[42] N. Tremlett and N. Banerji, *The 1992 Survey of Industrial Tribunal Applications*, Department of Employment Research Series No. 22 (London: Department of Employment, 1994), ch. 8.

[43] J. Macmillan, 'Industrial Tribunals—A Defence and Some Proposals for Reform', *Law Society's Gazette*, 30 November 1983, 3901.

[44] Reported in Department of Employment, *Employment Gazette*, March 1984, 127.

[45] W. Hawes and G. Smith, *Patterns of Representation of the Parties in Unfair Dismissal Cases: A Review of the Evidence*, Department of Employment Research Paper No. 22 (London: HMSO, 1981).

Figure 15.2. **Representation in employment tribunals (including only expert representation)**

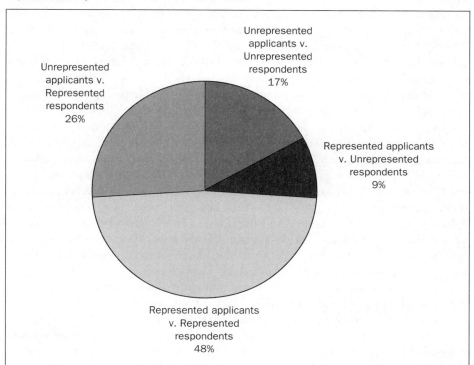

of the applicant succeeding is increased from 30 per cent to 48 per cent. Where the applicant has no representation and the respondent is legally represented the applicant's probability of success is reduced to 10 per cent. Where the applicant is represented by a non-lawyer, and the respondent is represented by a lawyer the probability of the applicant succeeding is 18 per cent.[46]

The Royal Commission on Legal Services' treatment of tribunals was lamentably weak.[47] The only issue discussed in any detail was that of representation. The Commission expressed concern at the figures showing that the unassisted lay person was at a disadvantage: 'Whatever the tribunal and however informal its procedure, representation, whether by lawyer or a skilled layman, in the majority of cases confers an advantage on the represented party'.[48]

The Commission's task in tackling this problem was complicated by the generous provisions of the rules of procedure of adjudicatory tribunals as to rights of

---

[46] The Genn Study, *supra* n. 22, p. 99.
[47] *Final Report of the Royal Commission on Legal Services (Benson Commission)* (London: HMSO, 1979, Cmnd. 7648). [48] Ibid., para. 2.17.

audience. Whereas representation before the civil and criminal courts is normally limited to solicitors and barristers, adjudicatory tribunals allow anyone to act as representative. As we have seen, representation other than by lawyers has become an important form of representation before tribunals. A major factor accounting for this development is the absence of legal aid for representation before tribunals. It is important to have a clear understanding of the impact of legal aid on tribunal representation. Save for the exceptional case of Mental Health Review Tribunals, legal aid does not cover representation before tribunals of first instance. The Green Form Scheme will provide two hours' work by a solicitor on a case (more with an extension), but the solicitor cannot recover the cost of appearing before a tribunal to argue a case under this component of legal aid. Unless the solicitor is prepared to act without charge, at the point at which the client most needs a lawyer, the lawyer apparently abandons the case. At best a written submission for presentation to the tribunal will be prepared, but this is not normally an adequate substitute for the interactive process of actual appearance before the tribunal. Few parties before tribunals have the resources to fund the use of a lawyer. It will therefore come as no surprise that empirical research confirms the low level of activity in welfare benefits and tribunal work among solicitors.[49] Finally, it should be noted that legal aid only remunerates lawyers and not other representatives.

The Royal Commission made three recommendations to tackle the problem of representation: the simplification of tribunal procedures, the development of lay advice and representation, and the extension of legal aid. On the first limb of the response, the Royal Commission rather lamely noted that the procedures of some tribunals have become 'legalistic', mainly because the law governing their work has become more complex, and recommended that procedures be reviewed 'to ensure that applicants in person are able to conduct their own cases wherever possible'. The work of advice agencies was praised and it was recommended that public funds should be available for their development. Parties to tribunal proceedings should be sent a list of agencies in the area offering advice and representation. No effort was made to quantify the need or to address a major issue with public sector legal services generally. At present, there are not enough specialist lay advisers to meet the demand for their services. As a consequence, such agencies are selective in the cases they will represent. In some cases all that is offered is advice; in the busiest agencies even the amount of advice and assistance offered may be rationed.

The third limb of the Royal Commission's policy was the recommendation that legal aid be extended. It was accepted that there are some cases before all tribunals where legal representation is needed. This being so, it was necessary to establish an appropriate merits test. The traditional requirement that there be reasonable grounds for taking the proceedings was accepted, and to this was added the subsidiary test that it must be reasonable to employ a legal representative. In applying the second limb of the merits test, the Royal Commission felt that the relevant criteria should be:

---

[49]   R. Lawrence, 'Solicitors and Tribunals' [1980] JSWL 13.

- does a significant point of law arise?
- is the evidence so complex or specialised that the average lay person could reasonably wish for expert help in assembling and evaluating the evidence and in testing or interpreting it?
- is it a test case?
- is deprivation of liberty or the person's occupation at stake?
- is the amount at stake, though small, significant in relation to the financial circumstances of the applicant?
- is suitable lay representation available?
- are there any special circumstances making legal representation desirable or would hardship follow if it was withheld?

The Government response was to accept these recommendations in principle 'subject to further consideration being given to timing and the availability of resources'.[50] Unanswered questions relate to how the complementarity of roles of lay and legal advisers will operate, and when, in the current climate of Lord Chancellor's concern about legal aid expenditure, resources for an extension of legal aid to tribunals are likely to be available. Nor has any attempt been made to establish criteria for distinguishing those cases where applicants might reasonably be expected to represent themselves from those where representation either by specialist lay adviser or by lawyer is appropriate. The newly elected Labour Government indicated in 1997 that it has no plans to extend legal aid to tribunals.

Outcomes

The most common remedy granted is compensation. Awards after a hearing are significantly higher than those agreed by conciliation.[51] The Tremlett and Banerji study reported median awards following tribunal hearings in unfair dismissal cases of £1,900,[52] compared with £999 for conciliated settlements. Research is needed to establish whether the level of conciliated settlements is fair to applicants or whether applicants simply prefer the bird in the hand to that in the bush. There are suggestions that conciliated settlements are finalised without conciliation officers taking a view on the equity of the monetary settlement they conciliate. The Dickens Study concluded that the prime reason for the relatively low amounts awarded by way of compensation is the statutory rules for determination of compensation and the exercise of the tribunal's discretion in areas where this is open to them, such as in the consideration of future loss of earnings. The study also found tribunals frequently willing to attribute some contribution to the dismissal to the employee, which operates like a finding of contributory negligence to reduce the compensation payable. Overall the study considers that a low price is set on unfair

---

[50] *The Government Response to the Report of the Royal Commission on Legal Services* (London: HMSO, 1983, Cmnd. 9077).   [51] The Dickens Study, *supra* n. 2; and the Genn Study, *supra* n. 22.
[52] N. Tremlett and N. Banerji, *The 1992 Survey of Industrial Tribunal Applications*, Department of Employment Research Series No. 22 (London: Department of Employment, 1994), ch. 10.

deprivation of a job and that unfair dismissal compensation has little deterrent value for most employers wishing to dispense with the services of employees.

The employment tribunal has no enforcement powers of its own. If an employer defaults on an award of compensation, then the employee must register the tribunal's decision with the county court and use the enforcement powers available in the county court to recover the award. If the applicant (or respondent) has avoided being required to pay a deposit at a pre-hearing review, there is little risk of costs being awarded. The only basis on which costs can be awarded is that a party has acted 'frivolously, vexatiously, abusively, disruptively or otherwise unreasonably'.[53] Parties and witnesses are entitled to allowances for loss of earnings, subsistence and travel to and from the tribunal.

Streamlining Procedure

Provisions of the Employment Rights (Dispute Resolution) Act 1998 are designed to enable justice in the tribunals to be delivered more speedily and efficiently. Much of the material is technical, but the theme of proportionality of procedure introduced by Lord Woolf in his Interim and Final Reports on civil procedure[54] can also be discerned in them. So provision is made for the determination of some cases without a hearing or by a chairman alone. Assistance with more routine decision-making will be provided by 'legal officers'.[55] What qualifications will be required of such personnel is not clear from the Act, which merely refers to those appointed in accordance with regulations to be made under the Act.

In order to encourage early and proper use of dispute resolution mechanisms within employment, provision is made for any award of compensation for unfair dismissal by a tribunal to be reduced by such amount as appears just and equitable where the complainant has not used an internal appeal procedure provided by the employer.[56]

A further reflection of the favour with which alternative dispute resolution is currently viewed can be found in the provisions for formal ACAS arbitration as an alternative to tribunal adjudication.

Part II of the Employment Rights (Dispute Resolution) Act 1998 provides for the introduction of ACAS arbitration. ACAS is empowered to prepare a scheme to run alongside ACAS conciliation which litigants can choose as an alternative to tribunal adjudication. So the role of ACAS will become more central. In addition to suggesting a settlement, they will also be able to advise on the relative merits of arbitration and adjudication. The new arbitration scheme is initially available only in unfair dismissal claims. The *Fairness at Work* White Paper[57] indicates that the new scheme should be up and running in the Spring of 1999. The object of

---

[53] Rules of Procedure, *supra* n. 12, r. 12.   [54] See Chs. 10–12.   [55] See s. 5 of the 1998 Act.
[56] Employment Rights (Dispute Resolution) Act 1998, s. 13, inserting a new s. 127A in the Employment Rights Act 1996.   [57] DTI, *Fairness at Work,* White Paper (London: HMSO, 1998, Cm. 3968).

encouraging arbitration is twofold: to provide a dispute settlement process which is more likely to result in complainants returning to their work, and to reduce the incidence and costs of 'high profile, hostile disputes'.

An Assessment of Employment Tribunals

Both the law and procedure for unfair dismissal claims are complex. The money figures at stake can be high. The employment tribunals have become arenas in which there is inequality between applicant and respondent. At present many more employers than employees are legally represented, and it is not unknown for counsel to appear for employers. Furthermore non-legal representatives of employers, including in-house representatives, may well be highly trained personnel with considerable experience of employment law.[58]

No legal aid is available to provide representation for employees. The law is far too complex to justify a policy of allowing only advice and assistance. The understanding of the interaction of statute and case law required in this area is no different from that required in many cases pursued in the county courts and High Court. Nor is the law as self-contained as social security law; many employment cases require a command of principles of contract law. When this difficulty is coupled with the inequality of unrepresented applicant facing represented respondent, the case for the extension of legal aid, or some other form of assistance with representation, is overwhelming. Because there is no general regime of costs, it is difficult to see how conditional fees could operate in this area. No procedural devices can accommodate such an imbalance of skills within what is a procedure requiring party presentation of the issues and the testing of evidence by process of cross-examination. This is not a criticism of the tribunals themselves, which contain some valuable devices to assist employees, but of the failure to provide the required assistance to employees to enable them to pursue their claims effectively.

Entrusting the decision in unfair dismissal cases to tribunals was a conscious decision designed to include as part of the decision-making process the industrial experience of employers and employees. There was some mistrust of mainstream court-based methods of determining these types of dispute. The presence of lay members would also, it was believed, contribute to informality. The Dickens Study reports that the contribution of lay members on matters of industrial and practical knowledge are tempered by the carefully constructed legal framework within which unfair dismissal applications must be considered. In general lay members did not see their role as an enabling one and do not play a particularly active role in hearings. The research identified an 'underlying accusatorial model of hearings and a tendency towards legalism.'[59] The JUSTICE Report defines legalism in

---

[58] J. Macmillan, 'Industrial Tribunals—A Defence and Some Proposals for Reform', *Law Society's Gazette*, 30 November 1983, 3901; and the Dickens Study, *supra* n. 2.

[59] The Dickens Study, *supra* n. 2, p. 84.

two ways. The first refers to the manner in which the tribunals interpret and a pply employment legislation, though the Report recognises that the complex language and structure of the controlling legislation contributes to the potential for legalism. The second refers to the degree of formality in the physical arrangements and courtroom atmosphere; the major obstacle here is seen as the adversarial system of examining and cross-examining witnesses.[60] The Genn Study is even more forthright:

Industrial tribunals are totally adversarial. They are courts of first instance and their purpose is to adjudicate disputes between employers and employees, arising under employment protection legislation.[61]

Review of Tribunal Decisions

Employment tribunals enjoy a power to review their own decisions on application of either party within fourteen days of notification of the tribunal's decision. The grounds for such a review are circumscribed by the tribunal's rules of procedure. Five grounds are listed:

- the decision was wrongly made as a result of an error on the part of the tribunal staff; or
- a party did not receive notice of the proceedings; or
- the decision was made in the absence of a party entitled to be heard; or
- new evidence has become available which could not have been reasonably known about or foreseen; or
- the interests of justice require a review.[62]

The procedure seems to work well, providing a balance between finality of decision-making and the interests of justice in allowing the re-opening of certain decisions. It is a simple and relatively cheap procedure for remedying mistakes or obvious injustices, which complements the work of the Employment Appeal Tribunal which can only deal with questions of law.[63]

Appeal to the Employment Appeal Tribunal (EAT)

The Employment Appeal Tribunal (EAT) is the indirect successor to the National Industrial Relations Court, which was so unloved by trades unions that it could

---

[60] JUSTICE, *Industrial Tribunals* (London: JUSTICE, 1987).
[61] The Genn Study, *supra* n. 22, p. 198.   [62] Rules of Procedure, *supra* n. 12, r. 11.
[63] J. McMullen, 'An Analysis of the Power of Review by Industrial Tribunals of Their Own Decisions' (1984) 3 CJQ 12.

not survive in its original form the repeal of the Industrial Relations Act 1971.[64] After a short interregnum in which appeals went to the Divisional Court of the Queen's Bench Division, the EAT was established to hear appeals on points of law from employment tribunals. The EAT is staffed by High Court judges who normally sit with two additional members representative of employers and employees. The procedure lacks the ritual formality of the High Court, but there can be no doubt that serious legal issues are being considered. Legal representation is common and legal aid is available to meet the cost of this. A party aggrieved by a decision of an employment tribunal has forty-two days in which to file an appeal. The Employment Appeal Tribunal Rules 1993[65] set out standard forms for appealing. Even at this stage conciliation is encouraged and the EAT is enabled to take such steps as it thinks fit to enable the parties to avail themselves of the opportunity for conciliation. The EAT has proved to be of major importance in clarifying and elaborating the rules contained in the statutory material. Their decisions are binding on employment tribunals and have had a significant impact on managerial practices by major employers. The sensitivity of employment law issues may perhaps be gauged by the frequency with which employment cases go to the Court of Appeal and House of Lords, though this may also have something to do with the looseness of the statutory language used in the legislation.[66]

Alternative Proposals

The Dickens Study offered as an alternative to the current system an arbitral system as a way of overcoming the perceived disadvantages of the employment tribunal system.[67] The focus would move from the determination of who is legally right and from consideration of the reasonableness of the employer's action in the circumstances of the individual dismissal to the location of the dispute firmly in the realms of industrial relations, rather than employment law, where the search would be for a workable and acceptable solution which took account of the wider context. It was argued that such a system would generally be more favourable to employees and would be more likely to curb 'the exercise of managerial prerogative in the interests of individual job retention as well as avoiding the tendency to legalism'.[68]

The JUSTICE Report takes a different tack. It recommends the introduction of two different procedures for determining unfair dismissal disputes: the investigative model and the adversarial model.[69] For nine out of every ten cases, the

---

[64] See now Part II of the Employment Tribunals Act 1996.   [65] S.I. 1993 No. 2854.
[66] See further J. Wood, 'The Employment Appeal Tribunal as it Enters the 1990s' (1990) 19 ILJ 133.
[67] The Dickens Study, *supra* n. 2, ch. 9.   [68] Ibid., p. 299.
[69] JUSTICE, *Industrial Tribunals* (London: JUSTICE, 1987). For a similar proposal, see R. Lewis and J. Clark, *Employment Rights, Industrial Tribunals and Arbitration* (London: Institute of Employment Rights, 1993).

investigative model would be sufficient. The tenth case would require an adversarial approach backed by equality of representation and access to resources to enable the dispute to be presented effectively and efficiently. Such cases would go to a higher body, described as an upper-tier Industrial Court staffed by senior chairmen and members. The criteria for transferring cases to the Industrial Court would be:

- where a significant point of law arises;
- where the case has important implications beyond the interests of the individual parties;
- where the evidence is highly complex or specialised and raises difficult questions of evaluation.

For such cases the Report argues that legal aid should be available as in the lower courts.

For those cases dealt with by the investigative procedure, a chairman would direct, after reading the Originating Application and Notice of Appearance, preliminary investigations by an officer of the tribunal. It is envisaged that the investigation officer would be a legal officer in the Civil Service with special training, who would take full statements from parties to the dispute and any key witnesses and inspect all the documentation relevant to the case. The investigation officer would then prepare a full dossier to be sent to both sides prior to the hearing. The investigative role would not supplant the conciliation stage, which would remain with ACAS.

The tribunal members would read the dossier in preparation for the hearing and would take the initiative at the hearing by indicating the issues of fact and law on which evidence and submission remained necessary. The tribunal would itself take the lead in questioning, reducing the reliance of parties on representatives with the forensic skills of questioning and cross-questioning. The parties would have a secondary opportunity to ask questions of any witnesses and to make submissions on the law.

Conclusion

The employment tribunals represent the tribunals whose practice and procedure is most like that of the traditional courts. There can be little doubt that they have now become the forum for the expert. The evidence is overwhelming that the unrepresented party suffers serious disadvantage in this forum. The issue now facing policy-makers is whether the tribunals are equated with the county courts and legal aid extended to them or whether structural changes are made which enable unrepresented litigants to have a fair chance to present their cases in a manner which gives them a fair chance of success.

16

REVIEW AND SUPERVISION

Introduction

The parties to litigation, whether before a court or a tribunal, which results in trial and judgment have resisted strong encouragement to settle the claim along the road to trial. Both parties will have been convinced of the correctness of their arguments on the facts and law. The party who loses will inevitably be disappointed. Sometimes the loser will not only be disappointed but also aggrieved because the trial judge or tribunal has taken some view of the facts and the law, which are believed to be wrong. Alternatively one party may be arguing for a significant change or development in the law, and might actually be expecting to lose at first instance. That party knows that only a higher court is likely to push forward the boundaries of some legal rule. For these cases the appellate process provides the remedy. In civil cases the rights of appeal are not ungenerous, though the overall system of civil appeals has been described as a 'hotchpotch' needing rationalisation.[1] It is usual to be able to take one appeal as of right with a second appeal being possible with leave. Appeals are not re-trials, but considerations of whether the trial judge erred in some way. This chapter is concerned, first, with the practice and procedure of appeals from courts and the appellate tribunals, and, secondly, with an introduction to the general objectives of appeals in civil cases.

From what follows it will be clear that the Court of Appeal, Civil Division, is at the heart of the civil appeal process.[2] The House of Lords may be the highest court in the land, but it hears comparatively few appeals each year. Its contribution is particular rather than general, and some have questioned whether there is a need for two levels of appeal court.

---

[1] H. Woolf, 'A Hotchpotch of Appeals—The Need for a Blender' (1988) 7 CJQ 44.

[2] Though this might change if the recommendations contained in the Bowman Report are implemented: see *Review of the Court of Appeal (Civil Division): Report to the Lord Chancellor (Bowman Report)* (London: Lord Chancellor's Department, 1997), cited in this chapter as 'the Bowman Report'.

The Processes of Review and Supervision

Two separate functions of appeals have been identified, which have been labelled **review** and **supervision**.[3] Review is the process by which defects in the trial process are corrected. These may typically be errors of practice and procedure, incorrect conclusions on the facts and inferences to be drawn from them, improper exercises of judicial discretion or an incorrect application of established legal principles. Supervision is the process of the laying down by the courts of guidelines for the development of legal principles. The process may involve a critical re-consideration of an area of law in the light of changing social conditions or an authoritative interpretation of a statutory provision. Review is about due process of law;[4] supervision is about the generation of new legal rules.

There is one type of appeal which falls in the grey area between review and supervision. This is the appeal which involves a review of an existing line of authority without any re-consideration of it. The Court of Appeal exercises the functions both of review and of supervision.

Drewry's analysis of the grant and refusal of leave to appeal to the House of Lords in 1971 demonstrated that leave was routinely refused in cases where the second appeal raised issues of review, that leave was granted in cases involving issues of supervision, and that there was a mixture of refusals and grants in cases falling in the grey area of re-consideration of authority without critical re-appraisal of the cases.[5] It also seems that the work of the Court of Appeal is predominantly the determination of appeals involving review. The grounds of appeal to the Court of Appeal most frequently relate to issues of fact or practice and procedure. The Court of Appeal is a very busy court which has to ration its time and manage its business carefully to avoid unacceptably long delays in the determination of appeals.

By contrast the House of Lords, though not short of cases, has a small workload of key cases. Time and the most careful deliberation of the issues raised are available in the House of Lords. It is the system of requiring leave to appeal which rations the caseload of the House of Lords and filters out cases for attention which involve issues of supervision. Once the distinction between review and supervision is understood, the reasoning behind the conditions required for leap-frog appeals[6] becomes more readily understandable. The conditions are designed to distinguish cases involving issues of supervision from those involving issues of review.

Judicial Control and Supervision of Tribunals

Some tribunals, like the social security appeal tribunals and the employment tribunals, are part of a two-tier system with separate tribunals enjoying appellate jurisdiction.

---

[3] L. Blom-Cooper and G. Drewry, *Final Appeal—A Study of the House of Lords in its Judicial Capacity* (Oxford: Clarendon Press, 1972), and G. Drewry, 'Leapfrogging—and a Lords Justice's Eye View of the Final Appeal' (1973) 89 LQR 260.

[4] Which is taken here to include the proper application of well-established substantive legal rules.

[5] G. Drewry, 'Leapfrogging—and a Lords Justice's Eye View of the Final Appeal' (1973) 89 LQR 260.

[6] See below.

The constituent legislation of other tribunals contains provisions allowing access to the High Court, whereas some tribunals have to fall back on the appeals contained in section 11 of the Tribunals and Inquiries Act 1992. Indeed the decisions of some tribunals are not subject to any appeal. An example is the Vaccine Damage Tribunals[7] to review questions of the extent and cause of disablement by persons claiming to be entitled to payments under the Act as a result of disabilities arising from vaccination damage. The provision of appeals through separate tribunals enjoying appellate jurisdiction is generally more satisfactory than where reliance must be placed on the High Court. Making an appeal to a specialist appellate tribunal is cheaper, quicker and easier than using the High Court. Examples of appellate tribunals are the Social Security Commissioners and the Employment Appeal Tribunal.[8] But review by the High Court of decisions of tribunals is a common feature of many other tribunals.

Section 11 of the Tribunals and Inquiries Act 1992 provides two forms of appeal to the High Court from specified tribunals. It is important to realise that this is not a general power in respect of all tribunals. To enjoy these types of appeal there must be specific statutory authority. Section 11 provides that a person dissatisfied with a decision of a specified tribunal on a point of law may either appeal against that decision to the High Court, or require the tribunal to state a case for the opinion of the High Court. The section further provides that rules of court may regulate and restrict the appeal in particular cases to one or other form of appeal.[9] In addition to the tribunals to which section 11 applies, there are a number of tribunals whose constituent legislation provides that a person aggrieved by a decision of the tribunal may require the tribunal to state a case for the opinion of the High Court. This is the same process as the stating of a case under section 11. The distinction between an appeal on a point of law and the requiring of a tribunal to state a case is important.

The appeal operates like any other appeal; it will be for the appellant to formulate the grounds of appeal and to present the arguments in favour of the appellant's view to the High Court. The respondent may also adduce argument. The tribunal itself need do nothing to further the appeal, other than making available the notes of evidence and the chairman's record of the hearing. The appeal will be restricted to the point or points of law raised in the notice of appeal.

By contrast requiring a case to be stated, just like the appeal by way of case stated from a decision of a magistrates' court or the Crown Court,[10] obliges the tribunal to set out its decision and the reasons for it together with a formulation of the questions to be considered by the High Court. The parties will, of course, have the opportunity to address argument to the court on these questions. Unlike the position in criminal proceedings, the procedure may be used to enable a tribunal to obtain a preliminary ruling on a point of law which arises during the hearing of the case. The hearing will be adjourned pending the delivery of the High Court's opinion, at which time it will be re-listed and a decision given on the merits in the light of the High Court's opinion on the law. This procedure is rarely used.

---

[7] Established under the Vaccine Damage Payments Act 1979, s. 4.   [8] See Chs. 14 and 15.
[9] See RSC Ord. 56 and Ord. 94.   [10] See Ch. 7.

Appeals to the High Court from tribunals number around 200 a year,[11] most of which are tax appeals. Once 'plugged in' to the High Court, the possibility arises of using the ordinary system of civil appeals to challenge the decision of the High Court. Thus, ordinarily appeals will be available with leave to the Court of Appeal and thereafter to the House of Lords. Those tribunals with their own appellate tribunal do not enjoy the appeal to the High Court, but appeals on points of law lie with leave to the Court of Appeal from the Employment Appeal Tribunal, and Social Security Commissioners, and thereafter to the House of Lords.

Judicial Review

In addition to the statutory procedures described above, the Queen's Bench Division of the High Court enjoys a common law power to control the operation of inferior courts and tribunals in certain circumstances by way of judicial review. Judicial review is the preferred remedy for settling public law disputes. The High Court may grant one of the three prerogative orders: certiorari, prohibition or mandamus. Certiorari quashes a decision which is found to be invalid because it is outside the powers granted to the court or tribunal (*ultra vires*), or has been given in proceedings in which the principles of natural justice were not observed, or where there has been an error of law on the face of the record. Prohibition lies to prevent some unlawful action by a tribunal on the same grounds as the granting of an order of certiorari. Whereas certiorari quashes past unlawful conduct, prohibition prevents future or continued unlawful conduct. Mandamus is a royal command to secure the proper performance of a tribunal's functions. It is usually sought in addition to an order of certiorari and is designed to ensure the performance of a public duty. For example, mandamus would lie to compel a tribunal to hear a case which it had mistakenly decided was not within its jurisdiction. The details of the availability, scope and grounds for such orders need not detain us here because they form part of substantive administrative law.[12]

All these remedies are now sought by a single application for judicial review.[13] Because the granting of a prerogative order is discretionary in nature, leave of the High Court must be obtained to make application for them. The distinction between appeal and judicial review is an important one to grasp. Appeal is

---

[11] *Judicial Statistics 1996* (London: HMSO, 1997, Cm. 3716).

[12] See generally R. Gordon, *Judicial Review: Law and Procedure*, 2nd edn. (London: Sweet and Maxwell, 1996) and G. Aldous and J. Alder, *Applications for Judicial Review: Law and Practice* (London: Butterworths, 1985). See also Law Commission, *Administrative Law: Judicial Review and Statutory Appeals*, Law Com. No. 226 (London: Law Commission, 1994), and R. Cranston, 'Reviewing Judicial Review' in G. Richardson and H. Genn (eds.), *Administrative Law and Government Action: The Courts and Alternative Mechanisms of Review* (Oxford: Clarendon Press, 1994), p. 45.

[13] Supreme Court Act 1981, s. 31; RSC Ord. 53; *O'Reilly* v. *Mackman* [1983] 2 AC 237; and *Cocks* v. *Thanet DC* [1983] 2 AC 286.

concerned with the merits of the decision being appealed, while judicial review is concerned with the legality of the process by which that decision was reached. In the latter case the jurisdiction is described as being supervisory. If a bad decision on the law was made or the court or tribunal took a view of the evidence that no reasonable tribunal could take which does not appear as an error of law on the face of the record, that is a matter for appeal rather than judicial review. Equally a perfectly proper decision on the law and facts taken in proceedings which did not meet the required standards of procedural regularity (for example, a decision of a social security appeal tribunal where no reasons for the decision were given) could be quashed by means of judicial review. With the development of rights of appeal against tribunal decisions, the significance of judicial review is diminishing in relation to such tribunals. This is particularly so where tribunals have their own appellate tribunal. Very often the appeal to the appellate tribunal can cover matters that might be raised on judicial review. For example, the Social Security Commissioners will regard a failure to have regard to the principles of natural justice as an error of law which can form the basis of an appeal to them. Such a deficiency in the first instance tribunal's deliberations would also, of course, ground an application for judicial review. It is noticeable that, where the decisions of the appellate tribunal are not appealable to the Court of Appeal, as is the case with the Immigration Appeal Tribunals, more frequent use is made of judicial review. Nevertheless judicial review remains an important process for curing illegality.

In 1996 there were 3,604 applications for leave to seek judicial review in all civil cases of which 1,257 were allowed to proceed to consideration of their merits.[14] Finally, it should be noted that section 12 of the Tribunals and Inquiries Act 1992 provides that no provision in legislation prior to 1958[15] should be taken as ousting the supervisory jurisdiction of the High Court, thus making clear the Government's intention that all statutory tribunals should be subject to this jurisdiction regardless of whether other remedies are provided.

The overall importance of judicial review is reflected in the words of Sir Jack Jacob:

The introduction in 1977 of the remedy of judicial review was a milestone in the history of English civil justice. It constituted one of the most beneficent, significant and effective innovations and improvements in the fabric of English civil justice. It restored credence in the creativity of the system of English justice; it provided a virile and vigorous procedure for remedies in the public law area to replace those which were in a weary and withering state.[16]

Judicial review is expected to play a major role following the incorporation of the European Convention on Human Rights, since the process lends itself so well to considering the legality of State action.

---

[14] *Judicial Statistics 1996* (London: HMSO, 1997, Cm. 3716).
[15] The year the Tribunals and Inquiries Act 1958 was passed, which established the appeal to the High Court.　　　　[16] J. Jacob, *The Fabric of English Civil Justice* (London: Stevens, 1987), p. 180.

Rights of Appeal

Getting advice on appealing

Parties to litigation in the High Court or a county court do not receive a full written judgment containing the trial judge's reasoning. The official court documentation will simply deal with the disposition of the case. Initially the parties will rely on the notes made by solicitors and counsel when the trial judge gave the reasons for his decision when delivering judgment in open court. In the High Court, if the case justifies the expense, a transcript of the judgment may be ordered from the shorthand writer who has kept the verbatim record of the proceedings. Of course, in the High Court, a case of particular significance may be reported, but the law report will almost certainly not appear before the time allowed for appealing has passed. In the county court, apart from the judge's own note, there will only be the lawyer's notes of the decision. By contrast, litigants before tribunals, the Social Security Commissioners or the Employment Appeal Tribunal are entitled to receive a full written decision. Losers may be aggrieved for a number of reasons: they may disagree with the findings of fact, statements of the law, award of damages, or even the way the case was conducted. In considering an appeal all these avenues will need to be explored.

Though not expressly so stated as in the case of criminal appeals where there is a criminal legal aid order, it seems that a civil legal aid certificate will also cover advice on appeal. If an appeal is merited, application can be made for an extension of the legal aid certificate to cover the appellate proceedings. This can be done expeditiously, though initially the extension will probably only cover the obtaining of any necessary transcripts and a formal opinion of counsel on the likelihood of a successful appeal. Once these papers are to hand there can be a proper consideration of whether or not there are good grounds for extending legal aid to cover the arguing of an appeal. If the litigant was not assisted at first instance, or before one of the appellate tribunals, a full application for a legal aid certificate must be made. In either case it is unlikely that all the legal formalities will have been completed in the time allowed for filing an appeal. The Court of Appeal has intimated that such cases are appropriate cases for the grant of extensions of the time allowed for appealing.[17]

From the county courts

There is a right of appeal to the Court of Appeal, Civil Division, from decisions of the county courts in contract and tort where the claim is for £5,000 or more. If the claim is for less, then leave of either the county court judge or of the Court of Appeal is required, unless the decision includes or preserves an injunction.[18] The notice of

---

[17] *Legal Aid Handbook, 1997/98* (London: Sweet & Maxwell, 1997), pp. 137–8.
[18] County Courts Act 1984, s. 77; County Courts Appeal Order 1981, S.I. 1981 No. 1749, as amended by S.I. 1993 No. 2131.

appeal, or application for leave to appeal, must be filed within four weeks of the date the judgment was entered, unless an extension of time has been allowed either by the county court or the Court of Appeal. The correct procedure is to apply first to the county court judge for leave, but if leave is refused, the application may be renewed before the Court of Appeal. A single judge of the Court of Appeal may dispose of the application and there is no appeal against such a decision.[19] If the point raised is particularly complex, the single judge may decide to refer the matter to a court of two or more judges.

In *Smith* v. *Cosworth Casting Processors Ltd,*[20] the Court of Appeal set down the test to be applied in considering an application for leave to appeal. An application would only be refused if the court was satisfied that the applicant had no realistic prospect of success. It would, however, be open to the court to grant leave even if it was not so satisfied, for example, where the issue was one which the court considered that it was in the public interest. The opportunity may be presented to clarify an area of law in need of attention, which should be taken.

From the High Court

In actions in contract and tort, there is a general right of appeal to the Court of Appeal,[21] which is excluded in relation to particular matters of which the only significant one for our purposes is the exclusion of a right of appeal against a decision of the High Court allowing an extension of time for appealing. The Court of Appeal may also allow an extension of time for appealing. The notice of appeal must be filed within four weeks of the date on which the judgment was entered.

From the Social Security Commissioners

There is no general right of appeal, since this will be the second appeal following the decision of the social security appeal tribunal, disability appeal tribunal or medical appeal tribunal. The appeal lies only where a point of law is involved. Leave to appeal must be obtained from the Commissioner or, failing that from the Court of Appeal.[22] There is a three-month time limit, which can only be extended for good reasons.

From the Employment Appeal Tribunal

Again the appeal to the Court of Appeal is only available where a point of law is involved. Application is made initially to the Employment Appeal Tribunal, but if that fails, it may be renewed before the Court of Appeal.[23]

---

[19] Supreme Court Act 1981, s. 54(6).   [20] Judgment of 26 February 1997, LEXIS transcript.
[21] Supreme Court Act 1981, s. 16.   [22] Social Security Administration Act 1992, s. 24.
[23] Employment Tribunals Act 1996, s. 37.

The grounds of appeal

The notice of appeal must set out clearly and completely, shortly and simply, the grounds of appeal. The Court of Appeal has very wide powers to remedy deficiencies in the decision under appeal and the grounds of appeal are not restricted in any way. They must show the error in the court below or the tribunal and the relief being sought. It is important that the grounds of appeal are full because any omission can only be cured with the leave of the Court of Appeal. The detailed rules governing appeals to the Court of Appeal in civil cases can be found in Order 59 of the Rules of the Supreme Court.

The Powers of the Court of Appeal

In general terms the Court of Appeal has all the authority and jurisdiction of the court or appellate authority from which the appeal is brought.[24] Indeed it is now clear that the Court of Appeal may on appeal even exercise a power conferred on the court below after the date of the judgment against which the appeal is lodged.[25] Though the appeal is said to be 'by way of rehearing', it is not a re-creation of the trial with witnesses giving evidence again before the appeal court. The appeal will be limited to the matters raised in the notice of appeal, and normally only legal argument will be presented. In theory it is possible to raise new points not dealt with in the pleadings or argument in the trial, but the Court of Appeal is reluctant to exercise the power to admit them, since it smacks of allowing the running of alternative arguments where those run at trial have failed. Where evidence is relevant, the court almost always relies on the chairman's notes of evidence in tribunal proceedings, on the county court judge's note, or on the transcript. It is difficult to persuade the Court of Appeal to alter a finding of direct fact by the trial judge. The court takes the view that it has not had the benefit of seeing the witnesses, hearing their evidence and forming opinions as to the weight to be attached to it. Accordingly, they will not lightly interfere. There is more chance of persuading the court to substitute its own finding of inferential fact from the direct facts, because this goes to the conclusions drawn by the trial judge from direct facts. The best example is a conclusion that direct facts do or do not amount to contributory negligence, which will always be an inference drawn in the light of the facts found.

It is possible to appeal against the amount of damages awarded by the trial judge and here the Court of Appeal will amend the amount if the trial judge has applied an incorrect principle of law or has awarded a sum which is clearly inconsistent with awards in comparable cases. The appeal court will only interfere if there is a significant divergence from the norm; here again they allow the trial judge a margin of appreciation because that judge has seen the parties and heard the evidence.

---

[24] Supreme Court Act 1981, s. 15.   [25] *Attorney-General* v. *Vernazza* [1960] AC 965.

Different principles apply to awards by juries, which are used only rarely in civil cases, usually in defamation cases. There is here the traditional reluctance to interfere with decisions of jurors.[26] The unpredictability of damages awards in defamation cases led to the passing of section 8 of the Courts and Legal Services Act 1990 which enables the Court of Appeal to vary jury awards on the basis that the damages are 'excessive or inadequate'.[27]

The Court of Appeal has power to receive fresh evidence only on special grounds. The test for the admission of fresh evidence is laid down in *Ladd* v. *Marshall*[28] and was approved by the House of Lords in *Skone* v. *Skone*.[29] Three conditions must be satisfied:

- the evidence could not have been obtained with reasonable diligence at the trial, and
- if given at the trial, the evidence would probably have had an important influence on the result of the case, and
- the evidence is apparently credible, though it need not be incontrovertible.

These rigorous tests mean that the Court of Appeal hears fresh evidence only rarely; it will certainly need to be satisfied that the appeal is not being used merely as an attempt to argue the case in a different way. If the matter cannot be resolved by the Court of Appeal, it has power to order a re-trial.

The civil division of the Court of Appeal enjoys wide powers to order a re-trial. Some have already been mentioned; others relate to jury trial. In addition to these the Court of Appeal has powers to order the re-trial of a case tried before a judge alone in the following cases: first, where there has been improper admission or exclusion of evidence; secondly, where there has been surprise, as where the trial judge allows the case to proceed on a basis other than that pleaded without giving the other side an opportunity to consider the new material; and thirdly, where there have been irregularities in the course of the trial, as where the judge intervened so much that proper cross-examination was precluded.[30]

The final power to mention is not a power exclusive to the Court of Appeal, nor is it a power whose exercise disposes of the appeal. This is the power to make a reference to the Court of Justice of the European Communities seeking an authoritative interpretation of a point of European Community law relevant to the determination of the dispute before the court.[31] Any court or tribunal may make such a reference, and final appeal courts must make a reference where the point of European Community law is relevant to its decision.[32] The effect of a reference is to suspend the proceedings before the referring court until the Court of Justice has handed down its opinion which is then applied by the referring court to the dispute before it.

---

[26] *Cassell* v. *Broome* [1972] AC 1027.
[27] See also RSC Ord. 59, r. 11(4) and *Rantzen* v. *Mirror Group Newspapers Ltd* [1993] 2 WLR 953.
[28] [1954] 1 WLR 1489.   [29] [1971] 1 WLR 812.
[30] *Jones* v. *National Coal Board* [1957] 2 QB 55.   [31] RSC Ord. 114.
[32] Art. 177, EC Treaty. See also ch. 2.

Managing the Business of the Court of Appeal

Significant changes were made by the Supreme Court Act 1981 in the arrangements for the management of the business of the Civil Division of the Court of Appeal. Prior to the implementation of the Act the Civil Division had no staff of its own except the clerks to the Master of the Rolls and the Lords Justices of Appeal. As a result much judicial time was taken up with administrative matters and with interlocutory matters which did not justify the use of the time and expertise of the judges. In December 1978 the unpublished report of a Working Party headed by Lord Scarman recommended the establishment of a Registrar of Civil Appeals having both judicial and administrative functions.[33] The Act made provision for such an office, which has now been established and has already contributed to increased efficiency in the Division.[34] The Act also made provision for some appeals to be disposed of by courts composed of two judges rather than three. There is now a clear hierarchy of powers exercisable by the Registrar, and by one, two or three judges of the division. The most important points to note are as follows. The Registrar has power to deal with most interlocutory matters arising on appeal, though there is provision for review of his decisions by a single judge with the possibility of appeal with leave to a full court. The single judge may review decisions of the Registrar and make interim orders outside the Law Terms. Most importantly, of course, the single judge may decide applications for leave to appeal. Refusals of leave by a single judge are final.

Two-judge courts will normally deal with appeals concerning interlocutory matters and may hear any final appeals with the consent of the parties. In addition two judge courts are competent to hear many appeals.[35] Where the court consists of an even number of judges who are equally divided, the case must be re-argued before an uneven number of judges being not less than three[36] before appeal to the House of Lords is possible. The principal work of three judge courts will now be the determination of appeals from the High Court where the amount of the claim or counterclaim exceeds the relevant county court limits. Of course, it will remain open to the court to list any appeal which involves important points before a court of three or more judges.

The importance of the role of the Master of the Rolls as head of the Civil Division of the Court of Appeal should not be overlooked. The Master of the Rolls sets the tone of the court and can control the distribution of business among his colleagues. The matching of judges to cases can, of course, have an effect on the outcome of appeals. It will be the Master of the Rolls who decides whether an appeal is so important that it should be referred to a court composed of more than three judges, even though decisions of such courts formally have no greater weight than those of three judge courts. A good modern example is the decision of the former

---

[33] For a summary of its impact see the Bowman Report, *supra* n. 2, App. 3.

[34] The Bowman Report, *supra* n. 2, recommends the replacement of this office by two senior legal officers who would carry out the judicial functions of the office. The administrative functions would be taken over by the Head of the Civil Appeals Office.   [35] Supreme Court Act 1981, s. 54(4).

[36] Ibid., s. 54(5).

Master of the Rolls, Lord Denning, to convene a special court of five judges to hear the appeal in *Davis* v. *Johnson*[37] concerning the scope of the county court's jurisdiction under the provisions of the Domestic Violence and Matrimonial Proceedings Act 1976 to exclude a person from premises in which that person has a proprietary interest. The problem was that there were two previous decisions of the Court of Appeal, by which the court would normally be bound, which would, contrary to the justice of the case, have denied a remedy in the case before the court. The device of a court of five judges was adopted to add weight to the reconsideration of the earlier cases. The case was taken on appeal to the House of Lords, who upheld the decision of the Court of Appeal on the merits, but rebuked the Court of Appeal for not following its own previous decisions. We shall return later in this chapter to the doctrine of precedent.

As part of the campaign to increase the efficiency of the Civil Division of the Court of Appeal, the Master of the Rolls of the day, Sir John Donaldson (as he then was), has introduced a number of innovations following the recommendations of Lord Scarman's Working Party[38] The first is the early listing of cases in which it appears that the only purpose of the appeal is to secure some advantage by preserving the status quo pending the outcome of the appeal. The example given was of a tenant against whom an order for eviction had been made securing further time in residence by appealing. Early listing is seen as likely to remove the incentive for such appeals.

The second innovation is more interesting and raises wider issues. In a *Practice Note* in April 1983[39] Sir John recommended the submission shortly before the hearing of the appeal of 'skeleton arguments' by counsel for the parties. These would also be exchanged between counsel. The contents of the skeleton arguments should be a list of numbered propositions expressed in no more than one or two sentences which counsel proposed to argue. References to authorities and to documents, to which counsel intends to refer in his or her submissions to the court, should be annexed to the skeleton arguments. Counsel should also ensure that there is annexed any material which counsel would expect the court to note in detail. The judges hearing the appeal will read the skeleton arguments prior to the hearing along with the notice of appeal and the judgment appealed. The benefits of skeleton arguments are seen to be:

- the saving of time because the need for longhand notes is obviated;
- the elaboration of the substance of the appeal which is not usually apparent from the notice of appeal;
- the provision of an aide-memoire for convenience of reference for counsel.

The Practice Note emphasised the informal nature of the arrangements and stated that counsel should not be inhibited from departing from the skeleton arguments.

---

[37] [1979] AC 264.
[38] Practice Note (Court of Appeal: New Procedure) [1982] 1 WLR 1312, as amended by Practice Note (Court of Appeal: New Procedure (No. 2) [1983] 1 WLR 598.
[39] Practice Note (Court of Appeal: Skeleton Arguments) [1983] 1 WLR 1035.

Their use was not envisaged in every case; express reference is made to the submission in simple appeals only of material counsel would expect the court to note in detail.

The use of skeleton arguments has been popular with the Court of Appeal, but met with some resistance from some members of the Bar.[40] Their use has now been refined and extended. The current guidance is contained in a 1995 Practice Statement and Direction.[41] Skeleton arguments are now compulsory in all appeals before the Court of Appeal except in cases of urgency or where the court otherwise directs. The Practice Direction emphasises that the purpose of a skeleton argument is to identify points and not to argue them. Succinctness is the order of the day. In the case of points of law, the skeleton argument should state the point and cite the principal authority or authorities in support with references to the particular page(s) where the principle concerned is enunciated. In the case of questions of fact, the skeleton argument should state briefly the basis on which the Court of Appeal can interfere with the finding of fact concerned, with cross-references to the passages in the transcript or notes of evidence which bear on the point.

The skeleton arguments must be accompanied by a chronology of events, which must be contained in a separate document for ease of consultation. Skeleton arguments are normally to be exchanged between the parties and four copies delivered to the court fourteen days in advance of the hearing.[42]

The Bowman Report proceeds on the basis that skeleton arguments have proved to be a helpful innovation, but concludes that they are delivered too late to assist in judicial case management in the Court of Appeal. The Report recommends that skeleton arguments should be submitted with every application for leave to appeal or notice of appeal. Provision would be made for them to be amended or resubmitted nearer to the hearing date if this proved necessary.

The issue raised by the introduction of skeleton arguments is whether the principle of orality upon which English trials and appeals proceed is the best way of dealing with appeals. The English requirement of oral presentation of the whole of the case stands in marked contrast to the rules obtaining in other jurisdictions. The judges have repeatedly rejected the introduction of written briefs into English civil procedure, but the introduction of skeleton arguments is a step in the direction of a written stage in appellate procedure, despite the somewhat ambivalent caveat added at the end of the original Practice Note:

It cannot be over-emphasised that skeleton arguments are not formal documents to the terms of which anyone will be held. They are simply a tool to be used in the interests of greater efficiency. Experience shows that they can be a valuable tool. The judges of the court all hope that it will be possible to refine and extend their use.

---

[40] L. Blom-Cooper, 'The Changing Nature of the Appellate Process' (1984) 3 CJQ 295.

[41] Practice Statement (Court of Appeal: Procedural Changes) [1995] 1 WLR 1188; and Practice Direction (Court of Appeal: Procedure) [1995] 1 WLR 1191, together with Practice Direction (Court of Appeal: Amended Procedure) [1997] 1 WLR 1013.

[42] For the detail on timetabling of skeleton arguments and the rules which apply in more complex appeals, see Practice Direction (Court of Appeal: Procedure) [1995] 1 WLR 1191, paras. 40–50.

This caveat is echoed in the statement in the explanatory introduction to the 1989 Practice Direction that the Court of Appeal remains 'firmly wedded to its long established tradition of oral argument in open court'.

In *Mardas* v. *Official Receiver*[43] Lord Donaldson said:

One of the points of skeleton arguments is this. Judges ought, when they are pre-reading a case, to be able to pick up the skeleton argument, and they ought actually to be able to start with the skeleton argument, which would tell them in very succinct form the background facts and what the points are.

Appellate procedures in the USA rely on the submission of written briefs by each side followed by limited oral argument, upon which a strict time limit is placed. The Evershed Committee[44] in 1953 considered the introduction of such procedures in the Court of Appeal but rejected them. The principle of orality was considered to contribute to unanimity in decision-making because of the thorough sifting and testing of argument in unrestricted oral argument. This team-work aspect of the work of the Court of Appeal would be lost if written briefs were read individually by judges prior to limited oral argument. The strongest objection raised by the Evershed Committee was that the system would not fit easily into the division of labour between solicitors and barristers. It was stated that solicitors would not find it possible to prepare the written briefs, and that it would be unfair to expect them to do so. If barristers were to be instructed to prepare written briefs, they would need to be remunerated fairly for the work and there would be a resulting rise in costs. The conclusions of the Evershed Committee, particularly with regard to the division of work between solicitors and barristers, are open to challenge. The real problem is that if solicitors prepare the written brief, there is much less of a case for denying them the right of audience to argue that brief before the court. Indeed to suggest that solicitors might not be equipped to prepare written briefs is rather odd, since much of the paperwork in litigation is done by solicitors, though traditionally counsel settle documents to be used in court.

The rejection of written briefs was repeated by Lord Evershed in 1962.[45] An interesting attempt was made in 1966 by Michael Zander, acting as solicitor for the appellant, to introduce a written brief into the Court of Appeal. Though received in the case before it, Danckwerts L. J. said that the submission of such a document was 'wholly irregular and contrary to the practice of the court and . . . should not be allowed as a precedent for future proceedings'.[46] Lord Scarman's Working Party also rejected the introduction of written briefs. If the introduction of skeleton arguments works well, and the indications are that it does, then the case against fuller written briefs becomes less easy to answer. The principle of orality clearly belongs to an age in which the speedy production of multiple copies of documents was a slow labour-intensive exercise. In the age of photocopiers and word processors, the case against written procedures is more difficult to sustain.

---

[43] *New Law Journal*, 24 November 1989, 1597.

[44] *Final Report of the Committee on Supreme Court Practice and Procedure (Evershed Committee)* (London: HMSO, 1953, Cmd. 8878).   [45] Practice Note (Reading Documents) [1962] 1 WLR 395.

[46] *Rondel* v. *Worsley* [1967] 1 QB 443, 509.

To save time when judgment is given, the practice has been adopted of stating the disposition of the case in open court, but of providing printed copies of the full judgments to the parties' lawyers and to the representatives of the press in court. This is a further, but eminently sensible, erosion of the principle of orality.

The Court of Appeal receives about 3,000 applications for leave to appeal each year and deals with around 1,700 appeals. The county courts and the Queen's Bench Division of the High Court account for over half the business of the Court of Appeal. About one in three applications for leave succeeds, and about three in ten appeals.[47]

The Bowman Report, if implemented, will redraw the civil appellate structure. The Report recommends that leave should always be required for an appeal. Most significantly it will dramatically increase the appellate jurisidictions of certain courts and judges by providing that appeal in fast-track cases[48] will lie to the Circuit judge if the trial judge is a district judge, or to a single High Court judge if the trial judge is a Circuit judge. A number of situations are envisaged in which an appeal which would normally lie to a lower level should be heard by the Court of Appeal:

- where an important point of principle or practice is raised;
- where there is some special reason why the Court of Appeal should hear the appeal;
- when the Master of the Rolls directs that appeals in certain cases or groups of cases giving rise to similar issue should be heard by the Court of Appeal;
- when Parliament sanctions that a particular class of appeals should lie directly to the Court of Appeal.

Appeals in multi-track cases would lie to the Court of Appeal.

Experience in other countries, such as Canada and New Zealand, following the incorporation of human rights charters has been that the business of the appellate courts increases significantly as a result. In Canada, about one-quarter of appeals concern human rights points. It follows that the Court of Appeal is likely to play a central role in deciding issues in the national courts on the application of the rights contained in the European Convention. It can be expected that guidance will be provided not only on the substantive rights but also on the interpretation of legislation in the light of the requirements of the Human Rights Act 1998.[49]

Appeal to the House of Lords

From the Court of Appeal

In civil cases a precondition to any appeal from the Court of Appeal to the House of Lords is the obtaining of leave from either the Court of Appeal or the Appeal Committee of the House of Lords, which consists of three Law Lords. Leave will

---

[47] Bowman Report, *supra* n. 2, App. 9.   [48] See Chs. 11 and 12.   [49] See Ch. 2.

only be granted if the appeal involves a point of law of general public importance. In those cases where no time for appealing is fixed by statute or by order of
the House, the time for appealing is three months from the date the judgment of
the Court of Appeal was handed down. The proper procedure is to apply first
to the Court of Appeal, but if leave is refused, the application may be renewed
before the Appeal Committee within one month of the refusal of leave by the Court
of Appeal. The Appeal Committee will hear oral argument before deciding whether
leave should be given.

The criteria which seem to be applied by both the Court of Appeal and the
House of Lords in deciding whether leave should be granted are:[50]

- does the case raise a point of law of general public importance?
- does the appeal appear likely to succeed?
- has the case resulted in significant differences of opinion in the courts below?

It is common for conditions to be attached to the grant of leave. The most
common condition is that the appellant must bear the costs of the appeal whatever the outcome. This is almost standard in appeals by the Inland Revenue. The
justification is that a respondent should not be put at further risk of costs by virtue
of the Revenue's wish to have final authority on some aspect of taxation law, which
will inevitably be of general application.

The use of a written procedure was pioneered in the House of Lords where
each party has for some years been required to lodge a 'Case' with the court which
is very similar to the skeleton arguments more recently introduced in the Court
of Appeal. The Case did not appear to play an important part in the process of
decision-making in the House of Lords during the period under review (1957 to
1973) in Alan Paterson's book *The Law Lords*, which indicates that both counsel
and the Law Lords in practice diminished the effect of the written Case in the
arguing of the appeal.[51] A similar conclusion had been reached in an earlier study
covering the period 1952 to 1968.[52] If this remains true today, it is probably because
the House does not have the same pressures placed on its time as the Court of
Appeal and is able to devote as much time as it wishes to oral argument.

Appeals to the House of Lords are heard by the Appellate Committee of the
House, which consists of those members of the House qualified to deal with its
judicial business. This should be distinguished from the Appeal Committee which
considers applications for leave to appeal. Following oral argument the Law Lords
inevitably take time to consider their opinions. The opinions are printed and
handed down to the parties rather than being read aloud. The House has no power
to implement its own decisions, which are transmitted to the trial judge to be
converted into enforceable judgments or orders.

---

[50] L. Blom-Cooper and G. Drewry, *Final Appeal—A Study of the House of Lords in its Judicial Capacity*
(Oxford: Clarendon Press, 1972).   [51] A. Paterson, *The Law Lords* (London: Macmillan, 1982).
[52] L. Blom-Cooper and G. Drewry, *Final Appeal—A Study of the House of Lords in its Judicial Capacity*
(Oxford: Clarendon Press, 1972).

From the High Court

In some cases appeals may proceed directly from the High Court (not from county courts or tribunals of first instance) to the House of Lords. Part II of the Administration of Justice Act 1969 introduced the procedure universally known as the 'leap-frog' procedure to deal with those cases where determination by the Court of Appeal might not be the most effective way of disposing of the case. The conditions to be met before a leap-frog appeal can take place indicate the type of case the legislature had in mind. Two conditions must be met before there can be such an appeal:

- the trial judge must grant a certificate which is only available where:
  (a) the parties consent, and
  (b) a point of law of general public importance is involved (i) which relates to the construction of legislation, or (ii) in respect of which the trial judge was bound by a decision of the Court of Appeal or House of Lords and which in either case was fully considered by the trial judge or in the previous decisions by which the trial judge was bound; and
- the House of Lords must give leave on the basis that the case is one which ought to be heard by the House.

It should be noted that both the trial judge and the House of Lords have discretions. Trial judges are not required to grant certificates where the conditions are met; they simply have power to grant certificates. The restrictive conditions governing the leap-frog appeal reflect the usual caution over the introduction of innovations and the real misgivings some members of the judiciary had over the introduction of the procedure. These were that the House would be inundated with appeals relating to the interpretation of statutes and that the House would not have the benefit of the careful consideration of the case before it went up to the House.[53] The conclusions drawn by Drewry in 1973 remain apposite today. The use of the leap-frog appeal has been surrounded by considerable caution and the very stringent conditions to be met before such an appeal can be taken has meant that there have been very few such appeals. In 1996 one such appeal was determined.[54] A further reason for the small number of appeals is that there is only a small pool of cases involving principally the interpretation of legislation or the resolution of conflicting cases. There is also the problem of breaking with tradition; the House of Lords is accustomed to having the assistance of judgments from the Court of Appeal following full and careful consideration of detailed argument on the points of principle involved in an atmosphere which, though busy, is not quite so frenetic as that of the High Court.

It is not clear why the consent of the parties should be a precondition to leap-frog appeals, and the issue was contentious when the Bill was debated in Parliament.

---

[53] G. Drewry, 'Leapfrogging—and a Lords Justice's Eye View of the Final Appeal' (1973) 89 LQR 260.

[54] *Judicial Statistics 1996* (London: HMSO, 1997, Cm. 3716). There are no more than three or four such cases in any year.

If it is appropriate for a case to go direct to the House of Lords it seems wrong that a litigant should be able to frustrate what appears to be a proper course. No doubt if such a condition were not written into the Act, the trial judge and the House of Lords would have regard to the significance of the adoption of the procedure for litigants and to their wishes in exercising their respective discretions to grant a certificate or leave to appeal. It seems that the absence of transcripts of evidence, argument and judgment in the county court explains why the leap-frog procedure does not apply to decisions of county courts. This is surely right, even though in cases like *Davis* v. *Johnson*, which began in the county court, situations can arise in which there is not only an important point of interpretation to be decided, but also binding decisions of the Court of Appeal to be considered. Such cases could be met by adopting for civil cases a procedure similar to the Attorney-General's reference in criminal proceedings. Such a procedure would allow the Attorney-General to refer a point of law of general public importance arising in any litigation to the Court of Appeal or House of Lords. References to the House of Lords would be available following a decision of the Court of Appeal, but could also be allowed from either the county courts or the High Court where the Attorney-General was satisfied that the criteria for the grant of a certificate under Part II of the Administration of Justice Act 1969 were met. To grant a power to make references on points arising other than in connection with litigation would present difficulties in the selection of points for reference. Furthermore the judges have never relished answering hypothetical points.

The caseload

The House of Lords is not overworked. The number of civil appeals in England and Wales is small. In 1996 there were 174 petitions for leave to appeal. Of these 122 were refused and thirty were allowed. In the same year forty appeals were determined including one leap-frog appeal.[55] It is fair to say that 1996 was a typical year for the House of Lords.

The Functions of Civil Appeal Courts

The Bowman Report

Comparatively little has been written on the purposes of appeals in civil cases.[56] The Bowman Report, however, devotes a brief chapter to the principles underlying a civil appeals system. Civil appeals should operate in a manner which is consistent with the principles recommended by Lord Woolf for the civil justice system as a whole.[57] Appeals are said to serve a dual purpose: there is the private

---

[55] *Judicial Statistics 1996* (London: HMSO, 1997, Cm. 3716).
[56] But see above on the distinction in some academic writing between review and supervision.
[57] See Ch. 10.

purpose of doing justice in particular cases by correcting wrong decisions, and there is the public purpose 'which is to ensure public confidence in the administration of justice by making such corrections and to clarify and develop the law and to set precedents'.[58] The distinction is close to that between Drewry's supervision and review functions of appellate processes. The Report goes on to import the notion of proportionality to the appeal system, which Lord Woolf argued was so important to first instance cases. Normally only one level of appeal would be available, and that should be with leave. Uncertainty and delay should be reduced to a minimum.

The impact of the doctrine of precedent

The doctrine of precedent ensures that decisions of the Court of Appeal and House of Lords are of the greatest importance for lawyers and litigants alike. The doctrine of precedent requires that trial judges follow decisions of the Court of Appeal and House of Lords. The Court of Appeal itself is, subject to limited exceptions, bound by its own previous decisions and is always bound by decisions of the House of Lords. The House of Lords is, as we shall see, no longer bound by its own previous decisions and enjoys a unique power to re-shape legal principles established by an accumulation of case law. With his tongue firmly in his cheek, Mr Justice Murphy, the colourful former judge of the High Court of Australia (roughly the equivalent of our Court of Appeal), has described the doctrine of precedent as follows:

Then there is the doctrine of precedent, one of my favourite doctrines. I have managed to apply it at least once a year since I've been on the Bench. The doctrine is that whenever you are faced with a decision, you always follow what the last person who was faced with the same decision did. It is a doctrine eminently suitable for a nation overwhelmingly populated by sheep. As the distinguished chemist, Cornford, said: 'The doctrine is based on the theory that nothing should ever be done for the first time'.

To state that trial judges are bound by decisions of the Court of Appeal and House of Lords seems remarkably straightforward, but the multiple judgments of the Court of Appeal and of the House of Lords immediately make the issue more complex. The solution has been to separate the propositions made in judgments into two categories: those of binding authority and those of persuasive authority. Indeed some propositions falling into the second category are of such little weight as to amount to virtually no authority at all, while others are so significant as to be more important than those apparently of binding authority. Only that part of the judgment classified as binding authority is required to be followed in a similar later case. The key to unlocking the secret of the system of precedent is the ability to unravel lengthy individual judgments in order to identify the key propositions of law relevant to the essential facts of the litigation. This will reveal the reason for

[58] Bowman Report, *supra* n. 2, ch. 2, para. 9.

the decision, known among lawyers as the '*ratio decidendi*' (reason for deciding) of the case. This is the binding authority of the decision. Unravelling cases is not, as some commentators have suggested, a formalistic process. It is rather one which results from the process of 'legal reading', that is, the reading of the text against the background of 'the legal reader's access to a store of specifically legal relevant contexts'.[59]

Attempts have been made to offer formulae for determining the *ratio decidendi* of cases, but few have proved to be really satisfactory. Too much emphasis on the search for the *ratio decidendi* of cases can be misleading. Though it is the ratio that will be binding, the significance of other statements (*obiter dicta*) which have only persuasive authority may be considerable. For example, it is clear that, faced with the ratio of a two to one majority decision in the Court of Appeal as against dicta of three judges in the House of Lords agreeing with the dissent in the Court of Appeal and casting doubt on the correctness of the majority opinion, but not expressly overruling it, the Court of Appeal must follow the dicta of the House of Lords rather than the ratio of their earlier decision, so paradoxically preferring the persuasive to the binding authority. Courts also avoid the slavish copying of earlier decisions by the technique of distinguishing cases. The judge in the later case finds some relevant fact in that case of sufficient importance to justify a different approach from that adopted in the first decision.

The use of cases as precedents therefore involves an evaluation of the weight of propositions, both of binding and of persuasive authority, and of their application to the facts of the instant dispute. In evaluating the weight of propositions, the following factors will be relevant:

- Greater weight is given to propositions by judges of courts higher in the hierarchy of courts.
- Greater weight is given to propositions contained in judgments where the judges took time to consider their judgments. This is indicated in the law reports by the abbreviation *cur. adv. vult*[60] at the end of the judgments. Judgments in the House of Lords are always reserved, but in the much busier Court of Appeal many judgments are delivered extemporaneously after very brief deliberations.
- Greater weight is given to propositions which have been repeated by judges in a number of cases.
- Greater weight is given to propositions in cases where the decision was unanimous.
- Greater weight is generally given to propositions which have stood the test of time.
- Greater weight is given to propositions which appear to be broadly consistent with the general law governing the area in which the proposition arises.

[59] M. Davies, 'Reading Cases' (1987) 50 MLR 409. See also P. Goodrich, *Reading the Law: A Critical Introduction to Legal Method and Techniques* (Oxford: Basil Blackwell, 1986), ch. 6.
[60] *Curia advisari vult* which translates as 'the court wishes to be advised'.

- Greater weight will usually be given to propositions which have met with general approval among lawyers and commentators. But if, for example, the Law Commission in a law reform proposal has suggested that a proposition is ripe for alteration by statute, that would seriously erode the importance of the proposition.

The doctrine of precedent depends upon courts lower in the hierarchy respecting the authority of previous cases. As an intermediate appellate court the Court of Appeal is bound by its own previous decisions and by decisions of the House of Lords. It now seems clearly established that the Court of Appeal may only depart from one of its own previous decisions if five circumstances. The first three exceptions were spelled out by a six judge Court of Appeal in *Young v. Bristol Aeroplane Co. Ltd*:[61]

(1) When faced with two conflicting decisions of its own, the Court of Appeal is entitled and bound to decide which it will follow.
(2) The Court of Appeal is bound to refuse to follow a previous decision of its own which, even though not expressly overruled, cannot in its opinion stand with a subsequent decision of the House of Lords.
(3) The Court of Appeal is not bound to follow a decision of its own if it is satisfied that the decision was given *per incuriam*. A decision is given *per incuriam* if it appears to have been made in ignorance of relevant statutory provisions or binding case law.[62]
(4) The Court of Appeal is not bound to follow an interlocutory decision made by two judges of the Court of Appeal which it considers to be wrong.[63]
(5) The Court of Appeal may disregard a decision which it regards as a 'manifest slip or error'.[64]

Lord Denning as Master of the Rolls fought long and hard to persuade his colleagues that the Court of Appeal should free itself from the fetter of being bound by its own previous decisions just as the House of Lords had done in the 1966 Practice Statement,[65] and also suggested that the Court of Appeal was free to refuse to follow decisions of the House of Lords which were considered to be clearly wrong.[66] Lord Denning and the few colleagues agreeing with him met with little success in either case. In *Cassell v. Broome*[67] and *Miliangos v. George Frank (Textiles) Ltd*[68] the House of Lords made it clear that the Court of Appeal is bound by decisions of the House of Lords whatever its views as to the correctness of those decisions. Lord Denning's views on the liberation of the Court of Appeal from the obligation to follow its own previous decisions were crushingly rebuffed in *Davis v. Johnson*[69]

---

[61] [1944] KB 718.   [62] *Morelle v. Wakeling* [1955] 2 QB 379.
[63] *Boys v. Chaplin* [1968] 2 QB 1.
[64] *Rickards v. Rickards* [1989] 3 All ER 193; such instances will be very rare indeed.
[65] See below.
[66] H. Carty, 'Precedent and the Court of Appeal: Lord Denning's Views Explored' (1983) 1 *Legal Studies* 68.   [67] [1972] AC 1027.
[68] [1976] AC 443.   [69] [1979] AC 264.

in which the authority of *Young* v. *Bristol Aeroplane Co Ltd* was re-affirmed. With the retirement of Lord Denning, it seems that the issue has been laid to rest for some time, since none of his successors and most of the current Lords Justices of Appeal do not appear to share the views of the former Master of the Rolls.

Until 1966 the House of Lords was also bound by its own previous decisions having so decided in *London Street Tramways* v. *London County Council.*[70] But in 1966 the Lord Chancellor, Lord Gardiner, with the concurrence of the Law Lords, announced that in future the House would regard itself as free to 'depart from a previous decision when it appears right to do so'. A principal justification for the change was said to be that it unduly restricted the proper development of the law.[71] The decision to change the rules of precedent in the House of Lords was not a sudden one. By 1960 the judicial approach in the House of Lords, which has been summed up by Paterson as 'be fair, be consistent, don't legislate', was beginning to be seen as too restrictive and the potential conflicts between the requirements of fairness, consistency and creativity were being recognised. By a process described by Paterson as 'Dissimulation', the Law Lords began to violate one of the three expectations of judicial activity necessary to do justice in individual cases while nevertheless appearing to uphold all three expectations. The years 1962 to 1966 immediately prior to the issuing of the Practice Statement were marked by considerable judicial creativity.[72]

It was always envisaged that the House of Lords would use the freedom to depart from its own previous decisions sparingly, but in the years following the Practice Statement the potential impact of the new freedom was narrowed by the addition of a series of riders. The effect of these riders was to stress the need for certainty in decision-making. Thus it was considered inappropriate to overrule a previous decision if:

- this would defeat the legitimate expectations of those who had acted in some way in reliance on the old authority; or
- this would change the interpretation to be given to particular statutory provisions; or
- the House could not foresee all the consequences of the change proposed; or
- the whole area of law in which the question arose is in need of comprehensive reform.

The main types of case appropriate for the application of the Practice Statement appear to be those which will rectify some uncertainty which has arisen in the case law or which are outmoded or unjust in relation to some broad issue of principle. The sparing use of the Practice Statement is confirmed by the statistics: the use of the Statement was made thirty-nine times between 1966 and the end of 1989, but in only twelve cases was it been applied to overrule a previous decision. The main importance of the change of practice in 1966 is that it allowed the Law

---

[70] [1898] AC 375. [71] Practice Statement (Judicial Precedent) [1966] 1 WLR 1234.
[72] A. Paterson, *The Law Lords* (London: Macmillan, 1982).

Lords to accept an innovatory role and to avoid the practice of 'Dissimulation'. The removal of the shackles of the doctrine of precedent also confirms the special role of the House of Lords as a court of supervision.

Do we need two levels of appeal court?

The distinction between supervision and review and the discussion of the differing roles of the Court of Appeal and House of Lords provide part of the answer to this question. But the small caseload of the House of Lords and the expense of bringing a second appeal have produced suggestions that there is no need for the second appeal if the Court of Appeal were to be free to re-consider its own previous decisions. In considering the merits of such suggestions, it is important to realise that the House of Lords is also the final appeal court for cases originating in Scotland and Northern Ireland which have their own legal systems. Without the House of Lords there would be no institutional link between these legal systems in which there is considerable overlap of legal rules. Blom-Cooper and Drewry concluded that there was a role for the House of Lords and argued that the House of Lords was neither unfitted to retain its present judicial role nor prohibitively expensive to use. Such conclusions are surely right. Once the distinction between review and supervision is grasped, there is surely sense in having a special type of final appeal for cases involving issues of supervision, which allows more leisurely consideration of the issues than is possible in the Court of Appeal. Though the Court of Appeal is also a court of supervision, it appears to be too busy to be able to devote as much time and thought as is needed to such cases. But what is also clear is that it is unfair to litigants that they should meet the cost of a second appeal one of the principal purposes of which is to resolve issues of law of general public importance. Such issues should, as currently occurs in most tax cases, always be litigated at the public expense. The discretionary nature of the grant of leave to appeal to the House of Lords avoids any suggestion that there might be abuse of such an approach.

Are the judges fitted for the task of making law?

It will be clear from the description of the functions of the Court of Appeal and House of Lords that they make law to meet the needs of cases arising before them and lay down guidelines for judges in courts below. Even in cases involving the interpretation of legislation the judges' choices between competing or differential readings of the words of the statutory material involve judicial creativity or innovation. The doctrine of precedent restrains tribunals and the trial judges in the county courts and in the High Court from digressing into frolics of legal innovation, but even the trial judge will be presented from time to time with issues upon which there are no binding precedents. After all, every great House of Lords decision, which does not involve a departure from precedent, began with the presentation of issues at first instance. So to a limited extent all judges are involved in the process of supervision and the gradual accretion of legal rules by layer upon layer of precedent. All judges face choices in the process of adjudication. Nevertheless the overwhelming majority of trials turn on the establishment of facts and the matching of those facts to well settled legal rules. Simon Lee has argued that judges' creativity ought to vary according to four factors:[73]

(1) Does the case involve statutes or common law (the latter allowing more freedom)?
(2) Where is the judge in the courts' hierarchy (the higher up, the more creativity is suitable)?
(3) Is the subject-matter such that creativity or justice is more important?
(4) What is the likelihood of other institutions of government correcting any injustice?

Given the greater creative role of the judges in the appellate courts, it is appropriate to question whether they are fitted for the task of supervision. Today appellate judges, apart from the Lord Chancellor, are in practice recruited exclusively from among the best High Court judges, who after serving the Court of Appeal may be elevated to the House of Lords. This is a quite extraordinarily narrow group within the legal profession. Until the passing of the Courts and Legal Services Act 1990, only barristers could become High Court judges. Not only will the years at the Bar have moulded the barrister, but 'judicial qualities' will have been noted under the Lord Chancellor's system for recording the progress of barristers. Dossiers on barristers (and presumably now solicitor advocates) are kept by the Lord Chancellor's Department which record the progress of the barrister or solicitor advocate and judges will pass on comments, both favourable and unfavourable, about those appearing before them. By the time a barrister or solicitor is considered for judicial appointment, the dossier will contain considerable information on him or her. In addition there will be discreet enquiries about the candidate's personal life. Finally there will be an interview with the Lord Chancellor.[74] Historically, no applications have been invited for High Court judgeships, though they are for Circuit judgeships.[75] In October 1997, the new Lord Chancellor, Lord Irvine, announced that he had shelved consideration of a Judicial Appointments Commission, but would be opening up High Court judgeships to the application procedure.[76] The Lord Chancellor will, however, continue to collects the views of the judiciary and the legal profession on potential candidates. The historical system of selection for elevation to the High Court bench and for promotion to the Court of Appeal and House of Lords has tended to result in the character of the judiciary seeming to be self-perpetuating. Whether the modest changes announced

---

[73] S. Lee, *Judging Judges* (London: Faber & Faber, 1988).
[74] Or, for lesser judicial appointments, a judicial appointing panel consisting of a judge, lay member and senior member of the Lord Chancellor's Department.
[75] S. Shetreet, *Judges on Trial* (Amsterdam: North Holland, 1976).
[76] Lord Chancellor's Department, Press Release 220/97.

by Lord Irvine, coupled with an increase in solicitor High Court judges, will change that must be doubted.

The system secures a marked uniformity among the puisne judges and consequently among the appellate judges. It would also seem to discriminate against women and ethnic minorities.[77] The time spent on the High Court bench will also impose its further stamp upon the potential appellate judge. The typical appellate judge will be at least sixty years of age, white, male, and educated at public school and at Oxford or Cambridge and have lived in the insular world of the Bar for more than thirty years. There is clearly much scope and a very strong case for broadening the representation of the legal profession, both practising and academic, on the appellate bench. Where issues of supervision are involved, the necessity for practice in trial advocacy as a qualification for office are much harder to sustain than in relation to trials and appeals involving review.

Against this background, it is hardly surprising to find assertions made that judges consistently support the conventional established and settled interests and that this role of preserving stability is in conflict with the role of the judiciary as protectors of the liberties of the individual.[78] Professor Griffith's book *The Politics of the Judiciary* first published in 1977 caused a considerable stir in documenting such assertions with many examples. On judicial creativity Professor Griffith was worried that judges' emotional and personal prejudices became, perhaps unconsciously, a part of their decision-making process, and therefore lacked impartiality. The perceived need to ensure stability in society took precedence over fairness and justice. But no recipe for remedying the perceived deficiency was offered.

In an article responding to the gauntlet hurled down by Professor Griffith, Lord Devlin does not deny the homogeneity of attitudes of the appellate judges, but goes on to argue that this is probably inevitable. Lord Devlin concludes:

To my mind none of the evidence, general or specific adds much to the inherent probability that men and women of a certain age will be inclined by nature to favour the status quo. Is it displeasing to the public at large that the guardians of the law should share this common tendency?[79]

But in the context of a consideration of judicial creativity, or perhaps lack of it, the selection of the judiciary and their 'politics' in the sense used by Professor Griffith seem to be marginal considerations. Even in the United States Supreme Court with its overtly political processes of appointment, it seems that, in deciding landmark cases embodying sweeping reforms of the law, the justices do not always fully appreciate the significance and social consequences of their decisions.[80] This is despite, in addition to the special process of appointment, the presentation of elaborate written briefs and in appropriate cases 'Brandeis briefs' containing detailed economic and social data pertinent to the issue being litigated.

---

[77] P. Cohen, 'Born to Judge' *LAG Bulletin*, August 1982, 8.
[78] J. Griffith, *The Politics of the Judiciary*, 5th edn. (London: Fontana Press, 1997).
[79] P. Devlin, 'Judges, Government and Politics' (1978) 41 MLR 501, 509.
[80] D. Horowitz, *The Courts and Social Policy* (Washington DC: The Brookings Institution, 1977).

The role of domestic judges in interpreting and applying the provisions of the European Convention on Human Rights, following the incorporation of the Convention into domestic law,[81] is likely to place what have traditionally been regarded as political questions before judges. They may well be called upon to determine whether some provision of English legislation which limits a freedom protected by the Convention goes beyond what is regarded as 'necessary in a democratic society'. In undertaking this task, they will, of course, have the guidance which the European Court of Human Rights has provided to national courts through its own decisions.

In the English appellate courts it may be true to say that change that can be based on reasoning by analogy and the evolutionary development of legal rules is the most that can be expected, and that major changes of direction require legislation which, to overcome the bias of judges in favour the status quo, must be unequivocally expressed. While permitting a degree of creativity, the doctrine of precedent, even in the House of Lords, operates to limit the changes in the law which the judges are willing to make. The judges can develop the law, but major exercises in 'judicial legislation' are not perceived as appropriate. Indeed if there is any validity in the argument that the narrow background and insularity of judges renders them unfitted to make decisions with significant broad social consequences, there is some merit in a system which limits their ability to change the law and reserves such questions for full consideration by a democratically elected legislature. But there is scope for innovation and change both in the composition and procedures of appellate courts. The greater use of written procedures has been mentioned. Other possibilities are the use of a broader range of amicus curiae briefs in cases involving issues of supervision. For too long the modernisation of the appellate courts has been geared towards the management of caseloads rather than with equipping the appellate judges better for the task of the development of legal rules.

---

[81] See Ch. 2.

PART 4

THE PROVISION OF
LEGAL SERVICES

17

LEGAL SERVICES: THE LEGAL PROFESSION

Introduction

There is no statutory restriction on the giving of legal advice, but the professions of solicitor and barrister have become synonymous with the legal profession. Their predominance as the providers of legal services flows from their having succeeded in securing protected rights to undertake certain types of work. There are, however, a substantial number of other professions which give legal advice: accountants constantly give advice on matters of revenue law, while advice centres throughout the land are staffed by those without any professional legal qualification who advise on matters of law. This chapter is, however, primarily about solicitors and barristers, and those who work with them.[1]

Today, there are around 70,000 solicitors with practising certificates,[2] and 9,000 barristers in independent practice in England and Wales. Of the solicitors, eighty-five per cent are in private practice[3] and twenty-six per cent are women. Half of all admissions are of women. But in the profession as a whole, seventy-nine per cent of men, and fifty-three per cent of women are partners.[4] This reflects the tripling in size of the solicitors branch of the profession since the early 1960s. Though women lawyers were known in medieval times, they were excluded from the profession in the nineteenth century and it was not until 1922 that women were admitted as solicitors. The barristers profession was similar, with women admitted as barristers in 1920.

Solicitors historically enjoyed only two monopolies: drafting a deed which transferred ownership in land,[5] and beginning court proceedings on behalf of another.[6]

---

[1] Particularly legal executives in solicitors' offices and barristers' clerks.

[2] Solicitors engaged in active practice are required to hold a current practising certificate which is renewable each year.

[3] Those not in private practice are likely to work in commerce and industry, local and central government, the Crown Prosecution Service, in law centres and Citizens Advice Bureaux, in the magistrates' courts service and in other courts, and for trades unions and charities. See R. Woolfson et al., *Solicitors in the Employed Sector*, Law Society Research Study No. 13 (London: the Law Society, 1994).

[4] B. Cole, *Trends in the Solicitors' Profession: Annual Statistical Report 1997* (London: the Law Society, 1997).

[5] Commonly known as 'the conveyancing monopoly'.

[6] Commonly known as 'the litigation monopoly'.

Correspondingly, barristers have historically enjoyed the single monopoly of appearing as advocates in the higher courts.[7]

The period since the mid-1970s has been a turbulent one for the legal professions. They have been under constant scrutiny. Perceptions of high cost and poor service have abounded. They have been accused of not meeting the needs of all citizens, of performing shoddy and negligent work, and of making off with their clients' money in unprecedented amounts. The ground swell of concern led the Labour Government of the day to establish a Royal Commission to examine the structure, training and regulation of the legal profession and to recommend those changes that would be desirable in the interests of justice.[8]

Over the years Royal Commissions have been noted for the lack of impact made by their recommendations, but there can be no doubt that the profession was frightened by the Benson Commission. They feared structural change and the loss of monopolies on property transfer work, in probate, and in the conduct of litigation. In particular, the threat to conveyancing work was viewed as undermining the main fee earning activity of many practices. It was a source of great satisfaction to both branches of the profession when the Benson Commission's Report in 1979 did not propose any radical change, though the Report was generally unpopular with other commentators. One commentator said, 'The arguments with which it supports its more important conclusions are lame beyond orthopaedic help'.[9]

The Report of the Benson Commission did not, however, disperse the gathering storm clouds and three events can be identified which led to what might be termed the great reform of the legal profession, which is still continuing.

The first event was the scandal which has come to be known as the Glanville Davies affair. The failure of the Law Society to act effectively in dealing with complaints against a solicitor and respected member of the Council of the Law Society, Mr Glanville Davies, attracted enormous publicity and led to a complete breakdown of public confidence in the Law Society's ability to regulate professional conduct. Mr Davies did not contest an application by the aggrieved client, Mr Parsons, that he should be struck off the roll of solicitors following the reduction on taxation of a grossly inflated and inaccurate litigation bill from £197,000 to £67,000. The litigation and the subsequent enquiries by the Lay Observer and by the Law Society (known as 'the Ely Report') revealed an appalling catalogue of errors, insensitivity, and lack of sound judgement.[10] Despite radical revisions of the complaints procedures, there remains dissatisfaction about the handling of

---

[7] Commonly known as 'the advocacy monopoly', though it should be noted that solicitors have rights of audience in the lower courts and tribunals.

[8] *Final Report of the Royal Commission on Legal Services (Benson Commission)* (London: HMSO, 1979, Cmnd. 7648) cited in this chapter as 'the Benson Commission'.

[9] Lord Goodman, *Evening Standard*, 4 October 1979.

[10] 'The Lay Observer's Letter to Mr Leslie Parsons Regarding Mr Glanville Davies' *Law Society's Gazette*, 14 December 1983, 3203; and the Law Society, *Report of The Law Society's Council's Committee of Enquiry into The Law Society's Treatment of the Complaints of Mr L. A. Parsons against Mr G. Davies and Mr C. Malim (The Ely Report)* (London: the Law Society, 1984).

complaints similar to those concerning police complaints procedures considered earlier in this book.[11]

The second event was the ending of the conveyancing monopoly. In 1983 Austin Mitchell introduced a Private Member's Bill proposing the establishment of licensed conveyancers able to undertake residential conveyancing in competition with solicitors. This Bill failed but the Government undertook to introduce its own legislation on conveyancing in the Parliamentary session 1984–85 with the same objective. The Government honoured its undertaking and included the extension of the conveyancing monopoly to licensed conveyancers in the Administration of Justice Act 1985. The effect of this change has not been as dramatic as had been feared. Conveyancing work has become more competitive, but solicitors have not lost substantial amounts of work to the modest number of licensed conveyancers who have set up in practice. Much more fear was engendered by the proposal that banks and building societies be allowed to offer conveyancing services. Such bodies have a very large, almost captive, clientele since many of those buying houses will go first to the bank or building society to arrange to borrow the money to buy the house.

The third event was the liberalisation of the restrictions on advertising, which had previously permitted only institutional advertising of the profession as a whole. This took the form of a series of 'See a Solicitor' leaflets. The removal of restrictions was, in part, a reaction to the threat of competition from licensed conveyancers. From a position where individual advertising was considered inconsistent with the professional image of solicitors and where there were rules determining the size and style even of the name of the practice on its premises, the Law Society moved speedily to a virtually de-regulated advertising regime. The sole remaining restraint is the requirement that the advertising must not impair the solicitor's independence and integrity and must not bring the profession into disrepute. Sending brochures and leaflets to clients, and advertising in local newspapers and some specialist journals are now common, though larger well-established firms seem to do less advertising than smaller and newer practices. Many solicitors still obtain business through 'networking', that is, establishing a network of friends and business contacts likely to refer business to the solicitor. It is common for solicitors to build cordial relationships with estate agents, building societies and even with the custody officer at the police station, in order to secure referrals. Solicitors also participate in social activities likely to get them and their firms known to potential clients. In 1967 Abel-Smith and Stevens asserted that 'solicitors tend to be active members of rotary clubs, golf clubs, rugby football clubs and to become freemasons and leading churchmen'.[12] More recent empirical research tends to confirm this assertion.[13]

---

[11] A. Newbold and G. Zellick, 'Reform of the Solicitors' Complaints Procedures: Fact or Fiction?' (1987) 6 CJQ 25; and National Consumer Council, *The Solicitors Complaints Bureau: A Consumer View* (London: National Consumer Council, 1994); and V. Lewis, *Complaints against Solicitors: the Complainants' View*, Law Society Research Study No. 19 (London: the Law Society, 1996).

[12] B. Abel-Smith and R. Stevens, *Lawyers and the Courts* (London: Heinemann, 1967), pp. 142–3.

[13] D. Podmore, *Solicitors and the Wider Community* (London: Heinemann, 1980).

These three events also coincided with a period when the character of legal work was changing. The 1980s saw an explosion in corporate, commercial and financial services work, and the creation of very large law firms to meet the needs of large corporate clients.[14]

There is no doubt that the professions are today under attack. Privileges and self-regulation are no longer accepted as necessary corollaries of professional status. For some, the chill wind of competition is again blowing through their offices coupled with a dismantling of the traditional legal aid system. Small firms are threatened by the need for specialisation, and the resources needed to secure economies of scale in the running of a modern practice.

Nor is the Bar immune from change. Here it is the changes to the legal aid scheme and to rights of audience which threaten traditional ways of working.

The Great Reform of the Legal Profession

The great reform of the legal profession is the result of three major enquiries into the legal profession. The first was the Benson Commission, which has already been mentioned. The second was joint committee set up by the General Council of the Bar and the Law Society, chaired by Lady Marre, which reported in July 1988.[15] It is more noted for its failure to address issues of modernising the profession than for its contribution to change. The third and by far that most important was the trio of Green Papers[16] issued by the Lord Chancellor in January 1989 followed by a White Paper[17] in June 1990 and culminating in the Courts and Legal Services Act 1990.

The Benson Commission

The Benson Commission, which was chaired by a lay person and had a majority of lay members, devoted three years to its study of legal services. It took voluminous evidence, undertook its own research studies, and engaged in lengthy consultation and deliberation. The Report published in 1979 runs to four volumes. There is much of value in the Report and implementation of many of its recommendations would undoubtedly have resulted in improvements in the system for delivering legal services.

---

[14] See also J. Lewis and J. Keegan, *Defining Legal Business: Understanding the Work of the Largest Law Firms*, Research and Policy Planning Unit Research Paper No. 27 (London: the Law Society, 1997).

[15] *A Time for Change: Report of the Committee on the Future of the Legal Profession (Marre Committee)* (London: the General Council of the Bar and the Law Society, 1988).

[16] *The Work and Organisation of the Legal Profession* (London: HMSO, 1989, Cm. 570); *Conveyancing by Authorised Practitioners* (London: HMSO, 1989, Cm. 571); and *Contingency Fees* (London: HMSO, 1989, Cm. 572).   [17] *Legal Services: A Framework for the Future* (London: HMSO, 1990, Cm. 740).

The Benson Commission's unpopularity with commentators (though not with lawyers)[18] is based on its recommendations that the status quo be retained in three areas seen by the profession as crucial: the retention by barristers of a monopoly on rights of audience in the higher courts, the retention by solicitors of the monopoly on conveyancing work, and the division of the profession into solicitors and barristers. In 1983 the Government accepted the Report,[19] though it has never been debated in Parliament. The Government indicated that implementation of a number of recommendations was subject to resources becoming available or would need to await an appropriate legislative opportunity.

The Marre Committee

When solicitors lost the conveyancing monopoly with the enactment of the Administration of Justice Act 1985, they turned their attention to the advocacy monopoly enjoyed by barristers in the higher courts. The absurdity of the monopoly was brought to public attention when Cyril Smith MP's solicitor sought the leave of the High Court to read out an agreed statement in settlement of a libel action, because he considered the fee proposed by counsel for doing this to be 'unnecessarily expensive'. Leave was refused at first instance and in the Court of Appeal, though a few months later a Practice Direction[20] was issued indicating the collective view of the judges that solicitors should be permitted to appear in the High Court or Court of Appeal in formal or unopposed proceedings.

There followed a public and acrimonious debate between representatives of solicitors and barristers on the issue of rights of audience. The General Council of the Bar responded by proposing a joint committee with the Law Society to consider the future of the legal profession. The Marre Committee[21] was born, but its report was a great disappointment. Its deliberations had been hurried, its request for evidence stressed the need for a brevity viewed by many as excessive and it lacked sufficient resources to produce a credible alternative to any government proposals. The credibility of the final report was further damaged by the Note of Dissent attached by the barrister members and some independent members on the proposed extension of rights of audience.

The Marre Committee concluded that unless the professions themselves initiated change, it would be forced upon them. Commercial considerations should not alone determine the future supply of legal services and the profession should retain only those rules which are 'essential for the maintenance of professional standards in the public interest'. The biggest area of unmet need was identified as the provision of social welfare law, particularly in rural districts, in parts of London and in

[18] See P. Thomas, 'Introduction' in P. Thomas (ed.), *Law in the Balance: Legal Services in the Eighties* (Oxford: Martin Robertson, 1982), p. 1.

[19] *The Government Response to the Report of the Royal Commission on Legal Services* (London: HMSO, 1983, Cmnd. 9077).   [20] Practice Direction: Rights of Audience [1986] 2 All ER 226.

[21] *A Time for Change: Report of the Committee on the Future of the Legal Profession (Marre Committee)* (London: the General Council of the Bar and the Law Society, 1988).

the urban conurbations of the midlands and the north of England. Realism was needed in providing new services because of resource constraints. Informational and education initiatives were encouraged.

On legal aid, the Committee essentially recommended the status quo, but did recommend the extension of legal aid to tribunal proceedings. Law centres and other advice agencies should receive funding from the Legal Aid Board, but the idea of a national legal service and of a public defender system were disapproved. The controversial part of the report related to rights of audience, where the majority recommended the creation of a Rights of Audience Advisory Board which would recommend to the Law Society the licensing of suitably qualified solicitors to act as advocates in the Crown Court. Employed lawyers should also be entitled to rights of audience in the courts.

Lord Mackay's proposals

In January 1989, the then Lord Chancellor, Lord Mackay issued three Green Papers: *The Work and Organisation of the Legal Profession, Conveyancing by Authorised Practitioners*, and *Contingency Fees*. The Green Papers were short, sharp and to the point. They seemed to depend more on policy preferences than research and to reflect the Government's preference for action not words, for speedy response rather than lengthy debate, and perhaps also a deep disregard for the theoretical overview. Notions of 'value for money', 'efficiency' and 'market forces' are firmly embedded in these reports. They stated that the Government believed that free competition between the providers of legal services would, through the discipline of the market, ensure that the public is provided with the most efficient and effective network of legal services at the most economical price. The mood of deregulation is tempered only by reference to the need to assure the public of the competence of providers of legal services.

The debate which the Green Papers generated has been fully chronicled elsewhere,[22] but the response to the proposal that rights of audience should in future depend on certificates of competence in advocacy rather than membership of a particular branch of the profession met a predictably hostile response from the Bar and a response verging on the intemperate from the judges. The subsequent White Paper, *Legal Services: A Framework for the Future*, adopted a different tone referring rather more to the requirement for legal services to be responsive to clients' needs than to notions of competition and the discipline of the market but in content the proposals actually gave little ground on key points.

Extended rights of audience were to be permitted, both for current advocates in more courts and for new classes of advocates. For certain classes of work (small claims, debt cases and housing cases in the county courts) there would be no restrictions at all on rights of audience; the only control would be the court's discretion to restrict the involvement of unruly or corrupt representatives. The Government

---

[22] F. Cownie, 'The Reform of the Legal Profession or the End of Civilisation as We Know It' in F. Patfield and R. White (eds.), *The Changing Law* (Leicester: Leicester University Press, 1990), p. 213.

believed that it was for the professional bodies and other organisations whose members provide legal services to satisfy the courts and the public that their members are competent to undertake representation. Professional bodies would produce rules of conduct for such activity having regard to advice from an Advisory Committee to be set up by the Lord Chancellor.

The concession to the Bar was that any person called to the Bar would have rights of audience in all courts on completion of pupillage, dependent only on their compliance with rules of conduct made by the Bar. Any change to the rules relating to education training and conduct would be subject to the concurrence of the Lord Chancellor, Lord Chief Justice, Master of the Rolls, President of the Family Division and Vice-Chancellor, who would act having regard to advice received from a new Advisory Committee on Legal Education and Conduct.

The Law Society would become a recognising authority under the new scheme and so would be able to recognise a solicitor as qualified as an advocate in a particular court or courts, again subject to rules on education, training and conduct which would parallel the arrangements for the Bar. Again there would be no loss of existing rights of audience; solicitors would be recognised as having competence to be advocates in the lower courts. The gain for the Law Society was that they would be able to certificate solicitors who have undertaken further training entitling them to rights of audience in the higher courts. This in turn would open the way to appointment to the High Court bench for solicitors.

The new Act would remove the monopoly on starting and conducting litigation. The Government considered that this unnecessarily hindered the ways in which the provision of legal services might develop. Anyone suitably qualified would be permitted to undertake this work. The Government would licence authorising bodies which might include bodies other than the Law Society and the General Council of the Bar.

The Advisory Committee on Legal Education and Conduct would play a central role in the revised arrangements for supervising legal education and ensuring satisfactory standards of conduct by those entitled to undertake legal services. The functions of the Advisory Committee would be to advise on questions that arise as to what qualifications are necessary for providing legal services connected with litigation and what requirements are necessary to ensure proper standards of conduct. An annual report would be presented to the Lord Chancellor and would be laid before Parliament. Professional bodies would be placed under a statutory duty to have regard to advice from the Advisory Committee in preparing rules of competence and conduct for their own members.

The Courts and Legal Services Act 1990

The proposals which required legislative change for their implementation were included in Part II of the Courts and Legal Services Act 1990.[23] This lays down a

---

[23] See generally R. White, *A Guide to the Courts and Legal Services Act 1990* (London: Fourmat Publishing, 1991).

general statutory objective of making provision for new or better ways of providing legal services and a wider choice of person providing them, while maintaining the proper and efficient administration of justice. The Advisory Committee on Legal Education and Conduct is established. Chaired by a judge of the High Court or a higher court, it has sixteen members, a majority of whom must be persons other than practising or academic lawyers. The system of advocacy licensing is also detailed in the Act. There are a multitude of other very significant changes on specific matters relating to monopolies and styles of practice. But these do not impact dramatically on the overall work of the profession.

The Labour Government's policies

The Labour Government elected in May 1997 looks set to continue broadly the policies of the previous Government on legal services. The Government's policies were set before solicitors in a keynote address by Lord Irvine of Lairg, the Lord Chancellor, in October 1997.[24] The unifying theme was the need for modernisation of legal institutions. The reforms recommended by the Woolf Reports into civil justice were coupled with the need to modernise the legal aid scheme. It was clear that public funding would be reined in and that the targets for spending would change. Access to justice would be secured by increased emphasis on conditional fee arrangements, by block contracting for legal services rather than the traditional fee indemnity through legal aid, and by the development of a community legal service.[25]

The Organisation of the Profession

The Benson Commission's concept of a profession

What is clear to anyone reading the Report of the Benson Commission is that it accepted that the practice of law was a professional activity and that professions display a number of common characteristics:

- the existence of a central organisation or governing body representing the profession and having powers of control and discipline over its members;
- the function of giving specialist advice and services in a specialised field of knowledge;
- entry and training are controlled by the profession itself and are dependent on a formalised system of education and training;
- the activity is self-regulated, enabling the requirement of high standards in relations with clients, usually higher than that imposed by the general law;

---

[24] Keynote address by the Lord Chancellor to the Solicitors' Annual Conference, 'Civil Justice and Legal Aid Reforms', 18 October 1997.
[25] On legal aid changes and the community legal service, see below and Ch. 18.

• the first and paramount responsibility of the members of the profession is to act in the best interests of their clients.

The existence of these characteristics required the independence of the profession from interference by government. Without independence, the interests of the client cannot be a first and paramount consideration. The self-regulation of the profession and the high standards demanded of its members are said to be the justification for the monopolies enjoyed by those engaging in the activity and for the restrictive practices permitted. These issues have dominated debates about the role of solicitors and barristers in a modern legal system.

A divided profession

The legal profession in England and Wales is divided into solicitors and barristers, with the latter being considered the senior branch of the profession. The solicitor gives advice and has the conduct of the business of the client from day to day and will retain a barrister to carry out a specific task in handling the client's business. Though there is a system of direct access to barristers for a number of professions, most clients will need to see a solicitor before they can gain access to counsel, who will be called in as the occasion demands to give specialist advice, to draft documents or to act as advocate in the higher courts. There is a small number of solicitors with rights of audience in the higher courts, but these work in-house for large firms, and do not hold themselves out as trial advocates for hire in the same way as barristers. Each branch of the profession has its own system of entry and training, its own governing body and its own rules of conduct and discipline.

The distinction between the two branches of the profession is an artificial one. There are, in fact, no tasks, exclusive to one branch. Solicitors regularly appear as advocates in the lower courts and, by special fiat of the Lord Chancellor, in some Crown Courts which are geographically remote from barristers' chambers. Some now have rights of audience in the higher courts. Equally, there are many barristers who do not appear in court, spending all their time on oral and written opinions on the law. Over the years there has been much debate on the fusion of the two branches of the profession. Though this has not happened, and is unlikely to happen for many years, there is some convergence between the two branches of the profession.

The issue of fusion was considered by the Benson Commission which unanimously concluded that the legal profession should continue to be divided. Advocates of fusion, who represented a minority among those who submitted evidence to the Benson Commission, criticised the divided profession on a number of grounds: duplication, inefficiency, delay, and inaccessibility. Duplication of effort arises because convention demands the involvement of both solicitor and barrister where only one need be involved. Barristers do not appear in court alone; the solicitor, or a representative of the practice, must also be present. Clients must consult solicitors[26]

---

[26] Or where direct access is permitted, another professional adviser.

even if their only need is for an opinion from counsel. No convincing answer has been given to this criticism; all that is offered is the general argument in favour of a specialised division of the profession which is free from hour to hour to engage in advocacy and other specialist work. Inefficiency obviously arises because of the necessity to reduce everything to written instructions. Conferences at an early stage are only common in major litigation. Very frequently counsel will only begin to prepare on the night before the case is to be heard and will only meet with the client on the morning of the hearing. If the brief has been badly prepared, there cannot be effective representation. Nor does the system guarantee that the barrister of the solicitor's choice will be able to take the case, and in minor cases last minute changes of barrister are fairly common. The Benson Commission's response to this criticism was to note that fusion might not improve matters and to suggest that a more detailed set of standards should be prepared for both solicitors and barristers on the preparation and handling of briefs. The argument in favour of a divided profession which found favour with the Benson Commission was that the existence of a separate branch of the profession ensured that there was a body of specialist advocates available to all solicitors, which would be dispersed if the two branches were fused.

There is some merit in the Benson Commission's reasoning, but it does not seem to warrant so total a separation of the two branches of the profession as exists currently. Ultimately the issue may not be that important, because the impact of fusion for clients might well be minimal. In order to allow time for attendance in court to represent the client, office administration probably demands that there be separation of preparation and advocacy. Furthermore even in a fused profession, the barristers in chambers in the Inns of Court and elsewhere would undoubtedly enter into partnership as specialist trial advocates and do agency work for other solicitors, whose own staff were unable to act as advocates in every case or where the complexity of the case justified bringing in a specialist advocate. On the other hand, there would be much greater flexibility for clients and lawyers, and much more control by the instructing client who would have direct access to the advocate in the case. No party would be able to shelter behind the barriers inevitably created by the divided profession.

Often ill-informed and repetitive, the debate has tended to ignore the interests of the client and has frequently been conducted by those whose minds are already made up on the issue. Increasingly, the distinction is being blurred and fusion will eventually arrive in some form. The provisions on advocacy rights in the Courts and Legal Services Act 1990 provide a further blurring of the distinction. Proposals from the Lord Chancellor's Advisory Committee on Legal Education and Conduct bring together much of the formal training for admission as a solicitor and barrister.[27]

---

[27] The Lord Chancellor's Advisory Committee on Legal Education and Conduct, *First Report on Legal Education and Training* (London: ACLEC, 1996), chs. 5 and 6.

Solicitors

Solicitors are increasingly becoming the dominant branch of the profession despite the historical recognition that they are the junior part of the legal profession. Solicitors are governed by the Law Society, established by Royal Charter in 1831, which also acts as the main professional association of solicitors.[28] The Law Society acts through its Council which is composed of seventy solicitors, fifty-six of whom are elected by members of the Society with the remaining fourteen being elected by the Council itself. There are also 121 autonomous local law societies, which have an important role to play in the formulation of policy by the Law Society.

Admission to practice requires the completion of three stages of training: the academic stage, the vocational stage and the apprenticeship. The academic stage of training is satisfied by completion of a qualifying law degree which meets the Law Society's requirements for demonstrating the foundations of legal knowledge, including an ability to research the law, in seven subject areas or by passing the Common Professional Examination. The seven foundation subjects are Contract, Tort, Criminal Law, Equity and Trusts, the law of the European Union, Property Law and Public Law. The second stage of training is the Legal Practice Course taken after a further year of study at one of the professional schools. This is known as the vocational stage of training, which is designed to provide a bridge between the academic stage of training and what might be labelled the clinical stage of training in a solicitor's office under a training contract.

Though the subjects available as part of law degree courses have increased enormously in range in recent years, the balance of courses offered is still weighted considerably in favour of 'practical' subjects reflecting traditional private law concepts of property rather than the 'new property' in the many entitlements deriving from the public law that regulates the welfare state.[29]

The final stage is two year's apprenticeship to an established solicitor, known as a training contract,[30] which can be regarded as the clinical stage of training during which the skills of managing an office, interviewing clients, writing letters, instructing counsel and handling client money are learned. Trainee solicitors are paid salaries, which have in recent years become increasingly attractive, at least in firms in the big cities. The salary will naturally depend on the size and range of work of the practice in which the trainee solicitor is articled, but the Law Society sets down recommended minimum salaries and can refuse to register training contracts where the salary is less than this figure. Trainee solicitors must complete the Professional Skills Course, which is designed to provide formal instruction alongside the practical experience of the training contract in personal work management,

---

[28] See generally D. Sugarman, *A Brief History of The Law Society* (London: the Law Society, 1995).

[29] R. Abel, 'The Politics of the Market for Legal Services' in P. Thomas (ed.), *Law in the Balance: Legal services for the 1980s* (London: Martin Robertson, 1982), p. 6; and M. Zander, *Legal Services for the Community* (London: Temple Smith, 1978); and F. Cownie and A. Bradney, *English Legal System in Context* (London: Butterworths, 1996), ch. 7.

[30] Formerly, articles of clerkship. Trainee solicitors are still frequently referred to as articled clerks.

accounts, advocacy and oral communication skills, investment business and professional conduct. On satisfactory completion of the period of apprenticeship, trainee solicitors are entitled to be formally admitted as solicitors and to describe themselves as such. They may not set up in practice on their own account for a further three years.[31]

Once admitted, the solicitor is required to maintain a practising certificate, for which a substantial annual fee is charged. The solicitor must also contribute to the compensation fund, which makes good any losses suffered by clients when a dishonest solicitor makes off with their money. All solicitors other than employed solicitors are also required to take out compulsory professional indemnity insurance as a condition of the grant of the annual practising certificate.

Barristers

The barristers' governing bodies are more complex than those of solicitors. They are the barrister's own Inn of Court, the Senate of the Inns of Court and the General Council of the Bar, often known simply as the Bar Council. In order to become a barrister it is necessary to become a member of one of the Inns of Court: the Inner Temple, the Middle Temple, Lincoln's Inn or Gray's Inn. Each Inn is governed by benchers appointed by existing benchers. The Inns are very powerful and wealthy institutions which rent chambers (offices) for the large majority of London barristers. There is also a collegiality within each Inn which maintains for the members dining and library facilities and, some would argue, a retreat from the real world.[32]

The Senate of the Inns of Court consists of 101 barristers (some of whom will be judges) representing the profession of barrister; some are appointed by the benchers of each Inn, some are *ex officio* members like the leaders from each of the six circuits, and some are elected by members of the Bar. The Senate's powers are essentially supervisory and policy-making, enabling the four Inns to speak with one voice on matters of common interest.

Though admission to the Bar is still largely the domain of the individual Inns, the formal education of the trainee barrister is centralised through the Inns of Court School of Law run by the Council of Legal Education, which is a committee of Senate. The other governing body for barristers is the Bar Council whose membership derives much less from the Inns; it is the barristers' elected representative body. The Bar Council is responsible for the maintenance of professional standards and represents the general interests of the Bar in its relations with outsiders. There

---

[31] For a valuable longitudinal study of law students, see D. Halpern, *Entry into the Legal Profession: The Law Student Cohort Study—Years 1 and 2*, Law Society Research Study No. 15 (London: the Law Society, 1994); M. Shiner and T. Newburn, *Entry into the Legal Profession: The Law Student Cohort Study—Years 3*, Law Society Research Study No. 18 (London: the Law Society, 1995); and M. Shiner, *Entry into the Legal Profession: The Law Student Cohort Study—Years 4*, Law Society Research Study No. 25 (London: the Law Society, 1997).

[32] See generally R. Cocks, *Foundations of the Modern Bar* (London: Sweet & Maxwell, 1983).

is considerable overlap in membership of the Senate and Bar Council. The establishment of the Senate does not yet appear to have resulted in any discernible shift of power away from the individual Inns.[33]

The training of barristers can, like that of solicitors, be divided into the same three stages: academic, vocational and apprenticeship. The requirements of the academic stage are common to both branches of the profession. The vocational stage for the barrister consists of a year at the Inns of Court Law School followed by Bar Finals. Success in Bar Finals entitles the candidate to admission to the Bar, known as call to the Bar provided that they have completed the quaint requirement of eating the necessary number of dinners in their Inn. Following call, candidates can call themselves barristers but may not yet practise as such. A one year period of apprenticeship to an established barrister must be undertaken. In marked distinction to the solicitors' branch of the profession, the pupil barrister may not earn any money during the first six months of pupillage and there are only limited opportunities for earning in the second six months of pupillage. This places financial constraints on qualification as a barrister which do not exist for intending solicitors. The award of bursaries and scholarships can mitigate the difficulties the system causes and in recent times the Bar has taken on board the need to change the system so that the equivalent of salaries can be offered during pupillage.

Barristers in private practice are all sole practitioners, though they work in sets of offices (called sets of chambers) in groups ranging in number from just a few barristers to around sixty sharing central services, notably of a clerk but also secretarial and other support staff.[34] Each set of chambers is required to have at least one clerk, who performs the functions of office administrator and accountant, business manager and agent. Work coming in from solicitors is allocated among members of the chambers by the clerk, who also negotiates the fee for the brief. The clerk therefore has some control over the flow of work for each barrister in the chambers. A senior clerk takes a commission of between five and ten per cent of the brief fees rather than a salary, which can exceed the earnings of many of the barristers in the chambers.[35] More recently the practice has developed of employing salaried practice managers rather than clerks on commission.

After around ten to fifteen years in practice, successful barristers can consider applying for promotion to Queen's Counsel, known as 'silk' from the material of which the QC's formal gown is made. Queen's Counsel are appointed by the Queen on the advice of the Lord Chancellor, who will normally consult senior members of the judiciary. Being a Queen's Counsel brings status, high income, and relief from some of the more tedious paper work done by barristers. It may also often be a step on the way to judicial appointment in the High Court, though the earnings of many silks exceed that of a High Court judge and there have been

[33] R. Hazell, 'Introduction to the Bar' in R. Hazell (ed.), *The Bar on Trial* (London: Quartet Books, 1978), p. 1.

[34] See generally J. Morison and P. Leith, *The Barrister's World and the Nature of Law* (Milton Keynes: Open University Press, 1992).

[35] J. Flood, *Barristers' Clerks* (Manchester: Manchester University Press, 1983).

numerous reports of the offer of appointment to the High Court bench being turned down.[36]

Socialisation

Socialisation refers to the mechanisms by which the profession reproduces the motivations and attitudes regarded as appropriate for the practice of law. The lengthy period of training required for admission to either branch of the profession has a socialising effect on entrants to the profession. The character of the profession is thus maintained. Since the standard route of entry is graduate entry, the social profile of graduates is the starting point for consideration of the social profile of the profession. The social composition of undergraduate law students is predominantly middle-class in origin and outlook.[37] The social composition of admitted solicitors is remarkably similar to the profile of law students, but the socialisation process involved in qualifying to practise at the Bar dramatically increases the preponderance of persons from professional and managerial backgrounds. The process in both branches of the profession has tended to impact adversely on women and ethnic minorities, who, even when they do enter the profession, tend to be relegated to lower status work.[38]

The traditions and customs of each branch of the profession influence the form of education and training rather than any objectively determined educational needs. The eating of dinners as a pre-condition to call to the Bar and the serving of pupillage as a pre-condition to practice at the Bar are the most obvious examples of socialisation processes. For potential solicitors the apprenticeship to an experienced solicitor in the form of a training contract performs the same function. The apprenticeship is the period when the motivations and attitudes important for the practice of the law are inculcated and reinforced.

It seems inevitable that the social profile of lawyers is going to be markedly different from that of society at large because the social profile of persons attaining the level of educational achievement required for admission to higher education does not itself correspond with that of the whole community. The differences, however, go beyond this, most notably at the Bar. This has important consequences for the delivery of legal services, which are only now being slowly realised. The social class composition of lawyers compared with particular client groups appears to make it easy for some to consult lawyers while presenting barriers to other sections

---

[36] In addition to a reduction in salary, the working conditions, particularly the practice of judges going 'on circuit' to try cases in provincial Crown Court centres has been cited as an unattractive feature of the work of a High Court judge.

[37] P. McDonald, 'The Class of '81—A Glance at the Social Class Composition of Recruits to the Legal Profession' (1982) 9 J of Law and Soc. 267.

[38] See generally R. Hazell (ed.), *The Bar on Trial* (London: Quartet Books, 1978); D. Podmore and A. Spencer, 'The Law as a Sex-Typed Profession' (1982) 9 J of Law and Soc. 21; and R. Abel, *The Legal Profession in England and Wales* (Oxford: Basil Blackwell, 1988). For a comparison with other professions, see the United Kingdom Inter-Professional Group, *Women in the Professions* (London: the Law Society, 1990). On ethnic minorities, see M. King et al., *Ethnic Minorities and Recruitment to the Solicitors' Profession* (London: the Law Society, 1990).

of the community. Poorer working class groups do not seem to perceive lawyers as providing a service for them. Law centres have tried to address this problem, but it is difficult to isolate the factors which make law centres more accessible to working class clients. The offering of a free service and the ability to advertise have obviously been key factors having little to do with questions of social class composition, though they have much to do with socialisation since law centres perceive their role very differently from those in private practice.

Monopolies

One common feature of professions is the claim that their services are more than business transactions and that this aspect of the delivery of professional services justifies in the public interest monopolies that would not be acceptable in the ordinary industrial and commercial arena. The traditional monopolies applicable in the legal profession are under attack and some are on the point of disappearing. There have always been surprisingly few monopolies though they have become principal protectors of the exclusivity of the legal profession. These are the conveyancing and probate monopolies, restrictions on instituting litigation and on rights of audience. There is no general monopoly on the giving of legal advice, but the monopolies that do exist have been very effective in reserving most legal work for solicitors and barristers. There has been some encroachment in specific areas such as employment law advice and welfare benefits advice, where tribunals with their generous rights of audience are major institutions. In addition more generous rights have been accorded for certain proceedings in the county courts.[39]

Barristers and solicitors, together with certificated notaries (who are normally also solicitors) and licensed conveyancers, enjoy a statutory monopoly which makes it an offence for any other persons to draw up or prepare documents connected with the transfer of title to property for payment. This is commonly known as the conveyancing monopoly.

Solicitors, barristers and certificated notaries enjoy a statutory monopoly over the drawing up or preparation of the executor's affidavit and account; these are formal documents which must be obtained before probate can be granted. Like the conveyancing monopoly, the probate monopoly affects only a small part of the work involved in the administration of the estate of a deceased person. In both cases the practical effect of the monopolies is in most cases to reserve all the work for solicitors (and in the case of property transfer, licensed conveyancers). By practice rule barristers do not undertake conveyancing and probate work falling within these monopolies. Despite popular opinion to the contrary there is no monopoly over the preparation of wills.

Restrictions connected with litigation cover two situations. First, only solicitors may begin and conduct litigation on behalf of others. Secondly, there are rules

---

[39] Courts and Legal Services Act 1990, s. 11, and Lay Representation (Rights of Audience) Order 1992, S.I. 1992 No. 1966.

restricting rights of audience. Obviously individuals may begin litigation on their own account and represent themselves in those proceedings, but otherwise only solicitors and barristers have the right to act as advocates in courts. Other than on formal or unopposed business, rights of audience in the higher courts are only available to solicitors with additional advocacy qualifications, and to barristers. Legal executives and lay advisers have rights of audience before judges in chambers and in certain proceedings before Masters and district judges, as well as in designated county court proceedings. It is important to note in this context that courts have an inherent power to permit anyone to act as advocate. Rights of audience before tribunals are much wider, as noted in Chapters 14 and 15.

Restrictions on rights of audience ensure that persons appearing as representatives before courts have a minimum level of competence as advocates. Most of the argument has related to the divided profession's respective rights of audience discussed above, with much of the argument centring on solicitors being granted full rights of audience before the higher courts, especially the Crown Court.[40]

The monopoly over the initiation of proceedings has proved to be most contentious in relation to claims assessors, who deal with accident claims on a contingency basis taking part of the compensation as remuneration. Because few such cases proceed to trial it was argued that claims assessors should be able to issue proceedings on behalf of their clients. These claims were rejected and the rule that a solicitor be involved was seen as protecting the client who might otherwise be advised to settle too early or for too little to maximise the claims assessors' cash flow.[41]

The Work of the Profession

This section focuses on solicitors since they remain the initial point of contact for those seeking legal services from the profession. With around 14,000 outlets in England and Wales for their businesses,[42] solicitors are likely to remain for some time the principal providers of legal services even if there is considerable expansion of alternatives to the use of solicitors for some legal work. What follows is a description of a typical general practice, but this description should be set against the increasing stratification of legal practice in England and Wales.[43] For example, sixty per cent of all solicitors now practice in London, many doing commercial and financial services work for corporate clients in very large firms, some with over

---

[40] There is also argument concerning the proper extent of rights of audience for employed barristers.

[41] *Report of the Committee on Personal Injury Litigation (Winn Committee)* (London: HMSO, 1968, Cmnd. 369).

[42] 10,120 head offices and 3,799 branch offices: see B. Cole, *Trends in the Solicitors' Profession: Annual Statistical Report 1997* (London: the Law Society, 1997), p. 22.

[43] In addition there is a significant number of solicitors working in central and local government and as in-house solicitors for commerce and industry: see B. Cole, *Trends in the Solicitors' Profession: Annual Statistical Report 1997* (London: the Law Society, 1997), p. 15.

400 lawyers in post.[44] There is also an increasing focus on European law.[45] Outside London, there has also been a trend towards larger practices seeking to soak up the commercial work which remains in the provincial cities of England and Wales. Yet there are still large numbers of small modestly supported and equipped practices. These are where the ordinary citizen goes for the help of a lawyer.[46]

The type of practice which the ordinary citizen is most likely to encounter is the practice of between two and ten solicitors, working with up to around fifteen support staff.[47] Over half of all firms of solicitors fall within this profile. But interestingly the significant areas of growth have been the sole practitioner and the multi-partner firm.

For many years solicitors' practices have employed non-lawyers to do professional work. Formerly known as managing clerks, this body of employees has been known as legal executives since 1963 when the Institute of Legal Executives was established; they are also increasingly called paralegal staff. The Institute has worked hard to ensure recognition of the professional work done by such staff and operates its own qualification procedures. Associates of the Institute must have served in a solicitor's office for three years and have passed four examination papers in law and Fellows must be over twenty-five, have served eight years in a solicitor's office and have passed a further three examinations from a list of subjects offered by the Institute. These three papers are said to be of the same standard as papers on the Legal Practice Course. There is no requirement that a person holds a qualification from the Institute in order to be employed as a legal executive. It is estimated that over half the legal executives working in solicitors' practices hold no formal qualification in law at all. Late in 1997 suitably qualified Fellows of the Institute of Legal Executives were granted rights of audience in certain proceedings before magistrates' courts and the county courts.

There are likely to be as many paralegal staff in an office as there are qualified solicitors. Paralegal staff undertake a wide range of work, often said to be of lesser complexity than the work undertaken by admitted staff. In one survey it was found that in all but the largest firms, almost sixty per cent of paralegal staff were women. It is suggested that a phenomenon in recent years has been the increase in the number of graduates who have become paralegals. It seems likely that the work of paralegals in solicitors' offices will increase in the coming years.[48]

The Benson Commission commissioned a survey into the use of lawyers services and the matters upon which they consulted lawyers. The survey did not include use of lawyers by business clients. In so far as the typical client can be identified

---

[44] See R. Lee, 'From Profession to Business: The Rise and Rise of the City Law Firm' (1992) 19 J of Law and Soc. 31.

[45] See C. Whelan and D. McBarnet, 'Lawyers in the Market: Delivering Legal Services in Europe' (1992) 19 J of Law and Soc. 49.

[46] See K. Economides, 'The Country Lawyer: Iconography, Iconoclasm, and the Restoration of the Professional Image' (1992) 19 J of Law and Soc. 115.

[47] B. Cole, *Trends in the Solicitors' Profession: Annual Statistical Report 1997* (London: the Law Society, 1997), ch. 4. See also B. Cole and J. Sidaway, *The Panel: A Study of Private Practice 1995/96*, Law Society Research Study No. 24 (London: the Law Society, 1997), ch. 3.

[48] J. Sidaway and T. Punt, *Paralegal Staff in Solicitors' Firms* (London: the Law Society, 1997).

Figure 17.1. **Benson Commission survey on the work of solicitors***

	Percentage
Conveyancing and related matters	35
Wills and probate	21
Matrimonial work	12
Crime (including motoring)	7
Personal injury claims	7
Consumer problems (including insurance)	4
Employment rights	1
Welfare rights	<0.5

* Source of data: *Final Report of the Royal Commission on Legal Services.*

from the survey information, he is likely to be a male owner-occupier aged between twenty-five and thirty-four and be himself a member of the professional or employers and managers socio-economic group. Incidence of lawyer use drops off dramatically for those over forty-five, for those renting their homes, and is markedly less for those from the skilled manual and own-account and semi-skilled or unskilled manual socio-economic groups. There was no significant regional variation in the incidence of lawyer use, despite earlier evidence of considerable regional variations in the concentration of solicitors.[49]

The enquiry into matters about which the public had consulted lawyers in 1977 confirmed the generally accepted division of work by lawyers. The results are set out in Figure 17.1.

The survey did not include work for the business client. A different kind of survey conducted among 103 West Midlands practices showed that company and commercial advice and taxation advice often associated with the drafting of wills were regarded as important categories of work.[50] The results are reproduced in Figure 17.2. Firms were asked to rank categories of work on a seven point scale; from 0 representing 'not important at all' to 7 representing 'extremely important'.

The Podmore survey indicated that on average fifteen per cent of a practices' time would be taken up with company and commercial work. The survey is perhaps also significant for the total absence of any importance being placed on welfare law work.

Research conducted by the Law Society has consistently shown that commercial work, probate, and personal injury work (including medical negligence cases) were seen as the most profitable types of work. The middle ground was occupied by personal finance work, family law, crime and employment law, while residential conveyancing,[51] consumer law and personal debt work were regarded as low profitability work. Welfare benefits cases were seen as the least profitable area of work.[52]

---

[49] K. Foster, 'The Location of Solicitors' (1973) 36 MLR 153.
[50] D. Podmore, 'The Work of Solicitors in Private Practice', *Law Society's Gazette*, 20 July 1977, 636.
[51] Residential conveyancing entered the category of low profitability for the first time in 1995.
[52] B. Cole and J. Sidaway, *The Panel: A Study of Private Practice 1995/96*, Law Society Research Study No. 24 (London: the Law Society, 1997).

Figure 17.2. **Podmore survey on the work of solicitors***

	Mean score
Conveyancing	6.65
Wills and probate	5.41
Matrimonial work	5.18
Personal injury claims	4.60
Crime	4.52
Company and commercial	4.03
Tax advice	3.60

* Source of data: D. Podmore, 'The Work of Solicitors in Private Practice' *Law Society's Gazette*, 20 July 1977, 636.

Paying for Legal Services

The basis of charging and the control of fees

The income of solicitors and barristers in private practice comes from the fees paid by clients. Solicitors and barristers in private practice are in business and must make a profit to survive. This section will focus on solicitors' charges but will only consider them in outline. There are two important distinctions to make: that between contentious and non-contentious business, and that between private payment of fees and legal aid.

Contentious business is work involving litigation, while non-contentious business is the rest of the solicitor's work of which the most important component will be conveyancing and probate work. The broad basis of all private charges of fees is what is fair and reasonable having regard to the complexity of the matter and its importance to the client. This translates in reality into the use of time charging at cost plus a mark-up for the profit element and for the care and conduct of the matter. For the private client, actual hourly charges[53] in the range of £50 to £150 are not uncommon; in addition a mark up for 'care and conduct' is also allowed. It follows that legal fees can quickly grow into substantial sums. Clients are often aggrieved by the size of the bill delivered at the conclusion of the business brought to the solicitor and, save perhaps recently for conveyancing work, advance estimates of total costs are still not standard practice. It is now regarded as best practice for a solicitor, on receiving instructions, to send the client a care letter setting out the best estimate of the total cost of the work at that time.[54]

There are three ways clients can challenge the fees charged. First, they can always return to the solicitor to seek more details of the basis of charging; many bills are uninformative about this. Secondly, they can require the solicitor to obtain a remuneration certificate from the Law Society to show whether the fees are fair and reasonable. This involves the solicitor submitting full details of the transaction for

[53] To which VAT will be added.

[54] See P. Stevens, *Keeping Clients: A Client Care Guide for Solicitors* (London: the Law Society, 1997). This guide was prepared by the Office for the Supervision of Solicitors and endorsed by the Law Society.

consideration by the Office for the Supervision of Solicitors.[55] If the fees certified by the Law Society are lower than those in the bill, only the lower sum is recoverable by the solicitor. No solicitor can sue for fees unless the client has been told about the remuneration certificate procedure. The use of the procedure is free and the bill can only be lowered; it can never be increased. In 1997, 1,008 remuneration certificates were issued, and more than half resulted in a reduction in favour of the client.[56] At any time, even after requiring a remuneration certificate, the client may apply to a High Court taxing master for taxation of the bill. Taxation is a formal process of verification of the fairness and reasonableness of the charges. The applicant pays the costs of taxation if the bill is reduced by less than twenty per cent, whereas the solicitor normally pays if the reduction is twenty per cent or higher. Neither procedure is commonly used, but taxation is hardly used at all, which is not surprising in view of the costs risk.

Costs in contentious cases are more complicated because a successful party may normally recover some of the costs from the losing party. In this context formal taxation of costs on the standard basis has a major role to play, though in minor cases costs may be agreed between the parties without the need for taxation.

Finally, in cases involving legal aid, legal aid rates are established by regulations and it will be these which determine the amount payable to the solicitor out of the Legal Aid Fund for work done whether contentious or non-contentious. It is a breach of the legal aid regulations for a solicitor to receive money for fees from a client who is legally aided other than the contribution payable under the advice and assistance scheme.[57]

Legal aid

Fear of costs is one of the major inhibitions which prevents clients from consulting lawyers. It is a fear which often arises out of ignorance, because for those on low to middle incomes, some assistance may be available under the various components of the legal aid scheme. The legal aid scheme is currently in transition. The overall costs had, in the view of the current Government and its predecessor, exceeded what the State could afford on subsidising the use of lawyers. Its structure also precluded the imposition of cash limits. Total legal aid expenditure grew from £682 million in 1990/91 to £1.56 billion in 1997/98. The numbers assisted had increased by twenty-five per cent in this period, but the average cost of a case supported by civil legal aid had increased by eighty-nine per cent, far outstripping the rate of inflation for the period.[58]

---

[55] Which operates the scheme on behalf of the Law Society. The work of the Office for the Supervision of Solicitors is considered below.

[56] Office for the Supervision of Solicitors, *Annual Report 1996/97: The First Year* (Leamington Spa: Office for the Supervision of Solicitors, 1997), p. 10.

[57] Usually referred to as the 'Green Form scheme'.

[58] Lord Chancellor's Department, *The Legal Aid System—An Overview*, http://www.open.gov.uk/lcd/justice/leg-aid.htm (November 1997).

A number of choices was made on the introduction of legal aid after the Second World War, which have affected its development. These came to be considered fundamental principles and it is important to bear them in mind when looking at the limitations of the legal aid scheme. The enshrining of these principles in the scheme explains, in part, the fierce reaction of solicitors to the Lord Chancellor's proposals for 'modernisation' of the system in October 1997. The fundamental principles are:[59]

(1) There should be free access to all courts within the jurisdiction and to legal services to make such access effective, including access to assistance which avoids the need to resort to litigation.
(2) Persons receiving legal aid should make such contribution to the cost of legal services as they are deemed able to afford having regard to their resources.
(3) Persons eligible for legal aid should have a free choice of lawyers and the services provided should be of the same quality as those available for fee-paying clients.
(4) Lawyers offering legal services under the legal aid scheme must remain professionally independent.
(5) Lawyers should be fairly and reasonably remunerated for work done under the legal aid scheme.

The obvious impact of these principles has been to graft the legal aid scheme onto the existing structure of private practice. Persons within the scheme are provided with an indemnity against the cost of legal services subject only to the payment of the contribution. The legal aid scheme developed over the decades as a means of paying for a lawyer in connection with litigation work. Its impact has been greatest in personal injuries litigation and matrimonial proceedings and in the defence of those charged with serious criminal offences. These aspects of the legal aid schemes were discussed in the parts of the book on the civil and criminal justice systems.

An attempt was made in the Legal Advice and Assistance Act 1972[60] to extend the scope of legal aid beyond the confines of civil and criminal litigation. Since April 1973 the advice and assistance scheme has been available. This is the simplest component of legal aid, but alterations and adjustments to it make it best to think of it as encompassing a number of different types of help.

Standard advice and assistance work is the basic part of the scheme. Any person is entitled to ask for advice on any question of English law except one concerning conveyancing services, wills, or a step in proceedings. Those over seventy and certain other vulnerable groups are entitled to receive advice and assistance connected with wills. The solicitor or some other member of the practice will conduct a simplified means test using a green form and a key card to determine financial eligibility. If the client is happy to pay any contribution required, the solicitor is

---

[59] S. Pollock, *Legal Aid—The First Twenty-Five Years* (London: Oyez, 1975).
[60] Now consolidated in the Legal Aid Act 1988.

authorised to provide up to two hours of work. The work which can be done is any work a solicitor normally does other than representation in a court or tribunal. It is even possible for the solicitor to draft a submission for the client to present personally in a court or tribunal. Obviously the time limit may not be enough to enable the solicitor to complete the client's business. If this is so, the solicitor may seek an extension from the Legal Aid Board, who, if satisfied that there is a need to spend further money, will authorise further expenditure. There is no limit to the number of different problems which can be taken to a solicitor under the scheme. In undefended divorce cases a higher initial time limit of three hours' work applies.

Assistance by way of representation (ABWOR) is best thought of as a simple and easily administered type of civil legal aid for particular types of litigation. ABWOR covers certain civil litigation, but is administered on arrangements more like the advice and assistance scheme than civil legal aid. Potentially ABWOR can be used for any proceedings. Currently the main cases for which it is used are:

- applications to the domestic panel of the magistrates' court for various kinds of matrimonial relief;
- representation of parents in care proceedings;
- applications to Mental Health Review Tribunals;
- applications concerning certain prisoners before Prison Visitors.

The intention behind the introduction of the advice and assistance scheme was to extend the range of services offered by solicitors which would be covered by legal aid. Unfortunately this expectation has not been fulfilled. Three-quarters of advice and assistance work is made up of advice on divorce and family matters and on criminal cases. It is also often used to pay for the preliminary work involved in making applications for civil and criminal legal aid. New ways of delivering legal advice and assistance are being explored by the Legal Aid Board including schemes which will franchise certain work to specific firms or agencies rather than making such advice available from any solicitor.[61]

Looking at the legal aid scheme overall, it is clear that it offers nothing new in the system for the delivery of legal services. The scheme is neatly dovetailed into the established system of private practice. No attempt has been made to see the needs of legally aided clients as different from those of fee-paying clients. Yet as we shall see in the next chapter, with poorer clients the problem is not simply one of providing lawyers for people who cannot afford them from their own resources.

For the areas of work traditionally offered by lawyers, the legal aid scheme can provide very good coverage for the poor. For the rich the cost of legal services is not a barrier to the use of lawyers. But the legal aid financial limits all have cut-off points. Income above the prescribed figures operates as a bar. This has left a section of the community without effective access to legal services for expensive

---

[61] R. Smith, 'The Board, the Future and the Franchise', *New Law Journal*, 19 May 1989, 687. See further below on franchising.

litigation. A number of alternatives have been suggested. The use of contingent fees was initially rejected despite the ability to operate such schemes alongside legal aid and the English system of costs,[62] but has now found favour in the guise of conditional fee agreements.[63] They seem to have worked well for personal injury claims and, as a consequence, legal aid was removed for most of these claims in October 1998. There are now plans to extend such arrangements for all litigation involving money claims, which would dramatically reduce the scope of civil legal aid.

Another alternative which is attracting increasing attention is the development of legal expenses insurance against such risks, which has been welcomed and sponsored by the Law Society.[64] Indeed, the expectation is that insurance will cover most litigation which was formerly covered by legal aid. People will either take out before-the-event insurance to provide a fund for taking a case to court if it arises at some time in the future, or after-the-event insurance against the risk of having to pay the other side's costs in litigation conducted under a conditional fee agreement. Of course, insurers will only provide after-the-event insurance for those cases where the chances of success are high. The premium will increase with both the complexity of the case and the predicted risk of losing until the point is reached where the insurer will be unwilling to underwrite the risk. This threshold is likely to be considerably higher than that traditionally required for support from the legal aid scheme. This is reflected in the planned change in the required prospect of success from reasonable grounds for taking the action to a seventy-five per cent prediction of success as a condition of entitlement to legal aid.

Franchising

Legal aid franchises are unlike the High Street fast food outlets with which most people are familiar, and which cater for those anxious for a predictable ambience and product from city to city and even country to country. Legal aid franchises are quality-controlled contracting arrangements for the supply of legal services. The Legal Aid Board has granted franchises to firms which can show that they have approved practice management systems, and whose quality is assured.[65] The immediate benefit to the holder of a franchise is that it will hold a quality kitemark which should make it attractive to clients, while the Legal Aid Board can increase its efficiency by entrusting decisions that would otherwise need to be taken by itself to the firm holding the franchise.[66] The next step is to remove the need for individual authorisations on a client by client basis; the Legal Aid Board contracts for a block of legal services which the law firm will deliver. This will enable the firm to operate within economies of scale which will reduce the overall cost of the service while retaining its quality. Currently firms may be franchised in one or more of the following categories: personal injuries, employment, consumer, crime, debt,

---

[62] R. White, 'Contingent Fees—A Supplement to Legal Aid? (1978) 41 MLR 286.
[63] See Ch. 11.   [64] R. White, 'Legal Expenses Insurance' (1984) 3 CJQ 245.
[65] Legal Aid Board, *Franchising Specification* (London: Legal Aid Board, 1995).
[66] For example, to exceed the two hour limit under the advice and assistance scheme.

family, housing, immigration, and welfare benefits. Though franchising arrange-ments are still very new, it is not difficult to envisage legal aid being limited to firms with franchises and the introduction of a bidding process for certain types of work. Indeed consultation has been completed on the introduction of such schemes.[67] For example, the Legal Aid Board may choose to contract with a particular firm for all welfare benefits advice under the advice and assistance scheme in a particular area. The firm would know that all clients wanting help in this area would have to come to them, but would also know the fee it would receive for this work and could plan its service delivery within those constraints in order to meet its obligations under the contract with the Legal Aid Board. In this context, the observation of practice management standards and client care requirements become the essential protec-tion against any suggestion that the firm might maximise its profit by minimising its service to clients. This is the basis of some of the criticisms levelled against block contracting in this way.

Complaining about Lawyers

Key distinctions

The history of complaints mechanisms relating to solicitors' work has not been a happy one. Despite the creation in September 1996 of a new semi-autonomous body, the Office for the Supervision of Solicitors (OSS),[68] there remains dissatis-faction both on the part of solicitors and their clients with the machinery for the redress of grievances.[69] A key distinction is made between complaints of negligence and of other deficiencies, which determines whether the OSS will investigate com-plaints. The Law Society takes the view that the remedy for negligent work is to sue the negligent solicitor for compensation. Because of difficulties experienced in the past over finding one solicitor prepared to take negligence actions against other solicitors, the OSS has established Negligence Panels. These are essentially lists of independent solicitors experienced in negligence claims, who will offer an initial one hour consultation free of charge. There is also an arbitration scheme under which many negligence claims are settled. The distinction between professional mis-conduct and negligence has been blurred by a middle category of complaint, that of 'inadequate professional service', where the OSS does have jurisdiction to consider complaints and may award up to £1,000 in compensation. This is clearly intended to exclude negligent work, but it is not easy for the lay person[70] to define the bound-ary between inadequate and poor service and negligent work. Despite this point,

---

[67] See Legal Aid Board, *Civil Advice and Assistance Scheme. Exclusive Contracting—The Way Forward* (London: Legal Aid Board, 1998).

[68] Replacing the Solicitors Complaints Bureau, on which see National Consumer Council, *The Solicitors Complaints Bureau: A Consumer View* (London: National Consumer Council, 1994).

[69] See V. Lewis, *Complaints against Solicitors: the Complainants' View* (London: the Law Society, 1996).

[70] Or indeed the lawyer.

the introduction of a jurisdiction for the OSS to consider poor or inadequate work which leads to moderate financial loss is a welcome development.

The Office for the Supervision of Solicitors

The Solicitors Complaints Bureau set up in September 1986 was the Law Society's answer to critics of the complaints machinery. It had an unhappy time in its ten-year history and this led to its rebirth in September 1996 as the Office for the Supervision of Solicitors. The OSS is funded by the Law Society, but enjoys a quasi-autonomous status, operating at arm's length from the Law Society. But its honourable attempts to demonstrate that independence have already resulted in complaints from solicitors that it is too pro-client and that there is no readily accessible machinery by which solicitors can complain about the way in which a complaint against them has been handled.[71]

The OSS is based in Leamington Spa and has a staff of over 200 and cost £12.5 million to run in its first year.[72] The OSS is concerned with both client-related matters and regulation of the profession. The Office for Client Relations deals with most complaints from clients. This office also runs the remuneration certificate procedure described above. The Office for Professional Regulation is responsible for dealing with matters relating to solicitors' compliance with the profession's practice and conduct rules.[73] This office is also responsible for running the Law Society's Compensation Fund which makes good any defalcations of client money by solicitors. It is funded by a levy on all practising solicitors.

The starting point for consideration of any complaint about the service provided by a solicitor is Practice Rule 15, which requires every principal in private practice to operate a complaints handling procedure and to ensure that clients know how they should raise any concern about the firm's standard of work. It is rightly believed that firms which have effective in-house complaints machinery will generate few complaints which need to be taken outside the firm. The OSS will not deal with complaints unless the matter has first been raised directly with the firm concerned.

Where a client finds it necessary to refer a complaint to the OSS, the client will normally be asked to complete a complaint referral form, and to send it in together with any relevant documentation.[74] From January 1998 a fast-track procedure has been introduced, which will apply to most complaints. On receipt of the complaint, a member of the OSS staff will contact the complainant by telephone to agree the exact nature of the complaint. A process of conciliation will then take place for

---

[71] N. Rose, 'Council to Vote on OSS Fast Track Plan', *Law Society's Gazette*, 10 December 1997, 1; and N. Rose, 'Cleaning up the Act', *The Law Society's Gazette*, 10 December 1997, 12.

[72] Office for the Supervision of Solicitors, *Annual Report 1996/97: The First Year* (Leamington Spa: Office for the Supervision of Solicitors, 1997), p. 16.

[73] See the Law Society, *The Guide to the Professional Conduct of Solicitors*, 7th edn. (London: the Law Society, 1996), which runs to some 746 pages.

[74] This description assumes that the complaint is about the client's own solicitor, but it is possible to complain about another solicitor.

fourteen days in an attempt to resolve the grievance. If conciliation does not succeed, the solicitor is given three weeks in which to produce a formal written response to the complaint. The OSS will then make a decision on the documentation it has; so a failure by the solicitor to respond in time will result in the decision being based on the client's account of events.

The outcome of an investigation by the OSS can be:

• reduce the solicitor's bill in whole or in part;
• order the solicitor to pay compensation not exceeding £1,000;
• require the solicitor to correct the mistake at their own expense;
• discipline the solicitor for misconduct;[75] or
• intervene in the solicitor's practice in extreme cases.[76]

In its first year, the OSS received 22,305 complaints, but half of these came from solicitors and organisations[77] and only half from clients. About 6,000 appear to have been settled by conciliation.[78]

The Solicitors Disciplinary Tribunal

The Solicitors Disciplinary Tribunal is wholly independent of the Law Society and its members are appointed by the Master of the Rolls.[79] The Tribunal sits in groups of three: two lawyer members and one lay member. The principal function of the Tribunal is to determine applications in respect of allegations against solicitors of unbefitting conduct or breaches of the rules relating to professional practice, conduct and discipline. Most applications are made by the OSS, but it is open to anyone to make application to the Tribunal without recourse to the Law Society. The penalties available to the Tribunal include striking a solicitor off the roll of solicitors, suspension from practice, the imposition of a money penalty not exceeding £3,000, and payment of all or part of the costs of the application. The Tribunal heard 207 cases in 1996/97, which resulted in forty-five solicitors being struck off the role; a further thirty-two were suspended from practice and sixty-eight were fined.[80]

Complaints about barristers

The Bar only offered a fully fledged complaints mechanism from April 1997. Previously, the complaints system was primarily a disciplinary system. The Bar scheme

---

[75] This can include the imposition of an internal sanction, or prosecution before the Solicitors Disciplinary Tribunal, discussed below.

[76] This, in effect, closes the firm down. In its first twelve months, the OSS intervened in seventy-eight practices, twenty-five for suspected dishonesty and fifty-three for 'difficulties not related to honesty'.

[77] Including the Legal Aid Board.

[78] Office for the Supervision of Solicitors, *Annual Report 1996/97: The First Year* (Leamington Spa: Office for the Supervision of Solicitors, 1997). The Report is not very informative on the outcome of complaints.

[79] See D. Swift, *Proceedings before the Solicitors' Disciplinary Tribunal* (London: the Law Society, 1996).

[80] Office for the Supervision of Solicitors, *Annual Report 1996/97: The First Year* (Leamington Spa: Office for the Supervision of Solicitors, 1997), p. 16.

now deals with inadequate service and the new system can require barristers to reduce, refund or waive fees where there has been inadequate service. Where financial loss has resulted from the poor service, up to £2,000 can be ordered by way of compensation.

A new post of Complaints Commissioner has been created; this post is held by a lay person who has wide powers to accept or reject complaints. Conciliation is to be encouraged. The Commissioner acting with the Professional Conduct and Complaints Committee will determine how complaints are to be dealt with. Matters of professional discipline can be dealt with by way of an informal hearing or by summary procedure, with the most serious cases being referred to the Disciplinary Tribunal.

Many of the complaints relating to professional conduct emanate from judges rather than members of the public and relate to conduct in court. Complaints are investigated by the Professional Conduct and Complaints Committee of the Bar, which considers a written report from a barrister who has been given the task of investigating the complaint. Adjudication panels consist of two barristers and two lay representatives, one of whom is the Commissioner, who acts as chairman of the panel but without a casting vote. Any split panels result in the decision most favourable to the barrister taking effect. Substantiated complaints may result in applications to the Bar Disciplinary Tribunal, which can disbar the barrister, suspend from practice, order to repay or forego fees, or order various types of rebuke to be administered.

The Legal Services Ombudsman

The Legal Services Ombudsman, who must be neither a solicitor nor a barrister, is appointed by the Lord Chancellor to consider the investigation of complaints about lawyers. The Legal Services Ombudsman makes an annual report to Parliament.

The Legal Services Ombudsman has been critical of the operation of the complaints mechanisms, and questions whether self-regulation is proving to be adequate. Unless the new systems reverse the 'disastrously low level' of consumer satisfaction with the work of the Solicitors Complaints Bureau, the Ombudsman warns that 'the pressure for a major shake-up in the system are likely to become irresistible'.[81]

The Legal Services Ombudsman hopes that the new system for handling complaints against barristers will result in a more flexible approach to customer service by barristers who are criticised for taking too legalistic a view of complaints handling. The Ombudsman says, 'A complaints system is not a legal process. It provides a forum for alternative dispute resolution'.[82]

---

[81] *Sixth Annual Report of the Legal Services Ombudsman 1996*, HC24 (1996–97) (London: HMSO, 1997), but note that the report covers the work of the Solicitors Complaints Bureau rather than the OSS. The *Seventh Annual Report of the Legal Services Ombudsman 1997*, HC793 (1997–98) (London: HMSO, 1998) indicates, in relation to both the OSS and the Bar Council's new procedures, that there has been some progress since the *Sixth Report*, but that the professional bodies 'will need to put on some speed if they are to make it in time for the Millennium'. [82] Ibid., para. 3.28.

Professions—an Outmoded Concept?

There has been much criticism of the theoretical framework within which the enquiries of the Benson Commission proceeded, which has been characterised as 'functionalist' and criticised as being 'discredited in contemporary sociology of law'.[83]

Abel has offered an alternative analysis of legal services.[84] Building on the work of other sociologists, he notes that professions as producers of services can only really control supply of those services by controlling the supply of members of the profession. By the turn of the last century, law and most of today's major professions had acquired this control by the system required for entry to the profession and by securing monopolies over certain types of work. But since around 1945 the gateway to the legal profession has changed. It has ceased to be effectively wholly within the control of solicitors and barristers through the system of articles of clerkship and pupillage, for which premiums and pupillage fees were paid and which were generally obtained by the exercise of patronage, and through professional examinations conducted by the profession.

The growth of universities and polytechnics teaching for law degrees has led to expectations, which have been largely fulfilled, that a law degree provides a gateway to professional qualification. Though non-graduate entry to the profession is still possible, it is very much the exception to the more normal graduate entry. This loss of control over supply resulted in dramatic increases in the numbers of lawyers, noted at the start of this chapter. The increase in numbers led the profession to turn its attention to the stimulation of demand for legal services, called by Abel 'demand creation'. It seems that private demand is almost fully met, and so the focus of attention has been in public demand creation. Major initiatives have been the growth of the legal aid schemes and duty solicitor schemes, support for generalist advice services like the Citizens Advice Bureaux and legal advice centres, which generate work for lawyers, and the serious attempt made by the profession to recover control over law centres, which is described in the next chapter.

The dilemma presented by all these initiatives is that they affect the homogeneity of the profession. A heterogeneous profession is not nearly as powerful. The market initiatives can also backfire, particularly in the private sector, where alternatives to the use of professional advisers or self-help are seen as viable. The claim to exclusive competence also becomes harder to sustain in an environment of market competition, as is evidenced in the area of conveyancing. Abel even suggests that, whereas the latter half of the nineteenth century saw the rise of the professions, the latter half of the twentieth century will see their demise. He concludes with a new image for the lawyer:

The lawyer today, and even more tomorrow, is an entrepreneur selling his services in an increasingly competitive market, an employee whose labour is exploited, an

---

[83] P. Thomas (ed.), *Law in the Balance: Legal services for the 1980s* (London: Martin Robertson, 1982).
[84] R. Abel, 'The Politics of the Market for Legal Services' in P. Thomas (ed.), *Law in the Balance: Legal Services for the 1980s* (London: Martin Robertson, 1982), p. 6.

employer exploiting subordinates—all increasingly dependent upon state or capital for their business and therefore increasingly subject to their control. Although the ideal of professionalism will undoubtedly linger on as an ever more anachronistic warrant of legitimacy the profession as an economic, social and political institution is moribund.[85]

Another eminent commentator on the legal profession takes a less gloomy view than Abel. Glasser draws attention to the move away from complete self-regulation, the increasingly heterogeneous rather than homogeneous character of the legal profession and changing ideologies about the delivery of legal services, and suggests that a new type of professionalism is emerging. He says:

In a recent major study of professional society since 1800, Professor Harold Perkin has produced an altogether different analysis. He sees much of the structure of modern British politics as a battle between 'the public sector ideal of an egalitarian, compassionate and caring state run by well paid professionals and the private sector ideal of equal opportunity for those who are able to climb the corporate ladder of success and compete in the struggle for survival of the fittest corporation'. He argues for a new professional society for late twentieth century Britain which does not fall into the rival pits of corporate neo-feudalism and the authoritarian state.[86]

Concluding Comment

There can be little doubt that the typical practice is still populated by middle class lawyers catering largely for the needs of middle class clients. It will be located in or near the centre of commercial activity in a town or in a prosperous suburb with a high incidence of owner-occupation.[87] The bulk of the work and income will come from conveyancing and related matters, but there is likely to be some degree of specialisation within the firm in three areas: litigation, business and commercial work, and wills and probate. It is likely that much routine conveyancing will be conducted by unadmitted staff, that is, legal executives, with minimum supervision, leaving the solicitors free for more complex conveyancing and for the specialist work. This typical profile is not intended as a criticism, nor should it come as a great surprise. A concentration on profitable work is perfectly natural if the provision of legal services is seen as a business activity. Practice seems at variance here with the pious noises sometimes emanating from the Law Society that solicitors' practices provide a service equally attractive to all sections of the community. We can also conclude that, though legal aid provides valuable support for traditional legal work, it does not break new ground in ensuring that poorer sections of the community receive adequate delivery of legal services.

[85] R. Abel, 'The Politics of the Market for Legal Services' in P. Thomas (ed.), *Law in the Balance: Legal Services for the 1980s* (London: Martin Robertson, 1982), 48.

[86] C. Glasser, 'The Legal Profession in the 1990s—Images of Change' (1990) 10 *Legal Studies* 1, 9.

[87] K. Foster, 'The Location of Solicitors' (1973) 36 MLR 153.

18

LEGAL SERVICES: DELIVERY SYSTEMS

Introduction

The great challenge for the legal system, for an independent legal profession and for policy-makers is to ensure that legal services are available to all who need them at a cost they can afford. The continuing erosion of the legal aid scheme is leading lawyers to abandon work under it and the private practice of law in the competitive era of the 1990s is tending to concentrate on the more profitable areas of work to the exclusion of work for poorer sections of the community. The two areas targeted for expansion in a survey of public use and perception of legal services in 1989 were legal and financial advice connected with pensions and with setting up businesses.[1]

There are gaps in the provision of legal services. Divorce and crime are the only two areas of private practice where the poorer sections of the community have any significant contacts with lawyers. These types of work are, of course, not exclusive to the poor. This chapter will consider other needs and the difficult concept of the unmet need for legal services. The attempts made by law centres and other agencies to fill the gap will be discussed, together with the issue of who should manage delivery of legal services to ensure that an adequate service is available to all who need it.

Unmet Need for Legal Services

The phrase 'unmet need for legal services' has been surrounded by controversy and confusion. There is disagreement about the precise meaning of virtually every word, and even disagreement about whether the phrase is capable of meaningful definition. Though most commentators accept that there is unmet need, there is little agreement on its extent or about appropriate responses to it.

---

[1] J. Jenkins, E. Skordaki and C. Willis, *Public Use and Perception of Solicitors' Services* (London: the Law Society, 1989).

First it is necessary to consider what is meant by 'legal services'. The Royal Commission on Legal Services[2] construed the expression as referring to those services: 'which should be available to any person or organisation requiring advice or assistance of a legal character whether payment for the service is made from public or private funds'.

Unfortunately the Report immediately goes on to qualify this broad definition by making it clear that it had in mind only services provided by qualified lawyers and excluded from the definition advice by 'lay persons'.[3] A preferable definition of legal services is to be found in the Report of the Royal Commission on Legal Services in Scotland where the wide role of non-lawyers in providing legal services is recognised and such a service is characterised as 'no less a legal service than when it is done by a solicitor'.[4] This Report adopts a much more consumer-oriented approach and defines legal services as:

advice information or assistance involving a knowledge of rights and obligations conferred by law, and of legal procedures, whether provided by a lawyer or otherwise. These services may include action taken on behalf of a client, or facilities used by a client (whether the client is an individual, a group or an organisation).[5]

Lord Mackay's Green Paper *The Work and Organisation of the Legal Profession* rather blandly states that: 'legal services are concerned with the advice, assistance and representation required by a person in connection with his rights, duties and liabilities'.[6] But it is clear that Lord Mackay was not limiting himself only to the work done by solicitors and barristers.

Armed with these definitions, few would argue with the following examples of situations in which there is a need for legal services:[7]

- where a person fails to recognise a problem as having a legal aspect to it and so takes no further action to seek out legal services;
- where a person recognises a problem as having a legal aspect but is ignorant either about the existence of a relevant legal service or about his or her own eligibility to make use of it;
- where a person recognises a problem as having a legal aspect and identifies a legal service as relevant and available but, because of some barrier, such as fear of costs or ignorance of legal aid, chooses not to make use of the service;
- where a person recognises a problem as having a legal aspect and as requiring legal services, but finds no developed legal services available; no legal action is taken because no service is available.

---

[2] *Final Report of the Royal Commission on Legal Services (Benson Commission)* (London: HMSO, 1979, Cmnd. 7648) cited in this chapter as 'the Benson Commission'. [3] Ibid., paras 2.1–2.4.
[4] *Report of the Royal Commission on Legal Services in Scotland (Hughes Commission)* (London: HMSO, 1980, Cmnd. 7846), para. 2.2. [5] Ibid., para. 2.2.
[6] *The Work and Organisation of the Legal Profession* (London: HMSO, 1989, Cm. 570), para. 2.1.
[7] R. White, 'Lawyers and the Enforcement of Rights' in P. Morris, R. White and P. Lewis (eds.), *Social Needs and Legal Action* (Oxford: Martin Robertson, 1973), p. 15.

The obvious solutions to these various needs will differ. In the second and third cases, strategies which increase public awareness of the legal aid schemes would resolve some of the difficulties. The last case requires changes in the services and skills offered by lawyers and legal advisers while the first case is particularly problematic because it begs the questions of what constitutes a legal problem and what constitutes need.

These are the two areas where confusion has been injected into the debate. The definition of a 'legal problem' is highly dependent upon the perceptions of the definer. If legal services are seen as contributing to the amelioration of the situation, it will be defined as a legal problem, but if the problem appears rather to be shortage of money or some lack of competence in the individual, the problem will be defined as a social problem. Many lawyers in private practice have categorised problems concerning the range of rights deriving from the public law that regulates the welfare state, most notably in the area of welfare benefits, as social problems simply because they have typically had no involvement in these areas. Others who see law and legal strategies as a means of giving power to a section of the community lacking in power and influence would adopt a very wide definition which almost subsumes both legal and social problems under one heading.

As though this was not confusing enough, we then find very obvious difficulties with the definition of 'need'. The term is often used without any regard to the fact that need is a relative concept. Need tends to be related to resources available and to be constantly re-defined and adjusted with the ebb and flow of resources. The acuteness of need is also relative to the circumstances of the individual. The poor person in low quality rented housing where the landlord allows the roof to fall into disrepair and let in water can only hope to secure a weather-proof roof by reliance on the landlord's obligation to repair. Rich people whose luxury rented houses develop leaking roofs have the wealth to choose to pay for the repair and argue about the matter afterwards. They may even choose not to pursue the matter further. The poor person's need may be said to be more acute. There is then the question of how the need is satisfied. Is it always necessary to have the advice of a qualified lawyer? In many welfare law areas alternatives to lawyers are being used increasingly to give advice on legal rights and to negotiate claims for clients. Because of the monopolies given to lawyers, they often need to be brought in for the difficult case where litigation is involved and representation is needed.

The increasing use of lay advisers has also raised questions as to whether the appropriate solution is always the legal solution. This can be encapsulated in the question of whether the poor tenant with the leaky roof needs a lawyer or a ladder.[8] If the relative costs of public provision of a lawyer and of a roofing contractor were the same, it may be better to pay the roofer rather than the lawyer. This would leave unresolved the problem of what, if any, action should be taken against the defaulting landlord. Perhaps the State could have a right to recover the roofer's costs from the landlord.

---

[8] P. Lewis, 'Unmet Legal Needs' in P. Morris, R. White and P. Lewis (eds.), *Social Needs and Legal Action* (Oxford: Martin Robertson, 1973), p. 73.

Attempts to quantify unmet need for legal services are problematic, but a number of attempts have nevertheless been made. An early study which matched individuals own recognition of their need for advice in a number of areas with the action they actually took produced evidence of considerable perceived unmet need. There was also a clear correlation between high incidence of taking advice and those matters which we saw in the last chapter to be important areas of solicitors' work.[9] Virtually every respondent who identified the need for advice in buying a house consulted a solicitor, but in relation to employment problems only four per cent took advice from a solicitor. Thirty-four per cent took advice from some other source while sixty-two per cent took no advice at all. For social security problems the figures were even worse: three per cent consulted solicitors, sixteen per cent took advice elsewhere and eighty-one per cent took no advice despite their own perceived need for some advice. The study of need in personal injury cases discussed in Chapter 11 provided similar evidence of alarming cases where no action had been taken by victims of accidents who felt someone else was to blame for their injuries.[10]

The Benson Commission's own Users' Survey sought information about matters not taken to solicitors even though respondents felt that advice from a solicitor might be useful. One in eleven respondents identified such matters. The most common matter was neighbour disputes, and the other commonly mentioned matters were consumer complaints and problems with employment and social security. In a number of cases the respondents resorted to advice from friends, the local council or from a Citizens Advice Bureau. One third of respondents identified cost as the major reason they had not taken advice from a solicitor.

These findings led the Benson Commission to conclude that there were two main reasons why legal services 'are, in some areas and for certain classes of society, not available'. The first was the inadequacy of legal aid for certain types of work, notably those involving tribunal representation. The second was a combination of ignorance, powerlessness and a shortage of resources. Five factors were identified as principal contributors to this unmet need:

- a lack of knowledge of the rights offered by the law and of the remedy offered by the use of legal strategies;
- a lack of lawyers working in the areas of law where the problems arise;
- a lack of information about lawyers working in the areas of law where the problems arise;
- a reluctance to consult a lawyer about the problem for fear of what might be involved, particularly cost;
- the public image of lawyers inhibits approaches to lawyers by poorer sections of the community.

In a report which is devoid of any express theoretical framework, it is difficult to identify the reasons underlying particular conclusions. The Benson Commission seems to accept as the causes of unmet need a combination of the 'poverty'

[9] B. Abel-Smith, M. Zander and R. Brooke, *Legal Problems and the Citizen* (London: Heinemann, 1973).
[10] H. Genn, *Meeting Legal Needs* (Oxford: Centre for Socio-Legal Studies, 1982).

theory and the 'legal incompetence' theory. The first simply asserts that poverty is the major cause of unmet need, but empirical studies do not seem to bear this out. For the poor do use solicitors on marriage breakdown and for criminal defence work, both substantial parts of lawyers' practices. Equally the middle classes do not use lawyers very much for advice with employment or consumer problems.

The legal competence theory suggests that unmet need arises predominantly among the poor because they do not recognise their problems as legal nor do they perceive lawyers as a resource available for them save in very specific areas. Because they are almost always 'one-shotters' arguing cases against 'repeat-players' they also lack power. For repeat-players the matter is routine and they are used to using the law and lawyers, while for the one-shotter the matter is traumatic and unfamiliar at every stage.[11]

Zander rejects both these explanations.[12] He prefers, but does not totally accept, the 'social organisation' theory of Mayhew and Reiss,[13] because this provides a better explanation of the incidence of lawyer use by rich and poor alike. This theory links particular types of work with networks of social contacts. Thus acquisition of real property, or divorce, or writing a will, or administering an estate become areas where lawyer use is taken for granted by all sections of the community and where lawyers have responded by providing the service expected. In other areas the social links and networks are not as well developed and the incidence of lawyer use will not be as high. Examples would be personal injuries litigation and minor crime. For Zander the key to variations in the incidence of lawyer use is contact with a knowledgeable and trusted lay person who identifies, or confirms the identification of, the problem as requiring the services of a lawyer. But this alone is not enough, because the referral needs to be backed by sympathetic, relevant and fruitful help from a lawyer.

A further difficulty is that the interpretation of data may suggest different results. We have seen in Chapters 14 and 15 that those who are represented are more likely to succeed in their claims before the employment tribunals and the social security tribunals. If it is accepted that this indicates a problem which needs to be addressed, a number of hypotheses can be constructed which might explain the research findings. It may be that representatives select stronger cases; it may be that those with weaker cases do not seek out such help as is available for representation; it may be that it is the way in which the tribunals handle represented and unrepresented cases which accounts for the variation. If the latter is the 'real' reason for the variation, then a solution which focuses on increasing representation rather than tackling the way in which the system of adjudication works may not be the most effective use of resources. If the 'real' reason is selection of cases for representation, it could be argued that there was no a problem at all.

---

[11] J. Carlin, J. Messenger and S. Howard, 'Civil Justice and the Poor—Issues for Sociological Research' (1966) 1 Law and Soc. Rev. 9; and M. Galanter, 'Why the "Haves" Come out Ahead: Speculation on the Limits of Legal Change' (1974) 9 Law and Soc. Rev. 95.

[12] M. Zander, *Legal Services for the Community* (London: Temple Smith, 1978).

[13] L. Mayhew and A. Reiss, 'The Social Organisation of Legal Contacts' (1969) 34 Am. Soc. Rev. 318.

Whatever the disagreements about the definition of unmet need, there is general agreement that there is a gap between certain new rights that are legally recognised and their observation and enforcement. These rights have arisen principally in the areas of welfare law, a generic label referring to the law relating to housing, social security benefits, mental health, discrimination, employment, immigration and nationality, and the welfare of children. One solution to the problem is commitment to making these rights effective by ensuring genuinely accessible legal services in all these areas.[14] Many of these rights have a special significance for the poor because they are rights relating to basic human needs: housing, a source of income and respect for the dignity of the person. It is precisely in these areas that law centres have made a major contribution. They have also developed a system of trusted referral and effective response which has been the source of their success in getting clients to use their services. This process is sometimes called 'mobilising' a clientele. Law centres and those working for the poor are often labelled public sector legal services to distinguish them from solicitors in private practice.

It is possible to classify the trends in the response to the problem of unmet need since 1945 into four overlapping phases. The first was the development of the legal aid scheme, the second was the perception of legal services as a social service using recognised legal strategies in order to make rights effective, the third was the questioning of whether traditionally accepted legal strategies are the most appropriate response to particular problems or the development of public interest law, and the fourth is the development of a legal services delivery system based on a partnership between a cash-limited public sector and delivery in the private sector through new methods of funding legal services.[15] I will label this fourth phase 'the new realism'.

The Development of Legal Aid

The role of legal aid in funding advice and representation by lawyers has been well chronicled in earlier chapters, notably in Chapter 17. Legal aid in its traditional form simply provided lawyers in private practice with a costs indemnity in respect of the costs and disbursements incurred on behalf of legally-aided clients. The underlying theory was that there would be no distinction in the level of service provided for such clients. Sociologists point to this as an example of successful demand creation by the legal profession.[16] Demand creation refers to the ability of a professional group—particularly one enjoying a monopoly position—to generate new areas of business for themselves. A recent research paper has concluded

---

[14] M. Cappelletti (ed.), *Access to Justice*, 4 vols. (Alphen aan den Rijn: Sitjhoff and Noordhoff, 1978).

[15] On the first three phases, see A. Paterson and D. Nelken, 'Evolution in Legal Services: Practice without Theory' (1984) 3 CJQ 229.

[16] R. Abel, 'The Politics of the Market for Legal Services' in P. Thomas (ed.), *Law in the Balance: Legal Services for the 1980s* (London: Martin Robertson, 1982), p. 6.

that the monopoly power enjoyed by lawyers is the only explanation which fully accounts for the continuing growth in legal aid expenditure.[17]

Under legal aid, lawyers are re-imbursed, as with private clients, retrospectively for the work they do. Access to legal aid for representation in court is, however, restricted both in terms of the work it covers and in terms of the need to satisfy a means and merits test in each particular case. The means test is designed to determine whether legal aid should be provided without contribution, subject to a contribution towards the costs involved, or not at all because the person is considered to have sufficient means to fund their own legal costs. The merits test is designed to determine whether the case has a reasonable prospect of success.

In England and Wales, components of the legal aid scheme were extended and came to include advice and assistance, in addition to the provision of representation for certain actions in court. The scheme was generally regarded as among the best in the world. Nevertheless, there were both limits and limitations. The grafting of legal aid onto legal services provision by private practice limited the way in which the service was provided. The scheme was essentially reactive; indeed the scheme matured before the relaxation of the rules on advertising.[18] It did not seek to deliver legal services in new ways. Its coverage remained limited. Perhaps most significantly, the budget for legal aid was open-ended. At a time when many government budgets were cash-limited, the legal aid budget was not so limited. Cash was guaranteed to meet the costs incurred by the lawyers in providing services for those who were held to be eligible to receive help. This provided little incentive for the profession to argue that the public money might better be used in other ways.

Provision had been made in 1949 for a salaried component, though it was never implemented. In its evidence to the Rushcliffe Committee,[19] the Law Society had argued strongly for a salaried component as part of the scheme. It was proposed that there should be a network of advice centres employing solicitors which would provide advice and assistance in those parts of the country with only sparse provision of solicitors' offices.

By 1958 the Law Society had changed its mind and proposed that advice and assistance could be more economically provided by solicitors in their own offices rather than by salaried lawyers. The new proposals were accepted and eventually came to fruition with the introduction in April 1973 of the Green Form scheme. When proposals for the new scheme were first introduced in 1968, the Law Society also proposed the appointment of salaried Advisory Liaison Officers to ensure that all sections of the community would get to know about the facilities offered by the legal aid scheme and where these facilities were available. In essence Advisory Liaison Officers were to be a salaried taskforce within the legal

---

[17] M. Hope, *Expenditure on Legal Services*, Lord Chancellor's Department Research Series No. 9/97 (London: Lord Chancellor's Department, 1997), ch. 4.   [18] See Ch. 17.

[19] *Report of the Committee on Legal Aid and Advice (Rushcliffe Committee)* (London: HMSO, 1945, Cmnd. 6641). This report formed the basis of the Legal Aid and Advice Act 1949, which established the foundations of the modern legal aid scheme.

aid scheme drumming up legal aid business for lawyers in private practice. It was envisaged that the Liaison Officer would, for example, hold referral sessions at Citizens Advice Bureaux to discover the nature of clients' problems and to provide introductions to solicitors in private practice. Seton Pollock puts it very frankly in his history of the first twenty-five years of legal aid:

For solicitors in private practice to be diverted by undertaking 'missionary' activities to attract work to themselves would be wasteful, would be a recipe for professional problems and would reduce their availability to do the very work so attracted. What is needed is a link between them and those who need, but would otherwise not obtain, those services and this would be the basic function that the Advisory Liaison Officer would perform.[20]

Following the publication of the Society of Labour Lawyers pamphlet *Justice for All*,[21] the Law Society amended its proposal to include the use of Advisory Liaison Officers to set up permanent salaried offices and to offer a broader range of work including litigation in the magistrates' and county courts. Provision was made in the Legal Advice and Assistance Act 1972, and later included in the consolidating Legal Aid Act 1974, for the establishment of the scheme but it was never brought into force. The idea was probably sound in 1949, but by 1972 it was an idea whose time was past. To understand why it is necessary to consider what was happening elsewhere in the development of legal services.

Making Rights Effective

A new approach

By the early 1970s, it was becoming clear that simply making private sector lawyers available to poorer clients was limited in its ambition. In the 1960s in the USA, President Lyndon Johnson had announced his 'War on Poverty' and the Economic Opportunity Act 1964 had established the Office of Economic Opportunity (OEO) which in turn established a 'Legal Services Program' which set up several hundred neighbourhood law offices at public expense. The policy of these law offices was not simply to provide legal services on an individual basis but also, and principally, to secure law reform. The Director of the OEO Legal Services Program put it thus:

We cannot at the same time provide every indigent with a lawyer, treat all his problems legal and personal, work devotedly to change the statutes and court holdings that have placed our clients in a disadvantageous position, and develop the theories to win the battles of tomorrow as well as today . . . [T]he primary goal of the Legal Services Program should be law reform, to bring about changes in the structures of the world

---

[20] S. Pollock, *Legal Aid—The First Twenty-Five Years* (London: Oyez, 1975), p. 125.   [21] See below.

in which the poor people live in order to provide on the largest scale possible consistent with our limited resources, a legal system in which the poor enjoy the same treatment as the rich.[22]

In 1966 and 1967 the Lord Chancellor's Advisory Committee on Legal Aid considered, and rejected, proposals for a similar system of neighbourhood law firms of salaried lawyers.[23] The idea was, however, enthusiastically embraced by the Society for Labour Lawyers, whose pamphlet *Justice for All* recommended a pilot project on the feasibility of neighbourhood law firms in England, and the Conservative Political Centre's pamphlet *Rough Justice* also expressed cautious approval of experiments in the area.

The recommendations were again rejected by the Law Society and the Government.[24] Undaunted, independent groups of young lawyers and community workers, inspired by the American experience, began planning new means of delivering legal services. Some began by setting up legal advice centres where lawyers from private practice offered their services as volunteers to provide surgery style consultations in the evenings without charge. Some later matured into fully-fledged law centres.[25]

The emergence of law centres

The first law centre to open was the North Kensington Neighbourhood Law Centre in 1969.[26] Between 1969 and the late 1980s there was a steady growth of law centres. No official figures are kept because law centres have been set up on local initiative and on a number of different models. But they probably reached around seventy in number, before falling back to their current level of just over fifty. Most are funded by a mixture of charitable funding, and local and central government funding. The development of law centres occurred outside the control of the Law Society and initially without its official encouragement. Though solicitors in private practice have been and continue to be involved in the management of law centres, the Law Society has no policy control over the operation of law centres. Its only involvement arises because it is the regulator of professional conduct and is the body responsible for granting the waivers of the Solicitors Practice Rules needed to accommodate law centres' working methods.

The Law Society's rejection of the idea of neighbourhood law firms was based upon considerations of expense and its commitment to ensuring that expansion of legal services took place in the context of the legal aid scheme, which, of course,

---

[22] E. Johnson, *Justice and Reform: The Formative Years of the OEO Legal Services Program* (New Brunswick: Transaction Books, 1989), p. 133.

[23] M. Zander, *Legal Services for the Community* (London: Temple Smith, 1978).   [24] Ibid.

[25] J. Cooper, *Public Legal Services: A Comparative Study of Policy, Politics and Practice* (London: Sweet & Maxwell, 1983).

[26] A. Byles and P. Morris, *Unmet Need—The Case of the Neighbourhood Law Centre* (London: Routledge & Kegan Paul, 1977); and J. Cooper, *Public Legal Services: A Comparative Study of Policy, Politics and Practice* (London: Sweet & Maxwell, 1983).

channels work to solicitors in private practice. The language of the rejection of the idea was surprisingly strong at times. For example the Law Society said that the new scheme:

contemplates a radical departure from the concept of legal aid as so far developed in this country and, by introducing a separate and distinct legal service, it would exercise a divisive social influence.[27]

To test the hypothesis that a legal aid practice could be set up and work effectively, the Law Society in co-operation with the Greater Manchester Legal Services Committee set up the experimental firm of Cooper and Pearson in Manchester in May 1977. The firm was set up on traditional lines and was not allowed to advertise. The object of the project was to assess the demand for welfare law practices in inner city areas and the commercial viability of meeting the need by the establishment of new practices in such areas. The firm experienced problems from the outset in mobilising a clientele in areas of work other than the traditional legal work of solicitors. Very little welfare law work was received. The partners felt that the prohibition on advertising was a major inhibition in this respect. It also seems that remuneration for legal aid work makes it unattractive and forces practices to take on traditional work to secure an acceptable cash flow. This is confirmed by other figures produced by legal aid practices elsewhere.[28] Cooper and Pearson lost money and in May 1980 the firm was taken over.[29]

The initial hostility of the Law Society to law centres has happily long since evaporated. Law centres are now accepted as making an important contribution to the provision of legal services and the Law Society made a concerted effort in its evidence to the Benson Commission to persuade it to recommend that the Law Society should have control over law centres. They did not succeed, nor do they seem likely to do so in the foreseeable future. The Law Society's early opposition to law centres was based on two grounds. First, that the creation of salaried lawyers in law centres was expensive and unnecessary: a cheaper way of meeting the same objective was to raise the profile of legal aid work in private practice and to use Advisory Liaison Officers. The second was undoubtedly the fear of competition. Experience has shown that, far from taking work from solicitors in private practice, law centres generate work from clients who have not previously used lawyers. Evidence given to the Benson Commission confirms this and the Law Society in its own evidence concedes the point. Indeed in some areas private practices have become established in the shadow of law centres and receive considerable work on referral from the nearby law centres. The Law Society is also involved with law centres in its capacity as regulator of the profession.

[27] The Law Society, *Legal Advice and Assistance* (London: the Law Society, 1968), para. 20.
[28] M. Zander, *Legal Services for the Community* (London: Temple Smith, 1978); and J. Cooper, 'Public Interest Lawyers in England and Wales' in J. Cooper and R. Dhavan (eds.), *Public Interest Law* (Oxford: Basil Blackwell, 1986), p. 161.
[29] J. Cooper, *Public Legal Services: A Comparative Study of Policy, Politics and Practice* (London: Sweet & Maxwell, 1983).

Individual law centres have been set up on local initiative. There is no stand-ard structure or style of work. It will be for the local group to identify the style of practice for its law centre. This represents one of the major differences between law centres and the private profession. Whereas partners in private practice decide the work that the firm will do and the resources that will be devoted to each de-partment within the firm, in law centres it is the management committee, which is usually representative of the community from which the clients are drawn who determine the allocation of resources and priorities. In effect the clients control the practice rather than the lawyers. The Law Centres Federation (LCF), formerly the Law Centres Working Group, does attempt to monitor the development of law centres and enables law centres belonging to the LCF to speak with one voice on matters of common concern.[30] Though it offers advice and information to groups trying to set up law centres, the LCF is careful to avoid plugging one particular ideo-logy of law centres. Many, it seems, have not really thought about such matters prior to starting work and only develop a particular style of practice in the light of experience.

The Law Centres Federation, the nearest thing to a national body representing law centres, describes law centres as follows:

A Law Centre is a community legal practice. It is based in, belongs to, and works for the community within a defined locality. It will be managed by an independent group elected from that community.

Law Centres are non-profit making organisations providing legal advice and rep-resentation at no cost to their users. They also use training, education and other forms of group work to make oppressed people and groups aware of what their rights are and how they can be used to improve their lives. When appropriate, Law Centres will assist in defending these rights in the courts. Law Centres will also strive locally, through their national Federation, and internationally to achieve change to unjust laws and to make justice more accessible.[31]

John Hendy of the Newham Rights Centre, a London law centre, made a major contribution to the debate on styles of practice by identifying five different approaches to legal services for the economically underprivileged. These are not necessarily mutually exclusive, though each has its own unique attributes and con-siderable implications for the allocation of resources within the law centre.[32]

The first approach, which is also the most conservative, argues that poverty is no longer really a problem and so there are few, if any, problems peculiar to the poor. Therefore no change is required in systems for the delivery of legal services. This approach has few supporters. Not even the Law Society adheres to this view.

---

[30] Solicitors may not practice in an organisation described as a law centre unless it is a member of LCF: *The Guide to the Professional Conduct of Solicitors*, 7th edn. (London: the Law Society, 1996), p. 126.

[31] Law Centres Federation, *Is Justice Back on the Agenda/Annual Report 1996/7* (London: Law Centres Federation, 1997), p. 5.

[32] Newham Rights Centre, *Report and Analysis of a Community Law Centre 1974–5* (London: Newham Rights Centre, 1975).

The second approach accepts that there is a gap between the promise and reality of rights for the underprivileged and the need to make those rights effective. It goes on to argue for genuine access to legal services for the poor by an expansion of legal services. The traditional solicitor-client relationship is retained, though some flexibility of approach is possible to include the use of community workers and the permissibility of educational outreach activities. Nevertheless the emphasis remains on the provision of legal services to individual clients.

The third approach follows from the recognition that the legal problems of the poor do not exist in isolation from their social problems. The poor not only suffer from legal deprivation but also from social grievances. To respond to individual cases is to ignore the underlying disease by merely providing relief for a symptom. Once this is accepted it becomes more important to focus on the social grievance as a whole and to direct attention to the class of clients suffering the grievance rather than to respond to the individual complainant. Securing a remedy for the individual may do little for the class. This approach is still rooted in the use of traditional legal remedies but on a group basis rather than on an individual basis. Equally where the law does not recognise a social grievance, a legitimate strategy will be to lobby for changes in the law.

The fourth approach seems rather more radical because it appears to move away from the traditional practice of law. It certainly does so in regarding the legal remedy or strategy as only one of a number of possible solutions to a grievance. In doing so, it accepts the limited capacity of the law to secure significant change. It recognises that the poor lack power and seeks to assist in giving them power to secure change by programmes of community development, community organisation and self-help. Law centres adopting this approach will frequently be found advising on the legal form an organisation should take, writing constitutions for groups and advising them on how best to achieve the objectives and goals they have chosen for themselves. Though often challenged as overtly political, in terms of function law centres adopting this approach have much in common with lawyers advising large corporations. Provided that the law centre lawyers avoid domination of the groups they are involved with and simply serve their needs as perceived by them, their action is clearly not political.

The fifth approach is based on a Marxist analysis of society and rejects the capacity of law and legal services to effect any redistribution of wealth. Since law is seen as a tool of the capitalist classes designed to secure power and wealth for the ruling class, it would be futile to expect the law to contribute to the alleviation of poverty. Most subscribers to this view join the revolution rather than law centres!

Most law centres adopt the third or fourth approaches, or a combination of the two. It is sometimes suggested that law centres become involved in group work as a forced alternative to work with individuals because they are inundated with individual cases. An appreciation of the above approaches shows that this is a fallacy. Unfortunately this fallacy is not always recognised. As we shall see shortly, the Benson Commission does not appear to have understood the importance of the group work approach.

The Benson Commission's proposals

Law centres were well established when the Benson Commission called for evidence and there was a massive volume of evidence submitted about their work and potential. The response of the Benson Commission is disappointing because the Commissioners failed to understand the importance of the new initiatives which seek to release enterprise within communities to enable them to solve their own problems. A distinction which separates the practice of law in law centres from that in private practice is that between reactivity and proactivity.[33] This is an abbreviated way of referring to the five approaches discussed above. The reactive approach is that of private practice: the lawyer remains passive and only responds to the legal problems of clients who seek out the lawyer's services. The proactive approach goes beyond the traditional lawyer-client relationship and reaches into communities 'to encourage collective and concerted action by neighbourhood groups'.[34] The notions of reactivity and proactivity can be seen as opposite ends of a spectrum of operational philosophy. There is, of course, an element of hypocrisy in the distinction between proactivity and reactivity. As was noted in Chapter 17, solicitors have always had ways of mobilising clients through networks of private contacts even before advertising was allowed. The distinction is more one of degree than absolutes.

The Benson Commission was unhappy with a proactive approach to the provision of legal services. While acknowledging the beneficial work of law centres generally, the Commission regarded the decade from 1969 to 1979 as one of experimentation. For the Commission the time for experimentation was over; it had a model for law centres which it proposed should become the official model. The security of central funding would only be available to those law centres complying with all the criteria laid down for the official model. These new law centres were called Citizens Law Centres. Most notably an embargo would be placed on 'general community work'. Law centres doing this type of work are described in the Report as follows:

[These centres] like to work for the community at large or sections of it, rather than for individuals. They often seek to attack the roots of problems by organising groups to bring pressure to bear on landlords, local authorities and central government either to improve working, housing or living conditions or to urge changes in priorities of public expenditure so as to meet urgent needs or to promote changes of a similar character.[35]

Such work is said to be inappropriate for a legal service for three reasons, which clearly indicate that the Commission failed to understand the function of group work. The reasons put forward are:

---

[33] M. Stephens, 'Law Centres and Citizenship: The Way Forward' in P. Thomas (ed.), *Law in the Balance: Legal Services for the 1980s* (London: Martin Robertson, 1982), p. 107.   [34] Ibid., p. 109.
[35] Benson Commission, *supra* n. 2, para. 8.19.

- that the purpose of a legal service is to bring legal advice to all those in its area who would not otherwise receive them;
- that general community work involves only sections of the community served whereas a legal service should be seen as willing to act for anyone who needs its services;
- that general community work cannot be done while maintaining a position of providing an independent service.

Citizens Law Centres would offer legal services of the same type and on the same terms as private practice, being obliged to use the legal aid scheme and to require the payment of any assessed contributions from clients. Though many law centres use legal aid where they feel it is appropriate, many waive the payment of contributions.[36] Nor did the Commission seem to like the pluralism which exists in law centres both in their structure and organisation. They proposed considerable national standardisation and to this end recommended the creation of a new national agency which would hold the purse strings and be able to direct certain aspects of centres' work and organisation. There would still be local committees, but the role of 'local advisory committees', by contrast with existing management committees, is considerably reduced. The carrot of financial security is dangled before existing law centres to entice them into the new structure.

The proposals have been described as 'corporatist' by which is meant disguised State regulation,[37] as leading to 'the emasculation of the current law centre movement'[38] and as 'seeking to nurture and support these important innovatory schemes by bludgeoning them into a rigidly centralised bureaucracy'.[39] There is no doubt that implementation of the Benson Commission's proposals would mean that the poor would only be offered individual case work subject to all the restrictions of the legal aid scheme, even though the Commission elsewhere proposes significant extensions to the legal aid scheme. Given the evidence by law centres of their being inundated by individual cases, this would be both expensive and ineffective for the reasons given above. Law centres made it clear that they would have nothing to do with the new system, and the Government quietly shelved the proposals.

Law centres today

Law centres have shown a remarkable ability to survive, confirming the Benson Commission's statement that they have an influence out of all proportion to their numbers. The Law Centres Federation reports that there are fifty-two law centres in membership as at mid-1998. The survival of law centres is the more remarkable given their general lack of national organisation:

---

[36] See *British Waterways Board* v. *Norman* (1993) 26 HLR 232; and D. Hartley, 'Acting for Clients who Cannot Pay', *The Law Society's Gazette*, 19 January 1994, 40.

[37] M. Elliott, 'The Royal Commission on Legal Services: The Theoretical Background' [1980] JSWL 1.

[38] M. Stephens, 'Law Centres and Citizenship: The Way Forward' in P. Thomas (ed.), *Law in the Balance: Legal Services for the 1980s* (London: Martin Robertson, 1982).   [39] Law Centres Federation, 1980.

Law centres, whilst working a system that has many exciting possibilities for radical public interest development, are dogged by underfunding, a failure to keep experienced lawyers, inequitable distribution, very bad public relations and publicity output, and an almost lack of co-ordinated back-up systems.[40]

Law centres appear to be searching for a new strategy and focus; whether that will emerge from the Labour Government's proposal for a community legal service remains to be seen.[41] There is a paradox in their role. On the one hand they wish to retain their strong local links and responsiveness to local communities. On the other hand they wish to be seen as the focus of a new national salaried element with a network of law centres in all major urban areas.[42]

Public Interest Law

The third phase is a period of questioning whether traditionally accepted legal strategies are the most appropriate responses to particular problems. The strategies of some law centres as described in the preceding section show strong evidence of a recognition that a legal service specifically designed to be responsive to the needs of local people of limited means will not alone achieve strategic change. The emergence of the notion of public interest law perhaps best characterises the third phase.

The label 'public interest law' was devised in the USA and imported into the United Kingdom[43] where it was 'a compendium phrase to gather together a cluster of movements seeking to mobilize law and legal services on behalf of the disadvantaged'. It encompasses the espousal of the public interest by any person or group. The concept has had an important effect on the debate on the provision of legal services, especially concerning the practice of law in law centres. Dhavan concludes:

Public interest law is not just concerned with giving the disadvantaged access to lawyers but with creating a greater consciousness about entitlements and devising ways and means in which these entitlements can be won. Accepting that the life of law is larger than litigation, it seeks to use a combination of skills and community involvement to develop the law and restructure legal processes to benefit the disadvantaged. Despite considerable opposition and a low-key public law system, public interest law has been established as an important emerging part of the English legal system.[44]

One conclusion to emerge from consideration of the notion of public interest law is that the legal aid scheme only has a limited role to play in bringing legal services to all sections of the community. This system of funding legal services, whereby solicitors in private practice provide the same service for legal aid clients

---

[40] J. Cooper, 'Public Interest Lawyers in England and Wales' in J. Cooper and R. Dhavan (eds.), *Public Interest Law* (Oxford: Basil Blackwell, 1986), pp. 161, 189.

[41] On the community legal service, see below.

[42] See R. Campbell, 'The Inner Cities: Law Centres and Legal Services' (1992) 19 J of Law and Soc. 101.

[43] R. Dhavan, 'Whose Law? Whose Interest?' in J. Cooper and R. Dhavan (eds.), *Public Interest Law* (Oxford: Basil Blackwell, 1986), p. 17.   [44] Ibid., p. 38.

as for private clients but with payment of their fees coming from the public purse, fails to see the problems of the poor and disadvantaged as collective problems. The problem is an individual problem brought by an individual client to an individual solicitor. That solicitor then deals with the case on an individual basis. In truth, the problem may reflect a group problem which will not be solved by providing an individual remedy for the client. An example will give life to this notion. Suppose that a client comes to an individual solicitor complaining that the house let to the client's family by the local council is damp and in poor repair. The client wishes to secure a transfer to a house in better condition. The solicitor, under the Green Form scheme, collects evidence of the state of the house and writes to the local council, who ultimately agree to transfer the family to another house. The client is naturally pleased, but only the symptoms and not the cause of the problem have been tackled. The local council subsequently relets the damp house to another family, who may take no action. Though the case may be put forward as a success for legal aid, the public interest in improving the quality of housing stock has not been tackled. Public interest law involves more than servicing individual cases. It can also involve community legal education, law reform, negotiation on behalf of interest groups, lobbying, involvement in alternative methods of dispute resolution, legal research, monitoring the efficacy of enforcement procedures, and publicity.

Public interest law is also the province of the very many 'one-issue' groups, such as the Child Poverty Action Group, Release,[45] and Liberty.[46] All these organisations as well as law centres have made significant use of judicial review as a means of challenging government action.[47]

Law centres have sought to tackle both the individual needs of clients and the collective needs of the community in the work that they do. Single issue groups have used similar strategies for their constituencies. They have also brought into the arena other providers of legal services which have not previously been recognised as part of the network of legal service delivery. Principal among these institutions are the Citizens Advice Bureaux, but there are a host of other agencies providing both general and specialist advice both to individuals and groups.

The New Realism

In an era in which restraint in public spending has been the order of the day under both a Conservative and more recently a Labour Government,[48] it was inevitable that the open-ended legal aid budget would come under scrutiny despite the

---

[45] Which is concerned with drugs-related issues.

[46] Formerly the National Council for Civil Liberties.

[47] For an example of the use of judicial review in connection with access to justice, see R. English, 'Wrongfooting the Lord Chancellor: Access to Justice in the High Court' (1998) 61 MLR 245.

[48] See *Review of Civil Justice and Legal Aid: Report to the Lord Chancellor by Sir Peter Middleton GCB* (London: Lord Chancellor's Department, 1997).

overall cost being modest by reference to overall government spending. In 1991 total legal aid expenditure was £682 million; by 1998 this had more than doubled to £1.6 billion.[49] Ninety per cent of the money represents lawyers' fees. The Lord Chancellor reported[50] that the bill had risen faster than the number of cases handled. Average costs had increased by forty-three per cent while the number helped had decreased by nine per cent. His conclusion was that the taxpayer was paying more for less. No reduction is planned in legal aid expenditure, though the growth of expenditure is to be curbed. The Government's proposals are for the redirection of the current spend on new targets.

The Lord Chancellor has coupled constitutional reform[51] with the civil justice reforms flowing from the Woolf Reports with a root and branch reform of the legal aid scheme. The demand-led system will be converted to a supply-led system. The current 'bill paying machine for the work of lawyers' is to be replaced by 'a positive system for buying the services that people need'.[52] There are a number of ingredients to this new system.

One of the most significant, the introduction of conditional fee agreements, has already been discussed in relation to personal injury claims.[53] The rise of after-the-event insurance represents a privatisation of part of the civil legal aid scheme. The long-term plan is that all money claims will be handled through conditional fee agreements rather than civil legal aid, though in the short term medical negligence claims will be excluded, and there is to be a transitional legal aid sum earmarked for other high value claims which attract significant early costs from expert witnesses in the early stages.

Though it is accepted that those earning reasonable wages can afford the cost of the after-the-event insurance policy and other out-of-pocket expenses the solicitor will incur, the Government has recognised that not everyone with a money claim will be in a position to do so. The response has been to suggest that solicitors fund this expenditure as part of the conditional fee agreement, recouping the expenditure from the damages awarded. There is much debate concerning the cash flow demands this could place on law firms; one survey estimates that for a firm of average size which does a significant volume of personal injury work a sum of £450,000 will need to be set aside in order to carry the costs of insurance premiums and out-of-pocket expenses.[54] Another concern is whether the client is paying too much for the risk the solicitors' firm will carry.[55] Finally, there is some scepticism that the successful use of conditional fee agreements in personal injuries cases can be transplanted to all money claims.

---

[49] Which might be compared with £21 billion spent on defence, £35 billion on health and £77 billion on social security: *Public Expenditure: Statistical Analysis 1998–99*, (London: HMSO, 1998, Cm. 3901).

[50] Lord Irvine of Lairg L.C., 'Civil Justice and Legal Aid Reforms', Keynote Address to the Law Society Annual Conference, 18 October 1997.

[51] Scottish and Welsh devolution and the incorporation of the European Convention on Human Rights.

[52] Geoff Hoon M.P., 'Justice—Addressing the Balance' Speech at the Legal Action Group's Conference, 6 November 1997.   [53] See Ch. 11.

[54] See 'Conditional Fees and Personal Injury', *New Law Journal*, 1 May 1998, 613.

[55] See generally S. Yarrow, *The Price of Success: Lawyers, Clients and Conditional Fees* (London: Policy Studies Institute, 1997).

The funding of all money claims through conditional fee agreements will leave legal aid to provide representation for non-money claims,[56] family matters, crime, and public interest litigation. For all these cases, it is proposed that a higher likelihood of success than in the past will be required. The Lord Chancellor initially spoke of a requirement for 75 per cent chance of success, but later statements took a somewhat more generous view. But it is clear that it will be harder than at present to satisfy the merits test. Public interest litigation will include support for judicial review cases to challenge State action. As noted in Chapter 16, actions resulting from the incorporation of the European Convention are likely to increase the demand for legal aid for such challenges.

The second limb is the complete re-shaping of the Green Form scheme. Proposals out for consultation indicate that the Government is considering entering into exclusive franchise agreements with firms for the provision of advice and assistance in designated areas. Some of these franchises could be awarded to not-for-profit organisations. This refers to law centres and advice centres rather than solicitors' firms. The use of exclusive contracts is also likely to impact upon the provision of representation in both civil and criminal cases. The use of such contracts in criminal cases could lead to something akin to a public defender system.

The third limb is the creation of a 'community legal service'; to date the details of what is meant by a community legal service are far from clear. The Lord Chancellor has said that its principal aim will be 'to help people decide if their problem is really a legal one'.[57] This begs many questions which were addressed earlier in this chapter. What appears clear is that it is not a proposal for a national legal service, or for the central funding of existing law centres.[58] Detailed proposals are expected to be available for public consultation at the beginning of 1999.[59]

Policy is to be shaped by a network of regional legal services committees set up in December 1997 under the auspices of the Legal Aid Board. A Committee has been set up for each of the Board's thriteen areas and is chaired by a member of the Legal Aid Board. This immediately leads to questions concerning their independence. Their functions are essentially advisory. A leaflet issued by the Legal Aid Board[60] lists their functions as follows:

- assessing the need for legal services;
- gathering information on the supply of legal services;
- prioritising geographical areas, categories of work and type of individuals most in need of legal services;

---

[56] For example, where the remedy being sought was specific performance or an injunction.

[57] Lord Irvine of Lairg L.C., 'Civil Justice and Legal Aid Reforms', Keynote Address to the Law Society Annual Conference, 18 October 1997.

[58] Though a very rough and ready estimate suggests that the 52 law centres affiliated to the Law Centres Federation could be fully funded for less than £25 million.

[59] On the community legal service, see R. Smith, 'CLS: Threatening Opportunity?' *Legal Action*, May 1998, 6; and National Consumer Council, *A Community Legal Service: The First Steps* (London: National Consumer Council, 1998).

[60] *Regional Legal Services Committees: Shaping the Future of Legal Aid*, May 1997.

- developing regional strategies to meet the need for legal services in consultation with appropriate organisations; and
- monitoring the implementation of the strategies.

Evaluation of the New Realism

It is far too soon to make firm judgments on whether the Lord Chancellor's proposals are a bold new approach to legal services or merely an ornate facade for a crumbling system. But the overall message is clear: contracted and salaried services will take over from the indemnity provided to private practice. Predictably the Law Society and the Bar have reacted strongly to the new proposals. The move to purchasing services rather than indemnifying lawyers in the private sector is part of a worldwide movement with the most obvious parallels being found in the USA.[61] This movement is designed to secure 'value for money' which means the cheapest price per case for a guaranteed quality of work. Goriely[62] identifies five problems with salaried schemes. The first is overload, as case work increases beyond the capacity of the staff and resources provided. This can be addressed by the establishment of guidelines on maximum workloads, but these have proved difficult to enforce. The second is the need for constant vigilance to ensure independence from the funding agency. This is sometimes converted into a stated need for the paramount obligation to be to provide 'zealous and quality representation'. This is of particular importance in salaried criminal defence schemes. The third is that restriction of choice to the salaried sector can lead to loss of confidence in the publicly-funded scheme. The fourth is that there appears to be an advantage for those living nearer to the publicly-funded outlet, with a corresponding disadvantage for those who live at some distance from the service. Finally, publicly-funded schemes tend to generate bureaucracy and can develop inefficiencies. There appears to be an emerging consensus that a mixed legal aid and salaried system can overcome these difficulties. There appear to be few parallels in other countries to the national contracting scheme currently proposed by the Legal Aid Board. Most such schemes in the USA cover very small populations.[63] There is some indication that initial savings as lawyers compete for the contracts are lost in later years by competitors not wishing to enter the market, leaving the initial contract holders able to increase the contract price as the only tenderer for the work.[64]

---

[61] See generally T. Goriely, *Legal Aid Delivery Systems: Which Offer the Best Value for Money in Mass Casework? A Summary of International Experience*, Lord Chancellor's Department Research Series No. 10/97 (London: Lord Chancellor's Department, 1997); and R. Smith, 'Contracted and Salaried Services', *Legal Action*, June 1998, 6.

[62] T. Goriely, *Legal Aid Delivery Systems: Which Offer the Best Value for Money in Mass Casework? A Summary of International Experience*, Lord Chancellor's Department Research Series No. 10/97 (London: Lord Chancellor's Department, 1997).   [63] 50,000 or less.

[64] Ibid.

Significant advances have been made in our understanding of legal services delivery systems by the experience and reflection of law centres, but all have struggled over the issue of funding. Law centres cannot generate in fees from clients the sums necessary to become self-financing. The public subsidy has been vital to survival, but has been volatile and subject to political whim. There can be no doubt that financial stability for public sector legal services is a major precondition to their development.

It is interesting that the idea of a national legal service in some guise will not go away. The earliest calls which accompanied the introduction of legal aid in the late 1940s were for a national legal service paralleling the national health service. This evolved into the Citizens Law Centres proposed by the Benson Commission, and now finds official endorsement in the proposed community legal service.

Alternatives to Lawyers

The notion of paralegal advisers

New initiatives in legal services have not only involved qualified lawyers. The rise of lay advisory agencies has been phenomenal, so much so that it has been described as 'a new social service'.[65] Much of the advice available from this new service is related to social welfare law and to consumer law. The agencies giving this advice are likely to be trades unions, Citizens Advice Bureaux, welfare rights teams, consumer advice centres, money advice centres, housing aid centres, neighbourhood centres run by social services departments and a whole host of specialist agencies. What they have in common and what distinguishes them from law centres is that generally advice is given by lay advisers who are not under the direct or indirect supervision of a qualified lawyer. Many such services devote the whole of their time to the provision of legal advice; they frequently appear as advocates before tribunals and are increasingly being granted rights of audience in county courts. The term paralegal adviser has grown up in the literature to describe those giving legal advice and doing legal work who are not qualified as solicitors or barristers.

The principal feature of many lay advisory agencies is that they give routine free legal advice on a massive scale to members of the public at very low cost.[66] They act as an important filter for both private practice and for law centres to whom cases of difficulty are frequently referred. It would, however, be wrong to assume that such agencies only deal with the routine. For example, it is becoming standard practice for welfare rights advisers to argue cases with great competence before the Social Security Commissioners, and specialist agencies like MIND (National

---

[65] National Consumer Council, *The Fourth Right of Citizenship: A Review of Local Advice Services* (London: National Consumer Council, 1977).

[66] E. Kempson, *Advice Services in Oldham: A Review of Current Provision and Patterns of Use* (Oldham: Oldham Metropolitan Borough, 1987); and E. Kempson, *Legal Advice and Assistance* (London: Policy Studies Institute, 1989).

Association for Mental Health) employ lay advisers whose knowledge of mental health law is a match for any lawyer.

There is little wrong with this pluralism in the delivery of legal services. However, two problems can be identified. The first is the issue of quality control. Because the legal profession enjoys no monopoly on the giving of legal advice, there is no restriction on the establishment of a legal advice service and no formal check on the competence of advisers. Many agencies are scrupulous in their internal requirements for proper training before advisers are let loose on clients, but other are more casual. It is difficult for the consumer of legal services to discern the competence of the adviser. The client group most likely to use the free services of a lay adviser may not realise that the general principles of tort law on professional negligence apply to all such advisers and may not take action in the face of negligent advice which causes loss. The second problem is the price paid for pluralism. Faced with the multiplicity of agencies, how does the client choose where to go and which agency is most appropriate for his or her problem? There is something of a lottery about whether the right client gets to the right agency at the right time to be best dealt with. Attempts at the co-ordination of services seem doomed to failure. There is such a wide range of funding bodies and philosophies that it would be impossible to bring them all together. It may be that such co-ordination would result in the loss of the varied skills and traditions which make such agencies popular.

The diversity of agencies and advisers indicates how multi-faceted the provision of legal services is. Consumers of such services may be in the best position to judge their worth; consumers of legal services have proved remarkably astute in sifting the good from the bad and the fruitful from the useless.

Citizens Advice Bureaux

The Citizens Advice Bureaux (CABx) are seen as having an important role to play in the future delivery of general legal advice. There is a national network of independent bureaux in all major towns and in some rural areas with some 900 outlets. Local bureaux are members of the National Association of Citizens Advice Bureaux (NACAB). The CABx provide front-line advice on a range of matters, but increasingly they are delivering legal advice and conducting representation before tribunals. Some employ a community lawyer who will handle more complex matters in-house. They typically operate from well-located, open-fronted offices near a central shopping district. There is no means test and no matters excluded from their range of services. They are extremely cheap to run because most of their work is done by trained volunteers. Salaried staff often includes only a manager, deputy manager and some secretarial support. Funding of individual bureaux is commonly a combination of NACAB funding and funding from local authorities in its catchment area.[67]

---

[67] J. Citron, *Citizens Advice Bureaux: For the Community by the Community* (London: Pluto Press, 1989); and J. Richards, *Inform, Advise and Support: The Story of Fifty Years of the CAB* (London: Butterworth Press, 1989).

NACAB provides some finance, which it receives from government, and a wide range of support for local CABx, including a superb information system upon which advisers can rely in giving advice and which is designed to be easy to use for the trained lay adviser. NACAB also lays down national standards for the service, which includes guidance on opening hours, staffing, training and suitability of premises. It is also the national voice for the CABx.

The development of legal advice through the CABx is, however, patchy. The best approach law centres in their expertise and innovation. The worst remain rather amateurish in their work. Until recently, NACAB has not viewed itself as a central player in the legal services debate, but it does have the largest national coverage of advice provision. It is certain to be an influential actor in the development of a total strategy for the delivery of legal services. It may, indeed, become the logical first point of contact for anyone with a legal problem as the Legal Aid Efficiency Scrutiny had suggested. The proposal failed on two grounds: the paucity of funding on offer and the lack of maturity of the CABx network for the task.

Managing the Delivery of Legal Services

The need for an overview

The Benson Commission had recognised the need for some body having overall responsibility for the management of legal services. The Commission proposed the establishment of a Council on Legal Services, whose functions would be:

- to review and to carry out research on the provision of legal services;
- to prepare proposals for the more effective provision of legal services of any description;
- to review implemented proposals and, if so directed, to accept responsibility for the implementation of proposals;
- to carry out any other functions in connection with the provision of legal services assigned to it.

The upward reporting, and receipt of direction, would be to and from the Lord Chancellor. It is unfortunate that the Government has rejected this proposal.

Looking at the experience in other countries there does seem to be a broad consensus that the management of legal services requires the participation of both consumers and providers of legal services. There is evidence of this process of democratisation in this country with increasing participation by lay people in the work of regulation of the profession. No one is suggesting that a central body should take over the control of the powerful private profession. To do so would erode the sacred notion of the independence of the profession. However, legal services are increasingly a matter of public provision and even the private profession draws considerable fee income from the public funds of legal aid. There is clearly room for some body to oversee and comment on all public sector spending on legal services. The creation of a Council on Legal Services would have been the first step towards the creation of such a body in this country. There is the Legal Aid Board and its network of Regional Legal Services Committees, but its independence of thought is constrained by the budgets available to it.

To suggest the need for some central policy-making body is not to suggest the bureaucratisation of legal services. It is possible to develop a national policy which accommodates local or regional policy variations. But without some national co-ordination it is possible for some regions to be inadvertently starved of the resources and ideas needed for appropriate provision of legal services while other regions are favoured.

A Ministry of Justice?

There is an arguable case that the time has come to create a Department of Justice. The idea was first floated in 1918 by the Haldane Committee, because of the problems caused by issues of law being covered by a number of ministries. That position has got much worse as regulation has penetrated more and more activities. There are now at least eight government departments charged with various aspects of the administration of justice, with the nearest to an overall remit being the Lord Chancellor's Department. Though the Lord Chancellor's Department has increased its role in determining policy for the administration of justice, the situation remains unsatisfactory. The creation of a single Department of Justice in which responsibility for justice matters would be concentrated would also serve to make the Government more readily accountable to Parliament because there would be a Minister of Justice in the House of Commons. Government legal business could be co-ordinated through the Department of Justice, who would take over responsibility for the drafting of legislation and break the Parliamentary draughtsmen's stranglehold on out-dated legislative drafting techniques which result in legislation barely comprehensible to lawyers let alone members of the public.

There are two areas of the administration of justice where there is concern to secure a degree of independence from the government of the day. The first is judicial appointments and the second is the administration of legal aid. These functions could be handed over to a Judicial Commission and a Legal Services Commission respectively. These would be independent Commissions voted funds by Parliament to enable them to carry out their functions. The idea of a Legal Services Commission has been part of the policy of the Legal Action Group since at least 1974. The Legal Action Group, an influential group which campaigns for greater access to justice, identified as shortcomings of the existing system:

- the legal rights of many citizens were going by default because of ignorance of those rights and an inadequate legal aid system;
- the uneven geographic distribution of existing legal services, both in the form of solicitors' practices and advice agencies;

- the concentration of solicitors' practices in the commercial centres of towns and in wealthier suburbs;
- the absence of subsidies to encourage practices to set up in 'unpopular' areas;
- the absence of a national policy on law centres;
- a reluctance by some sections of the community to use solicitors in private practice because of fear of cost, inconvenience of location and office hours, and cultural and psychological barriers.

The Group's response was to call for a fresh approach to the provision of legal services based on:

- a definition of need for legal services from the consumer's point of view, rather than leaving it to the lawyers to choose the services they are prepared to provide and to lobby for funds to pay for them;
- legal services being seen as a branch of the social services, with a category of essential legal services identified for which non-means-tested legal services would be available to all;
- a move away from viewing legal services as the parochial concern of solicitors and barristers.

The Legal Action Group called for a complex mix of more lawyers, greater use of paralegals, active encouragement of self-help, new specialist courts and tribunals, and simplified procedures, and a new administrative structure. Essential legal services would include matters relating to occupation of residential accommodation, custody and care of children, personal injuries, protection against arbitrary action by employers, defence of persons accused of crime, income maintenance, immigration and discrimination.

The proposed Legal Services Commission would be an independent body funded by government grant and responsible for all publicly financed legal services. Its remit would be wide, including:

- the monitoring of legal services;
- the efficient allocation of public funds to ensure adequate provision of legal services to all sections of the community;
- the allocation of funds to a salaried sector;
- the running of the legal aid scheme;
- the investigation of the scope for savings by changes in, and simplification of, legal procedures;
- to provide information for the public on the availability of legal services;
- to promote an active policy for improving the quality of legal services by remaining continually responsive to consumer needs.

In the exercise of its functions the Legal Services Commission would be advised by a network of regional advisory councils composed of both providers and consumers of legal services from both the private and public sector. The broad idea was attractive to the Benson Commission, whose report in November 1979 proposed the establishment of a Council on Legal Services.[68]

The proposal for a Legal Services Commission was restated in 1992 as Legal Action Group policy,[69] though it appears to be presented as a function which a modified Legal Aid Board could perform. However, the thrust of the argument in a 1997 publication[70] appears to be that a semi-independent Legal Aid Board would work with a statutory Community Legal Services Authority and the Lord Chancellor's Department in managing legal services. The Community Legal Services Authority is clearly the new name for what was formerly described as a Legal Services Commission.

One consequence of this sort of recognition of the significance of public sector legal services is that the role of the Law Society, and to a limited extent, the General Council of the Bar, would be restricted to that of professional associations of solicitors and barristers. They would provide just one input, representing the private sector, rather than the sole input, into issues involving the delivery of legal services. That is, of course, an important input because the nature of legal services, especially corporate legal services, is such that they will always be a privately funded sector.

Conclusion

In terms of the numbers of lawyers working in law centres and other advisory agencies, their significance is minimal. There are around 70,000 solicitors in private and corporate practice compared with no more than about 250 solicitors in law centres. Yet the importance of the public sector cannot be ignored. Why should this be so? The main reason is that the law centre movement has marked a shift away from reliance upon the legal profession to identify the legal needs of the public and to respond to them. The impetus for law centres and public provision of legal services outside the legal profession and liberated from the constraints of legal aid came from consumers rather than providers of legal services.

The mood of the late 1960s and early 1970s undoubtedly acted as a catalyst. The question of the provision of legal services has ceased to be an issue just for lawyers. The public sector will undoubtedly grow, but the private sector will not wither and die. Michael Zander points out that the ratio of private sector to public sector lawyers in 1978 was 340:1 in England and Wales but only 80:1 in the USA. The private sector will continue to be the main source of legal services for most people. The permanence of law centres, however, also seems certain. Despite

---

[68] See above.

[69] See Legal Action Group, *A Strategy for Justice: Publicly Funded Legal Services in the 1990s* (London: Legal Action Group, 1992).

[70] R. Smith, *Justice: Redressing the Balance* (London: Legal Action Group, 1997).

perennial worries about funding and severe cuts in public expenditure, law centres have survived.

One heartening development in recent years has been the forging of under-standings between the private profession and law centres. Initial scepticism and hostility, coupled with fears of losing legal aid clients to law centres, have tended to evaporate as law centres have become established and as the private profession sees them meeting different needs and actually generating work for the private profession. There is surely nothing wrong with a system which offers different styles of practice to different types of clients. The need being met by the private sector is that of the wealthy and middle class clients and of businesses, together with civil and criminal litigation for all sections of the community supported by legal aid. The public sector is tackling the needs of the poorer communities and is contribut-ing to the movement to make rights effective.

These developments have coincided with a more critical mood on the part of consumers and providers, so that deficiencies in the operation of the legal system are highlighted and the role of law in achieving social policy goals becomes more overt. These issues tend to be unsettling; yet in the long term they are a sign of a healthy system. The result will be evolutionary change in the systems for the delivery of legal services in this country. In criticising the Report of the Benson Commission it is sometimes forgotten that it proposed a considerable increase in public spending on the provision of legal services. Few would deny that legal ser-vices remain comparatively underfunded. The argument is about the best alloca-tion of funds and the most cost-effective system of delivery. What is missing from the debate is a sound foundation of principles upon which the provision can be based and perhaps also a tone which is less critical of the traditional provision of legal services than the mood of the times demands.

Many analyses of the role of lawyers stress the role of looking after the interests of clients. This involves fighting for clients, counselling them, constructing power-ful and persuasive arguments for their cases whether in litigation or otherwise, influencing decision-makers and presenting clients with choices and information about the consequences of those choices. To these must be added the skills of man-aging and organising transactions.[71] These are skills which will always be needed in both the public and private sectors, and so both are likely to flourish.

[71] D. Podmore, *Solicitors and the Wider Community* (London: Heinemann, 1980).

PART 5

RECURRING THEMES

19

RECURRING THEMES

Introduction

At many points, this book has presented a gloomy picture of the achievements of institutions which form part of the English legal system. Questions have been raised about the fairness of outcomes, about the cost of justice, and about the performance of lawyers. The focus has been on the experience of the system by the citizen caught up in it either as defendant in the criminal process or litigant in the civil courts and in tribunals. The view has been selective. Nothing has been said of the many thousands of day to day transactions effectively and efficiently managed for their clients by solicitors. Nothing has been said of the work of lawyers in avoiding disputes which come to the courts. Yet it is surely fair to measure the effectiveness of the most public institutions of the legal system in handling the business of the ordinary citizen. When this is done, the rhetoric of the system is frequently found to be hollow. Excessive cost and delay, unjust results and denial of access seem to abound. There are, however, promising signs of a freshness of approach to the resolution of these deficiencies.

This chapter seeks to draw together some recurring themes from the welter of information presented so far in order to see whether the English legal system is evolving into more than a haphazard collection of public institutions.

Appropriate Dispute Resolution

Both public and private enquiry has concluded that there is a need for matching dispute resolution methods more closely to the nature of the dispute and the amount at stake. Nowhere is this more clearly articulated than in the principle of proportionality which pervades the Reports into civil justice by Lord Woolf. It is also at the heart of the access to justice philosophy which has been referred to at a number of points in discussing the performance of the English legal system. It has even resulted in suggestions that there needs to be greater co-ordination between adjudication in the courts and the use of private alternative dispute resolutions systems.

These developments must result in some erosion of the adversarial system to which the English system has had a long historical attachment. The English legal system adopts the adversarial system of dispute resolution even where it seeks to provide assistance for those who come before the courts and tribunals of the system without an advocate to speak for them. This often leads to suggestions that all the deficiencies of the English system could be removed by the adoption of inquisitorial procedures. The principal difference is that whereas the adversary system places the onus of collecting and presenting evidence on the parties, the inquisitorial system places a duty upon the judge to investigate and inquire into the facts and the law upon which the claim is based. In terms of civil procedure this results in the absence of a concentration on the ultimate trial of the issue that pervades the English system, even though trial is a rare occurrence.

The process in countries with civil law traditions is more diffuse. Typically there are three stages. First, there is the preliminary stage at which pleadings less formal than in the English system are filed and a hearing judge is appointed. Secondly, there will be the evidence-taking stage at which the hearing judge takes evidence and prepares a written report on the case. Thirdly, there is the decision-taking stage at which a bench of judges, of whom one will be the hearing judge, consider the report on the case together with the lawyers' written submissions on the law. They will hear oral argument only on selected issues and make a decision as to the outcome of the claim before them.[1] Written procedures play a large part.

In France the procedures in civil cases are as follows. The lawyers (*avocats*) file their pleadings (*conclusions*), following which a hearing judge (*juge des mises*) is appointed. At the evidence taking stage, the *juge des mises* supervises the collection of evidence which is placed in a *dossier* which includes a summary of the evidence and report on the case prepared by the *juge des mises*. *Conclusions* continue to be exchanged throughout the case, particularly on legal issues raised. The *juge des mises* may pursue avenues of enquiry not suggested by the parties' *avocats*. He may not make any conclusions as to facts or law, but he does have a continuing supervisory role and does prepare the *dossier*, which is the written record on the basis of which the bench of three judges (the *juge des mises* will be one of the three) will decide the case following the final hearing (*audience*). The *audience* rarely lasts more than an hour or two. It will be seen that there is no culminating event equivalent to the English trial; there is rather a continuing trial with evidence presented early in the process.

As Sir Jack Jacob has noted,[2] both systems assume the contradictory character of the dispute they are called upon to determine, but employ different ways to reach that determination. It is possible to envisage the adversary system operating with a high degree of intervention from the judge. The essence of the adversary system is that it is for one of the parties to prove certain facts crucial to the claim. Often, especially where one of the parties is unrepresented, there will be a startling

---

[1] J. Merryman, *The Civil Law Tradition* (Stanford: Stanford University Press, 1969).
[2] J. Jacob, *The Fabric of English Civil Justice* (London: Stevens, 1987).

inequality between them. An interventionist approach from the judge can reduce that inequality. The unanswered question is whether it can remove the inequality. Only if such strategies can remove the inequality is it right to say that litigation without representation is possible. Few would dispute the need for courts and tribunals to be friendlier places for litigants to use whether with or without lawyers.

The Woolf Reports have suddenly made judicial case management an acceptable means of seeking to reduce excessive cost in the civil justice system and to speed up decision-making. This invariably erodes the adversarial nature of the process, since the parties will have to adopt a much more 'cards on the table' approach in their dealings with the procedural judge. An adversarial approach is also not entirely consistent with the exhortation to use alternative dispute resolution methods. The parties cannot currently be compelled to discard adjudication in court, and so they must see some advantage in adopting a process of dispute resolution other than competitive adjudication. The Woolf reforms are not yet up and running, but it would be surprising if their implementation did not lead to some unexpected results. If the fast-track works as it should and if conditional fees become a popular form of funding litigation, the result may well be an increase in adjudication which, in turn, might put at risk the ability to keep to the timetable which makes the procedure attractive.

Elsewhere in the legal system, particularly in some tribunals and in the handling of small claims, the hands-on approach already calls into question whether it is appropriate to describe the process as adversarial. In a climate where the selection of an appropriate or proportional dispute resolution method is the touchstone test, there is likely to be continuing erosion of the adversarial approach.

The Concept of Due Process of Law

In English law there is no formal legal rule requiring the resolution of disputes to be by due process of law. Though there are similarities, care should be taken not to confuse the concept with that contained in the Fourteenth Amendment to the United States Constitution, which ordains that no State in the Union 'shall deprive any person of life, liberty or property, without due process of law'. Professor Atiyah concludes that the concept of due process of law in this country is a combination of three ideals:

- that adjudication is open;
- that each party has a right to be heard (that is, to adduce evidence and to present argument); and
- that the decision-maker is impartial.

He notes that due process of law involves more than merely a trial by 'process authorised by a law validly made by Parliament', because in a formal sense Parliament is free to pass any law it wishes and this would include a law abolishing the ideals of due process in the judicial settlement of disputes. But Professor Atiyah considers it 'unthinkable that the concept . . . could be swept away like this'.[3]

The incorporation of the European Convention on Human Rights adds a new dimension in that the complex requirements of Article 6 can now be applied in domestic courts and tribunals.[4] The Convention sets high and developing standards for both for the criminal trial and for the determination of civil rights and obligations in the courts and tribunals of England and Wales.

However a full-blown trial is a rarity in the English legal process in both criminal and civil matters. The bulk of criminal cases is disposed of by guilty plea in both magistrates' courts and the Crown Court. Such proceedings cannot be said to display in any meaningful sense the ideals of due process. Openness is lacking in that important processes are hidden, masked behind the single word 'guilty' which is almost the limit of the defendant's right to be heard. In these cases impartiality of the judge is an irrelevance. In civil cases dealing with major personal injuries claims, the impact of insurance and the settlement of so many claims by negotiation dramatically reduces the significance of adjudication. In contract claims there is seldom any consideration of, or challenge to, the merits of the claim. In small claims in the county court the requirements of due process are ineffective. The adjudication of the dispute may claim to be open, fair and impartial, but if the procedures are too complex and legal aid provides no assistance, the right to be heard becomes illusory.

Does all this mean that yet again there is a gap between the rhetoric of due process and the actuality of the experience of those caught up in the legal process? Not necessarily. But it is necessary to extend the focus of due process to include not just the final adjudication of the dispute but also every preliminary stage leading up to adjudication. This requires a broadening of the ideals of due process. The key must be the requirement at every stage that those involved in the process make choices freely and on an informed basis. The notion of informed choice requires the availability of an independent adviser whenever someone is faced with a choice but lacks the knowledge upon which to base an informed and genuine choice. The requirement is of special importance in a legal system where the adversarial tradition means that party initiative is required throughout the whole process. It is in the nature of the adversarial process constantly to confront participants with the need to make choices concerning the preparation and conduct of their cases. For this reason mere simplification of procedures without any fundamental change in the responsibilities of litigants for the presentation of their cases is unlikely to secure lasting benefits.

The adoption of inquisitorial procedures does not mean the redundancy of the lawyer or legal adviser, though any process of dispute settlement designed to be used without a lawyer or legal adviser must be genuinely inquisitorial in function if it is to be fair to the parties. It may be more fruitful to consider due process more in terms of information and informed choices throughout the process than in terms

[3] P. Atiyah, *Law and Modern Society* (Oxford: Oxford University Press, 1983).   [4] See Ch. 2.

of the qualities of the rare final determination of a dispute by contested adjudication before a court or tribunal. In addition to asking 'has there been due process?' we should also ask the broader question 'has there been access to justice?'

The concept of access to justice is far wider than that of due process, which is subsumed within this concept. The concept is argued and developed in the major Florence Access to Justice project whose results are published in six volumes.[5] Access to justice involves focus on two basic purposes of the legal system. First, the legal system must be equally accessible to everyone, and that access must be effective. Secondly, access to the system must lead to results that are individually and socially just. The emphasis on individual and social justice does not allow the problems of, for example, the litigant seeking redress following the purchase of a defective radio for £5 to be ignored.

The access to justice approach has developed as a consequence of the modern notion of the equality of all citizens and has grown out of developments in the provision of legal aid for the poor and of the growth of identifiable group interests for the protection of, for example, the rights of employees, of consumers, of ethnic minorities and of women. The access to justice approach moves beyond merely providing representation to consideration of 'the need to relate and adapt the process to the type of dispute'. Though the access to justice project was concerned with the civil process, its underlying philosophy can easily be transferred to the criminal process. It requires an examination of processes to determine whether there are structural imbalances or inequities in the system and to effect change to redress any imbalances, inequities or insufficiencies. It accepts a pluralism in methods of dispute resolution, but above all focuses on the needs of participants in the process. The report does not demand the abolition of the full adversarial trial, but would reserve it for disputes where so slow, expensive and formal a process is warranted.

Advice and Representation

The complexity of the law and the techniques used in its application mean that there will be few occasions where the citizen can use the law without assistance of some sort.[6] Again the current touchstone is proportionality, under which the style and cost of the resource provided must be matched to the nature of the legal issue. Current government policy emphasises choice and self-reliance, as well as prudence in planning for the need for legal services by taking out legal expenses insurance. But it is also recognised that in some circumstances advice and assistance will need to be provided at public expense.

---

[5] M. Cappelletti (ed.), *Access to Justice*, 4 vols. (Alphen aan den Rijn: Sitjhoff and Noordhoff, 1978).

[6] See, for example, L. Bridges, *The Provision of Duty Advice Services in County Courts* (London: Legal Aid Board, 1991).

Though the legal profession is made up only of solicitors and barristers, the practice of law is increasingly stratified. The diversification of the practice of law may have reached the stage at which it can be said that there is not a single profession of solicitor, but many professions. Furthermore, legal advice is no longer simply the province of the professionally qualified. There are thousands of lay advisers meeting perfectly adequately the need for advice on questions of law. More recently, there has been some encroachment on legal representation, where the work of knowledgeable lawyers who are not professionally qualified is of considerable significance. Solicitors can now call upon legal executives in their own firms to undertake certain business in court if they hold the appropriate right of audience. The Crown Prosecution Service can use its non-professionally qualified staff for certain matters in the magistrates' courts. This raises the perennial question of whether it is simply a sensible choice applying the principle of proportionality, or whether it is a de-skilling of certain work in order to reduce public expenditure.

Attempts have been made to develop processes where legal representation is not required, but in every such case research has shown that represented parties do better than unrepresented ones. As noted in the last chapter, a number of hypotheses can be offered to explain this phenomenon. It is impossible, however, to discount the possibility that quality representation makes a difference no matter how user friendly the process is. It can also, rather patronisingly, devalue what individuals want.[7]

The final issue which makes representation such a difficult question is that of the style of representation. It is axiomatic to say that the style of representation should be appropriate to the forum, but the pluralist approach to representation, particularly as observed in tribunals, means that a tribunal is likely to see all types and styles of representation from the confrontational aggressive approach adopted by some Claimants Union representatives to the highly formalised performance of a lawyer used to appearing before the courts. Both would seem to be inappropriate. Studies have shown that claimants prefer proceedings in which they are involved and participate.[8] The lower levels of formality before tribunals do mean that claimants are less stage-managed and can become far more involved in the presentation and argument of their cases. This has led experienced tribunal advocates to argue in favour of a style of 'joint representation' or 'co-operation'.[9] This means working with the claimant, advising on the legal framework within which the decisions are made, and avoiding reducing the claimant to the status of a passive participant in the process, whose only role is to give evidence. It is difficult to achieve joint representation, requiring time and patience in the preparatory stages. This style is contrasted with that of 'co-option', which occurs when the adviser takes over the

---

[7] See T. Tyler, 'Procedure or result: what do disputants want from legal authorities' in K. Mackie, *A Handbook of Dispute Resolution: ADR in Action* (London: Routledge, 1991), p. 19.

[8] K. Bell et al., 'National Insurance Local Tribunals—A Research Study' [1974] 3 J Soc. Policy 289 and [1975] 4 J Soc. Policy 1; and K. Bell, *Research Study on Supplementary Benefit Appeal Tribunals: Review of Main Findings: Conclusions; Recommendations* (London: HMSO, 1975).

[9] R. Lawrence, *Tribunal Representation* (London: Bedford Square Press, 1980).

claim and does not involve the claimant save to take instructions and to give evidence at the hearing. Claimants represented effectively using the co-operative style
of representation are likely to have a far higher opinion of the process regardless
of the outcome when compared with the litigant who has understood little of what
is going on and has hardly participated in the decision-making process. But too
much is sometimes made of this issue of style. The co-operative style is obviously
preferable whatever the forum. A common division of responsibilities is to reserve
factual issues for the claimant and legal issues for the representative.

Effective advice and representation in tribunals will undoubtedly result in more
sittings of tribunals, but under the present system seems to be the only way of ensuring that claimants' cases are put fully to, and more importantly considered fully
by, tribunals. In the long term it may well prove to be quicker and cheaper than
changing to a fully inquisitorial system designed to be used by claimants without
advice and representation.

It seems unlikely that there will be major changes in the general requirement
of party initiative in all areas of the legal system. If this is so, advice, assistance and
representation are of considerable importance in helping litigants to cope with the
system. Yet we have seen that there are enormous gaps in the provision of legal services both in the criminal and civil process. In proceedings before magistrates' courts
large numbers of defendants are unrepresented and alarmingly few defendants
receive any legal help prior to charge or summons. For major civil claims matters
are not quite as bad, though in debt cases debtors seem all too readily to submit
to the claims of creditors. In the areas of small claims and of tribunal adjudication
which were designed for use without representation, there is inadequate assistance available and the dramatic differences in the success rates of represented and
unrepresented litigants indicates a failure in the design of the system. The solution
for these difficulties is the ready availability of advice and assistance, and, in many
cases, also of representation. Such representation must be of a quality and price to
match the dispute. For less complex matters the use of paralegal workers is a real
possibility. An optimistic view of the reshaping of legal aid under current proposals
is that it will at long last offer hope of offering a national system of representation
for those appearing before tribunals.

There is a need for a broader consideration of the means of delivering legal
services which encompasses both the public and the private sectors and which does
not ignore the important contribution of paralegals. At present the Law Society
and the Bar seem to regard the non-professionally qualified as irrelevant in considering policies for the delivery of legal services. The need for a more representative body to oversee such policies is urgent. More public money needs to be spent
on legal services. There is much merit in the argument for increased spending
on law centres, but there is also a need for a salaried public litigation service. Such
a service could be split into criminal and tribunals divisions. A salaried body of
solicitors, barristers and paralegal workers could then be available to represent
individuals with claims before criminal courts and a wide range of tribunals. Small
claims are excluded because, with increased funding, lawyers and others working

with consumer groups and in consumer advice centres could take on this work. A major contribution of increased use of paralegals is that the background and social composition of the providers of legal services is likely to be dramatically widened. The issue of the competence of paralegals would need to be addressed, but, just as the profession of legal executive has developed within the private sector, there is no reason why paralegals should not develop an organisation similar to the Institute of Legal Executives with the ability to certificate its members.

The law has become too complex, even when unnecessary mystification is removed, for all members of society to act for themselves in claims which reach the stage of formal adjudication. Where help is available, for many people it unfortunately tends to be too little and too late, except for serious criminal offences and major civil claims. For this reason more resources should be devoted to legal education in schools and to the provision of effective advice and assistance at the earliest stages of claims. The concept of access to justice for all demands greater recognition of the need to inform individuals of their rights and of the choices available to them in securing enjoyment of those rights.

The Role of Lay Persons as Decision-Makers

The use of lay men and women as adjudicators in the legal system is widespread and is not unique to the English system. The use of lay persons has consequences for the operation of the system. There must be a clear understanding of the role of the lay members who cannot be expected to have a complete command of the law relevant to the issue before them. Professor Stein concludes that 'the association of laymen in the legal process tends to limit the issue to a clear-cut question which they can readily answer without having to give reasons'. He adds that a similar limitation applies to the remedies open to a lay court.[10] The English legal system uses lay members as adjudicators in both criminal and civil cases. Justices of the peace deal with the bulk of criminal cases. Juries determine issues of fact in trials on indictment and are used on rare occasions in civil cases. Expert lay members can be called upon to sit with High Court judges in Admiralty and commercial cases. Finally, lay members sit alongside lawyer chairmen and women in tribunals.

The consequences of their involvement are considerable. Professor Stein considers that lay adjudicators are superior to professional judges in the application of general standards of conduct and gives as examples the notions of reasonableness, fairness and good faith. He also considers an important contribution by them to be the provision of 'an antidote against excessive technicality' and 'some guarantee that law does not diverge too far from reality'. Because they are not experts lay decision-makers present a very real danger that the dispute may not be resolved

---

[10] P. Stein, *Legal Institutions—The Development of Dispute Settlement* (London: Butterworths, 1984).

in accordance with the prescribed rules of law, but rather by some general notion of fairness between the parties. In some circumstances the decisions made by lay adjudicators may not be appealable. The making of decision in accordance with the prescribed rules of law is an inherent aspect of due process of law. Many criticisms of the old supplementary benefit appeal tribunals, often at that time composed wholly of lay members, was that adjudication of claims was based on whether the claimant was seen as deserving rather than on the legal rules of entitlement.

The modern tribunal composed of lawyer and two lay members[11] presents an opportunity to develop a model of adjudication that combines the merits of lay decision-making with legal competence. The participation of lay members does seem to lead to general public confidence in the fairness of the process. It can also dramatically widen the social experience represented by the decision-makers. What is important here is the broadest representation consistent with the demands of the task. Appointments of lay members of tribunals seems currently too locked into the system for the appointment of justices of the peace, which hardly seems likely to result in the representation of a wide cross-section of the community. The key role of lay members, apart from their breadth of experience, will be in ensuring that procedures do not become too full of mystery, and to ensure that litigants before them are not reduced to passive spectators in a process designed to resolve their disputes. Perhaps more than any other change, moves to ensure that parties under-stand what is going on will increase effective access to justice. Lay members sitting regularly will obviously, and rightly, become familiar with the legal framework within which they are operating. Perhaps to ensure that the lay input is always well represented, it would be worth considering limiting the appointment of lay members (and possibly also lawyers as chairmen and women) to terms of five years with a compulsory period before reappointment. Such a move may also encourage broader representation since more lay members would be needed.

If the pattern of joint decision-making can be made to work effectively in tribunals, then it might be extended to adjudication in the magistrates' courts where the role of clerk would be taken over by a lawyer in the chair sitting with two lay justices. Reasons for decisions could then be required, as they are currently required of tribunals. Again to reduce the incidence of the 'professional' lay adjudicator, there might be an embargo on holding more than one lay 'judicial' appointment at any given time. Of course, if the tribunal model becomes widely accepted, then adjudication of small claims would seem to be an obvious candidate for disposal in this manner, though a change to an inquisitorial procedure genuinely accessible to litigants in person would be the most beneficial change. But changes in structures even as dramatic as those suggested will not alone be enough if abandonment of claims continues to be of major significance because the process and law are too difficult to understand alone.

---

[11] Though this is clearly no longer entrenched, since both employment tribunals and the social security appeal tribunals may now be composed of a single legal qualified person.

Concluding Comment

Implementation of the Government's plans for the civil justice system and legal aid will bring major changes to these areas of the legal system. For the future, whatever changes are planned will be implemented against the constitutional background of the European Convention. The procedural due process requirements of Article 6 will take centre stage, but virtually all Convention rights are capable of having an impact upon the operation of the English legal system.

Greater coherence is being brought to the legal system over time, but it still remains a collection of institutions rather than a unified system. Parts of it are being unified, notably the civil courts where the triple track of small claims, fast-track, and multi-track procedures will operate across the county courts and the High Court. But it is more accurate to say that procedure is being streamlined rather than institutions coalescing into a single system.

It would be easy to end on too pessimistic a note and to leave the reader with a picture of a legal system which is rotten to the core. This is clearly not so. It is, however, wrong to be complacent and to accept that the current system offers individual and social justice to all who invoke its processes. There is a place for bold and innovative reform based on a clear understanding of the strengths and weaknesses of the present system. The seeds of ideas for innovation and experimentation can be found in the present system. If we build on its strengths and seek to remove its weaknesses, the legal system of tomorrow can be more effective, more equitable, more open and more understandable than the system of today.

Index